May 17–19, 2019
Chengdu, Sichuan, China

**Association for
Computing Machinery**

Advancing Computing as a Science & Profession

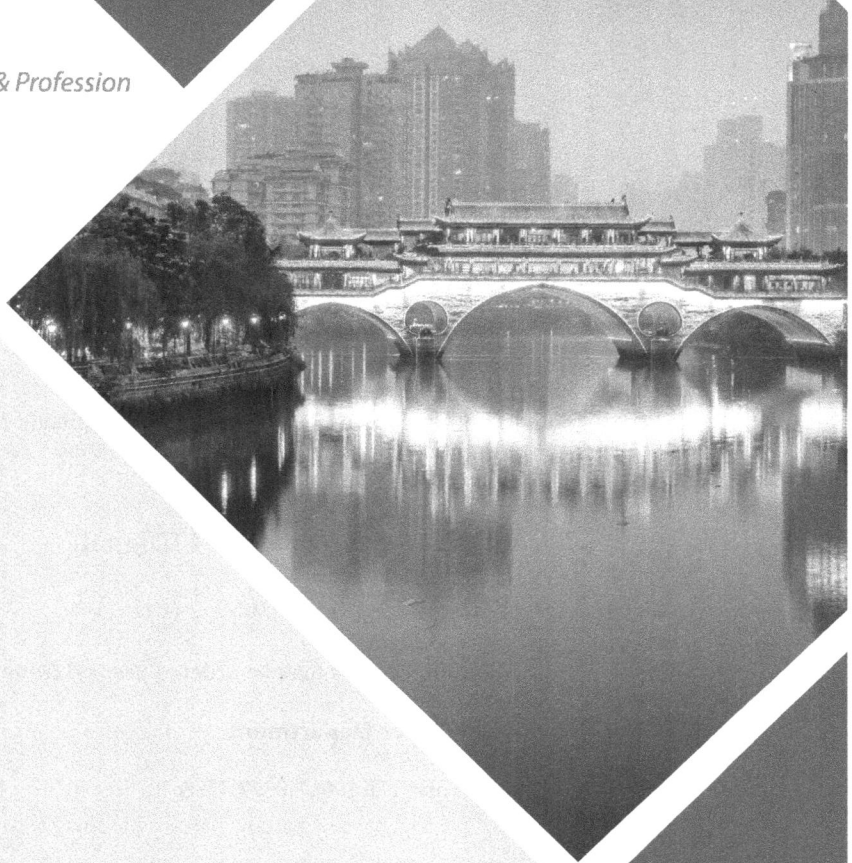

CompEd'19

Proceedings of the ACM Conference on
Global Computing Education

Sponsored by:
ACM SIGCSE

Supported by:
GitHub Education, and Google

**Association for
Computing Machinery**

Advancing Computing as a Science & Profession

The Association for Computing Machinery
2 Penn Plaza, Suite 701
New York, New York 10121-0701

ISBN: 978-1-4503-6259-7 (Digital)

ISBN: 978-1-4503-7059-2 (Print)

Additional copies may be ordered prepaid from:

ACM Order Department
PO Box 30777
New York, NY 10087-0777, USA

Phone: 1-800-342-6626 (USA and Canada)
+1-212-626-0500 (Global)
Fax: +1-212-944-1318
E-mail: acmhelp@acm.org
Hours of Operation: 8:30 am – 4:30 pm ET

Welcome from the SIGCSE Chair

Welcome to the inaugural Association for Computing Machinery (ACM) Global Computing Education Conference (CompEd). CompEd is sponsored by the ACM Special Interest Group for Computer Science Education (SIGCSE).

When it was created by the SIGCSE Board, CompEd was envisioned as an opportunity for SIGCSE to reach new audiences around the globe. The proposal was inspired by the very positive reaction to temporarily moving one of our other conferences from Europe to South America. That experience made it clear to the SIGCSE Board that there were people who wanted to be a part of our community but who could not travel to any of our existing conferences on a regular basis. It was our hope that CompEd would serve those people by expanding and connecting the computing education community around the globe.

It is difficult to imagine now, but the SIGCSE Board voted to create CompEd in February 2017. It is a testament to the dedication and hard work of the CompEd steering committee, organizing committee, and program committee that the conference has come together in the way that it has. I would especially like to thank steering committee chair Brett Becker, steering committee members Susan Rodger, Boots Cassel, Alison Clear, and Ming Zhang, conference co-chairs Ming Zhang and Bo Yang, and program co-chairs Steve Cooper and Andrew Luxton-Reilly. You have created something that was only a dream fifteen months ago, and I and the rest of the SIGCSE Board are in your debt.

As an attendee at the first CompEd you have a unique experience ahead of you. The conference offers all of the things you would expect at a SIGCSE conference, including paper, poster, panel, and birds-of-a-feather sessions, a keynote, and working groups taking place prior to the start of the conference. CompEd is also co-located with the 2019 ACM Turing Celebration Conference (TURC), which gives you the opportunity to see talks by Turing laureates and other notable computer scientists. Finally the conference offers the opportunity to see the Chengdu Research Base of Giant Panda Breeding, something that I highly recommend. I expect that we will all leave the conference energized about the experience.

CompEd 2019 is the first conference of its kind for SIGCSE. The conference organizers and the SIGCSE Board would appreciate hearing what you enjoyed about it, and you should complete your evaluation so that we can use your ideas to shape the next conference in 2021. We anticipate that this will be the first of many wonderful experiences in computing education communities around the globe.

Amber Settle
SIGCSE Chair, 2016-2019

CompEd 2019 Program Chairs' Welcome

Welcome to the inaugural ACM Global Computing Education Conference (CompEd 2019) being held May 17-19, 2019 in Chengdu, China! Slightly more than 20 years ago, SIGCSE made the decision to expand its successful annual US conference, the SIGCSE Symposium, and to offer an annual conference in Europe. The first Innovation and Technology in Computer Science Education conference (ITiCSE) was held in Barcelona, Spain, in June, 1996. Nearly 15 years ago, SIGCSE started supporting a third conference, the International Computing Education Research (ICER) conference. Held alternating years in the US, every fourth year in Europe, and every fourth year in Australasia, ICER focuses exclusively on computing education research. And now, SIGCSE is starting the offering of CompEd, to be held alternating years in different locations in the developing world. There is a growing worldwide interest in computing education, and we are thrilled with SIGCSE's decision to start regularly offering a fourth conference.

The CompEd conference, to be held May 17-19, 2019 (with working groups starting on May 14) will be a conference similar to ITiCSE and the SIGCSE Symposium. It will consist of paper, panel, working group, poster and birds of a feather (which will focus on international collaborations) sessions. The target audience for the conference will be both researchers in computer science education and practitioners. The conference will run approximately 2.5 days, with breaks for attendees to attend the Turing Award Celebration in China (TURC) keynote addresses. CompEd will be co-located with the TURC conference. The ACM SIGCSE China chapter traditionally meets at TURC and will instead be participating in CompEd. The Computing Curriculum 2020 task force (building from CC2005) will be held immediately prior to CompEd in Chengdu.

The topics of the new CompEd conference are:

1. Computing education research

2. Computing education experience reports and tools

3. New curricula, programs, and degrees

We quote from former SIGCSE Board chair Susan Rodger's original note to the SIGCSE community, in August 2018 (with minor corrections since in August 2018, the new conference had yet to be named):

"Think about attending CompEd, SIGCSE's newest conference. That's right, the SIGCSE Board is starting SIGCSE's fourth conference. CompEd will be held in Chengdu, China May 17-19, 2019. Chengdu is the capital of China's Sichuan province. CompEd will be co-located with the annual ACM Turing Celebration Conference - China (ACM TURC). If you are not familiar with ACM TURC, it usually has several Turing award winners as keynote speakers. CompEd will overlap with ACM TURC so that CompEd attendees can attend ACM TURC keynote sessions.

Why start another SIGCSE conference? First, our other three conferences are quite healthy. The SIGCSE Symposium in 2018 had over 1500 attendees, its largest number ever. The ICER conference has more than doubled in size since it started back in 2005. And the ITiCSE conference has been steady with around 200 or more attendees each year.

Second, the SIGCSE Board would like to reach the computer science education community in all parts of the world. The SIGCSE Symposium is only held in North America. ITiCSE is only held in or near Europe, with one exception. In 2016 ITiCSE was held in Peru with great success. With ITiCSE quite successful in Europe, we would like ITiCSE to stay in Europe. ICER is held in North America every other year, in Europe every fourth year and in Australasia every fourth year.

CompEd will be held in countries where SIGCSE does not have annual conferences. So it will not be held in North America or Europe. For its first three offerings, we are planning on holding CompEd every other year. The first CompEd will be held in China in 2019. We are considering India for the second CompEd conference in 2021. We'd love to hear from possible hosts for the third CompEd, perhaps in South America.

What is the focus of CompEd? We plan for it to focus on research and practice, and to have several ways to participate with papers (research, experience, curricula, position, etc), posters, working groups, birds of a feather sessions, and likely more. More information and the conference call for participation will be out soon."

We believe that Chengdu, China is the perfect location to host the first ever CompEd conference. Especially well known for its cooking and its Pandas, Chengdu is an old and historic city, and serves as the capital of Sichuan province, in southwestern China. While perhaps not as well-known as the cities of Beijing and Shanghai, Chengdu is a vibrant city that offers a multitude of sights and experiences for attendees to explore when not attending the CompEd conference.

The conference brings together the global computing education community with 125 total submissions. Authors of accepted papers come from Canada, China, Costa Rica, Finland, Hong Kong, Italy, Netherlands, New Zealand, Spain, Sweden, United States.

Table 1: CompEd 2019 Submission and Acceptance Statistics

Track	Submitted (N)	Accepted (N)	Acceptance Rate (%)
Papers	100	33	33%
Panels	3	2	67%
Birds of a Feather	4	2	50%
Posters	10	8	80%
Working Groups	8	3	38%

All papers were blind-reviewed by 5 reviewers, who then engaged in discussion led by one of the associate program chairs who also provided a meta-review and recommendation to the program chairs. In total, 87 reviewers and 13 associate program chairs contributed to a high-quality review process that ensured fair reviews for all papers.

This year, 33 papers (33%) were selected for presentation and inclusion in the proceedings, along with 3 panels, 4 birds of a feather sessions, and 10 posters. We were very pleased to be able to support 3 working groups immediately prior to the main conference. The working groups addressed topics related to online judge systems, barriers to adopting peer instruction, and teaching of computing ethics. As working group reports are among the most read and cited works published by the SIGCSE community, these groups are well positioned to make a valuable contribution. We anticipate that the working groups will be a major strength of the CompEd conference in future years and will continue to develop connections between computing education researchers globally.

The keynote address will be delivered by Dr Paul Denny from the University of Auckland. Typically, teachers and other subject experts create the learning resources that students use, such as textbooks, lecture notes, assignments and lab activities. However, there may be advantages in having students create some of these materials themselves. The keynote address will present the motivation for having students generate their own learning resources, discuss both practical challenges and measurable benefits, and summarise recent research involving tools such as PeerWise which hosts millions of student-generated practice questions.

Two awards were established to recognize the high quality of work published at CompEd. The Best Paper is awarded to An Exploration of Cognitive Shifting in Writing Code by Ilenia Fronza, Arto Hellas, Petri Ihantola and Tommi Mikkonen. The Program Chairs' Award goes to Impact of Open-Ended Assignments on Student Self-Efficacy in CS1 by Sadia Sharmin, Daniel Zingaro and Clare Brett. The Program Chairs' Award is given to the best paper in which the first author is a student.

The CompEd conference chairs would like to thank the SIGCSE community and the team of volunteers who have contributed to the organization and running of this event. We would particularly like to thank the steering committee for their tireless efforts, and the submission chair, Simon, for keeping the submissions and reviewing running so smoothly.

Steve Cooper
Program Co-Chair
University of Nebraska-Lincoln, USA

Andrew Luxton-Reilly
Program Co-Chair
University of Auckland, New Zealand

Table of Contents

Paper Session: Tools for Students

Paper Session: CS1 Practice

Panel Perspectives on Global Bachelor Computing Education

Paper Session: Upper Level CS

Paper Session: Tools for instructors

Paper Session: CS1 Observations Part 2

Birds of a Feather

Paper Session: Pre-college Part 2

Panel The Computing in Data Science

Paper Session: Upper Level CS Part 2

Paper Session: CS1 Metacognitive

Paper Session: CS1 Online

Posters

CompEd 2019 Conference Organization

Program Committee

Program Co-Chairs: Steve Cooper *(University of Nebraska-Lincoln, USA)*
Andrew Luxton-Reilly *(University of Auckland, New Zealand)*

Working Groups Chair: Judy Sheard *(Monash University, Australia)*

Panels and Posters Co-Chairs: Stephan Krusche *(Technical University of Munich, Germany)*
Carsten Kleiner *(Hannover University of Applied Sciences, Germany)*

BoFs and Evaluations Co-Chairs: Yanxia Jia *(Arcadia University, USA)*
Francisco J. Gutierrez *(University of Chile, Chile)*

Organizing Committee

Steering Committee Brett A. Becker *(University College Dublin, Ireland/ Beijing-Dublin International College, China)*
Lillian "Boots" Cassel *(Villanova University, USA)*
Alison Clear *(Eastern Institute of Technology, New Zealand)*
Susan Rodger *(Duke University, USA)*
Ming Zhang *(Peking University, China)*

General Chairs Ming Zhang *(Peking University, China)*
Bo Yang *(Linyi University, China)*

Local Chairs Xi Wu *(Chengdu University of Information Technology, China)*
Juan Chen *(National University of Defense Technology, China)*

Local Committee: Junlin Lu *(Peking University, China)*
Yu Zhang *(University of Science and Technology of China, China)*
Wenjun Wu *(Beihang University, China)*
Jianguo Wei *(Tianjin University, China)*
Hong Yu *(Dalian Ocean University, China)*
Shuang Zhou *(Chengdu University of Information Technology, China)*

Registrar: Cary Laxer *(Rose-Hulman Institute of Technology, USA)*

Submissions Chair: Simon *(University of Newcastle, Australia)*

Publications/Publicity Chair: John Impagliazzo *(Hofstra University, USA)*

Reviewers (Continued):   Meng Han *(Kennesaw State University, USA)*
Qiang Hao *(Western Washington University, USA)*
Arto Hellas *(University of Helsinki, Finland)*
Wendy Huang *(Nanyang Technological University, Singapore)*
Janet Hughes *(The Open University, UK)*
Sarah J Huibregtse *(Rochester Institute of Technology, USA)*
Petros Kefalas *(The University of Sheffield International Faculty City College, Greece)*
Tobias Kohn *(University of Cambridge, UK)*
Anastasia Kurdia *(Tulane University, USA)*
Lisa Lacher *(University of Houston - Clear Lake, USA)*
Juho Leinonen *(University of Helsinki, Finland)*
Zhigang Li *(Kennesaw State University, USA)*
Jingsai Liang *(Westminster College, USA)*
Zilu Liang *(Westminster College, USA)*
Matija Lokar *(University of Ljubljana, Slovenia)*
Ana Paula Ludtke Ferreira *(Universidade Federal do Pampa, Brazil)*
Nicholas Lytle *(North Carolina State University, USA)*
Stephen MacNeil *(University of North Carolina at Charlotte, USA)*
Raina Mason *(Southern Cross University, Australia)*
William Mason *(Southern Cross University, Australia)*
Xiannong Meng *(Bucknell University, USA)*
Jose Carlos Meireles Metrôlho *(Polytechnic Institute of Castelo Branco, Portugal)*
Christophe Meudec *(Institute of Technology Carlow, Ireland)*
Razvan Mezei *(Saint Martin's University, USA)*
Paul Mihail *(Valdosta State University, USA)*
Karina Mochetti *(Universidade Federal Fluminense, Brazil)*
Niema Moshiri *(University of California San Diego, USA)*
Brandon Myers *(University of Iowa, USA)*
Eldanae Nogueira Teixeira *(COPPE - UFRJ, Brazil)*
Emma Norling *(The University of Sheffield, UK)*
Suhaib Obeidat *(Bloomfield College, USA)*
Oluwakemi Ola *(University of British Columbia, Canada)*
Mehdi Oulmakki *(African Leadership University, Rwanda)*
Miranda Parker *(Georgia Institute of Technology, USA)*
Andrew Petersen *(University of Toronto Mississauga, Canada)*
Yizhou Qian *(Jiangnan University, China)*
Dapeng Qu *(Liaoning University, China)*
Keith Quille *(Institute of Technology Tallaght, Ireland)*
Luiz Antonio Lima Rodrigues *(Londrina State University, Brazil)*
Mazyar Seraj *(University of Bremen, Germany)*
Lenandlar Singh *(University of Guyana, Guyana)*
Yang Song *(University of North Carolina Wilmington, USA)*
Anna Sotiriadou *(University of Sheffield International Faculty City College, Greece)*
Kalpathi Subramanian *(University of North Carolina at Charlotte, USA)*
Maciej Syslo *(UMK Torun, Poland)*
Sheng Tan *(Florida State University, USA)*

CompEd 2019 Sponsors & Supporters

Sponsor:

SIG CSE

Platinum-Plus Supporter: GitHub Education

Platinum Supporter: Google

Four Million Questions and a Few Answers

Lessons From Research on Student-Generated Resources

Paul Denny
The University of Auckland
Auckland, New Zealand
paul@cs.auckland.ac.nz

ABSTRACT

Typically, teachers and other subject experts create the learning resources that students use, such as textbooks, lecture notes, assignments and lab activities. The quality of the content generated by experts is high, and teachers can leverage years of classroom experience to develop effective resources.

There are, however, some advantages in having students create learning materials for their peers. Distributing the work required to generate resources enables the creation of large repositories of content very quickly. There are also learning benefits associated with students reflecting on, and explaining, their understanding of relevant concepts as they create resources. A number of interesting research questions arise — how does the quality of resources generated by students compare with those created by experts, what do students think about the shift in responsibility for creating resources, how can students be motivated to engage in both creating and using the generated resources, and what evidence exists for the learning benefits of such activities?

This talk will present the motivation for having students generate their own learning resources, discuss both practical challenges and measurable benefits, and answer the research questions above by drawing upon data from tools such as PeerWise which hosts several million student-generated practice questions.

CCS CONCEPTS

• **Applied computing** → **Collaborative learning**; • **Social and professional topics** → **Computing education**.

KEYWORDS

student-generated resources, peer learning, educational technology, student engagement, PeerWise

ACM Reference Format:
Paul Denny. 2019. Four Million Questions and a Few Answers: Lessons From Research on Student-Generated Resources. In *ACM Global Computing Education Conference 2019 (CompEd '19), May 17–19, 2019, Chengdu, Sichuan, China*. ACM, New York, NY, USA, 1 page. https://doi.org/10.1145/3300115.3312507

1 BIOGRAPHY

Paul Denny is a Senior Lecturer in Computer Science at the University of Auckland, New Zealand. His research interests include developing and evaluating tools for supporting collaborative learning, particularly involving student-generated resources, and exploring the ways that students engage with these environments. One of his developments, PeerWise, hosts more than four million practice questions, with associated solutions and explanations, created by students in 90 countries. He has fostered a community of educational researchers around this project, more than 100 of whom have published their research as a result.

Dr. Denny has received Best Paper Awards at SIGCSE 2019 and ICER 2008, and has published several other award-winning papers at venues such as SIGCHI, ITiCSE and ACE. He has been recognized for contributions to teaching both nationally and internationally, receiving the QS Reimagine Education Overall Award and the "ICT Tools for Teaching and Learning" Gold Award (2018), the Association of Commonwealth Universities Jacky McAleer Memorial Fellowship (2017), New Zealand's National Tertiary Teaching Excellence Award (2009), the Australasian Association for Engineering Education Award for Innovation in Curricula, Learning and Teaching (2009) and the Computing Research and Education Association of Australasia Teaching Award for Outstanding Contributions to Teaching (2010).

Comparison of Learning Programming between Interactive Computer Tutors and Human Teachers

Ruiqi Shen, Donghee Yvette Wohn, Michael J. Lee
New Jersey Institute of Technology
Newark, New Jersey, USA
{rs858,donghee.y.wohn,mjlee}@njit.edu

ABSTRACT

People typically learn programming from teachers in in-person courses or online tutorials. Interactive computer tutors—systems that deliver learning content interactively—have become more prevalent in online settings for teaching skills such as computer programming. Research has shown the efficiency and effectiveness of learning programming from teachers, interactive computer tutors, and a combination of both. However, there is limited understanding of learners' comparative perspectives about their experience learning from these different resources. We conducted an exploratory study using semi-structured interviews, recruiting 20 participants that had experience learning programming from both teachers and interactive computer tutors. We identified factors that learners like and dislike from both learning methods and discussed the strengths and weaknesses of them. Based on our findings, we propose suggestions for designers of interactive computer tutors, and for programming educators.

CCS CONCEPTS

• **Social and professional topics** → **Computing education**.

KEYWORDS

Tutors; interactive computing tutors; student perspectives; computing education; teachers

ACM Reference Format:
Ruiqi Shen, Donghee Yvette Wohn, Michael J. Lee. 2019. Comparison of Learning Programming between Interactive Computer Tutors and Human Teachers. In *ACM Global Computing Education Conference 2019 (CompEd '19), May 17–19, 2019, Chengdu, Sichuan, China.* ACM, New York, NY, USA, 7 pages. https://doi.org/10.1145/3300115.3309506

1 INTRODUCTION

Learning programming is considered a difficult process that requires considerable practice just like learning a natural language. However, unlike natural languages that can be used in multiple contexts and modalities in everyday experience, learners typically program within the constraints of a computer screen [26]. The difficult nature of programming may contribute to the high dropout rates in related courses in both classrooms [18, 40] and massive open online courses (MOOCs) [28, 37]. Due to this difficulty, choosing the right learning tools and methods is important for programming learners, regardless of their prior experience.

Like all learning methods, however, each has benefits and drawbacks. One-on-one tutoring would be an ideal strategy to teach and learn programming—human tutoring is one of the most effective ways for students to overcome programming barriers [15], but the lack of teachers in computing education has always been a concern of researchers and educators [16], and many learners have limited access to tailored, in-person programming courses. Even for those who have access to courses, large lecture-based formats make individualized attention from the instructor for tailored instruction unlikely [2]. Besides traditional in-classroom lectures, MOOCs are an attractive, alternative educational resource for learners since they are more affordable, accessible, and can support more students simultaneously than traditional classrooms [36, 43]. However, the lack of interactions with instructors [31] and the lack of extrinsic motivations [10, 16] are major limitations for MOOCs and are development opportunities for the future.

For the purposes of this paper, we focus only on MOOCs that deliver instruction through a virtual agent, or *interactive computer tutor* (as opposed to those primarily giving instruction through text or video). Farrell et al. were the first to introduce an interactive computer tutor (ICT) for teaching programming [9]. They described it as a system with two components: a "problem solver" (which can interpret learners' code and give feedback), and an "advisor" (which provides tutorials that guide learners throughout the whole learning process) [9]. Systems for teaching programming such as Codecademy, Datacamp, and Treehouse, are much like the ICT described by Farrell, including a problem solver and advisor. We define ICTs as having these two features, and examine these types of systems in this paper. We choose to study ICTs rather than other types of MOOCs because literature has shown that these interactive tools are effective in delivering programming courses [7, 19] and are gaining more popularity with learners [25, 27].

While learning programming from either ICTs or teachers have shown positive student learning outcomes, there are few studies examining learners' perspectives on their experience using and comparing these two methods. Exploring these perspectives can lead to important insights for better designs and highlight effective techniques that learners look for while learning to program.

This paper describes an exploratory qualitative study examining the learning experience from the *learners' perspective*, contrasting their views on learning from an ICT and from a classroom teacher. By understanding the learners' perspective on instructors, we aim to find ways to improve current ICTs' and teachers' teaching methods, and to further improve learners' educational experience.

2 RELATED WORK

2.1 Learning from Interactive Computer Tutors

The key to successfully master programming skills is through extensive practice and making mistakes [1]. However, during the learning process, students have more difficulties in applying programming in practice than understanding basic programming concepts [35]. Many MOOC websites such as Codecademy and Khan Academy provide interactive learning environments for programming. They integrate tutorials with extensive exercises and code editors with feedback systems [30]. Empirical studies have found that students learning programming interactively through well-designed computer systems achieve good learning outcomes and increased self-efficacy [9, 19].

What are the good features of an ICT for delivering programming courses? Prior work has found that watching videos and solving multiple choice questions are not sufficient in learning hands-on skills or practical programming tasks [34], and that instant feedback for students' submissions are important in learning programming [20, 21, 34]. Staubitz et al. proposed five requirements for an ICT to deliver programming courses: Versatility (support multiple programming languages), Novice-Friendliness (UI catered for beginners), Scalability (support for many users), Security (secure students' submissions/assessments), and Interoperability (integrate into existing infrastructures) [34]. Pritchard & Vasiga summarized that embedded coding environments are beneficial for students' continuity in learning-by-doing [30]. While most educators will agree that a mentor is essential in the initial learning process for beginners, Liyanagunawardena et al. showed that in an online course, the learner's community itself can act as a mentor and could possibly mitigate the issue of not having enough teachers for students [22]. Users can also recognize the benefits of features such as intentional instructional design (well-designed instructions), learning analytics (information for self-reflection), and instant feedback [42]. Our study expands on these works, aiming to explore whether these commercial systems (e.g., Codecademy and Datacamp)—which include features such as the ones mentioned above—can be considered good ICTs, and what users of these systems think about them.

2.2 Learning from Teachers

Unlike computer tutors, which have a relatively short history in education, human teachers have been a part of education for centuries. Several studies have demonstrated the effectiveness of human teachers [4, 6, 24]. A teacher can guide students and can have them do as much thinking as possible before giving hints or answers [11]. Teachers can also intervene at the right moment to prevent students from becoming too frustrated [24], which is especially important in the early stage of learning, when learners have a higher likelihood of quitting [40, 41]. Teachers are also adaptable, with research showing that interventions in teaching styles can drastically improve teachers' effectiveness [38].

In addition to one-to-one teaching, there is also research about one-to-many teaching. Robins et al. [32] concluded that an effective programming class should stimulate students' interest and involvement, by setting clear goals and actively engaging participants in course materials and problem-solving activities [32]. However, what teaching approach contributes to an effective programming class remains a question. Pears et al.'s overview of programming classes found little systematic evidence to support any particular teaching approach that answers the question of how to teach programming effectively [29]. From a learner's perspective, Tan et al.'s survey study indicates that programming learners find the practical application of programming most difficult, and therefore lab sessions with consultation are considered more helpful than pure lectures [35]. However, questions such as what kind of lab sessions they like and whether they could get sufficient consultation opportunities remain largely unknown to us.

2.3 Learning From the Learners' Perspective

Based on our literature review, we found a gap in knowledge examining the learners' perspectives on receiving instruction from either ICTs or teachers. It is important to examine the learners' perspective on the difference(s) between computers and teachers, and what their preference are when interacting with either of these choices when learning to program. The learning method they choose may influence their perception of programming skills, and therefore, potentially affect retention rates and learning experiences. Therefore, we explore the following two research questions in this paper:

RQ1: What do learners (a) like, and (b) dislike, about learning programming from interactive computer tutors (ICTs)?

RQ2: What do learners (a) like, and (b) dislike, about learning programming from teachers?

3 METHOD

To answer these research questions, we conducted in-person, semi-structured interviews with 20 subjects. Interviews are a commonly used method for exploratory studies [8, 33, 39], especially to gain an in-depth perspective into subjects' views and experiences when there is limited research in the literature [13]. We recruited participants through snowball sampling [14], where each participant suggested at least one additional person that met our inclusion criteria and that they thought would be a good candidate for us to interview. The initial six participants were students from a mailing list that represented a wide range of demographics (e.g., gender, ethnicity, age, job/major) from two public universities in the northeast United States (US), with subsequent participants being classmates, alumna, or professional colleagues distributed across the US.

One researcher conducted all the interviews, either in-person (n=16) or on the phone (n=4). All interviews were recorded, averaging 29 minutes per interview. We required participants to have experience learning programming from both teachers and ICTs. We defined a *teacher* as a human instructor in a classroom setting, and used Farrell et al.'s two-component definition for *ICTs* (see introduction and [9]). We intentionally did not specify ICTs any further, so that our participants could talk broadly about the technologies they had used without being limited to a specific type of ICT.

The interview questions included two major parts: (1) behavioral questions that asked participants about their occupations, majors, coding experience, and coding-related behaviors (e.g., "In general, how long have you been programming?"); and (2) research-related questions that probed participants about their experiences learning programming from both ICTs and human teachers (e.g., "What problems did you encounter, and how did you resolve them?").

All of the recorded interviews were transcribed and coded using NVivo. Two researchers coded the interview transcripts using the three-stage coding process outlined by Cambell et al. in their work describing how to measure intercoder reliability for semi-structured interview studies [5]. This was done iteratively until the two researchers came to a consensus on codes and a sufficient level of intercoder reliability and intercoder agreement (stages 1 and 2); then the full set of transcripts were analyzed (stage 3) [5]. Since participants could state their likes, dislikes, and preferences in every research related question, we read through all the transcriptions and assigned tags to any emergent patterns (e.g., code editors, content design, flexibility, and efficiency). During the process, we read through those tagged texts, and consolidated similar tags into one tag (i.e., code families [5]), or split one tag into different tags. This resulted in 19 themes (each research question has several themes) and more than 50 tags. We analyzed all 20 interview transcripts, reaching a high level of intercoder reliability (.87) and intercoder agreement (.92)[1]. We present representative quotes from participants in our results to better explain our themes.

4 RESULTS

Our participants included 9 females and 11 males, ranging from 22 to 32 years old (median 26). Everyone was from a STEM field/major or job, consisting of 13 students (6 females and 7 males), and 7 working professionals (3 females and 4 males). Their experience in programming ranged from 1 to 15 years (median 4.5).

4.1 RQ1a: What Do Learners *Like* About Learning Programming from Interactive Computer Tutors?

4.1.1 Provides a Code Editor. A code editor allows learners to write and run their code directly on the ICT. Most of the participants considered this feature to be helpful, and there are three main reasons: First, a code editor dismisses the need to set up a local environment. 7 out of 20 participants mentioned that they did not need to set up local environment when they only wanted to learn some basics. The code editor saves time from having to set up a local programming/development environments.

Second, a code editor provides one-window convenience. Participants mentioned that they liked the code editor because they could see the tutorials, examples, and do the exercises in the same window, which was more convenient than switching windows between tutorials and coding tools. P9 told us how she found the code editor to be convenient: "*If I follow YouTube, it's not convenient because I code on my local computer, I watch the video, then switch to my software. But in Dataquest, the screen is separated in two parts. You can see the instruction and at the same time, you can type your code.*"

Third, a code editor provides a similar, but better-than-real environment. Two participants mentioned that they liked the code

editor because it was similar to the real coding environment but better in terms that the code editor in the ICT could give customized feedback while a real environment could not.

4.1.2 Content Design. This refers to the course materials and the way ICTs organize and deliver information. The content design can be grouped into three main features. First, ICTs organize and display lessons with a clear outline, which learners can use to see exactly where they are in the learning process (i.e., curriculum). P20 described how she found the organization useful in Dataquest: "*The lessons are very simplified [in Dataquest]. They are broken down into different modules, so it makes it very easy to consume.*"

Second, ICTs provide practice immediately after each tutorial, so learners can (re)apply whatever they learned quickly. P3 mentioned how the immediate practice was useful: "*for the W3 school, you'll first grab the same concept, but immediately you will use the 'try it yourself' demo page. You can put this knowledge into real world practice. That's why I like it.*"

Third, ICTs provide examples. Participants mentioned that the examples from ICTs were very helpful to understand the lessons. P5 is a novice programmer, and his biggest concern was that he could not visualize what his code would output. He described his experience of learning web development in Codecademy, and how it helped him with examples: "*It [Codecademy] has an example to show you the final version, you can test again and compare your code to the example, that will help you to improve your code.*"

4.1.3 Flexible. Participants enjoyed the flexibility in learning when using ICTs. Flexibility allows learners to go at their own pace whenever and wherever they want. 8 participants mentioned that they wished to learn at their own pace, and so learning from ICTs could satisfy their needs. P2 told us that he preferred online learning because he could learn at his own pace: "*For lectures [that are] 3 hours long, if you don't understand something an hour in, then you kind of waste two hours. Whereas you can make sure you understand it online before proceeding onto the next section or the next concept.*"

With an ICT, learners can learn whenever and wherever they want. P20 gave us her opinion on location flexibility: "*Like, I don't have Python installed on my phone and I can still do my lessons [on Dataquest] maybe if I'm in transit traveling somewhere.*" In the case of P8, he was a full-time student who also held a part-time job. He told us how time flexibility helped him learn. "*I could do it at 2am if I want. A teacher is not available at 2am,*" he said.

4.1.4 Efficient. Some participants compared the ICT with other resources and concluded that they liked the efficiency when learning from ICTs. 2 participants compared the time spent learning from an ICT and from a teacher in a classroom. They felt that being present in a physical classroom was time-consuming, just as P19 told us: "*Because if I want to go to school and take a class, that's going to be very time-consuming.*"

Four participants compared ICTs with textbooks. They thought that learning from ICTs helped them apply skills more efficiently than reading textbooks. For example, P7 told us: "*I think for textbook resource, one annoying thing for me is it doesn't show you like all the command[s] and what it does. So, you have to waste time reading it yourself, but for Codeacademy, they just teach you each command. It's a faster way to learn it.*"

---

[1]Scores were calculated using the proportion agreement procedure [5]. We note that while well-established in quantitative work, there is no community consensus about the applicability of inter -rater/coder reliability measures for qualitative studies [3, 17].

4.1.5 Provide Sufficient Help. Participants mentioned that they could use in-context resources within the interface to get assistance if needed. There are three specific features that provide sufficient help for learners: (1) hint systems, (2) staff help, and (3) discussion panels. A hint system is the basic feature providing help (usually generated automatically), and the very first help learners will receive. P14 gave us an example on a hint system: "*you can just get the hints and they'll give you a hint and then you can either get the answer or you can just continue trying, but you're not just stuck there if you really can't figure it out.*"

Although the next two kinds of help require some type of human intervention, we report them since they were emergent themes. Currently, it appears that ICTs do not have the capability to supply some types of help that learners want (but humans can provide). However, this may change with advancements in natural language processing and machine learning, where systems might better detect and understand the context of their users' need for help.

If the hint system fails to achieve learners' expectations, some ICTs provide staff help. Staff are real people who are course experts. P1 gave us an example: "*They have two or three hints that they give, after that, they even say if you have any issues, 'we have [real] people who would help you out,' and you can send your queries to them.*"

Built-in discussion panels also provide a place where learners can discuss their questions and ask for help. P9 liked discussion panels very much and she said: "*Because in Dataquest, they also have something called 'the community.' You can search [for] your questions in the community and the community members will post the answers. You can refer to their answers.*"

4.1.6 Designed for Various Learner Levels. Some ICTs provide different pathways based on skill-level. With these, learners can find courses matching their experience. P16 told us: "*For Codecademy, they have levels, like 'did you just start learning code,' 'you already have some experience,' 'you're an expert,' like that. So that really helps because if you already know coding you don't need a very simple example because it's too easy.*"

Interestingly, one participant mentioned that he liked the feature of Codecademy that locks access to later content until finishing the current module. He had one year of programming experience, and he emphasized many times his anxiety as a beginner. This feature forced him to learn step-by-step. Another participant mentioned that he liked the short video tutorials provided by Treehouse. Compared with a long video tutorial, these short videos relieve the cognitive load of learners.

4.2 RQ1b: What Do Learners *Dislike* About Learning Programming from Interactive Computer Tutors?

4.2.1 Content Design. This again refers to the course materials and the way ICTs organize and deliver information. While most people liked the content provided by ICTs, there were also participants who did not like the content design. Four participants thought that the tutorials and practice materials were too basic to be useful. They liked ICTs but wished they could provide more advanced content. P2 had 4 years of programming experience; he considered himself as having a good understanding of programming basics,

and expressed his concerns: "*I was doing C++, but I kind of stopped because I thought it was too easy and too basic [...] They just teach you such basic concepts and they don't go in-depth.*'

One participant disliked course content because the sections were redundant. He said: "*At the beginning, I will find they are pretty useful, but like 4-5 lessons after, I find the content to be very dry, meaning it's really the same thing over-and-over again, I'm not really learning a lot of things that weren't [covered] there before.*"

While some experienced learners considered the content covered by ICTs to be too basic, other junior-level learners mentioned that sometimes, information were too brief to understand. Some ICTs provide short introductions, but do not really explain the logic behind the material. P11 started programming 2 years ago, and was struggling to understand the complex logic behind concepts. "*For me, I don't like reading introduction[s online], because they want to simplify their content and the introduction is so brief. Sometimes I don't fully understand the [programming] language,*" she said.

4.2.2 Locks Access to More Advanced Concepts. Participants said that some ICTs required them to finish the current module before unlocking the next one. While we mentioned that one participant liked this feature earlier, four participants disliked this feature. They had prior experience and had clear goals on what they had to learn. This feature limited their learning efficiency. P13 was a working professional who had 2+ years of programming experience and learned programming for fun in his leisure time. He said: "*I know what this is, and I want to skip it to [go to] the next module. I'm not able to do that, because I got to complete the first module, and then go to the second module. So, I didn't find that to be very user-friendly.*"

4.2.3 Does not Provide Sufficient Help. Although some participants believed they could get sufficient help from ICTs, four participants disagreed. These participants did not believe that the tutor could guide them effectively to figure out the logic behind a problem. P5, a novice programmer, shared his experience getting stuck on a problem in Codecademy: "*They [Codecademy] will actually show me the right answer. I still don't know what's wrong with my answer and it didn't show me or highlight the mistakes that I made, so I still don't know the answer.*"

4.3 RQ2a: What Do Learners *Like* About Learning Programming from Teachers?

4.3.1 Has Real Life Experience in Programming. 7 out of 20 participants mentioned that they liked to learn from teachers who share their real-life experience in programming. These experiences include: how to avoid common mistakes, how to style the code, tips on interviews, and how to become a good programmer. P5 was a beginner in programming, he said: "*They [professors] always try to tell you how to avoid mistakes.*" P11 had 2 years of experience in programming, but she was anxious about being a novice. She enjoyed learning from her teachers. "*They teach some things about the languages and they also tell some real experience for coding, and even some tips about interview and future working. They told us how a good programmer should do their job,*" she said.

One participant observed that teachers are not only experienced in programming, but also in teaching. Teachers know and can focus on parts that students have the most difficulty understanding.

4.3.2 Provides Solid Learning Experience. Participants believed they could learn programming more concretely and systematically with teachers. Teachers introduce new concepts, but also provide more information and background about these concepts. Teachers also help students stay on the right track. P4 had 10 years of programming experience, and suggested beginners to start programming with a good teacher. He said: "*I believe a good teacher will teach you knowledge in a systematic way. If you have zero knowledge, the best way is to learn from a teacher, because if you learn from an online app, your knowledge is scattered, and it's not systematic. You learn piece-by-piece, [so] you might miss some bigger parts.*"

4.3.3 Has Conversations. Conversations with teachers are valuable to learners. Participants thought that they could discuss ideas and explain their problems better through conversations. P17 was experienced in programming and was full of project ideas that he would like to discuss with his advisor. He said: "*When you communicate with him, firstly you can solve your problem. And secondly if you have some ideas, you can talk with him and he is experienced, so he'll give you some feedback on your ideas and you know how to improve yourself or how to improve your program.*"

Another 3 participants felt conversations allowed teachers to better understand students' problems. Face-to-face conversation with experts is an easier way to get problems solved than sending emails or searching for answers elsewhere, because learners can use various methods to express themselves in-person (e.g., drawing, writing, gesticulating). P10 told us that she could show her work directly to teachers when communicating face-to-face, so that the teachers can better understand her questions with real examples.

4.3.4 Provides Real-Time Help. Participants mentioned that they could have their questions answered immediately when they were in class with teachers. When learners program, it is common to encounter errors. However, if these errors are not solved immediately, it may lead to other issues, causing the learner to get stuck. ICTs usually cannot provide real-time help for specific questions, while teachers can. When asked why they like to learn programming from teachers, P11, a beginner said: "*I think it is better with a teacher. Because if there are any questions you can immediately ask for help.*" Another more advanced programmer, P16, said: "*So, in-person it's more instant and I can do some things right away and get out the way whatever question I have.*"

4.3.5 Displays Code Example. Three participants liked teachers who showed code examples in class. P2 had 4 years of programming experience; he had some teachers who would just lecture for hours and teachers who showed code examples. He thought that he got little from the former because he could not understand the lecture content without any examples. He had a teacher who made class easier by showing code examples. He said: "*She basically taught and then she had her code that helped us, whereas other professors were just lecturing for three hours.*"

4.4 RQ2b: What Do Learners *Dislike* About Learning Programming from Teachers?

4.4.1 Not Efficient. Most participants thought that learning from teachers was not efficient. Teachers typically take time in providing assignments and giving feedback. In contrast, online tools do these

immediately and on-demand. As P2 told us: "*Because at the same time a teacher, you don't get assignments as quickly as you would online. So, the feedback comes in once a week as opposed to maybe you could literally do the whole course in a day if you want.*"

The lecturing style of the teacher may also be less efficient than reading the course materials. P6 had 15 years of programming experience. Most of the teachers he had would just read from the textbooks. He expressed his frustration with these types of teachers since he could just read from the textbook himself at home.

In addition, three participants felt online materials were easier to access than teachers. For example, P13 stated that online materials could be accessed quickly, while for teachers, he needed to register and pay for a course, and even be physically present in class.

4.4.2 Does Not Have Same Pace with Students. Teachers' speed of instruction was also a large concern for learners. 9 out of 20 participants had the experience of being unable to keep up with the teachers' pace. This happened when the teacher delivered the content too quickly, or when students had difficulties understanding some points, but the teacher kept moving forward. For example, P20 had a fast-paced programming course. As a novice programmer with little experience, she could not catch up with the progress, so she turned to online courses for help. She said: "*And with class, things go by so quickly, we meet only once a week and we have to cover so much. So, I feel like I'm lagging behind, I'm not catching up fast enough with the professor in the class, so I went to do something online where it can go at my own pace.*"

Two participants had the opposite experience—they found classes too slow. P16 was a student who always learned things quickly, and so, when she took a class but was ahead of the teacher's pace, she felt bored. She said: "*The class gets boring, because you already know. [...] there are students around you that are still asking questions and they don't get it, it's very hard for them to understand.*"

4.4.3 Provides Inflexible Curriculum. Sometimes, the content provided in a course were not what learners wanted. P12 had learned programming for years. When he was in college, he selected a C++ course, wishing to learn some advanced topics. However, the course he attended only covered basic concepts. He told us how disappointed he was: "*what he taught during lecture, I already know, and what he taught was just the basic syntax, but he did not introduce those advanced [content] which [...] I already learned from another way. That's why I say he is not very helpful.*"

While P10, who was less experienced than P12, told us that she wished to learn some basics, but what the teacher taught was more advanced. She said: "*I figured I will get a tutor to teach me the basics, because he [professor] didn't teach us the basics.*"

4.4.4 Teaching Competency. Some of the participants questioned their teachers' programming competence. Three participants thought their teachers were not experienced in programming, and believed that a good programming teacher should be a good programmer. P9 was disappointed with her programming teacher when he could not explain example code in detail. She said: "*he is not experienced in programming. All of his code is just copy-paste from another website, and then sharing it to you. He can't explain any details to you.*"

Programming skills and new technologies are constantly changing, but participants had concerns that their teachers' skills were not up-to-date. For example, P12 had a solid foundation in programming; his goal was to learn new technologies. He found that teachers in school did not satisfy his needs. "*I think the teacher is usually far behind the current progress [...] But what I want to learn, is always something new,*" he said.

4.4.5 Is Not Responsive. Some participants felt that they lacked teacher attention in large classes. "*They [professors] are always busy; your problems might not be solved in time,*" P18 said.

Lack of responsiveness may also be attributed to a teacher's personal style. P17 told us one of his teachers who never replied their emails, he said: "*one of my professors never replied [to] my e-mails. The only way you'll find him is in his class. So, I will only have limited chances to ask questions.*"

5 DISCUSSION

We identified many features that make learners like or dislike learning from ICTs and teachers. Efficiency and practice were the two main factors that learners care about. Since most of our participants learned programming with the goal of applying it quickly into work or study, learning efficiency was their biggest concern. Most of the participants thought that learning-by-doing was the best way to master programming skills, so immediate practice was also a consideration when choosing learning methods. In addition, our participants were not satisfied with single-media instructions such as textbooks or video. Our findings have implications for designers of ICTs and teachers who teach programming.

For ICTs, the biggest strengths that most participants mentioned were code editors and additional practice, while a major weakness was the content design (too basic, repetitive, or brief). To address this issue, designers could provide more advanced, practice-oriented tutorials by taking advantage of the availability of code editors.

The existence of both basic and advanced experience levels leads to another problem we identified during interviews. Two participants liked the features that some ICTs separate the content for different level of learners; one beginner programmer liked the features that the computer forced him to learn step-by-step (by locking content until finishing the current activity), whereas four, more experienced learners, did not like this feature. A key design consideration is to gauge a learner's experience at the beginning of the course/tutorial/activity so that the teacher or ICT can deliver content in a manner consistent with one's experience.

According to our findings, ICTs were good at delivering content with related exercises in an efficient manner, while teachers did a better job in providing customized help with real life experience. Both ICTs and teachers can gain benefits from each other. First, teaching applications can hire experts, who can provide help for questions when requested by online learners. Experts can also be present in the system's online learning community to have conversations with learners.

Second, one of our findings suggests that teachers were experienced in delivering knowledge, so they knew what parts of the course content might be most difficult to students, so that they could pay extra attention when teaching those parts. ICTs can achieve this feature by gathering data about different sections of their course content (e.g., how many tries does someone take to write the correct code, or how much time do they spend on a concept) and provide extra instruction, help, or practice for the parts that most learners have difficulties with.

Third, most participants indicated that they valued the opportunity to have conversations with teachers. Reasons include gaining coding tips, real life experience as programmers, exchanging project ideas, and getting help with questions. Listening to long lectures without interactions were disliked by students. There is potential to combine ICTs into programming classes to compliment teachers. Our findings suggest that existing ICTs do a good job in delivering basic concepts and exercises. Therefore, teachers may be able to have ICTs deliver basic information, and spend the time saved having more conversations with students regarding problems, projects, and real-life experience in programming.

6 LIMITATIONS & FUTURE WORK

Our study has limitations that present opportunities for further research. First, our recruitment method may have introduced a sampling bias. However, we found that our participants represented a wide variation of demographic factors and years of experience with coding. Second, we had a total of 20 participants in our study, which may raise questions about the representativeness of our sample and generalizability of our findings. We reached data saturation [12, 23] on our 16th interview and verified that our additional participants did not provide substantially different information from prior participants. Third, we identified that factors such as learning environment (e.g., summer camp, college course, vocational training) and learning objectives (e.g., learning for work, school practice, or personal interest) may affect how learners evaluate their learning experience. We will conduct further research to explore whether learning environments and learning objectives, or even other factors (e.g., gender, age, job, level of experience, order of learning from a specific type of tutor), affect how learners evaluate their learning experience(s). Lastly, we used participants' self-reported number of years in programming to describe them in our study (e.g., "P11 had 2 years of experience in programming."). However, self-reported years of experience may not reflect participants' actual programming ability or expertise. Future studies can examine the relationship between years of experience and programming ability. Other objective measures (e.g., test of knowledge) can be used to gauge learners' programming ability and experience level.

7 CONCLUSION

In this paper, we explored learners' perspectives on receiving instructions from human teachers versus interactive computer tutors when learning programming. We found that efficiency and practice are the two main factors that learners care about when choosing between these two types of instruction. Our findings also suggest the strength and weakness of learning from interactive computer tutors and teachers, which we use as a basis for design suggestions for these types of instruction.

ACKNOWLEDGMENTS

This work was supported in part by the National Science Foundation under grant IIS-1657160. Any opinions, findings, conclusions or recommendations are those of the authors and do not necessarily reflect the views of the National Science Foundation.

REFERENCES

[1] Carlos Alario-Hoyos, Carlos Delgado Kloos, Iria Estévez-Ayres, Carmen Fernández-Panadero, Jorge Blasco, Sergio Pastrana, and J Villena-Román. 2016. Interactive activities: the key to learning programming with MOOCs. *European Stakeholder Summit on Experiences and Best Practices in and Around MOOCs, EMOOCS* (2016), 319.

[2] John R. Anderson and Edward Skwarecki. 1986. The automated tutoring of introductory computer programming. *Commun. ACM* 29, 9 (1986), 842–849.

[3] David Armstrong, Ann Gosling, John Weinman, and Theresa Marteau. 1997. The place of inter-rater reliability in qualitative research: an empirical study. *Sociology* 31, 3 (1997), 597–606.

[4] Benjamin S Bloom. 1984. The 2 sigma problem: The search for methods of group instruction as effective as one-to-one tutoring. *Educational Researcher* 13, 6 (1984), 4–16.

[5] John Campbell, Charles Quincy, Jordan Osserman, and Ove Pedersen. 2013. Coding in-depth semistructured interviews: Problems of unitization and intercoder reliability and agreement. *Sociological Methods & Research* 42, 3 (2013), 294–320.

[6] Peter A Cohen, James A Kulik, and Chen-Lin C Kulik. 1982. Educational outcomes of tutoring: A meta-analysis of findings. *American Educational Research Journal* 19, 2 (1982), 237–248.

[7] Brian LF Daku and Keith Jeffrey. 2000. An interactive computer-based tutorial for MATLAB. In *Frontiers in Education Conference (FIE)*, Vol. 2. IEEE, F2D–2.

[8] Kathleen DeMarrais. 2004. Qualitative interview studies: Learning through experience. *Foundations for research: Methods of inquiry in education and the social sciences* 1, 1 (2004), 51–68.

[9] Robert G Farrell, John R Anderson, and Brian J Reiser. 1984. An Interactive Computer-Based Tutor for LISP.. In *AAAI*. 106–109.

[10] Gerhard Fischer. 2014. Beyond hype and underestimation: identifying research challenges for the future of MOOCs. *Distance Education* 35, 2 (2014), 149–158.

[11] Barbara A Fox. 1991. Cognitive and interactional aspects of correction in tutoring. *Teaching knowledge and intelligent tutoring* 01 (1991).

[12] Jill J Francis, Marie Johnston, Clare Robertson, Liz Glidewell, Vikki Entwistle, Martin P Eccles, and Jeremy M Grimshaw. 2010. What is an adequate sample size? Operationalising data saturation for theory-based interview studies. *Psychology and Health* 25, 10 (2010), 1229–1245.

[13] Paul Gill, Kate Stewart, Elizabeth Treasure, and Barbara Chadwick. 2008. Methods of data collection in qualitative research: interviews and focus groups. *British Dental Journal* 204, 6 (2008), 291.

[14] Leo A Goodman. 1961. Snowball sampling. *The Annals of Mathematical Statistics* (1961), 148–170.

[15] Philip J Guo. 2015. Codeopticon: Real-time, one-to-many human tutoring for computer programming. In *ACM Symposium on User Interface Software & Technology*. ACM, 599–608.

[16] Mark Guzdial. 2014. Limitations of MOOCs for Computing Education-Addressing our needs: MOOCs and technology to advance learning and learning research (Ubiquity symposium). *Ubiquity* 2014, July (2014), 1.

[17] Kevin A Hallgren. 2012. Computing inter-rater reliability for observational data: an overview and tutorial. *Tutorials in quantitative methods for psychology* 8, 1 (2012), 23.

[18] Päivi Kinnunen and Lauri Malmi. 2006. Why students drop out CS1 course?. In *ACM International Computing Education Research*. ACM, 97–108.

[19] Kris MY Law, Victor CS Lee, and Yuen-Tak Yu. 2010. Learning motivation in e-learning facilitated computer programming courses. *Computers & Education* 55, 1 (2010), 218–228.

[20] Michael J Lee and Andrew J Ko. 2011. Personifying programming tool feedback improves novice programmers' learning. In *International Workshop on Computing Education Research*. ACM, 109–116.

[21] Michael J Lee, Andrew J Ko, and Irwin Kwan. 2013. In-game assessments increase novice programmers' engagement and level completion speed. In *ACM Conference on International Computing Education Research*. ACM, 153–160.

[22] Tharindu R. Liyanagunawardena, Karsten O. Lundqvist, Luke Micallef, and Shirley A. Williams. 2014. Teaching programming to beginners in a massive open online course. (2014).

[23] Kirsti Malterud, Volkert Dirk Siersma, and Ann Dorrit Guassora. 2016. Sample size in qualitative interview studies: guided by information power. *Qualitative health research* 26, 13 (2016), 1753–1760.

[24] Douglas C Merrill, Brian J Reiser, Michael Ranney, and J Gregory Trafton. 1992. Effective tutoring techniques: A comparison of human tutors and intelligent tutoring systems. *Journal of the Learning Sciences* 2, 3 (1992), 277–305.

[25] Briana B Morrison and Betsy DiSalvo. 2014. Khan academy gamifies computer science. In *ACM Technical Symposium on Computer Science Education*. ACM, 39–44.

[26] Robert Moser. 1997. A fantasy adventure game as a learning environment: why learning to program is so difficult and what can be done about it. In *ACM SIGCSE Bulletin*, Vol. 29. ACM, 114–116.

[27] Robert Murphy, Larry Gallagher, Andrew Krumm, Jessica Mislevy, and Amy Hafter. 2014. Research on the use of Khan Academy in schools: Research brief. (2014).

[28] Daniel Fo Onah, Jane Sinclair, and Russell Boyatt. 2014. Dropout rates of massive open online courses: behavioural patterns. *EDULEARN* (2014), 5825–5834.

[29] Arnold Pears, Stephen Seidman, Lauri Malmi, Linda Mannila, Elizabeth Adams, Jens Bennedsen, Marie Devlin, and James Paterson. 2007. A survey of literature on the teaching of introductory programming. In *ACM SIGCSE Bulletin*, Vol. 39. ACM, 204–223.

[30] David Pritchard and Troy Vasiga. 2013. CS circles: an in-browser python course for beginners. In *ACM Technical Symposium on Computer Science Education*. ACM, 591–596.

[31] Liana Razmerita, Kathrin Kirchner, Kai Hockerts, and Chee-Wee Tan. 2018. Towards a Model of Collaborative Intention: An Empirical Investigation of a Massive Online Open Course (MOOC). In *Hawaii International Conference on System Sciences*.

[32] Anthony Robins, Janet Rountree, and Nathan Rountree. 2003. Learning and teaching programming: A review and discussion. *Computer science education* 13, 2 (2003), 137–172.

[33] Herbert J Rubin and Irene S Rubin. 2011. *Qualitative interviewing: The art of hearing data*. Sage.

[34] Thomas Staubitz, Hauke Klement, Jan Renz, Ralf Teusner, and Christoph Meinel. 2015. Towards practical programming exercises and automated assessment in Massive Open Online Courses. In *Teaching, Assessment, and Learning for Engineering (TALE)*. IEEE, 23–30.

[35] Phit-Huan Tan, Choo-Yee Ting, and Siew-Woei Ling. 2009. Learning difficulties in programming courses: undergraduates' perspective and perception. In *Computer Technology and Development*, Vol. 1. IEEE, 42–46.

[36] Terry Tang, Scott Rixner, and Joe Warren. 2014. An environment for learning interactive programming. In *ACM Technical Symposium on Computer Science Education*. ACM, 671–676.

[37] Colin Taylor, Kalyan Veeramachaneni, and Una-May O'Reilly. 2014. Likely to stop? predicting stopout in massive open online courses. *arXiv preprint arXiv:1408.3382* (2014).

[38] Arto Vihavainen, Jonne Airaksinen, and Christopher Watson. 2014. A systematic review of approaches for teaching introductory programming and their influence on success. In *Conference on International Computing Education Research*. ACM, 19–26.

[39] Robert S Weiss. 1995. *Learning from strangers: The art and method of qualitative interview studies*. Simon and Schuster.

[40] Aharon Yadin. 2011. Reducing the dropout rate in an introductory programming course. *ACM Inroads* 2, 4 (2011), 71–76.

[41] An Yan, Michael J Lee, and Andrew J Ko. 2017. Predicting abandonment in online coding tutorials. In *Visual Languages and Human-Centric Computing (VL/HCC)*. IEEE, 191–199.

[42] Ahmed Mohamed Fahmy Yousef, Mohamed Amine Chatti, Ulrik Schroeder, and Marold Wosnitza. 2014. What drives a successful MOOC? An empirical examination of criteria to assure design quality of MOOCs. In *Advanced Learning Technologies (ICALT)*. IEEE, 44–48.

[43] Li Yuan, Stephen Powell, JISC CETIS, and others. 2013. MOOCs and open education: Implications for higher education. (2013).

CodeSport: Increasing Participation in Programming Using Coding Tournaments as an Alternative to Hackathons

Michael J. Lee and James Geller
New Jersey Institute of Technology
Newark, New Jersey, USA
{mjlee,james.geller}@njit.edu

ABSTRACT

Though hackathons are successful in attracting large crowds, they may not be sufficiently effective for broadening participation in computing, because they lack appeal for underrepresented groups in computing, and for people with family and job obligations. We propose a contrasting model for creating interest in computing, by making coding a spectator sport. We present an experience report on the design and implementation of a coding tournament, including survey results that informed the design of the system along with post-event questionnaire data from participants, exploring their attitudes towards different coding events. We find that coding tournaments can be an effective and engaging alternative to hackathons, and that they can motivate some audience members to pursue more coding activities, and possibly even participate as competitors in future tournaments.

CCS CONCEPTS

• **Social and professional topics** → **Computing education**.

KEYWORDS

Hackathons; Broadening Participation; Computing Education

ACM Reference Format:
Michael J. Lee and James Geller. 2019. CodeSport: Increasing Participation in Programming Using Coding Tournaments as an Alternative to Hackathons. In *ACM Global Computing Education Conference 2019 (CompEd '19), May 17–19, 2019, Chengdu, Sichuan, China.* ACM, New York, NY, USA, 7 pages. https://doi.org/10.1145/3300115.3309505

1 INTRODUCTION

Hackathons are typically multi-day events, where teams are challenged to create applications containing specific features within a given amount of time (these events are also called game jams when the focus is on creating games) [8, 23, 31]. Many people and organizations are using hackathons to increase exposure to coding, in hopes of generating excitement and broadening participation in computing (as well as networking with potential job candidates for programming jobs). Researchers anticipate that these kinds of events will attract women [26] and people with limited technical

background [33]. However, hackathons also have some features that can be discouraging. Johnson [14] highlights three potential impediments [32], specifically discussing potential causes for the low participation in hackathons by certain groups [7, 30]. Individuals from underrepresented groups 1) fear that they will be treated differently from others, 2) lack self-confidence and/or self-efficacy in their technical abilities, and 3) with job and/or family obligations cannot or do not want to participate in coding events that last too long (but many hackathons are multi-day events).

Due to these issues, we propose an alternative coding event in this paper – making programming a one-on-one spectator sport where individuals can choose to be competitors or spectators. This may help minimize the three problems above as follows:

First, team activities (such as competing in a hackathon) can lead to negative treatment (or micro-aggressions) of minority team members, by *any* definition of minority. One-on-one competitions can help minimize these group biases, since they are largely solo activities. Furthermore, because it is a spectator sport, even if it were to be organized as multi-member teams playing against each other, the public nature of the event with an audience would reduce the opportunity for micro-aggressions that might occur in teams working in a more secluded environment.

Second, research has shown that females and minorities may not prefer participating in competitive events themselves (which may draw unwanted attention) [3, 5], but that they are satisfied *watching* competitive events [11]. Therefore, individuals interested in programming, but with (justified or unjustified) lack of confidence or self-efficacy in their own abilities, can self-select to be spectators instead of competitors. Watching may eventually lead to increased willingness to learn more about programming for some of these individuals (even if they do not choose to be participants themselves), especially if they see other people similar to themselves participating and succeeding as competitors.

Third, as a spectator sport, the length of a tournament is limited by the game rules. Consequently, organizers can approximate total times fairly accurately (while keeping them at a reasonable limit), and participants can plan their schedules accordingly.

In this paper, we explain the background behind our vision, and describe results from a questionnaire demonstrating that people would be willing to participate in (competing/watching) coding tournaments. We then present an experience report of an actual coding tournament, including setup, rules, and results.

2 BACKGROUND

Why make programming a spectator sport? We are interested in increasing the participation of underrepresented groups in computing education and in computing careers. We propose this approach based on the observation that many young people are attracted by spectator sports to become more active in the sport disciplines of their role models themselves.

Lardinoit [16] explored how watching sporting events on television might influence subsequent desires, and found that 16% of French viewers of the Olympic Games reported that they felt more inspired to get active after watching the competitions. Relatedly, watching a sport has long been associated with encouraging children to participate in the sport themselves (in the popular press), although we are not aware of any rigorous study supporting this approach [19]. Meredith [19] lists *watching* as one of nine possible methods for achieving this outcome.

There is a precedent for making intellectual activities into a spectator sport. In 2014, the Millionaire Chess Open debuted in Planet Hollywood and was broadcast on television (TV) with the organizers expressing their desire to turn "chess into a spectator sport" that replicates the "atmosphere of the World Series of Poker" [27]. High profile chess games are already a TV spectacle, with the World Chess Championship Organization stating that televised chess matches are "expected to attract a global online and TV audience of more than 1 billion fans" [15, 27].

Similarly, Go has extremely high viewership numbers, particularly in East Asian countries [1]. In a match between DeepMind's AlphaGo Artificial Intelligence program and the world-class player Lee Sedol, Chinese-language coverage reached up to 60 million viewers [21], while English-language coverage reached 100 thousand viewers [32]. Moreover, Hikaru-no-Go, a Japanese animation series about Go (from the early 2000s), dramatically increased the popularity of Go worldwide, particularly among children [28, 29].

Computer gaming as a spectator sport, or eSport, has gained tremendous attention in recent years, even appearing in the Asian Games (organized by the Olympic Council of Asia). Tournaments for popular games such as Starcraft and League of Legends, both fast-paced real-time strategy games, can draw thousands of spectators at large arenas. In these competitions, the sports consist of using a complex real-time graphics game program. Our approach is to make programming itself a spectator sport.

Finally, we subscribe to the theory of situated learning [17, 20], which states that people learn through observation and interacting with others. We provide participants with an authentic experience [13] in the spectator event – creating, editing, and testing real code to satisfy specific requirements.

3 TOURNAMENT ENVIRONMENT

3.1 Hackathon Alternative? – A Viability Study

We created a survey to get a generalized view of people's opinions about hackathons and viability of our proposed coding tournament. First, we provided an objective description of each type of event, with information about the style and format of how the different types of events are run. Next, we asked a series of 5-point Likert scale questions [25] to determine how agreeable (with 1 being least agreeable, and 5 being most agreeable) participants would be to attend different types of competitive events as a spectator, and also how comfortable they would be in competing in these events with others watching them. Finally, we asked if they had ever attended

a hackathon, if they have a computing-related job, and about their age and gender.

We report the range and median of our responses (since we collected ordinal data). In addition, since our data is not normally distributed, we use nonparametric Chi-Squared tests (which are commonly used to analyze ordinal data [9]) with $\alpha = 0.05$ confidence to compare participants' responses based on their demographic categories. We report all of our (Pearson) Chi-Squared statistics in Table 1.

We surveyed 200 people on Amazon Mechanical Turk (MTurk), limiting our participants to people living in the USA, and between the ages of 18-35 years old (the primary age range of hackathon participants [2]). We chose to use MTurk because we wanted to get responses from a wide range of people who might be better representative of the general public (as opposed to using a mailing list at our STEM-focused university, where more than half the student population are enrolled in engineering or computing-related fields). Our goal is to understand what types of computing events people would be willing to participate in as a spectator or competitor.

The task took a mean time of 3.12 minutes, and we paid each participant US$1.00 to complete the task. Our sample included 107 females and 93 males, was ethnically diverse (79 White/Caucasian, 46 Hispanic/Latino, 33 Black/African-American, 28 Asian/Pacific-Islander, and 14 multi-ethnic or other), and 87 people reported they had a computing-related job. Also, 19 people reported that they had been to a hackathon in the past (5 females and 14 males; all with computing-related jobs).

Table 1 shows the summary of all the statistics, including the median and range, calculated for each of our questions. For each question, we compared across five categories (gender, age, ethnicity, computing-job, and hackathon experience (H-Exp)) to see if there were any differences in responses by measure.

When asked if they would be willing to attend a 48-hr hackathon, a 12-hr hackathon, or a 3-hr coding tournament as a *spectator*, our participants had a median response of 2, 3, and 3, respectively. There was no statistically significant difference detected by gender, age, ethnicity, or job for either of the hackathons. However, we found a significant difference by participants' job and H-Exp for 3-hr tournaments. Those with computing-related jobs and H-Exp were more likely to report they would attend a 3-hr coding tournament as a spectator compared to those in non-computing-related jobs and people without H-Exp.

To the question whether they would be willing to attend a 48-hr hackathon, a 12-hr hackathon, or a 3-hr coding tournament as a *competitor*, our participants had a median response of 1, 2, and 3, respectively. There were no statistically significant differences detected by gender, age or ethnicity in participants' responses. However, we found a significant difference by participants' H-Exp (and trending by participants' job for hackathons). Those with H-Exp were more likely to report that they would attend a 48-hr hackathon, 12-hr hackathon, or a 3-hr coding tournament as a *competitor* compared to those without H-Exp.

Lastly, we attempted to establish baseline measurements by asking questions about chess and poker. When asked if they would attend a *chess tournament* or a *poker tournament* as either a spectator or competitor, our participants had a median response of 1 for all questions. There was no statistically significant difference detected by gender, age, ethnicity, job, or H-Exp for those questions.

In summary, we found that our participants were generally not enthusiastic about attending any of the proposed types of competitive events as a spectator or competitor (the highest median value was 3, which indicates they neither agree nor disagree that they would attend an event as a competitor or spectator). This was not completely unexpected, as the general public might not be interested in these types of events overall.

However, we did find that people who had computing-related jobs or previous experience with hackathons were more likely to report that they would attend hackathons (as a spectator or competitor) and coding tournaments (as a spectator and as a competitor). This is also not unexpected, as those who are more familiar with computing might be more open to attending computing-related events. Moreover, our data indicates that people are more willing to attend 48-hr/12-hr hackathons and coding tournaments as spectators (medians were 2, 3, and 3, respectively) than spectating a chess or poker tournament (medians were 1 and 1, respectively).

While we did not compare events directly against each other, these results (medians and statistical results) are good indicators that a coding tournament can be at least as attractive as hackathons (which do attract high numbers of attendees [2]) for the general public, those with computing-jobs, and/or past hackathon experience. Additionally, the shorter time-investment required by coding tournaments compared to hackathons may be attractive to more people. Finally, we were concerned that minorities and females may not be attracted to these competitive events. However, we did not find any differences by gender, ethnicity, or age for any of our questions, indicating that members of these groups might be willing to watch, or even possibly compete in these types of events.

We acknowledge the limitation of our sample, as our MTurk workers may not be representative of the general public. Nevertheless, MTurk workers are generally tech-savvy (as evidenced by the high number of our participants who self-reported that they have computing-related jobs and had attended hackathons), and may be a good representation of the people that are aware of these types of events and might consider attending. For example, we found that those who attended hackathons in the past were more likely to say that they would attend other hackathons and coding tournaments. We conclude from our survey results that there is sufficient interest to explore the viability of coding tournaments further.

3.2 Participants and Audience

Now that we had some evidence that people would attend a coding tournament, we brainstormed how to organize the activity and what the participants' experience should be. We realized that not every kind of programming activity can be adapted into a competitive sport, especially if audience members cannot judge the results and cannot compare the outcomes of two competitors.

However, we determined this matter is less of an issue if programming problems are limited to graphical programming tasks. Even audience members with no technical background can judge the similarity of pairs of graphical displays. We converged on a one-on-one tournament design concentrating on small, well-defined

I would attend a...	Statistic		p-val
48hr hackathon as a *spectator* Median: 2 (disagree), Range 1-5	Gender: Age: Race: Job: H-Exp:	$\chi^2(4,N=200)=0.757$ $\chi^2(8,N=200)=11.008$ $\chi^2(16,N=200)=18.340$ $\chi^2(4,N=200)=4.240$ $\chi^2(4,N=200)=3.223$	.946 .201 .304 .375 .521
12hr hackathon as a *spectator* Median: 3 (neutral), Range 1-5	Gender: Age: Race: Job: H-Exp:	$\chi^2(4,N=200)=3.182$ $\chi^2(8,N=200)=5.522$ $\chi^2(16,N=200)=15.956$ $\chi^2(4,N=200)=5.255$ $\chi^2(4,N=200)=4.863$	.528 .701 .456 .262 .302
3hr coding tournament as a *spectator* Median: 3 (neutral), Range 1-5	Gender: Age: Race: Job: H-Exp:	$\chi^2(4,N=200)=1.780$ $\chi^2(8,N=200)=14.267$ $\chi^2(16,N=200)=14.456$ $\chi^2(4,N=200)=10.466$ $\chi^2(4,N=200)=11.262$	.776 .075 .565 *.048** *.043**
chess tournament as a *spectator* Median: 1 (s.disagree), Range 1-5	Gender: Age: Race: Job: H-Exp:	$\chi^2(4,N=200)=3.065$ $\chi^2(8,N=200)=7.242$ $\chi^2(16,N=200)=7.020$ $\chi^2(4,N=200)=7.082$ $\chi^2(4,N=200)=4.130$	.547 .511 .973 .132 .389
poker tournament as a *spectator* Median: 1 (s.disagree), Range 1-5	Gender: Age: Race: Job: H-Exp:	$\chi^2(4,N=200)=2.345$ $\chi^2(8,N=200)=7.492$ $\chi^2(16,N=200)=17.319$ $\chi^2(4,N=200)=0.648$ $\chi^2(4,N=200)=1.886$	.673 .485 .365 .958 .757
48hr hackathon as a *competitor* Median: 1 (disagree), Range 1-5	Gender: Age: Race: Job: H-Exp:	$\chi^2(4,N=200)=1.548$ $\chi^2(6,N=200)=5.403$ $\chi^2(12,N=200)=17.554$ $\chi^2(4,N=200)=9.312$ $\chi^2(4,N=200)=10.625$	.818 .493 .130 *.054* *.047**
12hr hackathon as a *competitor* Median: 2 (disagree), Range 1-5	Gender: Age: Race: Job: H-Exp:	$\chi^2(4,N=200)=4.715$ $\chi^2(8,N=200)=6.570$ $\chi^2(16,N=200)=9.997$ $\chi^2(4,N=200)=9.351$ $\chi^2(4,N=200)=17.127$	.318 .584 .867 *.053* *.032**
3hr coding tournament as a *competitor* Median: 3 (neutral), Range 1-5	Gender: Age: Race: Job: H-Exp:	$\chi^2(4,N=200)=4.504$ $\chi^2(8,N=200)=6.911$ $\chi^2(16,N=200)=6.766$ $\chi^2(4,N=200)=10.234$ $\chi^2(4,N=200)=10.419$	.342 .546 .978 *.037** *.034**
chess tournament as a *competitor* Median: 1 (s.disagree), Range 1-5	Gender: Age: Race: Job: H-Exp:	$\chi^2(4,N=200)=3.090$ $\chi^2(8,N=200)=7.081$ $\chi^2(16,N=200)=22.849$ $\chi^2(4,N=200)=3.603$ $\chi^2(4,N=200)=1.070$	.543 .528 .118 .463 .900
poker tournament as a *competitor* Median: 1 (s.disagree), Range 1-5	Gender: Age: Race: Job: H-Exp:	$\chi^2(4,N=200)=3.275$ $\chi^2(8,N=200)=7.870$ $\chi^2(16,N=200)=20.450$ $\chi^2(4,N=200)=1.942$ $\chi^2(4,N=200)=1.610$	.513 .446 .201 .746 .807

Table 1: Survey results for participants.

graphics coding problems that would potentially be exciting to watch for non-programmers.

3.3 Programming Environment

The strong connection between computer graphics and programming education has a long history, going back to the Logo language [22] from 1967 and its use of turtle graphics. We chose to use the *Processing* language[1] for our tournaments, which its developers describe as being designed "for learning how to code within the context of the visual arts" [10]. It is based on a simplified version

---

[1]The Processing language website: https://www.processing.org/

of Java, which is the major teaching language for programming in many US colleges and has a large established user base, especially among the visual arts community [10].

We considered using other popular (block) programming environments such as Scratch [24] and Alice [6]. However, we determined that using a textual language would offer more benefits to those interested in learning programming (e.g., learning the language *Processing* would enable a user to relatively quickly advance to Java) and that the animation capabilities of these other environments go beyond what is currently intended for this project. While animated graphics would provide interesting visuals for the audience, it creates challenges with respect to fair evaluation of the results of two competitors.

3.4 Setup and Procedure of a Game

We implemented the "CodeSport" tournament system in Java, requiring three computers (one for the referee, and one for each player) with internet connections. The referee's view contains a list of pre-arranged graphics programming problems, each consisting of a collection of shapes that we call *diagrams*. The referee sets a time limit on the screen, typically 5 minutes, and a required overlap percentage. A round of the game ends either at the time limit or when one of the players reaches the desired overlap percentage between her/his solution and the referee's diagram. To allow for more sophisticated shapes and fast-paced rounds, the referee may choose to provide players with parts of the solution code, requiring them to edit (i.e., debug) existing code instead of starting with a blank coding pane (which may be beneficial for less-experienced coders [18]). The referee's screen is projected on a large screen so that audience members can see the countdown timer and the players' current progress.

The players' view (see Figure 1), contains a code editing pane, the target image, the program/image the code generates, the timer, and the overlap percentage score. Each player's screen is projected on large screens so audience members can follow the player's coding progress and state of their diagrams. Many of the diagrams include repeated shapes and/or patterns, which would be most effectively solved by using arrays (e.g., to store information such as color) and loops (e.g., to repeat commands and cycle through arrays).

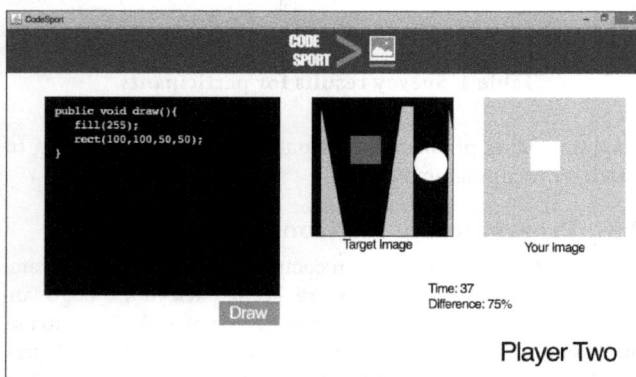

Figure 1: A player's screen showing the code pane (left), goal shapes (center), and current output (right).

We designed the tournament rules to be fast-paced, flexible, and to accommodate different time constraints and numbers of competitors. The winner of a best-of-three rounds wins the game. Each round has a recommended time limit of 5 minutes (±1-2 minutes, depending on task difficulty), making each game approximately 15 minutes. In an elimination tournament, players compete in one-on-one elimination games, with the winners advancing in their bracket. For longer tournaments, referees can choose to provide brief intermissions to give players and the audience a brief rest and to allow for announcements.

3.5 Features

In a CodeSport tournament, the basic procedure of one *round* of a game is as follows:

- The referee selects a diagram and displays it on the public screen (e.g., a half circle in red, slanted by 30 degrees with a black fill, as in Figure 2). This is the target shape that the two participants must match as closely as possible by *writing a program* in the Processing language.
- The referee clicks a button to activate both players' screens with the newly selected diagram.
- The two players attempt to reproduce the target diagram by writing the necessary code on their computers. This may require the use of different types of data structures, looping, and/or conditional statements.
- Players can push a button to execute their current code and display their current solutions.
- Once they are sufficiently satisfied with their progress, players can push a button to send the referee their diagram.
- The referee's computer performs a pixel-by-pixel comparison between the target shape/color and the player's diagram and returns the current overlap percentage.
- The audience sees the correct solution and the players' solutions at the same time on the public screens.
- Players can continue to submit their solutions until the referee's computer determines a winner.
- The referee's computer decides the winner of the round when a player's solution sufficiently overlaps with the goal solution, or the round reaches the time limit. We define "sufficient" as a numerical threshold parameter with a value between 95%-100%, to be set by the referee and/or organizers before the tournament begins. The referee predetermines the time limit for each round and players can see a countdown timer at all times. For rounds that reach the time limit, the player with a higher overlap percentage at the time of the deadline is the winner.
- The referee's computer displays the winner and shows the final outputs of both players at the end of the round. It also displays the overlap percentages and the winner's code.

4 CODESPORT EXPERIENCE REPORT

We ran a CodeSport tournament at a local STEM-focused university, recruiting participants through mailing lists and word-of-mouth. We offered free food and US$120 in prize money as incentive ($50 for 1st, $30 for 2nd, and $20 each for two 3rd place winners).

We had a total of 26 spectators (6 females, 20 males) and 16 players (2 females, 14 males) compete in the tournament. These 16 players were randomly grouped into eight pairs, and competed one-on-one, in single-elimination brackets. Each pair played one game (i.e., three rounds), with the eight winners advancing to the quarter-finals where they competed for the top four spots. These four winners played in the semi-finals and the two winners of these games were the finalists. When not competing, competitors stayed to watch others compete along with the other spectators. The tournament consisted of 15 games in total. Our first-place winner was a fourth-year, Asian, female student majoring in mathematics.

To determine the effectiveness of our coding tournament, we surveyed our 16 players exploring their attitudes towards participating in different kinds of competitive events. We e-mailed our players an online questionnaire two weeks after the event to minimize any novelty bias, and make a fairer comparison to past hackathons they may have participated in. Unfortunately, we had only collected the e-mail addresses of competitors (to distribute prizes), so were unable to contact those who were just spectators. We received a total of 12 responses—our sample had 1 female and 11 males, was ethnically diverse (4 White/Caucasian, 3 Hispanic/Latino, 5 Asian/Pacific-Islander), and included those with part/full time jobs (4 did not have jobs). Our respondents were composed of undergraduate upper-classmen (3+ years in college), and they were all in STEM-related majors with some prior programming experience.

We asked a series of 5-point Likert scale questions to determine respondents' 1) preference between hackathons and coding tournaments (with 1 meaning highly preferring hackathons, 3 preferring hackathons and coding tournaments equally, and 5 highly preferring coding tournaments), and 2) agreeability to statements regarding their experience with coding tournaments (with 1 being least agreeable, and 5 being most agreeable). We report the range and median of our (ordinal) responses. We use nonparametric Chi-Squared tests (likelihood ratios) with $\alpha = 0.05$ confidence to compare participants' responses based on their demographic categories with the understanding that our sample size is small (which is why we report likelihood ratios) and that the resulting statistics may not be widely generalizable. We report all of our Chi-Squared statistics in Table 2.

4.1 Hackathons vs. Coding Tournaments

Our first set of questions was designed to learn more about the participants' preference(s) between hackathons and coding tournaments. We provided objective definitions and examples of both types of events to remind participants of the differences.

When asked which type of event they would prefer being a *spectator*, our participants were split with a median response of 3 (range 1-5). When asked which type of event they would prefer being a *competitor* in, our participants leaned towards coding tournaments with a median response of 4 (range 1-5). There were no statistically significant differences detected by gender or ethnicity.

When asked which type of event motivated them to be a *competitor in the future*, our participants had a slight preference for coding tournaments with a median response of 3.5 (range 1-5). When asked which event type motivated them to *learn more about programming*, our participants leaned towards coding tournaments with a median

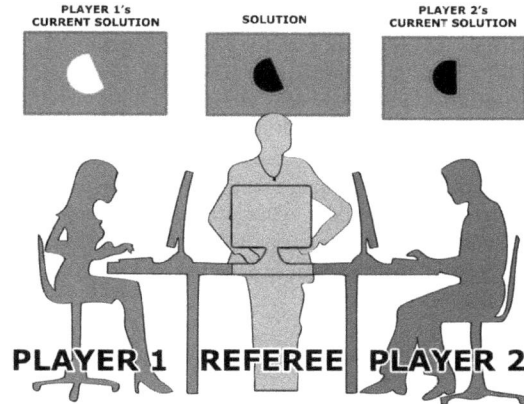

Figure 2: Stage setup with two players and a referee at their stations. The screens behind the referee display the goal shape and the players' current solutions.

response of 4 (range 1-5). There were no statistically significant differences detected by gender or ethnicity for any these measures.

4.2 Enjoyment of the Codesport Tournament

The next set of questions was designed to evaluate participants' experience with the CodeSport tournament, and whether they would consider attending in the future.

When asked about being a *spectator* for the coding tournament, participants indicated they enjoyed it with a median response of 4 (range 3-5). Although not quite statistically significant, Asians/Pacific Islanders and Hispanic/Latino players were more likely to report they enjoyed being a *spectator* compared to their Caucasian/White counterparts (see Table 2). Additionally, participants agreed they would consider attending a coding tournament as a *spectator* in the future, with a median response of 4 (range 3-5). There were no statistically significant differences detected by gender or ethnicity for these measures.

Hackathon vs Coding Tournament	Statistic		p.val
I would prefer to be a *spectator* at Hackathons ←→ C.Tournaments	Gender:	$\chi^2(2,N=12)=2.385$	.665
	Race:	$\chi^2(4,N=12)=11.998$	.151
I would prefer to be a *competitor* at Hackathons ←→ C.Tournaments	Gender:	$\chi^2(2,N=12)=3.065$	.547
	Race:	$\chi^2(4,N=12)=7.133$	.522
_____ motivates me to consider being a *competitor* in the future.	Gender:	$\chi^2(2,N=12)=6.884$	.142
	Race:	$\chi^2(4,N=12)=7.133$	.522
_____ motivates me to learn more about computer programming.	Gender:	$\chi^2(2,N=12)=3.065$	.547
	Race:	$\chi^2(4,N=12)=9.905$	.272
I enjoyed being a *spectator* for the coding tournament.	Gender:	$\chi^2(2,N=12)=1.142$	.564
	Race:	$\chi^2(4,N=12)=9.168$	*.057*
I enjoyed being a *competitor* in the coding tournament.	Gender:	$\chi^2(2,N=12)=0.856$	.652
	Race:	$\chi^2(4,N=12)=7.50$	.112
I would consider *spectating* at a coding tournament in the future.	Gender:	$\chi^2(2,N=12)=2.385$	.303
	Race:	$\chi^2(4,N=12)=3.175$	.529
I would consider *competing* at a coding tournament in the future.	Gender:	$\chi^2(2,N=12)=1.880$	.598
	Race:	$\chi^2(4,N=12)=12.401$	*.054*

Table 2: Post survey results for event participants.

To the question about being a *competitor* in the coding tournament, participants reported that they highly enjoyed the tournament, with a median response of 5 (range 3-5). Moreover, participants agreed they would consider attending another coding tournament as a *competitor* in the future, with a median response of 4 (range 2-5). Although not quite statistically significant, Asians/Pacific Islanders and especially Hispanic/Latino players were more likely to report they would consider being a future *competitor* compared to their Caucasian/White counterparts (see Table 2). There were no statistically significant differences detected by gender or ethnicity for any of the other measures.

5 DISCUSSION

5.1 Lessons Learned

We found that participants reported that they preferred coding tournaments over hackathons. Participants consistently reported that the CodeSport tournament was enjoyable, that they wanted to learn more about programming, and that they would consider attending future events as competitors or spectators. Although our post-tournament sample size was small, we found that our Asian/Pacific Islander and Hispanic participants' responses trended towards significance in reporting that they enjoyed being spectators (while not competing) and that they would also consider being competitors in future tournaments, compared to their Caucasian/White counterparts. Although our results are not conclusive, we saw some evidence that coding tournaments may be able to attract spectators who might later consider learning more about programming (and a subset of these people may possibly consider becoming competitors themselves). These are promising outcomes and something we will continue to investigate with more tournaments.

5.1.1 What Worked and Did Not Work. Overall, the CodeSport application worked well and the tournament succeeded in engaging the people who came out to participate in the tournament. However, this is also an issue, as we only collected survey data from the competitors, who are likely the most representative of the types of people who already have an interest in computing and attend events such as hackathons, and may be different from the people who came just to spectate. For future events, we will survey non-competitors, and we will try to appeal to a wider audience in our advertisements, focusing on recruiting people who are not in computing or closely related STEM fields.

5.1.2 Adoption by Others. The CodeSport software is compatible across many operating systems and is free to download and use. We would like to collaborate with others who are interested in using, adapting, and evaluating the system to further test the viability of coding tournaments as a way to attract a more diverse group of participants into computing.

5.1.3 Limitations and Future Work. There are several limitations to our experience report that limit its generalizability. First, our initial survey was conducted on Mechanical Turk, so our participants may not be representative of the general public. However, people did attend our coding tournament and indicated that they enjoyed the tournament and would attend again.

We also realize that the prizes and free food are factors that may have incentivized people to spectate and/or to compete in the tournament. However, these types of incentives are also common in hackathons and related events, so we assume the effects of these were minimal, and therefore a reasonable comparison.

Next, our post-tournament questionnaire had a small sample size and only represented those who participated as competitors, which limits how we can interpret the results. Moreover, the participants were all from the same university with some prior programming experience. Although our winner was a female, the tournament mostly consisted of college-aged males, which reflects the gender demographics of the university, and typical makeup of hackathon participants [2]. It would have been better for a larger, more diverse audience to witness the winner's achievements at the tournament.

We will attempt to address these issues by running more events and getting more feedback from our participants (especially from spectators). We will specifically try to recruit more female and/or minority participants, and include more collaborative elements (as opposed to competitive elements) to be more gender-inclusive and appeal to a wider audience [3–5]. We also plan to host middle/high school students to participate in CodeSport tournaments to learn how these types of events might appeal to and engage these younger students (and possibly contrast with older participants).

6 CONCLUSION

Educators and researchers have tried many different approaches to increase participation in computing education and in the computing professions [12]. Recently, hackathons have become popular and touted as an effective mechanism in broadening participation in computing-related activities. However, evidence suggests that certain people might feel uncomfortable or have other constraints that prevent them from participating in hackathons.

In this paper, we presented an alternative method for broadening participation in computing. We aimed to increase the public's interest in programming by making it a spectator sport, since there is evidence that a percentage of sport spectators will eventually take up that activity [16].

First, we conducted a survey that confirmed that people would attend and participate in coding tournaments. Next, we created the CodeSport system and tournament rules. We ran a tournament with 16 participants and received feedback from 12 of them. Participants reported that they highly enjoyed the coding tournament, that they preferred coding tournaments over hackathons, and that they would continue to attend future coding tournament events. Likewise, participants agreed that the event motivated them to learn more about programming and take part as competitors in the future. Given these results and feedback, we are encouraged about the viability of coding tournaments as an alternative to hackathons that may be able to attract additional people into computing through spectating and possibly competing.

ACKNOWLEDGMENTS

This work was supported in part by the National Science Foundation under grant DRL-1837489. Any opinions, findings, conclusions or recommendations are those of the authors and do not necessarily reflect the views of the National Science Foundation.

REFERENCES

[1] Steven Borowiec and Tracey Lien. 2016. AlphaGo beats human Go champ in milestone for artificial intelligence. *Los Angeles Times* 12 (2016).

[2] Gerard Briscoe. 2014. Digital innovation: The hackathon phenomenon. (2014).

[3] Margaret M Burnett, Laura Beckwith, Susan Wiedenbeck, Scott D Fleming, Jill Cao, Thomas H Park, Valentina Grigoreanu, and Kyle Rector. 2011. Gender pluralism in problem-solving software. *Interacting With Computers* 23, 5 (2011), 450–460.

[4] Margaret M Burnett, Elizabeth F Churchill, and Michael J Lee. 2015. SIG: Gender-Inclusive Software: What We Know About Building It. In *ACM Conference Extended Abstracts on Human Factors in Computing Systems*. ACM, 857–860.

[5] Anne Campbell. 2004. Female competition: Causes, constraints, content, and contexts. *Journal of Sex Research* 41, 1 (2004), 16–26.

[6] Tebring Daly. 2013. *Influence of alice 3: reducing the hurdles to success in a cs1 programming course*. University of North Texas.

[7] Adrienne Decker, Kurt Eiselt, and Kimberly Voll. 2015. Understanding and improving the culture of hackathons: Think global hack local. In *Frontiers in Education Conference (FIE)*. IEEE, 1–8.

[8] Allan Fowler, Foaad Khosmood, Ali Arya, and Gorm Lai. 2013. The global game jam for teaching and learning. In *Conference on Computing and Information Technology Research and Education New Zealand*. 28–34.

[9] J Frost. 2016. Best Way to Analyze Likert Item Data: Two Sample T-Test versus Mann-Whitney. (2016).

[10] B Fry and C Reas. 2017. A short introduction to the Processing software and projects from the community. (2017).

[11] Walter Gantz. 1981. An exploration of viewing motives and behaviors associated with television sports. *Journal of Broadcasting & Electronic Media* 25, 3 (1981), 263–275.

[12] James Geller. 2016. Building, Recruiting, And Inclusion for Diversity. (2016). Retrieved March 7, 2017 from https://web.njit.edu/~geller/braid/Main.html

[13] Mark Guzdial. 2015. Learner-centered design of computing education: Research on computing for everyone. *Synthesis Lectures on Human-Centered Informatics* 8, 6 (2015), 1–165.

[14] Phil Johnson. 2014. Why hackathons are a boys' club and how to change that. (2014). Retrieved March 26, 2017 from https://www.itworld.com/article/2700151/networking/why-hackathons-are-a-boys--club-and-how-to-change-that.html

[15] Tovin Lapan. 2014. Chess as a spectator sport? Organizers of big-money tourney say yes. (2014). Retrieved March 26, 2017 from http://lasvegassun.com/news/2014/oct/15/chess-spectator-sport-organizers-big-money-tourney/

[16] Thierry Lardinoit. 2014. Watching the world cup: can TV encourage physical activity? (2014). Retrieved March 26, 2017 from http://knowledge.essec.edu/en/sustainability/watching-world-cup-can-tv-encourage-physical-activ.html

[17] Jean Lave and Etienne Wenger. 1991. *Situated learning: Legitimate peripheral participation*. Cambridge University Press.

[18] Michael J Lee, Faezeh Bahmani, Irwin Kwan, Jilian LaFerte, Polina Charters, Amber Horvath, Fanny Luor, Jill Cao, Catherine Law, Michael Beswetherick, et al. 2014. Principles of a debugging-first puzzle game for computing education. In *Visual Languages and Human-Centric Computing (VL/HCC)*. IEEE, 57–64.

[19] Janis Merideth. 2014. 9 fun ways to motivate your child in sports. (2014). Retrieved March 26, 2017 from https://blogs.usafootball.com/blog/693/9-fun-ways-to-motivate-your-child-in-sports

[20] Sharan B Merriam, Rosemary S Caffarella, and Lisa M Baumgartner. 2012. *Learning in adulthood: A comprehensive guide*. John Wiley & Sons.

[21] Cade Metz. 2016. The sadness and beauty of watching Google's AI Play go. *Wired* (2016).

[22] Seymour Papert. 1980. *Mindstorms: Children, computers, and powerful ideas*. Basic Books, Inc.

[23] Jon A Preston, Jeff Chastine, Casey O'Donnell, Tony Tseng, and Blair MacIntyre. 2012. Game jams: Community, motivations, and learning among jammers. *International Journal of Game-Based Learning (IJGBL)* 2, 3 (2012), 51–70.

[24] Mitchel Resnick, John Maloney, Andrés Monroy-Hernández, Natalie Rusk, Evelyn Eastmond, Karen Brennan, Amon Millner, Eric Rosenbaum, Jay Silver, Brian Silverman, et al. 2009. Scratch: programming for all. *Commun. ACM* 52, 11 (2009), 60–67.

[25] Melanie A Revilla, Willem E Saris, and Jon A Krosnick. 2014. Choosing the number of categories in agree–disagree scales. *Sociological Methods & Research* 43, 1 (2014), 73–97.

[26] Gabriela T Richard, Yasmin B Kafai, Barrie Adleberg, and Orkan Telhan. 2015. StitchFest: Diversifying a College Hackathon to broaden participation and perceptions in computing. In *ACM Technical Symposium on Computer Science Education*. ACM, 114–119.

[27] Oliver Roeder. 2016. The World Chess Championship comes to New York City. (2016). Retrieved March 8, 2017 from https://fivethirtyeight.com/features/the-world-chess-championship-comes-to-new-york-city/

[28] Charles Scanlon. 2002. Young Japanese go for Go. (2002). Retrieved March 8, 2017 from http://news.bbc.co.uk/2/hi/asia-pacific/2164532.stm

[29] Yoko Shimatsuka. 2005. Do Not Pass Go. (2005). Retrieved March 15, 2017 from http://www.asiaweek.com/asiaweek/magazine/nations/0,8782,132162,00.html

[30] Shuba Swaminathan. 2014. Why don't more women go to hackathons? (2014). Retrieved March 26, 2017 from https://www.quora.com/Women-in-Technology-1/Why-dont-more-women-go-to-hackathons

[31] Jeremy Warner and Philip J Guo. 2017. Hack. edu: Examining how college hackathons are perceived by student attendees and non-attendees. In *ACM Conference on International Computing Education Research*. ACM, 254–262.

[32] Frank Wunderlich-Pfeiffer. 2016. Künstliche Intelligenz: Alpha Go spielt wie eine Göttin. (2016). Retrieved March 26, 2017 from https://www.golem.de/news/kuenstliche-intelligenz-alpha-go-spielt-wie-eine-goettin-1603-119646.html

[33] Jorge Luis Zapico, Daniel Pargman, Hannes Ebner, and Elina Eriksson. 2013. Hacking sustainability: Broadening participation through green hackathons. In *International Symposium on End-User Development*.

Five Years of Graduate CS Education Online and at Scale

David A. Joyner
College of Computing
Georgia Institute of Technology
Atlanta, GA, USA
david.joyner@gatech.edu

Charles Isbell
College of Computing
Georgia Institute of Technology
Atlanta, GA, USA
isbell@cc.gatech.edu

Thad Starner
College of Computing
Georgia Institute of Technology
Atlanta, GA, USA
thad@cc.gatech.edu

Ashok Goel
College of Computing
Georgia Institute of Technology
Atlanta, GA, USA
goel@cc.gatech.edu

ABSTRACT

In 2014, Georgia Tech launched an online campus for its Master of Science in Computer Science program. The degree, equal in stature and accreditation to its on-campus counterpart, offered a notably lower cost of attendance. Its design emphasized flexibility in both geography and time, allowing students from around the world to earn a highly-ranked MSCS without taking time off work or moving to campus. Five years later, the program enrolls over 8000 students per semester and has graduated 1500 alumni. It is believed to be the largest program of its kind and has received recognition from national organizations on professional education. Existing research on the program has focused on challenges and opportunities to scale that are agnostic to the content itself. In this reflection, we look at the creation and growth of the program as it relates to graduate-level CS instruction. In particular, we note a unique and powerful unity of content and platform: the online delivery of the program dovetails with the technical skillsets of the professors and students that it draws, putting both in the position to contribute and innovate.

ACM Reference Format:
David A. Joyner, Charles Isbell, Thad Starner, and Ashok Goel. 2019. Five Years of Graduate CS Education Online and at Scale. In ACM Global Computing Education Conference 2019 (CompEd '19), May 17–19, 2019, Chengdu,Sichuan, China. ACM, New York, NY, USA, 7 pages. https://doi.org/10.1145/3300115.3309534

1 Introduction

Higher education in the 2010s has been characterized in large part by two major trends. The first has been the arrival and widespread deployment of Massive Open Online Courses, or MOOCs. MOOCs first appeared in 2010 and quickly rose in visibility, culminating in New York Times dubbing 2012 the "Year of the MOOC" [28]. That early hype was met with early skepticism as well, and MOOCs have since followed a traditional hype cycle, but in more recent years they have begun to find applications in for-credit educational environments [16][17][28].

A second well-documented trend has been the rising cost of college [18], and the accompanying meteoric rise in student debt burdens [25]. On the surface, it appears that one of these trends may address the other: MOOCs aim to make higher education far more accessible and affordable.

It is against the backdrop of these two trends that in 2014, Georgia Tech, a major public research university in the United States created the first MOOC-based graduate degree. By design, the program was more like traditional distance learning than MOOCs: students applied for admission, paid to enroll in semesters, were evaluated by human graders, received letter grades, and earned a fully-accredited diploma. The program capitalized on the strengths of MOOCs; however: instruction was delivered on a popular MOOC platform and designed to be consumed asynchronously, and enrollment cost was lowered to less than one-ninth of the out-of-state cost (one-third of the in-state cost), regardless of the state or country in which the student resided.

Five years later, the program has thrived. It has grown to over 8,000 students in the Fall 2018 semester, and it is projected to increase the world's output of MSCS graduates by 8% annually [10]. It was recognized by the University Professional and Continuing Education Association for program excellence, and has spawned numerous similar programs, both at the university and on other platforms such as edX and Coursera.

In this paper, we trace back the motivation and creation of this new curriculum initiative. While much has already been written about the program, most existing research has focused on elements of the program that are domain-neutral. In this overview, we will concentrate as much as possible on those elements of the program unique to its nature as a computer science graduate degree. Of special note will be the frequency with which innovative initiatives occur specifically due to the technical backgrounds of the students and instructors in the program.

2 Program Motivation

As noted above, the primary context under which the program was developed was the rise of college prices and the emergence of

MOOCs as a possible means through which to deliver education affordably by leveraging scale. These trends may address any similar affordable online program, and indeed some of the new initiatives that have followed on this program's success are in less technical fields like public health, business administration, and accounting. Specifically with regard to computer science education, however, two additional trends contributed to the inception of this program.

The first is the increasing need for additional lifelong learning, especially within technical fields. The "fourth industrial revolution" as it has been dubbed [32] has seen an explosion in job opportunities in computing-oriented fields [22]. This trend, coupled with automation and outsourcing driving additional changes in the job market [2], has led to a dramatic increase in computing as a new career choice. Even for those already within technical fields, the rapid changes in the technology industry mean that employees need to re-skill regularly to stay current. A Bachelor's degree in Computer Science from many schools in the early 2000s would likely not have covered machine learning, cloud computing, computer vision, and more topics that are spawning entire new job categories today. These learners, however, are often in the middle of their careers with families: they cannot afford the opportunity cost of going two years without a salary to obtain a graduate degree, let alone the high price of enrollment.

There was thus a demand for rigorous, respected lifelong education specifically in computing from both students and industry, but too much friction in the existing mechanisms to meet either demand. Startups have been quick to provide bootcamps, MOOCs, and other non-traditional credentials to address this gap, but research has found that these alternate methods typically focus only on a small subset of the skills delivered by traditional programs [35].

A second significant motivating trend in the program's inception was a more straightforward desire to continue to innovate in the emerging area of online learning. Georgia Tech had been at the forefront of these initiatives, highlighted by its early participation in one of the first MOOCs as well as its decades-old distance learning division. Given the nature of the delivery mechanism, an initial focus on computer science was logical as the individuals involved in teaching in the program could also contribute to its technological development.

Thus, the program can be seen as largely motivated by four trends: the rising cost of higher education; the emergence of MOOCs as a possible new delivery mechanism; the increasing need for lifelong CS education (driven by both student and industry demand); and the desire to continue to innovate on technological mechanisms for delivering high-quality for-credit education. This motivation, of course, is in some ways teleological: the full nature of the motivation behind the program's inception is more complex; however, these motivations were all present, and moreover, all directly connect to the program's eventual success.

3 Program Development

It is useful to think of the development of the program in terms of three major stages. The first stage, creation, occurred before the initial students began the program and provided the initial foundation. The second stage, experimentation, covered the first few years and saw expansion coupled with experimentation in production and delivery methods to find the procedures most effective for scale and quality. The third stage, normalization, began within the past year and sees an increasing focus on standardizing practices, maintaining growth, and optimizing existing systems. Although there are formal milestones that may be marked along the way—such as the matriculation of the first class in January 2014 and the graduation of the first students in December 2015—these stages are interpretive. Experimentation continues in the program today, but now there exists a set of principles and practices for delivery that did not exist when the program began and were derived based on that early experimentation.

3.1 Creation

Creation of the program began in the summer of 2013. The university partnered with a startup specializing in creating MOOCs to develop its initial set of five courses to launch in Spring 2014, including one taught by one of this paper's co-authors, Isbell. Courses were generally developed by three-person teams: a professor, a course developer, and a video producer. The professor was responsible for authoring and filming all course content. The course developer worked with the professor to convert the content to work in the traditional MOOC presentation style, characterized by short videos, frequent interspersed exercises, and pen-based presentation (wherein professors would write on a virtual "whiteboard" while narrating for students). The course developer also assisted the professor in developing the syllabus and assignments, authoring autograding tools, and typically served as the course's teaching assistant during its inaugural semester. The video producer filmed and edited sections of the course where professors were on camera, as well as edited the virtual whiteboard portions of the course.

The majority of course content was presented in this virtual whiteboard format, which carried several benefits. First, because the recording setup required only a single pre-configured setup, professors were able to film on their own schedules rather than coordinate with the video editor to be present and working during every filming session. This approach allowed professors more autonomy over production scheduling and maximized video producers' time. Second, because the professor was typically not on screen, content could be filmed in very small chunks. A professor could attempt a sentence several times until they were satisfied, and then move on to the next sentence. A single bad take meant re-filming only a few seconds, not multiple minutes, allowing the finished product to be more professional.

Pre-production allowed additional benefits as well. In one course from the original set of five, Isbell presented the course along with a prominent colleague from another university. In an on-campus class, it would be entirely infeasible to have another professor—especially from another university—co-teach a class every semester for five years, but by pre-producing the material and delivering it online, those different perspectives could not only be included, but included in a conversational style. The asynchronous and remote nature of the course could allow another professor to be involved in the delivery as well, an opportunity realized to a greater extent during the subsequent experimentation phase.

3.2 Experimentation

The experimentation phase began with the inaugural semester of the program in spring 2014, where 300 students enrolled in that initial batch of classes. This semester was intentionally constructed as a "beta" semester to ensure the feasibility of the program under optimal conditions, with classes no larger than their on-campus counterparts. Upon the success of the initial semester, the program was opened more broadly in fall 2018, including students deferred from the first semester. In the lead-up to this semester, five additional courses were developed, including one by two additional co-authors of this paper (Goel and Joyner).

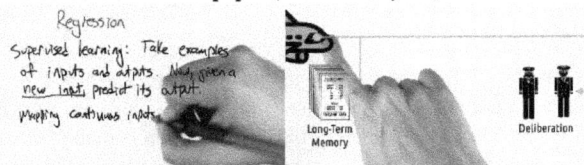

Figure 1. A still from one of the early courses produced in the program (left), and one from a later course (right). Over time, the production workflow shifted from the virtual whiteboard with a working pen to an emphasis on produced diagrams, visuals, and animations.

As course delivery began, experimentation focused on ways to address the myriad of challenges to scaling a program while keeping all of the rigors and procedures associated with an accredited degree. Likely the most significant development, though, was the discovery that online students could be relied upon to work as teaching assistants to support the program's growth. Early semesters relied upon on-campus students, but not enough such students were available to support the program's growth, and the cost of their tuition waivers and stipends was prohibitively expensive compared to the inexpensive price paid by online students. We hypothesized that online students would be too occupied with work, family, and coursework obligations to work in the role, but found that enough were interested to support the program's growth. Additionally, they were more suited to give better feedback given their professional backgrounds, and they were motivated by more intrinsic and altruistic factors than extrinsic [15]. Compounding this benefit was the realization that online students never truly "leave" campus: students may consider working as teaching assistants after graduation. Of the 250 teaching assistants hired for fall 2018 at time of writing, 19% are alumni of the online program, and 43% are present students in the program. 28% of the remaining teaching assistants are on-campus MS students, and 10% are on-campus PhD students. This ability to hire alumni—and apparent interest from alumni in being hired—provides a pool of potential teaching assistant candidates that will continue to grow over time even as program enrollment ultimately stabilizes.

Additionally, early feedback from students in the initial semesters led to changes in the course production process. One course in this second phase of development experimented with avoiding the virtual whiteboard and instead pre-producing all course visuals.

During recording, the professor retained the ability to point to elements on the screen with a recorded hand, similar to an instructor pointing at elements on a slide. Although there was skepticism that this change would lead to a dry presentation of bullet-point slides, the approach was ultimately successful as it allowed significant resources to be invested into producing high-quality, previously reviewed, engaging visuals [27]. This approach has since become the standard approach for creating new courses for the program, and video producers—previously responsible solely for post-production—began to take on the roles of graphic designers and artists. Course developers, in turn, began focusing more attention on translating the professors' vision into descriptions of visuals for the video producers to create even without subject matter expertise. This change then freed professors to focus entirely on their manner of presenting during recording rather than having to attend to screen layout, virtual ink color, and other distractions from speaking. Figure 1 shows typical visuals from an early course and a more recent course produced for the program.

Other areas of experimentation include forum management, office hour delivery, and grading management. These early experiments have given way to a "toolbox" of approaches to delivering different classes based on the specific requirements of their content, students, and teaching teams. A comprehensive view of the variety of different approaches developed through this phase is available in prior work [16]. The initiatives described in section 4 below also took place during this phase.

In many ways, this experimentation phase is a growth phase as well: Figure 2 shows the growth of the program during these semesters, measured in seats. A seat is a single student enrolling in a class: if one student takes two classes, they count as two seats. The figure portrays seats because a single student taking two classes requires no less work for the professors and teaching assistants than two students each taking one class. Thus, the program has grown from 10 courses and 1,828 seats in its first open semester in fall 2014 to 29 classes and 8,911 seats in spring 2018.

3.3 Normalization

The current phase in the program is modeled here as normalization. This label is not to suggest that experimentation has ended, but rather that a technological and procedural foundation has been laid. There are still challenges to be addressed and improvements to be made, but unlike in the experimentation phase, those are no longer seen as existential: whereas inability to scale feedback and assessment would threaten the very viability of the program, the challenges to be addressed now concern improving student outcomes and experiences, maintaining growth, and leveraging emerging opportunities.

Supporting that notion, the program continues to grow: this term, over 1500 students are expected to begin the program, more than the total number of alumni the program has generated so far. Graduation numbers have risen each semester since the inaugural class graduated in December 2015, and it is likely that matriculation and graduation numbers may ultimately balance out as they do on-campus (where the total enrollment capacity is dictated more strictly by housing and lecture hall capacity). That point has not been reached yet, however.

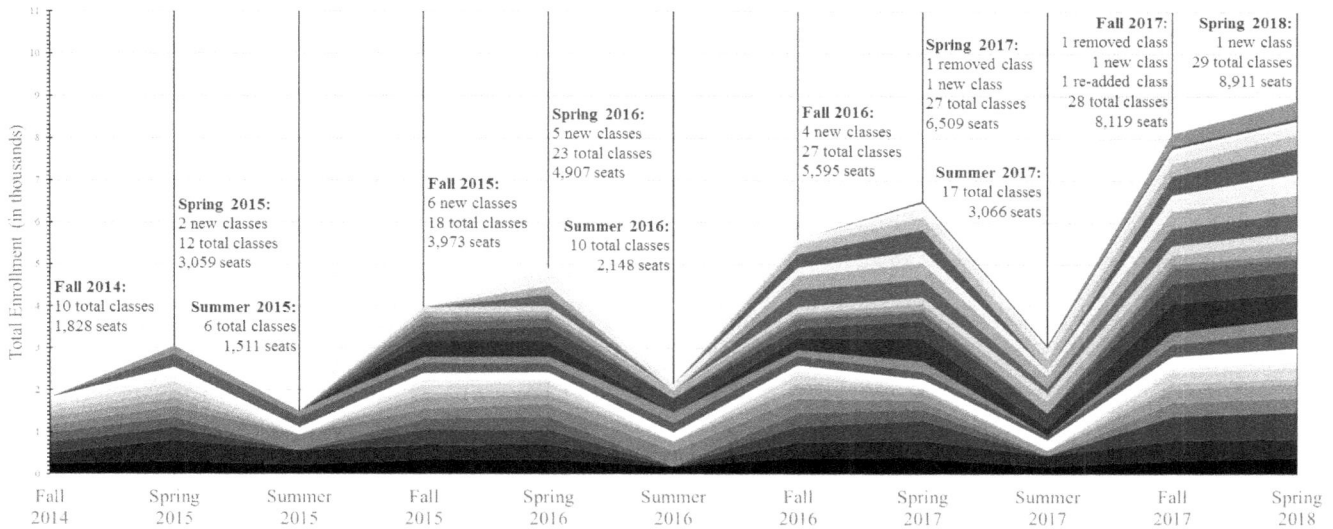

Figure 2. Growth of the program over time. Summer semesters are shorter, and thus some courses are not offered during summer. Each color represents a different course; color families represent the semester of launch for each course.

Thus, normalization focuses pedagogically on setting and communicating best practices across the program, and administratively on building out the supporting infrastructure behind the program. On the administrative side, the later years of the program's history have seen the hiring of a half-dozen academic advisers; multiple associate directors ded icated to topics like admissions, grievances, and the student experience; and greater relationships with other departments of campus covering academic integrity, student life, and alumni relations.

Pedagogically, much of this initial success is owed to the entrepreneurial nature of the courses and their professors: each has been active in experimenting and revising their own classes, discovering procedures and developing technologies that likely would never have been realized had requirements been communicated in a more top-down fashion. However, enough has been learned that a set of best practices has emerged: these may be challenged by future experiments, but such experiments should build from the experiences of these previous semesters. Moreover, there are specific details that must be filled in for every course: every course has its own deadlines, late policy, regrade policy, and so on. We are encouraging more standardization across these criteria so students may spend less time learning a course's specific delivery policies and more time learning the course's content.

The experimentation focuses now on building from that solid and shared foundation, but experimentation is underway. In fall 2018, for example, the program's peer review tool has been adjusted to share reviews across all reviewers of a particular assignment to gauge whether that shared foundation sparks more conversation or if the quality of students' feedback rises due to any perceived social pressure. In spring 2019, work is planned to quantify the biases that may emerge based on the name attached to a student in peer review; this controlled experiment would be able to quantitatively answer the extent to which a name associated with

a certain gender or demographic group is prone to receive systematically better or worse numeric evaluation and feedback.

Other ongoing experimentation looks at the potential use of virtual reality to facilitate social presence in online learning and the increasing role that AI serves in providing students rapid feedback and answers to their questions. Those initiatives bring the program's development full circle back to one of its original motivations: the desire to innovate, and the unique ability of computing professors and students to contribute to both the program's content and its platform. This innovation echoes one of the major new opportunities in the program: how do we scale research opportunities for online students as we have scaled learning opportunities?

4 Technological Initiatives

Significant research has already been done on this program. However, much of that research has focused on elements of scale that are not unique to a computer science program, such as scaling human grading, office hours, peer grading, and forum management [3][12][15][16][19]. In teaching CS, however, there are unique additional demands absent from other fields, such as increased technological needs (e.g. cloud computing resources), unique types of integrity violations (e.g. code plagiarism), and increased focus on projects.

Those needs have given way to one of the program's distinct features: a unity of platform and skillset. As an online program, all elements of instruction and assessment are delivered via technology. As a CS program, all faculty members and students are (or must become) proficient with the design and development of technology. As a result, we note that several of the solutions to the demands documented above have come from students or faculty teaching in the program rather than external partners, and moreover, that there are several opportunities in teaching online that these professors and students have been uniquely positioned to exploit.

4.1 AI for Forum Administration

Significant attention has been paid to forum administration, whether it be in for-credit online courses (e.g. [23]), MOOCs (e.g. [26]), or non-academic settings (e.g. [5]). Like MOOCs, for-credit at-scale courses have a massive number of interactions, but like for-credit courses, they carry the expectation that all questions will receive answers from official course staff. As graduate-level CS courses, these questions are often back-and-forth discussions to debug errors or expand knowledge, not solely isolated questions with singular answers.

While non-technical human-based solutions have been developed [16], several projects have applied AI to this challenge. In one of Goel's projects, an AI agent was developed based on previous semesters' Q&A patterns as well as a structured knowledge representation of course information to proactively answer student questions when a certain level of confidence in the answer could be achieved [9]. Starner has developed a tool that intelligently recommends related questions to students based on new questions they are asking in order to offload responsibility for finding repeated questions from students or teaching assistants. Both projects aim to allow students to get answers more quickly, either by proactively delivering an answer or making an existing answer easier to find, while also reducing the number of questions teaching assistants must answer individually.

Forums play an additional role regarding community-building in online courses and may be analyzed to signify overall student sentiment or identify students in need of individual intervention. For a class project, two students in the program individually leveraged sentiment analysis to accomplish these two tasks: one AI system flags individual students whose tone is seen trending negatively for instructor intervention, while another gauges overall classroom sentiment to synthesize for instructors points of contention or difficulty in the semester [31]. Another student used sentimental analysis to evaluate longitudinal changes in discourse in one of the program's courses [3].

4.2 Code Plagiarism Detection & Deterrence

Detecting code plagiarism is a commonly referenced problem in computer science education that has given rise to several projects (e.g. [1][4][21], among many others). While many are narrowly tied to a particular programming language or context, MOSS [29] covers multiple languages. However, detecting if two code files are similar is only the last stage of plagiarism detection at scale. The ubiquity of tools like Github for sharing work demands that plagiarism detection occur across semesters rather than just within singular assignment submissions, but these courses at scale retain thousands of submissions after multiple semesters. To support organizing and filtering the results for only pertinent pairs, one student for her class project developed a tool specifically for organizing archives of previous submissions, deliberately uploading pertinent sets for evaluation, and presenting results for efficient confirmation and action [32].

Detecting plagiarism relies on possessing both the original and the copied material, but no plagiarism detection solution can address the case of homework-for-hire services where the original is never available to anyone but the student ultimately submitting it as their original work. To combat this tactic, Starner has led a project to construct an AI agent to proactively identify suspected requests for homework-for-hire on a popular freelancing web site, with plans to extend that work to other services as well.

As an international program, the courses are also notably impacted by the documented difference in cultural perceptions of plagiarism [11]. To address this dynamic, one course has—in addition to employing MOSS to detect plagiarism and proactively having public code repositories removed—authored content with embedded formative assessment to instruct students on what behaviors are permitted and forbidden.

4.3 Peer Evaluation and Participation

Peer assessment has been heavily used in MOOCs, for both summative (e.g. [33]) and formative feedback (e.g. [20]). Research on this program, however, has noted the need—for accreditation and reputation—to rely on expert review rather than peer review for generating grades [15]. Peer review may nonetheless play a pedagogical or supporting role, however. Isbell has led a project wherein peer review of short answer responses is seeded with responses whose assessment is known. A probabilistic graphical model is then constructed to establish individual students' proficiency in evaluation, which can be used to generate grades for their peers or to evaluate those students directly [19]. Joyner led a project to modify an existing peer review platform to equip graders with the results of a round of peer review while grading, finding that doing so increased students' perceptions of the quality of feedback they received [12].

As part of a graduate-level CS program, the program also has courses focused on design or evaluation of interfaces. Toward this end, students may need to conduct surveys, interviews, or demonstrations and gather feedback. Classmates' participation in these is encouraged and scored for course credit. To support this process, a student under the direction of Joyner developed a platform for students to create surveys or evaluations and share them with classmates, whose participation is then recorded automatically for inclusion in their grade.

4.4 Automated Evaluation and Feedback

One major area of opportunity in online learning is the opportunity for AI-driven automated feedback. As instruction and assessment are already occurring in a computational interface, the platform is present to give students immediate evaluation in support of a rapid feedback cycle. To realize this potential, Goel and Joyner developed the notion of nanotutoring, wherein small, highly specialized AI agents are developed for specific problems [6]. These nanotutors, inspired by the broad literature on intelligent tutoring systems, address problems narrow enough that the entire potential answer space may be mapped to feedback, but broad enough that student answers may have hundreds of variations. Goel and Joyner constructed from scratch over 100 such nanotutors in their course and have received positive feedback on the role this feedback plays in students' learning [7].

On the other end of the spectrum, automated evaluation is also possible on much larger projects of the outcome measures are objective. In one class taught by Goel and Joyner, students are asked to construct cognitive agents that attempt a human intelligence test [8]. Upon submission to the autograding platform, the students' agents are tested against a battery of problems they did not see while writing the agent. Students are then given the results of this test immediately so they may continue to iterate on and improve the agent. This project was used before in the course's on-campus counterpart, but the scale of the online program provided the incentive and resources to develop a sophisticated solution.

The platform on which this solution resides is general and available for use by other classes as well, which has given way to several new opportunities for innovation. Goel and Joyner capitalized on the formal structure and automated execution to study crowdsourced ideation for complex problems featuring novel solutions from students [13]. In Starner's course, students construct separate agents for search and for game-playing, the latter of which are then matched against each other in a tournament. Similar to crowdsourced ideation, this infrastructure combined with the program's scale and the instructors' research background has given rise to valuable research on the content itself. Notably, this infrastructure was all constructed by program staff for the program; no out-of-the-box solutions are used.

4.5 Student-to-Student Advising

Professors in this online program have noted the significant impact that the online platform allows individual students to have [14]. The forum-based environment allows every student to effectively have unlimited time "in front of" the class to share their thoughts without taking time away from the planned lecture. As a result, a powerful student community has emerged. While this community could be present in any similar program regardless of subject matter, the technical ability of these students has given rise to projects to support their classmates. The most significant among these is an unofficial student-run web app in which students review courses and read reviews of other students. The site evolved from a collaborative spreadsheet shared in the early days of the program, and although similar sites exist (e.g. RateMyProfessor), this site's close tie with the program's structure and student body drive significantly more traffic. To date, the site has received over 2,700 reviews, most connected with numeric assessments of the quality, difficulty, and workload for quick summarization. Students may filter reviews by semester, rating, and difficulty, and the course pages automatically pull from the school's publicly-available grade database to augment the reviews. The entire effort has been performed completely independently by the student community with no support from the school, and the project has changed hands multiple times since its inception. The platform has even served as the target for follow-up studies; one student used sentiment analysis on the platform's reviews and compared them to official university reviews, finding that these public classmate-targeted reviews showed more negative sentiment than private professor-targeted reviews [24].

5   Persistent Challenges

While the program has largely addressed existential threats, there are still challenges and opportunities. One major issue is course maintenance. Most courses in the program are built on top of a MOOC with hundreds of videos. Over 14,000 individual videos have been produced, most around 3 minutes in duration. Most professors will record a lecture (which is then split into smaller videos) in a single sitting, lending continuity to the presentation. If later content is to be added or revised, the process typically demands re-recording the entire lecture. Joyner experimented with focusing on video independence and modularity and has found the course easier to maintain. This solution requires a fundamental shift in the initial development paradigm that is less natural than the standard presentation style.

Forum administration remains an issue. Although the forum workflows documented in prior work [16] and the AI tools described in section 4 help, forums for large classes still become difficult for both students and teaching teams. While AI may find duplicate questions within a semester or proactively answer routine questions, a graduate CS program is characterized in part by discussion. Constructing an AI to participate in discussion is more difficult challenge than clustering or pairing answers to questions. Developments are underway to create a forum built with the needs of a large, for-credit online course in mind.

Finally, much of this analysis has focused on delivery of individual courses. However, the program exists as part of a broader ecosystem, from which it draws value. Elements of that broader ecosystem are strained by the program's growth. Academic advising, for example, is needed by the program's students. Institute policies exist for documenting family emergencies or illnesses, tracking and investigating integrity violations, and addressing students' grievances. In many cases, technological solutions are possible, but many of these require a human's direct involvement in each case. Scaling these processes remains a challenge.

6   Conclusion

This paper has recounted the motivation, creation, expansion, and normalization of an online graduate program in computer science. While in some ways it is a straightforward evolution of traditional distance learning, it is distinct in its approach to leveraging the lessons learned from the rise of MOOCs and the extent to which it takes advantage of the online environment to improve the student experience. In many ways, the scale, asynchronicity, and remoteness of the program have proved to be opportunities rather than obstacles: they allow the creation of a 24/7 classroom where students may interact with one another any without permanently missing any lecture or discussion.

REFERENCES

[1] Aleksi Ahtiainen, Sami Surakka, and Mikko Rahikainen (2006). Plaggie: GNU-licensed source code plagiarism detection engine for Java exercises. In *Proceedings of the 6th Baltic Sea Conference on Computing Education Research: Koli Calling 2006*, 141-142. ACM Press.

[2] Marc Beylerian & Brian H. Kleiner (2003). The downsized workplace. *Management Research News, 26*(2/3/4), 97-108.

[3] Ida Camacho & Ashok Goel. (2018, June). Longitudinal trends in sentiment polarity and readability of an Online Masters of Computer Science course. In *Proceedings of the Fifth Annual ACM Conference on Learning @ Scale*. ACM Press.

[4] Georgina Cosma & Mike Joy (2012). An approach to source-code plagiarism detection and investigation using latent semantic analysis. *IEEE Transactions on Computers, 61*(3), 379-394.

[5] Kushal Dave, Martin Wattenberg & Michael Muller (2004, November). Flash forums and forumReader: navigating a new kind of large-scale online discussion. In *Proceedings of the 2004 ACM conference on Computer-Supported Cooperative Work*, 232-241. ACM Press.

[6] Ashok Goel & David A. Joyner (2016). An Experiment in Teaching Cognitive Systems Online. In Haynes, D. (Ed.) *International Journal for Scholarship of Technology-Enhanced Learning 1*(1).

[7] Ashok Goel & David A. Joyner (2017). Using AI to Teach AI: Lessons from an Online AI Class. *AI Magazine 38*(2), 48-59.

[8] Ashok Goel, Maithilee Kunda, David A. Joyner & Swaroop Vattam (2013). Learning about Representational Modality: Design and Programming Projects for Knowledge-Based AI. In *Fourth AAAI Symposium on Educational Advances in Artificial Intelligence*, 1586-1591.

[9] Ashok Goel & Lalith Polepeddi (2016). Jill Watson: A Virtual Teaching Assistant for Online Education. Georgia Institute of Technology Technical Report. Retrieved from https://smartech.gatech.edu/handle/1853/59104

[10] Joshua Goodman, Julia Melkers & Amanda Pallais (2019). Can online delivery increase access to education? *Journal of Labor Economics, 37*(1), 1-34.

[11] Niall Hayes & Lucas D. Introna (2005). Cultural values, plagiarism, and fairness: When plagiarism gets in the way of learning. *Ethics & Behavior, 15*(3), 213-231.

[12] David A. Joyner, Wade Ashby, Liam Irish, Yeeling Lam, Jacob Langston, Isabel Lupiani, Mike Lustig, Paige Pettoruto, Dana Sheahen, Angela Smiley, Amy Bruckman, & Ashok Goel (2016). Graders as Meta-Reviewers: Simultaneously Scaling and Improving Expert Evaluation for Large Online Classrooms. In *Proceedings of the Third Annual ACM Conference on Learning at Scale*. Edinburgh, Scotland. ACM Press.

[13] David A. Joyner, Darren Bedwell, Chris Graham, Warren Lemmon, Oscar Martinez & Ashok Goel (2015). Using Human Computation to Acquire Novel Methods for Addressing Visual Analogy Problems in Intelligence Tests. In *Proceedings of the Sixth International Conference on Computational Creativity*. Provo, Utah.

[14] David A. Joyner, Ashok Goel & Charles Isbell (2016). The Unexpected Pedagogical Benefits of Making Higher Education Accessible. In *Proceedings of the Third Annual ACM Conference on Learning at Scale*. Edinburgh, Scotland.

[15] David A. Joyner (2017). Scaling Expert Feedback: Two Case Studies. In *Proceedings of the Fourth Annual ACM Conference on Learning at Scale*. Cambridge, Massachusetts. ACM Press.

[16] David A. Joyner (2018). Squeezing the Limeade: Policies and Workflows for Scalable Online Degrees. In *Proceedings of the Fifth Annual ACM Conference on Learning at Scale*. London, United Kingdom. ACM Press.

[17] David A. Joyner (2018). Toward CS1 at Scale: Building and Testing a MOOC-for-Credit Candidate. In *Proceedings of the Fifth Annual ACM Conference on Learning at Scale*. London, United Kingdom. ACM Press.

[18] Rita Kirshstein (2013). Rising tuition and diminishing state funding: An overview. *Journal of Collective Bargaining in the Academy*, (8), 14.

[19] Pushkar Kolhe, Michael L. Littman & Charles L. Isbell (2016, April). Peer Reviewing Short Answers using Comparative Judgement. In *Proceedings of the Third Annual ACM Conference on Learning at Scale*. Edinburgh, Scotland. ACM Press.

[20] Chinmay E. Kulkarni, Michael S. Bernstein, & Scott R. Klemmer (2015, March). PeerStudio: rapid peer feedback emphasizes revision and improves performance. In *Proceedings of the Second (2015) ACM Conference on Learning @ Scale*, 75-84. ACM Press.

[21] Cynthia Kustanto & Inggriani Liem (2009, May). Automatic source code plagiarism detection. In *Proceedings of the 10th ACIS International Conference on Software Engineering, Artificial Intelligences, Networking and Parallel/Distributed Computing*, 481-486. IEEE.

[22] Frank Levy & Richard J. Murnane (2005). *The new division of labor: How computers are creating the next job market*. Princeton University Press.

[23] Margaret Mazzolini & Sarah Maddison (2003). Sage, guide or ghost? The effect of instructor intervention on student participation in online discussion forums. *Computers & Education, 40*(3), 237-253.

[24] Heather Newman & David A. Joyner (2018). Sentiment Analysis of Student Evaluations of Teaching. In *Proceedings of the 19th International Conference on Artificial Intelligence in Education*. London, United Kingdom. Springer.

[25] Elvira Nica & Catalina-Oana Mirica (2017). Is higher education still a wise investment? Evidence on rising student loan debt in the US. *Psychosociological Issues in Human Resource Management, 5*(1), 235.

[26] DFO Onah, Jane E. Sinclair & Russell Boyatt (2014, November). Exploring the use of MOOC discussion forums. In *Proceedings of London International Conference on Education*, 1-4.

[27] Chaohua Ou, Ashok Goel, David A. Joyner & Daniel Haynes (2016). Designing Videos with Pedagogical Strategies: Online Students' Perceptions of Their Effectiveness. In *Proceedings of the Third Annual ACM Conference on Learning at Scale*. Edinburgh, Scotland.

[28] Laura Pappano (2012, November 4). The Year of the MOOC. The New York Times (p. ED26).

[29] Cathy Sandeen (2013). Integrating MOOCs into traditional higher education: The emerging "MOOC 3.0" era. *Change: The Magazine of Higher Learning, 45*(6), 34-39.

[30] Saul Schleimer, Daniel S. Wilkerson & Alex Aiken (2003, June). Winnowing: local algorithms for document fingerprinting. In *Proceedings of the 2003 ACM SIGMOD International Conference on Management of Data*, 76-85. ACM Press.

[31] Michael Schubert, Damian Durruty, & David A. Joyner (2018). Measuring Learner Tone and Sentiment at Scale via Text Analysis of Forum Posts. In *Proceedings of the 8th Edition of the International Workshop on Personalization Approaches in Learning Environments (PALE)*. London, United Kingdom.

[32] Klaus Schwab (2017). *The fourth industrial revolution*. Crown Business.

[33] Dana Sheahen & David A. Joyner (2016). TAPS: A MOSS Extension for Detecting Software Plagiarism at Scale. In *Proceedings of the Third Annual ACM Conference on Learning at Scale*. Edinburgh, Scotland.

[34] Hoi K. Suen (2014). Peer assessment for massive open online courses (MOOCs). *The International Review of Research in Open and Distributed Learning, 15*(3).

[35] Leslie Waguespack, Jeffry Stephen Babb & David Yates (2018). Triangulating Coding Bootcamps in IS Education: Bootleg Education or Disruptive Innovation?. *Information Systems Education Journal, 16*(6), 48.

Undergraduate CS Curricula in the U.S. and China

Comparison Using a Selected Set of Data

Xiannong Meng
Department of Computer Science
Bucknell University
Lewisburg, PA, U.S.A.
xmeng@bucknell.edu

Jianming Deng[†]
School of Computer Science and Engineering
Southeast University
Nanjing, China
jmdeng@seu.edu.cn

ABSTRACT

Computing science and information technology are playing an increasingly important role in our economy and society. In one listing of publicly traded companies, the U.S. and China captured the top 10 spots with eight U.S. companies and two Chinese companies, all of which are tech companies. It is of great interest to examine and compare the undergraduate computing science education in the two countries. The U.S. has about 1,500 academic units that offer undergraduate computing related programs. China has 2,850 such programs. We selected 16 programs in the U.S. and eight programs in China in our study. The data collected include titles, the number and the hours of computer science courses as well as the required math, sciences, and engineering courses. We found that Chinese degree programs often require more courses in CS and math and more overall credit hours to graduate. We also found that a typical CS student in China takes more courses per semester.

CCS CONCEPTS

• Social and professional topics • Computer science education

KEYWORDS

Curriculum; Undergraduate CS education; China; U.S.A.

ACM Reference format:

Xiannong Meng and Jianming Deng. 2018. Undergraduate CS Curricula in U.S. and China: Comparison Using a Selected Set of Data. In *Proceedings of ACM Global Computing Education Conference (CompEd'2019). May 17-19, 2019, Chengdu, China. ACM New York, NY, USA, 7 pages.*
https://doi.org/10.1145/3300115.3309526

1 Introduction

Computing science and information technology are playing an increasingly important role in our economy and society. They also

[†]Jianming Deng is also a Professor of Computer Software at Jinling Institute of Technology in Nanjing, China

CompEd '19, May 17–19, 2019, Chengdu,Sichuan, China
© 2019 Association for Computing Machinery.
ACM ISBN 978-1-4503-6259-7/19/05$15.00
https://doi.org/10.1145/3300115.3309526

have a great impact on many aspects of the world. As such both the U.S. and China place emphasis on computing science undergraduate education. The U.s. has about 1,500 academic units that offer computing related programs [6] with 64,450 bachelor's degrees conferred in 2016 [14]. On the other hand, China has 2,850 computing related degree programs that have 902,000 students [19]. Besides numbers, both the U.S. and Chinese computing science students and graduates who go to industry or graduate schools are very competitive in many measures. For example, in the last three years (2016, 2017, 2018) of International Collegiate Programming Contest (ICPC), student teams from China won a total of eight top medals (two gold, five silver, one bronze) while teams from the U.S. won four top medals (one gold, one silver, two bronze) [4], [18]. Outside academics, the graduates of computing science contribute to the economy of their country significantly. In one listing of publicly traded companies, the U.S. and China captured the top 10 spots with eight U.S. companies and two Chinese companies, all of which are tech companies [17]. The super-computers made by China and the U.S. dominate the top-500 fastest computer competitions. If we consider the top 10 winners in each of last 10 listings, the Chinese-made super-computers placed 16 spots in the total 100 spots, claiming first in nine of the 10 listings; while the U.S. placed 51 spots, claiming one first spot [15]. It is of great interest to examine and compare the undergraduate computing science education in the two countries. The motive of this study is to help us better understand the CS education in the U.S. and China. We also hope the two systems will learn from the strengths of each other so that we can better educate next generations of computing scientists and engineers.

We selected 16 programs in the U.S. and eight in China in this study, based mostly on the recent *U.S. News* ranking. The data collected includes computing science core requirement, math and science requirement, credit hours required to graduate, among some other subjects. The rest of the paper is organized as follows. Section 2 reviews related work in the area of CS education in China and the U.S. Section 3 explores some historic notes of CS curriculum in the two countries. Section 4 discusses the methods used and the type of data collected in the study. Each of the Section 5 and Section 6 presents the data and a summary of the computing science course requirement and other course requirement including math, science, and engineering in the programs under study, respectively. We present some observations in Section 7, followed by some concluding remarks in Section 8.

2 Related Work

We first examine the related study of CS curriculum in China and in the U.S. Though the computing science education in China started in late 1950s [21], it is relatively recent to see any English publication on the study of Chinese computing science education. Li and Lunt [12] discussed a brief history of CS education in China, indicating that the Ministry of Education in China (MOEC) started a systematic review of the status of CS education in China around 2005, aiming to improve the CS education. Zhang and Lo [20] reviewed the status of the CS education in China at the time. The paper reported some important statistics such as the number of departments or colleges offering CS related degrees, the pyramid model of CS education, i.e., technology-oriented, engineering-oriented, and science-oriented. The paper also listed major course requirement for the CS degrees. Huang and Hang [8] presented the result of their study to improve the "entrepreneurial spirits" of Chinese computing undergraduates, as the country moves towards applying CS and IT in many aspects of everyday life. Jiang [9] studied and compared three CS programs each in China and in the U.S. The paper by Douglas et al. [7] reported an initiative to explore internationalization of computing science education. The authors reported a Pacific Rim community of computing science departments and high tech firms to explore a new model of computing science education focusing on the knowledge, skills, and competencies necessary for professional success and leadership in a global context. On the U.S. side, CS curriculum has long been a subject of research and discussion in SIGCSE, IEEE-CS, or ASEE sponsored forum. The publications are abundant. We will briefly review the evolution of CS curriculum in the U.S. and China in next section.

3 Curriculum Development in U.S. and China

In the U.S., the computing curricula have been evolving and documented since 1960s. The first ACM computing curricula guideline was published in 1968 [2]. Since then every 10 years or so, the computing curricula were revised. The subsequent curricula revisions took place in 1978, 1991, 2001, and most recently in 2013 [3], [16], [10], and [11]. A group of computing education experts initiated and revised the curricula in the early years. Now a joint task force of ACM and IEEE-CS is in charge of the task of revising the curricula. We can see two highlights from the evolution of the computing curricula in the U.S. from these documents. One is that the CS curricula show a strong mathematics influence. The other is that the recent (2013) guidelines provide flexibility in core requirement by splitting content into Knowledge Units, rather than in courses, to accommodate the ever-growing amount of new content in the field.

The evolution of computing education in China can be divided into four stages according to [21], 1958 to 1966, 1966 to 1976, 1977 to 1994, and 1995 to current. These stages of development reflect various changes in the goals of computing education and thus the curricula. Curricula in Chinese higher education institutes are usually proposed and set by a group of filed experts organized by MOEC, see for example [5] for a set of curricula guidelines that include computing science. Most recently started in 2015 and completed in 2016, MOEC and a working group created a set of guidelines for undergraduate curriculum of applied computing majors such as software engineering, network engineering, and internet of things. An example is the guidelines for software engineering [19]. An overwhelming strategy is to divide computing majors into more specific areas such as AI, computing security, software engineering, among others. For example, the MOEC initiated "national exemplary" colleges of software engineering in 2001. More recently, under the guidance of MOEC, many universities established more "application"- or "industry"-oriented majors such as AI, computing security, and internet of things. According to [13], more than 70 Chinese universities and colleges have introduced AI-related majors. Over 20 AI colleges or schools have been established in various universities since May 2017. At the same time, we can see that the Chinese higher education institutes are paying more attention to what the U.S. universities are doing in CS curricula. For example, in 2015 the ACM China Committee on Education translated and published the ACM Computer Science Curriculum 2013 [1].

4 Methods of Study and Data Collected

With huge number of computing science programs and students in the U.S. and in China, it is difficult, if not impossible, to conduct a comprehensive study. We selected a few programs from the U.S. and China in our study. The selection is based on the ranking of undergraduate computing science programs published by the *U.S. News* in 2017. On the U.S. side, we picked eight national universities and eight undergraduate engineering colleges. On the Chinese side, we chose eight Chinese national universities. All data are collected from public websites of the respective schools, in English or in Chinese. A few excellent Chinese CS programs were not included because we cannot find their data on the web. The U.S. programs include those from MIT, Berkeley, Stanford, CMU, UIUC, Georgia Tech, University of Michigan, University of Texas at Austin, Harvey Mudd, Rose Hulman, West Point, Air Force Academy, Naval Academy, Bucknell, Cal Poly, and Milwaukee School of Engineering. The Chinese programs include those from Tsinghua University (Tsinghua), Peking University (PKU), Shanghai Jiao Tong University (SJTU), University of Science and Technology of China (USTC), Beihang University (BUAA), Harbin Institute of Technology (HIT), Beijing University of Post and Telecommunications (BUPT), and Southeast University (SEU). See Appendix A for a complete list.

The data collected include the required computing science courses, the required math, science, and engineering courses, as well as the hours for each of these courses and the total semester hours required for graduation. One of the challenges in comparing semester hours is that every school may use a different mechanism to define their hours. We take the following approach. If the credit is defined for a course, we take its face value. For example, a calculus course in one school may be defined as 4 credits, another school may have it as 5. We take them as declared. A second challenge is that the length of the semester is not all the same across different schools. The Chinese universities usually have 16-18 weeks of instructions per semester, while the U.S. universities typically have 14 weeks of instructions in semester-based systems and 10 weeks of instructions in quarter-based systems. We take a simplistic approach by assuming all semesters have 16 weeks of instructions in Chinese universities, 14 weeks of instructions in U.S. universities with semester systems, and 10 weeks in quarter systems. Another challenge is that some courses, especially those in Chinese programs list the lab associated with a course separately. Whenever possible, these lab hours are combined with the lecture for the course. All these factors alert us that the comparison, especially in specific credit hours or course hours, is an approximation.

5 Computing Science Course Requirement

We first examine the computing science course requirement in these degree programs. The "computing science course requirement" include the core courses and the elective courses of which students are required to take certain number for their degree program. While it is difficult to discuss the exact content of the courses, we infer the course content from its title. We compare the total credit hours required to graduate, the number of courses, credit hours, and the number of hours for all computing science courses, including required number of hours for electives. As discussed earlier, the hours assigned to a course vary widely across different schools. We use the "normalized hours" in our comparison. Some schools designate some commonly recognized math courses as computing science courses, i.e., giving them CS course titles. We took the liberty to move such courses to the math course category. Examples include discrete math, probability and statistics, and modern algebra. In addition, some schools list the lab or project portion of the course separately from the course; while others do not. In such cases, we combined the lecture hours with the project/lab hours in the normalized hours. Table 1 shows the four pieces of data from the eight Chinese universities. The credit hours as well as the total hours are the summation of all computing science courses for a particular school. Table 2 shows the same information for the eight U.S. national universities.

Table 1: Count, credits, hours of CS, total credits for degree

Chinese national	CS courses			Credits for graduation
	Count	Credits	Hours	
Tsinghua	18	51	616	172
PKU	18	53	832	150
SJTU	13	48	648	165
USTC	27	85	1208	162.5
BUAA	15	58	792	140
HIT	22	54	1072	167.5
BUPT	20	54	696	153
SEU	14	46	640	150

In Table 1 (and Table 2), the "Credits for graduation" is the total number of credits required of the degree. For example, the CS degree in Tshinghua University requires 18 computing science courses including both required core courses and elective courses. These courses add up to 51 credits, or about 30 percent of the total

credits for the degree. The number of CS courses required range from 13 in SJTU to 27 in USTC, the difference is huge!

Table 2: Count, credits, hours of CS, total credits for degree

US national	CS courses			Credits for graduation
	Count	Credits	Hours	
MIT	10	39	399	128
Berkeley	8	32	336	120
Stanford	12	36	360	180
CMU	12	46	504	120
UIUC	14	47	588	128
GA Tech	14	44	588	124
Michigan	11	36	399	128
Texas	13	41	546	127

The number of required courses, the CS credits, and the total credits required of the degree programs in the U.S. national universities does not appear varying as widely compared to those in the Chinese universities.

Not all US universities specify the hours of study for their courses. Some use very different way of counting the hours. In Table 2 and Table 3, we normalize all course hours as follows. For semester based universities, every full course is counted as 42 hours (half course would be 21 hours) based on the reason of 14 weeks of instructions and three hours of meeting per week. For quarter-based universities, every full course is counted as 30 hours for the same reason because a quarter is 10 weeks long (at least among the schools under our study.) Note Stanford is the only one in this group of U.S. and Chinese national universities running a quarter system. It requires 180 credits to graduate.

The same information is shown in Table 3 for the eight U.S. undergraduate engineering colleges that grant none or at most limited number of master's degrees.

Table 3: Count, credits, hours of CS, total credits for degree

US undergraduate	CS courses			Credits for graduation
	Count	Credits	Hours	
HarveyMudd	14	40	560	128
RoseHulman	20	66	600	192
West Point	14	40	588	120
Air Force	13	39	546	116*
Naval	15	38	602	137
Bucknell	12	46*	483	136*
CalPoly	20	76	570	180
Milwaukee	23	90	690	192

Note *: Air Force Academy and Bucknell University use course count or course credits as their graduation requirement, not credit hours. Air Force requires 29 academic courses, Bucknell 34 course credits. For comparison, the degree credit hours in these two schools are counted as 1 full course = 4 credit hours.

Among the eight undergraduate engineering colleges listed, Rose Hulman, Cal Poly, and Milwaukee School of Engineering run on a quarter system. The rest are on a semester system. That is the reason why the course count in these three schools are higher.

We now compare the computing science courses that each of these schools require. While the exact titles of the course for each school vary, we use some commonly recognized course titles. Table 4 uses course title abbreviations to make a clean presentation. Table 5 gives the complete list of course titles. Because the large number of universities involved in this table, we use letters and digits to represent the schools. Letters represent U.S. universities, while digits represent the Chinese universities. Table 4 contains only U.S. and Chinese national universities. U.S. undergraduate engineering colleges are listed in Table 6. See Append A for a complete mapping of schools.

Table 4: Required computing science courses

	a	b	c	d	e	f	g	h	0	1	2	3	4	5	6	7
C1	x	x	x	x	x	x	x	x	x	x	x	x	x	x	x	x
C2	x	x		x	x	x	x	x	x	x	x	x	x	x	x	x
Or	x	x	x			x	x	x	x	x		x	x		x	x
Os				x		x	x	x	x	x	x	x			x	x
SE	x		x	x	x			x				x		x	x	x
PL			x	x												
CP									x	x		x	x	x	x	x
Al	x		x	x		x		x		x	x	x	x	x	x	
Ar				x	x			x			x	x		x		
Db												x		x	x	x
Nt						x						x		x	x	x
Th	x			x	x	x		x				x		x	x	
Sy	x		x	x	x									x		

Table 5: Mapping the abbreviated CS course titles

C1	Introduction to computer science I
C2	Introduction to computer science II
Or	Computer organization
Os	Operating systems
SE	Software engineering
PL	Programming languages
CP	Compiler
Al	Algorithm
Ar	Computer architecture
Db	Database
Nt	Computer networks
Th	Theory of computation
Sy	Computer systems

Table 6: Required CS courses in U.S. undergraduate colleges

	i	j	k	l	m	n	o	p
C1	x	x	x	x	x	x	x	x
C2	x	x	x	x	x	x	x	x
Or		x	x	x	x	x	x	x
Os		x	x	x	x	x	x	x
SE	x	x	x	x	x	x	x	x
PL	x	x	x	x	x	x	x	x
CP								
Al	x	x	x	x	x	x	x	x
Ar		x			x	x		
Db								
Nt								
Th	x	x	x		x		x	
Sy	x							

Examining Table 4 and Table 6, we can see that Chinese programs require more CS courses compared to the U.S. programs in general. We can find that all schools require CS1 and CS 2 except Stanford (**c** in Table 4) which has an algorithm design course. In addition, many Chinese programs require courses such as compiler, database, and computer networks, while these courses would be electives in the U.S. programs. This phenomenon can be explained from two perspectives. One is that Chinese programs emphasize more on engineering. Unlike most of the U.S. computing science programs, which have math origins, most, if not all, Chinese computing science programs came out of engineering departments in the early years of computing. The second reason is that Chinese higher education is highly regulated. The universities follow closely the guidelines from MOEC, which list these courses as required components.

6 Math, Sciences, and Engineering Course Requirement

We follow a similar pattern to examine the math, sciences, and engineering course requirements. We first look at the math requirement of Chinese universities, the U.S. national universities, and the U.S. undergraduate engineering colleges in Tables 7, 8, and 9, respectively. The values listed in the tables are semester hours. "Cnt" is for the count of math courses, and "CR" is for the total math course credits. We use abbreviations of course titles in these tables to make a clean presentation. The mapping of the title abbreviations is in Table 10.

Table 7: Math requirement of Chinese universities

	M1	M2	PS	AG	DS	OT	Cnt	CR
Tsinghua	80	80	48	96	96	80	9	30
PKU	80	80	48	64		144	7	26
SJTU	96	68	51	48	32	51	6	21
USTC	120	120	60	80		266	11	35
BUAA	96	96	48	96	96		6	24
HIT	88	88	56	64		168	8	29
BUPT	80	80	64	48	80	32	7	24
SEU	64	64	48		80	80	7	23.5

Table 8: Math requirement of U.S. national universities

	M1	M2	M3	PS	AG	DS	OT	Cnt	CR
MIT	42	42				42		3	12
Berkeley	42	42	42	21	21	21	21	5	20
Stanford	30	30	30	30		30	60	7	26
CMU	42	42		42	42	42		5	16
UIUC	42	42	42	42	42	42		6	20
GA Tech	42	42	42	42	42	42	84	8	24
Michigan	42	42	42	42	42	42		6	24
Texas	42	42	42	42	42	42		6	21

Table 9: Math requirement of U.S. undergraduate engineering colleges

	M1	M2	M3	PS	AG	DS	OT	Cnt	CR
HarveyMudd		42	42	42	42	42	84	7	12
RoseHulman	30	30	30	30	30	60		7	31
West Point	42	42		42		42	42	5	19
Air Force	42	42		42		42		4	12
Naval	42	42	42			42		4	12
Bucknell	42	42	42	21		42	63	7	24
CalPoly	30	30	30	30	30	30	30	7	28
Milwaukee	30	30	30	30	30	60	30	8	27

Table 10: Mapping the abbreviated math course titles

M1	Calculus I
M2	Calculus II
M3	Calculus III
PS	Probability and statistics
AG	Linear algebra
DS	Discrete mathematics
OT	Other math courses

The Calculus I and Calculus II in Chinese universities typically mean single variable calculus and multi-variable calculus, which are different from those of most U.S. universities in which multi-variable calculus are treated in a Calculus III course. This is why none of the Chinese universities under study has a Calculus III course. In the U.S. universities, Calculus I and II are required. Harvey Mudd does not list Calculus I as requirement for its CS degree because it is a college-wide requirement. The subject of discrete mathematics is a foundational building block of computing science majors. All U.S. universities explicitly require such a course, so do many of the Chinese universities. The three Chinese universities that do not explicitly list the discrete math course requirement have the subject covered in other courses. PKU has three separate courses, "Sets and graphs," "Algebra and combinatorics" and "Mathematical logic." HIT has "Sets and graphs" and "Mathematical logic." USTC has "Graphs." All these courses are listed under "Others." Overall, the Chinese CS programs require more math courses than those of the U.S. programs. The average number of math courses in the Chinese universities is 7.63. The number for all 16 U.S. schools is 5.94. Note that all Chinese universities are in semester system, while a number of U.S. universities are in quarter system including Stanford, Rose Hulman, Cal Poly, and Milwaukee School of Engineering. Considering this factor, the effective average number of math courses for the U.S. schools would be even lower. Also, note that the Chinese universities have longer semesters, typically in 16-18 weeks of instruction, while the U.S. schools have 14 weeks and 10 weeks of instruction in semester and quarter system, respectively.

Now let us examine the science and engineering course requirement among all schools under study. The case for science courses is relatively simple. The CS programs in Chinese universities all require a Physics I course (a few require a Physics II course) with no other science course requirement. The U.S. universities typically require more science courses in addition to a sequence of two physics courses. The reason that the Chinese programs do not require more science courses is that the MOEC guideline only specifies physics as the science requirement. As for the comparison of engineering courses, please see Table 11, 12, and the discussion of the U.S. national universities in the next paragraph. The semester hours are listed in the tables. We use the same conversion as described before if the original program does not specify the semester hours. Tables 11 and 12 list the values of semester hours for courses including "Analog circuits," "Digital logic," "Analog and digital circuits," and other engineering courses.

From Tables 11 and 12, we can see that all Chinese CS programs require circuits or digital logic or both with the exception of BUAA. Six of the eight programs require additional engineering courses. On the other hand, very little of engineering content is required in the CS programs of the U.S. national universities. Among the eight schools under study, Berkeley requires a 2-course sequence on information device and system design (EE16A/B); Stanford requires an introduction to making course (ENGR 40M); Georgia Tech requires a digital design lab

(ECE2031); and Michigan requires an introduction to engineering (ENGR 100). These required engineering courses are more on the introduction to engineering or engineering system with the exception of Georgia Tech that has a digital lab requirement. Because of the sparse amount of information, we do not make a separate table for the engineering course requirement of the U.S. national universities.

Table 11: Engineering requirement of Chinese universities

	Analog	Digital	AandD	Others
Tsinghua		64		128
PKU	80	48		48
SJTU			80	64
USTC			120	390
BUAA				
HIT		56		
BUPT	32	64		40
SEU			96	144

Table 12: Engineering requirement of U.S. undergraduate engineering colleges

	Analog	Digital	AandD	Others
HarveyMudd				42
RoseHulman				
West Point		42		84
Air Force				168
Naval			42	
Bucknell	42	42		
CalPoly				
Milwaukee				

From Table 12 we can see even the CS programs in U.S. undergraduate engineering colleges do not necessarily all require engineering courses. Overall, the CS programs in Chinese universities require more engineering courses than those in the U.S. universities. This probably is because the Chinese CS programs have their roots in engineering colleges or departments, more so compared to the U.S. CS programs.

7 Some Observations

We summarize our findings from the data presented in the previous sections as follows.

The semesters in Chinese universities are longer so effectively Chinese students complete more hours in their four-year undergraduate study. Chinese programs also typically require more credit hours to graduate than those in the U.S. The average credit hours to graduate for the eight Chinese programs is about 158. The average for the programs of the eight U.S. national universities is 132. For the eight U.S. undergraduate engineering

schools it is 150. Note that among the 16 U.S. universities, Stanford, Rose Hulman, Cal Poly, and Milwaukee School of Engineering use quarter systems. Chinese students often take more courses per semester than American students do. For example, a sample curriculum shows that students of USTC in China take 11 courses worth 27.5 credits in their first semester. Most U.S. students would take 4-6 courses of 16-20 credits at a time, during a semester or a quarter. Note that course count alone does not necessarily reflect the actual workload of a student. Other factors such as the amount of programming, course related research, writing and presenting papers and other course-related activities all play important role in student workload.

The CS programs in China seem emphasizing more on engineering and applications, indicated by the facts that courses such as compiler, database, and computer networks are often required in these Chinese programs, while they are typically electives in the U.S. schools. In addition, the Chinese CS programs actually require more engineering courses on average. They also require more math courses or hours, compared to the U.S. programs. The Chinese programs require very little science component beyond Physics I.

8 Conclusions

In this paper, we examine and compare the undergraduate computing science curricula in a selected group of U.S. and Chinese universities. In addition to eight Chinese programs, a total of 16 U.S. programs are chosen, including eight national universities and eight undergraduate engineering colleges. A few excellent Chinese programs were not selected because their data are not readily available over the internet, either in Chinese or in English.

We compared the total courses and semester hours of three sets of courses across these 24 programs, computing science, math and sciences, and engineering. We found that the Chinese programs require more total courses and hours in CS, math, and engineering, though the U.S. programs require more science courses. The degree programs in these Chinese universities also require more credit hours to graduate.

Challenges and future work remain in such a study. For example, how to take into account the fact that the Chinese programs require more hours and more courses for their degree programs? What are the meanings of "credit hours" exactly in different universities? Would it be possible to conduct a statistical analysis? How can we make meaningful comparison in student workload? What are the general impact of the curricula on the CS education in the two countries? How can we as computing science educators make use of the data found in this study?

We hope the study helps better understand the commonality and differences between the U.S. and Chinese undergraduate computing science education. Further, we hope the study will spark interest in discussions and in conducting further studies in these areas.

REFERENCES

[1] ACM China Committee on Education. (2015). *Computer Science Curricula 2013 (Chinese translation)*, Original by ACM and IEEE, Translated by ACM China Committee on Education and The Computer Science Curriculum Advising Committee of the Ministry of Education of China.

[2] W.F. Atchison *et.al.* (March 1968). Curriculum 68: Recommendations for academic programs in computer science: a report of the ACM curriculum committee on computer science. *Communications of the ACM, 11(3), 151-197.* ACM:New York.

[3] R.H. Austing et.al. (March 1979). Curriculum '78: recommendations for the undergraduate program in computer science: a report of the ACM curriculum committee on computer science. *Communications of the ACM, 22(3), 147-166.* ACM:New York.

[4] Baylor University, "ACM International Collegiate Programming Contest Results 2016," https://icpc.baylor.edu/community/results-2016. [Accessed Sept. 10, 2018].

[5] College Education Guidance Committee, Ministry of Education of the People's Republic of China, (2018). *National standards for all undergraduate majors in universities (1)*, Beijing:Higher Education Publishing. Original in Chinese, 普通高等学校本科专业类教学质量国家标准（上）. 高等教育出版社.

[6] Computing Research Association. (2017). Generation CS: Computer Science Undergraduate Enrollments Surge since 2006. https://cra.org/data/Generation-CS/ [Accessed Oct 15, 2018].

[7] S. Douglas, A. Farley, G. Lo, A. Proskurowski, and M. Young. (2010). Internationalization of computer science education. In *Proceedings of the 41st ACM technical symposium on computer science education, Mar 10-13, 2010, Milwaukee, USA, 411-415.* ACM:New YorK.

[8] J. Huang and L.L. Hang, L. L. (2011). A Comprehensive Approach for Improving Chinese Computing Undergraduate Entrepreneurial Spirits. In *Proceedings of International Conference on Information and Management Engineering, Part V, Wuhan, China, September 17-18, 2011, 268-274.* Springer:Berlin.

[9] E.P. Jiang. (2014). A Comparative Study on Undergraduate Computer Science Education between China and the United States. In *International Education and the Next-Generation Workforce: Competition in the Global Economy. pp. 208-223.* IGI Global:Hershey.

[10] The Joint Task Force on Computing Curricula. (2001). Computing curricula 2001. In *Journal on Educational Resources in Computing (JERIC), 1(3).* ACM:New York.

[11] The Joint Task Force on Computing Curricula. (2013). *Computer Science Curricula 2013: Curriculum Guidelines for Undergraduate Degree Programs in Computer Science.* ISBN: 978-1-4503-2309-3. ACM:New York.

[12] X. Li and B. Lunt. (2006). Undergraduate computer education in China - a brief status and perspective. In *Proceedings of the 7th conference on Information technology education, Minneapolis, MN, USA, October 19 - 21, 2006, 35-38.* ACM:New York.

[13] Medium (June 2018). "China's AI Schools Are Accepting Applications: Here's a List." https://medium.com/syncedreview/chinas-ai-schools-are-accepting-applications-here-s-a-list-5a568e1e31a1. [Accessed Sept 11, 2018].

[14] National Center for Education Statistics. (2017). Degrees in computer and information sciences conferred by postsecondary institutions, by level of degree and sex of student: 1970-71 through 2015-16. In *Digest of Education Statistics 2017.* https://nces.ed.gov/programs/digest/d17/tables/dt17_325.35.asp. [Accessed Sept 22, 2018].

[15] Top500 LISTS. https://www.top500.org/lists/. [Accessed Sept 10, 2018].

[16] A.B. Tucker. (June 1991). A Summary of the ACM/IEEE-CS Joing Curriculum Task Force Report (Computing Curriculum'91). *Communications of the ACM, 34(6), 68-84.* ACM:New York.

[17] Wikipedia. (2018). "List of public corporations by market capitalization." https://en.wikipedia.org/wiki/List_of_public_corporations_by_market_capitalization. [Accessed Sept 10, 2018].

[18] Wikipedia. (2018). "ACM International Collegiate Programming Contest." https://en.wikipedia.org/wiki/ACM_International_Collegiate_Programming_Contest. [Accessed Sept. 10, 2018].

[19] Working Group for Software Engineering Curriculum. (2016). *Guidelines for undergraduate curriculum of applied software engineering majors.* Original in Chinese, 高等学校本科软件工程专业应用型人才培养指导意见 2016 年.

[20] M. Zhang and V.M. Lo. (2010). Undergraduate computer science education in China. In *Proceedings of the 41st ACM technical symposium on computer science education. March 10-13, 2010, Milwaukee, Wisconsin, USA, 396-400.* ACM:New York.

[21] X. Zhou. (March 2005). Some historic notes of Chinese computer science education and their enlightenment. In *Computer Education, March 2005, 15-18.* Original in Chinese, "我国计算机教育的回顾与启迪"《计算机教育》2005 年第 3 期 作者：周兴社.

APPENDIX A: List of Universities in the Study

1. U.S. programs

a. MIT	e. UIUC	i. Harvey Mudd	m. Naval
b. Berkeley	f. GA Tech	j. Rose Hulman	n. Bucknell
c. Stanford	g. U of Michigan	k. West Point	o. Cal Poly
d. CMU	h. U of Texas	l. Air Force	p. Milwaukee School of Engineering

2. Chinese programs

0. Tsinghua University	4. Beihang University
1. Peking University	5. Harbin Institute of Technology
2. Shanghai Jiao Tong University	6. Beijing U of Post & Telecommunications
3. University of Science and Technology	7. Southeast University

Quantifying the Effects of Prior Knowledge in Entry-Level Programming Courses

David H Smith IV
Western Washington University
smithd77@wwu.edu

Qiang Hao
Western Washington University
qiang.hao@wwu.edu

Filip Jagodzinski
Western Washington University
filip.jagodzinski@wwu.edu

Yan Liu
University of British Columbia
yan.liu@ubc.ca

Vishal Gupta
University of British Columbia
vishal.gupta@alumni.ubc.ca

ABSTRACT

Computer literacy and programming are being taught increasingly at the K-12 level with more students than ever matriculating in college with prior programming experience. Accurately assessing student programming skills acquired in high school can inform college faculty about the range of competencies in introductory programming courses. The tool predominantly-used for assessing past CS knowledge and skills is a survey, which lacks quantitative rigor. This study aims to (1) quantify the effects of prior knowledge in entry-level programming courses and (2) compare the different measurement approaches of student prior knowledge in programming, including surveys and aptitude tests. The results of this study reveal that a discrepancy exists between the results of surveys and aptitude tests. Consistent with prior survey studies, our survey results showed that the effects of student prior programming knowledge faded gradually during the course period. In contrast, the aptitude test results indicated that the effects of student prior knowledge did not weaken over time. The accuracy of both measurements and implications for instructors were further discussed.

CCS CONCEPTS

• **Applied computing → Education**;

KEYWORDS

CS1; prior knowledge; assessment; performance prediction

ACM Reference Format:
David H Smith IV, Qiang Hao, Filip Jagodzinski, Yan Liu, and Vishal Gupta. 2019. Quantifying the Effects of Prior Knowledge in Entry-Level Programming Courses. In *ACM Global Computing Education Conference 2019 (CompEd '19), May 17–19, 2019, Chengdu,Sichuan, China*. ACM, New York, NY, USA, Article 4, 7 pages. https://doi.org/10.1145/3300115.3309503

1 INTRODUCTION

K-12 students today have unprecedented, and ever increasing, access to Computer Science (CS) courses and resources. A recent poll conducted by Gallup and Google concluded that 76% of U.S. schools offered some form of CS learning opportunity, 60% offered at least one CS course, and 40% offered a class that involved programming [1]. From this, it can be expected that an increased proportion of students enrolling in undergraduate computer science courses have some prior knowledge related to programming and/or CS fundamentals. However, the survey also noted that although many computer science related activities are offered in modern high schools, great variances exist in terms of what is offered by such activities, including general computer classes, introductory programming courses as well as a wide variety of clubs [1]. Furthermore, considering the lack of curricula consistency across K-12 in the United States, students' prior knowledge in computer science is likely to be heterogeneous and challenging to measure [2].

Studies investigating this topic generally divide the broader concept of "prior knowledge" into a number of factors asking students to self-evaluate their abilities and/or experiences. These factors are then compared to students' scores with the goal of determining which play the largest role in predicting students performance. Previous studies have found that students with prior CS or general STEM related knowledge are more likely to outperform their peers [3–6]. Other factors explored by these studies include factors such as "personal comfort", and how a student perceives their own programming abilities. Students exhibiting a strong sense of personal comfort as well as confidence in their own abilities have been shown to outperform their peers [6, 7].

Despite the relatively consistent findings, it is worth noting that all the prior studies used self-answering surveys as their primary means of data collection. Such data collection methods are only effective for determining where a student first came in contact with a subject, how long they stayed in contact with it, as well as a self-evaluation of their abilities. Such surveys neither validate nor quantify a student's perceived abilities. Given the great variance of computing education at the high school level, successful completion of a high school CS course may mean very different things to students from different schools or school districts (e.g., whether students have taken a CS course in high school is a frequently-used survey question). Consequently, the reliability and generalizability of the survey results might be questionable. To the best of our knowledge, alternative measurements to surveys, such as validated aptitude tests, are rarely used to measure student prior knowledge in programming.

To fill this gap, this paper aims to investigate different measurements of prior programming knowledge on student performance in the context of introductory programming courses (CS1). This study also explores using a validated aptitude test to measure prior knowledge. The results of this study provide insights into the accurate quantification of student prior knowledge in programming. These insights could be used by instructors to gain the most accurate view of their classes' prior knowledge and thus aid them in their course design and calibration.

2 RELATED WORK

Students develop their knowledge by interpreting incoming information through the lens of their existing knowledge, beliefs, and assumptions [8]. As a result, sufficient, appropriate and accurate prior knowledge aids in the learning process, whereas insufficient, inappropriate and inaccurate prior knowledge may have the opposite effect [9]. These aforementioned studies further discuss why teachers should take into consideration the extent of students' prior knowledge and structure their courses appropriately with the goal of building new knowledge atop that which already exists. Research conducted in a variety of fields on the impact of prior knowledge has concluded that prior knowledge is a key factor in student learning [10–14].

Factors involving or related to prior knowledge, and its effectiveness in predicting CS1 students' performance, explored by prior studies include:

- Exposure to and performance in math classes
- Exposure to and performance in core science classes (chemistry, physics, biology, etc.)
- Previous exposure to computer programming and CS concepts (high school, college, online, club, etc.)
- Previous non-programming computer experience
- Student programming comfort levels
- Perception of personal ability

The roles of both mathematical prowess and prior programming experience have been the most investigated by far with nearly all studies pointing to their significance in predicting students success. Bergin and Reilly [7] performed a replication study seeking to reproduce the significance of existing math, science, and programming knowledge in predicting students performance in a CS1 course. Their findings corroborate previous studies where math and/or prior programming experience were found to influence most future perfromance [6, 15–18]. Wilson and Shrock [6] investigated 12 factors, with math and science courses included among them, that might affect the learning ability of students in introductory computer science courses. They concluded that each of these factors plays a significant role in predicting student performance. Hagan and Markham investigated the effects of prior programming experience as measured by the number of programming languages a student had previously used [18]. Their findings point to students previous knowledge as having initially positive performance benefits. The level to which students with prior experience outperformed their peers was related to the number of programming languages a student had experience with.

There is a long-standing belief that there exists a correlation between student lecture attendance and their subsequent course performance[4]. Veerasamy *et al.* investigated the connection between prior programming knowledge, lecture attendance, and course performance and compared their results against the longstanding idea that lecture attendance plays a significant role in predicting student performance[4]. Their results not only show that students with prior programming knowledge outperformed their peers, but that those same students had significantly lower lecture attendance.

In addition to simply looking at the level of a student's prior experience, many studies investigate the impacts of factors such as self-efficacy and student comfort levels. The effects of student cognitive skills and self-efficacy were investigated alongside prior knowledge by Bergin and Reilly [7]. They found a student's perception of their own abilities to be the most significant factor in predicting their performance, even above that of prior knowledge. In Wilson and Shrock's investigation of 12 factors that may affect learning ability, they also investigated the effects of self-efficacy [6]. Their findings corroborate with that of Bergin and Reilly in that a student's perception of their own abilities had a significant impact on their performance throughout thea course.

The effects of prior knowledge and experience by separate genders has also been investigated by multiple studies [5, 15, 19]. Wilcox and Lionelle administered surveys prior to the start of term and as well as after the term's completion with questions primarily focusing on prior programming experience and personal comfort levels within the entire student body as well as between genders [5]. Their findings reaffirm the significance of student's comfort levels and prior knowledge in performance prediction. Female students were shown to have lower rates of both when compared to their male peers. A study also investigating the roles of aptitude in math and science as well as prior programming knowledge in student performance found that female students achieved scores consistent with their male peers [15]. It should be noted the student body consisted of male and female students with similar levels of prior knowledge which may have skewed results. With regard to the student body as a whole, students with prior programming knowledge significantly outperformed their peers. Additionally, the link between aptitude in math and science and performance in introductory programming courses was reaffirmed.

Given the significance of prior knowledge related to STEM concepts in predicting student performance in CS1 courses, the question arises as to the duration of their effects. Morrison [20] investigated this with regard to prior knowledge gained through high school computer science courses. Their findings show that students who had completed high school level computer science courses significantly outperformed their peers on both the courses' validated pretest as well as assessments performed throughout the course. The performance gap between students with high school experience and those without had narrowed to the point of obsolescence by CS2. Wilson and Shrock [6] suggest the effects of prior knowledge may be even more short-term than suggested by Morrison[20]. Their study showed the effects of prior programming experience to be limited to the midterm, disappearing by the time of the final exam.

All prior studies discussed in this section used self responding surveys as their primary means of data collection. Although this means of evaluation is effective for establishing the means by which a student initially came in contact with concepts, as well as a self evaluation of their skills, it does not quantify their current knowledge. This study seeks to add to the literature on this subject by using both a survey and a validated assessment to evaluate a student body and compare their results to their exam performance.

3 RESEARCH DESIGN

3.1 Participants and Contexts

This study was conducted on a group of students enrolled in a large university in the North American Pacific Northwest. A total of 62 students taking a CS1 over a regular academic term participated in this study. Students were expected to complete a set of programming assignments individually and two comprehensive programming projects collaboratively. In addition, two exams, including one midterm and one final, were administered.

CS1 in this study is being used in consistency with most prior computing education studies conducted in North America, which refers to the first core programming course [21, 22]. At the institution in question, students taking CS1 typically have declared their major intentions as CS, but are not yet in the CS major. Whether a student can be admitted to the CS major is dependent on their performance in CS1 and a set of sequential core courses. Many CS departments also offer a set of elective CS courses aiming at growing student interests in CS, such as "computer science and society" and "computational thinking", which involve little to no learning and teaching of programming. Such courses are referred to as "**college-level CS courses prior to CS1**" in this study. It is worth noting that college-level CS courses prior to CS1 are not necessarily more advanced than computer science courses being offered in high school.

3.2 Measurements

Both a survey and an aptitude test were given to students at the beginning of the semester to measure their prior knowledge in programming. The survey, composed of seven questions, was adopted from a study done by Wilcox and Lionelle [5].

The aptitude test, known as Programming Aptitude Test (PAT), was developed and validated by Tukiainen and Monkkonen [23]. The PAT evaluates a students grasp of fundamental programming concepts as well as conceptual solution design, but does not involve actual programming. There have been many efforts in developing language-independent assessments of CS1 knowledge in the last decade, such as Foundamental CS1 Assessment (FCS1) and Second CS1 Assessment (SCS1) [21, 24]. However, such instruments were developed to serve the goal of measuring student learning performance after taking CS1, but not prior to taking CS1. To our best knowledge, PAT developed by Tukiainen and Monkkonen [23] is the only instrument aiming at student prior knowledge before taking CS1. Different from FCS1 and SCS1 that involve complex programming concepts, PAT measures mainly generic problem solving strategies and capabilities. Given the specific goals of this study, PAT was chosen to measure student prior programming knowledge prior to taking CS1.

In addition, student performance on the midterm and final exams were collected and regarded as their academic performance.

Both midterm and final exams were developed by the instructor. Although neither midterm nor final exam was validated, both of them carefully mapped the tested concepts of FCS1 developed by Tew and Guzdial [21] to language-dependent questions.

4 RESULTS

4.1 Descriptive Summary

Participants consisted of 71% male and 29% female students ranging in age from 18 to 43 years old (male: M = 20.20, SD = 3.90; female: M = 19.67, SD = 1.50). Students largely consisted of young adults under the age of 20 with numbers dwindling as age increased. In terms of prior experience, it was found that, of the pool of 17 female students enrolled in the class, 64.7% had no high school CS experience with the remaining 35.3% having had taken one or more classes. As for the college experience, all had taken at least one or more prior CS elective courses (e.g., computational thinking). Male participants showed slightly higher participation in high school CS courses with 44.2% having taken at least one or more. Male students also showed a high level of participation in prior college-level CS courses with 93.0% of male participants having taken one or more.

There were 48 course participants at or under the age of 20 with the remaining 14 falling above that age line. Students at or under the age of 20 tended to have had more experience via high school courses with 47.9% having taken at least one or more compared to only 28.6% of those over 20. Both groups had high levels of participation in college-level computer science courses with 93.8% of those under the age of 21 having completed at least one or more.

4.2 Results of Survey Responses

Linear regression was applied to examine the effects of surveyed factors on student midterm exam performance. As is seen in Table 1, the surveyed factors in total accounted for 18.32% of the variance in academic performance. Student completion of high school level computer science courses (t = 2.434 , p < 0.05) as well as amount of time dedicated to self study (t = 2.253, p < 0.05) were found to be significant factors in the linear model. The completion of college-level computer-science-related courses or a students level of confidence prior to beginning the course were not found statistically significant.

Table 1: Linear Regression of Survey Responses on the Midterm Exam

	R^2	R^2_{adj}	Δ F	β	t
Midterm	0.2636	0.1832	3.281		
CS in College				-2.932	-1.155
CS in High school				5.974*	2.434
Self Learning Time				5.813*	2.253
Confidence				2.202	0.779
Age				-3.823	-1.544
Gender				5.443	1.021

* p <0.05; **p <0.01; ***p <0.001

When the same factors were applied to a linear model for final exam performance, it was found that the surveyed factors only explained 8.068% of the observed variance in student performance (Table 2). None of the factors, however, were found to have any significance in predicting the exam's results. In other words, the influences of the surveyed factors became much weaker on student final exam performance than their midterm performance.

Table 2: Linear Regression of Survey Responses on the Final Exam

	R^2	R^2_{adj}	ΔF	β	t
Final	0.1711	0.08068	1.892		
CS in College				-3.473	-1.172
CS in High school				1.170	0.409
Self Learning Time				5.483	1.822
Confidence				2.272	0.689
Age				-5.472	-1.894
Gender				6.302	1.014

* $p < 0.05$; ** $p < 0.01$; *** $p < 0.001$

4.3 Results of the Programming Aptitude Test

Same as the analysis on student survey responses, linear regression was applied to explore student PAT performance on their midterm and final exam performance. Age and gender were controlled for analysis consistency (Table 3). The results showed that student PAT performance along age and gender explain 22.54% of the variance in midterm performance. Student PAT performance was found to be highly significant in predicting their midterm performance (t = 3.903, $p < 0.001$).

Table 3: Linear Regression of PAT Performance on the Midterm Exam

	R^2	R^2_{adj}	ΔF	β	t
Midterm	0.2635	0.2254	6.918		
PAT				9.091***	3.903
Age				-5.326*	-2.308
Gender				-1.487	0.291

* $p < 0.05$; ** $p < 0.01$; *** $p < 0.001$

When the same factors were tied to final exam results (Table 4) the model was found to explain 18.49% of the variance in performance. Student PAT performance was once again found to be a highly significant predictor of their final exam performance (t = 3.317, $p < 0.01$). Different from the surveyed factors, the predictive power of student PAT performance was found consistently strong on both their midterm and final exam performance.

Table 4: Linear Regression of PAT Performance on the Final Exam

	R^2	R^2_{adj}	ΔF	β	t
Final	0.225	0.1849	5.612		
PAT				8.7147**	3.317
Age				-5.9625*	-2.290
Gender				0.6099	0.106

* $p < 0.05$; ** $p < 0.01$; *** $p < 0.001$

4.4 Correlation Analysis

Given the significant differences in predictive power between survey factors and PAT performance on student learning, correlational analysis among survey factors and PAT performance was further conducted (Table 5).

Surprisingly, the correlations between PAT performance and any other survey factor is below 0.2, and none of them were found to be significant. In other words, taking CS courses (prior to CS1) in high school or college does not necessarily have a positive effects on the mastery of programming-language-independent problem solving. In contrast, confidence was found significantly correlated with both taking CS courses prior to CS1 in college (r = 0.353, p < 0.01) and self-learning time (r = 0.361, p < 0.01). In other words, taking CS courses prior to CS1 and self-study may boost student confidence in successful completion of CS1.

Table 5: Pearson Correlations Between Survey Factors and PAT Performance

	CSC	CSH	Confid	SLT	PAT
CS in College	1				
CS in High school	0.0190	1			
Confidence	0.353**	-0.111	1		
Self Learning Time	0.0910	0.0698	0.3607**	1	
PAT	-0.0897	0.0522	-0.0393	0.1130	1

CSC: CS in College, CSH: CS in High school, Confid: Confidence, SLT: Self Learning Time

5 DISCUSSION

5.1 Consistency of Findings

Surveys, as the conventional measurement approach of student prior knowledge, have been used widely in prior studies. Overall, these studies [5, 15, 20] have found that student prior knowledge in programming significantly influences their performance. However, the significance of these influences became smaller over time, whether it is over the course of one semester or across two different entry-level courses.

Such findings were consistent with those of the survey results of this study. It was found that the number of computer science courses taken at high school and self-learning time had significant influences on student midterm exam performance, but the effects were no longer detectable for their final exam performance. Although the findings on the gradually weakened effects of student prior knowledge were consistent with that of prior studies, it is worth noting that such factors had limited power in predicting student academic performance. If survey results are to be trusted and used as guidance for course design, instructors can rest assured that given some time every student will catch up and perform equally well. However, considering the low predictive power of the survey factors, the conclusion that students with all levels of prior knowledge can perform equally well might not be so easily reached.

5.2   Which Measurement Approach is Better?

The second research focus of this study was to compare the results of both surveys and aptitude tests. As opposed to surveyed factors, student PAT performance was found to be the most significant influencing factor in midterm and final exam performance.

The significance of these results could indicate the PAT as being a more accurate measurement of student prior knowledge in programming when compared to survey. A fundamental source of error existing within the survey collection method is the ambiguity held within its answers. For instance, in the question of self-study time, there exists no objectively quantifiable amount of time that would constitute "a lot". Even the question of prior courses is open to ambiguity as it fails to consider two important factors, course content and student performance in the course. The validated aptitude test eliminates such errors by providing students with a range of question on fundamental programming concepts, all with objectively correct or incorrect answers, and grading their performance.

The correlation analysis seems to corroborate that PAT is a more accurate measurement of student prior knowledge in programming. Taking CS courses prior to CS1 in college has low correlation with student PAT performance but high correlation with confidence in successfully completing CS1. One possible explanation for this finding is that taking courses such as computing and society or computational thinking can help boost student overall confidence in CS, but does not necessarily help improve their problem-solving capabilities in programming. The variations and lack of consistency of such courses may further contribute to such a result.

Though the PAT proved to be a superior predictor of performance it lacks the indications of where students acquired prior knowledge that surveys provide. The combined use of the PAT and survey results as a means of prior knowledge evaluation produces a more complete picture of the various factors that influence expected performance. The collection of such data affords instructors a better idea of their class's overall prior knowledge and therefore their expected performance. This information can then be used to better calibrate course content/structure to the given student bodies expected capabilities.

6   LIMITATIONS AND FURTHER DIRECTIONS

A few limitations may hinder the generalizability of this study. First, this study was conducted on a sample of 62 students at a single institution. The findings may be different if multiple classes taught by different instructors from different institutions are involved. Future studies may consider replication at a larger scale. Second, the adopted validated test, Programming Aptitude Test,

was developed and validated in 2002 [23]. Considering the curriculum development in computer science in the last two decades, the results of this test may not provide an accurate portrayal of student capabilities today. Future studies may investigate the necessity of developing a new instrument to accurately measure student prior knowledge in programming. Furthermore, this study did not investigate the influences of student prior programming knowledge in their long-term performance (e.g., performance in sequential programming courses). To provide a complete picture of the impacts of student prior programming knowledge on their achievement, the understanding of both its short-term and long-term impacts are both necessary. Longitudinal studies adopting both surveys and validated tests may serve this purpose in the future.

7   CONCLUSIONS

Although the effects of prior knowledge have been examined in a variety of fields, most such studies opted to use self-reported surveys as the only measurement approach. The survey can indeed shed light as to whether or not a student has been previously exposed to related topics, but may not accurately measure the amount of knowledge a student has retained. This is especially true given that great variance exists in terms of what students may have previously learned, as happens to be the case with introductory programming courses. This study seeks to bridge this gap by comparing two measurements of student prior programming knowledge, including both surveys and aptitude tests. Although prior findings through surveys were consistent with those in this study, we detected a significant difference between the survey responses and aptitude test results. Survey results show the effects of previous experience, specifically that gained from high school, to have an impact only on midterm performance. Aptitude test performance, however, was shown to have significant impacts on both the midterm and final. Given the importance of student prior knowledge in course design and delivery, more studies exploring its role should be conducted using a standardized test as a means of evaluation.

8   APPENDIX

A   PROGRAMMING APTITUDE TEST

Question 1:
The company has information of their employers in three different lists. You have acquired all three lists, which all have little bit different information depending in the purpose of the list. The lists have following information of the employees:

- List 1: the number, the name, the occupation and the department (*List 1 is ordered by the number of employee to ascending order*)
- List 2: the name, the number, the address, the phone number, and the SSN (*List 2 is organized to alphabetic order by the name*)
- List 3: the number, the SSN, salary and some secret information (*List 3 is ordered by the number to ascending order*)

Your job is to make a report of those employees whose salary is greater than $2,000. The report has to display the name, the address, the department and the salary of the employees. Describe how you would solve the problem.

Question 2:
Let i and j be both integers between 0 and 10 (inclusive). List all values of i and j, that make the expression to be always true:

- (i>=1) and (i<=5)
  The expression is true when i has values:
- (j>=7) or (j<=3)
  The expression is true when j has values:

Question 3:
Try to determine the general form of the series by the given series of words, and write a word sequence, that is next on the series.

- bce , bbcde , bbbcdde , ...
- bcace , bcacacace , bcacacacace , ...
- abcccdd , abbccccdd , abbbccccdd ...

Question 4:
Your job is to sum up 50 numbers and at the end report the sum and the count of numbers that were positive numbers (>0). Describe how you would solve the problem or write in a pseudo-code.

B SURVEY

Question 1:
Did you take computer science related courses in college?

- I took one CS related course in college
- I took more than one CS related courses in college
- Never

Question 2:
Did you take computer science courses in high school?

- I took one CS course at high school
- I took more than one CS courses at high school
- Never

Question 3:
How much time did you spend on self-learning & teaching of programming outside of school?

- A lot of time
- Some time
- Little time

Question 4:
How would you like to describe yourself in terms of programming?

- Have a lot of experience in programming
- Have some experience in programming
- Have very limited experience in programming

Question 5:
How confident are you in your ability of programming?

- Very confident
- Somewhat confident
- Not confident at all

Question 6:
What is your gender?

- Male
- Female
- Other

Question 7:
What is your age?

REFERENCES

[1] Google Inc. & Gallup Inc. Trends in the state of computer science in u.s. k-12 schools. 2016. URL http://goo.gl/j291E0.
[2] André Schäfer and Rainer Brück. Teaching strategies for undergraduate laboratories with students having heterogeneous prior knowledge. In Global Engineering Education Conference (EDUCON), 2013 IEEE, pages 112–117. IEEE, 2013.
[3] Anya Tafliovich, Jennifer Campbell, and Andrew Petersen. A student perspective on prior experience in cs1. In Proceeding of the 44th ACM Technical Symposium on Computer Science Education, SIGCSE '13, pages 239–244, New York, NY, USA, 2013. ACM.
[4] Ashok Kumar Veerasamy, Daryl D'Souza, Rolf Lindén, and Mikko-Jussi Laakso. The impact of prior programming knowledge on lecture attendance and final exam. Journal of Educational Computing Research, 56(2):225–253, 2018.
[5] Chris Wilcox and Albert Lionelle. Quantifying the benefits of prior programming experience in an introductory computer science course. In Proceedings of the 49th ACM Technical Symposium on Computer Science Education, SIGCSE '18, pages 80–85, New York, NY, USA, 2018. ACM.
[6] Brenda Cantwell Wilson and Sharon Shrock. Contributing to success in an introductory computer science course: A study of twelve factors. In Proceedings of the Thirty-second SIGCSE Technical Symposium on Computer Science Education, SIGCSE '01, pages 184–188, New York, NY, USA, 2001. ACM. ISBN 1-58113-329-4. doi: 10.1145/364447.364581. URL http://doi.acm.org/10.1145/364447.364581.
[7] Susan Bergin and Ronan Reilly. Programming: Factors that influence success. ACM Sigcse Bulletin, 37:411–415, 01 2005. doi: 10.1145/1047124.1047480.
[8] James V Wertsch and C Addison Stone. The concept of internalization in vygotsky's account of the genesis of higher mental functions. Lev Vygotsky: Critical assessments, 1:363–380, 1999.
[9] Marie K. Norman, Marsha C. Lovett, Michael W. Bridges, Michele di Pietro, Susan A. Ambrose, and Richard E. Mayer. How Learning Works: Seven Research-Based Principles for Smart Teaching. Jossey-Bass, 2010.
[10] Jeffrey Alan Greene, Lara-Jeane Costa, Jane Robertson, Yi Pan, and Victor M. Deekens. Exploring relations among college studentsâĂŹ prior knowledge, implicit theories of intelligence, and self-regulated learning in a hypermedia environment. Computers & Education, 55(3):1027 – 1043, 2010.
[11] Gregor Kennedy, Carleton Coffrin, Paula de Barba, and Linda Corrin. Predicting success: How learners' prior knowledge, skills and activities predict mooc performance. In Proceedings of the Fifth International Conference on Learning Analytics And Knowledge, LAK '15, pages 136–140, New York, NY, USA, 2015. ACM.
[12] R. M. Rias and W. K. Yusof. Animation and prior knowledge in a multimedia application: A case study on undergraduate computer science students in learning. In 2012 Second International Conference on Digital Information and Communication Technology and it's Applications (DICTAP), pages 447–452, 2012.
[13] Stergios Tegos and Stavros Demetriadis. Conversational agents improve peer learning through building on prior knowledge. Journal of Educational Technology & Society, 20(1):99–111, 2017.
[14] Belle Selene Xia and Elia LiitiÃďnen. Student performance in computing education: an empirical analysis of online learning in programming education environments. 42:1–13, 11 2016.
[15] Pat Byrne and Gerry Lyons. The effect of student attributes on success in programming. SIGCSE Bull., 33(3):49–52, June 2001.
[16] R. R. Leeper and J. L. Silver. Predicting success in a first programming course. SIGCSE Bull., 14(1):147–150, February 1982.
[17] Laurie Honour Werth. Predicting student performance in a beginning computer science class. pages 138–143, 1986.
[18] Dianne Hagan and Selby Markham. Does it help to have some programming experience before beginning a computing degree program? SIGCSE Bull., 32(3):25–28, July 2000.
[19] University of Kent. Computer programming aptitude test. https://www.kent.ac.uk/ces/tests/computer-test.html, 2018.
[20] Briana B. Morrison, Adrienne Decker, and Lauren E. Margulieux. Learning loops: A replication study illuminates impact of hs courses. In Proceedings of the 2016 ACM Conference on International Computing Education Research, ICER '16, pages 221–230, New York, NY, USA, 2016. ACM.
[21] Allison Elliott Tew and Mark Guzdial. The fcs1: a language independent assessment of cs1 knowledge. In Proceedings of the 42nd ACM technical symposium on Computer science education, pages 111–116. ACM, 2011.
[22] Cynthia Taylor, Daniel Zingaro, Leo Porter, Kevin C Webb, Cynthia Bailey Lee, and Mike Clancy. Computer science concept inventories: past and future. Computer Science Education, 24(4):253–276, 2014.

[23] Markku Tukiainen and Eero Monkkonen. Programming aptitude testing as a prediction of learning to program. In *Proceedings of PPIG*, pages 45–57, 2002.

[24] Miranda C Parker, Mark Guzdial, and Shelly Engleman. Replication, validation, and use of a language independent cs1 knowledge assessment. In *Proceedings* of the 2016 ACM conference on international computing education research, pages 93–101. ACM, 2016.

Developing Feedback Analytics
Discovering Feedback Patterns in an Introductory Course

Richard Glassey
KTH: Royal Institute of Technology
Stockholm, Sweden
glassey@kth.se

ABSTRACT

Feedback plays a vital role in learning. The earlier misconceptions are identified and corrected, the better for the development of a student's knowledge. Whilst this primarily benefits the student, this paper investigates the value of developing feedback analytics in order to discover new insights, patterns or issues within a course. To facilitate this, issue tracking was used within a large introductory computer science course to capture weekly feedback between teaching assistants and students. Key areas of feedback analytics were identified in terms of the amount of interaction and volume of discussion generated for weekly assignments over a twelve week period. These areas were further divided by focusing on the difference between weekly assignments and the teaching assistants. Applied to two years of data, feedback analytics revealed novel and useful insights about the course, its assignments and the interaction between students and teaching assistants, which helped to highlight areas for deeper course analysis and improvement.

CCS CONCEPTS

• **Social and professional topics** → **Computing education**;

KEYWORDS

Feedback, Analytics, CS1, Issue Tracking, Teaching Assistants

ACM Reference Format:
Richard Glassey. 2019. Developing Feedback Analytics: Discovering Feedback Patterns in an Introductory Course. In *ACM Global Computing Education Conference 2019 (CompEd '19), May 17–19, 2019, Chengdu, Sichuan, China.* ACM, New York, NY, USA, 7 pages. https://doi.org/10.1145/3300115.3309519

1 INTRODUCTION

As students encounter new topics feedback helps to elaborate upon assessment outcomes, with much richer details about what might have went wrong, what was good, and where to go next. Good feedback will enable a student to reflect upon their own work and provide information on where to take action for improvement [12, 18]. On the flip side, bad feedback is not helpful, does not benefit the student in understanding their performance [11], and is ultimately not worth the extra effort for teachers to produce [1, 14]. In both cases,

if feedback data is digitised, consistent, and accessible, there is an opportunity to build and analyse a feedback dataset, which might lead to a better understanding of feedback patterns, whether positive or negative, and as a means to identify areas of improvement. The aim of this paper is to investigate whether feedback analytics can provide additional value and insights for course leaders.

The following questions guide this work: (1) Are issue trackers a viable platform for feedback? (2) Do amount of interaction and volume of discussion provide insights as feedback analytics? and (3) Can feedback analytics provide insight into differences between weekly assignments and differences between teaching assistants? In order to answer these questions, the first challenge is to ensure that feedback data is captured in a digital format for convenient archival and retrieval, consistent in terms of metadata that is recorded, and accessible in a programmatic manner to simplify aggregation and analysis. In terms of platforms for feedback, oral and hand-written modes of delivery do not meet these criteria. Email satisfies the first two criteria, but falters on the third as multiple teachers may be involved, making it challenging to aggregate the data. Learning management systems do a better job on the accessibility criteria, by centralising feedback into a gradebook structure, however they typically provide a limited application programmers interface (API) to access such data. A final promising option is the use of an issue tracking system for feedback, typically used in software development projects to track bugs, features and enhancements. Such platforms export a rich API that provides convenient retrieval of any aspect regarding an issue, and are increasingly being positively received as part of the learning environment in CS courses [4, 6, 9].

To investigate the value of these feedback analytics, a two year feedback dataset for an introductory computer science course was analysed. The enrollment for the course is roughly 200 students, making it a reasonably large course. Students must attempt weekly assignments spread over a 12 week period. Assignments are managed via version controlled repositories, and feedback is delivered via the related issue tracker. This process generates a large amount of effort, in terms of grading assignments and providing feedback. To manage this effort, a team of teaching assistants is employed to take responsibility for smaller groups of students — a common strategy for large courses [5]. However, this division of labour also creates the challenge of differing levels of consistency between teaching assistants, which potentially has an effect upon the feedback that students receive.

Using issue tracker data, it was possible to analyse the amount of feedback interaction that was generated for each assignment, as well as by each assistant. This provided a clear view on the differences that emerged across the duration of the course. Furthermore, it was possible to measure the volume of discussion that was generated within the feedback interaction. These two feedback analytics allowed observations to be made across two years of the course, revealing common patterns, inconsistencies and varying efforts between assistants; providing signals for more investigation, e.g. why does this particular assignment provoke more (or less) conversation within the issue tracker than others?

Taking a wider perspective, this work provides a starting point for the study of feedback analytics. Other courses that use issue tracking (or have access to feedback datasets) can take advantage of this method for analysing feedback, and adopt or develop new feedback analytics for their own course design. However, it is critcally important to stress that quantative analysis should be a replacement for qualitative analysis of feedback; these analytics are merely indicators for further study. Ultimately, this approach provides a unique view on what is happening in a course in terms of its feedback, and reveals unseen feedback patterns, problems and opportunities that can help improve the quality of feedback within a course.

The remainder of the paper is as follows: Section 2 presents related literature on feedback, teaching assistant consistency and use of version control; Section 3 describes the use an issue tracker to manage the feedback. Section 4 shows the findings in terms of amount of interaction and volume of discussion in relation to both assignments and teaching assistants. Finally, the paper ends with the implications and practical contributions of this work.

2 BACKGROUND

A central challenge for a large introductory course in Computer Science is managing scale, whilst maintaining quality. All aspects of course administration, distribution of course material and assignments, assessment and feedback can become problematic. In particular, delivering quality feedback at the right time is often overlooked in relation to the other aspects, despite its importance. Observations such as, "...for students to be able to improve, they must develop the capacity to monitor the quality of their own work during actual production" [18], and "...quality external feedback is information that helps students troubleshoot their own performance and self-correct: that is, it helps students take action to reduce the discrepancy between their intentions and the resulting effects" [12], underline the importance of quality and timely feedback in theory. However, in practice, student surveys across the world indicate that students are dissatisfied with their feedback [11], and academics themselves find it difficult to determine the effectiveness of feedback in spite of their efforts to produce it on time and to a high standard [1, 14].

One negative effect of scale is that the feedback itself becomes limited to a one-way monologue [11], without any opportunity for dialogue to emerge between teacher and student. Students are predominantly left with a single shot of feedback that they must take the time to interpret and recognise the benefits [14], which leaves the question of, 'what happens next?', very much up to chance. Despite the recent positive advances in the development of systems that automate the production of feedback, especially in the context of introductory programming situations [2, 7, 16, 20], they still lack the value, depth and nuances that dialogue can bring to the quality of feedback [3, 11]. Consequently, limited resources

means that finding strategies to deliver quality and timely feedback demands compromise and external support.

The use of teaching assistants provides much needed division of labour for managing larger courses. The approach of using teaching assistants has been used throughout the explosion in popularity of Computer Science, as reported in [17] in 1995 to help deal with enrollments in the order of 1000 students at Stanford University, to more recent discussions on the growing role of using undergraduates as teaching assistants [5]. The benefits of this strategy include reduced cost, increased instruction quality, emergence of a teaching assistant community, and the experience that teaching assistants acquire in their role as teacher [15]. However, in spite of the benefits, there are new challenges that emerge when relying on a team of teaching assistants.

One of the main challenges with teaching assistants, is the question of how to ensure that the consistency of instruction, assessment and delivery of feedback meets the expectations of the course. [19] found that within a small study of consistency between 12 teaching assistants when reviewing code, teaching assistants were self-consistent, however they all assessed code quality in different ways. The authors recommended the need for criteria to help manage the variation in consistency. Beyond the challenge of consistency, the role itself is also one of many tensions, where the teaching assistant must be teacher, employee and student simultaneously [10]. Finally, there is evidence to suggest that the drive and motivation of teaching assistants (important to ensure sustained levels of quality) is negatively affected, as they are often left with the feeling of being the "donkey in the department", because of their heavy workload, sizeable responsibility, and limited autonomy [13].

Whilst using teaching assistants to contribute to the task of providing timely and quality feedback is one concern, a second concern is how best to manage the delivery of feedback, such that it is closely connected to the submissions, and also provide the ability to move from a monologue to a dialogue between teacher and student. One trend in Computer Science courses has been to adopt version control systems (e.g. Subversion[1], Git[2], and Mercurial[3]) to help manage course content [6], distribute assignments [4] or manage group projects [9]. Whilst the use of version control platforms have had successes within these aspects, the closely related technology, the issue tracker, has not received as much attention, despite its opportunity to be a platform for communication. In [8], an issue tracker was used to help facilitate the development of professional communication skills, whilst in [21] an issue tracker was used to help evaluate individual contributions within a group project. One area that seems ripe for investigation is whether an issue tracker could be a useful platform for managing feedback, as well as providing the opportunity to centralise feedback such that it could be analysed in order to gain insights on how consistent teaching assistants were in its use.

3 USING AN ISSUE TRACKER FOR FEEDBACK

In 2014, the Introduction to Computer Science course (CS1) at KTH Royal Institute of Technology (Sweden) made use of a mixture of

---
[1]https://subversion.apache.org/
[2]https://git-scm.com/
[3]https://www.mercurial-scm.org/

digital and paper submissions for assignments. Because the university had already had an enterprise license for Github[4], the decision was made to use it as the platform for managing course assignments. As the students were first years, substantial efforts were made to streamline the experience of using Github as part of the learning environment. Furthermore, technical issues were not held against students if it prevented their work being submitted, and every effort was made to communicate clearly what was required and how help could be found on any topic relating to the use of Github.

The Github platform provides a rich set of resource management and information tools for software engineers to collaborate on project work. The central component is the repository, a version control system that tracks all changes to any resource that is added. In the context of this work, each student in the course received a repository for each weekly assignment. Linked to each Github repository is an issue tracker, a simple ticket system that allows one or more developers to communicate bugs that need to be fixed, features that should be added, and any other notice that is relevant to a project. In the student context, teaching assistants were instructed to use the issue tracker to give feedback to students on their assignments. Finally, a web interface integrates these systems, so that the assignment resources (repository) and feedback (issue tracker) can be viewed by students and teachers.

Before the assignments began, students received a week of training in basic computer survival skills, which included using the command line as well as elementary version control tasks. These mandatory labs ensured that students became familiar with simple Git commands (`clone`, `status`, `add`, `commit`, `push`), as well as navigating the Github interface. As a safety measure, teaching assistants were instructed to provide extra support in overcoming any initial problems with using version control[5]. After basic training, students in subgroups of ~15 were assigned to a teaching assistant, who led weekly exercises and graded their assignments.

For each weekly assignment, students had an individual repository automatically created for them. This contained the assignment text and any other resources they might need. Each repository was private, and only the student, teaching assistants and the course leader could access it. To successfully submit an assignment, students needed to push all of their commits before the weekly deadline. During the weekly exercise, students met with their teaching assistants and orally explained their solutions, and received oral feedback as a group. After this, teaching assistants graded individual assignments and posted more feedback via the issue tracker.

In terms of feedback, the main convention was that teaching assistants should post an issue that indicated if a student had passed, required correction, or had directly failed the task (typically this only occurred through non-submission). However, teaching assistants were also encouraged to experiment with the platform. For example, some teaching assistants preferred to use the issue tracker in an authentic fashion, and created separate issues per correction. Others used issue commenting to engage in discussions with students that expanded and clarified the original feedback.

The original intent to use Github did not focus upon the use of the issue tracker, however it became clear after the first course iteration

in 2015 that it was a well adjusted platform to centralise and digitise feedback. The remainder of the work will consider the data from the second and third years of implementation of this process, as the first year was mostly experimental and ad-hoc. Furthermore, from anecdotal evidence, both students and teaching assistants approved of the issue tracker usage, especially as it provided first year students with an authentic experience of a communication system widely used in software engineering. Through successive course iterations, it also became clear that the feedback dataset itself could provide deeper insights into how the course was running and identify possible areas for improvement.

4 RESULTS

The first result concerns the suitability of the issue tracker to be a valid platform for managing feedback. The basic criteria of digitising feedback, consistent metadata (who posted what and when and why) and providing a programmatic interface to the dataset were all satisfied. Where the issue tracker really excelled is in its issue / comment feature. For each issue, there is an associated comment thread that both students and assistants can use to continue discussing the feedback. This meant that both the amount of feedback that was provided per assignment was measurable, but also the extent to which that students and assistants made use of comments to continue the discussion. This made it trivial to establish the following metrics of interest about the feedback dataset:

Commits — Number of times a repository is updated
Issues — Number of issues present in a repository
Comments — Number of comments attached to an issue
Interactions — Sum of issues and comments in a repository
Issue Wordcount — Count of words in the text of an issue
Comments Wordcount — Count of words in the text of all comments for an issue
Volume of Discussion — Sum of Issue Wordcount and Comments Wordcount for a repository

Both the repository and issue tracker can be accessed via a well documented Application Programmers Interface (API) for Github[6]. To access and retrieve the data for this work, the following API calls were made via HTTP using the Python `requests`[7] module and responses were converted using Python's built-in `json` module:

```
/repos/:owner/:repo/commits
/repos/:owner/:repo/issues
/repos/:owner/:repo/issues/:number/comments
```

Table 1 provides a summary of the dataset for two successive years. Whilst the course accepts about 200 students, the average valid repositories (over 12 weeks) is lower due to students dropping out, teaching assistants not using the issue tracker as instructed, or students opting not to complete an assignment. The number of interactions for each assignment is the sum of issues that an assistant opened (potentially one or more per repository), and the subsequent comments from either the student or assistant as they engage in further discussion. The volume of discussion is the sum of all words that occur in the interactions occurring for each assignment.

---

[4]http://www.github.com
[5]The most problematic recurring issue has been the successful generation of SSH Keys in order to work on repositories outside of the university network.

[6]https://developer.github.com/v3/
[7]http://docs.python-requests.org/en/master/

Table 1: Summary of dataset extracted from issue tracker over two years

	2016	2017
Enrolled Students	200	180
Average Valid Repositories	128	123
Repository Commits	9975	9404
Issues	2186	1858
Comments on Issues	1262	1058
Interactions (issues + comments)	3448	2916
Issue Wordcount	88474	102084
Comments Wordcount	38252	34452
Volume of Discussion (in words)	126726	136536

The following sections will expand upon the detail that lies behind these totals, by considering the amount of interaction and volume of discussion that occurred in the issue tracker from the perspective of the assignment and teaching assistant.

4.1 Amount of Interaction

One way that data from the issue tracker can be useful is if it is viewed as a dialogue — teaching assistants post issues and students reply with comments, which then evolves into a conversation. This expansion upon the original issue potentially increases the overall value of the feedback, and at the very least, shows engagement from the student in their feedback. To look deeper at this particular theme, it was helpful to look at the difference in interactions per assignment as well as by assistant.

Figure 1 shows the number of interactions (issues and comments) per assignment over two years. Each assignment is represented as a boxplot, where the box depicts the interquartile range (IQR) or middle 50% of observations, the horizontal bar represents the median value, and the whiskers represent the minimum and maximum values, excluding the outliers, represented as dots. Across all assignments the majority of boxplots do not have a Q_3 (top edge of box) above 3 interactions. This is somewhat expected as passing assignments does not generate many interactions. However, the more interesting results occur above Q_3 in the whiskers and outliers. In some cases the number of interactions is in the range 5 to 15. Whilst this may not be a regular occurance, it does show real evidence of discussion emerging between students and teaching assistants around their feedback. Also of interest is why assignments 3, 8, 9, 11 and 12 all have such a narrow spread compared to the other assignments. In contrast, assignment 4 has a larger spread. This finding could be a stimulus to investigate these assignments and their feedback in a more qualitative manner to understand why these patterns occur.

An alternative view of amount of interactions is to consider the differences between teaching assistants. Figure 2 shows that for each year, there is at least one assistant that engages above and beyond the other teaching assistants. The remaining assistants in both years have less dramatic variation, but it still exists. In 2016, assistant 7, and in 2017, assistants 1 and 11 are all barely registering more than 100 interactions. Explanations here are difficult, as an

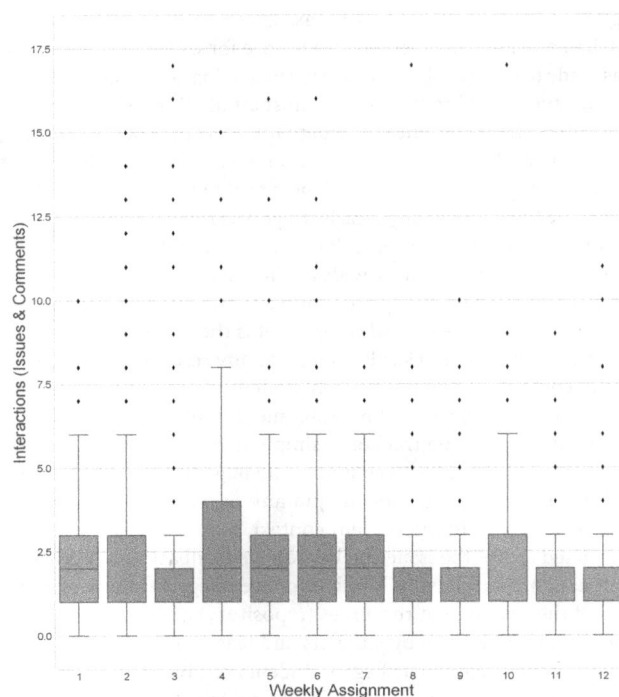

Figure 1: Number of interactions (issues and comments) within issue tracker by each assignment over two years.

assistant might have decided to focus more on oral feedback during the weekly exercises they lead, and simply relied on the issue tracker to register that a student had passed the assignment. Alternatively, they simply happen to have a smaller group, or not very active group in terms of posting comments. This does reveal an important limitation with an analytic approach to feedback that does not take into account the finer details. However, in 2016, with a factor of 8 times difference between the most active and least active assistant, there is perhaps a need to aim for a middle ground. Whilst more feedback might seem positive here, not at the cost of a teaching assistant that is overworking themselves.

4.2 Volume of Discussion

Whilst the amount of interactions provides some insights on the engagement between student, teaching assistant and feedback, it is also helpful to consider the volume of discussion that is occurring across these interactions.

Figure 3 shows the volume of discussion data for each assignment. In these boxplots, the mean value is represented as a black diamond on each box. For each week, the average volume of discussion is close to 100 words. Once again, it is the upper whiskers and outliers that reveal in some cases at least, the volume of discussion is becoming quite large, up to 800 words in some extreme cases. Whilst this may not be occurring for the majority, it is encouraging to believe that those students engaging in their feedback or needing more support are receiving it. Also, compared to Fig. 1 there are many more outliers here indicating that whilst there are not so

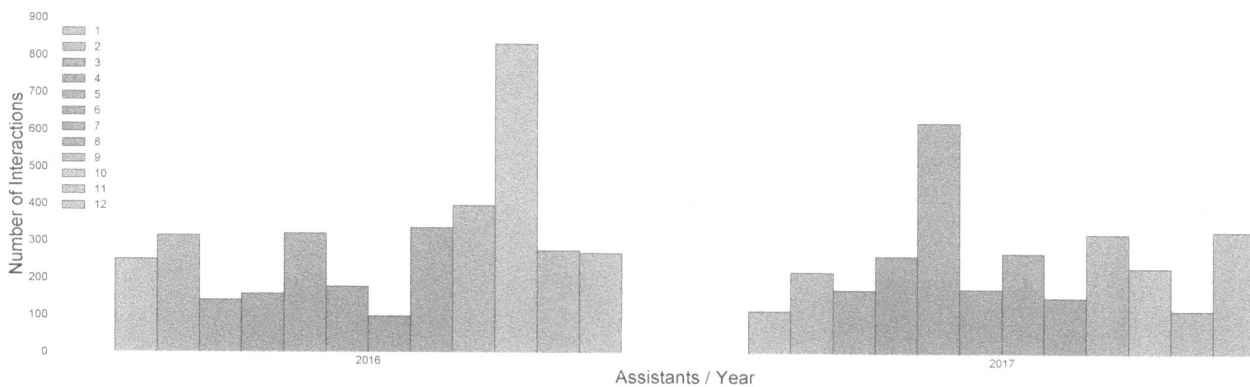

Figure 2: Number of interactions (issues and comments) in issue tracker by assistant.

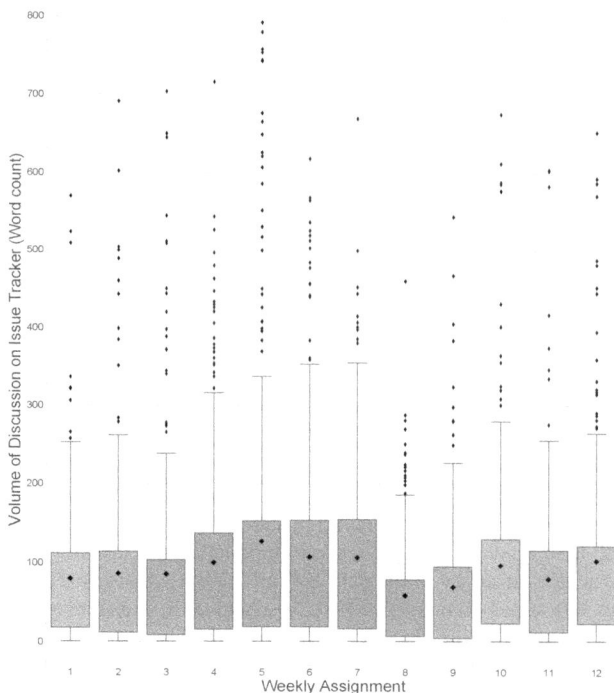

Figure 3: Volume of discussion (word count of issues and comments) in issue tracker by assignment over two years.

many interactions, they are typically longer. The other interesting feature here is the drop in discussion overall for assignments 8 and 9, having the most compact spread of observations. Here there is a clear signal to investigate what it is about these assignments that leads to such an outcome. For the sake of curiosity, assignment 8 was development of a simple game and assignment 9 was on testing. Despite this, it is encouraging to observe that there is not a downward trend of feedback towards the end of the course, and that assignments 8 and 9 are the anomalies.

In Fig. 2, the data mostly showed that teaching assistants were not too far apart in terms of interactions, however in Fig. 4, there is a much wider spread in terms of the volume of discussion when viewed from the assistant perspective. It is worth remembering at this point that volume of discussion can come from both teaching assistant and student, so this result must be treated with caution, and not indicating some lack of effort from the assistant. It is interesting to note that in Fig. 2 in terms of amount of interaction, assistant 10 (2016) and assistant 5 (2017) having the most interaction, whilst in Fig. 4 in terms of volume of discussion, it is assistant 9 (2016) and assistant 7 (2017) having the most volume of discusion, indicating that different conditions and approaches to feedback are at play. Ultimately, looking at the issue tracker via analytics should provoke insights into a course, rather than motivate pejorative action. Once again, there is probably a happy average, however the differences in student groups and teaching assistant approach are difficult to control and must be remembered when looking at the data presented here.

5 DISCUSSION

In terms of an issue tracking system being a viable platform for student feedback, three years of experience with a reasonably large course of first year students has made a convincing case for its continued use. Besides satisfying the basic requirements (digitised, consistent, accessible) it provides additional features, like comment threads around feedback, that make it superior to existing feedback delivery mechanisms. Importantly, this experience has not met any resistance from students, and even when not directly asked about it in student evaluation, positive opinions emerge: "*Worked really well with feedback and examination*", as well as those reflecting some results here: "*It worked nicely. Would be better if the programming assistants would give more consistent feedback.*".

This work has only begun to scratch the surface of developing feedback analytics, namely in the form of counting interactions and measuring the volume of discussion that emerge between assistants and their students. In terms extracting feedback analytics, this work illustrates some useful starting points that others can reuse and build upon. Whilst every course will have its own unique approach to production of feedback, there will be common aspects

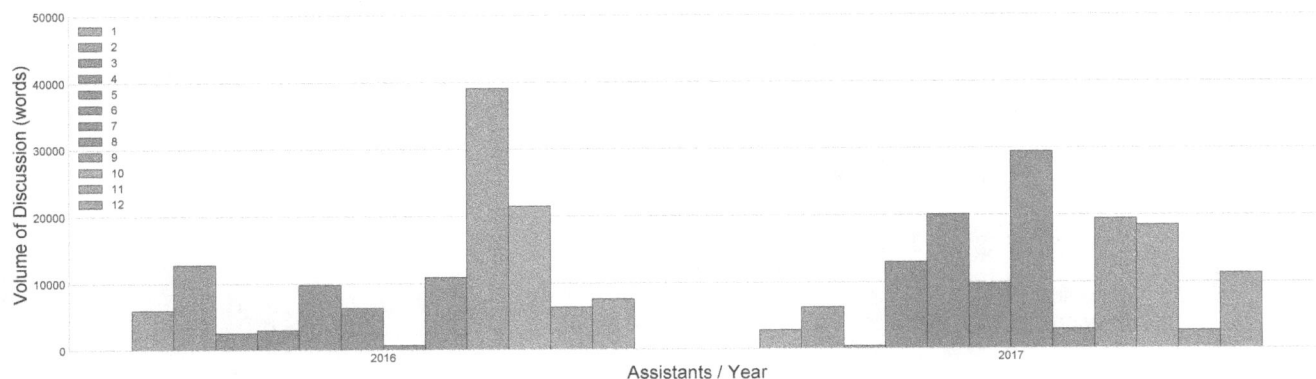

Figure 4: Volume of discussion (word count of both issues and comments) in issue tracker by each assistant over two years.

in feedback data that can be exploited to offer new insights. Both amount of interaction and volume of discussion are trivial to model and measure, yet they provide useful insights that were previously unknown about this particular course studied here.

Perhaps the most intriguing insights revealed the differences between teaching assistants. Both for amount of interactions and volume of discussion, there were large differences between teaching assistants. Whilst this cannot provide an explicit answer, it does provide an awareness for a course leader that the amount of effort needs to be managed in such a way that assistants do not operate as silos, and instead should be aware of how it is going in other groups. This may provoke further investigation in order to provide some suggestions on how to better standardise the expectations of what is considered an adequate amount of feedback, which echoes the recommendations from the study in [19].

The data presented here showed the inconsistencies all too clearly, and this knowledge will help to motivate action to design better criteria to guide feedback. Beyond these differences, the findings here also suggest an approach to facilitate and investigate feedback as a dialogue [3, 11]. Whilst developing feedback dialogues was not specified nor expected, the data here showed that both students and teaching assistants were taking advantage of the support for conversations afforded by the issue tracker. However, whilst this data is valuable in how it can inform course leaders, great care must be taken in the interpretation, otherwise teaching assistants may feel a new burden to satisfy. An unfortunate consequence could be that certain amounts of interaction and discussion become abstract targets to meet, rather than the use of careful judgement of when and where feedback is most needed.

Finally, taking a quantitative viewpoint only provides a signal; it does not provide a definite answer. Furthermore, the comparison across years only has limited value, as the group of teaching assistants is changing, and there is very little in the way of clear guidelines to ensure that the feedback is consistent across the course offerings. However, the quantitative approach feels appropriate given the scale of the data in order to gain a high-level overview. A key limitation of this work is that quantity certainly does not guarantee quality. This is a critical and contextual aspect of feedback that should not be undermined by taking a purely data analytic perspective. Rather, these are complimentary investigations that both aim to look deeper into feedback as a dataset that should be given more focus. Whilst the analytics presented here represent a starting point, future work will take a more qualitative, content-based approach that will attempt to investigate more sophisticated measures, taking inspiration from natural language processing topics such as sentiment, topic and discourse analysis.

6 CONCLUSION

This work has reported on the use of feedback analytics to help develop new perspectives on how feedback data can be utilised to provide value to course leaders. Feedback is a crucial component of a student's development. It can be both good and bad in terms of its effectiveness. By analysing feedback, course leaders can gain new insights into their courses. In this case, two basic feedback analytics were proposed (amount of interaction and volume of discussion) and evaluated in the context of a large first year course in computer science. The findings revealed that students did engage with their feedback, both in terms of interaction and discussion. Of particular interest was the data around the outliers and extremes, which revealed quite a lot of effort being spent in engagement and production of feedback.

Furthermore, this work also highlighted the use of an issue tracking platform to both manage course feedback and develop analytics from the resulting dataset. Whilst issue trackers are not designed for pedagogical purposes, they represent a very sophisticated platform for managing feedback. In the context of feedback analytics, the issue tracker was the ideal platform for creating the dataset, then providing a detailed interface to access all of the relevant metadata and content that normally would be challenging to access via other feedback mechanisms. In terms of implications, any teacher who is using a modern version control platform or issue tracking system in their course can take advantage of the ideas and findings presented here in order to develop deeper insights into course feedback. This is an overlooked dataset and there is value in there to be uncovered. By increasing the value of feedback, for both students and course leaders, it may be possible to further promote its production, quality and analysis.

REFERENCES

[1] Richard Bailey and Mark Garner. 2010. Is the feedback in higher education assessment worth the paper it is written on? Teachers' reflections on their practices. *Teaching in Higher Education* 15, 2 (2010), 187–198. https://doi.org/10.1080/13562511003620019

[2] Hannah Blau and J Eliot B Moss. 2015. FrenchPress Gives Students Automated Feedback on Java Program Flaws. *ITiCSE '15* (2015), 15–20. https://doi.org/10.1145/2729094.2742622

[3] Tony Dowden, Sharon Pittaway, Helen Yost, and Robyn McCarthy. 2013. Students' perceptions of written feedback in teacher education: Ideally feedback is a continuing two-way communication that encourages progress. *Assessment and Evaluation in Higher Education* 38, 3 (2013), 349–362. https://doi.org/10.1080/02602938.2011.632676

[4] Joseph Feliciano, Margaret-Anne Storey, and Alexey Zagalsky. 2016. Student experiences using GitHub in software engineering courses: a case study. *Proceedings of the 38th International Conference on Software Engineering Companion - ICSE '16* (2016), 422–431. https://doi.org/10.1145/2889160.2889195

[5] Jeffrey Forbes, David J. Malan, Heather Pon-Barry, Stuart Reges, and Mehran Sahami. 2017. Scaling Introductory Courses Using Undergraduate Teaching Assistants. *Proceedings of the 2017 ACM SIGCSE Technical Symposium on Computer Science Education - SIGCSE '17* (2017), 657–658. https://doi.org/10.1145/3017680.3017694

[6] Lassi Haaranen and Teemu Lehtinen. 2015. Teaching Git on the Side: Version Control System As a Course Platform. In *Proceedings of the 2015 ACM Conference on Innovation and Technology in Computer Science Education.* 87–92. https://doi.org/10.1145/2729094.2742608

[7] Hieke Keuning, Johan Jeuring, and Bastiaan Heeren. 2016. Towards a Systematic Review of Automated Feedback Generation for Programming Exercises. *Proceedings of the 2016 ACM Conference on Innovation and Technology in Computer Science Education - ITiCSE '16* March (2016), 41–46. https://doi.org/10.1145/2899415.2899422

[8] Chang Liu. 2005. Using issue tracking tools to facilitate student learning of communication skills in software engineering courses. In *Proceedings - 18th Conference on Software Engineering Education and Training, CSEE and T 2005.* 61–68. https://doi.org/10.1109/CSEET.2005.40

[9] Ivan Milentijevic, Vladimir Ciric, and Oliver Vojinovic. 2008. Version control in project-based learning. *Computers and Education* 50, 4 (2008), 1331–1338. https://doi.org/10.1016/j.compedu.2006.12.010

[10] Valbona Muzaka. 2009. The niche of graduate teaching assistants (GTAs): Perceptions and reflections. *Teaching in Higher Education* 14, 1 (2009), 1–12. https://doi.org/10.1080/13562510802602400

[11] David Nicol. 2010. From monologue to dialogue: Improving written feedback processes in mass higher education. *Assessment and Evaluation in Higher Education* 35, 5 (2010), 501–517. https://doi.org/10.1080/02602931003786559

[12] David J. Nicol and Debra Macfarlane-Dick. 2006. Formative assessment and self-regulated learning: a model and seven principles of good feedback practice. *Studies in Higher Education* 31, 2 (2006), 199–218. https://doi.org/10.1080/03075070600572090

[13] Chris Park and Marife Ramos. 2002. The donkey in the department? Insights into the graduate teaching assistant (GTA) experience in the UK. *Journal of Graduate Education* 3, 2001 (2002), 47–53. http://eprints.lancs.ac.uk/121/

[14] Margaret Price, Karen Handley, Jill Millar, and Berry O'Donovan. 2010. Feedback: All that effort, but what is the effect? *Assessment and Evaluation in Higher Education* 35, 3 (2010), 277–289. https://doi.org/10.1080/02602930903541007

[15] Stuart Reges. 2003. Using undergraduates as teaching assistants at a state university. *ACM SIGCSE Bulletin* 35, 1 (2003), 103. https://doi.org/10.1145/792548.611943

[16] Kelly Rivers and Kenneth R. Koedinger. 2013. Automatic generation of programming feedback: A data-driven approach. In *CEUR Workshop*, Vol. 1009.

[17] Eric Roberts, John Lilly, and Bryan Rollins. 1995. Using undergraduates as teaching assistants in introductory programming courses. *ACM SIGCSE Bulletin* 27, 1 (1995), 48–52. https://doi.org/10.1145/199691.199716

[18] D. R. Sadler. 1989. Formative assessment and the design of instructional systems. *Instructional science* 18, 2 (1989), 119—-144. https://doi.org/10.1007/BF00117714

[19] Michael James Scott and Gheorghita Ghinea. 2015. Reliability in the Assessment of Program Quality by Teaching Assistants During Code Reviews. *Proceedings of the 2015 ACM Conference on Innovation and Technology in Computer Science Education - ITiCSE '15* 85, 6 (2015), 346–346. https://doi.org/10.1145/2729094.2754844

[20] Rishabh Singh, Sumit Gulwani, and Armando Solar-Lezama. 2013. Automated feedback generation for introductory programming assignments. *Proceedings of the 34th ACM SIGPLAN conference on Programming language design and implementation - PLDI '13* (2013). https://doi.org/10.1145/2491956.2462195

[21] P. Young, V. Yip, and R. B. Lenin. 2012. Evaluation of Issue-tracker's Effectiveness for Measuring Individual Performance on Group Projects. In *Proceedings of the 50th Annual Southeast Regional Conference (ACM-SE '12).* ACM, New York, NY, USA, 89–94. https://doi.org/10.1145/2184512.2184534

LP Based Integration of Computing and Science Education in Middle Schools

Yuanlin Zhang
Texas Tech University
y.zhang@ttu.edu

Fox Bolduc
Texas Tech University
Fox.Bolduc@ttu.edu

Jianlan Wang
Texas Tech University
jianlan.wang@ttu.edu

William G. Murray
Texas Tech University
William.G.Murray@ttu.edu

ABSTRACT

There is a consensus on integrating computing with STEM teaching in K-12. However, very little is known about the integration. In this paper, we propose a novel framework for integrating science and computational thinking teaching using Logic Programming. We then develop and implement two 8-session integration modules on chemistry and physics for 6th and 7th graders. Pre- and post- tests, class observations and interviews show the feasibility of the framework in terms of 1) development and implementation of the modules, and 2) the students' learning outcomes on science content and Computational Thinking, and their acceptance of the integration.

CCS CONCEPTS

• **Social and professional topics** → **Computational thinking**; **K-12 education**; • **Computing methodologies** → **Logic programming and answer set programming**.

KEYWORDS

Logic Programming, Middle School Science, Computing

ACM Reference Format:
Yuanlin Zhang, Jianlan Wang, Fox Bolduc, and William G. Murray. 2019. LP Based Integration of Computing and Science Education in Middle Schools. In *ACM Global Computing Education Conference 2019 (CompEd '19), May 17–19, 2019, Chengdu, Sichuan, China*. ACM, New York, NY, USA, 7 pages. https://doi.org/10.1145/3300115.3309512

1 INTRODUCTION

There is consensus on the need of integrating computing, integral to the practice of all other STEM disciplines, in STEM teaching and learning in K-12 (Kindergarten to 12th grade in the US education system) (see, e.g., [31, 41]). However, little is known about how best Computational Thinking (CT) can be taught and how to integrate it with STEM disciplines to improve STEM and CT learning in K-12 in general and middle schools in particular.

To develop effective, integrative curriculum, it is desirable to have frameworks on how CT can be integrated to STEM education to support both CT and STEM curricular topics and students' learning outcomes.

In this paper we propose a Logic Programming (LP) based framework for integration, called *LPK12*. LPK12 achieves a deep integration of CT and STEM education by building computer models for STEM problems through Answer Set Programming (ASP) [15] – a modern LP paradigm. LPK12 is based on the following arguments. First, LP has low floor and high ceiling [32]. It allows students to start developing computer models for interesting, non-trivial STEM problems after a very short introduction and yet it is a full-fledged programming paradigm. Second, LP facilitates a unified treatment of the fundamental skills and topics in STEM and Computing thanks to the fact that LP is based on discoveries and ideas of Logic which forms an important base for learning and problem solving in all STEM disciplines. The LP modeling methodology allows a natural and seamless connection of subject-matter concepts and reasoning to computer model development. Thirdly, middle school students are cognitively ready for LP based approaches. By Piaget [33] and Vygotsky [44], children at age 11 to 15 demonstrate substantial knowledge of natural language and the logical use of symbols related to abstract concepts. Finally, for STEM, LPK12 facilitates students to develop fundamental skills, as defined in next generation science standards (NGSS) [30], such as *asking questions* and *defining problems, constructing explanations, engaging in argumentation*, and *communicating information*. For Computing, students will get abundant opportunities to learn and practice *various levels of abstraction, problem solving, programming* and *communication* as identified in the K-12 Computer Science Framework [22].

The rest of the paper is organized as follows. We present the LPK12 framework in Section 2 before the discussion of the related work in Section 3. In Section 4, we introduce the design of the study of the feasibility of LPK12 and the procedure of data collection and analysis. In Section 5, we present the data in alignment with our research questions. The paper is concluded by the last section.

2 THEORETICAL FRAMEWORK

2.1 LP Based Integration of Computing and Science Teaching

To integrate STEM and Computing teaching, we employ a methodology with two (often iterative) sequential components: (1) **Problem Description**. Teach students a new or learned STEM topic (problem). Students are expected to answer basic questions in this topic and understand why. (2) **Modeling.** Ask students to build a computer model using LP. The model is expected to answer the questions in the problem descriptions.

We will use food chain as an example to illustrate both the methodology and LP.

Problem description. Food chains are a science topic taught in middle school. Consider a chain with carrots, rabbits, snakes and eagles. Typical questions include "Q1: do eagles eat snakes?" and "Q2: what would happen to eagles if snakes become extinct?" Students are expected to review or learn food chains and how these questions can be answered.

Modeling. To design a computer model to answer the questions above, we follow an LP modeling methodology which consists of two steps. (1) Identify *objects* and *relations* in the problem. (2) Identify *knowledge* in the problem and write *LP rules* for this knowledge. The final LP rules, also called a *program*, form the model of the problem.

Objects of the food chain problem. The objects here are four species of organisms, which can be represented in LP by the following sort declaration:

```
#species = {eagle, snake, rabbit, carrot}.
```

Note that each species is taken as an object here. #species is called a *sort name*.

Relations in the food chain problem. From question Q1, we identify a relation of the form $feedsOn(X, Y)$ meaning that *members of species X feed on those of species Y*. In question Q2, we introduce a relation $extinct(X)$ which means that *species X is extinct*.

Knowledge and LP Rules. In this part, we explicate the science knowledge needed to answer the questions in English and then "translate" that knowledge into LP rules. The *declarative nature* of LP allows for a natural translation. For example, in the given food chain, we know that "rabbits feed on carrots", which can be translated, using the relation introduced earlier, into

$r1 : feedsOn(rabbit, carrot)$.

which is called a *fact*, a simplest form of an *LP rule*. $r1$ is the label of the rule which may be referred to later. Similarly, we have the knowledge that "snakes feed on rabbits" and "eagles feed on snakes" which are translated respectively into the facts: $r2 : feedsOn(snake, rabbit)$ and $r3 : feedsOn(eagle, snake)$. The collection of rules above forms an *LP program* which can be used to answer question Q1. A query $feedsOn(rabbit, X)$, where X is a variable (in the standard sense of a variable in algebra/math), asks the program to find an organism (X) that the rabbits in the chain feed on. The correct answer is carrot. Figure 1 gives an idea of *onlineSPARC*, an online LP programming environment (http://goo.gl/ukSZET) [34]. Area 1 (in red ellipse) is an editor containing the program above, and area 2 contains the query $feedsOn(rabbit, X)$. When the "submit" button is pressed, the answer is shown in area 3.

To answer question $Q2$, we add the knowledge that snakes are extinct which is represented as $r4 : extinct(snake)$. We also need some more general knowledge: "a species will be extinct if what it feeds on is extinct." This knowledge can be represented by an LP rule of the form: $r5 : extinct(X) :- feedsOn(X, Y), extinct(Y)$ where the symbol ":-" is understood as "if." The rule is read from left to right as *for any species X, X is extinct if X feeds on Y and*

Y is extinct. (Note: the rule is an accurate representation of the knowledge in food chains, but needs to be refined when a food web is modeled.) With these newly added rules, the LP program concludes that eagles are extinct too.

We have covered almost all major constructs of ASP. We hope the examples demonstrate the simplicity of ASP and the naturalness of the modeling and how the modeling focuses on domain knowledge. One can also see that LP, together with its modeling methodology, produces a seamless integration of Science and Computing.

2.2 LPK12 Facilitates STEM and CT Learning

Model-based learning is well accepted in science education. It is anticipated to help students' "attainment of 'conceptual understanding' in science at a level that goes beyond memorized facts, equations, or procedures" [5]. It is well recognized that building computer models for STEM problems helps STEM education too [10, 16, 19, 21, 35, 40, 45]. In fact, Harel and Papert [19] pointed out that learning computing together with another subject can be more effective than learning each separately.

To illustrate how LP-based integration will facilitate STEM learning, we use the framework for K-12 science education[11]. The framework articulates a vision of the scope and nature of K-12 education in *Science, engineering*, and *technology*. It has been implemented by NGSS (Next Generation Science Standards) which has been adopted by 16 states in US.

The NGSS framework divides the fundamental, core skills for science, engineering and technology into eight practices. SP1: asking questions and defining problems. SP2: developing and using models. SP3: planning and carrying out investigations. SP4: analyzing and interpreting data. SP5: using mathematics and Computational Thinking. SP6: constructing explanations and designing solutions. SP7: engaging in argument from evidence. SP8: Obtaining, evaluating, and communicating information.

LPK12 is able to cover the majority of the eight practices. As shown in our integration example in Section 2, students have to ask and answer questions before building a computer model. Hence, $SP1$ is in a prominent position in LPK12. LPK12 is driven by developing computer models for STEM problems and thus $SP2$ will be practiced intensively under our integration methodology. In LPK12, as shown in Section 2.1, students are encouraged to identify the knowledge and represent it as rules for computer models. Hence, $SP3$ and $SP6$ (solution design) are addressed in our integration. When testing and debugging their computer models, students have to re-examine the program and apply logical reasoning to explain the program behavior. Therefore, $SP6$ (explanation) and $SP7$ are well represented in our integration. As required in LP modeling methodology, students have to identify the knowledge used in modeling, express it in English and then translate it into rigorous rules. Hence, our integration helps students to practice $SP8$ (communicating information). Practice $SP5$ will be elaborated below on mathematics and computing separately.

As for mathematics, our integration helps address some core practices as identified in the Common Core State Standards for Mathematics [20]. MP2: reason abstractly and quantitatively. MP3: construct viable arguments and critique the reasoning of others. MP6: attend to precision. As argued before, when developing and

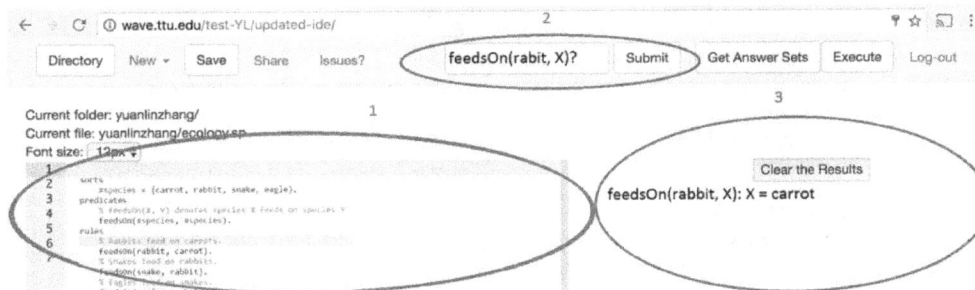

Figure 1: Screenshot of onlineSPARC

testing the computer models (e.g., that for food chain), all these practices are explicitly involved.

As for computing, LP covers the core practices of *abstracting, problem solving, programming* and *communicating*, as defined in an AP course [8] and standards ([12, 22]). The identification of relations and knowledge and the translation of knowledge into rules are a clear practice of *abstracting*. As a programming paradigm, LP offers the practice of all aspects of *programming*: model (program) design, program editing, (informal yet rigorous to a great extent) syntax and semantics, coding, testing and debugging. As shown in Section 2.1, model development starts from problem description. Hence *problem solving* is at the core of our integration. As argued for STEM, *communicating* is well covered by LPK12.

2.3 Appropriateness for Middle School Students

By Piaget [33] and Vygotsky [44], children from 11 to 15 demonstrate logical use of symbols related to abstract concepts. LPK12 also supports learning progression across multiple years as required in both STEM and CT [2, 9, 39] because of the easy integration with STEM topics. LPK12 also lends itself to well-accepted pedagogies such as *scaffolding* (because LP methodology explicates the knowledge and skills needed in problem solving in STEM) and *inquiry based learning* (because LP integration is driven by building computer models for answering questions – see Section 2 and 4.2). Due to space limitation, we are not able to elaborate on the above here.

3 LITERATURE REVIEW

Logic Programming Research and Its Use in Education. Born in the 1960s, Logic Programming is a meeting point of Thinking, Logic and Computing [24, 26]. It has been studied for teaching children since the 1980s [25] because it is supposed to allow a declarative (i.e., logical) reading and understanding of a program (and thus easy for children) [17, 29]. Unfortunately, the strong *procedural component* of classical LP systems such as PROLOG [29, 43] has prevented LP from reaching a wider audience although there have been efforts in the last two decades to include it in high school curriculum [3, 38, 42] and undergraduate teaching [27]. A major breakthrough in the last two decades is the establishment of Answer Set Programming – a *purely declarative* LP paradigm [15]. ASP is now a major paradigm in Knowledge Representation and Logic Programming community [24] with numerous applications

across many areas [14]. This breakthrough merits a revisiting of LP in teaching because it eliminates the *procedural component*.

Programming Systems in K-12. The mainstream systems used in K-12 is based on visual programming environments such as Scratch and Alice [23, 28]. The majority of systems encourage and facilitate tinkering and fit the needs of students who prefer *tinkering* to *logic and planning* [32, 36]. These languages and environments have been very successful in reaching a large K-12 population. However, more research is needed to understand how CT occurs as students are tinkering while using visual programming languages [17, 28]. The majority of the teaching modules, based on the visual programming languages, adopt open-ended contexts such as game design and storytelling for ad hoc STEM topics [2], which makes the alignment with curricular topics difficult.

Integration of Computing and STEM Teaching. Some challenges for integrating computing into STEM in K-12 are how to align with STEM and CT curricula topics and how to support students' learning progression (usually across multiple years) in both STEM and CT [2, 9, 39]. To develop effective integration curriculum, it is desirable to have integration frameworks to support curricular alignment and learning progression. One of the few works in this direction is [40] which proposes the use of agent-based computation to integrate CT and science. We also note a rigorous study on how the integration may improve students' learning of a specific topic in mathematics [37]. However, this study does not present a general framework on the integration.

Our Contribution. As far as we are aware, we are the first to propose the use of LP, a purely declarative programming paradigm, to integrate computing and STEM. The majority of integration (including [40]) is based on *imperative programming paradigms*. We note functional programming, also declarative, is used in integration, e.g., [37]. However, the work in [37] is on a specific topic but not on a general framework. The main advantages of LP over imperative languages are as follows: 1) LP is simple in both syntax and semantics (see Section 2); 2) the fact that LP is based on discoveries and ideas of *Logic* which also forms an important basis for learning and problem solving in all other disciplines provides a more straightforward connection between LP based models and STEM problem solving; and 3) the high level of abstraction of LP allows one to "hide" many machine-related details when solving a problem. It is also observed that text-based languages have the advantage over visual languages of "taking students deeper into both programming and science" [13, 39]. LP is a text-based language.

4 STUDY DESIGN

To study the feasibility of LPK12, we developed two LP-integrated modules and applied the exploratory case study method to pilot the exploration of the efficacy of the modules [1].

4.1 Participants and Context

This study took place in an elective course, with the name "STEM", of a middle school with 900 students in grades 6th - 8th which is located in a middle-south city in the United States. The participants were one STEM teacher and her four sections of 96 6th-graders and three sections of 71 7th-graders. Among the 6th (and 7th respectively) graders, there were 61 (and 51) males and 36 (and 20) females. The ethnographic composition of 6th graders was 60 Whites, 28 Hispanics, 5 Blacks, 2 Asians, and 1 American Indian; and that for 7th graders was 43 Whites, 22 Hispanics, 3 Blacks, and 3 Asians.

4.2 LP Based Integration Modules and Implementation

We developed a chemistry module (periodic table) for 6th graders and physics module (motion) for 7th graders.

4.2.1 Chemistry Module. Lesson 1 introduces computer science in general and computer models in particular. Part 1 includes motivating videos such as *Computer Science is Changing Everything* by code.org (2016) and discussions following these videos. In part 2, by asking students questions about their classroom, school, and a family, we introduce the concept of models that human beings may use to answer questions. Using human thinking as an analogy, we introduce the concept of LP based computer models for problem solving. Students would interact with a model by asking the same questions they were asked in the lesson and extending the model with new knowledge.

Lesson 2 introduces LP concepts of *relations, facts,* and *queries* using examples. It first reviews the chemical symbols for elements. Students will then extend a given model by adding facts, e.g., on the symbol for Hydrogen. They first type a comment "% The symbol for Hydrogen is H" and then the fact "symbolFor(hydrogen, h)." *Queries* are introduced to answer questions to the model. Students then extend the model with knowledge from other elements including carbon and phosphorous, and test the model using queries.

Lesson 3 reviews new topics of *atomic number* and *mass number.* The teacher will introduce relations needed to answer questions in those topics. Students will then expand a given model with facts about the new knowledge on atomic number and mass number, and then test the model using queries.

Lesson 4 introduces *variables* using queries. E.g., for question "what is the chemical symbol for the element silicon?', we need a query "symbolFor(silicon, What)?" where What is a variable. Students practice variables by writing queries for similar questions about other elements. A new relation $protonsOf(E, N)$ is introduced to denote that the number of protons of the atom of element E is N. Finally, students are challenged to extend a given model with facts representing the knowledge of the protons of hydrogen.

Lesson 5 introduces *rules.* It reviews knowledge relating proton number to atomic number: the number of protons of the atom of an element E is N if N is the atomic number of the element E. It then shows the rule for representing it:

```
protonsOf(E, N) :- atomicNumber(E,N).
```

Students extend a given model by this rule and test it. They then practice by writing a rule for knowledge on getting atomic number from proton number and to test it.

Lesson 6 and 7 introduce more complexity to the rules. It reviews domain knowledge relating the number of neutrons to mass number and proton number: N is the number neutrons of an atom E if M is the mass number of the atom E, and $N = M - P$. It is represented as

```
neutronsOf(E, N) :- massNumber(E, M),
              protonsOf(E, P), N = M - P
```

where "," between relations means conjunction. The students extend a given model with the rule and further by a rule defining the mass number of an element using its number of neutrons and protons.

Lesson 8 continues the practice of writing rules and reviews domain knowledge relating the number of electrons of an atom to that of protons or the atomic number. Students are asked to write and test a rule for this knowledge. Another exercise is to represent the knowledge on getting neutron number from proton and mass numbers.

4.2.2 Physics Module. This 8-lesson module has a similar structure to the chemistry one. Due to lack of space, here we only give the physics problem involved and its modeling information. The physics concepts covered are *target object, reference object, distance change* between two objects and the target object's *motion relative to* the reference object. They are introduced by an experiment where one student will move a chair with another student on it. During and after the experiments, questions about the concepts are asked, discussed and explained. To model the problem, we introduce the relations *isTarget(X)* (i.e., X is a target object), *isReference(X)* (i.e., X is a reference), *distanceChange(X, Y)* (the distance changes between X and Y), and *moving(X, Y)* (X is moving relative to object Y). One piece of knowledge used is: an object X is moving relative to object Y if the distance between X and Y changes. (This knowledge may need to be refined in a rigorous setting or multiple dimensions.) We also introduce the classical negation ¬ in this module.

4.2.3 Implementation. Each class session consists of one or several cycles. Each cycle consists of two components: concept understanding (by lecturing and discussion with a duration of 5-10 minutes) and programming practices. Slides are designed to facilitate the lecturing and discussion, and workbooks are designed to contain detailed information to guide the students on their programming practices. Programming involves too much information and any ignorance of any information by students will frustrate them and interrupt the class flow. The workbooks make it easy for students to review or find information they need.

4.3 Research design

This study lasted for four weeks of totally 8 50-minute long periods in spring 2018. Due to the exploratory nature of this study, we selected topics that the participating students had learned prior to the intervention. The goal is to measure students' learning outcomes in science content and computational thinking.

4.4 Data collection and analysis

We administered pre- and post-surveys to examine the learning outcomes. They contain multiple-choice questions assessing students' scientific content knowledge of interest and computer science skills. The science questions have been previously validated. Since LP is new in teaching CT, the questions are designed by the researchers by following the guide in [4]. Each question is graded as either 1 (correct) or 0 (incorrect). The total score is the sum of scores from all question. The questions from the pre- and post-surveys are substantially the same and vary only in different context. For instance, the questions in the pre-survey for the 7th-graders are about a boy on a swing and those in the post-survey are about a car leaving a garage. The purpose of not using the same questions in the post-survey is to suppress the possibility of students answering questions through memorization.

Here are some questions for physics. Pre-question. A boy is playing on a swing in a park. His mom stands still by the swing. There are several other kids playing on a slide in the same park. In reference to the boy, is the swing moving? A. Yes, B. No, C. Not sure, more information is needed. Post-question. A boy is sitting in a car. His mom is reversing from the garage. His dad is standing still in the garage and saying bye to them. In reference to the boy, is the car moving? A. Yes, B. No, C. Not sure, more information is needed. Here is a question for measuring abstraction in Computing. We know protonNumber(E, N) means that the proton number for element E is N, electronNumber(E, N) means that the electron number for element E is N. Write a rule to represent the following knowledge: the electron number of E is N if the proton number of E is N. A. the electron number of E is N if the proton number of E is N. B. protonNumber(E, N) :- electronNumber(E, N). C. electronNumber(E, N) :- protonNumber(E, N). D. None of the above.

Besides descriptive statistics, we applied paired t-tests on the surveys for the pre-post comparison. Meanwhile, we calculated Cohen's d [7] and normalized gain [18] to measure the effect size. Cohen's d describes the width of the impact on students from the integration modules (small 0.2, medium 0.5, large 0.8) and normalized gain describes the magnitude of the impact in terms of the ratio of the actual progress made by students to the maximum progress that students could make (small <0.3, medium 0.3-0.6,large >0.7).

We also carried out one post group interview for each grade to gauge the students' feedback to their experience with the integration modules. The interviews were semi-structured. We recruited volunteer 6th and 7th graders with a diverse background in terms of gender, race, science content knowledge and CT understanding (so that they are representative to the greatest extent – See Table 1).

Table 1: Background information of the interviewees

	S7-1	S7-2	S7-3	S7-4	S7-5	S7-6	S7-7	S7-8	S6-1	S6-2	S6-3	S6-4	S6-5	S6-6	S6-7
G	7	7	7	7	7	7	7	7	6	6	6	6	6	6	6
S	M	F	M	M	M	M	F	M	M	M	M	M	F	F	M
R	A	W	W	W	H	W	W	W	W	H	W	W	H	W	W
Sc	3	4	1	2	3	4	4	3	2	3	3	2	2	1	1
CT	3	3	3	2	3	4	4	3	2	3	2	4	3	2	3

G: grade; S: sex; R: race; M: male; F: female; Sc/CT: Science/CT score out of 4; S7-i, S6-i: pseudo code for students; A: Asian; H: Hispanic; W: White.

The interviews were audio-recorded and transcribed later. Codes were developed to identity students' feedback to the integration modules. We coded the interviewees' comments from three perspectives: *module being interesting, computing being impactful to science learning*, and *science being impactful to computing learning*. For each category, we coded an interviewee's response as "Yes" (i.e., admitting that statement), "No" (denying that statement), and "N/A" (i.e., not mentioning it in the interview).

5 FINDINGS

5.1 Q1. How did the integration modules affect the students' learning?

We summarized in Table 2 the data about pre-post comparison. Both the 6th- and 7th-grade students developed their CT (abstraction) significantly with Cohen's d being large and normalized gain being medium, which indicates that the modules have helped most of the participating students make considerable progress in CT skills. Similarly, the 7th graders' physics content knowledge increased significantly. The effect size indexes (Cohen's d=1.15,<g>=0.61) suggest that most students developed their understanding about the relative nature of motion to a considerable extent after the integration modules. However, the 6th graders' chemistry content knowledge decreased from 1.55 to 1.35. This decrease might happen by chance because it is not statistically significant. Some possible reasons might be that the students had different statuses while answering those questions, and students may be more serious to answer the questions in pre-survey. Some extra instruments may be needed to figure out the reasons in the future study.

Table 2: Paired t-tests of assessments on science and CT

	Pre	SD	Post	SD	|t|(df)	p	C-d	<g>
6-C	1.55	0.95	1.35	0.88	0.89(73)	ns	-0.22	-0.08
6-CT	1.14	1.02	2.51	0.99	10.46(70)	***	1.36	0.48
7-P	1.62	1.37	3.07	1.16	6.71(55)	***	1.15	0.61
7-CT	1.73	1.17	2.61	1	4.37(56)	***	0.82	0.39

ns: not significant; ***: p<0.001; Pre and Post: mean score with a max score of 4; 6-C: chemistry; 7-P: physics; C-d: Cohen's d; <g>: normalized gain

The quantitative data does not cover students' learning of programming and communication. They are examined by class observations and the interviews. For programming, students are expected to repeat given models and extend them with new knowledge and rules during class. According to the class observation by the teacher and researchers, a majority of the students are able to complete both types of tasks. We will discuss next the interview results on the programming and communication aspect of CT.

From the interviews, students show positive experience with programming and LP. For example, "*I think it was really easy. Because you're basically just saying it in English, but just like a different. Well.. It's like pretty much the same thing*" by S7-7. "*I really liked the questions for the query because if you get your answer yes your like hard work paid off or if it didn't you need to like go through all your steps again*" by S6-5 (and similarly S6-4). The favorite part of the class is "*the coding part*" by S7-3 (and agreed by S7-1, S7-4, S7-5 and S7-6). "*My favorite part is I think just learning new coding styles in general is cool to me because we went from symbol forward to atomic* number to number of neutrons to protons and I'm just excited for what we learned" by S6-7. When comparing other programming paradigms such as drag and drop, "this time around, we actually we had to learn what to say to do it. I mean in fourth grade all we did was pretty much move like right forward back but here we actually had to learn is like protons, neutrons, electrons stuff like that for sparc [LP system used in our implementation], which I think is actually better on that because we can learn more .... I mean it's a lot harder and more informative if you actually do [LP programming]" by S6-2.

Debugging is an important element of programming. Students seem to be able to do debugging and appreciate its value. Here are example excerpts. Comment by S6-5 above on programming. "When it [the model/program] just doesn't give you an answer and then you realize you did something wrong and you go back and you look over it [program]" by S6-6. "when you make a mistake you get to go back and then while you're retyping something or redoing something you can look and make sure that you get like if I got let's say lithium and I went back next to and accidentally only put a top or a symbol for it is as LI can go back and put it as li and that helps me more because the more and more I do it and the more I make mistakes the more I will know to put the right or correct answer" by S6-7. When something is wrong, "I got through all the steps that I took and if I missed a step or something I would go back and fix it and it would work again" by S6-6. When asked if they tried to find errors when their program does not answer a query correctly, S7-1, S7-2, S7-3 and S7-4 answered yes while S7-5 no. As for locating errors, "ask a query of a certain line of code. And if it [LP system] comes up ... the opposite [to the expected] response then ... you can go through that specific line of code and see what's wrong" by S7-2.

For CT practice communication, in our teaching, we always start from English description of knowledge and then write rule(s) to represent the knowledge. As a result, we observed that majority of students always write English description before writing any rules. When commenting about this methodology "I think they help ... because you're actually reading it and if you don't understand something you can read it again maybe ask a couple questions" by S6-6. Another example is the comment by S7-7 above. Given the precision needs of computer models, the writing of the description and translating it into rule(s) will improve students' rigorousness in communication.

5.2 Q2. How the participants reflect on their experience with the LP based integration?

Most of the interviewees commented positively on their experience with the integrated modules. 13 out of 15 interviewees thought that the modules were interesting (S7-7 was coded as "No" and S7-6 as "N/A"). 14 out 15 interviewees believed that computing impacted science learning (S7-3 is coded as "No"), and vice versa (S7-6 is coded as "No"). Thus, the LP based integration of science and CT is accepted by the students. S6-4 commented that science and computing can support each other: "I think it can be fun just like learning about new like elements that like mean this is technology, but we're also learning about like other stuff in our world not just kind of ... it's like a win-win." "instead of just learning it [motion], but putting it into something you can do like teaching the computer, that makes it more fun" by S7-7. "[computing] makes it more interesting

because you're not just looking at a whole lot of boxes on a piece of paper [periodic table]" by S6-5. "[Computing is interesting] when we had to do the like the number of neutrons equals the number of protons like you add both of those to get the uh, atomic mass" by S6-3. "You don't really notice you are learning the chemistry and stuff until you are done with it [modeling] ..." by S6-1. When talking about modeling chemistry problems, "you might feel more professional because you're doing something that professionals would do" by S6-4.

6 CONCLUSION

We propose an LP based framework to integrate computing and STEM teaching in K-12. To test its feasibility, we have developed two integration modules for 6th and 7th grades. By our experience, the framework allows a rather straightforward development of the modules (see Section 4.2). We conjecture that the development of modules for other topics in science, based on our modules, will also be straightforward. Our survey data show that students' learning has been improved on physics and CT (abstraction) significantly. Class observations and interviews show that students are doing well in the other aspects of CT: programming and communication. Interviews also show the LP based integration is accepted by students: the modules are interesting and there is a positive impact of computing and science to each other.

In summary, LP based integration seems to be promising in terms of the development and implementation of the two 8-session modules, the students' learning outcomes.

There are some limitations in this preliminary study. 1)It is difficult to test students' development of problem solving capacity, a CT practice, because the short duration of the project. Our framework allows a curriculum with much longer duration (see Section 2.3). We will plan experiments with longer duration in future. 2) Other variables are not controlled. For example, we did not control the students' access to resources of both science and computational science. Thus, we cannot ascribe the observed pre-post differences solely to the LP-integrated modules as there might be other variables that took effects. 3) Our survey data did not show improvement on students' learning outcome on chemistry. One explanation is that two of the four test questions involve complex relations and calculations. One question is "How many protons, neurons and electrons are present in an atom of hafnium, Hf, with a mass number of 178, and an electron number of 72?" We focus on the declarative knowledge, but it may still be challenging for 6th graders to calculate the right answer from their knowledge. In future, clinical interviews will be used to understand students' performance change. 4) We do not have a quantitative measurement on students' learning outcomes on programming and communication of CT practices. In future, we will develop and validate quantitative assessment and rubrics to more rigorous measurement of students' outcomes on these CT practices. Finally, our future work will be exploring how to integrate the LP-integrated method into core STEM courses seamlessly.

ACKNOWLEDGMENTS

We thank Michael Gelfond and Michael Strong for numerous discussions on this topic, and Edna Parr, Wendy Staffen and Jeremy Wagner for their support in our implementation.

REFERENCES

[1] Donald Ary, Lucy Cheser Jacobs, Christine K Sorensen Irvine, and David Walker. 2018. *Introduction to research in education*. Cengage Learning.

[2] Satabdi Basu, Gautam Biswas, Pratim Sengupta, Amanda Dickes, John S Kinnebrew, and Douglas Clark. 2016. Identifying middle school studentsâĂŹ challenges in computational thinking-based science learning. *Research and Practice in Technology Enhanced Learning* 11, 1 (2016), 13.

[3] Silvio Beux, Daniela Briola, Andrea Corradi, Giorgio Delzanno, Angelo Ferrando, Federico Frassetto, Giovanna Guerrini, Viviana Mascardi, Marco Oreggia, Francesca Pozzi, Alessandro Solimando, and Armando Tacchella. 2015. Computational Thinking for Beginners: A Successful Experience using Prolog. *Proceedings of the 30th Italian Conference on Computational Logic* (2015).

[4] Philip Sheridan Buffum, Eleni V Lobene, Megan Hardy Frankosky, Kristy Elizabeth Boyer, Eric N Wiebe, and James C Lester. 2015. A practical guide to developing and validating computer science knowledge assessments with application to middle school. In *Proceedings of the 46th ACM technical symposium on computer science education*. ACM, 622–627.

[5] John Clement. 2000. Model based learning as a key research area for science education. *International Journal of Science Education* 22, 9 (2000), 1041–1053.

[6] code.org. 2016. Computer Science is Changing Everything. Video retrieved from https://www.youtube.com/watch?v=QvyTEx1wyOY on September 4 2018.

[7] Jacob Cohen. 1988. Statistical power analysis for the behavioral sciences. 2nd.

[8] CollegeBoard. 2017. AP Computer Science Principles: course and exam descriptions. Retrieved from https://apcentral.collegeboard.org/pdf/ap-computer-science-principles-course-and-exam-description.pdf on September 4 2018.

[9] Thomas B Corcoran, Frederic A Mosher, and Aaron Rogat. 2009. Learning progressions in science: An evidence-based approach to reform. (2009).

[10] National Research Council et al. 2011. *Report of a workshop on the pedagogical aspects of computational thinking*. National Academies Press.

[11] National Research Council et al. 2012. *A framework for K-12 science education: Practices, crosscutting concepts, and core ideas*. National Academies Press.

[12] CSTA. 2017. CSTA K-12 computer science standards. Computer Science Teachers Association.

[13] Betsy DiSalvo. 2014. Graphical qualities of educational technology: Using drag-and-drop and text-based programs for introductory computer science. *IEEE computer graphics and applications* 34, 6 (2014), 12–15.

[14] Esra Erdem, Michael Gelfond, and Nicola Leone. 2016. Applications of answer set programming. *AI Magazine* 37, 3 (2016), 53–68.

[15] Michael Gelfond and Yulia Kahl. 2014. *Knowledge Representation, Reasoning, and the Design of Intelligent Agents*. Cambridge University Press.

[16] Mark Guzdial. 1994. Software-realized scaffolding to facilitate programming for science learning. *Interactive Learning Environments* 4, 1 (1994), 001–044.

[17] Mark Guzdial. 2004. Programming environments for novices. *Computer science education research* 2004 (2004), 127–154.

[18] Richard R Hake. 1998. Interactive-engagement versus traditional methods: A six-thousand-student survey of mechanics test data for introductory physics courses. *American journal of Physics* 66, 1 (1998), 64–74.

[19] Idit Harel and Seymour Papert. 1990. Software design as a learning environment. *Interactive learning environments* 1, 1 (1990), 1–32.

[20] Common Core State Standards Initiative et al. 2010. Common core state standards for mathematics. *http://www. corestandards. org/assets/CCSSI_Math% 20Standards. pdf* (2010).

[21] Kemi Jona, Uri Wilensky, Laura Trouille, MS Horn, Kai Orton, David Weintrop, and Elham Beheshti. 2014. Embedding computational thinking in science, technology, engineering, and math (CT-STEM). In *future directions in computer science education summit meeting, Orlando, FL*.

[22] K-12 Computer Science Framework. 2017. http://www.k12cs.org. Retrieved on September 4 2018.

[23] Caitlin Kelleher and Randy Pausch. 2005. Lowering the Barriers to Programming: A Taxonomy of Programming Environments and Languages for Novice Programmers. *ACM Comput. Surv.* 37, 2 (June 2005), 83–137.

[24] Robert Kowalski. 2014. Logic Programming. *Computational Logic, Volume 9 (Handbook of the History of Logic)* (2014).

[25] Robert A Kowalski. 1982. Logic as a computer language for children. In *ECAI*. 2–10.

[26] Robert A Kowalski. 1988. The early years of logic programming. *Commun. ACM* 31, 1 (1988), 38–43.

[27] Hector J. Levesque. 2012. *Thinking As Computation: A First Course*. The MIT Press.

[28] Sze Yee Lye and Joyce Hwee Ling Koh. 2014. Review on teaching and learning of computational thinking through programming: What is next for K-12? *Computers in Human Behavior* 41 (2014), 51–61.

[29] Patrick Mendelsohn, TRG Green, and Paul Brna. 1991. Programming languages in education: The search for an easy start. In *Psychology of programming*. Elsevier, 175–200.

[30] NGSS Lead States. 2015. Next generation science standards: For states, by states. National Academies Press.

[31] NSF. 2018. STEM+C Program. https://www.nsf.gov/funding/pgm_summ.jsp?pims_id=505006, retrieved on October 10 2018.

[32] Seymour Papert. 1980. *Mindstorms: Children, computers, and powerful ideas*. Basic Books, Inc.

[33] Jean Piaget. 1972. Intellectual evolution from adolescence to adulthood. *Human development* 15, 1 (1972), 1–12.

[34] Christian Reotutar, Mbathio Diagne, Evgenii Balai, Edward Wertz, Peter Lee, Shao-Lon Yeh, and Yuanlin Zhang. 2016. An Online Logic Programming Development Environment.. In *AAAI*. 4130–4131.

[35] Alexander Repenning, David Webb, and Andri Ioannidou. 2010. Scalable game design and the development of a checklist for getting computational thinking into public schools. In *Proceedings of the 41st ACM technical symposium on Computer science education*. ACM, 265–269.

[36] Mitchel Resnick and Eric Rosenbaum. 2013. Designing for tinkerability. *Design, make, play: Growing the next generation of STEM innovators* (2013), 163–181.

[37] Emmanuel Schanzer, Kathi Fisler, Shriram Krishnamurthi, and Matthias Felleisen. 2015. Transferring skills at solving word problems from computing to algebra through Bootstrap. In *Proceedings of the 46th ACM Technical symposium on computer science education*. ACM, 616–621.

[38] Zahava Scherz and Bruria Haberman. 1995. Logic programming based curriculum for high school students: the use of abstract data types. In *ACM SIGCSE Bulletin*, Vol. 27. ACM, 331–335.

[39] Pratim Sengupta, Amanda Dickes, Amy Voss Farris, Ashlyn Karan, David Martin, and Mason Wright. 2015. Programming in K-12 science classrooms. *Commun. ACM* 58, 11 (2015), 33–35.

[40] Pratim Sengupta, John S Kinnebrew, Satabdi Basu, Gautam Biswas, and Douglas Clark. 2013. Integrating computational thinking with K-12 science education using agent-based computation: A theoretical framework. *Education and Information Technologies* 18, 2 (2013), 351–380.

[41] STEM education act. 2015. Public Law No: 114-59.

[42] Jurriën Stutterheim, Wouter Swierstra, and Doaitse Swierstra. 2013. Forty hours of declarative programming: Teaching Prolog at the Junior College Utrecht. *arXiv preprint arXiv:1301.5077* (2013).

[43] Josie Taylor and Ben Du Boulay. 1987. Studying novice programmers: why they may find learning Prolog hard. In *Computers, Cognition and Development: Issues for Psychology and Education*. John Wiley, 153–173.

[44] Lev S Vygotsky and Lev Seminovitch Vygotski. 1987. *The collected works of LS Vygotsky: Volume 1: Problems of general psychology, including the volume Thinking and Speech*. Vol. 1. Springer Science & Business Media.

[45] Uri Wilensky and Kenneth Reisman. 2006. Thinking like a wolf, a sheep, or a firefly: Learning biology through constructing and testing computational theoriesâĂŤan embodied modeling approach. *Cognition and instruction* 24, 2 (2006), 171–209.

Computability and Algorithmic Complexity Questions in Secondary Education

Rafael del Vado Vírseda
Universidad Complutense de Madrid
rdelvado@mat.ucm.es

ABSTRACT

Theoretical computing is a difficult area to teach in university courses due to different causes. Many students who begin computing subjects have little mathematical or theoretical background. It is important that students acquire an intuitive knowledge of these theoretical concepts before they finish their secondary education. In this work we describe how to bring computability and complexity questions in secondary education to address classic issues raised in the curriculum about the limits of mathematics and its formal systems, and subsequently, their algorithmic and algebraic complexity. We report a complete educational experience for enhancing the algorithmic curriculum of pre-university computing and mathematics courses to know what computability and algorithmic complexity questions may be introduced into secondary education, how to teach these concepts, and train teachers to do it. The good experimental results obtained are compared with the results in standard high school courses in which these questions about theoretical computing are not addressed. The conclusions obtained are exposed, as well as the pros and cons of the educational experience carried out, so that they can be taken into account in the future design for the curriculum of an official subject in computing on a global scale, or be included in the curriculum of pre-university courses.

CCS CONCEPTS

• **Social and professional topics** → **K-12 education**; *Model curricula*; • **Mathematics of computing**; • **Theory of computation** → *Computability*; *Complexity theory and logic*;

KEYWORDS

Computability theory; algorithmic complexity; computing curricula; curriculum issues; undergraduate studies

ACM Reference Format:
Rafael del Vado Vírseda. 2019. Computability and Algorithmic Complexity Questions in Secondary Education. In *ACM Global Computing Education Conference 2019 (CompEd '19), May 17–19, 2019, Chengdu, Sichuan, China.* ACM, New York, NY, USA, 7 pages. https://doi.org/10.1145/3300115.3309507

1 INTRODUCTION AND MOTIVATIONS

Theoretical computing is a very broad discipline, which includes concepts and questions that contribute to the creation of a computer identity, which, in turn, try to identify the big ideas that underlie a science, especially those related to the study of computability and complexity in solving problems, and the scope and limitations of formal systems [7, 13, 23, 28]. Unfortunately, while theoretical computing is a very difficult area to teach in university courses, computing at high school often focuses on programming, and consequently many students who enter the university computing courses have very little theoretical or mathematical background. It is important that students obtain an appreciation of these theoretical concepts before they finish high school. For these reason, and anticipating that these questions on theoretical computing will not be incorporated into an official subject, we describe in this paper how to bring theoretical computing concepts into secondary education, so that students can perform better in some areas of mathematics and be increasingly prepared and motivated for their university science and engineering studies. We report a complete educational experience including introductory computability theory questions in secondary education to address the classic questions raised in the curriculum about the limits of mathematics and its formal systems, and subsequently, their algebraic complexity. We provide arguments to stimulate debate and discussion on whether or not to introduce the concepts of computability and algorithmic complexity in the pre-university education system. We believe that this educational approach can be useful and applicable on a global scale in many secondary school settings and could be useful for enhancing the algorithmic curriculum of pre-university computing and mathematics courses.

The paper is structured as follows. The following section reviews prior and related work on teaching theoretical computing at the pre-university level. Then, we analyse what the questions related to the limits of mathematics are that are already included in the last two courses in secondary education and which allow us to introduce preliminary questions about computability and algorithmic complexity. Then follows a discussion of how to address the introduction of more specific questions related to the existence of non-computable problems, based on the scope and limits of formal systems, logical paradoxes, and problems of high computational and algebraic complexity. Finally, the experimental results obtained with the introduction of all these questions are analysed.

2 RELATED WORK AND CONTRIBUTIONS

Most of the previous work on teaching theoretical computing at the undergraduate level dates to the 1980s [8, 30, 34] and early 1990s [11, 17, 31]. For an overview, [34] provides experiences, observations, and proposals to be added to existing computing curricula to cultivate within students their 'mathematical maturity'. Similar attempts were presented more recently in [4–6, 22, 24, 25]. As concrete examples, [25] describes an innovative methodology for teaching theoretical computing by completing a game-building assignment, and [5] describes the design of videos and classroom activities on various theoretical topics of computing. However, the lack of a concrete educational experience with a detailed collection of selected problems, questions, puzzles, and riddles, designed from high school mathematics and introductory logic to be added to the current secondary mathematical curriculum, weakens and demotivates their real application. For this reason, in this work we report a detailed educational experience presenting concrete and specific questions from Complexity and Computability in secondary education for enhancing the algorithmic curriculum of pre-university computing and mathematics courses. Unlike the *CS Unplugged* approach [4, 24] (a collection of free learning activities, games and puzzles to introduce students to Computational Thinking [1, 7, 14, 24] where no programming is required), our activities and questions are designed on the basis of the classic mathematical and logical limits in the last courses of a secondary school curriculum, where we can work with students with programming languages like Python [26, 27]. The main novelty of our work with respect to all these previous approaches is to address typical questions raised in the curriculum about the limits of mathematics and its formal systems, intuitively presenting theoretical computing concepts from classic textbooks [10, 15, 18, 29, 32, 36, 39] in secondary education. The first contribution is that the education community can know what concepts of theoretical computing, conveniently adapted to students' capability, may be introduced into their secondary courses, how and when to teach these questions, and then train teachers to do it. The second contribution is to stimulate debate and provide arguments for changing the current computing standards to incorporate theoretical computing questions into official subjects of secondary education on a global scale.

3   THE CLASSIC LIMITS OF MATHEMATICS

The subjects of Mathematics in secondary education raise questions about the classic limits of mathematics that constitute the perfect moment to introduce to the student questions of interdisciplinary motivation that allow him/her to distinguish between computable and non-computable problems, and within the computable problems, to understand better their algorithmic complexity in order to approach them adequately by means of a computer [9, 32, 40]. The first contact with these 'mathematical obstructions' in computation is obtained by the student at the beginning of high school when studying *irrational numbers*, understanding that there are real numbers that can present infinite decimal numbers, which makes them impossible to represent in a computer, having to be satisfied only with mere approximations. For example, for $\sqrt{2} \approx$ 1.414213562373... the following simple program in Python contradicts the intuition of the student, since it seems that it should always return True, but it is not because of the error of the representation of real numbers:

```
def paradox(a):
    b = math.sqrt(a)
    return a == b * b
```

The students of the first year contemplate the use of irrational numbers by means of estimations and approximations, controlling the margins of error. However, the most important limitation faced by students is the *resolution of algebraic equations*, through the impossibility of obtaining by means of a formula in radicals the solutions of the equation of the fifth degree, and in general the solutions of equations of degree greater than four in terms of radicals. Students also understand that, although solutions have been obtained from lower degree equations, such as the third grade equation using the *Cardano method* [38], when they try to program them in Python, due to the complexity of the calculation of these equations and the errors introduced in the approximations of real numbers, it is necessary to find methods that approximate their roots with a certain precision. Although not included in the high school math curriculum, it is the right time to use it with students for root approximation, for example, *Newton's method* $x_{i+1} = x_i - \frac{f(x_i)}{f'(x_i)}$, where except for a few x_0 elections this succession converges at a root of $f(x) = 0$. This method of dealing with the problem of computability and complexity in the resolution of algebraic equations is easy for students to program in Python [27]:

```
def newton_method(f, derf, x0, max_iter):
    epsilon = 1e-10
    x = x0
    fx = f(x)
    i = 0
    while i < max_iter and abs(fx) > epsilon :
        x = x - fx / derf(x)
        fx = f(x)
        i += 1
    return x
```

Another classic limitation of mathematics that students encounter, in the case of students in the last year of high school, appears in the study of the *normal distribution*. A random variable follows the so-called standard normal distribution $\mathcal{N}(0, 1)$ if its density function is $f(x) = \frac{1}{\sqrt{2\pi}} e^{-\frac{x^2}{2}}$. The probability that the random variable with such a normal distribution will take its value in an interval $[a, b]$ is given by the area under the Gaussian bell curve between the extremes a and b, i.e., by the defined integral $\int_a^b e^{-\frac{x^2}{2}} dx$. In the last year of high school, students are taught to calculate the area under the graph of a $f(x)$ function between the extremes a and b by using the *primitive calculus* $\int_a^b f(x)dx$. However, the limitation that students face is that the function $f(x) = e^{-\frac{x^2}{2}}$ does not admit primitive in terms of elementary functions (exponentials, sines, cosines, logarithms, solutions of algebraic equations, etc.), that is, there is no function that can be expressed as a combination of elementary functions such that its derivative is $e^{-\frac{x^2}{2}}$. Our students naturally ask if there is an algorithmic method to recognize whether a given function is 'elementary integrable' or not. However, [33] has proved that no such algorithm exists, so for its calculation they use tables or computer programs. As in the case of solving algebraic equations, it is the right time to motivate the student to know how to deal with this impossibility or difficulty of performing the integration in an analytical way, approximating the numerical value of a defined integral $\int_a^b f(x)dx$ through, for example, the *midpoint rule* [26]:

```
def midpoint_rule(f, num, a, b):
    div = (b - a) / num
    approx = 0
    for m in range(num) :
            approx += f((a + div / 2) + m * div)
    approx *= div
    return approx
```

In relation to other subjects in the pre-university level, similar questions can also be addressed in an introductory way in physics classes of the first years as a complement to those already seen in the mathematics classes. *The Three-Body Problem* [40] consists in determining, at any moment, the positions and velocities of three bodies, of mass m and distance r, subjected to the force F of mutual gravitational attraction $F = G\frac{m_1 \times m_2}{r^2}$ (G is the constant of universal gravitation), and starting from a given position and velocity. The Earth-Moon-Sun system is a familiar case of the problem. The evolution of the system is extremely chaotic, since a very small variation in the initial state of any of the bodies, for example, due to measurement errors, however small, could lead to completely different results (the phenomenon known as the *butterfly effect*). The computability problems to determine a stable solution lie in the fact that this problem again lacks an analytical solution, that is, the integral solution that must be solved to obtain a function that represents the position of each one of the bodies as a function of time, does not exist as an expression in terms of the usual functions that we all know, namely, polynomials of any degree, even fractional, circular, exponential and logarithmic functions, as in the case of the normal distribution. However, it is possible for the students to obtain numerical approximations in Python with any precision we want, with which we can calculate and predict trajectories.

Additionally, a numerical approximation that high school students enjoy is based on the *Monte Carlo methods* [35, 36]. The increasing computing power and speed of computers has made them one of the basic tools for simulation and research in recent years to solve the 'unsolvable'. As an illustration of the method, students compute in Python an approximation of the irrational number π by launching darts [27]:

```
def approximate_pi(darts):
    dartboard = 0
    i = 0
    while i < darts :
        a = random.uniform(-1,1)
        b = random.uniform(-1,1)
        if a * a + b * b <= 1 :
            dartboard += 1
        i += 1
    return 4 * (dartboard / darts)
```

4 NON-COMPUTABLE PROBLEMS

One of the most surprising and motivating questions that can be asked of students during high school is the discussion of whether computers can be capable of solving any kind of problem [35, 40]. Although this question is not dealt with in the curriculum of secondary education, the contents taught in the mathematic subjects do make it possible to answer this question in a simple and clear way through the concept of cardinality of a set, and the paradoxes of infinity. The first of the paradoxes of infinity that high school students face is the demonstration that there is the same cardinality of even numbers as natural numbers, which contradicts her/his intuition that the whole is greater than the part. This idea may lead to suppose that every infinite set can be matched to its elements one by one with natural numbers, that is, apparently, all infinite sets seem to have infinity as cardinality. The surprise in the middle and high school students comes to show them that this statement is not true, since there are cardinalities superior to the infinity of the natural ones. In particular, real numbers (which include numbers as exotic as the irrational ones $\sqrt{2}$ and π already seen in the previous section) are more than the natural numbers. Using the famous *Cantor's diagonal argument* [10, 38] they are taught that the set of real numbers $\mathbb{R}$ is not countable, and that its cardinality is superior to that of $\mathbb{N}$: $card(\mathbb{N}) < card(\mathbb{R})$.

This is the right time to show secondary school students the relevance of this result, in order to intuitively prove the existence of non-computable problems. In all the known computation models and programming languages that have been developed, it is easy to demonstrate to the students that the number of programs that can be written by them is at most infinite and numerable, that is, the cardinality of the natural numbers. Therefore, there are no more programs than natural numbers. On the other hand, every program calculates a certain mathematical function: given some input data, it produces a result that is a function of that input. In order for students to understand this, they can suppose that the input and output are two natural numbers. Consequently, the number of problems that are candidates to be soluble by means of a computer program are the functions $f : \mathbb{N} \rightarrow \mathbb{N}$, at least as many as the cardinality of $\mathbb{R}$. We conclude that there are many more problems than computer programs to solve them; therefore, there must be undecidable and non-computable problems. In fact, there is a huge number of problems that are not computable.

At this point, students want to know concrete examples of problems that a computer cannot solve. A good point to start is to discuss with them the problem of the *continuum hypothesis*: Is there some infinite set X such that $card(\mathbb{N}) < card(X) < card(\mathbb{R})$? In 1938 Kurt Gödel demonstrated that if set theory is consistent (i.e., it does not imply contradiction), then set theory is also consistent with the continuum hypothesis. In 1963 Paul Joseph Cohen demonstrated that if set theory is consistent, set theory is also consistent with the negation of the continuum hypothesis. Consequently, the hypothesis of the continuum can be accepted or denied without contradiction. From this fact, students learn how the hypothesis of the continuum is *undecidable* in set theory. But in a more practical way, students need to know a more concrete problem. Here is another of the classic undecidable problems related to the knowledge they have acquired during high school: it is undecidable to know if an arbitrary *Diophantine equation* (an algebraic equation with integer coefficients) has integer solutions. In 1970 the mathematician Yuri Matiyasevic demonstrated there is no computer program that can solve this problem.

However, the problem that has provided best results to students through this educational experience is the so-called *Tiling Problem* [40], the problem of deciding whether a particular finite tile collection admits a valid tile covering of the plane. This problem was proved undecidable by Robert Berger in 1966. To work with

Table 1: First year pre-university mathematics curriculum with computability and algorithmic complexity questions

Schedule	Mathematics Curriculum	Computability and Complexity Questions	Results
1EV	Decimals and Irrational numbers	Representation of irrational numbers on a computer, Estimating irrational numbers with Monte Carlo dart throws.	
	Real numbers	Cantor's diagonal argument, Uncountable infinity, The Continuum Hypothesis.	6.75 on 6.71
2EV	Algebraic equations and Complex numbers	Impossibility of obtaining solutions by means of a formula in radicals of an equation of the fifth degree. Undecidable diophantine equations, Using approximation methods to find a root (Newton's method).	6.33 on 6.29
3EV	Exponential functions and series	Legend of chess and Legend of the horse and hawk, Towers of Hanoi.	7.10 on 6.15
4EV	Trigonometry, triangles, polygons	Tiling puzzles: *Mathekreis* and *Mathe Quadrat*.	7.25 on 5.43
FINAL	2D Geometric transformations	On the undecidability of the tiling problem.	7.50 on 6.57

this problem, we previously used a series of mathematical puzzles with the students. Deciding whether a specific set of shapes can tile a floor is one of many problems that are harder than the *Halting Problem*, and hence undecidable [36]. It would be wonderful if there were some way of entering different sets of shapes into a computer that would be able to tell if those shapes are able to tile a large floor without gaps. However, no such computer program can ever exist. This is a surprising result for a secondary school student.

5   LOGICAL PARADOXES

The second part of our educational experience aimed to introduce into secondary schools questions related to the limitations of formal systems. It consisted of working with the students with the so-called *logical paradoxes*, starting with the well-known *paradox of Bertrand Russell's barber* [9]. It should be noted that, several centuries before, the Spanish writer Miguel de Cervantes Saavedra had already left the same paradox written in his work *Don Quixote* (*Liar's paradox, Part II, Chapter* 51), which has allowed us to work with our high school students in an interdisciplinary way in other subjects that are not the usual ones of the sciences.

These kinds of logical paradoxes have also allowed us to raise very interesting questions among middle and high school students, especially in philosophy classes: Is mathematics *complete*, in the sense that every mathematical statement can be proven or refuted? Is mathematics *consistent*, in the sense that you will never be able to reach a contradictory statement like $2 + 2 = 5$? Is mathematics *decidable*, in the sense that there is a computer program that allows us to determine, for any mathematical affirmation, if it is demonstrable or not? To illustrate the discussion, in addition to recalling the questions introduced in the previous sections, it was very helpful to begin by introducing the problem of *The Fifth Postulate of Euclid*. The most important knowledge of Greek mathematics is collected in Euclid's work entitled *The Elements*, which contains the five postulates or axioms on which his development of Geometry is based. The fifth postulate is known as the *parallel postulate* and it seems to correspond to the physical nature of the three-dimensional space in which we live, so it would not be necessary to postulate it, but it should be possible to demonstrate it on the basis of the other four axioms, which are obvious. Nowadays it is known that this system

of postulates is *incomplete* due to the independence of the postulate of the parallels from the other postulates of Euclidean geometry. Although in a very intuitive way, the students reach at this point of the academic year a fairly approximate idea of the so-called *Gödel Incompleteness Theorem* [37].

6   ALGORITHMIC COMPLEXITY

The third and last part of our educational experience focused on demonstrating to high school students how the limits of computing stated in the previous sections are even greater. Many problems that admit algorithmic solution cannot be delegated to a computer either because it would take too much time to solve them. We started working with the students on the following *Legend of the Horse and the Hawk*, a Spanish medieval legend behind which is the famous Indian tale that explains the invention of chess at the beginning of the 5th century BC. This little-known historical version in the form of a poem also allows us to link better with the contents developed in other subjects such as History, Language, and Literature. Fernán González, Count of Castile (931-970) had a horse and a hawk that fascinated the King of Leon, who did not hesitate to ask him for them. Fernán González assures that he will lend them for a certain period of time, but after the deadline, the first day will mean the loss of a small piece of land (the unit of measure for length was displayed in feet); for each successive day of delay in the return of the animals, that feet of land increases "*al gallarín*", that is, exponentially. Broken the commitment to return, the monarch sees that the territory to be ceded is as wide as the County of Castile (over 18 quintillion feet!):

$$1 + 2 + 4 + 8 + \cdots + 2^{63} = \sum_{i=0}^{63} 2^i = 2^{64} - 1 = 18.446.744.073.709.551.615$$

Students understand this exponential complexity much better when they work with the well-known mathematical game or puzzle *Tower of Hanoi* [29, 36, 39], first manually through the mathematical game developed by the mathematician Édouard Lucas, and then through its simple recursive implementation in Python [21, 27]:

```
def hanoi_towers(n, a, b, c):
    if n > 0 :
        hanoi_towers(n - 1, a, c, b)
        print('Move disk from', str(a), 'to', str(b))
        hanoi_towers(n - 1, c, b, a)
```

Table 2: Second year pre-university mathematics curriculum with computability and algorithmic complexity questions

Schedule	Mathematics Curriculum	Computability and Complexity Questions	Results
1EV	Mathematical problem solving	The barber paradox and the liar's paradox,	
		An intuitive explanation of Gödel's incompleteness theorems,	
		The continuum hypothesis is undecidable in set theory,	
		Existence of non-computable problems.	
	Linear algebra and matrices	What is the fastest algorithm for matrix multiplication?	
	Optimization problems	Travelling salesman problem and knapsack problem,	
		An intuitive explanation of the P versus NP problem.	**5.88 on 4.12**
2EV	Foundations of Geometry	The Parallel Postulate cannot be proved from the other postulates.	
	3D Geometry	An approach to the three-body problem and chaotic systems.	**5.29 on 3.96**
3EV	Differentiation and Integration	Numerical integration of functions that does not admit primitive in	
		terms of elementary functions.	**5.08 on 3.50**
FINAL	Combinatorics and Probability	Combinatorial problems and games (Hamilton's icosian game).	
	Statistics	Monte Carlo simulations.	
	Binomial and Normal Distributions	Numerical approximations to the normal distribution (Galton board),	
		The indefinite integral of the normal probability density function	
		cannot be expressed in finite elementary terms.	**6.42 on 5.81**

It is also possible to demonstrate to a pre-university student with the mathematical knowledge of high school why the problem of the towers of Hanoi is considered 'untreatable' by increasing the number of disks n. The minimal number of moves required is

$$\mathrm{hanoi}(n) = \begin{cases} 0 & \text{if } n = 0 \\ 2 \cdot \mathrm{hanoi}(n-1) + 1 & \text{if } n > 0 \end{cases} = \sum_{i=0}^{n-1} 2^i = 2^n - 1$$

Finally, the third question discussed with the students was the following. For a great number of problems (many of them of great practical interest) we only know impractical algorithms, that is, we have exponential complexity, and we do not have any information on lower complexity levels that allows us to classify such problems. Concrete examples of these problems that were presented to students in the final year of high school were *Travelling Salesman Problem* and *Knapsack Problem* [29, 39]. The students were very surprised to learn that it has not been possible to find a simple algorithm so far, and it has not been proven that such an algorithm exists. At this time, without formally defining the classes *P* and *NP*, students may be asked the question *P vs. NP* [36].

7 EXPERIMENTAL RESULTS

The questions of computability and algorithmic complexity presented in this educational experience have been compiled and applied in several public and private high schools since the academic year 2011-2012. However, until the academic year 2017-2018 it has not been possible to design a realistic model based on all these previous experiences that could be evaluated as a *proof of concept* in a complete educational experience of one year's duration. The secondary school has been carefully chosen among students with a special lack of motivation in the learning of mathematics, so their academic results have often been low. The educational experience was carried out in the last two courses of which the European pre-university education is currently legislated in Spain [3, 19, 20], introducing the questions addressed in the previous sections of this paper. The results obtained have been compared with the average

results obtained in the three previous academic years in which the students were taught without introducing questions of computability and algorithmic complexity. The results obtained in the academic year 2017-2018 and in the three previous years are shown in the statistical graph of **Figure 1** for the first year of the Spanish high school, with students aged 16 to 17, and the statistical graph of **Figure 2** for the second year, with students aged 17 to 18. In the first year there were 52 students who had the new educational experience (the results are shown in dark grey in **Figure 1**). The same groups that followed the studies in the usual way in previous academic courses were formed by a similar number of students (in white in **Figure 1**). In the case of the second year, 49 students have undergone the new educational experience (in dark grey in **Figure 2**), and a similar number of students have followed the traditional method in the three previous years (in white in **Figure 2**). Each course consists of three/four quarterly evaluations and a final evaluation.

8 METHODOLOGY

The selected questions have been progressively introduced on the basis of the didactic units in which the two pre-university mathematics courses are structured. The activities carried out for each of the contents of the current curriculum, when and where to address each question in the theory, the required student background, as well as the results obtained for each of them in comparison with the experimental results obtained in previous years, are graphically described in **Table 1** and **Table 2**. Each theoretical question has been introduced starting with historical and biographical anecdotes, always in a very pleasant and visual way, until arriving at the formal approach to the activities as described in this paper. The level of previous knowledge of our students is the reason why sometimes, these questions had to be introduced only in a very intuitive and merely experimental way, but always sufficiently rigorous so that they could perceive by themselves the theoretical concepts that underlie them. In order to follow this methodology, sufficient time

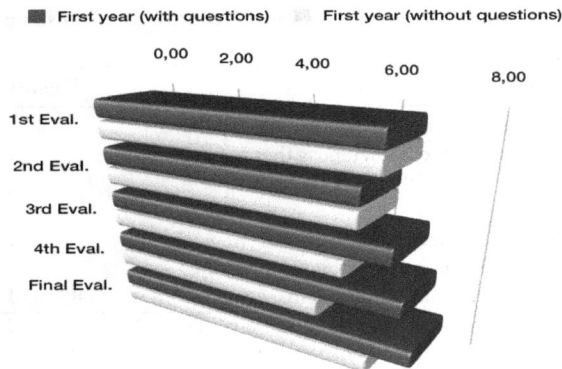

Figure 1: Results in the first pre-university year.

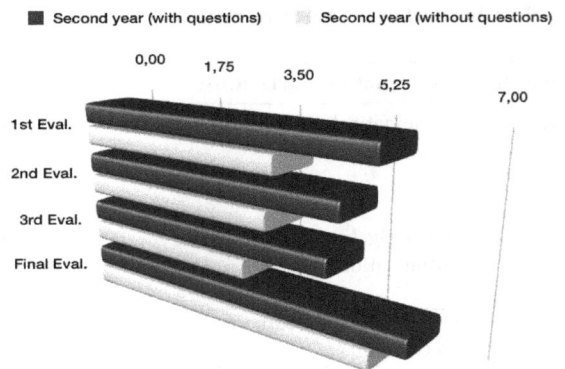

Figure 2: Results in the second pre-university year.

has been reserved in the weekly schedule, at least one hour of class per week, so that the students could practice with the puzzles, riddles and logical paradoxes, and actively participate in the debates proposed during the development of these educational activities.

9 DISCUSSION

The experimental results obtained show that the students who have undergone this innovative educational experience have obtained a higher qualification than those who have followed the course in its traditional form. The students who have followed this new educational experience had difficulties in learning mathematics because of their negative motivational pattern. Although the grades have not been excessively high (the scores are established on a scale of 0 to 10 points through the completion of practices, exercises and exams throughout each evaluation), 91.7% of the students in the first year who underwent the new educational experience passed the course with an average of 5.65 points, while in the three previous courses the average was 3.95 points. In the last year of high school, 88.5% of students who experienced the educational experience passed their courses with an average of 6.42 points, while the average in the previous three courses was 5.19.

10 HOW THE ASSESSMENT WORKED

The evaluation of the results obtained by the students has been carried out mainly by means of exams, practices, and similar exercises to those proposed in the three previous academic courses. The students were evaluated on the same usual math topics, so that the comparison of the new results would be carried out in the same conditions to those of the previous courses. The good results obtained show that the mathematical capacity of the students in the comprehension of classical mathematical concepts and in the resolution of the usual exercises was increased thanks to the increase of their curiosity to deepen and understand better the learned knowledge. To obtain more discussion of the assessment with the new computability topics, specific questions on computation and complexity were also part of the general examination. For example, first-year students were asked an extra question in the first evaluation about the use of irrational numbers, such as Euler's number e, through the use of estimates and approximations, controlling the margins of error. By the second year students, small

programming practices were also carried out in Python, such as the approximation of areas under a curve using the Monte Carlo simulation methods. In terms of capability, a high student score in **Figure 1** and **Figure 2** means that thanks to these activities, the curiosity of the students to deepen and investigate in diverse subjects has grown before beginning their university studies.

11 CONCLUSIONS

The difficulties that students find in their university studies of Science and Engineering when faced for the first time with questions related to theoretical computing in the resolution of problems had opened the debate on whether or not it is appropriate to introduce such questions in the pre-university education system, conveniently adapted to students' capability, either in their own specific subject or through inclusion in the official curriculum of existing subjects [2, 3, 16, 19]. The good results obtained with this educational experience show that the introduction of questions about computability and algorithmic complexity in pre-university courses affects the motivation of students with learning difficulties positively. However, despite the good results obtained, some of the difficulties encountered in the development of this educational experience are the following: the limited time available to address these kinds of questions, specific training courses for teachers would be required, and it would be necessary to create and adapt curricular programming using resources that may not always be available. Despite these difficulties, we believe that this educational experience can guide and be used to let the educational computing community know how to teach the introduction of theoretical computing topics at the pre-university level and train teachers to do it on a global scale.

12 FUTURE WORK PERSPECTIVE

The implications for future work are to collect more data on the success of this enhanced algorithmic curriculum of pre-university computing and mathematical courses so that the reported experience can be based on more academic years. We are currently working in the 2018-2019 academic year [12] to provide more classroom activities and detailed information on the evaluation and on meshing current curriculum with computability theory, to demonstrate that the possible adoption of this approach does not depend on the educational contexts of different countries.

REFERENCES

[1] Alfred V. Aho. 2011. Computation and Computational Thinking. *Ubiquity symposium* (2011). https://doi.org/10.1145/1922681.1922682

[2] Michal Armoni. 2016. COMPUTING IN SCHOOLS: Computer Science, Computational Thinking, Programming, Coding: The Anomalies of Transitivity in K-12 Computer Science Education. *ACM Inroads* 7, 4 (nov 2016). https://doi.org/10.1145/3011071

[3] A. Balanskat and K. Engelhardt. 2015. *Computing our future: Computer programming and coding. Priorities, school curricula and initiatives across Europe.* Technical Report. European Schoolnet.

[4] Tim Bell, Jason Alexander, Isaac Freeman, and Mick Grimley. 2009. Computer science unplugged: school students doing real computing without computers. *New Zealand Journal of Applied Computing and Information Technology* 13, 1 (2009), 20–29.

[5] Tim Bell, Caitlin Duncan, Sam Jarman, and Heidi Newton. 2014. Presenting Computer Science Concepts to High School Students. *Olympiads in Informatics* 8, January (2014), 3–19.

[6] Jonathan Black, Jo Brodie, Paul Curzon, Chrystie Myketiak, Peter W. McOwan, and Laura R. Meagher. 2013. Making Computing Interesting to School Students: Teachers' Perspectives. In *Proceedings of the 18th ACM Conference on Innovation and Technology in Computer Science Education (ITiCSE '13).* ACM Press, New York, NY, USA, 6. https://doi.org/10.1145/2462476.2466519

[7] Stefania Bocconi, Augusto Chioccariello, Giuliana Dettori, Anusca Ferrari, Katja Engelhardt, Panagiotis Kampylis, and Yves Punie. 2016. Developing Computational Thinking in Compulsory Education. Implications for policy and practice. *EUR - Scientific and Technical Research Reports* (12 2016). https://doi.org/10.2791/792158

[8] Ricky Carter, Wallace Feurzeig, John Richards, and Nancy Roberts. 1988. Intelligent Tools for Mathematical Inquiry. In *Proceedings of the 9th Annual National Education Computer Conference, Dallas TX.*

[9] Paul Cockshott, Lewis M. Mackenzie, and Gregory Michaelson. 2012. *Computation and Its Limits.* Oxford University Press, Inc.

[10] Nigel Cutland. 1980. *Computability: An Introduction to Recursive Function Theory.* Cambridge University Press, Boston, MA, USA.

[11] Robert B. Davis, Carolyn A. Maher, and Nel Noddings. 1990. Constructivist Views on the Teaching and Learning of Mathematics. *Journal for Research in Mathematics education. Monograph.* 4 (1990). https://www.jstor.org/stable/i230382 Published by: National Council of Teachers of Mathematics, Reston, Virginia.

[12] Rafael del Vado Vírseda. 2019. Introducing Theoretical Computer Concepts in Secondary Education (Poster Session). In *Proceedings of the 2019 ACM SIGCSE Technical Symposium on Computer Science Education, Minneapolis, Minnesota, USA, February 27th - March 2nd, 2019.* https://doi.org/10.1145/3287324.3293784

[13] Peter Denning and Craig Martell. 2015. *Great Principles of Computing.* The MIT Press.

[14] Peter J. Denning. 2017. Remaining Trouble Spots with Computational Thinking. *Commun.* 60, 6 (may 2017). https://doi.org/10.1145/2998438

[15] Gilles Dowek. 2011. *Proofs and Algorithms: An Introduction to Logic and Computability* (1st ed.). Springer Publishing Company, Incorporated.

[16] Joint Informatics Europe and ACM Europe Working Group on Informatics Education. 2013. *Informatics education: Europe cannot afford to miss the boat.* Technical Report. http://www.informatics-europe.org/images/documents/informatics-education-europe-report.pdf.

[17] Michael R. Fellows. 1993. Computer science and mathematics in the elementary schools. In *Mathematicians and Education Reform 1990–1991. Providence RI.* Amer. Math. Society.

[18] Maribel Fernández. 2009. *Models of Computation: An Introduction to Computability Theory.* Springer London.

[19] Anusca Ferrari. 2013. *DIGCOMP: A Framework for Developing and Understanding Digital Competence in Europe* (institute for prospective technological studies, joint research centre, comision europea ed.). Publications Office of the European Union.

[20] FECYT Google and Everis. 2016. *Educación en ciencias de la computación en España 2015.* Cultura científica e-NIPO: 720-16-173-3. Ministerio de Ciencia, Innovación y Universidades, España.

[21] Tina Götschi, Ian Sanders, and Vashti Galpin. 2006. Mental Models of Recursion Revisited. In *Proceedings of the 11th Annual SIGCSE Conference on Innovation and Technology in Computer Science Education (ITiCSE '06).* ACM SIGCSE Bulletin, ACM, NY, USA, 138–142. https://doi.org/10.1145/1140123.1140162

[22] Orit Hazzan. 2002. Reducing abstraction level when learning computability theory concepts. In *Proceedings of the 7th Annual Conference on Innovation and Technology in Computer Science Education (ITiCSE '02).* ACM, New York, NY, USA, 156–160. https://doi.org/10.1145/544414.544461

[23] Orit Hazzan, Tami Lapidot, and Noa Ragonis. 2011. *Guide to Teaching Computer Science: An Activity-Based Approach* (1st ed.). Springer Publishing Company, Incorporated.

[24] Maria Knobelsdorf, Christoph Kreitz, and Sebastian Bohne. 2014. Teaching Theoretical Computer Science Using a Cognitive Apprenticeship Approach. In *Proceedings of the 45th ACM Technical Symposium on Computer Science Education (SIGCSE '14).* ACM Press, New York, NY, USA, 67–72. https://doi.org/10.1145/2538862.2538944

[25] Laura Korte, Stuart Anderson, Helen Pain, and Judith Good. 2007. Learning by Game-building: A Novel Approach to Theoretical Computer Science Education. In *Proceedings of the 12th Annual SIGCSE Conference on Innovation and Technology in Computer Science Education (ITiCSE '07).* ACM Press, New York, NY, USA, 53–57. https://doi.org/10.1145/1268784.1268802

[26] Hans P. Langtangen. 2012. *A Primer on Scientific Programming with Python* (5th ed.). Springer Publishing Company, Incorporated.

[27] Svein Linge and Hans P. Langtangen. 2016. *Programming for Computations - Python: A Gentle Introduction to Numerical Simulations with Python* (1st ed.). Springer Publishing Company, Incorporated.

[28] Michael McCracken, Yifat B-D. Kolikant, Vicki Almstrum, Cary Laxer, Dianne Diaz, Lynda Thomas, Mark Guzdial, Ian Utting, Danny Hagan, and Tadeusz Wilusz. 2001. A Multi-national, Multi-institutional Study of Assessment of Programming Skills of First-year CS Students. In *Working Group Reports from ITiCSE on Innovation and Technology in Computer Science Education (ITiCSE-WGR '01).* ACM Press, New York, NY, USA, 125–1804. https://doi.org/10.1145/572133.572137

[29] Christos H. Papadimitriou. 1994. *Computational Complexity.* Addison-Wesley.

[30] Seymour Papert. 1980. *Mindstorms: Children, Computers, and Powerful Ideas.* Basic Books, Inc., New York, NY, USA.

[31] Viera K. Proulx. 1993. Computer Science in Elementary and Secondary Schools. In *Informatics and Changes in Learning, Proceedings of the IFIP TC3/WG3.1/WG3.5 Open Conference on Informatics and Changes in Learning, Gmunden, Austria, 7-11 June, 1993.* North-Holland, 95–101. https://dblp.org/rec/bib/conf/ifip3-1/Proulx93

[32] Bernhard Reus. 2016. *Limits of Computation: From a Programming Perspective* (1st ed.). Springer Publishing Company, Incorporated.

[33] Daniel Richardson. 1968. Some undecidable problems involving elementary functions of a real variable. *The Journal of Symbolic Logic* 33, 4 (1968), 514–520. https://doi.org/10.2307/2271358

[34] Gabriel Robins. 1988. Teaching Theoretical Computer Science at the Undergraduate Level: Experiences, Observations, and Proposals to Improve the Status Quo. *University of California, Los Angeles. Computer Science Department* 88, 63 (02 1988).

[35] Marcus Du Sautoy. 2016. *What We Cannot Know: Explorations at the Edge of Knowledge* (1st ed.). 4th Estate.

[36] Michael Sipser. 2012. *Introduction to the Theory of Computation* (3rd ed.). Cengage Learning.

[37] Peter Smith. 2013. *An Introduction to Gödel's Theorems* (2nd ed.). Cambridge University Press.

[38] John Stillwell. 2018. *Yearning for the Impossible: The Surprising Truths of Mathematics* (2 ed.). CRC Press.

[39] Herbert S. Wilf. 2002. *Algorithms and Complexity* (2nd ed.). A. K. Peters, Ltd.

[40] Noson S. Yanofsky. 2016. *The Outer Limits of Reason: What Science, Mathematics, and Logic Cannot Tell Us.* The MIT Press.

CEO: A Triangulated Evaluation of a Modeling-Based CT-Infused CS Activity for Non-CS Middle Grade Students

Nicholas Lytle, Veronica Cateté, Yihuan Dong, Danielle Boulden, Bita Akram, Jennifer Houchins,
Tiffany Barnes, Eric Wiebe
{nalytle,vmcatete,ydong2,dmboulde,bakram,jkhouchi,tmbarnes,wiebe}@ncsu.edu

ABSTRACT

With the increased demand for introducing computational thinking (CT) in K-12 classrooms, educational researchers are developing integrated lesson plans that can teach CT fundamentals in non-computing specific classrooms. Although these lessons reach more students through the core curriculum, proper evaluation methods are needed to ensure the quality of the design and integration. As part of a research practice partnership, we work to infuse research-backed curricula into science courses. We find a three-pronged approach of evaluation can help us make better decisions on how to improve experimental curricula for active classrooms. This CEO model uses three data sources (student code traces, exit ticket responses, and field observations) as a triangulated approach that can be used to identify programming behavior among novice developers, preferred task ordering for the assignment, and scaffolding recommendations to teachers. This approach allows us to evaluate the practical implementations of our initiative and create a focused approach for designing more effective lessons.

CCS CONCEPTS

• **Social and professional topics** → **Computational thinking**; *K-12 education*;

KEYWORDS

Computational Thinking, Modeling and Simulation, Assessment

ACM Reference Format:
Nicholas Lytle, Veronica Cateté, Yihuan Dong, Danielle Boulden, Bita Akram, Jennifer Houchins, Tiffany Barnes, Eric Wiebe. 2019. CEO: A Triangulated Evaluation of a Modeling-Based CT-Infused CS Activity for Non-CS Middle Grade Students. In *ACM Global Computing Education Conference 2019 (CompEd '19), May 17–19, 2019, Chengdu,Sichuan, China.* ACM, New York, NY, USA, 7 pages. https://doi.org/10.1145/3300115.3309527

1 INTRODUCTION

Computer science and computing technologies have become recognized vehicles for economic growth and development across the globe. In order to meet the demands of this growing workforce with well-qualified employees, more countries are focusing on increasing their primary and secondary grade computing courses.

Computational knowledge has far-reaching benefits beyond standard technology companies. Computational thinking (CT) [17] and other aspects of computing are being used to solve advanced, multi-faceted, problems around climate change, marine ecosystems, and beyond. Introducing computing into the science classroom provides equitable access to computing training as well as demonstrates to students the usefulness of computing in outside fields.

Previous research has examined teacher preparedness and professional development on the impact of classroom implementation and teacher confidence [3, 5, 13]. Studies show that students with teachers more interested in facilitating CT exhibit higher levels of time on task and engagement than those with disengaged teachers. While previous research focuses primarily on teacher outcomes, more research is needed on student outcomes (i.e. learning and programming behaviors) in order to successfully gauge the curriculum and support materials.

We propose a CEO model to assess the implementation of a CT-infused science curriculum. The model examines student **C**ode traces, **E**xit tickets, and field **O**bservations in order to triangulate the effectiveness of curriculum implementation and student learning outcomes. In order to effectively infuse computing, students must achieve both an understanding of computer programming as well as reinforcement of the scientific concepts being taught in class.

Using the CEO model, we attempt to identify improvements for the existing curriculum, specifically:

(1) How are students completing the assignment tasks?
(2) What emergent behaviors or observations can we identify in order to better engage students in future iterations?
(3) How do students perceive the science vs CT learning goals?

2 BACKGROUND & RELATED WORK

Research practice partnerships (RPPs) are long-term collaborations between practitioners and researchers that are organized to investigate problems of practice and solutions for improving schools and school districts [4]. One type of RPP focuses primarily on design-based implementation research [6]. This research aims to study solutions implemented in real world contexts, typically utilizing a cycle of developing and testing instructional activities and curricula.

We detail the cycle of creating, piloting, and re-designing a life-sciences curriculum in a prior case study [8]. The grounding decisions for activity changes included realizations that the cognitive demands for learning both CT and science concepts could be too high for the diverse range of middle-grade students. Additionally, students without prior programming exposure would benefit from tutorials and scaffolded directions. Thirdly, interface distractions could derail students and cause extra demands to cognitive load[16]. Many of these realizations however, came from short lab-controlled settings or subjective team reflections and discussion.

As Fishman points out, there is a broad challenge to gather and interpret evidence of effectiveness in the field as this differs greatly from a controlled setting [6]. Strategies for gathering evidence include student assessments, self-report surveys, rigorous observations [11], along with trace data analyses and video-recorded sessions. Although many of these practices are common in the field of educational research, they are often difficult to set up and take place primarily in closed lab environments [14, 15].

Upon entering the implementation cycle of design-based research, additional data collection methods should be used. In a previous report, educational researchers described the implementation of computing oriented science activities in middle grades classrooms [3]. This research focused primarily on the teacher's willingness to adopt the activity and effects of just-in-time professional development, noting that teacher buy-in had a large impact on student perception of usefulness and active on-task engagement. Although this research is well documented, it relied solely on qualitative data, including teacher interviews and observations. The report did little to convey the student learning outcomes or other evidence of student success.

Conversely, work by Grgurina et al. focuses on assessing modeling activities in a secondary grade computing classroom [7]. The assessment uses a combination of the Revised Bloom's Taxonomy [9] and SOLO taxonomy [2] to evaluate students' written answers to a number of questions regarding their models on multiple dimensions ranging from prestructural (information makes no sense) to extended abstract (generalization and transfer) for areas of design, experimentation, and reflection on the model. This assessment, however, is summative in nature using a multi-week modeling and research homework assignment as it's main vessel. The assessment provides less formative feedback on their specific skills and knowledge and instead measures larger concepts.

As our current research concerns middle grades students who are still developing their scientific knowledge and coding abilities, more formative feedback is needed. Consequently, we need to be able to better assess their programming behaviors so that we may provide more support or scaffolding for emergent behaviors in future iterations. Prior research in assessing science and modeling activities in secondary classrooms have focused on teaching, adoption, and summative assessments. In our new research, we look at evaluating an experimental curriculum through both empirical and qualitative evidence of student understanding.

3 METHODS

We created and utilized a CEO model to assess student outcomes, our curriculum as a whole, and the effectiveness of our implementation. Each of the elements of CEO describe a different data set and methodology for curricula analysis. Code Traces (C) describe the actions within the coding environment used by the students, Exit Tickets (E) describe post-activity written responses, and Observations (O) are researcher notes taken during implementation. In the following sections, we describe the curriculum and implementation, followed by our data collection methods.

3.1 Curriculum & Implementation

The curriculum development team, composed of educational psychologists and computing education researchers, created an 8th-grade life science lesson on Epidemic Diseases infused with computational thinking. The lesson was designed to be aligned to national and state-level science standards as well as the k12cs.org Computational Thinking Framework. This five-day unit focused on modeling the spread of epidemic diseases like the flu, see Figure 1.

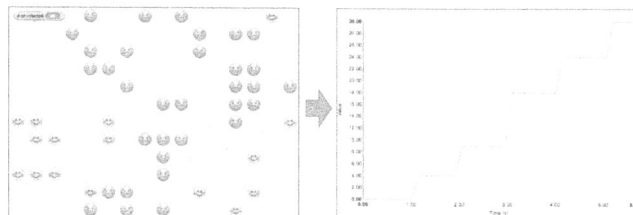

Figure 1: A Cellular representation of an epidemic.

Individual activities are described as "plugged" if students used a programming environment, or "unplugged" if students were learning without a computer. Students were given a block-based programming tutorial prior to the run of the unit. The unit features 2 unplugged days focused on modeling agent-host relations in the transmission of disease. There were also 3 plugged days: 2 of which had students develop a simulation based off the model discussed on the "unplugged" day using the block-based programming environment, Cellular [1], and 1 day where students used the environment to solve scientific research questions about the spread of diseases. An overview of the activities are shown in Table 1.

Table 1: Epidemics outline, P: plugged, U: unplugged

Day	Learning Goals
1: U	Able to explain a simple model. Understand Hosts and Agents share properties with modified values.
2: P	Define infection and infection rate. Demonstrate understanding of agent properties. Understand and use loops and conditionals.
3: P	Understand disease spread and rate of transmission/infection. Use variables to maintain count. Analyze trends in data to identify patterns. Demonstrate understanding of how interaction properties can affect simulations.
4: U	Understand Morbidity/Mortality rates and their influence on spread. Understand and use Finite State Machines to model logic flow. Model algorithmic thinking through transition modeling.
5: P	Understand how environmental factors affect disease spread; Learn experimental procedure for hypothesis testing. Visualize data; Use simulations to test hypotheses.

We tested the 5-day Epidemics activity with two 8th grade science teachers at a local middle school. Each teacher taught 5 sections of students with class sizes ranging from 20 to 25 students. Each of the teachers' classes were presented the same activity on the same day. Teachers taught every class period on unplugged days of the unit. On plugged days (2, 3, and 5), teachers had one observation period at the start of the day where they experienced the content as a student, following along as the researchers led the first class. They then taught the remaining 4 periods of the day, guiding students through program implementation. 61 students returned consent forms for us to analyze their data.

3.2 Code Traces

On days 2 and 3, students' actions within the Cellular environment were logged in a database for later examination. We focus our analysis on the actions that make changes to their code. Specifically, we call a student's code at any point a *code state*, and the sequence of code states that leads to the final solution a *code trace*.

For days 2 and 3, students were given instructions with individual tasks to complete within the environment. These tasks were presented sequentially, but the order in which students could complete the assignment did not have to match the intended order. These tasks are outlined in Tables 2 and 3. In examining student code traces, we can identify whether or not a specified task has been completed at any given point in the code trace. We refer to the instance in which a specified task has been completed as a *task completion state*. The second column of Tables 2 and 3 provides one of the many solutions that would result in the completion of that task.

Table 2: Task milestones for day 2 of the epidemics activity

Task/Feature	Example Solution
(1) Write a program that moves your sprite to an empty neighbor cell.	
(2) Use a control loop to have your sprites move to empty neighbor cells forever.	
(3) Add an if control block to your main script that checks whether your sprite is healthy before checking its neighbor cells for an infected sprite.	
(4) Add a script to your forever loop that makes your sprite infected if an infected sprite (a sprite with infected costume) is in a neighbor cell.	
All	

Task completion states were individually tagged by a member of the research team and build sequentially as students complete additional tasks. When a student has a task completion state with all tasks present, they have fully completed the assignment. To illustrate, take two students who completed day 2's activity, one by entering completion state "1234" and another by entering completion state "1243". The presence of all four tasks (i.e. tasks 1,2,3,4)

in both states signify both students completed the full assignment. The order of the numbers in the state tells the sequence of tasks the students completed in the assignment (notice the order difference in how they completed the last two tasks - 3 and 4).

Using code traces to identify student programming behaviors gives light to RQ1 as they can illustrate common solution strategies, most difficult tasks, and common pitfalls in student implementations. As these states and actions are also time-stamped, specific strategies by students can be compared to see whether or not certain strategies are easier (i.e. faster to complete) than others.

To complement our task completion state analysis, we went through traces and made qualitative observations of other behaviors in the environment we found interesting. These included behavior taken by the students after the assignment was complete, resets of the environment (giving up and starting over again), spots where students found difficulty in completing tasks, and off-task behavior.

Table 3: Task milestones for day 3 of the epidemics activity

Task/Feature	Example Solution
(1) Create a variable to hold number of infected sprites and name it # of diseased. Set this variable to zero in the beginning of your program (just after the "when green flag clicked" block)	
(2) Write a script that increases the value of the infected people by one when a sprite gets infected.	
(3) Write a script that restarts your simulation when you hit space. The restart script should make all sprites healthy and set the number of infected to 0. Add your restart script to this part of the code on the screen.	
(4) Write a script that changes the value of the variable: # of diseased when you click on a sprite.	
(5) Remove the set # of diseased from your main script (the script after "when green flag clicked")	
All	3,4, and 5 all co-present.

3.3 Exit Tickets

On plugged days, students were asked to take an end of class "Exit Ticket". This series of questions measured self-reported affect, student engagement, and perception of what they learned. The 61 consenting students generated 127 responses over three days of activity. The relevant questions are listed below:

(1) What did you learn today?
(2) What was the most helpful to you: the tutorials, your classmates, your teacher?
(3) Did you find anything difficult or frustrating? Please explain.
(4) Did the lesson go too fast, too slow, or just right?
(5) Do you have any suggestions to improve the activities?

For question 1, our aim was to answer RQ3 by analyzing student perception of the intent of the activity. As this was a CT-infused science lesson, we aimed to see whether or not the perception of the activity leaned more towards computing or science. Our approach consisted of having two researchers individually tag responses as being more focused on computing, science, both, or neither. After individual tagging, the researchers compared their tags and discussed cases where conflict existed until agreement could be reached. For questions 2 and 4, our aim was to see which of the three choices or combinations thereof were most present within an assignment. Finally, for questions 3 and 5, researchers counted and grouped the most common answers to use as feedback for the next development cycle.

3.4 Observations

During the implementation, at least one member of the research team acted as an observer on each plugged day. Each observer had prior classroom experience leading computing activities with middle and secondary age students (with three of the observers having 5+ years of experience). Our goal with classroom observations was to experience and record how the activity was conducted across different classrooms and to gather both insights for improving teacher training practices as well as improving the actual activity and its implementation environment. In most activity sessions, we assigned one observer to watch the teacher, and others to observe the students. We also had additional support to help students stuck on programming tasks, so that observers could stay focused on the field. Observers recorded student affect, behaviors, and interactions of note. After each session, observers conferred and noted interesting results to follow up with.

4 RESULTS

4.1 Code Traces

In Figures 2 and 3, we represent the paths students took to complete the assignment as a transition of progressive task completion states. These states correspond to the subset of tasks that have been completed thus far (e.g. state "12" represents finishing task 1 and then 2). The size of the shape corresponds to the number of individuals who entered that specific task completion state, and the size of the edges corresponds with the number of individuals who made that unique transition. Task completion states can often be stuck states (octagons in this representation) meaning that some students made no further progress in the assignment after reaching

this state. This representation was adapted from a similar analysis of student programming paths(see [18]).

4.1.1 Day 2. The code traces for 61 participants on day 2 are shown in Figure 2. The task completion was mostly uniform, with participants only differing on whether or not they completed task 3 or 4 first. Most students, 33, completed the tasks in the intended order of 1234 while 22 completed the ordering as 1243. The third feature was the most missed (7 students omitted).

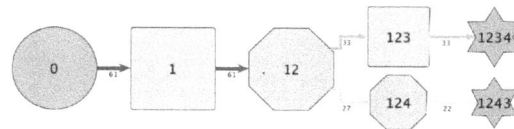

Figure 2: Task completion strategies for day 2.

Timing trends were also recorded and analyzed within the environment. The average time spent in the environment was 36 minutes. However, average time in environment varied considerably by class period. Periods 2 and 3 spent the most amount of time (41 and 39 minutes respectively) and period 4 spent the least (31 minutes). The last two periods spent 36 and 33 minutes within the environment. This difference in timing is important as all students within period 4 completed the features in the order 1243.

In looking through the traces, there is clear evidence for student confusion. 14 students reset the environment and started over at least once. Many students tried to complete their implementation with *distractor blocks* (blocks not useful in final solution). The most common distractor block was the "Touching" block, which was used to check if two sprites were overlapping, instead of checking if an agent was in a "neighboring cell". Another common block that students attempted to use in the solution was the "Move Step" block which was used in lieu of the "move to empty neighbor cell" block.

Students largely were able to complete the assignment with relative ease as there was 17 minutes on average left from the last feature was completed to close of the system. Due to the amount of time left at the end, many students elected to complete additional extension features with the most common (39/61) being a "reset functionality" that resets the simulation to its initial position.

4.1.2 Day 3. Among the 59 code traces, the average time spent in the environment was 39 minutes, ranging from 34 to 42 minutes. There were markedly fewer resets (only 6 students) than the previous day's programming assignment and many of these occurred after students made an error such as creating a new sprite (and losing track of their current sprite).

What is easily apparent by comparing the graphs of this assignment with the other is the incredibly varied paths that students take through the assignment. 11/59 students were unable to finish the assignment with five of these students missing all but Task 5. The 48 students who did finish the assignment took a myriad of paths. The majority of these solutions (34) did NOT include tasks 1 and 5. In fact, 44 students did not complete task 1 at all and of the 15 that did, nearly half (7) did not complete task 5 afterwards (and thereby not having correct final code).

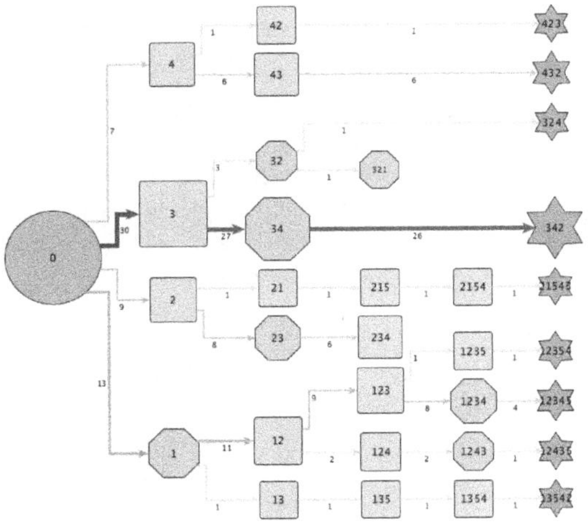

Figure 3: Task completion strategies for day 3.

Students who completed the assignment had less time on average (10 minutes) between finishing and close of the environment than those working on assignment 2, but this split also varied by solution strategy with those who did tasks 1 and 5 having less time (around 8.5 minutes) than those who just did only tasks 2, 3, and 4 (around 11 minutes). With the remaining time, students attempted a number of self-created extensions. Some students attempted to make other sprites in their model such as hospitals. Others attempted to extend the logic of their modeling by either stopping the simulation once the entire population was infected or keeping track of and graphing the remaining healthy population. Another student attempted to add interactivity into their model with key press events.

4.2　Exit Tickets

In addition to the main breakdown of students reporting learning science vs computing (see Table 4), we also wanted to examine how students articulate their new computing knowledge. We classified their learning statements by whether they mention a computing term or mention the term in connection to a specific goal. On day 2, 15 students mention sprites and costumes, 10 with specific goals in mind. Seven students mention programming blocks, but only two with a specific use in mind. On day 3, 23 students mention variables and plotting, 13 of which with a specific goal for use. This time, only four students mentioned sprites or costumes. Day 5, showed the biggest swing with most students reporting science, though 5 students also mention programming in general.

Most students on each day reported that they did not find anything frustrating with the activity. Of those that did, eight found programming errors and debugging frustrating, while five students found system related errors (problems saving, crashing, etc.) each day frustrating to deal with. Five students on day 2 and day 3 specifically mentioned adding the hospital was difficult, but this was an extension activity not explicitly supported in the curriculum. Finally, day 5's specific activity brought new challenges for five students as some were frustrated and confused about the terms introduced (e.g. independent variable) as well as using the tools in order to find the relationships in the assignment.

Table 4: Student responses to Exit Ticket questions 1, 2, and 4. Answers of none are omitted from the table.

Day	Balance	Most Helpful	Pacing
2 N=39	Computing: 23 Science: 3 Both:12	Teacher: 28 Tutorial: 5 Classmates:2	Perfect: 29 Slow: 5 Fast: 3
3 N=49	Computing: 34 Science: 5 Both:7	Teacher: 32 Tutorial: 8 Classmates:6	Perfect: 30 Slow: 13 Fast: 2
5 N=39	Computing: 0 Science: 26 Both: 7	Teacher: 24 Tutorial: 3 Classmates:6	Perfect: 23 Slow: 4 Fast: 5

Finally, students had a number of suggestions on how to improve the curriculum. Suggestions can be broadly categorized as having to do with the instruction (providing more support or improving the pacing); fixing technical problems with the programming environment (e.g. crashes, bugs); and activity-related suggestions (e.g. more extensions, time for group work, creative time).

4.3　Observations

Observers identified general patterns on all three days. First, concerns were raised about the task sequence in both days 2 and 3. For day 3, observers noted that the action of setting # of diseased to 0 under the Green Flag in task 1 didn't seem to serve a purpose and caused confusion in some cases. In later periods, teachers skipped this step entirely.

Observers noted that the ordering of tasks in day 2 was off. When comparing periods, the class seems to run smoother when students work to iteratively solve a problem and the nested-if (task 3) does not produce any visible change. Observers also noted that teachers adopted different strategies in different periods, resulting in the difference in pacing of the assignments. In some periods, the activities were led in an incredibly instructionist manner, leading students through each step. As teachers got more comfortable with the assignment, they began to add their own pacing and scaffolding approaches such as having students explain previous days code or creating parsons problems [12] for students to reason through as a group. Towards the end periods, teachers found ways to explicitly connect science concepts into the programming instruction.

Researchers observed the majority of students actively engaged during all three days of instruction with minimal off-task behavior. While students were generally able to code within the environment, some confusion was observed during day 5 of the activity. Students struggled to setup the simulation environment in a way needed to answer their group's research questions. This was alleviated in later periods with deliberate instructor support.

5　DISCUSSION & LIMITATIONS

In addressing the question "*How are students completing the assignment tasks?*", we examined the connection between code traces and observations. Overall, day 2 and 3 completion rates were strong with 55/61 and 42/59 students fully completing the assignment respectively. Those that completed the assignment tended to have extra time left, suggesting mid to high performing students need additional activities and extensions. Initial observer concerns about task sequencing were corroborated by examining students progression through the completion states. For day 2, the quicker completion time as well as observations suggest that the task sequencing should be 1243 instead of 1234. Task 4 is the behavior that actually visually changes the sprites to infected, which as observers noted, is critical in engaging students. Moreover, task 3 requires a doubly nested if, while task 4 only requires a single if, which is a better scaffolding strategy and smoother sequence than the original task sequence (as noted by field observations of teachers guiding the instruction). The final recommendation for day 2's sequence is informed by the large number of field observed and code trace observed end of day behaviors of adding in the reset functionality. This should be explicitly added as a day 2 task, as the behavior and functionality is necessary for day 3's activity.

In examining day 3's sequencing, the most apparent result was that the placing of the set block under the green flag in task 1 and the removal of this block in task 5 were unnecessary additions to the assignment. Not only did it impede progress in many cases as evident by the code traces, observations from researchers showed that teachers and students would often forego actually completing the tasks at all. This lead to faster overall completions of the assignment as well as fewer stuck states. As the plurality of students completed the task by completing task 3 first and without doing tasks 1 and 5 fully, the results strongly support removal and reordering of the tasks.

In answering the question *"What emergent behaviors or observations can we identify in order to better engage students in future iterations?"*, we identify several behaviors of actionable interest. First, blocks that are identified as distractors impede progress and can lead to student frustration and confusion, noted by both observers and exit tickets. Within the stuck states, it is also observable when students don't know which block to use. Since the goal of the curriculum is for the student to build the correct logic for the epidemics model instead of identifying the difference between blocks, we will hide the distractor blocks in future iterations in order to focus attention solely on blocks necessary for completing the assignment. Second, student exit tickets, observations and code traces all support the idea that students want more opportunities for open-ended exploration. With many extensions attempted in the extra time on days 2 and 3, the curriculum should explicitly provide additional scaffolding for students to be able to complete these extensions, including the reset functionality completed by the majority of students on day 2. Supporting these extra activities will also alleviate pacing issues with students finishing early and displaying disruptive/bored behavior.

In answering the question *"How do students perceiving the science vs computational learning goals?"*, we primarily examine exit tickets and observations. Students self-reported learning topics correlate strongly with the amount of programming on a particular day. On days 2 and 3, which focused creating the simulation to determine rate of infection, the majority of students reported learning computing (89.7% and 83.7% respectively). On these days, students were able to articulate the connections between the sprites/costumes and the resulting agent behavior in the simulation as well as the usefulness of variables in being able to track the rate of infection.

On day 5, which focused on solving research questions within the simulation the majority of students (84.6%) reported learning science. This trend in perceived learning, is further supported by observations that suggest teachers make deliberate breakpoints to connect the computing to science concepts previously covered in class as teachers introduced more guided reflections and connections with material as the day progressed. These moments of connection, created by teachers, should be explicitly supported within the curriculum in order to be able to truly promote the lesson as an infused activity.

Furthermore, several students reported the tutorial being helpful for each day, however, the majority of students report help from the teacher being most useful. Observers noted the teacher had a good sense of pace of the students on programming days, and helped students construct hypotheses and explain terms like susceptibility which they only briefly covered prior. The teacher also provided logical reasoning and discussions for students to understand why the simulation behaved they way it did.

The scope of this study is limited by mainly focusing on plugged days and not unplugged. We also did not record the action logs of students during the final day as no coding occurred in the environment. An issue that was not addressed in this study was student assessment of scientific concepts as this was also beyond the scope of our research. Finally, as is the case in much classroom research, an observer effect may have influenced findings.

6 CONCLUSIONS & FUTURE WORK

In this analysis of a CT-infused life science lesson, we created and used the CEO model to triangulate data from code traces, exit tickets, and field observations to evaluate the success of student outcomes in the experimental curriculum. Using these data measures, we identified popular student programming pathways that lead to successful completion of the assignment and pathways that lead to stuck states. The code traces provide empirical support for the subjective field observations and student exit tickets.

Other observations and suggestions corroborated by code traces include staging tasks in such a way that each milestone has a visual component or perceivable outcome by the students. Additionally, on days where students complete the main tasks quickly, additional content can be included, specifically, the functionality (such as reset) that most students already take upon themselves to complete. In general, these findings suggest a role for code traces as a initial attempt to empirically corroborate purely qualitative-based evidence. Thus, promoting a more robust pathway for iteratively improving computing-infused activities for non-computing students. While this process was done through inspection by a member of the research team, this process could be automated through the creation of unit tests for intended code behavior for each task.

A natural progression of this work is to investigate the transferability of these activities. Following Means and Penuel 2005, we want to further identify, "what works where, when, and for whom" [10]. We have piloted the epidemics curriculum in two additional schools within the same county. However, we would like to investigate if the lessons will also work at another institution, with a different school culture at differing times in the school schedule (i.e. before/after lesson plan; exploration vs. review activity).

ACKNOWLEDGMENTS

This material is based upon work supported by the National Science Foundation under 1742351 and 1742332. Any opinions, findings, and conclusions or recommendations expressed in this material are those of the author(s) and do not necessarily reflect the views of the National Science Foundation.

REFERENCES

[1] Bernd Meyer Aidan Lane and Jonathan Mullins. 2012. *Simulation with Cellular A Project Based Introduction to Programming* (first ed.). Monash University, Melbourne, Australia. Online: https://github.com/MonashAlexandria/snapapps.

[2] John B Biggs and Kevin F Collis. 2014. *Evaluating the quality of learning: The SOLO taxonomy (Structure of the Observed Learning Outcome)*. Academic Press, New York, New York, USA.

[3] Veronica Cateté, Nicholas Lytle, Yihuan Dong, Danielle Boulden, Bita Akram, Jennifer Houchins, Tiffany Barnes, Eric Wiebe, James Lester, Bradford Mott, and Kristy Boyer. 2018. Infusing Computational Thinking into Middle Grade Science Classrooms: Lessons Learned. In *Proceedings of the 13th Workshop in Primary and Secondary Computing Education (WiPSCE '18)*. ACM, New York, NY, USA, Article 21, 6 pages. https://doi.org/10.1145/3265757.3265778

[4] Cynthia E Coburn, William R Penuel, and Kimberly E Geil. 2013. *Practice Partnerships: A Strategy for Leveraging Research for Educational Improvement in School Districts*. Technical Report. William T. Grant Foundation, New York, New York, USA.

[5] National Research Council et al. 2011. *Report of a workshop on the pedagogical aspects of computational thinking*. National Academies Press, Washington, DC.

[6] Barry J Fishman, William R Penuel, Anna-Ruth Allen, Britte Haugan Cheng, and NORA Sabelli. 2013. Design-based implementation research: An emerging model for transforming the relationship of research and practice. *National society for the study of education* 112, 2 (2013), 136–156.

[7] Natasa Grgurina, Erik Barendsen, Cor Suhre, Bert Zwaneveld, and Klaas van Veen. 2018. Assessment of Modeling and Simulation in Secondary Computing Science Education. In *Proceedings of the 13th Workshop in Primary and Secondary Computing Education (WiPSCE '18)*. ACM, New York, NY, USA, Article 7, 10 pages. https://doi.org/10.1145/3265757.3265764

[8] J. K. Houchins, D. C. Boulden, B. Akram, E. Wiebe, V. Cateté, Y. Dong, N. Lytle, A. Milliken, T. Barnes, J. Lester, B. Mott, and K. E. Boyer. 2019. Designing a Computational Modeling Unit for Middle Grades Science Classrooms: Grounding Decisions in Practice. In *2019 American Educational Research Association Annual Meeting*. AIED, Toronto, Canada, 15.

[9] David R Krathwohl. 2002. A revision of Bloom's taxonomy: An overview. *Theory into practice* 41, 4 (2002), 212–218.

[10] Barbara Means and William R Penuel. 2005. Scaling up technology-based educational innovations. *Scaling up success: Lessons learned from technology-based educational improvement* . (2005), 176–197.

[11] Jaclyn Ocumpaugh. 2015. *Baker Rodrigo Ocumpaugh monitoring protocol (BROMP) 2.0 technical and training manual*. Teachers College, Columbia University.

[12] Dale Parsons and Patricia Haden. 2006. Parson's Programming Puzzles: A Fun and Effective Learning Tool for First Programming Courses. In *Proceedings of the 8th Australasian Conference on Computing Education - Volume 52 (ACE '06)*. Australian Computer Society, Inc., Darlinghurst, Australia, Australia, 157–163. http://dl.acm.org/citation.cfm?id=1151869.1151890

[13] Thomas W. Price, Veronica Cateté, Jennifer Albert, Tiffany Barnes, and Daniel D. Garcia. 2016. Lessons Learned from "BJC" CS Principles Professional Development. In *Proceedings of the 47th ACM Technical Symposium on Computing Science Education (SIGCSE '16)*. ACM, New York, New York, USA, 467–472. https://doi.org/10.1145/2839509.2844625

[14] Jonathan P Rowe, Scott W McQuiggan, Jennifer L Robison, and James C Lester. 2009. Off-Task Behavior in Narrative-Centered Learning Environments.. In *Proceedings of the 14th International Conference on Artificial Intelligence in Education, AIED 2019*. IOS Press, Brighton, UK, 99–106.

[15] Robert Sawyer, Andy Smith, Jonathan Rowe, Roger Azevedo, and James Lester. 2017. Enhancing Student Models in Game-based Learning with Facial Expression Recognition. In *Proceedings of the 25th Conference on User Modeling, Adaptation and Personalization (UMAP '17)*. ACM, New York, NY, USA, 192–201. https://doi.org/10.1145/3079628.3079686

[16] John Sweller. 1988. Cognitive load during problem solving: Effects on learning. *Cognitive science* 12, 2 (1988), 257–285.

[17] Jeannette M Wing. 2006. Computational thinking. *Commun. ACM* 49, 3 (2006), 33–35.

[18] Rui Zhi, Thomas W Price, Nicholas Lytle, Yihuan Dong, and Tiffany Barnes. 2018. Reducing the State Space of Programming Problems through Data-Driven Feature Detection. In *Educational Data Mining in Computer Science Education (CSEDM) Workshop @EDM 2018*. Educational Data Mining, New York, United States, 7.

An Exploration of Cognitive Shifting in Writing Code

Ilenia Fronza
Free University of
Bozen-Bolzano
Bolzano, Italy
ilenia.fronza@unibz.it

Arto Hellas
University of Helsinki
Helsinki, Finland
arto.hellas@helsinki.fi

Petri Ihantola
University of Helsinki
Helsinki, Finland
petri.ihantola@helsinki.fi

Tommi Mikkonen
University of Helsinki
Helsinki, Finland
tommi.mikkonen@
helsinki.fi

ABSTRACT

Programming is considered a demanding task that requires focusing on detail at code level. Students learning to program need to learn to think like a programmer, which involves coming up with plans needed to solve problems, and they need to learn to write the code that corresponds to the plans that they have thought of. The use of multiple files creates additional overhead to the process, as part of the code is not visible to the student. If a student does not remember the contents of a particular file, she needs to consciously move from writing code in one file to reading code in another file. This conscious transition of attention from one location to another is known as *cognitive shifting*. Using key-level data collected from a programming exam, we analyze students' movements within files and between files, and relate these movements with students' performance in the course. Our results indicate that frequently moving from one file to another may lead to worse performance than more focused actions, but no such effect exists when analyzing movements within an individual file.

CCS CONCEPTS

• **Applied computing** → **Education**;

KEYWORDS

Cognitive shifting, Educational data mining, Learning analytics, Programming process, Movement in source code.

ACM Reference Format:
Ilenia Fronza, Arto Hellas, Petri Ihantola, and Tommi Mikkonen. 2019. An Exploration of Cognitive Shifting in Writing Code. In *ACM Global Computing Education Conference 2019 (CompEd '19), May 17–19, 2019, Chengdu,Sichuan, China.* ACM, New York, NY, USA, 7 pages. https://doi.org/10.1145/3300115.3309522

1 INTRODUCTION

Programming is considered a demanding task, where the focus is placed on detail at code level. Therefore, students who learn to program need to not only figure out solutions to given problems in their mind, but also write the programs that correspond to the solutions they have thought of; this needs to be done according to a specified set of rules and procedures. Moreover, as students proceed in their programming courses, they must learn how to manage several files at the same time, as code in larger programming assignments can be (and typically is) partitioned into multiple files. Indeed, multiple files are much easier to read, maintain, and manage than a single large file; the downside is the creation of additional overhead to the design process.

There exists a large body of research regarding how students learn programming. For example, previous knowledge influences programming behavior; if students know how to solve a problem, they can write the solution line by line [14, 37]. However, when faced with a problem for which the students have no solution, they resort to experimentation and means-end analysis [41]. While the previous examples are from over 25 years ago, the recent interest towards mining student data in programming courses has increased the availability of data sets that can be used for such research [23].

In this work, we have studied how students move their attention in code and how students move between files. This conscious transition is called *cognitive shifting*, which is the mental process of consciously directing attention from one area to another [39]. If the attention is directed unconsciously, the process is called task switching. Both cognitive shifting and task switching are a part of cognitive flexibility, an executive function vital for learning [10].

Our work differs from code navigation studies [25, 26] as they typically focus on software professionals who work on a larger code base. In our case, the focus is on novice programmers who need to re-read their code in order to remember what they previously wrote, who typically work on a very small code base and, in our case, who have built all the code that they are working on. In our data, moving attention from one location to another can happen due to multiple reasons, ranging from student fixing a previous issue to revisiting code to check how a particular piece of code was written. Understanding movements within a file and between files can bring insight into how novices learn to program, and consequently help providing to students better learning resources. Such resources could include, for example, tools that are able to identify topics that students struggle with, and provide practice opportunities with challenging topics.

In this article, we report an analysis of cognitive shifting measured through students' movements within and between files. We study the relationship of the movements and students' performance in the programming exam and the course. The analysis is conducted using key-level data collected from a programming exam, which stores both writing into files and movements between files.

The rest of this paper is structured as follows. In Section 2, we provide background for the work. In Section 3, we introduce our research approach and methods. In Section 4, we present the results of the study. In Section 5, we give an extended discussion regarding the results. Finally, at the end of the paper, in Section 6, we draw some final conclusions.

2 BACKGROUND
2.1 How novices develop code

Experts and novices differ in a number of characteristics, such as skills, expertise, experience level, and knowledge. As a consequence, they also differ in their program comprehension process and programming strategies. For example, novices are typically limited to surface knowledge of programs, while expert programmers can "see the forest" [30], which means that they are able to integrate the parts of a program into a coherent structure. In comparison to experts, novices lack detailed mental models, and fail to apply relevant knowledge [50]. Moreover, experts mostly use a top-down approach (following the control flow) while novices generally adopt a bottom-up approach (sequentially, reading code line by line in the physical order) to understand a program [7, 32]. While reading, experts can even make larger jumps to focus on relevant source code elements [12]. Additionally, novices have been shown to paste relatively often when writing their first programs [47], and this is one of the reasons why they have long plateaus of no coding activity, during which they browse other code for useful pieces [9], or they look for information using a browser [21].

Novices also differ from one another. For example, Perkins and his co-authors classified novice programmers as *stoppers* and *movers* based on their learning styles [34]. Stoppers are novices who tend to give up when they are not able to proceed with a problem. Movers, instead, try different approaches in order to solve a problem. Extreme movers are called *tinkerers*: they try to make small (even random) changes in the hopes of getting the problem solved.

2.2 Schemas and plans

In cognitive science, the term *schema* refers to a memory structure that can represent complex categories of information as well as the connections between these categories [22]. Schemas are an integral part of storing and retrieving knowledge from long-term memory, and as such, they also guide patterns of behavior [22]. Schemas evolve over time due to the acquisition of new information [35]: new information will either be interpreted and understood through existing schemas or, if this fails, existing schemas are adjusted or new ones are created to accommodate the new information. Most of the new information, however, is either ignored or forgotten [43].

As schemas guide behavior, they are an integral part of problem solving [41]. When faced with a problem, schemas for that particular type of problem are identified and then the problem-solving strategies corresponding to the particular schema are applied. If the problem is unknown, that is, there are no corresponding schemas, general problem-solving strategies are used [41], such as means-ends analysis. Overall, the growth of problem-solving expertise is interlinked with the acquisition and evolution of domain-specific schemas [42].

There exists a number of studies that suggest that schemas are intertwined with programming [14, 17, 37]. One of the most explored programming problems in this area is the *Rainfall problem* [38, 40], which is often used as an example of a seemingly simple problem that is challenging for novice programmers. The Rainfall problem is composed of multiple smaller tasks. These include reading input, filtering input, finishing reading, and calculating an average of the inputs. Some variants also ask the programmer to, for example, output the count of filtered inputs and the count of valid inputs. These smaller tasks correspond to smaller goals that the programmer needs to achieve in order to complete the full problem, and one of the challenges of the problem comes from merging the solutions to the smaller tasks together into the actual solution for the Rainfall problem [20, 38]. It has been suggested that, when programmers can apply an existing schema to a problem (or a part of the problem), they write the solution in a linear manner [14, 37]. When no existing schema is found, the solution is constructed through experimentation using schemas on related problems, i.e., means-ends analysis. Through the experimentation and learning process, new schemas are formed, and later, schemas for similar problems are available for use. One of the important parts of this learning process is generalization, through which learners learns to ignore minute details such as input and output during design, making it possible to direct attention to more challenging areas of the problem [37].

2.3 Cognitive shifting

Multitasking is the ability to stop working on a task, switch to another, and return eventually to the first one (as needed or as scheduled). Multitasking for programmers happens for example when moving away from one coding task, before it has been finished, and onto another. Although multitasking can bring advantages [1], it also has limitations [11] related to cognitive shifting. Indeed, multitasking is neurologically impossible: what is happening in reality is that attention is moved from one context to the other. This requires some retention of technical details, then refocusing on the new task, and later a recall of the previous activity [45]. Therefore, limitations are given by the fact that human brain has a limited amount of cognitive flexibility [27], which is the mental ability to switch from thinking about one concept to thinking about another one. This is related both to the number of concepts we can manage, as well as to the difficulty in switching between them [45].

Cognitive shifting introduces necessary time spent switching between the tasks, called "attention switching" [15], and reduces the amount of short-term memory dedicated to a single task [44]. Memory-for-goals [3] is one of the major cognitive theories on interruptions. According to this theory, moving the attention to another task suspends the goal of the primary task and activates the secondary task goal.

The usage of multiple files in order to create larger programs requires programmers to remember the main content of each file. Otherwise, cognitive shifting is necessary, which means moving the attention to another file in order to retrieve information and then come back to the current task. The ability to develop abstract representations (i.e., mental models [33]) of a process in the form of logic structures increases with programming experience [30, 36], therefore novices might incur in cognitive shifting more frequently than more experienced programmers.

3 RESEARCH QUESTIONS AND METHOD

Our initial hypothesis, based on the related work discussed in Sections 1 and 2, is that accumulated competence in programming implies that one can focus on one task at a time and therefore needs to move less back and forth in the code. Conscious moving, or cognitive shifting, can occur for example within a file and between files belonging to the same exercises. Therefore, our Research Questions are:

RQ1 How is cognitive shifting within a file related to programming performance?

RQ2 How is cognitive shifting between files of the same task related to programming performance?

Cognitive shifting can be related to code reading or code writing. To get an initial overview of the phenomena, we will focus on code writing, from where there is large scale data available. The data is collected from an introductory programming course at the University of Helsinki, where students use Test My Code [49], which is an instrumented development environment that captures all events down to typing level and provides automated feedback on the correctness of programming assignments in the course.

The course contains 140 programming assignments divided over seven weeks. Assignments are organized so that whenever a new topic is learned, students first practice the relevant syntactic commands with small assignments, learning to avoid the typical syntactic and semantic pitfalls. After practicing the basic constructs, assignments are used to scaffold students into building larger programs, concurrently demonstrating how programs are built using a divide-and-conquer approach. Finally, open-ended assignments are given to the students. This cycle of assignments leading to larger open-ended assignments is developed into each of the main themes of the course.

At the end of the course, there is a mandatory exam where students solve practical programming tasks in the same environments as with the weekly exercises. The grading of the course is based on both the assignments and the exam; 70% of the course mark comes from the assignments and 30% from the exam. To pass the course, the students must receive at least 70% of the total points and at least half of the points in the exam.

Cognitive shifting is studied using two questions of the course exam (analyzed programming assignment questions have been included in Appendix A). The exam had four assignments from which only one contained multiple files (Question 3 in Appendix A). Data from that task are used to capture both in-file and between files cognitive switches. In-file cognitive switches are collected also from the first assignment (Question 1 in Appendix A) which is a variant of the Rainfall problem [38]. Cognitive shifting within files (*file_switches*) is calculated as the number of cases where consequent edits were marked to different files. For within a file cognitive shifting, we considered three variables derived from the line numbers of consequent edits, separately for both selected exercises:

in_file_jumps_n The number of cases when consequent edits were not on the same line or lines next to each other. Cases where a student moved to the next/previous line were disregarded as they were considered natural movements, not jumping in the code.

in_file_jumps_avg For all cases counted in *in_file_jumps_n*, average of absolute values of how many lines were jumped. Absolute values were used to ignore the jump direction and

highlight how far a student moved from the original edit points.

in_file_jumps_variance variance of the in_file_jumps used to calculate the *in_file_jumps_avg*.

We estimate *programming performance* using points from weekly programming assignments and the exam questions. Programming performance is then correlated with the previously defined variables describing cognitive shifting. Holm's correction is used to counteract the multiple comparison problem – in our work, all reported p-values have been adjusted appropriately.

Based on the related work, our hypothesis was that skilled students would jump less in the code. However, partial solutions of any exercise are likely shorter and therefore contain also less movement. For example, a student might have stopped working on a difficult task after few edits, in which case there would also be a very small number of movements. Thus, *we focus on students who got roughly the same points from the selected assignment*. The distribution of the points is provided in Figure 1. As most students were finally able to get full points from both the selected assignments, we will focus on those sub-populations.

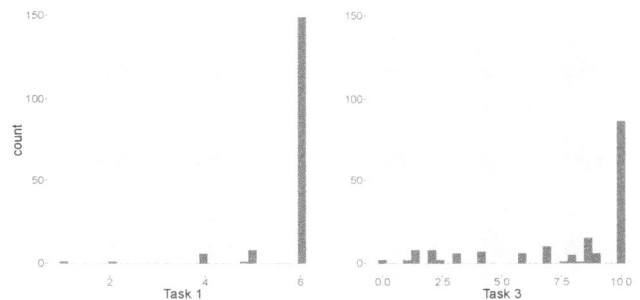

Figure 1: Histograms illustrating the distribution of points given from the exam questions.

Another challenge in our data set is that, although all the included students were able to solve the assigned task, the amount of cognitive shifting may still manifest through the amount of effort put into the task. For example, a student who spends more time with the assignment, and uses more keystrokes to solve it, is intuitively likely to do more jumping in the code as well. To control this, we calculated time between the first and last edit event, as well as the number of edit events related to the task, and will inspect their role as well.

4 RESULTS

4.1 Overview of the data

Our analysis focuses on those students who participated in the course exam, a total of 187 students. After removing students for whom the data collection failed for some reason (e.g., using an incorrect project in the editor) or who did not participate solving the weekly programming tasks, 166 students remained. From those 166 students, 149 got full points from the first exam question, and 87 got full points from the third exam question. Descriptive statistics of the variables analyzed in this section are provided in Table 1.

Table 1: Descriptive statistics of variables analyzed in this section. Time is reported in minutes. Assignment and exam grades are reported separately for both sub-populations.

Statistic	N	Mean	St. Dev.	Min.	Pctl(25)	Pctl(75)	Max.
Assignment 1: in_file_jumps_n	149	214.638	74.409	17	172	262	407
Assignment 1: in_file_jumps_avg	149	7.891	1.662	4.308	6.932	8.751	17.798
Assignment 1: in_file_jumps_variance	149	22.351	11.615	5.434	16.519	25.381	110.623
Assignment 1: eventcount	149	440.725	125.425	176	362	486	1,065
Assignment 1: time	149	16.743	27.798	2.733	5.298	9.684	122.873
Assignment 1: exercises	149	65.094	7.361	32	62	70	70
Assignment 1: exam_total	149	23.664	6.493	7	20.600	28.600	30
Assignment 3: in_file_jumps_n	87	518.816	249.546	32	315.500	668	1,369
Assignment 3: in_file_jumps_avg	87	10.109	3.315	3.955	8.284	11.286	25.008
Assignment 3: in_file_jumps_variance	87	128.934	76.977	28.462	86.383	151.362	431.791
Assignment 3: file_switches	87	11.690	6.066	3	8	14	46
Assignment 3: eventcount	87	2,043.908	755.941	758	1,641.500	2,194	6,020
Assignment 3: time	87	43.768	24.158	7.218	25.324	56.188	108.743
Assignment 3: exercises	87	66.701	6.515	32	66.500	70	70
Assignment 3: exam_total	87	27.744	2.062	20	26.800	29.300	30

4.2 Movement within a file

First, we studied the correlation between the within-file cognitive shifting – that is, moving from editing one location in the file to editing another location in the file – and programming performance. The analyzed exam question is a variant of the Rainfall problem [38], and the students work on the problem in a single file. When analyzing the variables and exam question performance, we use rank correlation as we are interested in understanding whether there is a monotonic relation between cognitive shifting and performance and as many of the variable pairs do not fulfill the assumptions of linear correlation. Performance correlations and related p-values of the first exam question and the within-file movement metrics are provided in Table 2.

Table 2: Spearman rank correlations between variables describing overall programming performance (i.e., exercises and exam grade) and cognitive shifting in the first exam task. p-values are corrected for multiple comparisons (Holm).

	exercises		exam total	
	r	p	r	p
in_file_jumps_n	-0.08	1.00	-0.09	1.00
in_file_jumps_avg	-0.01	1.00	-0.08	1.00
in_file_jumps_variance	0.10	1.00	-0.05	1.00
eventcount	-0.15	0.53	-0.13	0.71
time	-0.22	0.07	-0.27	0.01

As can be seen from Table 2, none of the correlations between the studied variables and the amount of completed exercises are statistically significant. When considering students' performance within the exam, none of the studied variables correlates statistically significantly with the exam total, except for the time spent on the question. There exists a small statistically significant correlation between the time spent on the question and total points from the exam, where time spent on the questions explains approximately 7.3% of the variance in the exam score.

4.3 Movement between files

Next, we studied correlation between moving across files and programming performance. We focused on the exam question where students are expected to work on multiple files (outlined in Appendix A, Question 3). Similar to the previous subsection, rank correlation was used for analysis. Performance correlations and related p-values of the third exam question and the within-file and across-file movement variables are provided in Table 3.

Table 3: Spearman rank correlations between variables describing overall programming performance (i.e., exercises and exam grade) and cognitive shifting in the third exam task. p-values are corrected for multiple comparisons (Holm).

	exercises		exam total	
	r	p	r	p
in_file_jumps_n	-0.27	0.14	-0.25	0.18
in_file_jumps_avg	0.05	1.00	-0.11	1.00
in_file_jumps_variance	-0.05	1.00	-0.14	0.93
file_switches	-0.26	0.14	-0.38	0.00
eventcount	-0.24	0.18	-0.24	0.19
time	-0.12	1.00	-0.23	0.20

Similar to the previous analysis, no statistically significant correlation between the exercise points and the studied variables exists. Almost none of the variables correlate statistically significantly with the exam total, except for the number of switches between the files, which explains 14.4% (r = −0.38) of the variance.

As discussed in the methodology, event count and time spent on the assignment can intuitively explain the variables. To investigate this, we calculated partial correlations for the variables where event count and time are given. The partial correlations, none of which are statistically significant after Holm-correction ($p > 0.1$), are presented in Table 4.

Table 4: Partial Spearman rank correlations between in-exercise Task 3, when time and eventcount are set.

	exercises	course_total
in_file_jumps_n	-0.17	-0.18
in_file_jumps_avg	0.12	0.07
in_file_jumps_variance	0.04	-0.00
file_switches	-0.16	-0.25
exercises	1.00	0.81
course_total	0.81	1.00

5 DISCUSSION

5.1 Cognitive shifting within file

The results presented in the previous section suggest that within file movements – that is, cognitive shifting within file – do not explain students' performance, when measured through completed course exercises or total points from exam. The only statistically significant correlation ($r = -.27$) was identified between the time spent on the exam question that was written within a single file and the total exam points.

We specifically observed that students' movements within the file was not correlated with the total exam points or the course assignments. One possible explanation for not observing a connection between movements and performance is that not many of the students struggled to complete the problem, having no need for means-ends analysis or experimentation. This is reflected also in the points received from the question (see Task 1 in Figure 1); 149 out of the 166 included students (89.8%) were able to solve the problem successfully. The problem, which is a variant of the Rainfall problem, draws us back to the original studies on schemas and plans in programming, as many of them were also conducted on the Rainfall problem. In those studies, the proportion of students who could complete the program was considerably lower [38].

The correlation between the time spent on the exam question and the overall exam performance, but not the course points, could be at least partially a result of some students having previous programming experience. Indeed, while all students, regardless of their programming background, seek to solve the programming assignments, students with previous programming background are able to write code faster on average [29].

5.2 Cognitive shifting between files

Upon analysis of cognitive switching in an assignment where students must complete multiple files, we noticed that the number of file switches correlates with exam performance ($r = -0.38$). None of the other variables, including the time spent on the assignment, was related to the selected performance metrics. When considering the jumps within file, it is possible that the question handout that has a listing of method names supports the students so that they can work in a more linear fashion.

Those students who switch between the files more perform worse in the exam than those who switch less between the files. It is possible that the analysis teases out students who have not yet reached a level of competency where they could ignore most of the details, and thus, need to jump between the files in an attempt to memorize the structure in the other file. Such phenomena are, however, complex. When performing partial correlations with time and events set, none of the movement-specific variables were no longer statistically significant. These results suggest that the time spent on the task and the number of events are also related to cognitive shifting; it is evident that those who work longer on the file also switch between the files more, but on the other hand, the amount of events cannot increase linearly over time.

5.3 Pedagogical differences

The results presented in the previous section are somewhat contradictory with the previous research on the topic. For example, many of the studies related to schemas and plans have been conducted on the already-mentioned Rainfall problem, which we also used in our study. In the studied context, however, students' performance was well above of students in the original Rainfall studies.

When comparing the pedagogical practices of the studied context to the original studies on program construction discussed in Section 2, it is possible that the way how programming is taught differs between the contexts. This can influence students' problem solving strategies [14] and overall course outcomes [46]. While the original studies do not report the pedagogical practices, which makes it impossible to compare the contexts, we highlight some of the pedagogical practices in the studied context which may have influenced the study outcomes.

First, timely and clear feedback can increase student learning [19]. Timeliness and clarity of feedback in the studied context is achieved through actionable automated tests that show students the cases that do not pass tests associated with the assignments they are working on. In addition, some of the tests provide students feedback on the steps that they should take next. Second, learning is largely dependent on practice [13] and distributing and interleaving practice over time can improve learning retention [18]. In the studied context, there are plenty of practice opportunities and the assignments are distributed over the duration of the course, where a set of assignments is given during each of the course weeks. Due to the amount of programming assignments, there also exists ample opportunity for rehearsal. Third, short term goals can improve student motivation [5], and the external motivation from the grading can improve student effort within the course [4]. The assignments in the course provided short term goals as they had weekly deadlines, and the course grading emphasized students' effort. Finally, the use of smaller tasks has been advocated within the computing education community (see e.g. [31, 48]). The use of smaller tasks has been shown to lead to students starting their work earlier, and subsequently, improving their overall performance [16].

5.4 Technology evolution

With the goal of finding effective teaching strategies, several studies have been dedicated to understanding the differences between novices and experts in writing code. The effort in this direction has generated, for example, several results on schema acquisition [37]. The idea of the work presented in this paper is to revisit those results, by taking into consideration the changes that have occured in writing code meanwhile. For example, larger screens and even multi-screen configurations have been proposed as a solution for multitasking [8, 24]. Some studies have been dedicated to exploring the effects of such a working configuration on developer's productivity, and large widescreen monitors have been shown to perform better than dual screen configurations [6]. While using multi-screens, developers need to switch their attention back and forth from one screen to the other one. Therefore, the perspective taken in this paper – cognitive shifting – and the presented approach can open new horizons to new studies in this field.

5.5 Blind men and an elephant, and other limitations

Following the line of thought presented in [2], by observing detail only in isolation can lead to misinterpretations of the whole[1]. As already pointed out above, intuitively there is a relation between the time spent on an assignment and associated keystrokes, and the amount of jumps in the code. To control this, in this paper we also calculated time between the first and last edit event, as well as the number of edit events related to the task and we have inspected their role as well. Ultimately, it is possible that the results simply amplify previous observations on how time and time-like metrics affect learning results [28].

The study presented in this paper is based on data from students' behavior only, and no reflection to their true intentions and concerns was made. Moreover, use of other resources was not monitored. This clearly introduces a risk that our interpretations regarding the data set simply do not match what the students were experiencing. Moreover, the data was gathered prior to performing the study, so we were bound to use only the data that was readily available, and there was no way to fine-tune the data collection process for more focused data and its analysis. Consequently, we can simply present correlations, not implications regarding students' behavior. Moreover, there is a clear selection bias, as we only focus on students that received full points from the selected tasks in the exam. Further limitations to this work are introduced by the fact that the studied programs are somewhat simple and straightforward in their nature. Hence, it is possible that the view to the data is overly simplified, and that with larger programs, the situation would be more fine-grained. Finally, the data set is fairly small, and consists of students of one course only, from a single university. Drawing conclusions on any single instance introduces a potential threat to external validity and generalizability of the study.

6 CONCLUSIONS

This work presents an analysis of students' cognitive shifting within and between files using key-level data collected from a programming exam. Two problems from the exam were analyzed; one a smaller one that can be implemented to a single file, and the other a larger one that must be implemented in multiple files. Students'

___
[1] Authors of [2] describe how three blind men observe an elephant differently depending if they touch the elephant's leg, tail, and so on.

data from these problems were contrasted with students' performance in the course, as evidenced by overall exam performance and completed course assignments.

Our analysis identified only small statistically significant correlations, between the time spent on a question and total points from the exam, and between the number of times the student moved across files and variance in the total exam points.

Nevertheless, the work presented in this paper opens several new avenues for future research. These include studying to which constructs novices jump to/from other files, i.e., understanding if they are jumping from control structures, print statements, etc. Furthermore, this can be done at multiple levels including methods, for instance. In addition, studying if novices return to the same location multiple times might introduce interesting insights in terms of which constructs require constant attention. Finally, as already mentioned, connecting this line of research to already existing studies on how novices solve their problems forms a potential future direction for further work.

A APPENDIX: EXAM QUESTIONS

The appendix outlines the exam questions that were included for analysis. For the purposes of this study, we focused on two assignments. The first problem (Question 1: Statistics) is a variant of the Rainfall problem [38] and is typically constructed within a single file; the second problem (Question 3: Emails) forces the students to use multiple files (static classes are not taught in the studied context and thus all students worked on the classes in separate files).

Question 1: Statistics

Write a program that reads in numbers from the user. When the user types in the number -1, the program should stop reading input and output (1) the count of the numbers, (2) the sum of the numbers, and (3) the average of the numbers.

Negative numbers should not be taken into account when analyzing the input. You may assume that the user always gives at least one valid number.

[Sample output of the program omitted]

Question 3: Emails

Your task is to write a program for handling email. The program must be composed of two classes, `Email` and `Mailbox`. Their expected functionality is as follows.

The class `Email` must have a constructor with which you can set the email topic, sender, and content. It must also have a `toString`-method, which is used to format the email accordingly for printing. In addition, the email must have the three following methods: `isNotRead()` returns `true` if the email has not yet been read and `false` otherwise; `setAsRead()` marks the email as read; and `setAsNotRead()` marks the email as not read.

The class `Mailbox` is used to handle the emails – use an `ArrayList` for storing the mails. The class `Mailbox` must have the following methods: `receive(Email mail)` adds the given email into the mailbox; `showUnreadMails()` prints all the mails that have not yet been read and marks them as read; `showMailsWithSender(String sender)` prints all the mails from the given sender (if any of the mails was marked as not read, the mail should be marked as read).

REFERENCES

[1] Rachel F Adler and Raquel Benbunan-Fich. 2012. Juggling on a high wire: Multitasking effects on performance. *International Journal of Human-Computer Studies* 70, 2 (2012), 156–168.

[2] Alireza Ahadi and Raymond Lister. 2013. Geek genes, prior knowledge, stumbling points and learning edge momentum: parts of the one elephant?. In *Proceedings of the ninth annual international ACM conference on International computing education research*. ACM, 123–128.

[3] Erik M Altmann and J Gregory Trafton. 2002. Memory for goals: An activation-based model. *Cognitive science* 26, 1 (2002), 39–83.

[4] Carole Ames. 1992. Classrooms: Goals, structures, and student motivation. *Journal of educational psychology* 84, 3 (1992), 261.

[5] Eric M Anderman and Christopher A Wolters. 2006. Goals, Values, and Affect: Influences on Student Motivation. (2006).

[6] James A Anderson, Janet Colvin, Nancy Tobler, and D Lindsay. 2003. Productivity and multi-screen displays. *CIC Report No 200351* (2003), 1–113.

[7] Christoph Aschwanden and Martha Crosby. 2006. Code scanning patterns in program comprehension. In *Proc. of the 39th Hawaii int. conf. on system sciences*.

[8] Russell Beale and William Edmondson. 2007. Multiple carets, multiple screens and multi-tasking: new behaviours with multiple computers. In *Proceedings of the 21st British HCI Group Annual Conference on People and Computers: HCI... but not as we know it-Volume 1*. British Computer Society, 55–64.

[9] Paulo Blikstein. 2011. Using learning analytics to assess students' behavior in open-ended programming tasks. In *Proceedings of the 1st international conference on learning analytics and knowledge*. ACM, 110–116.

[10] Stephanie R Boger-Mehall. 1996. Cognitive flexibility theory: Implications for teaching and teacher education. In *Society for Information Technology & Teacher Education International Conference*. Association for the Advancement of Computing in Education (AACE), 991–993.

[11] Jelmer P Borst, Niels A Taatgen, and Hedderik van Rijn. 2015. What makes interruptions disruptive?: A process-model account of the effects of the problem state bottleneck on task interruption and resumption. In *Proceedings of the 33rd annual ACM conference on human factors in computing systems*. ACM, 2971–2980.

[12] Teresa Busjahn, Roman Bednarik, Andrew Begel, Martha Crosby, James H Paterson, Carsten Schulte, Bonita Sharif, and Sascha Tamm. 2015. Eye movements in code reading: Relaxing the linear order. In *Program Comprehension (ICPC), 2015 IEEE 23rd International Conference on*. IEEE, 255–265.

[13] Guillermo Campitelli and Fernand Gobet. 2011. Deliberate Practice: Necessary But Not Sufficient. *Current Directions in Psych. Science* 20, 5 (2011), 280–285.

[14] Simon P Davies. 1991. The role of notation and knowledge representation in the determination of programming strategy: a framework for integrating models of programming behavior. *Cognitive Science* 15, 4 (1991), 547–572.

[15] Kerry Allison Delbridge. 2002. Individual differences in multi-tasking ability: Exploring a nomological network. (2002).

[16] Paul Denny, Andrew Luxton-Reilly, Michelle Craig, and Andrew Petersen. 2018. Improving Complex Task Performance Using a Sequence of Simple Practice Tasks. In *Proceedings of the 23rd Annual ACM Conference on Innovation and Technology in Computer Science Education (ITiCSE 2018)*. ACM, 4–9.

[17] Françoise Détienne. 1995. Design Strategies and Knowledge in Object-oriented Programming: Effects of Experience. *Hum.-Comput. Interact.* 10, 2 (Sept. 1995), 129–169.

[18] John Dunlosky, Katherine A Rawson, Elizabeth J Marsh, Mitchell J Nathan, and Daniel T Willingham. 2013. Improving studentsâĂŹ learning with effective learning techniques: Promising directions from cognitive and educational psychology. *Psychological Science in the Public Interest* 14, 1 (2013), 4–58.

[19] K Anders Ericsson, Ralf T Krampe, and Clemens Tesch-Römer. 1993. The role of deliberate practice in the acquisition of expert performance. *Psychological review* 100, 3 (1993), 363.

[20] Kathi Fisler. 2014. The recurring rainfall problem. In *Proceedings of the tenth annual conference on International computing education research*. ACM, 35–42.

[21] Ilenia Fronza, Alberto Sillitti, Giancarlo Succi, and Jelena Vlasenko. 2011. Understanding how novices are integrated in a team analysing their tool usage. In *Proc. of the 2011 Int. Conference on Software and Systems Process*. ACM, 204–207.

[22] Vanessa E Ghosh and Asaf Gilboa. 2014. What is a memory schema? A historical perspective on current neuroscience literature. *Neuropsych.* 53 (2014), 104–114.

[23] Petri Ihantola, Arto Vihavainen, Alireza Ahadi, Matthew Butler, Jürgen Börstler, Stephen H. Edwards, Essi Isohanni, Ari Korhonen, Andrew Petersen, Kelly Rivers, Miguel Ángel Rubio, Judy Sheard, Bronius Skupas, Jaime Spacco, Claudia Szabo, and Daniel Toll. 2015. Educational Data Mining and Learning Analytics in Programming: Literature Review and Case Studies. In *Proc. of the 2015 ITiCSE on Working Group Reports (ITICSE-WGR '15)*. ACM, New York, NY, USA, 41–63.

[24] Youn-ah Kang and John Stasko. 2008. Lightweight task/application performance using single versus multiple monitors: a comparative study. In *Proceedings of Graphics Interface 2008*. Canadian Information Processing Society, 17–24.

[25] Katja Kevic, Braden M Walters, Timothy R Shaffer, Bonita Sharif, David C Shepherd, and Thomas Fritz. 2015. Tracing software developers' eyes and interactions for change tasks. In *Proc. of the 2015 10th Joint Meeting on Foundations of Software*

Engineering. ACM, 202–213.

[26] Andrew J Ko, Brad A Myers, Michael J Coblenz, and Htet Htet Aung. 2006. An exploratory study of how developers seek, relate, and collect relevant information during software maintenance tasks. *IEEE Transactions on software engineering* 32, 12 (2006), 971–987.

[27] M Leinikka, A Vihavainen, J Lukander, and S Pakarinen. 2014. Cognitive flexibility and programming performance. In *Proc. of the Psychology of Programming Interest Group Annual Conference 2014*. 1–11.

[28] Juho Leinonen, Leo Leppänen, Petri Ihantola, and Arto Hellas. 2017. Comparison of time metrics in programming. In *Proceedings of the 2017 ACM Conference on International Computing Education Research*. ACM, 200–208.

[29] Juho Leinonen, Krista Longi, Arto Klami, and Arto Vihavainen. 2016. Automatic Inference of Programming Performance and Experience from Typing Patterns. In *Proceedings of the 47th ACM Technical Symposium on Computing Science Education (SIGCSE '16)*. ACM, 132–137.

[30] Raymond Lister, Beth Simon, Errol Thompson, Jacqueline L Whalley, and Christine Prasad. 2006. Not seeing the forest for the trees: novice programmers and the SOLO taxonomy. *ACM SIGCSE Bulletin* 38, 3 (2006), 118–122.

[31] Andrew Luxton-Reilly, Brett A. Becker, Yingjun Cao, Roger McDermott, Claudio Mirolo, Andreas Mühling, Andrew Petersen, Kate Sanders, Simon, and Jacqueline Whalley. 2017. Developing Assessments to Determine Mastery of Programming Fundamentals. In *Proceedings of the 2017 ITiCSE Conference on Working Group Reports (ITiCSE-WGR '17)*. ACM, New York, NY, USA, 47–69.

[32] Russell Mosemann and Susan Wiedenbeck. 2001. Navigation and comprehension of programs by novice programmers. In *Program Comprehension, 2001. IWPC 2001. Proceedings. 9th International Workshop on*. IEEE, 79–88.

[33] Donald A Norman. 2014. Some observations on mental models. In *Mental models*. Psychology Press, 15–22.

[34] David N Perkins, Chris Hancock, Renee Hobbs, Fay Martin, and Rebecca Simmons. 1986. Conditions of learning in novice programmers. *Journal of Educational Computing Research* 2, 1 (1986), 37–55.

[35] Jean Piaget. 1971. Biology and knowledge: An essay on the relations between organic regulations and cognitive processes. (1971).

[36] Vennila Ramalingam, Deborah LaBelle, and Susan Wiedenbeck. 2004. Self-efficacy and mental models in learning to program. In *ACM SIGCSE Bulletin*, Vol. 36. ACM, 171–175.

[37] Robert S Rist. 1989. Schema creation in programming. *Cognitive Science* 13, 3 (1989), 389–414.

[38] Otto Seppälä, Petri Ihantola, Essi Isohanni, Juha Sorva, and Arto Vihavainen. 2015. Do we know how difficult the rainfall problem is?. In *Proceedings of the 15th Koli Calling Conference on Computing Education Research*. ACM, 87–96.

[39] Lee S Shulman et al. 1968. Studies of the Inquiry Process; Inquiry Patterns of Students in Teacher-Training Programs. Final Report. (1968).

[40] Elliot Soloway. 1986. Learning to program= learning to construct mechanisms and explanations. *Commun. ACM* 29, 9 (1986), 850–858.

[41] John Sweller. 1988. Cognitive load during problem solving: Effects on learning. *Cognitive science* 12, 2 (1988), 257–285.

[42] John Sweller and Graham A Cooper. 1985. The use of worked examples as a substitute for problem solving in learning algebra. *Cognition and instruction* 2, 1 (1985), 59–89.

[43] Shelley E Taylor. 1981. Schematic bases of social information processing. *Social cognition* (1981), 89–134.

[44] Alexey Tregubov, Barry Boehm, Natalia Rodchenko, and Jo Ann Lane. 2017. Impact of task switching and work interruptions on software development processes. In *Proceedings of the 2017 International Conference on Software and System Process*. ACM, 134–138.

[45] Bogdan Vasilescu, Kelly Blincoe, Qi Xuan, Casey Casalnuovo, Daniela Damian, Premkumar Devanbu, and Vladimir Filkov. 2016. The sky is not the limit: multitasking across github projects. In *Software Engineering (ICSE), 2016 IEEE/ACM 38th International Conference on*. IEEE, 994–1005.

[46] Arto Vihavainen, Jonne Airaksinen, and Christopher Watson. 2014. A systematic review of approaches for teaching introductory programming and their influence on success. In *Proceedings of the tenth annual conference on International computing education research*. ACM, 19–26.

[47] Arto Vihavainen, Juha Helminen, and Petri Ihantola. 2014. How novices tackle their first lines of code in an ide: Analysis of programming session traces. In *Proceedings of the 14th Koli Calling International Conference on Computing Education Research*. ACM, 109–116.

[48] Arto Vihavainen, Matti Luukkainen, and Jaakko Kurhila. 2012. Multi-faceted Support for MOOC in Programming. In *Proc. of the 13th Annual Conf. on Information Technology Education (SIGITE '12)*. ACM, New York, NY, USA, 171–176.

[49] Arto Vihavainen, Thomas Vikberg, Matti Luukkainen, and Martin Pärtel. 2013. Scaffolding Students' Learning Using Test My Code. In *Proceedings of the 18th ACM Conference on Innovation and Technology in Computer Science Education (ITiCSE '13)*. ACM, New York, NY, USA, 117–122.

[50] Leon E Winslow. 1996. Programming pedagogy - a psychological overview. *ACM Sigcse Bulletin* 28, 3 (1996), 17–22.

Answering the Correct Question

Michelle Craig
University of Toronto
mcraig@cs.toronto.edu

Andrew Petersen
University of Toronto Mississauga
andrew.petersen@utoronto.ca

Jennifer Campbell
University of Toronto
campbell@cs.toronto.edu

ABSTRACT

The first step in writing code is understanding the problem to be solved. When this step is not properly completed, students can waste time developing a solution to the wrong problem. Arguably, this tendency is exacerbated by online automatically-tested code submission systems where students work in isolation and sometimes appear to focus more on passing the instructor testcases than on understanding the problem or its solution. We report on an randomized A/B test with 831 CS1 students using an online submission system. Students in the control group wrote small Python functions based on a written description including a docstring with one example. Before the treatment-group students solved the same exercise, they were given a description of the same functions and were asked to provide the corresponding output for three sets of input. We hypothesized that this would decrease the time and attempts required to correctly write the code because students in the treatment group would not waste time on an incorrectly-conceived problem. We found support for this hypothesis on one of the problems but not on the other, and we offer some suggestions as to how this might be explained.

CCS CONCEPTS

• **Social and professional topics** → *Computer science education*;

KEYWORDS

novice programming, CS1, tracing, test cases

ACM Reference Format:
Michelle Craig, Andrew Petersen, and Jennifer Campbell. 2019. Answering the Correct Question. In *ACM Global Computing Education Conference 2019 (CompEd '19), May 17–19, 2019, Chengdu,Sichuan, China.* ACM, New York, NY, USA, 6 pages. https://doi.org/10.1145/3300115.3309529

1 INTRODUCTION

In a study specifically focused on automated-assessment tools, Prather et al. [12] conduct think-aloud observations of 31 CS1 students attempting to solve a 35-minute programming exercise in an online programming environment. They report that the most common problem encountered by the 11 students who did not successfully complete the exercise was the students' "failure to build a correct conceptual model of the problem." They argue that, "This

breakdown shows perhaps the single greatest weakness in modern [Automated Assessment Tools]: the tools merely present the problem ... there are no measures between viewing the problem and submitting source code to ensure that the student understands what they're being asked to do."

In our CS1 course, we rely heavily on automated assessment tools. Inspired by Prather et al.'s observations, we considered our own questions and wondered how many students struggle with an incorrect conceptual model of the problems that we ask them to solve. Could we provide better feedback to students so that they could confirm that they had the correct conceptual model before they started to write code to implement a solution? With this research question in mind, we designed a controlled experiment where students were randomly selected to receive a small intervention on specific programming questions.

2 BACKGROUND AND RELATED WORK

Our CS1 approach involves teaching students a recipe for designing functions, inspired by the How to Design Programs (HTDP) work of Felleisen et al. [7]. We explicitly request that students construct (and include in the function's documentation) an example of calling the function that includes the corresponding output. These examples are written in the syntax of Python's doctest, and later in the term, students discover that the tests can be automatically executed. This step precedes writing code to implement the solution. Like Felleisen, we included this step in our recipe because we believed that crafting and documenting an example (a test case), would help students understand the problem they were being asked to solve.

This approach agrees with work on problem solving performed by Loksa et al. [10], who argue for the explicit inclusion of problem solving instruction in automated tools for teaching coding. Our example construction step corresponds to the first stage in Loksa's six-stage framework: *reinterpreting the problem prompt*. Loksa explains that in this stage programmers must "understand, interpret and clarify" the problem description to form a cognitive representation of the problem on which to base their steps toward finding a solution. It is during this stage that Prather's students struggle [12].

In a qualitative study of students learning using HTDP [4], Castro and Fisler observe that students do not see testing as part of their design process. Other instructors have advocated for writing tests first based on the Test-Driven Development movement in industry [2]. Some educators have even argued that instructing novices should begin from day one by introducing testing [8]. Both Spacco [13] and Buffardi [3] investigate students using online submission systems that provide opportunities for students to submit tests before writing code. Both researchers report that students are reluctant to write and submit tests unless they are incentivised to do so. Simply providing the mechanism and encouraging students to follow test-driven development is not enough motivation.

Karavirta, Korhonen and Malmi [9] investigated resubmissions in an automated-assessment system. They used clustering algorithms to group students based on numbers of resubmissions and total marks earned in the system. They observe a wide spread in the numbers of submissions per student. After removing outliers, they further divide the remaining students by submission pattern, but the subgroups are indistinguishable with respect to final exam performance. Karavirta concludes that in one of these groups students resubmit their work more carelessly than the others and suggests that instructors should consider limiting resubmission attempts or find an "alternative to guide students" by "improving the feedback to ... reduce inefficient reiteration."

Basu et al. [1] report on an automated tool called OK used in a large Python CS1 offering. When students first receive an online program to solve, the automatically-applied test cases are "locked". The OK tool presents test-case inputs and in order to "unlock" the tests and have them applied in the assessment of their solution, the student must demonstrate their understanding of the expected behaviour of the solution by either answering a related conceptual question or providing the correct test output. If the output provided by the student is incorrect or missing, the test remains locked and students cannot see the results of that testcase. The students are not required to unlock the tests before starting the coding, but the hope is that the system would help students to better understand the problem specification before they begin their implementation. Analyzing OK use in a 1300-student course, Basu reports that a large majority (between 70 and 99%) of the students are unlocking the test cases before they start coding. Basu also counts the related posts on the course discussion boards, and reports that in spite of a 27% increase in student submission numbers, the numbers of related posts decreased. He notes that the remaining questions appear to be primarily from students struggling with test-case unlocking rather than from students attempting to implement a solution to the wrong problem. Basu also evaluates the effectiveness of the system through a student survey, but does not directly examine the effects on the code submissions themselves. In other words, Basu's system may save time for instructors and students by discouraging students from advancing to the coding stage with a conceptual misunderstanding of the problem, but Basu doesn't directly measure the time students take on the actual coding process or the number of submissions they make.

3 METHODOLOGY

Our study was conducted in a CS1 course at a research-intensive North American public university. Our CS1 is taught as a flipped class to over 2000 students across three semesters each year. We also teach about 400 students in an online format, with only the final exam taking place on campus. Some students who enrol in CS1 intend to major in Computer Science (CS), while others take the course to fulfill a requirement for a non-CS program or simply as an elective. Our study takes place during the Fall semester, in which students planning to study CS typically account for up to half of the course enrolment.

Students use an online tool [14] to prepare for lecture by watching videos and completing multiple-choice and short-answer coding questions worth 5% of their course grade. Students use the same

Figure 1: Overdue Books Question

A library charges overdue fees for a borrowed book using the following fee schedule:

- less than 4 days late: 1 dollar per day
- 4 to 6 days late: 2 dollars per day (for all days, including the first 3 days)
- more than 6 days late: 3 dollars per day (for all days, including the first 6 days)

Borrowers of books are in one of these age groups: CHILD, ADULT, or SENIOR. A CHILD gets charged only half of the fees and a SENIOR gets charged only one quarter of the fees. An ADULT pays the full fee. Complete the following function according to the description above and the docstring below.

```python
CHILD = 'child'
ADULT = 'adult'
SENIOR = 'senior'

def overdue_fees(days_late: int, age_group: str) -> float:
    """Return the fees for a book that is days_late days late
    for a borrower in the age group age_group.

    >>> overdue_fees(2, SENIOR) # 2 days late, SENIOR borrower
    0.5
    >>> overdue_fees(5, ADULT) # 5 days late, ADULT borrower
    10.0
    """
```

Students receiving the intervention were presented with these three additional questions before writing the code.

(1) What should the function call overdue_fees(9, CHILD) return?

(2) What should the function call overdue_fees(4, ADULT) return?

(3) What should the function call overdue_fees(7, SENIOR) return?

tool to complete summative weekly exercises, worth 9% of the course mark, consisting of both multiple-choice and slightly larger code-writing tasks, such as implementing function bodies that are 5-10 lines long. Each week there are approximately ten summative exercises, most of which are reused from offering to offering. In addition to the exercises, there are three larger programming assignments, a midterm test, and a final exam.

For this study, we selected two programming tasks from one of the summative weekly exercises that had enough complexity that students may not fully understand the question and may attempt to solve the wrong question. One question involves implementing a function requiring a loop with conditional statements and the other involves implementing a function with a multi-branch conditional statement. Figures 1 and 2 show the exact wording of the questions used in the study.

We invited all students enrolled in our Fall 2018 offering of CS1 (n=1134) to participate in the study, and 71% consented (n=831). We randomly assigned all students to two treatment groups and a subset of those both gave consent and completed the coursework (group one n=372 and group two n=365). In each case, one treatment group received only the code-writing question and the second group saw the three new testcase-output questions before the code-writing

Figure 2: Password Validity Question

Complete the following function according to its docstring. Hint: try using boolean variables in your solution.

```
def check_password(passwd: str) -> bool:
    """A strong password has a length greater than
    or equal to 6, contains at least one lowercase letter,
    at least one uppercase letter, and at least one digit.
    Return True if and only if passwd is considered strong.

    >>> check_password('I<3csc108')
    True
    """
```

Students receiving the intervention were asked these three additional questions before they answered the coding question.

(1) According to the description above, what should the function call check_password('aA9bB') return?
(2) According to the description above, what should the function call check_password('a9_R99') return?
(3) According to the description above, what should the function call check_password('pkJzRoTTuJ') return?

Figure 3: Exercise structure by treatment group

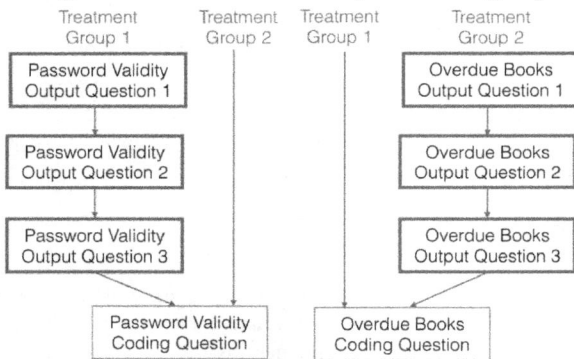

question. (See Figure 3). With this study design, each student is a member of the treatment group for one question and the control group for another. This design allowed all students to be asked the same number of questions to earn their grade. In addition, if the extra testcase questions benefit students, all students have the opportunity to benefit from them, since they were assigned testcase-output questions leading up to one of two coding questions.

For each question in the online tool, students can submit multiple attempts until they get the question correct. Therefore, a higher number of attempts on a question indicates poorer performance. Our research question considers whether we can provide better feedback to students before they attempt the problem to confirm that they have the correct model of the question. We hypothesize that students in the treatment group, which receives the three testcase-output questions, will take fewer attempts on the corresponding code-writing question.

Table 1: Submission counts and time spent on Overdue Books and Password Validity questions.

	Submissions		Time Spent (seconds)	
	Median	Mean	Median	Mean
Overdue Books:				
Control	3	4.27	79.5	6630
Treatment	3	3.80	51.2	6310
Password Validity:				
Control	5	8.27	361	12300
Treatment	5	9.35	464	19900

4 RESULTS

In this section, we examine the student submissions to the Overdue Books and Password Validity problems to determine if there is a noticeable difference between the behaviour of students in the control and treatment groups. The treatment group was provided with three testcase-output questions (short-answer questions that asked what output would be generated for a given input); the control group received no preparatory material before encountering the coding question. We first look at the number of submissions to each problem and time elapsed and then take a closer look at student performance on the testcases used to evaluate the coding questions.

4.1 Submission Counts

We investigated both the full submission data and filtered data where some students were removed. For the filtered data set, we removed all students (from the entire set) who completed the control question with a single correct attempt. We did so because, in past reviews of data produced by this tool, we had noticed issues with students who submitted correct submissions to coding problems on their first attempt. In some cases, the students were working outside of the online tool. In other cases, the students were obtaining answers to the questions from peers or other sources. Removing the students who submitted the control with a single, correct submission removes many of those students; it may also remove some very strong students, and we expect those students would not benefit as much from the treatment.

Table 1 provides both the submission counts and time elapsed for the full (not filtered) dataset for both coding questions studied. The dataset contains a total of 737 students (372 in one group and 365 in the other). The submission count refers to the total number of submissions made to each problem by a student. The elapsed time is calculated by subtracting the submission of the first correct submission from the time of the initial submission. As a result, it can be 0 if a student solves the problem with one submission; students who never correctly solved the problem are omitted from the elapsed time calculation.

The distributions of both submission counts and time elapsed are not normal (they had notable long tails), so we check for significance using Kruskal-Wallis H-tests (one-way ANOVA on ranks). The submission counts are not significantly different between the control and treatment groups for either the Overdue Books problem ($H(2)=0.55$, $p=0.46$) or Password Validity problem ($H(2)=0.85$, $p=0.36$). Similarly, the times elapsed are not significantly different

Table 2: Submission counts and time spent on Overdue Books and Password Validity questions after removing students with a single submission to the control problem.

	Submissions		Time Spent (seconds)	
	Median	Mean	Median	Mean
Overdue Books:				
Control	4	5.42	176	8977
Treatment	3	3.98	60	7066
Password Validity:				
Control	6	9.37	574	14214
Treatment	6	10.21	623	20537

Table 3: Submission counts on Testcase-Output Questions.

Overdue Books

Description	Median	Mean
child - 9 days	1	1.86
adult - 4 days	2	1.94
senior - 7 days	1	1.43

Password Validity

Description	Median	Mean
invalid - too short	1	1.28
valid	1	1.11
invalid - missing digit	1	1.07

Table 4: Rates at which testcases for the Overdue Books and Password Validity questions were failed. * indicates that the test was covered by a short answer question.

	Percent Incorrect	
Description	Control	Treatment
Overdue Books:		
*Adult, 3 days late	13.8	13.7
Adult, 5 days late	26.6	18.4
Adult, 7 days late	30.1	21.7
Child, 2 days late	17.1	18.4
Child, 5 days late	30.0	24.4
*Child, 7 days late	35.0	26.0
Senior, 3 days late	24.2	26.3
Senior, 5 days late	37.3	31.1
*Senior, 7 days late	40.3	34.1
Password Validity:		
*Too short	17.7	18.2
Empty string	16.3	20.8
*Legal, length 6	39.9	42.0
Legal, length 7	39.0	42.2
*Illegal, missing digit	42.2	40.1
Illegal, missing uppercase	41.5	39.4
Illegal, missing lowercase	41.4	38.7

between the two groups (H(2)=2.87, p=0.09 and H(2)=1.89, p=0.17). We also ran the Mann-Whitney U-test to determine if the mean submission counts were significantly different and found no difference in either (U=69993, p=0.23 and U=70544, p=0.18). We did not run the Mann-Whitney U-test on time elapsed, since the means were heavily impacted by long, multi-day breaks taken by some students. For this same reason, we report medians (in addition to means) in Table 1.

Table 2 provides both the submission counts and time elapsed for the filtered dataset. The filtered dataset contains 592 participants: 275 in one group and 317 in the other. Again, the distributions were not normal, so we use Kruskal-Wallis H-tests to test if the differences are significant. In this dataset, the difference in submissions in the Overdue Books problem is significant (H(2)=31.3, p<0.001), but the differences in the Password Validity problem (H(2)=0.36, p=0.55) remain not significant. We see the same pattern when looking at times elapsed (H(2)=44.77, p<0.001 for Overdue Books and H(2)=0.01, p=0.92 for Password Validity). Similarly, Mann-Whitney U-tests comparing the mean submission counts found a significant difference in the Overdue Books problem (U=55044, p<0.001) but not the Password Validity problem (U=42353, p=0.72).

In Table 3 we provide the average number of submissions made on the testcase-output questions by the students receiving the treatment. For all but one question, the median is one attempt. This means that most students predict the correct output of the test case on the first try. On average, the overdue books testcase-output questions take more attempts than the password ones. Because the students supply an answer by typing into a textbox, to answer the

testcase-output questions, they need to realize that the answer is either "True" or "False". A few students (5) made an error with the case of the answer, but once they correctly answer the first question, they have sorted this out. If they make a mistake on the second or third testcase-output question, they should immediately know the correct output – even if they don't understand why. Nobody should be taking more than two attempts. Perhaps the weaker students who are the very ones who might most benefit from the exercise are not actually thinking carefully about the function, but instead just providing the only remaining boolean answer.

The first two Overdue books testcase-output questions have means of almost 2. Students are spending more time on these. The question asking them to calculate the fine for an adult with a book overdue 4 days (a boundary condition on the number of days) was the most challenging, in terms of both median and mean submissions required to solve the problem, which suggests that calculating the fine is the more challenging part of the problem and also a task that students were able to practice with the provided problems.

4.2 Testcase Analysis

Table 4 contains the testcases for the two questions that were examined. We calculated the rate at which each testcase was failed *assuming at least one testcase passed*. This requirement removes code that failed with a syntactic or runtime error, as well as empty or trivial solutions. For the overdue books problem, we see that both groups spend similar amounts of submissions handling the different classes of person (adult, child, or senior at the base rate) but the treatment group spends relatively less time calculating the charges accrued per day. The short answer questions we provided to the treatment group asked them to consider both different classes of person as well as different numbers of days late.

For the password validity problem, where the control group did better in terms of number of submissions, we see that the control group spent relatively less time handling correct passwords but relatively more time dealing with incorrect passwords. The short answer questions provided covered both valid and invalid passwords, and none of the problems were found to be difficult. (Most students got the question correct in one try.) So while it's possible that the questions primed students to think about what might make a password invalid, we have no evidence that the questions were particularly helpful in preparing students to solve the problem.

5 DISCUSSION

5.1 Threats to validity

Students are not necessarily working solely within the tool. Many do write their code completely within the submission environment, so the number of submissions captures their every attempt to solve the problem. However, in the course students are also expected to complete work (their larger programming assignments) in a separate IDE (Wing101 IDE) and are taught to use its debugger. It is quite likely that some students write their solutions to the weekly exercises in Wing101, where they can run the code repeatedly and test on their own. Then, when they feel that have a potential solution, they copy and paste it into the submission system, perhaps making further changes when the automated tests report a failure.

In our analysis in Section 4.1, we removed students who solved their "control" problem with a single submission. The primary motivation for this change is to remove students who are simply pasting in solutions obtained from some other source, but this also will remove some – but not all – students who work offline. We don't have a good sense of the frequency of this behaviour, and while it impacts the absolute numbers (submission counts and times), it should not affect the conclusions since the students were assigned to treatment groups at random. As a result, there is no reason to suspect that one group would be more affected than the other by students working offline. However, the removal of these students had a secondary impact of removing high-performing students from consideration. This should be examined in a future study, both to verify that the result we have demonstrated holds in a different context and also to explore the impact of this intervention on students of varying experience and ability levels.

5.2 Students seeking help

One of the main claims of the work of Basu [1] on the OK system was the fact that having the students consider the test cases decreased instructor workload as measured by the number of discussion board posts on their class Piazza forum. We also use Piazza, but unlike Basu, who reports approximately 15 posts on each of the two topics before the intervention, we only had one and three posts on each of our questions in the previous course offering. This suggests that perhaps we chose too simple a problem on which to apply this intervention. In comparison to the assignment problems on which Basu reports, the small functions completed for our weekly exercises have relatively simple specifications. Additionally, our discussion board was shared with students in the control group

and the intervention group and participant identities were anonymous to the researchers who were therefore unable to identify the treatment group of any Piazza contributors.

5.3 Testcase output questions may help develop algorithms

In addition to gaining clarity on the problem to be solved, another potential benefit of having students provide testcase output is that it can help students develop an algorithm to use to solve the problem. For example, for the Overdue Books problem, to determine the testcase output given a particular input, students must perform the same calculations that they need to implement. They are implementing an algorithm on paper or in their minds that mirrors what they need to implement in order to solve the problem.

For the Password Validity problem, we suggest: "Hint: try using boolean variables in your solution." When evaluating a testcase involving a short candidate password, it is unlikely that students write down whether they have encountered the three required types of characters (uppercase letter, lowercase letter, and digit). Students can most likely keep track of that information in their heads and they may not make the connection between having that sort of a checklist and the hint suggesting they use Boolean variables in their implementation. If the Password Validity problem instead required four uppercase letters, six lowercase letters, five digits and minimum length of 20, there would be more information to remember and the students would be more likely to take notes as they consider the example function calls. Those notes would serve as hints for the local variables that might be needed and would translate more directly to the code to be implemented. Although testcase-output questions may provide clarity on the problem to be solved, in the case of the original Password Validity problem, the testcase questions may not help students to develop an algorithm for solving the problem. We suspect that testcase problems in which there are parallels between the algorithm used to determine the testcase output and the algorithm used to solve the problem, will be of greater benefit to students.

5.4 Understanding versus coding difficulty

We suspect that students find the code for the Password Validity problem to be more challenging to write. We reviewed the submissions for both problems to understand where students were encountering difficulty. In the Overdue Books problem, we found that students quickly adopted the use of if and else statements, and we did not see evidence that they had difficulty writing the numerical expression required to calculate the fines. However, they made frequent changes to the control structure of their solutions to make sure that the correct paths were implemented. In contrast, the student submissions to the Password Validity problem used more (and more difficult) structures: instead of relying on Python's standard string methods to test the entire password, many students tracked state through a for loop that examined each character individually. Loops were newly introduced, so students had less practice with them and appeared to struggle both with tracking state through the loop and in using string methods to check for uppercase and lowercase characters. This problem was more challenging to code, for our students, than it was to understand. This suggests that some problems are more amenable to this treatment than others; these questions may be helpful to focus student attention on border cases (or potential implementations) and less helpful when the code itself is the challenge.

5.5 When to develop, check, and mark testcases

In our intervention, we asked students to provide the output for instructor-developed testcases, but there are a wide range of possible approaches, including having students develop testcases themselves [5, 6]. For each student- or instructor-developed testcase, the testcase could also optionally be checked for correctness (automatically or by a human) and optionally counted towards a student's grade. Asking students to develop, determine the output of, and check the correctness of testcases is time consuming, so we need to identify the places where this extra work is most beneficial.

In our flipped classroom, where students work on not-for-credit worksheets during lecture, we sometimes ask students to fill in a docstring's example output before implementing the corresponding function. We suggest to students that they compare answers with their neighbouring classmates, which helps them to check their testcase output before they move on to solving the more complex problem. In our online CS1 offering, we also ask students to complete some docstring examples before solving the function, but that work is not corrected or counted towards students' grades. Students might skip the testcase questions with no apparent consequences or answer the testcase questions incorrectly, but they may then go on to solve the wrong problem. In future, we can explore whether students are completing the docstring examples in those online exercises and whether completing them improves performance. If providing the testcase output is beneficial, we could make the testcases separate questions, so students are more likely to solve them. However, if providing testcase output does not help for particular types of problems, we could also remove the testcases part of the problem entirely.

5.6 The difficulty of syntax

While removing submissions that failed to pass any testcase, we saw that we were consistently removing about 58% of submissions. These rates are relatively high, providing support for previous work suggesting that syntax is non-trivial for novices [11]. In case the high rate of syntax errors was hiding any benefits students might obtain from the preparatory short answer questions, we re-examined the submission counts of all problems after removing submissions with syntactic errors but found no change in any of the statistical results.

6 CONCLUSIONS

In our experiment, we found that having students provide output for instructor-provided testcases helped with one coding problem but not with the other. Closer analysis of the problems revealed that students find both problems challenging but that the particular challenges encountered are not the same. For one coding problem, the challenge is understanding the requirements of the problem and clarifying the boundary conditions. For this problem, the intervention was successful at reducing the number of submissions. The challenges in solving the second coding problem are not centred

on understanding what the function should do, but rather on how to write code for the task. Students quickly supplied the expected function output, but struggled to write code to do the same task.

Given that student and instructor time is limited, adding pre-coding testcases questions should be done selectively to problems where we expect students will get the most benefit. Instructors using automated testing tools should not only consider problems with high submission rates, but consider which of these high submission rates are due to students misunderstanding the problem itself. If individual testcase data is available, instructors could look at which testcases students are most often failing and create pre-coding testcase-output questions accordingly. In addition, problems where testcase-output questions can help students discover an algorithm to use are also good candidates for pre-coding testcases.

REFERENCES

[1] Soumya Basu, Albert Wu, Brian Hou, and John DeNero. 2015. Problems Before Solutions: Automated Problem Clarification at Scale. In *Proceedings of the Second (2015) ACM Conference on Learning @ Scale (L@S '15)*. ACM, New York, NY, USA, 205–213. https://doi.org/10.1145/2724660.2724679
[2] Beck. 2002. *Test Driven Development: By Example*. Addison-Wesley Longman Publishing Co., Inc., Boston, MA, USA.
[3] Kevin Buffardi and Stephen H. Edwards. 2014. A Formative Study of Influences on Student Testing Behaviors. In *Proceedings of the 45th ACM Technical Symposium on Computer Science Education (SIGCSE '14)*. ACM, New York, NY, USA, 597–602. https://doi.org/10.1145/2538862.2538982
[4] Francisco Enrique Vicente Castro and Kathi Fisler. 2017. Designing a Multi-faceted SOLO Taxonomy to Track Program Design Skills Through an Entire Course. In *Proceedings of the 17th Koli Calling International Conference on Computing Education Research (Koli Calling '17)*. ACM, New York, NY, USA, 10–19. https://doi.org/10.1145/3141880.3141891
[5] Stephen H. Edwards. 2003. Rethinking Computer Science Education from a Test-first Perspective. In *Companion of the 18th Annual ACM SIGPLAN Conference on Object-oriented Programming, Systems, Languages, and Applications (OOPSLA '03)*. ACM, New York, NY, USA, 148–155. https://doi.org/10.1145/949344.949390
[6] Stephen H. Edwards and Manuel A. Pérez-Quiñones. 2007. Experiences Using Test-driven Development with an Automated Grader. *J. Comput. Sci. Coll.* 22, 3 (Jan. 2007), 44–50. http://dl.acm.org/citation.cfm?id=1181849.1181855
[7] Matthias Felleisen, Robert Bruce Findler, Matthew Flatt, and Shriram Krishnamurthi. 2001. *How to Design Programs: An Introduction to Programming and Computing*. MIT Press, Cambridge, MA, USA.
[8] David S. Janzen and Hossein Saiedian. 2006. Test-driven Learning: Intrinsic Integration of Testing into the CS/SE Curriculum. *SIGCSE Bull.* 38, 1 (March 2006), 254–258. https://doi.org/10.1145/1124706.1121419
[9] Ville Karavirta, Ari Korhonen, and Lauri Malmi. 2006. On the use of resubmissions in automatic assessment systems. *Computer Science Education* 16, 3 (2006), 229–240. https://doi.org/10.1080/08993400600912426
[10] Dastyni Loksa, Andrew J. Ko, Will Jernigan, Alannah Oleson, Christopher J. Mendez, and Margaret M. Burnett. 2016. Programming, Problem Solving, and Self-Awareness: Effects of Explicit Guidance. In *Proceedings of the 2016 CHI Conference on Human Factors in Computing Systems (CHI '16)*. ACM, New York, NY, USA, 1449–1461. https://doi.org/10.1145/2858036.2858252
[11] Andrew Luxton-Reilly, Brett A. Becker, Yingjun Cao, Roger McDermott, Claudio Mirolo, Andreas Mühling, Andrew Petersen, Kate Sanders, Simon, and Jacqueline Whalley. 2017. Developing Assessments to Determine Mastery of Programming Fundamentals. In *Proceedings of the 2017 ITiCSE Conference on Working Group Reports (ITiCSE-WGR '17)*. ACM, New York, NY, USA, 47–69. https://doi.org/10.1145/3174781.3174784
[12] James Prather, Raymond Pettit, Kayla McMurry, Alani Peters, John Homer, and Maxine Cohen. 2018. Metacognitive Difficulties Faced by Novice Programmers in Automated Assessment Tools. In *Proceedings of the 2018 ACM Conference on International Computing Education Research (ICER '18)*. ACM, New York, NY, USA, 41–50. https://doi.org/10.1145/3230977.3230981
[13] Jaime Spacco and William Pugh. 2006. Helping Students Appreciate Test-driven Development (TDD). In *Companion to the 21st ACM SIGPLAN Symposium on Object-oriented Programming Systems, Languages, and Applications (OOPSLA '06)*. ACM, New York, NY, USA, 907–913. https://doi.org/10.1145/1176617.1176743
[14] Daniel Zingaro, Yuliya Cherenkova, Olessia Karpova, and Andrew Petersen. 2013. Facilitating Code-writing in PI Classes. In *Proceeding of the 44th ACM Technical Symposium on Computer Science Education (SIGCSE '13)*. 585–590.

Translation from Problem to Code in Seven Steps

Andrew D. Hilton
Duke University
Durham, NC, United States
adhilton@ee.duke.edu

Genevieve M. Lipp
Duke University
Durham, NC, United States
genevieve.lipp@duke.edu

Susan H. Rodger
Duke University
Durham, NC, United States
rodger@cs.duke.edu

ABSTRACT

Students in introductory programming courses struggle with how to turn a problem statement into code. We introduce a teaching technique, "The Seven Steps," that provides structure and guidance on how to approach a problem. The first four steps focus on devising an algorithm in English, then the remaining steps are to translate that algorithm to code, test the algorithm, and debug failed test cases. This approach not only gives students a way to solve problems, but also ideas for what to do if they get stuck during the process. Furthermore, it provides a way for instructors to work examples in class that focus on the process of devising the code—instructors can show *how to come up with the code*, rather than just showing an example. We describe our experience with this technique in several introductory programming courses—both in the classroom and online.

CCS CONCEPTS

• **Social and professional topics** → **CS1**.

KEYWORDS

CS1, introductory programming, from problem to code, metacognition, computational thinking

ACM Reference Format:
Andrew D. Hilton, Genevieve M. Lipp, and Susan H. Rodger. 2019. Translation from Problem to Code in Seven Steps. In *ACM Global Computing Education Conference 2019 (CompEd '19), May 17–19, 2019, Chengdu,Sichuan, China.* ACM, New York, NY, USA, 7 pages. https://doi.org/10.1145/3300115.3309508

1 INTRODUCTION

Novice programmers often struggle to take a problem statement and turn it into working code. This struggle arises from needing to both devise an algorithm to solve a class of problems, as well as to turn that algorithm into working code. This struggle is seen in a multi-national ITiCSE working group study [11] that showed students do not know how to program at the conclusion of an introductory programming course. Their study collected data on over 200 students from four institutions in which the average student score was 21%. Many students struggled to write any code at all. They were stuck on the algorithm design. Another multi-national

ITiCSE working group study [9] showed that some students in introductory courses may have a fragile grasp of the skills needed to problem solve. In this study they tested students on predicting the outcome of short code segments and on completing near-complete code from a small set of possibilities. Many students were weak at these tasks, especially the latter.

Some approaches to teaching programming instruct students to first devise an algorithm, and then write code. They may have several steps in their approach with the algorithm as only one of those steps [16, 19]. However, devising an appropriate algorithm is the more difficult part of the programming process. Students should not only be told *to* devise an algorithm, but also be instructed in *how to* devise an algorithm. In this paper, we present *The Seven Steps*—the approach we teach our students to devise and implement an algorithm. This process, which we describe in Section 3, not only describes how to develop an algorithm and turn it into code, but also gives students strategies for when they are stuck on a particular step. We use this approach with small problems in introductory programming courses. For larger problems, the problem could be broken down into components and our approach applied to each component.

The Seven Steps forms not only a way for students to work problems, but also a way for instructors to present material. Rather than showing students example code (which students are often prone to try to memorize), an instructor teaching with The Seven Steps can present an example of *how to come up with* a piece of code. The instructor can work through The Seven Steps, starting from a problem statement, and follow the steps to produce working code. In such an approach, students can understand the logical thinking that led to the algorithm and ultimately code to solve the example problem. Such an approach takes more instructional time than simply showing students working code but in our experience has far better results.

In the remainder of this experience report, we describe related work (Section 2), then describe The Seven Steps (Section 3), including some examples of its use. In Section 4 we discuss its usage in our in-person courses at Duke University, as well as in two online Coursera specializations. In Section 5 we evaluate The Seven Steps based on student anecdotes, as well as an end-of-semester survey. Finally, we conclude in Section 6.

2 BACKGROUND AND RELATED WORK

There are many practices to help novice programmers succeed in learning to program. Some practices provide support to learners, such as Peer Instruction [3] and Pair Programming [12, 20]. Some practices focus on the subject matter of the material as a motivating factor, such as Media Computation [5]. For example, Porter and Simon [15] showed that combining Peer Instruction, Pair Programming, and Media Computation resulted in a 31% improvement in

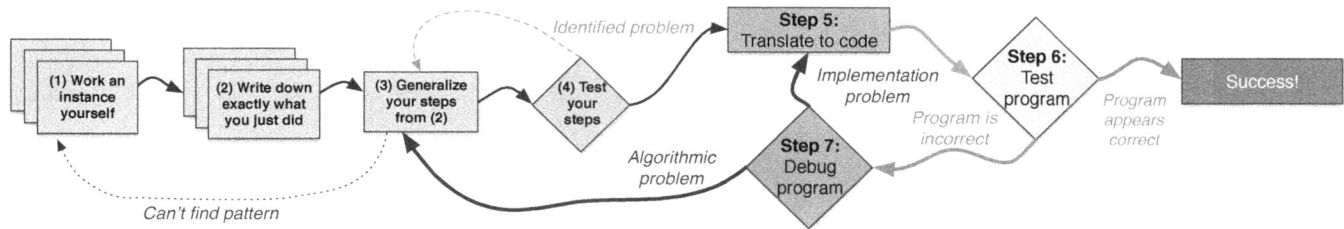

Figure 1: Diagram of The Seven Steps

retention of students in their CS1 course. Some practices provide a programming environment that aids the programmer in creating the code, such as the drag-and-drop interface in Alice [18] and Scratch [14]. Some practices focus on providing an environment for debugging the code, such as the program visualization tool Python Tutor [4]. All of these practices help the novice programmer in some way, but not in understanding how to develop an algorithm from a problem statement.

Problem solving in the context of introductory programming can be defined in many ways, and we list four such ways. First, computational thinking [21] includes the core concepts of abstraction, algorithmic thinking, decomposition, and generalization and pattern recognition—different meanings of it were discussed in two workshops [7, 8]. Second, Problem-Based Learning (PBL) was adapted to computer programming [13] with group work PBL sessions that involved seven steps: 1) examination of the case, 2) identification of problem, 3) brainstorming, 4) sketching explanatory model, 5) establishing learning goals, 6) independent studying, and 7) discussion. Third, the ITiCSE Working group [11] defined problem solving as the learning objectives for their assessment in a five-step process: 1) abstract the problem from its description, 2) generate sub-problems, 3) transform sub-problems into sub-solutions, 4) re-compose, and 5) evaluate and iterate. These three methods are very abstract. We were interested in defining concrete steps that students could more easily follow.

A fourth approach to problem solving in introductory programming is metacognition, being aware of and understanding one's own thought processes. In [10] the authors give explicit instructions on problem solving in stages that involve reinterpreting the problem, searching for similar solutions, evaluating those solutions and then implementing a solution. Our approach is different in that four of our seven steps focus on working out an algorithm with a sequence of small problems solvable by hand.

3 THE SEVEN STEPS

Because many students do not have much experience thinking about how they solve problems (they just do), we introduce The Seven Steps, shown in Figure 1 to give them a framework for thinking about solving a programming problem. Here is a summary of the explanation we give students:

Step 1: Work an example yourself. The first step is to work an example yourself by hand. If you cannot yet do that, it means either that you need to further specify the problem or that you need domain knowledge.

Step 2: Write down exactly what you just did. The next step is to write down the details of how you worked the problem by hand in Step 1. If you get stuck on this step because you "just knew it," you should try a more complex example that you cannot just solve by inspection.

Step 3: Generalize. Once you have worked at least one example by hand and written down the process, you can begin to generalize. Why did you do something a certain number of times? Where did you start? When did you stop? It is often necessary to have worked several examples by hand to generalize well. In fact, if you have trouble with this step, you should repeat Steps 1 and 2 on different instances of the problem.

Step 4: Test your algorithm. Now that you have a draft of a generalized algorithm, apply it to a new instance of the problem, and see if you get the correct answer. This is essential for catching generalization mistakes. Finding mistakes before translating to code avoids wasting time. You can go back to Step 3 if you identify a generalization mistake.

Step 5: Translate to code. Steps 1–4 can be done with pencil and paper and are independent of language. For Step 5, you need to know the syntax of a language and how to translate parts of the algorithm, such as counting or decision-making constructs. It is often helpful to start with your algorithm steps as comments before you write any code. If any of the lines in your algorithm do not immediately translate into one or two lines of code, they should be abstracted out into their own function: make a good name for the function, call it here, and make yourself a note about what it does. After you finish translating this algorithm, go implement that function. That function is itself a programming problem (for which you wrote the problem statement), so use The Seven Steps.

Step 6: Test. Another round of testing is important because you could have a correct algorithm and still have made mistakes in the implementation in code. You also can have the computer run many more test cases more quickly than you can do them by hand. Testing is the act of finding bugs, and you want to find as many as you can by writing a robust set of test cases. While it is not possible to know for certain that your program is correct, you can become more and more certain with good testing.

Step 7: Debug. Debugging is the act of fixing bugs you identified in the testing stage. Once you've identified a problem, you need to figure out if the issue is with the algorithm or code implementation and go back to Step 3 or Step 5, respectively. We teach debugging by the scientific method, rather than ad hoc, as many students would do otherwise.

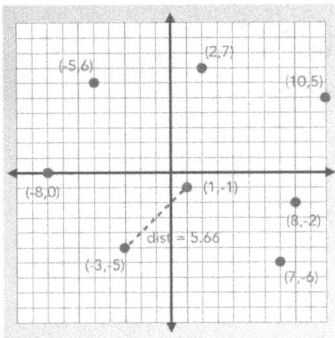

(a) Step 1: Working this example by hand

Write down exactly how you solved the problem:

(1) Computed $\sqrt{1^2 + 8^2} = 8.06$
(2) Started with best choice of $(2, 7)$
(3) Computed $\sqrt{9^2 + 6^2} = 10.82$
(4) Compared 10.82 to 8.06—8.06 is smaller
(5) Computed $\sqrt{7^2 + (-1)^2} = 7.07$
(6) Compared 7.07 to 8.06—7.07 is smaller
(7) Updated best choice to $(8, -2)$
(8) Computed $\sqrt{6^2 + (-5)^2} = 7.81$

(9) Compared 7.81 to 7.07—7.07 is smaller
(10) Computed $\sqrt{(-4)^2 + (-4)^2} = 5.66$
(11) Compared 5.66 to 7.07—5.66 is smaller
(12) Updated best choice to $(-3, -5)$
(13) Computed $\sqrt{(-9)^2 + 1^2} = 9.06$
(14) Compared 9.06 to 5.66—5.66 is smaller
(15) Computed $\sqrt{(-6)^2 + 7^2} = 9.22$
(16) Compared 9.22 to 5.66—5.66 is smaller
(17) Gave an answer of $(-3, -5)$

(b) Step 2: Write down exactly what you did

Figure 2: Steps 1 and 2 of the closest point example

We give examples on how we teach with this technique from two courses at Duke University. ECE 551 is an intensive introductory programming course in C and C++, for graduate students in Engineering. CompSci 101 is an introductory programming course in Python, for undergraduates.

3.1   Example 1 from ECE 551

From ECE 551 we give an example of executing The Seven Steps for the closest point problem—finding the closest point in a set of points to a given point in the plane. We use this problem, as it not only illustrates many algorithm concepts but is useful in a wide variety of applications: from maps to tagging data based on similarity.

Step 1. We pick a set of points S and single point P and find which point in S is closest to P

$$S = \{(2, 7), (10, 5), (8, -2), (7, -6), (-3, -5), (-8, 0), (-5, 6)\} \quad (1)$$
$$P = (1, -1) \quad (2)$$

We strongly encourage drawing a diagram. We also identify the domain knowledge needed to solve this problem, namely the Pythagorean theorem, rearranged into the distance formula: $d = \sqrt{\Delta x^2 + \Delta y^2}$. By hand, we calculate the distance between each point in S and P, finding that $(-3, -5)$ has a distance of 5.66, smaller than each of the other distances calculated, and shown in Figure 2a.

Step 2. We write down exactly what we did in Step 1, with a focus on being precise and complete. See Figure 2b.

Step 3. We generalize the results from Step 2, recognizing some key patterns: the "compute" and "compare" lines come in pairs; updating the best choice only happens sometimes, and some lines only happen at the start and end.

The resulting algorithm is

```
Compute the distance from S_0 to P--call it bestDist
Start with best choice of S_0
Count from 1 to the number of points in S exclusive,
    call each number i
    Compute the distance from S_i to P
    If currDist is smaller than bestDist,
        Then update bestChoice to S_i and
```

```
        update bestDist to currDist
Give an answer of bestChoice
```

Here is more explanation. Each compute uses Δx and Δy from point P to each point in S, so we generalize this to "Computed $\sqrt{(S_i\text{'s } x - P\text{'s } x)^2 + (S_i\text{'s } y - P\text{'s } y)^2}$, (call it currDist)." Each comparison always compares currDist to something. We realize that we are implicitly keeping track of the bestDist, and the update only happens when currDist is smaller than bestDist.

Step 4. We tested this code for several inputs, including the corner case where there are zero points in S. This reveals a problem with the algorithm, so we add the line

```
If S is empty, give an answer of "no answer exists"
```

Steps 5–7. This example was used in the first part of ECE 551, before students learned to write code, so we only practiced Steps 1–4. Later in the course, when students are learning about pointers and arrays, we revisit this problem. The students work through the translation to code, building their understanding of these concepts and how they relate to the algorithm that was designed earlier.

3.2   Example 2 from CompSci 101

In CompSci 101, we use The Seven Steps to solve the following problem (from the TopCoder website [17]). Given a word, translate it into a cryptic text message using the following rules. 1) If the word is only vowels, it is not changed. 2) If the word has at least one consonant, then write only the consonants that do not have another consonant immediately following them, and do not include any vowels. 3) Vowels are 'a', 'e', 'i', 'o', and 'u'.

Step 1. Work an example. The word is "please". We step through the word on paper, letter by letter, and end up with the result "ps".
Step 2. Write down exactly what you did. 1) Word is "please". Create empty answer. 2) First letter is "p", consonant, no consonant before, include it, answer is "p". 3) Next letter is "l", consonant with consonant before it, do not include it. 4) Next letter is "e", vowel, do not include. 5) Next letter is "a", vowel, do not include. 6) Next letter is "s", consonant, vowel before, include, answer is "ps". 7) Next letter is "e", vowel, do not include. Our answer is "ps".

Step 3. Generalize. In generalizing, we discuss how we find repetitive behavior and conditional behavior, as is typical of many algorithms. For this problem, we see how making the lines in the algorithm repetitive is done most easily by "pretending" that there is a vowel before the word—doing so removes special cases and makes the algorithm uniform. Generalization results in an algorithm that looks like this:

```
start with before being 'a'
ans is empty
for each letter in word
    If letter is a consonant, and before is a vowel,
        then add letter to ans.
    set before to the current letter
give back ans as your answer
```

Step 4. Test your algorithm. We follow the algorithm with the word "message" and get "msg". It works!

Step 5. Translate to Python code. Translation to code proceeds in a straightforward fashion: each line in the algorithm corresponds directly to one line of code. Checking if a letter is a vowel (or consonant) are logical choices to abstract out into another function. Students are familiar with the function isVowel(), so they can simply use it without solving another problem. The resulting code is:

```
before = 'a'
ans = ''
for ch in word:
    if not(isVowel(ch)) and isVowel(before):
        ans += ch
    before = ch
return ans
```

Step 6. Test. Testing shows that this algorithm works on many cases, but not on the string "a" (where the result should be "a", but is "").

Step 7. Debug. Debugging shows us that the problem was with our algorithm, so we return to Step 3. We note that repairing this algorithm likely requires working more examples, as none of the examples previously worked behave like the problematic test case. Once the algorithm is repaired, it can be translated back into code (repeating Step 5), and re-tested to find that it is now correct.

4 USAGE OF THE SEVEN STEPS IN COURSES

4.1 ECE 551

ECE 551 is an intensive programming class for Masters students in Electrical and Computer Engineering. This course builds fundamentals from the ground up, to take students from whatever their prior programming background might be (including nothing) to solid programmers ready to take graduate-level computer engineering courses the next semester. This course has pervasive use of The Seven Steps—we discuss it (and its importance) on day 1 of the course, and use it as the primary way to teach examples.

This course uses a flipped classroom, so the examples are not done in lecture. Instead, the students watch them in videos, which are part of the textbook [6] that we wrote for this course (which has embedded videos). This book includes 19 video examples where we use The Seven Steps to devise an algorithm and turn it into

code. Three of the early chapters are entirely devoted to detailed discussion of The Seven Steps (one focuses on Steps 1–4, one focuses on Step 5, and one focuses on Steps 6 and 7). This course also makes use of the Lego Lab, described in Section 4.3.

Furthermore, when students seek help, the instructors and TAs give assistance within the framework of The Seven Steps. For example, we respond to students saying "I'm stuck on this problem" with "Which step are you having problems with?" When students say "I cannot find the pattern in these steps," then we respond that it is quite good that they can precisely identify the problem they are having and work with them on how to find the pattern in the steps they wrote.

4.2 CompSci 101

CompSci 101 is an introductory Python programming course for undergraduates. This course is the first computer science course for the major, and typically 80% of the students have never programmed before. We integrate examples of The Seven Steps into the course and illustrate with those examples how this technique helps to write code. We introduce the technique in the fifth lecture and show them all of The Seven Steps for solving a particular problem. We work the first four steps with pencil and paper and then work Steps 5–7 on the computer. We ask them for input as we work through all seven steps. We spend a lot of time on this first example so students can see how we would solve each step. Writing an algorithm by hand and going through all seven steps in such detail takes a long time. For later examples, we built the problem solving steps into our lecture slides so that we could cover them more quickly and have time to go over more examples in detail. We used this technique in eight of the 26 lectures (30%), spread throughout the semester, and used it in the Lego Lab, described in Section 4.3. In the majority of the examples we focused on the first four steps, and in a few examples we worked through all seven steps.

In two consecutive lectures, we revisited a problem to show a different translation to code. In the first lecture for this problem we went through all seven steps to solve the problem, with the code resulting in a loop that iterates through all of the elements. In the next lecture we learned about indexing with a loop. Then we revisited the same problem from the previous lecture, but started with step 4, the same algorithm we had previously developed. This time we translated each line from that algorithm into different code that used indexing, resulting in a cleaner solution for the problem.

In another lecture, we were able to show the value in putting time into developing an algorithm before coding. In this lecture we worked through the first four steps for a problem. Then we translated each line of the algorithm with live coding with suggestions from students. We ran the program on several sets of test data and it worked correctly the first time! Students were very impressed. This really showed how investing a lot of time in the first four steps meant that little to no time was spent on debugging.

4.3 Lab with The Seven Steps

Both courses do a lab which focuses on Steps 1–4 of The Seven Steps, in which students determine and write down the algorithm used to place Legos on boards in a sequence of boards that defines a particular pattern. Patterns typically start with one lego on a board, then two legos on a board, then three legos on a board, etc. Students are suppose to identify an algorithm so that given a particular number, say 8, they could put down 8 legos on a board that following the pattern. The goal of this lab is to completely decouple Steps 1–4 from anything dealing with code (it can be done before students have even learned any syntax of any programming language).

An example Lego pattern is shown in Figure 3. This pattern would be appropriate when students have learned about repetition, conditionals, and modulus. This example uses two types of legos, square brown legos and orange rectangular legos that are twice the size of the square legos. The pattern is the following. The first board labeled 0 has one lego, a square lego in the bottom left corner. The second board labeled 1 uses two legos, a rectangular lego in the bottom left corner and a square lego that starts four columns over and one row up. Each consecutive board has one more lego. Students will need to make observations to help them in writing an algorithm that describes the pattern. They may notice the first lego on each board alternates from square to rectangle to rectangle, and then repeats. Meaning the seventh board would start with a square lego in the bottom left corner. They may notice that consecutive legos on a board are always four columns over and one row up. It can be a challenge for students to write an algorithm for the Nth board that describes the placement of the N legos on that board.

Prior to the lab, the instructors prepare two different patterns: the "A" and the "B" pattern. The algorithm one writes to explain a pattern is parameterized over one integer (N). The complexity of the algorithm should be appropriate to the amount of practice/skill the students have. The concepts involved should be appropriate to the material covered recently. Instructors (or TAs) execute the algorithm for $N = 0, 1, 2, 3, 4$ (more values of N if needed for a complex algorithm). Each parameter value is done on a separate Lego board. Boards are labeled with the value of N with a post-it note.

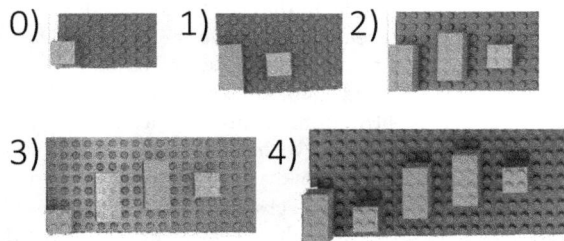

Figure 3: Example Lego boards for an algorithm with N=0–4.

For the actual lab session, students are divided into groups (approximately 4 students per group). The groups are then divided into "A" and "B" groups. Each "A" group is given a set of boards on which the "A" pattern is shown for e.g., $N = 0$ to 4 legos, and each "B" group is given a set of boards representing the "B" pattern. "A" groups should not be able to see "B" boards, and vice-versa. The students are then instructed to devise and write down an algorithm which would produce the pattern of Legos for any value of N. Each group has some spare Legos and boards so that they can work examples themselves.

After the students have had sufficient time to devise their algorithms, they are instructed to execute their own algorithm for the next value of N (e.g., if they were given $N = 0$–4, they are instructed to execute $N = 5$). When they complete this task, they swap algorithms (but not boards) with a group who had a different pattern ("A" swaps with "B").

The students are then instructed to execute the algorithm they *received* for a value of N, say $N = 5$ (or whatever value was just used). This means that an "A" group is executing a "B" group's algorithm, without having seen the "B" pattern or any of the "B" boards—the only information they have to go on is what is written in the algorithm.

When the groups finish executing the algorithm they received, they are told to compare results with the group whose algorithm they executed. The students are instructed to discuss the discrepancies in their results with each other, as well as any difficulties they had following the instructions.

This lab provides students with a lot of insight into Steps 2 and 3 of The Seven Steps (with Steps 1 and 4 being quite helpful in being successful). Often, students overlook important details (e.g., color, size, or orientation of their Legos) when writing their algorithms—this is the key skill of Step 2 and is critical to programming. Of course, finding the patterns in the Lego placement is key to writing a general algorithm, so students practice Step 3 as well. Sometimes students who struggle to find a pattern try to give instructions like "etc." "and then keep doing it similarly," or even "you know what I mean"—other groups struggle to follow such ambiguous steps and report their frustrations back to the group who wrote the poor algorithm. The fact that the algorithm is completely separated from writing code is crucial—the students can see that it is not a problem of remembering the syntactic details of a particular language, but rather that they are not being clear, and/or not finding patterns accurately.

4.4 Other uses

Beyond our use of The Seven Steps in our in-person courses, we have two different online introductory programming specializations in Java [1] and C [2], which make heavy use of The Seven Steps. In these courses, major examples are worked through with The Seven Steps, to go from a problem statement to working code. As with many in-class examples, we typically focus on Steps 1–5.

We are also seeing other instructors who are aware of The Seven Steps put it to use in their own courses. We are aware of a class at another University which makes use of the textbook [6] that we wrote for ECE 551. As previously mentioned, this textbook heavily emphasizes The Seven Steps.

5 EVALUATION

5.1 Student Anecdotes

One of the clearest indicators of the success of The Seven Steps in our classes is the stories that students tell us of their programming success. For example, one student in CompSci 101 wrote the following e-mail to Rodger towards the end of the semester:

> I just want to tell you that I tried the seven step method, and I worked on all of my code for one or two hours before I even looked at the computer. AND

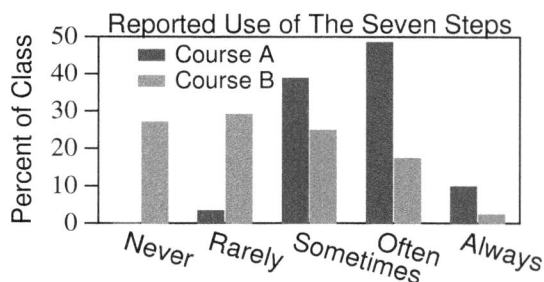

Figure 4: Students' use of The Seven Steps, by course.

> IT WORKED! I got all my code right on the first try! For the first time ever, I don't have to go to the help lab for hours on end. I just wanted to tell you how satisfied I am. Yay! Have a good day and thank you for re-teaching me the strategy.

We find this story particularly telling, as the student clearly has been struggling to write code on her own. However, when she follows The Seven Steps—and uses them to carefully plan before writing any code—she is able to write correct code on the first try. She is excited about the success and empowered by the ability to write working code without help.

A student in one of our online courses wrote the following:

> I have been programming for a couple of years. Learned from so many resources but none said how to write the algorithm, they just say you should write your algorithm first. The steps illustrated here are beautiful and definitely help to understand how to decompose a problem.

Even though this student has some experience programming, we find this story important—the student contrasts The Seven Steps with the approaches he has tried to use before. While he does not say what the prior approaches were or in what context they were used, he notes that "none said *how* to write the algorithm."

5.2 Survey Results

At the end of the semester, we conducted an anonymous, voluntary survey of both courses. We asked the students to report how often they used The Seven Steps, how useful they found various steps in the process, how important they thought various skills were (at start and end of course), and how confident they were in their programming ability. In total we received 132 responses from a total of 463 students (122 from ECE 551 and 341 from CompSci 101). Of these responses, 70 students reported their gender as "male," 61 reported their gender as "female," and 1 student did not report.

Figure 4 shows the percentage of students in each class who reported using The Seven Steps never, rarely, sometimes, often, or always. ECE 551 shows a remarkably higher rate of use of The Seven Steps than CompSci 101. One logical explanation is that The Seven Steps was emphasized much more strongly in ECE 551, as described in Section 4. However, other factors, such as the age and maturity of the students, may also contribute to these differences.

One set of these questions asked students to rate their perceived importance of four skills at the end and the start of the semester.

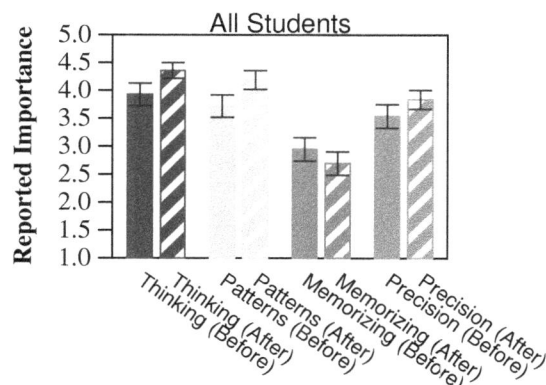

Figure 5: Mean student perceptions of skill importance

Three of these skills—Thinking before starting to write code, Finding patterns in a set of directions, and Being able to carefully and precisely articulate how you solved a problem—are important to programming, and we would hope students both learn them, and learn that they are important. The other skill—Memorizing example code that you have seen—is *not* important for programming, even though many students *think* that it is, based on prior academic success from memorization.

Figure 5 shows the average rating, on a scale of 1 ("not at all important"), 2 ("slightly important"), 3 ("neutral"), 4 ("very important"), and 5 ("extremely important"), for each of these four skills before the course (shown in solid bars) and after the course (shown in striped bars). We plot error bars for a 95% confidence interval around the mean on each bar.

The first observation is that the students' perception of what is important moves in the correct direction on all four skills: it increases for the three that are actually useful for programming and decreases on memorizing code. This change is statistically significant for the first two skills. Unfortunately, there is no control group available, so we cannot draw conclusions about whether these changes come from The Seven Steps in particular, or programming in general. However, The Seven Steps explicitly places emphasis on these skills. We also divided this data by gender, and found similar results and trends for both male and female students.

We also examined the relationship between how often students reported using The Seven Steps, and the level of confidence that they reported in their programming ability at the end of the course. While results were not statistically significant, those with more use of The Seven Steps reported higher confidence on average.

6 CONCLUSIONS

The Seven Steps provides students a step-by-step approach to work through programming problems, from problem statement to working code. It is important for instructors to integrate this technique into solving problems throughout the semester. We have had great success using this technique in a variety of courses, both in the classroom and online—and other faculty are beginning to adopt this technique. We highly recommend this approach to other CS instructors for use in their own classrooms.

REFERENCES

[1] Owen Astrachan, Robert Duvall, Andrew Hilton, and Susan Rodger. 2018. Java Programming and Software Engineering Fundamentals Specialization. (Dec. 2018). Retrieved December 12, 2018 from https://www.coursera.org/specializations/java-programming

[2] Anne Bracy, Andrew Hilton, Genevieve Lipp, and Liz Wendland. 2018. Introduction to Programming in C Specialization. (Dec. 2018). Retrieved December 12, 2018 from https://www.coursera.org/specializations/java-programming

[3] Catherine H. Crouch and Eric Mazur. 2001. Peer Instruction: Ten years of experience and results. *American Journal of Physics* 69, 9 (Sept. 2001), 970–977.

[4] Philip J. Guo. 2013. Online Python Tutor: Embeddable Web-based Program Visualization for CS Education. *SIGCSE 2013* (2013), 579–584.

[5] Mark Guzdial and Barbara Ericson. 2007. *Introduction to computing and programming with Java: A multimedia approach.* Pearson Prentice Hall, Upper Saddle River, NJ.

[6] Andrew Hilton and Anne Bracy. 2015. *All of Programming.* https://play.google.com/store/books/details/All_of_Programming?id=-zViCgAAQBAJ&hl=en, online book.

[7] Marcia Linn, Alfred Aho, M. Brian Blake, Robert Constable, Yasmin B. Kafal, Janet L. Kolodner, Lawrence Snyder, and Uri Wilensky. 2010. *Report of a Workshop on the Scope and Nature of Computational Thinking.* The National Academies Press, Washington, D.C.

[8] Marcia Linn, Alfred Aho, M. Brian Blake, Robert Constable, Yasmin B. Kafal, Janet L. Kolodner, Lawrence Snyder, and Uri Wilensky. 2011. *Report of a Workshop on the Pedagogical Aspects of Computational Thinking.* The National Academies Press, Washington, D.C.

[9] Raymond Lister, Elizabeth S. Adams, Sue Fitzgerald, William Fone, John Hamer, Morten Lindholm, Robert McCartney, Jan Erik Moström, Kate Sanders, Otto Seppälä, Beth Simon, and Lynda Thomas. 2004. A Multi-national Study of Reading and Tracing Skills in Novice Programmers, An ITiCSE 2004 Working Group Report. *SIGCSE Bulletin* 36, 4 (Dec. 2004), 119–150.

[10] Dastyni Loksa, Andrew J Ko, Will Jernigan, Alannah Oleson, Christopher J Mendez, and Margaret Burdett. 2016. Programming, Problem Solving, and Self-Awareness: Effects of Explicit Guidance. *CHI 2016* (2016), 1449–1461.

[11] Michael McCracken, Vicki Almstrum, Danny Diaz, Mark Guzdial, Dianne Hagan, Yifat Ben-David Kolikant, Cary Laxer, Lynda Thomas, Ian Utting, , and Tadeusz Wilusz. 2001. A Multi-national, multi-institutional study of assessment of programming skills of first-year CS students, An ITiCSE 2001 Working Group Report. *SIGCSE Bulletin* 33, 4 (Dec. 2001), 125–140.

[12] Charlie McDowell, Linda Werner, Heather E. Bullock, and Julian Fernald. 2006. Pair Programming improves student retention, confidence and program quality. *Commun. ACM* 49, 8 (Aug. 2006), 90–95.

[13] Esko Nuutila, Seppo Törmä, and Lauri Malmi. 2005. PBL and Computer Programming — The Seven Steps Method with Adaptations. *Computer Science Education* 15, 2 (2005), 123–142.

[14] Massachusetts Institute of Technology. 2018. Scratch website. (Dec. 2018). Retrieved December 12, 2018 from http://scratch.mit.edu

[15] Leo Porter and Beth Simon. 2013. Retaining Nearly One-Third more Majors with a Trio of Instructional Best Practices in CS1. *SIGCSE 2013* (2013), 165–170.

[16] Stephen Prata. 2013. *C Primer Plus* (6th ed.). Addison-Wesley Professional, United States.

[17] Topcoder. 2018. Topcoder Competitive Programming. (Dec. 2018). Retrieved December 12, 2018 from https://www.topcoder.com/community/competitive-programming/

[18] Carnegie Mellon University. 2018. Alice website. (Dec. 2018). Retrieved December 12, 2018 from http://www.alice.org

[19] Wikibooks. 2018. Five Steps of Programming. (Dec. 2018). Retrieved December 12, 2018 from https://en.wikibooks.org/wiki/The_Computer_Revolution/Programming/Five_Steps_of_Programming

[20] Laurie Williams and Robert Kessler. 2003. *Pair Programming Illuminated.* Pearson Education, Boston, Ma.

[21] Jeannette M. Wing. 2006. Computational Thinking. *Commun. ACM* 49, 3 (March 2006), 33–35.

IneqDetect: A Visual Analytics System to Detect Conversational Inequality and Support Reflection during Active Learning

Stephen MacNeil, Kyle Kiefer, Brian Thompson, Dev Takle, Celine Latulipe
The University of North Carolina at Charlotte
{smacnei2,kkiefer,bthomp57,dtakle,clatulipe}@uncc.edu

ABSTRACT

A series of recent studies have shed light on the existence of sociocultural inequities in collaborative learning environments. We present IneqDetect, a system which helps students reflect on the way that they communicate as a team. Conversations during collaborative learning activities are recorded using lapel microphones, processed to determine who spoke at a given time, and then visualized. The resulting dashboard visualization provides students with a timeline of when each student was speaking, a summary of how much they spoke, and an estimate of how equitable the conversation was between team members. Students reflect on this information at the end of the class period to identify and address issues, such as conversational inequality, within their groups. IneqDetect was deployed across four CS active learning classrooms. IneqDetect led students to discuss group dynamics, change their behaviors, and gain insights about themselves and their team. However, conversational equity within groups did not improve.

KEYWORDS

collaboration; group dynamics; reflective learning; active learning

ACM Reference format:
Stephen MacNeil, Kyle Kiefer, Brian Thompson, Dev Takle, Celine Latulipe. 2019. IneqDetect: A Visual Analytics System to Detect Conversational Inequality and Support Reflection during Active Learning. In *Proceedings of ACM Global Computing Education Conference 2019, Chengdu,Sichuan, China, May 17–19, 2019 (CompEd '19)*, 7 pages.
https://doi.org/10.1145/3300115.3309528

1 INTRODUCTION

Equity and inclusion are emerging as issues of critical importance in CS education research. A lack of diversity both in industry and in CS graduates has prompted many calls for broadening participation. In parallel, computing is increasingly being seen as a human literacy that should be shared by all [42]. Improving equity and inclusion in CS has been addressed with new pedagogical styles [20, 40], by changing the culture and environment through organizations and events [10, 30], or by improving the computing pipeline that leads to CS programs [7, 40]. In most of these cases, inclusion and equity

are considered from a representational or structural perspective with an emphasis on race, gender, or intersectional aspects [9]. Prior research has focused mostly on improving retention [20, 29], measures of self-efficacy and motivation [4, 40], or academic performance [20, 34, 40] for under-represented groups. Improving equity and inclusivity has understandably received a lot of attention and will continue to be a focus, especially as intersectionality challenges us consider diversity more holistically and in greater detail.

In this paper, we consider another aspect of equity and inclusion that is recently gaining attention in CS education, sociocultural equity. Sociocultural inequities are disparities between students in terms of how they communicate and interact with each other socially. Sociocultural inequities were observed in pair programming [22] and in group discussions [36]. Personality types and power dynamics within teams can serve to elevate the voices of some students while silencing the voices of others. To achieve 'CS for All', these social aspects need to be considered because students who do not have a sense of belonging and community have trouble identifying with their chosen field [11]. Inequitable social learning environments may also further propagate existing negative stereotypes about CS, such as it being competitive, singularly-focused, asocial, and primarily male [21]. These problems become especially relevant as CS classrooms increasingly adopt active learning and team-based pedagogies. Existing research helps to understand some of the dynamics that occur within groups and teams. However, few tools exist to help students reflect on group dynamics.

IneqDetect is a system that helps students reflect on their group conversations that occur during active learning activities. IneqDetect uses lapel microphones to record students' conversations and uses signal processing to determine who is speaking during a given time interval. These speech segments, the total talk time per speaker, and a measure of conversational equality within the group are presented as a dashboard visualization at the end of class. Students reflect on the visualization to identify trends or areas for improvement. We found that IneqDetect led students to discuss group dynamics, change their behaviors, and gain insights about themselves and their team. Despite these benefits, IneqDetect did not improve conversational equality. We also contribute insights about how students perceive collaboration. We conclude with suggestions to improve *Research Support Tools* (RSTs) for collaboration.

2 BACKGROUND

We present the social theory and related work that inspired the creation of IneqDetect and guided its development. We provide a brief overview of reflection and describe how it can be both an individual and collaborative effort. Finally, we explain why reflection may be an appropriate vehicle for improving equity within groups that also maintains the autonomy of the group members.

2.1 Group and Team Dynamics

Understanding and evaluating small group collaboration in education is challenging for a variety of reasons. First, language consists of both verbal and non-verbal cues [12, 17]. Verbal cues can mostly be transcribed whereas non-verbal cues are harder to represent due to their variety and subtly. Similarly, verbal cues can be identified in recorded audio. However, non-verbal cues are harder to capture automatically due to video camera occlusion. Second, verbal cues can be used to convey information but also to perform actions [1, 33, 41]. These two types of verbal cues contribute to different parts of the conversation, such as what is being said and how the conversation is being regulated. Third, social interactions are heavily shaped by the task, situation, and team structure [25]. Considering task, situation, and structure is non-trivial. Joseph McGrath describes eight different settings and six different task typologies [25]. Due to all of this complexity, connecting any of these aspects to performance is challenging. Even anecdotally, a team may have great off-topic conversations which do not translate to task performance.

Given this complexity, researchers analyze many different aspects of conversations. A simple measure that is often used is the amount or distribution of talk time [22, 24, 36]. The total talk time for each speaker can also be used to compute the amount of equality present within a group as a Gini Coefficient [24, 36]. While the quantity of a conversation doesn't equate to quality, it is a good starting point for automation. Stankiewicz and Kulkarni argue that quantitative measures may also encourage students' self-disclosure better than semantic or qualitative measures [36].

IneqDetect combines these popular metrics of total talk time and the Gini Coefficient with a scrollable timeline showing when voices were detected. By providing students with this visualization dashboard to reflect on at the end of class, students can negotiate what these measures mean in their own context. This novel adaptation is a first step to determine what is most relevant for the discussants themselves. This differs from previous conversation analyses which attempted to operationalize and evaluate social theory. Additionally, IneqDetect is robust to classroom noise which enabled these studies to take place in real active learning classrooms.

2.2 Reflection

In CS education, reflection has taken many forms, including collaborative discussions [31], diaries and journaling [13, 15] or portfolios [5]. Each of these provide scaffolding to help students to develop their reflective practice. Reflection can also be scaffolded using reflection support tools [14, 23]. *Reflection Support Tools* (RSTs) provide additional data about student's learning experiences or a digital scaffold to structure students' reflections. A review of RSTs by Kim and Lee include examples as early as 1993 [18]. Many examples of RSTs exist, such as the Subtle Stone which helps students reflect on their affective states [2]. Another example is the student activity monitor (SAM) which supports both students and instructors by visualizing learner's actions [16]. In many cases, the goal of RSTs is to make the implicit explicit through visual representations. This increases awareness, and challenges students to compare their perception with additional data about an experience. Ideally, this results in critical reflection, where students think critically about their assumptions and biases related to an experience [26].

2.3 Visualizing Conversations

Conversations consist of a series of verbal and non-verbal cues occurring over a period of time. This time-series data can have micro and macro patterns as topics change and discussants become more or less involved. Visualized conversations provide *an overview* of the conversation and *details on demand* about specific interactions between discussants [35]. Visualizations also afford exploration and discoverability which can promote sense-making.

For visualizing a single audio track, TimeNotes uses zooming techniques to explore audio at multiple points in time while maintaining an overview of the audio signal [39]. The *Conversational Clock* uses a clock metaphor to show recorded audio patterns in real-time that emerge in co-located groups [3]. It features a circular table with more recent parts of the conversation radiating out from the center of the table. This highlights recent discussions while preserving the overall conversation. Although real-time visualizations provide continuous feedback, they also increase cognitive load. Participants echoed this idea in a study that compared subtle to overt real-time visual feedback during conversation by indicating that they preferred the subtle feedback [32]. In learning settings, where students are being challenged to think, communicate, and remember concepts, this additional cognitive load may be less desirable. To this end, students use IneqDetect at the end of class to reflect.

VizScribe is a visual analytics tool for analyzing verbal protocols during design sessions [8]. It presents raw data about who spoke when. This encourages designers to explore the data to find their own meaning. IneqDetect also presents raw data to encourage students to engage in sense-making and find their own meaning. We also present aggregated representations to help scaffold exploration.

In educational contexts, Toyoura et al. have explored using both video and audio to classify student interactions, including group work, lecture, private work, presentation, and movement [38]. They visualize, temporally, the type of interaction that each group is having based on clustering and classifying the video and audio data. This technique helps instructors to see which groups are interacting in ways that weren't intended by the instructor. While helpful for instructors, this approach was not intended to support students.

3 INEQDETECT SYSTEM

IneqDetect is a system that was developed to support students as they reflect on conversations that they have had within their group. Students' verbalizations during conversations are recorded and then visualized for students to reflect at the end of class. The visualization highlights conversational inequality, but it also provides raw data such as when it detected a speaker. As seen in Figure 1, the visualization consists of three parts: a barchart of overall talk time for each speaker, an equity score that represents how even the distribution of speaking was within the team as measured by the Gini Coefficient, and a timeline which shows sections where each speaker was determined to be speaking. Students review this visualization after working in groups. Stickers attached to devices help students identify themselves while preserving anonymity. This addresses previous concerns about privacy and encourages self-disclosure [36]. Justifications for many of our other design decisions have already been presented in the background sections.

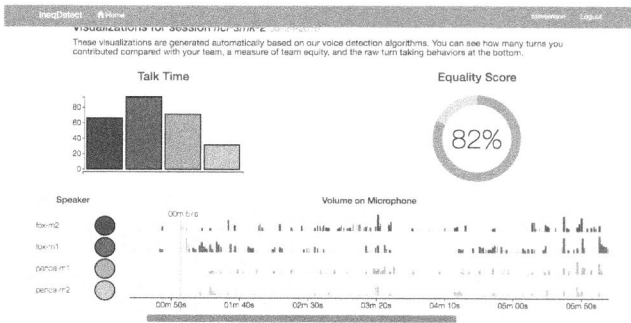

Figure 1: Visualization: A barchart summarizing each student's contribution (left), the equity score (right), and a timeline that displays when each student spoke (bottom).

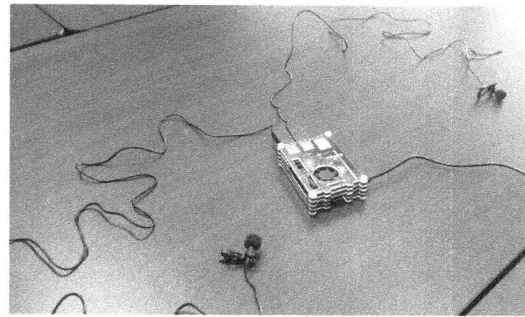

Figure 3: A Raspberry Pi Device connected to two lapel microphones to simultaneously record two speakers.

3.1 System Design and Speaker Recognition

The design of IneqDetect is shown in Figure 2. Students wear lapel microphones that are attached to Raspberry Pi devices, shown in Figure 3. Each device supported two microphones, recording two group members. In larger groups, multiple devices were used. An optional Twitter account can start and stop recordings if instructors want to use the devices without assistance. When a recording is ended, the audio is sent to the server to determine who spoke when. Students view the visualization in their web browsers.

Recording in classrooms is challenging because there is often a lot of background noise, which varies widely throughout the class period. Consequently, the audio was pre-processed before identifying the speakers. To denoise the audio signal, we used spectral whitening and a fast Fourier transform. The voice features are extracted from the audio signal as Mel-frequency cepstral coefficients (MFCC). As recommended [19], we used only the first 12 coefficients for voice activity detection (VAD). We computed the energy across these speech features during a given time interval which is a common energy-based approach for VAD [37]. The energy across all microphones was compared through a moving window and an adaptive threshold removed the lowest cluster using k-means clustering (elbow method). This effectively reduced the amount of cross-talk that was detected on the microphones. This last step was added after initial tests in classroom settings and it drastically improved our ability to distinguish between speakers even when speakers are very close (less than 3 feet apart) to each other.

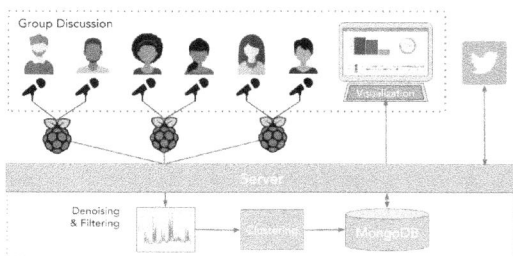

Figure 2: Raspberry pi devices are controlled by tweets and send recordings to the server for analysis.

4 IN-CLASS STUDIES

We used IneqDetect in four classes to evaluate its potential to improve equity and collaboration within teams. Consent was obtained in the first weeks of the course. For IneqDetect to be used by a group, all students in the group must have provided consent. If multiple groups were eligible to use IneqDetect then the groups were chosen at random but with a priority given to teams who had all students attend on the first day of the intervention where IneqDetect was used. Students from the groups that used IneqDetect were offered an opportunity to be interviewed about their experiences. Students received $5 each time they used IneqDetect and $15 for participating in the 30 minute interview.

4.1 Study Design and Protocol

We conducted a study that spanned four classes with two conditions: reflective writing and the IneqDetect intervention. Each class had 3-5 students per group. On the first day of class, students were introduced to IneqDetect and given a brief presentation about reflection. The presentation was tailored for each course to connect reflective practice to the course material or the instructor's intentions for reflection. The study began with a survey on the first day, four distinct reflection stages, and ended with an exit survey. In the first stage, students were given a reflective writing assignment that was related to high-level course concepts to engage them. In the second stage, students were asked to reflect on their teamwork at the end of class. In the third stage, the groups were placed into the two conditions. Some continued reflective writing and others used IneqDetect. In groups that were selected to use IneqDetect they followed the protocol displayed in Figure 4. In the fourth stage, all group members completed written reflections.

4.2 Study Context and Participants

The studies that we describe in this paper took place across four courses in Spring 2018 and both Summer Sessions I and II of 2018. The four courses were Introductory Programming II (CS1), System Integration (SI), Game Design and Development (GDD), and Human-Computer Interaction (HCI). These three courses each had opportunities for students to collaborate and work in groups. Our university (and our department in particular) has made efforts to encourage active learning across classrooms. The courses in which

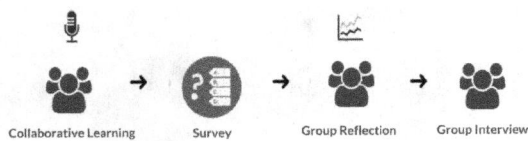

Figure 4: An overview of the in-class study.

we conducted our study were taught with a focus on active and collaborative learning experiences for the students.

The types of collaboration varied from discussion of clicker quiz questions to unstructured project work. Across classes, groups were formed randomly, and we didn't intervene with extant group formation practices. In every class except GDD, students worked in groups without formal roles. GDD had structured roles within teams. In each class, instructors rotated to help each group, but otherwise interactions were self-directed. Some groups were all-male, while others were mixed-gender. CS1 had two men and four women, all identified as white except one member who self-identified as African-American. The GDD group consisted of four men, all identified as white except one member who self-identified as Asian. The HCI group consisted of four men, all identified as white. A few groups in the SI class used IneqDetect, but none volunteered to be interviewed. The SI class was a graduate class with mostly international students with a roughly even gender distribution.

4.3 Data Collection

4.3.1 Survey Data. We collected survey data at the beginning and end of the semester. We also collected survey data each time students used the IneqDetect system, as shown in Figure 4. This data included Likert scale questions with questions such as "I find it useful to reflect on my learning process" and "IneqDetect helped me reflect on my learning." We analyzed the survey data using either inferential or descriptive statistics, depending on the amount of data and the need to generalize. Because Likert data is ordinal we applied Spearman's Rho (Rs). Spearman's Rank Correlation test is "appropriate when one or both variables are skewed or ordinal and it is robust when extreme values are present" [27].

4.3.2 Individual Interview Data. To gather more fine-grained information about students' experiences with IneqDetect we also conducted a series of interviews with participants in groups that used IneqDetect. Students were compensated $15 and interviews lasted about 30 minutes on average. We interviewed 6 students (5 men, 1 woman), across four teams, with at least one student from each of the four courses. For small project interviews, 6-10 people is the recommended number of participants to interview [6].

To analyze the interview data we had two independent coders review the interview recordings and take notes about interesting quotes and themes that emerged. After coding each recording, the coders met to discuss their codes. The codes that were common were kept and codes that didn't match were negotiated (followed by recoding), or they were removed if consensus wasn't reached. After coding all of the interviews, themes that appeared across sessions were merged and corresponding quotes were categorized into those themes. Quotes in the results section were taken from this analysis.

4.3.3 IneqDetect Data and Equity Scores. The visualization features two summative views of equity within the group. The first view is a bar chart which shows how much each group member spoke as aggregated by the total time that they were detected to be speaking. The second view was an equity measure based on the Gini Coefficient. The Gini Coefficient is a measure of equality that is often used in comparing economic data. In addition, we also elicited students' estimates of their own turn-taking behaviors after each learning activity in which they used IneqDetect.

5 RESULTS

To evaluate the effectiveness of IneqDetect and to evaluate our hypotheses, we conducted the study outlined above. We analyzed data generated during the study which included equity scores, survey data, and a thematic analysis of the transcribed interview recordings. This data provided some insights about how IneqDetect influenced equity and its ability to support reflection.

5.1 Triangulating Survey and Interview Data

Given the small sample size for this study, we present our results along with information from the interviews to provide some context and to provide additional evidence for our observations. Quotes used through this section were identified during the coding sessions and chosen to provide support where necessary. These quotes were not obtained after doing our statistical analysis on the survey data. While not completely unbiased, this was done to reduce the possibility of cherry-picking evidence to support our survey results.

5.1.1 Estimating Turn-Taking and Accuracy. We hypothesized that IneqDetect would improve conversational equality by challenging students' perspectives of how much they spoke. Students in our study were not able to estimate the relative amount of talk time they contributed to the conversation when compared to their peers. Spearman's Rho indicated no significant relationship between both variables. In the interviews, all but one participant indicated that they were surprised by the results of the visualization. GD-1 explained that they were "shocked at first. I didn't know that I talked that much". HCI-3 mentioned that they were "surprised ... [that] I think I talk a lot more than I do." HCI-3 described initial surprise followed by a reflection about how much he spoke, "when the equality score came up I was surprised at first how low it was [for me] but then I was like that's about right because I'm never like one of the super talkative ones." CS-1 was least surprised by the results but still indicated that on some days the results were unexpected "the amount of talking within each day you know sometimes I actually thought I was going to be an average speaker but then sometimes I notice sometimes, some days I'm talking more or less."

We didn't ask participants about how they interpreted the discrepancies between their expectations and the results as detected by IneqDetect. However, GD-2 gave one possible explanation, "There are instances where I thought I talked a lot more than others; essentially because of the high you get when you're talking, more so when you're leading the conversation." Another discrepancy is rooted in how students remember their interactions. Students appeared to prioritize some types of communication, explaining that higher quality contributions were perceived as being greater quantitatively as well.

5.1.2 Perceptions of Accuracy. As seen from the comments, students appear to estimate and value conversations differently. We've also seen initial evidence that students' estimates of conversational involvement are inaccurate. Some students described an awareness that their perception was not always accurate, and put forward interesting ideas about what accuracy might mean from a discursive standpoint. Overall, students described IneqDetect as accurate with HCI-3 describing the system as being "90-95%" accurate. GD-2 saying it was "100% accurate" at distinguishing who spoke but that "30% was irrelevant" and related to "jokes and side conversation."

Other students didn't provide an estimate but described how they knew that it was accurate. HCI-2 described its accuracy by his ability to identify events from the class period saying he was "pretty confident. That's where we all paused and we were working. That's where we were yelling about Star Wars." He went on to say, "Pretty accurate ... some points I couldn't place exactly." CS-1 explained that consistency was his way of evaluating IneqDetect's accuracy, "Because the result was consistent, constant results made me know."

5.1.3 Roles: Leaders and Non-Leaders. Across the classes in the study, only one group had defined roles provided by the instructor. Despite the lack of structured team work, there was evidence that students within groups defined roles for themselves. These roles were not always agreed upon explicitly, or even perceived in the same way by members within the group. The main roles that emerged were leadership roles. We asked students about their perception of themselves as leaders within the group. We found that the higher that students ranked themselves as a leader on a Likert scale, the more they estimated that they spoke ($Rs = 0.32$, $p < 0.05$) and the more they did speak as measured by IneqDetect ($Rs = 0.40$, $p < 0.05$). Furthermore, these self-perceived leaders strongly agreed with the statement that they spoke more than they would have liked to ($Rs = 0.55$, $p < 0.05$).

It is unclear from the survey whether these students took on the leadership role reluctantly and wanted more support from their team-members, which is why they said that they spoke more than they wanted to. Alternatively, as a leader, they may have wanted to speak less to ensure that the voices of others within the group were heard. Our interview data speaks to this aspect, GD-1 described his reluctant acceptance of the leadership role and he summarized his performance negatively saying that he didn't have enough experience with the course topics to lead the group, "As a leader, I didn't do a good job of assigning roles". His leadership role was assigned, though more generally he does prefer the role of leader, "I never say no to a leadership position." It is also interesting to note different types of leaders appeared in our groups. HCI-3 explained how two members of the group acted as leaders "HCI-2 talked most on hardworking days, HCI-1 talked more joking."

5.1.4 Motivation, Focus, and Behavioral Change. Students associated a variety of benefits with using IneqDetect. Most students cited general benefits, such as improved motivation and focus, but others provided very detailed accounts of how their teams changed over time. CS-1 talked about how IneqDetect helped him stay focused on the course material, "It motivated me to talk about the topic at hand." CS-2 also explained that it was "keeping me more focused." CS-2 indicated that students did more to explain ideas to each other so as to extend the amount they contributed. CS-2

said that previously they would just tell each other the answer. She speculated that this may have led peers to do the prep-work, "one or two of them might have even read the book even."

GD-2 indicated that wearing the lapel microphones "gave legitimacy, it made it all feel so real." He thought that IneqDetect "turned this into a fun activity to challenge ourselves to talk more." While fun, he also described it as "strangely competitive." He was in a group with four male students and described it thusly, "take four dudes give them all a microphone and you're going to find a competition." While the competition might be motivational he also described it as a potential stressor, "It was motivational and a kind of worry." In the same group, GD-1 did not experience any competition and described his experiment to get a group member more involved, saying "Our artist/designer didn't get as much time as I would like ... [and so] after the first project, I changed gears from leadership." He suggested that he took a back seat to give that partner more time "As you saw in the second time we recorded ... I took a backseat." He perceived his experiment as successful. We corroborated his perception using IneqDetect - his contributions did go down and that person's contributions went up.

An interesting change occurred in the HCI group. Initially, HCI-1 was the primary leader of the group. Both students interviewed described him as someone who cracked jokes and derailed the conversation away from the course topics. They enjoyed that about him, but they described how IneqDetect led to some changes. After reviewing the visualization, HCI-3 said his group observed that "HCI-2 talked most on hardworking days, HCI-1 talked more joking." After the group noticed this trend, HCI-3 said, "The group like unanimously decided and HCI-2 became the main worker ... HCI-2 took [the] leadership [role]", and as a result, "HCI-1 stopped talking." HCI-3 said this was motivational for him in his career and although he hadn't previously considered himself a leader, he wanted to "... take more of the [leadership] role HCI-2 did." When asking HCI-2 about whether he observed any changes within the group, he said "After? Honestly, no." It was interesting that both HCI-2 and HCI-3 had such different views of the same experience. The changes described by HCI-3 were also detected by IneqDetect with HCI-2 speaking more after the first session and HCI-1 speaking much less.

5.1.5 Equity and Changes in Equity. Based on analysis of the teams using data from IneqDetect, the inequality detected across teams with low initial inequality went up (0.12 => 0.38, 0.04 => 0.16 => 0.25, and 0.18 => 0.34) and the inequality in the one team with high initial inequality went down (0.60=>0.28). Furthermore, we observed high variability in terms of equality calculated for each team for the first time that they used IneqDetect ($n = 8$, *mean* = 0.25, *sd* = 0.21). IneqDetect was designed to improve equality within groups and so these results were surprising. These results were consistent with estimates made during group observations.

Equally surprising, equity was also not a theme that emerged when analyzing the interview data, which makes it harder to interpret these results. One possible explanation is that IneqDetect might be more helpful in teams that have a lot of inequality. HCI-2 suggested that easier classes don't need IneqDetect as much as in harder classes, saying "we were able to joke around and have a good time and still do the work that we need to do ... but there are some classes that require a lot more focus ... if I was sitting at a C or a D ... in that scenario it would be very useful for saying, dude, I need to stay on subject more cause I'm going to fail Calc 2."

5.1.6   IneqDetect as a Reflection Support Tool. The perceptions of IneqDetect as a RST were mixed. Seventy-one percent of students that used IneqDetect preferred it to reflective writing. GD-1 indicated that they preferred the structure present in reflective writing, "written reflections were a little better [than IneqDetect], they were specific." He suggested that IneqDetect could be improved "if you're given a set of tasks" adding that "reflection specifics help." CS-2 said that she received benefits from IneqDetect but explained that "writing might have had a similar effect" on improving the equity within their group. In regards to their perceived enjoyment, students that used IneqDetect indicated that they enjoyed IneqDetect more than reflective writing (4.3 > 3.7, with 5=Strongly Agree). Additionally, when comparing across both IneqDetect and non-IneqDetect users, students that used IneqDetect reported higher agreement (ID = 3.43, NO-ID = 3.13) for the statement "I enjoyed doing reflections." Neither of these two differences were statistically significant.

Qualitatively, some students discussed IneqDetect's role as a RST. HCI-2 indicated that IneqDetect resulted in "not a huge reflection. Made me think honestly that we should focus more in class." HCI-2 indicated that he wasn't a very reflective person to begin with, for example "I'm usually not overly mindful of what I'm saying" but also that the class was easy and that IneqDetect was would be more useful in harder class such as 'Calculus'. Some students were more positive about the reflective support that IneqDetect afforded for students. GD-2 described IneqDetect as "great tool to give feedback, the data it provided was great ... forced you to reflect on things."

6   DISCUSSION

Understanding the social dynamics of student groups is challenging because team formation, situation, and task each have a strong affect on collaboration [25]. We introduced IneqDetect into four CS courses, but did not make attempts to change the existing structure of those classrooms. Our data featured unstructured groups, a team with defined roles, and a mix of ages, genders, and races. This in-the-wild approach was adopted to capture the varied ways that collaboration happens in real classrooms. This makes generalization difficult, but our goal for this research was to take a first step in understanding how students interact with reflection support tools (RSTs) designed to help students reflect about collaboration.

IneqDetect was designed to make students more aware of their collaborations and inequalities present within their group. We expected that through reflection and positive reactivity [28], students would start conversing more equitably. While this didn't happen in the few groups that we studied, we did observe benefits for students. Students described instances of behavioral change that occurred within their groups. These changes included increased motivation, a renewed focus on course topics, and intentions to either take on leadership roles, speak more, or be more inclusive of team members. Not all students observed these changes and students in the same group often described very different perceptions of the same shared experiences. These profound differences in subjective interpretations were surprising.

Our results also suggest that students were unable to accurately estimate how much they contributed to a group conversation. Some students indicated an awareness that their perception may not reflect reality. They suggested that their perception changed depending on whether they were speaking or listening. Others suggested that high-quality contributions appeared to constitute more talking time. Others were confident that their estimates were accurate. Different students also ascribed value to different aspects of the conversation. In a single group, one student described silence as when the work happened, whereas another student equated more conversation to more productivity. Understanding students' perceptions of collaboration is an interesting area for future work.

Finally, we observed mixed, but mostly positive, results about IneqDetect's effectiveness as a RST. A few students created their own experiments based on the data and explored hypotheses in subsequent weeks. However, some students also indicated that they didn't know what patterns to look for or how to use the data. In particular, a few students struggled to interpret conversational inequality within their groups. Students requested additional scaffolding, such as specific tasks to perform. To improve IneqDetect as an RST, students asked for more information about conversational quality. This could be extracted from linguistic, paralinguistic, and gestural data to display conversation topics, the focus of each student's attention, and their affective states. Despite these challenges, IneqDetect improved motivation, focus, and awareness. Students also described intention to make changes, such as to take on leadership roles, participate more, or be more inclusive of others.

7   CONCLUSION AND FUTURE WORK

We present IneqDetect, a new RST for supporting reflection about collaboration and conversational equity within groups. Through our in-the-wild study across four classes, we found that students struggle to reliably estimate their contribution to the group. In addition, group members often have different, even conflicting, perceptions of the same experience and group dynamics. Despite these interesting challenges, students associated benefits with using IneqDetect and described instances of behavioral change that occurred within their groups. Results for IneqDetect as a RST were mixed. The majority of students preferred it to written reflections (71%), some students explicitly described how it supported reflection, but others said it would only be helpful in harder classes.

In this initial probe, we provided students with a mixture of raw and summarized data to reflect on. This information was based on the quantity of conversation, but students requested more information about quality of conversations. For future work, we have already extended IneqDetect to automatically transcribe the audio from conversations. From these transcripts, we plan to use natural language processing (NLP) to extract topics and sentiment from the conversations. Paralinguistic cues, such as pitch and resonance, and non-verbal communication, such as gestures and gaze, could eventually be included to track attention and emotion. In addition to supplementing the data presented, we can also provide more structure. For example, we didn't tell students how to reflect on the visualization or provide tasks. This open-endedness allowed some students to form and test hypotheses about group dynamics, but most students had difficulty knowing how to reflect on their collaboration. In the future, we plan to provide students tasks to complete while reviewing the visualization.

REFERENCES

[1] John Langshaw Austin. 1975. *How to do things with words*. Vol. 88. Oxford university press.

[2] Madeline Balaam, Geraldine Fitzpatrick, Judith Good, and Rosemary Luckin. 2010. Exploring affective technologies for the classroom with the subtle stone. In *Proceedings of the SIGCHI Conference on Human Factors in Computing Systems*. ACM, 1623–1632.

[3] Tony Bergstrom and Karrie Karahalios. 2007. Conversation Clock: Visualizing audio patterns in co-located groups. In *System Sciences, 2007. HICSS 2007. 40th Annual Hawaii International Conference on*. IEEE, 78–78.

[4] Sylvia Beyer. 2014. Why are women underrepresented in Computer Science? Gender differences in stereotypes, self-efficacy, values, and interests and predictors of future CS course-taking and grades. *Computer Science Education* 24, 2-3 (2014), 153–192.

[5] Madhumita Bhattacharya and Maggie Hartnett. 2007. E-portfolio assessment in higher education. In *Frontiers In Education Conference-Global Engineering: Knowledge Without Borders, Opportunities Without Passports, 2007. FIE'07. 37th Annual*. IEEE, T1G–19.

[6] Virginia Braun and Victoria Clarke. 2013. *Successful qualitative research: A practical guide for beginners*. sage.

[7] Amy Bruckman, Maureen Biggers, Barbara Ericson, Tom McKlin, Jill Dimond, Betsy DiSalvo, Mike Hewner, Lijun Ni, and Sarita Yardi. 2009. Georgia computes!: Improving the computing education pipeline. In *ACM SIGCSE Bulletin*, Vol. 41. ACM, 86–90.

[8] Senthil Chandrasegaran, Sriram Karthik Badam, Lorraine Kisselburgh, Kylie Peppler, Niklas Elmqvist, and Karthik Ramani. 2017. VizScribe: A visual analytics approach to understand designer behavior. *International Journal of Human-Computer Studies* 100 (2017), 66–80.

[9] J McGrath Cohoon and William Aspray. 2006. *Women and information technology: Research on underrepresentation*. Vol. 1. The MIT Press.

[10] Teresa Dahlberg, Tiffany Barnes, Kim Buch, and Audrey Rorrer. 2011. The STARS Alliance: Viable Strategies for Broadening Participation in Computing. *Trans. Comput. Educ.* 11, 3, Article 18 (Oct. 2011), 25 pages. https://doi.org/10.1145/2037276.2037282

[11] Regina Deil-Amen. 2011. Socio-academic integrative moments: Rethinking academic and social integration among two-year college students in career-related programs. *The Journal of Higher Education* 82, 1 (2011), 54–91.

[12] Paul Drew and John Heritage. 2006. *Conversation analysis*. Vol. 1. Sage London.

[13] Alan Fekete, Judy Kay, Jeff Kingston, and Kapila Wimalaratne. 2000. Supporting Reflection in Introductory Computer Science. In *Proceedings of the Thirty-first SIGCSE Technical Symposium on Computer Science Education (SIGCSE '00)*. ACM, New York, NY, USA, 144–148. https://doi.org/10.1145/330908.331844

[14] Angela Fessl, Oliver Blunk, Michael Prilla, and Viktoria Pammer. 2017. The known universe of reflection guidance: a literature review. *International Journal of Technology Enhanced Learning* 9, 2-3 (2017), 103–125.

[15] Susan E. George. 2002. *Learning and the Reflective Journal in Computer Science*. Vol. 24. IEEE Computer Society Press, Los Alamitos, CA, USA. 77–86 pages. https://doi.org/10.1145/563857.563811

[16] Sten Govaerts, Katrien Verbert, Erik Duval, and Abelardo Pardo. 2012. The Student Activity Meter for Awareness and Self-reflection. In *CHI '12 Extended Abstracts on Human Factors in Computing Systems (CHI EA '12)*. ACM, New York, NY, USA, 869–884. https://doi.org/10.1145/2212776.2212860

[17] Robert A Hinde. 1972. *Non-verbal communication*. Cambridge University Press.

[18] Dongsik Kim and Seunghee Lee. 2002. Designing collaborative reflection supporting tools in e-project-based learning environments. *Journal of Interactive Learning Research* 13, 4 (2002), 375–392.

[19] Tomi Kinnunen, Evgenia Chernenko, Marko Tuononen, Pasi Fränti, and Haizhou Li. 2007. Voice activity detection using MFCC features and support vector machine. In *Int. Conf. on Speech and Computer (SPECOM07), Moscow, Russia*, Vol. 2. 556–561.

[20] Celine Latulipe, Stephen MacNeil, and Brian Thompson. 2018. Evolving a Data Structures Class Toward Inclusive Success. In *Frontiers in Education Conference (FIE 2018)*. IEEE, 1–5.

[21] Colleen M Lewis, Ruth E Anderson, and Ken Yasuhara. 2016. I Don't Code All Day: Fitting in Computer Science When the Stereotypes Don't Fit. In *Proceedings of the 2016 ACM Conference on International Computing Education Research*. ACM, 23–32.

[22] Colleen M. Lewis and Niral Shah. 2015. How Equity and Inequity Can Emerge in Pair Programming. In *Proceedings of the Eleventh Annual International Conference on International Computing Education Research (ICER '15)*. ACM, New York, NY, USA, 41–50. https://doi.org/10.1145/2787622.2787716

[23] Stephen MacNeil. 2017. Tools to Support Data-driven Reflective Learning. In *Proceedings of the 2017 ACM Conference on International Computing Education Research (ICER '17)*. ACM, New York, NY, USA, 299–300. https://doi.org/10.1145/3105726.3105745

[24] Roberto Martinez, Judy Kay, James R Wallace, and Kalina Yacef. 2011. Modelling symmetry of activity as an indicator of collocated group collaboration. In *International Conference on User Modeling, Adaptation, and Personalization*. Springer, 207–218.

[25] Joseph Edward McGrath. 1984. *Groups: Interaction and performance*. Vol. 14. Prentice-Hall Englewood Cliffs, NJ.

[26] Jack Mezirow. 1998. On critical reflection. *Adult education quarterly* 48, 3 (1998), 185–198.

[27] Mavuto M Mukaka. 2012. A guide to appropriate use of correlation coefficient in medical research. *Malawi Medical Journal* 24, 3 (2012), 69–71.

[28] Rosemery O Nelson and Steven C Hayes. 1981. Theoretical explanations for reactivity in self-monitoring. *Behavior Modification* 5, 1 (1981), 3–14.

[29] Tia Newhall, Lisa Meeden, Andrew Danner, Ameet Soni, Frances Ruiz, and Richard Wicentowski. 2014. A support program for introductory CS courses that improves student performance and retains students from underrepresented groups. In *Proceedings of the 45th ACM technical symposium on Computer science education*. ACM, 433–438.

[30] Johanna Okerlund, Madison Dunaway, Celine Latulipe, David Wilson, and Eric Paulos. 2018. Statement Making: A Maker Fashion Show Foregrounding Feminism, Gender, and Transdisciplinarity. In *Proceedings of the 2018 Designing Interactive Systems Conference*. ACM, 187–199.

[31] Johanna Pirker, Maria Riffnaller-Schiefer, and Christian Gütl. 2014. Motivational Active Learning: Engaging University Students in Computer Science Education. In *Proceedings of the 2014 Conference on Innovation & Technology in Computer Science Education (ITiCSE '14)*. ACM, New York, NY, USA, 297–302. https://doi.org/10.1145/2591708.2591750

[32] Gianluca Schiavo, Alessandro Cappelletti, Eleonora Mencarini, Oliviero Stock, and Massimo Zancanaro. 2014. Overt or subtle? Supporting group conversations with automatically targeted directives. In *Proceedings of the 19th international conference on Intelligent User Interfaces*. ACM, 225–234.

[33] John R Searle and John Rogers Searle. 1969. *Speech acts: An essay in the philosophy of language*. Vol. 626. Cambridge university press.

[34] Robert M Sellers, Tabbye M Chavous, and Deanna Y Cooke. 1998. Racial ideology and racial centrality as predictors of African American college students' academic performance. *Journal of Black Psychology* 24, 1 (1998), 8–27.

[35] Ben Shneiderman. 1996. The Eyes Have It: A Task by Data Type Taxonomy for Information Visualizations. In *Proceedings of the 1996 IEEE Symposium on Visual Languages (VL '96)*. IEEE Computer Society, Washington, DC, USA, 336–. http://dl.acm.org/citation.cfm?id=832277.834354

[36] Adam Stankiewicz and Chinmay Kulkarni. 2016. $1 Conversational Turn Detector: Measuring How Video Conversations Affect Student Learning in Online Classes. In *Proceedings of the Third (2016) ACM Conference on Learning @ Scale (L@S '16)*. ACM, New York, NY, USA, 81–88. https://doi.org/10.1145/2876034.2876048

[37] Rong Tong, Bin Ma, Kong-Aik Lee, Changhuai You, Donglai Zhu, Tomi Kinnunen, Hanwu Sun, Minghui Dong, Eng Siong Chng, and Haizhou Li. 2006. The IIR NIST 2006 Speaker Recognition System: Fusion of Acoustic and Tokenization Features. In *presentation in 5th Int. Symp. on Chinese Spoken Language Processing, ISCSLP*.

[38] Masahiro Toyoura, Mayato Sakaguchi, Xiaoyang Mao, Masanori Hanawa, and Masayuki Murakami. 2016. Visualizing the lesson process in active learning classes. In *Frontiers in Education Conference (FIE), 2016 IEEE*. IEEE, 1–8.

[39] James Walker, Rita Borgo, and Mark W Jones. 2016. TimeNotes: a study on effective chart visualization and interaction techniques for time-series data. *IEEE transactions on visualization and computer graphics* 22, 1 (2016), 549–558.

[40] David C Webb, Alexander Repenning, and Kyu Han Koh. 2012. Toward an emergent theory of broadening participation in computer science education. In *Proceedings of the 43rd ACM technical symposium on Computer Science Education*. ACM, 173–178.

[41] Victor H Yngve. 1970. On getting a word in edgewise. In *Chicago Linguistics Society, 6th Meeting, 1970*. 567–578.

[42] Madeline Zug, Hanna Hoffman, Forest Kobayashi, Miles President, and Zachary Dodds. 2018. CS for All Academic Identities. *J. Comput. Sci. Coll.* 33, 4 (April 2018), 130–137. http://dl.acm.org/citation.cfm?id=3199572.3199590

Combining Analogies and Virtual Reality for Active and Visual Object-Oriented Programming

Tevita Tanielu, Raymond 'Akau'ola, Elliot Varoy and Nasser Giacaman
University of Auckland
Auckland, New Zealand
n.giacaman@auckland.ac.nz

ABSTRACT

Understanding object-oriented programming (OOP) and its underlying concepts is essential in any computing-related field. However, learning the OOP concepts is often daunting for novice programmers due to their abstract nature. This paper presents a systematic approach of creating interactive learning activities for OOP concepts aligned with fundamental learning outcomes and misconceptions. The strategy combines analogies and visualisation to deliver concepts without students feeling distracted or overwhelmed by the technicalities inherent in textual code. A virtual reality implementation was developed, to help promote immersion and engagement with the abstract OOP concepts. The app was evaluated with CS2 students (n=17), with the results showing a significant improvement in students' ability to visualise the targeted OOP concepts. Students responded positively and agreed it was an effective learning tool to complement lectures.

CCS CONCEPTS

• **Human-centered computing** → **Visualization**; • **Social and professional topics** → **Computer science education**; • **Software and its engineering** → *Object oriented languages*;

KEYWORDS

Object-oriented programming, misconceptions, analogies, visualisation, virtual reality

ACM Reference format:
Tevita Tanielu, Raymond 'Akau'ola, Elliot Varoy and Nasser Giacaman. 2019. Combining Analogies and Virtual Reality for Active and Visual Object-Oriented Programming. In *Proceedings of ACM Global Computing Education Conference 2019, Chengdu, Sichuan, China, May 17–19, 2019 (CompEd '19)*, 7 pages.
https://doi.org/10.1145/3300115.3309513

1 INTRODUCTION

Object-oriented programming (OOP) is a fundamental programming paradigm widely used in industry. Its application is a mandatory skill in any computer science related field, and is listed as a core topic for students to master [19]. However, learning OOP can be challenging as novice programmers find its concepts to be too abstract that require new ways of thinking and more depth to grasp them [7]. The textual complexities of standard programming languages add further challenges for students trying to grasp the underlying concepts. When it comes to correlating and applying OOP concepts into real-world problems, students struggle [28]. Students find it difficult for a number of reasons, such as having to learn OOP after procedural programming has been taught, the technicalities of the OOP language used and the teaching methods employed [2, 3, 10]. To make matters worse, students often conclude with developing misconceptions on various aspects of OOP [8, 18, 27]. This in turn leads to students dropping out, contributing further to decreased retention rates [1, 2].

A possible solution to this problem is to provide alternative learning experiences for students. *Analogies* can be effective in learning abstract concepts if they are carefully designed [24]; a good analogy can benefit a student's understanding of a concept, by making abstract information concrete [22]. Studies show that *visualisation* can also be helpful in understanding abstract concepts, as long as the visualisation actively engages the learner [16]. Caution still needs to be exercised, as analogies and visualisations carry the danger of being misinterpreted and may give rise to further student misconceptions [24]. To help mitigate these dangers, alignment of learning outcomes and misconceptions to the activities may help. This paper proposes a strategy supporting students learning abstract OOP concepts. The underpinning ideas include combining analogies and visualisation to provide an alternative learning experience. A virtual reality app was implemented and evaluated on a group of 17 students from a CS2 course. The rest of this paper is structured as follows. Section 2 discusses related work. The alignment of OOP learning outcomes, misconceptions and activities is presented in Section 3, followed by the analogy in Section 4. A virtual reality implementation is presented in Section 5, with its evaluation in Section 6 before sharing some thoughts on the experience in Section 7 and concluding in Section 8.

2 RELATED WORK

Greenfoot [11] provides an interactive and visual approach to teaching OOP concepts. It allows the visualisation of classes similar to that of UML but simplified to remove unnecessary features. BlueJ [12] is a development environment specifically designed to teach OOP concepts at an introductory level. The software enables the visualisation of classes as modifiable UML diagrams. BlueJ takes an object-first approach and visualises only the important abstraction entities of classes and objects which provide a different interaction style from other environments. Raptor [4], like BlueJ, is a programming environment designed to help students visualise classes and methods. Raptor programs are created visually using a combination of UML and flowcharts, which can later be converted to Java code. OOP-Anim [6] is an educational environment that aids students in visualising object-oriented programs. It essentially uses animation with 2D graphics to animate programs created in hopes to allow for a better understanding of how objects are created, message passing and program flow. The animation corresponds to the current-executed line of code and is shown side by side, allowing students to examine the current state of the program.

OOP-Anim visualises classes, objects and memory references separately using UML-like diagrams. AEIOU [14] takes a scaffolding approach and consists of three modules each indicating the level of difficulty: Novice, Intermediate and Advance. Each level is carefully designed to introduce new OOP concepts. It offers a graphical user interface for the creation of new classes and includes a graphical view of the existing classes in the project. Imsovison (IMmersive SOftware VISualisatION) [15] is a system for visualising object-oriented software programs in a virtual reality environment. It presents a visualisation language (COOL) that maps code to its corresponding visual representation and was designed to be used in an old virtual environment (CAVE). Imsovision's primary function allows users to visualise the relationship between classes, member functions and attributes as represented by their visual equivalents defined by COOL. The sizes of the visual components correlate to how big classes and methods are.

3 TARGETING OOP MISCONCEPTIONS

To ensure alignment of the activities (and subsequent support tool) with relevant learning outcomes, a process motivated by constructive alignment was undertaken. The OOP sub-topics and their relevant learning outcomes were first inspired by the ACM and IEEE Computer Science Curricula (CS2013) [19] guidelines. A literature review then identified concrete examples of misconceptions and difficulties that students faced in these sub-topics.

3.1 OOP Sub-Topics and Learning Outcomes

The CS2013 guidelines define topics that should be covered to gain a strong understanding of fundamental programming concepts. The *Object-Oriented Programming* knowledge unit is listed under the *Programming Languages* knowledge area, referred to as *PL/Object-Oriented Programming*. The following sub-topics have been selected for this project, all of which are core **Sub-Topics**:

[Core-Tier1]

- *Object-oriented design*
  - *Decomposition into objects with state and behavior*
- *Definition of classes: fields, methods, and constructors*
- *Dynamic dispatch: definition of method-call*

[Core-Tier2]

- *Object-oriented idioms for encapsulation*
  - *Privacy and visibility of class members*

Classes and objects are the most fundamental concepts in OOP, forming the foundation to more complex concepts (such as inheritance and polymorphism). While most of the learning outcomes

in this unit refer to those more complex concepts, this project specifically targets the following CS2013 **Learning Outcomes**:

[Core-Tier1]

  1. *Design and implement a class. [Usage]*
  3. *Correctly reason about control flow in a program ~~using dynamic dispatch~~. [Usage]*

[Core-Tier2]

  6. *Use object-oriented encapsulation mechanisms such as ~~interfaces and~~ private members. [Usage]*

While the evaluation will not specifically measure improvements in these learning outcomes at a usage level, the goal is to develop students' confidence in visualising the above sub-topics and scaffold them in working towards these learning outcomes. The above learning outcomes are also somewhat coarse-grained, and so finer-grained learning outcomes can also be spawned towards these collective goals (examples shown below).

3.2 Misconceptions and Difficulties

Due to the abstract nature of OOP concepts, students may initially face difficulties and develop misconceptions. Misconceptions are menacing as they act as barriers, through which subsequent teaching on the topic may be inadvertently distorted [8]. It is therefore important to be aware of these hindrances and how they impact the learner's ability to fully understand the topic. Several studies have looked at students' understanding and developed misconceptions based on students' design for a simple OOP program [20, 25], students' responses after an OOP course [21] and instructors' experience from teaching an OOP course [8]. Ragonis and Ben-Ari [18] conducted extensive, qualitative long-term research on novices' understanding of OOP concepts, presenting a defined list of difficulties and misconceptions that novice programmers encountered. Liberman et al. [13] undertook a study on computer science teachers to understand difficulties, while other studies looked at students' interpretation of OOP concepts [5, 26].

Collectively, these studies examine different areas of OOP but draw a consistent picture on the misconceptions that novices form when learning OOP concepts. After analysing this rich set of existing research, common themes of the misconceptions and difficulties were identified. These have been categorised into four sub-topics, and are summarised in Table 1. It is believed that an awareness of these misconceptions and difficulties will provide some scaffolding when designing the subsequent learning activities. By specifically targeting these issues, hopefully the explicit attention will help eliminate them. The next step involves developing small code snippets that will form the basis for the activities that students engage with. Table 2 presents a couple of example activities, along with the misconceptions and difficulties they are specifically targeting.

4 THE ANALOGY

This section describes the analogy used to visualise some OOP concepts. It is presented independently of any particular programming language to increase its relevance to OOP concepts in general, and as a useful teaching resource to help students. Careful alignments have been thought out between the specific technical concepts and the corresponding elements in the analogy. The selected analogy

Table 1: The targeted OOP misconceptions and difficulties.

Category	Misconception (M) & Difficulty (D)
1. Class and Object [5, 8, 18, 20, 21, 25, 26]	a. A class is a collection of objects rather than a template for creating objects (M) b. Difficulty in differentiating between class and object (D) c. Two objects of the same class cannot have equal values for their attributes (M) d. Difficulty in understanding the link between class and object
2. Instantiation and Constructors [5, 8, 18, 20, 21, 25, 26]	a. No need to invoke the constructor method, its definition is sufficient for object creation (M) b. Difficulty in understanding the chain of commands when an object is instantiated (D) c. Difficulty in understanding default constructors (D) d. Difficulty in understanding empty constructors (D)
3. Method and Program Flow [18, 25]	a. Difficulty in understanding the influence of method execution on the object state (D) b. Difficulty in understanding that a method can be invoked on any object of the class (D) c. Difficulty in understanding the flow of program execution (D) d. You can invoke the same method on an object only once (M) e. You can invoke different methods on an object only once (M)
4. Identifier and Attribute [8, 18, 20, 25]	a. A variable that references an object is part of the object attributes (M) b. Difficulty in understanding objects if their attributes are not explicitly stated (D) c. Two different variables (identifiers) must refer to two different objects (M)

Table 2: Two examples of activities aligned to OOP learning outcomes, misconceptions and difficulties.

Learning Outcomes	Activity Summary	Concepts Covered	Difficulties & Misconceptions (Based on Table 1)	Activity Code

Understand how an object is instantiated by passing parameters to its constructor.
 	
Understand the chain of commands in constructing an object.
	Construct an object by passing parameters to the constructor.
	
	Inside the constructor, set the instance fields.
		Classes
		Objects
		
		Constructors
		
		Program Flow
		
		Fields
			[1a][1b][1d]
			
			[2a][2b]
			
			[3c]
			
			[4a]
				```Person *p1 = new Person("John", 20);```
				
				```class Person {```
				    ```int age;```
				    ```string name;```
				
				    ```Person(string name, int age) {```
				        ```this->name = name;```
				        ```this->age = age;```
				    ```}```
				    `...`
				```};```

Understand how an instance method is invoked to change object state.
 	
Understand the flow of execution when an instance method is called.
 	
Understand that a method can be invoked on an object more than once.
	Modify an instance's field by calling the same instance method twice.	Classes
		Objects
		
		Methods
		Program Flow
		
		Fields
			[3a][3b][3c][3d]
			
			[4a]
				```Person *p1 = new Person("John", 20);```
				```p1->incrementAge();```
				```p1->incrementAge();```
				
				```class Person {```
				    ```int age;```
				    ```String name;```
				
				    ```public void incrementAge() {```
				        ```this->age++;```
				    ```}```
				    `...`
				```};```

revolves around *houses*, as this is a schema that would already be familiar to students. This analogy allows the expression of the targeted concepts in an easy-to-understand manner. The main OOP components, with their corresponding constructs in the analogy, are summarised in Table 3. Section 5 helps convey this more visually.

Since an object is instantiated from a class, the analogy represents this as a house being built from a blueprint. Multiple objects can be instantiated from a single class, just as multiple houses can be built from the same blueprint. This provides a significant differentiation between a class and an object and conveys the idea that a class is a template to create objects. An instance method (i.e. a non-static method) is represented as a room of the house[1], helping to visualise how instance methods operate on their own instance. Each house built has its own set of rooms, as was defined by the blueprint. Invoking and returning from a method call is represented by entering and exiting the room respectively. If an instance method requires parameters, a window sill next to the room's door will be present. On this window sill will be placed boxes to represent the required parameters.

---

[1]The analogy (necessarily) simplifies some language implementation technicalities, such as ignoring complexities of virtual function tables Stroustrup [23].

Table 3: Alignment of the analogy and technical components.

OOP Component	Analogy/Visual Construct
Class	Blueprint of a house
Instance	House
Instance method	Room within the house
Variables	Box labelled with name (value goes inside)
Method entry point	Door to room
Method arguments	Placed on window sill before entering room
Method parameters	Grabbed from window sill inside room
Accessibility of fields	In centre of house accessible from rooms
Instance's memory location	Plot of land with house on it
Instance's memory address	Mailbox with land's address on it
Encapsulation	House walls are solid

Variables themselves are visualised as small boxes. Boxes are thought to store items, just as variables store values or references. An instance identifier (variable) is itself also a box, only the value within the box is an "address" number to the actual object. This address, corresponding to the memory location of the instance, is portrayed as the house (instance) sitting on a plot of land (the space in memory) with a letterbox address (the memory location's address). The consistency of representing variables is applied to parameters, local variables within a method and fields of the instance. In the case of instance fields, (i.e. non-static fields), these variables should be accessible from any instance method of the same object; the analogy therefore represents fields as boxes placed in a central open area in the middle of the house, visible from any room within the house.

The setup of this analogy also promotes the representation of scope and encapsulation within an instance. For an example, when inside an instance method (room), the only accessible variables are the instance fields (in the central house space), variables passed in as parameters (on the window sill) and local variables declared within that method (in the room). The room walls are solid, hiding information within that room that can only be accessed when the room is entered (the door itself is visible). Methods that are private have no external door outside the house, and can only be accessed internally once inside the house.

5 OOPVR

OopVr is a virtual reality mobile application developed according to the activity guidelines (Section 3) and analogy (Section 4) previously presented. The focus is on helping students gain confidence in visualising the targeted OOP sub-topics. OopVr provides an alternative learning experience, and is intended to be used as a supplementary tool supporting other teaching methods. As such, it assumes that students have studied OOP concepts before using the app. By applying their OOP knowledge during the OopVr activities, it is hoped students get reinforcement on visualising the targeted concepts. Figure 1 presents select screenshots from an activity, namely the first activity defined in Table 2. This section discusses pedagogical design elements of the VR learning experience.

Active Visualisation: VR visualisation brings the analogy to life, but more importantly provides an opportunity for students to *actively engage* with the visualisation and analogy. The environment and its components are carefully designed to reduce potential misconceptions.

Aligning Visualisation to Code: When engaging with the VR activity, students need to know where they are and how their VR actions correspond to the underlying programming concepts. The notepad in OopVr bridges this gap, with explicit alignment of VR actions and program code. Additional scaffolding is provided to students, in the form of "blinking" relevant parts of the notepad. This signifies the next code bits that the student needs to action in the virtual world.

6 EVALUATION

OopVr was offered to students in a CS2 course teaching OOP, for engineers in non-computing majors. Although there were 250 students in this course, only 17 participated in the voluntary evaluation. The evaluation's aim was to understand if the house analogy and accompanying OopVr app helped students improve their confidence in visualising basic OOP concepts.

Threats to Validity: The ethics approval granted for this project was restrictive, therefore a number of factors affect internal and external validity. As a result, a true experimental design study (e.g. a two-group control design) was not performed. While the evaluation involved a one-hour workshop, this included explaining evaluation protocols and participants completing questionnaires – so interaction with the VR app was typically only 20 to 25 minutes. Due to the anonymous and voluntary aspects of the evaluation, reporting on impact was limited to self-reported improvements in visualisation (based on coded pre and post questionnaires). The sample size was quite small (17 participants), and the evaluation could not be correlated to a difference in exam or assignment results. Finally, the evaluation did not investigate the analogy and OopVr app independently, instead measuring their impact together.

6.1 Methodology

Participation by students was voluntary and involved attending a one-hour evaluation workshop to use the app and complete a pre and post questionnaire. The evaluation process was as follows:

- *Pre-Questionnaire:* This questioned students' incoming confidence in visualising various OOP aspects and students' preferred mode of learning. All questions used a 5-point Likert scale.
- *Analogy Explanation:* The analogy, as presented in Section 4, was explained with the aid of slides. This was to ensure students understood what to expect from interactions in the VR world, so they could complete the activities on their own.
- *OopVr activities:* Students were given a mobile VR headset with OopVr, and asked to complete seven activities at their own pace. All activities were completed in the same order, as only when one is completed will it unlock the next.
- *Post-Questionnaire:* This included the same confidence visualisation question as the pre-questionnaire, but also included additional questions around usability and overall experience.

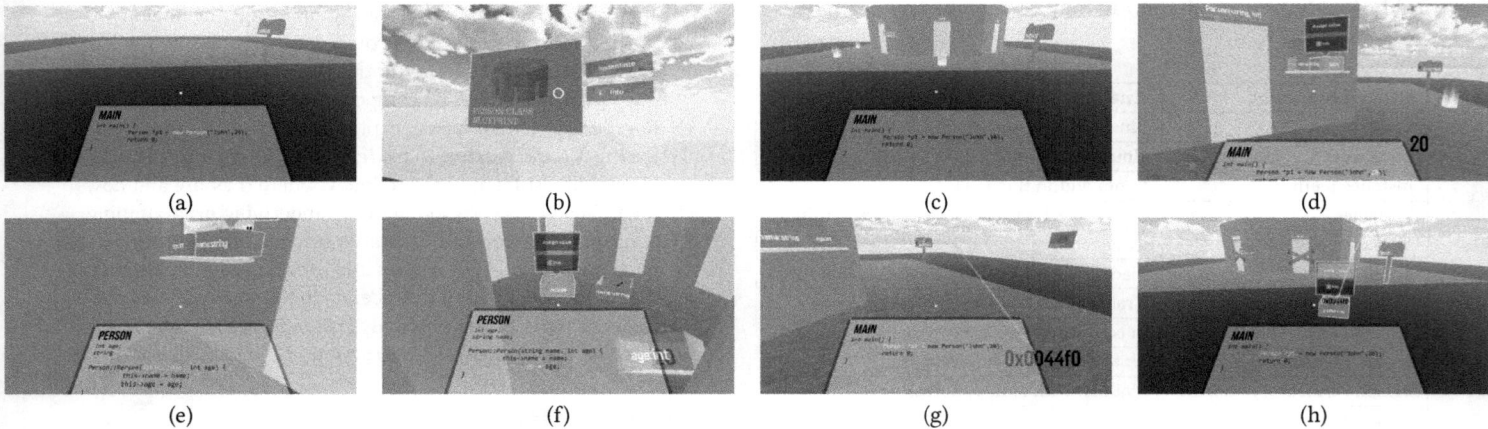

Figure 1: Screenshots from an OopVr activity, where an instance is created by calling the constructor with parameters: (a) no instance exists, so (b) the blueprint is used, (c) thereby creating the instance, (d) followed by placing values in the constructor's parameters. (e) Once inside the constructor, the parameters are copied and (f) placed inside the instance's central space for fields. (g) A reference to the instance is provided upon leaving the constructor, (h) to be assigned to the instance's identifier.

The questionnaires also included control questions on OOP concepts that were not explicitly targeted by the OopVr activities.

6.2   Results

In the pre-questionnaire, participants were asked how strongly they prefer *kinaesthetic* (need to be hands-on), *visual* (need to imagine things), or *textual* (need to read things) learning. Using a 5-point Likert scale (5 = Strongly Agree, ... , 1 = Strongly Disagree), the results were as follows:

Kinaesthetic:	$\overline{x} = 4.1$	$s.d. = 0.83$
Visual:	$\overline{x} = 4.1$	$s.d. = 0.90$
Textual:	$\overline{x} = 2.4$	$s.d. = 0.94$

The one-way repeated measures ANOVA calculation (F-ratio= 19.48, p<0.0001) confirms a statistical significance in the difference in means. Two-tailed paired samples t-tests between each type confirms that students equally-prefer kinaesthetic and visual learning over textual learning (kinaesthetic vs visual: t=0 p=1, kinaesthetic vs textual: t=5.6 p<0.0001, visual vs textual: t=4.4 p=0.0004). These results are not to be confused with learning styles [9], but rather emphasise that learning can be supported through multiple modalities. This reinforces the importance of combining visual *and* kinaesthetic opportunities for students in an otherwise inherently textual domain that is programming.

There were 16 questions in the pre and post questionnaires probing students for their confidence of visualising certain OOP concepts. This helps measure confidence improvements in visualising the concepts after immediately being exposed to the analogy and OopVr app. The results in Figure 2 are ordered by decreasing t-values from one-tailed paired-samples t-tests for each OOP concept (p-values < 0.001 for all, except the last question at p=0.035). While these results do not separately distinguish between the analogy or VR app, they do nonetheless confirm their collective impact together. This is particularly promising in that both were newly

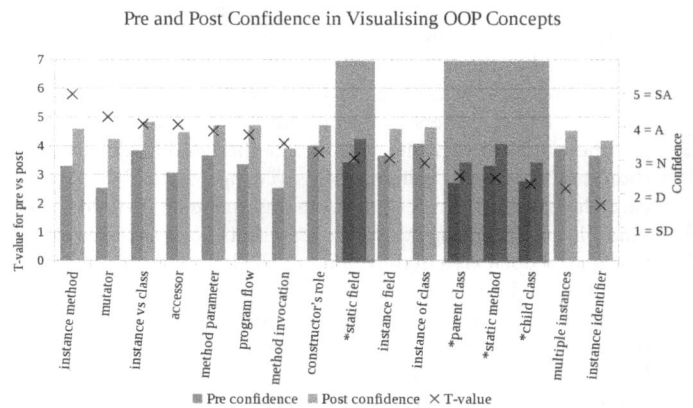

Figure 2: Visualisation confidence before and after exposure to the analogy and OopVr app. Concepts denoted with an *asterisk were control questions, not covered in the analogy or OopVr app.

presented to students within a one-hour workshop, thereby giving value to using this approach in a typical classroom setting.

A particularly interesting result is that students still felt visualisation improvements for concepts that were not present in the analogy and OopVr app. This might be a form of *transfer of learning*, where learning in one context enhances learning in another context [17]. While students were not taught how to visualise static fields or static methods, they were taught how to visualise (i) instance fields, (ii) instance methods, and (iii) the difference of classes versus instances. With these visualisation resources in place, students felt confidence in extending these to visualise other concepts not specifically covered. In fact, at the conclusion of the evaluation workshop, it was observed that students were immediately engaging in discussions regarding this very point.

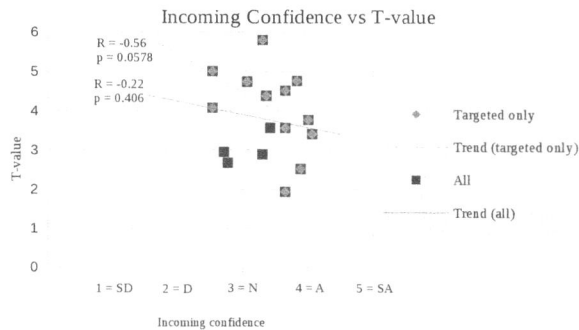

Figure 3: Spearman correlation of incoming confidence vs impact. The correlation is significant when analysing responses to targeted concepts, suggesting more impact on less-confidence concepts.

The concept that had the most impact in visualising was that of instance methods (t-value = 5.80), which is not to be confused with method invocations (coming in at 7th, with t-value = 4.08). It is unclear why this is the case, but it might be attributed to the visualisations helping more in the structural aspects of OOP, as the top five concepts are related to code structure rather than program flow. Another explanation is that these concepts were incorporated more heavily in the VR app experience; conversely, the concepts that were incorporated less with the app (or not at all) are shown to have less of an impact.

The Spearman correlation is used to determine if there is an association between incoming confidence and impact (as determined by the t-value from the above t-tests). Figure 3 shows no statistically significant correlation when looking at all questions covered by the study. However, when only the targeted questions are considered, the negative correlation is statistically significant. This suggests that the impact of the analogy and OopVr app is more powerful in helping students gain confidence for questions in which the students have less incoming confidence.

The post-questionnaire included a number of usability questions. Students' responses were overall very positive, commenting that OopVr was fun, engaging and immersive. When asked what they enjoyed most, 9 of the 17 students stated they liked the analogy used, and were curious to see how it would be extended to the more complex OOP concepts. This shows the potential of the analogy as a standalone teaching aid. In terms of shortcomings, some participants experienced slight dizziness or motion sickness. This could be attributed to a large amount of rotation and movement when performing the activities. Although this issue is common in VR-based applications, making movements more subtle might help.

This study has highlighted the importance of combining visual *and* kinaesthetic solutions for students in a dominantly-textual domain. Students reported improvements in their confidence visualising OOP concepts, crediting the combination of an analogy delivered through visual and interactive activities. It was also suspected that transfer of learning took place, as some students felt they were able to extend their newly-acquired visualisation skills to related OOP concepts. Students reported that virtual reality adds an element of fun, immersion and heightened engagement, while also

providing pedagogical value by helping them visualise otherwise abstract OOP concepts. Virtual reality not only brings an analogy to life, but it also allows students to interact with the analogy. It ultimately give students an alternative immersive experience to understand abstract OOP concepts. However, care needs to be exercised to avoid experiencing dizziness or motion sickness.

7 EXPERIENCE

7.1 Analogy Design

Despite the learning potential of analogies, extreme care needs to be exercised before releasing them to students. For the analogy to be useful to students, it needs to be simple enough that students can relate to it; however, it should also not be so simple that it incorrectly obscures vital details of the targeted technical concepts. The journey of moulding the analogy involves multiple repeat iterations of *contemplation* (by the analogy creator(s)), *alignment* (correlating analogy and target concepts as in Table 3), *critiquing* (by self and others – including colleagues and past students), and *informal testing* (exposing the analogy with current students). Even before attempting the VR app development, the analogy needs to be polished in its own right. If the analogy cannot be clearly imagined in the creator's mind, much like any story, then the VR implementation will suffer accordingly.

7.2 Challenges and Benefits

The remaining challenges include the extension of the analogy to more complex OOP concepts, such as inheritance, polymorphism and other visibility modifiers (e.g. `protected`). Seeing the response from students in the current version, this effort will be worthwhile and is already underway. Given that inheritance and polymorphism are even more difficult concepts, the benefits of these extensions are clear. Additional challenges will be in regards to accurately measuring the impact of the analogy and visualisations on actual student learning (rather than relying on self-reported improvements), both in terms of improved learning but also in terms of eliminating misconceptions.

8 CONCLUSIONS

Learning object-oriented programming (OOP) concepts is considered difficult for novice programmers due to its inherently abstract nature. Adding further complications is that programming is highly textual, while students are most dominantly visual *and* kinaesthetic learners – not textual learners. Visualisation and analogies have both been credited in promoting understanding of abstract concepts. However, to ensure pedagogical value, there needs to be engaging activities with clear learning outcomes and alignment to the underlying concepts being learnt. This paper presented a strategy to support the creation of effective and interactive learning activities for fundamental OOP concepts, along with an analogy to explain those concepts. OopVr is an implementation of the proposed analogy and activities, helping students better visualise the OOP concepts. Novice programmers from a CS2 course participated in the evaluation. Both the analogy and OopVr app were well-received by students as supplementary tools to help improve visualisation of OOP concepts.

REFERENCES

[1] Jens Bennedsen and Michael E Caspersen. 2007. Failure rates in introductory programming. *ACM SIGCSE Bulletin* 39, 2 (2007), 32–36.

[2] Susan Bergin and Ronan Reilly. 2005. The influence of motivation and comfort-level on learning to program. In *Proceedings of the 17th Workshop of the Psychology of Programming Interest Group*.

[3] Susan Bergin and Ronan Reilly. 2005. Programming: factors that influence success. In *ACM SIGCSE Bulletin*, Vol. 37. ACM, 411–415.

[4] Martin C Carlisle. 2009. Raptor: a visual programming environment for teaching object-oriented programming. *Journal of Computing Sciences in Colleges* 24, 4 (2009), 275–281.

[5] Anna Eckerdal and Michael Thuné. 2005. Novice Java programmers' conceptions of object and class, and variation theory. In *ACM SIGCSE Bulletin*, Vol. 37. ACM, 89–93.

[6] Micaela Esteves and António Mendes. 2003. OOP-Anim, a System to Support Learning of Basic Object Oriented Programming Concepts. In *Proceedings of the 4th International Conference Conference on Computer Systems and Technologies: E-Learning*. 573–579.

[7] Said Hadjerrouit. 1999. A constructivist approach to object-oriented design and programming. In *ACM SIGCSE Bulletin*, Vol. 31. 171–174.

[8] Simon Holland, Robert Griffiths, and Mark Woodman. 1997. Avoiding object misconceptions. In *ACM SIGCSE Bulletin*, Vol. 29. ACM, 131–134.

[9] Paul A. Kirschner. 2017. Stop propagating the learning styles myth. *Computers and Education* 106 (2017), 166 – 171.

[10] Michael Kölling. 1999. The problem of teaching object-oriented programming, Part 1: Languages. *Journal of Object-oriented programming* 11, 8 (1999), 8–15.

[11] Michael Kölling. 2008. Greenfoot: a highly graphical ide for learning object-oriented programming. *ACM SIGCSE Bulletin* 40, 3 (2008), 327–327.

[12] Michael Kölling, Bruce Quig, Andrew Patterson, and John Rosenberg. 2003. The BlueJ system and its pedagogy. *Computer Science Education* 13, 4 (2003), 249–268.

[13] Neomi Liberman, Catriel Beeri, and Yifat Ben-David Kolikant. 2011. Difficulties in learning inheritance and polymorphism. *ACM Transactions on Computing Education* 11, 1 (2011), 4.

[14] Guillermo Licea, Reyes Juárez-Ramírez, Carelia Gaxiola, Leocundo Aguilar, and Luis G Martínez. 2014. Teaching object-oriented programming with AEIOU. *Computer Applications in Engineering Education* 22, 2 (2014), 309–319.

[15] Jonathan I Maletic, Jason Leigh, Andrian Marcus, and Greg Dunlap. 2001. Visualizing object-oriented software in virtual reality. In *Program Comprehension, 2001.*

[16] Thomas L Naps, Guido Rößling, Vicki Almstrum, Wanda Dann, Rudolf Fleischer, Chris Hundhausen, Ari Korhonen, Lauri Malmi, Myles McNally, Susan Rodger, and J. Angel Velazquez-Iturbide. 2002. Exploring the role of visualization and engagement in computer science education. In *ACM SIGCSE Bulletin*, Vol. 35. 131–152.

[17] David N. Perkins, Gavriel Salomon, and Pergamon Press. 1992. Transfer of learning. *International encyclopedia of education* 2 (1992), 6452–6457.

[18] Noa Ragonis and Mordechai Ben-Ari. 2005. A long-term investigation of the comprehension of OOP concepts by novices. *Computer Science Education* 15, 3 (2005), 203–221.

[19] M Sahami, A Danyluk, S Fincher, K Fisher, D Grossman, E Hawthorne, R Katz, R LeBlanc, D Reed, S Roach, E Cuadros-Vargas, R Dodge, R France, A Kumar, B Robinson, R Seker, and A Thompson. 2013. Computer Science Curricula 2013: Curriculum Guidelines for Undergraduate Degree Programs in Computer Science. *Association for Computing Machinery (ACM)-IEEE Computer Society* (2013).

[20] Kate Sanders and Lynda Thomas. 2007. Checklists for grading object-oriented CS1 programs: concepts and misconceptions. In *ACM SIGCSE Bulletin*, Vol. 39. ACM, 166–170.

[21] Ronit Shmallo, Noa Ragonis, and David Ginat. 2012. Fuzzy OOP: expanded and reduced term interpretations. In *Proceedings of the 17th ACM annual conference on Innovation and technology in computer science education*. ACM, 309–314.

[22] PR Simons. 1984. Instructing with analogies. *Journal of Educational Psychology* 76, 3 (1984), 513.

[23] Bjarne Stroustrup. 1997. *The C++ Programming Language*. Addison-Wesley.

[24] Paul Thagard. 1992. Analogy, explanation, and education. *Journal of research in science teaching* 29, 6 (1992), 537–544.

[25] Benjy Thomasson, Mark Ratcliffe, and Lynda Thomas. 2006. Identifying novice difficulties in object oriented design. In *ACM SIGCSE Bulletin*, Vol. 38. ACM, 28–32.

[26] Stelios Xinogalos. 2015. Object-oriented design and programming: an investigation of novices conceptions on objects and classes. *ACM Transactions on Computing Education* 15, 3 (2015), 13.

[27] Stelios Xinogalos, Maya Sartatzemi, and Vassilios Dagdilelis. 2006. Studying students' difficulties in an OOP course based on BlueJ. In *IASTED International Conference on Computers and Advanced technology in Education*. 82–87.

[28] Lu Yan. 2009. Teaching object-oriented programming with games. In *Information Technology: New Generations, 2009. ITNG'09. Sixth International Conference on.* IEEE, 969–974.

VUC: Visualizing Daily Video Utilization to Promote Student Engagement in Online Distance Education

Huan He
SPKLSTN Lab, School of EIE
Xi'an Jiaotong University
Xi'an, Shaanxi, China
hehuan@mail.xjtu.edu.cn

Qinghua Zheng
SPKLSTN Lab, School of EIE
Xi'an Jiaotong University
Xi'an, Shaanxi, China
qhzheng@mail.xjtu.edu.cn

Bo Dong
School of Continuing Education
National Engineering Lab for Big Data Analytics
Xi'an Jiaotong University
Xi'an, Shaanxi, China
dong.bo@mail.xjtu.edu.cn

Guobin Li
Beijing National Center For
Open & Distance Education Co., LTD
Beijing, China
ligb@mail.open.com.cn

ABSTRACT

Online video is widely used in various courses in online distance education (ODE). For ODE students, it is challenging to study multiple online courses and keep track of the video viewing progress each semester. In this paper, we introduce a visualization tool called video utilization calendar (VUC) for promoting student engagement with the videos of multiple online courses. VUC is designed to visualize both the current viewing progress and the daily viewing history for all the courses in a semester for students to check their viewing progress for all videos and choose any course video to view directly. To evaluate VUC, we conducted a randomized controlled trial and a survey in an ODE school. Our results demonstrate that students may spend more days online and view more course videos with the support of VUC, whereas the total video viewing time does not increase significantly. In addition, course instructors identified two patterns of video utilization, which suggests that VUC may also be of assistance to instructors in understanding how students schedule their video viewing for multiple courses.

CCS CONCEPTS

• **Human-centered computing** → **Visualization**; • **Applied computing** → **Education**; E-learning;

KEYWORDS

Distance education; video utilization; visualization

ACM Reference Format:
Huan He, Bo Dong, Qinghua Zheng, and Guobin Li. 2019. VUC: Visualizing Daily Video Utilization to Promote Student Engagement in Online Distance Education. In *ACM Global Computing Education Conference 2019 (CompEd '19), May 17–19, 2019, Chengdu, Sichuan, China*. ACM, New York, NY, USA, 7 pages. https://doi.org/10.1145/3300115.3309514

1 INTRODUCTION

Online distance education (ODE) has become an important supplement to higher education in recent years, which provides students across the country with the opportunity to access high-quality educational resources [18]. In online learning and ODE, student engagement is considered a necessary prerequisite for learning, retention, achievement and graduation [12, 13, 20, 22]. Scholars have typically identified student engagement as a construct that consists of three components: behavioral engagement, emotional engagement, and cognitive engagement [10, 13]. Our work focuses on students' behavioral engagement and throughout this paper, "engagement" will refer to "behavioral engagement".

With the support of a learning management system (LMS), students' online activities (e.g., viewing and posting) can be recorded and saved as log data, which is a potential data source for measuring student engagement. By mining this log data, studies of student engagement in online learning environments have identified multiple factors that affect student engagement, such as video production [11], virtual achievement badges [1, 9], embedding discussion threads into video [26], and discussion activities [8]. Based on these findings, both student engagement and learning experience can be improved to achieve a better learning outcome. Moreover, several studies have demonstrated that improving the design or visualization function of the LMS may also have an impact on student engagement [2, 14, 20].

In this study, we describe our experience of using a visualization tool to promote student engagement with online video lectures for multiple courses. Since online videos are the main learning materials in the undergraduate program of our ODE school, each ODE student must view many videos on the LMS to obtain knowledge and skills (approximately 1,300 videos of 24 courses in 4 semesters over 2 years). Therefore, improving the LMS to promote student engagement with video lectures is of interest to the ODE school.

To address this issue, we developed a visualization tool called video utilization calendar (VUC), with reference to existing research on student engagement and visualization [2, 4, 11, 14, 24] in online learning environments. VUC is designed to help students understand their viewing progress for multiple courses by showing the video utilization from three aspects: the viewing progress for all courses, the daily viewing history during the semester, and the weekly viewing statistics. Moreover, we discussed the results of the experiment and the survey and analyzed the viewing histories of students in experiment with two course instructors.

The main contributions of this paper are as follows:

- We developed an online visualization tool for helping students understand and improve their video utilization for multiple courses in online learning environments.
- We conducted a randomized controlled trial and a survey to evaluate the effectiveness and usefulness of VUC.
- Two patterns of viewing history were identified in the visual analysis of video utilization using VUC.

2 RELATED WORK

In this section, we review the literature that is related to student engagement in online learning environments. Then, we summarize recent works on using visualization in online learning and discuss how our tool extends prior works.

2.1 Student Engagement

To measure student engagement in online learning environments, many metrics have been proposed from various perspectives. The most commonly used metrics for measuring student engagement are based on student interactions with functions and resources in the LMS. Guo et al. [11] used the time that a student spends on a video and whether a student attempts the follow-up problem after watching a video as proxies for engagement. Singh et al. [23] proposed a content engagement score for measuring the engagement by the students with specified content, which consists of cognitive, emotional, and behavioral engagement, using a comprehensive set of user activities. Van der Sluis et al. [24] used the dwelling time (how much time students spend watching a video) and the dwelling rate (how much of the video they watch) to measure student interaction with educational videos. Bote-Lorenzo and Gómez-Sánchez [4] defined 16 metrics for measuring student engagement in each chapter of an online course, such as the percentage of lecture videos that were totally or partially watched, the percentage of finger exercises that were answered, and the percentage of assignments that were submitted.

The promotion methods and the factors that influence engagement are also the focus of many studies. For example, Kovacs [17] found that in-video quizzes have the potential to improve engagement by making lectures more interactive. Van der Sluis et al. [24] proposed using the information rate to measure the video complexity and found there was a polynomial relationship between the video complexity and the student dwelling time. Brunskill et al. [5] suggested that providing a default option may encourage students to attempt to solve more practice problems. Zhao et al. [26] proposed reusing past high-value discussion threads in future lecture video and found that this approach was useful to students. Guo et al. [11] found that shorter videos, informal talking-head videos, high-enthusiasm videos and Khan-style videos are more engaging. Moreover, there are many other factors that may affect online learning engagement, such as cohort size of the forum [3], academic self-efficacy, teaching presence, perceived usefulness [16], the instructor's course preparation, guidance and assistance [21].

Previous studies have provided a variety of metrics that are related to course videos for measuring the student engagement. We plan to use viewing-related metrics in VUC with reference to existing metrics and methods [4, 11, 24] to improve the video utilization of ODE students.

2.2 Online Learning Visualization

Visualization tools have been widely used in online learning environments to improve the instructional design and the learning experience. On the one hand, instructors can use visual analytic tools to explore patterns in large-scale online learning. For example, Coffrin et al. [7] used bar charts, line charts and state transition diagram to help instructors understand learner behaviors. Chen et al. [6] developed a visualization system called PeakVizor to investigate viewing patterns in clickstream data. Xia and Wilson [25] developed a comparative heatmap tool that enabled instructors to explore and compare student video engagement.

Using visual aids can also support students' online activities. Ilves et al. [14] used a radar chart to support self-regulated learning and found that the lowest-performing students can benefit from this visualization. Ishizue et al. [15] presented a program visualization tool called PlayVisualizerC for novice C language programmers that facilitates learning the concept of memory management. Liu et al. [20] developed a learning analytic system called Tracer to promote student engagement by visualization feedback of behavioral patterns in writing activities. Auvinen et al. [2] used heatmap to show a prediction of students' success based on their behaviors. In addition, studies found that visual achievement badges have a positive impact on students' online learning activities [1, 2, 9].

In summary, these works apply a variety of visualization and interactive techniques in online learning, which inspires the design of VUC. However, these approaches are mainly designed for use in single courses, while ODE students take multiple courses at the same time. Hence, a multiview visualization tool must be developed to help ODE students understand their video utilization and viewing history for multiple courses.

3 OVERVIEW OF VUC

3.1 Video Utilization and Measurements

Students can access various learning resources on the LMS, including videos, slides, and textbooks. Among these learning resources, video is the main learning material. Consider the computer science and technology major in our ODE school as an example: There are 23 courses for each student to take in 4 semesters over 2 years, including foundation courses (e.g., English and discrete mathematics) and core courses (e.g., computer networks and operating systems), which involve 1,491 videos of 773 hours in total length. Therefore, each student must take 5-7 courses each semester.

However, the LMS that is currently used in our ODE school only provides the record of the last video that was viewed for a single course. Students can view neither the utilization of each video nor the viewing history for all of their courses. Therefore, we plan to develop a visualization tool that displays both the viewing progress and the daily viewing history for multiple courses to help students improve their video utilization. We use the following metrics to describe student video utilization as a proxy for student engagement and display them in VUC:

- *Video Attendance Rate (AR)* measures whether a student viewed a video or not. If a student viewed a video, the video AR is 1; otherwise, it is 0.
- *Video Utilization Rate (UR)* measures the proportion of a video that has been viewed by a student.
- *Course AR* measures the ratio of the number of viewed videos to the total number of videos in a course by a student.
- *Course UR* measures the ratio of the total time spent by a student viewing videos to the total video duration in a course.
- *Weekly viewing* measures the total number of videos a student viewed during a week.

3.2 System Architecture

As shown in Figure 1, the architecture of VUC consists of three components: a data analysis module, a data storage module, and a visualization module.

Data Analysis Module: This module includes two submodules: a data collection and preprocessing module, which collects data from the LMS, and a video utilization statistics module, which analyzes students' daily video utilization. We write several Python scripts that implement each submodule and deploy them as scheduled tasks on the VUC server. These scripts are executed automatically at 1:00 am every day to calculate the five metrics for the previous day.

Storage Module: In addition to saving the course data and cleared log data, this module also saves the statistical results to facilitate access from the visualization module.

Visualization Module: This module is a web-based application that enables students to check their viewing progress from various aspects. To facilitate students' use of VUC, we integrate the visualization module into the LMS by embedding the GUI as a panel called *My Viewing Calendar* on the student dashboard page. As a result, students will see their viewing progress immediately after login to the LMS. The GUI of this module is developed with HTML5, JavaScript and open-source libraries (including ECharts [19] and Vue.js[1]), and its source code has been opened as a standalone web application on GitHub [2] for demonstration.

3.3 VUC Design

To provide students with an intuitive impression of the progress in all courses, we design three visualizations that display video utilization from various aspects: a course progress table, a video viewing calendar and a weekly viewing chart. Figure 2 is a screenshot of the video utilization of a student who was involved in this study for six courses in one semester, which shows the interface of VUC.

Course Progress Table: As discussed in Section 3.1, each ODE student needs to observe the viewing progress for all courses in which he/she is enrolled in the semester. Therefore, we design a table that lists all the videos of the courses in which a student is

---

[1] An open-source JavaScript framework. https://vuejs.org/
[2] Source code of VUC: https://github.com/hehuan2112/VideoUtilizationCalendar

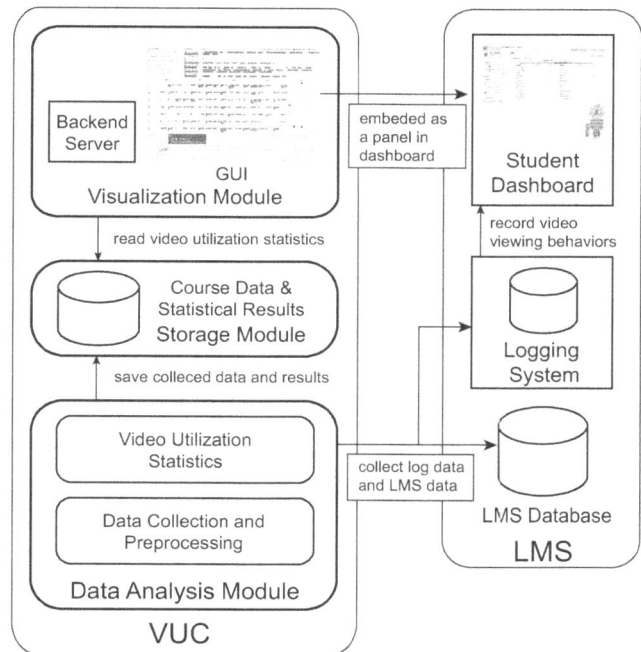

Figure 1: Overview of the VUC architecture

enrolled as cells (Figure 2(a)). We map the video utilization to the style of each cell with the AR and UR metrics, which are defined in Section 3.1. In this table, each course is assigned a color, which is used to distinguish the video cells in this table and the calendar below. The viewing progress of each course is displayed in each row, which contains three columns. The first column shows the course name. The second column shows the number of viewed videos and the course AR in a progress bar. The last column shows the utilization of each video in the course using a square cell of a different style, which is illustrated in Figure 2(d): an unwatched video is represented as a blank cell with a dashed border (the video AR is 0), while a watched video is represented as a cell with a solid border (the video AR is 1). The video UR is mapped to the width of the inner color block of the cell.

Video Viewing Calendar: As shown in Figure 2(b), we design a calendar-based layout for visualizing the daily video utilization, which shows a student's viewing history over the entire semester. The visual design of this interface is consistent with the printed version of curriculum calendar that students received in each semester. In each date cell, a check-in icon in the upper-right corner indicates that the student has viewed at least one video on that day. Meanwhile, all the videos that were viewed that day are listed in the date cell. When the course exam date is determined, there will be a black mark in the upper right corner of the corresponding date cell (as shown in the cells of July 8, 9 and 15 in Figure 2(b)).

Weekly Viewing Chart: Based on the detailed video viewing history, we use a line chart to illustrate the weekly viewing trend (the red line in Figure 2(c)). The horizontal axis of this chart represents the weeks in the semester, where each bin corresponds to a column in the calendar that is described above (e.g., as shown in Figure 2(c), the bin of week 2 corresponds to the week of March 5 to

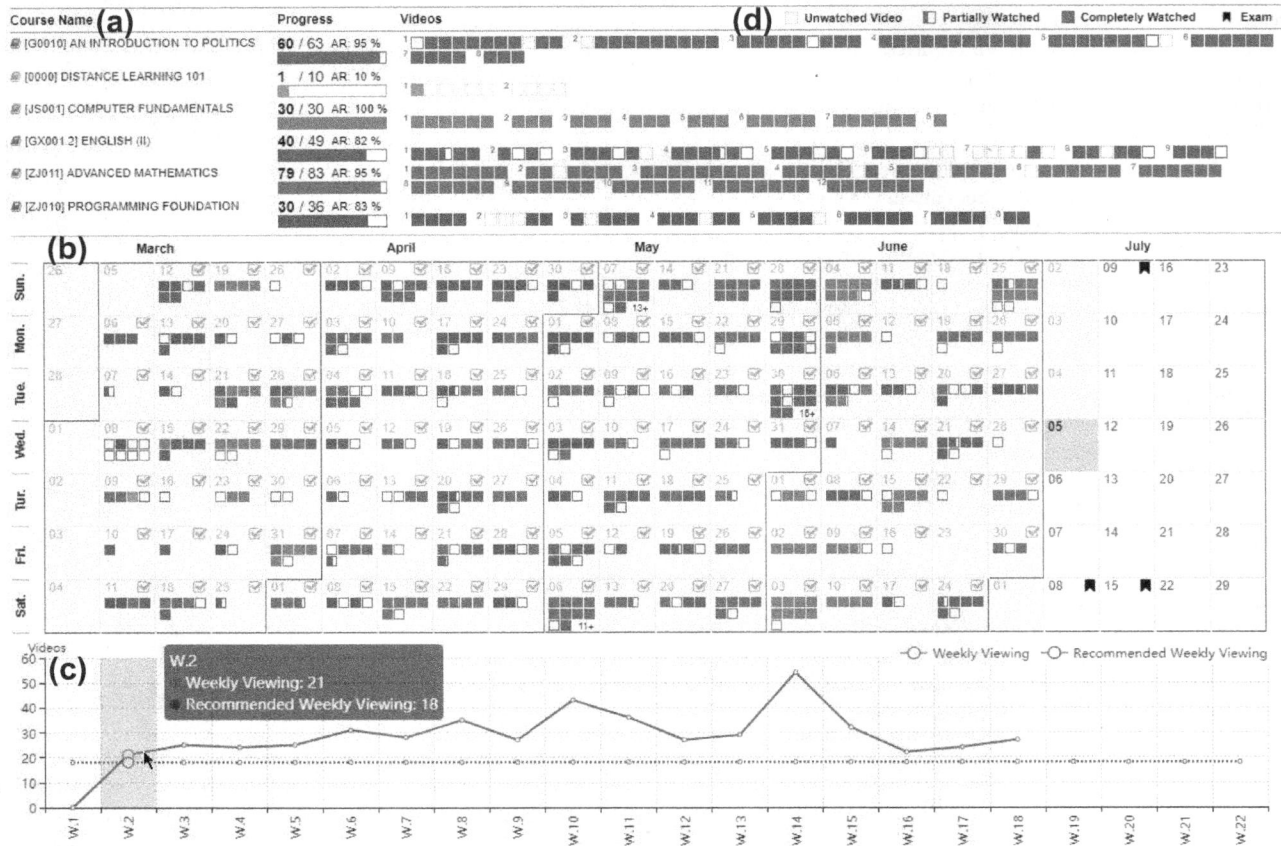

Figure 2: Screenshot of the visualization module of VUC, which includes: (a) a course progress table showing the viewing progress of all courses and all videos, (b) a video viewing calendar revealing viewing activities in each day, and (c) a weekly viewing chart showing something that is important for student to figure out learning history. (d) Legend of the cell and mark.

11 in the calendar). In addition, we add a reference line for weekly viewing in this chart (the blue dotted line in Figure 2(c)), the value of which is recommended by the ODE school.

4 EVALUATION

We investigate the following research questions (RQs):

- **RQ1** Does displaying the video viewing progress with VUC have a significant effect on students' video utilization?
- **RQ2** Is VUC useful for students who are taking multiple online courses?

A randomized controlled trail and a survey were conducted to evaluate VUC with respect to RQ1 and RQ2.

4.1 Context

The data that were used in this study come from the undergraduate program of computing in the ODE school of our university. This program runs from March 2017 to February 2019, with a total of 4 semesters. In the first semester, students must take 6 courses (which include English, computer fundamentals, and programming foundation, as shown in Figure 2 (a)). At the end of the semester, they must pass the course exams to earn credits.

In Spring 2017, 751 students were enrolled in this program, of whom 327 were included in this study. These students are aged between 20 and 45 ($M = 27.9$, $SD = 4.7$), and their academic qualifications at the time of enrollment are high school or equivalent. The remaining 424 students were excluded due to a restricted learning environment (e.g., a low-bandwidth network), in which they used offline videos for learning. VUC can neither collect their log data nor display their viewing progress. The 327 students were divided randomly into two groups: The control group consisted of 164 students who were not shown VUC and the treatment group consisted of 163 students who were shown VUC.

4.2 Method

At the beginning of the semester, few learning data have been recorded by the LMS since students spent approximately 2 weeks carrying out school affairs, such as entrance exams, payment, and receiving learning materials. Therefore, we enabled VUC in the LMS for the treatment group starting the 3rd week. Throughout the semester, the students in the treatment group can use VUC to view their video utilization at any time. At the end of the semester, we collected log data of all students in this study from the LMS and sent an online questionnaire to the students of the treatment group.

Table 1: Questions in the questionnaire about usefulness

#	Question
Q1	Do you think the visualization of videos and courses in VUC is easy to understand?
Q2	Do you think VUC is useful for checking your viewing progress and history of your courses?
Q3	Do you think VUC is helpful in promoting your viewing progress of multiple courses?

The questions in the questionnaire are listed in Table 1, which are evaluated on a scale from 1 (strongly disagree) to 5 (strongly agree). In addition, they were asked the following open-ended question: Please provide your comments or suggestions regarding VUC.

The following three metrics are used to measure the student engagement in the semester: *Semester AR*, *Semester UR*, and *Active Days*. *Semester AR* measures the mean course AR of each of the 6 courses over the semester; *Semester UR* measures the mean course UR of each of the 6 courses over the semester; and *Active Days* measures the number of days that were spent viewing videos online during the semester.

5 RESULTS AND DISCUSSION

5.1 Evaluation

Table 2 lists the statistical results of the three metrics for the control group and the treatment group. Figure 3 illustrates the distributions of the three metrics for the two groups. Figure 4 shows the distribution of students' answers to Q1-Q3 (131 of 163 responded), which are used to evaluate the usefulness of VUC.

RQ1: We conducted the Shapiro–Wilk test on each metric of two groups, which shows that none of the metrics follows a normal distribution ($p < 0.001$). Figure 3 and Table 2 show that the treatment group has higher semester AR and active days, on average, with higher standard deviations than the control group. Table 2 also shows the p-value between the two groups using the Mann–Whitney–Wilcoxon test. The differences in the semester AR and active days between the two groups are statistically significant ($p < 0.05$ and $p < 0.01$), while the difference in the semester UR is not statistically significant ($p = 0.152$). In addition,

The results demonstrate that although the overall engagement is low, using VUC does promote the engagement slightly. The treatment group viewed more videos and spent more days online than the control group. However, the total viewing time did not increase significantly as the number of views increased. This difference may imply that although students of the treatment group opened more videos when using VUC, they only viewed them for a short time. Since the activities after opening videos are beyond the scope of VUC, this finding suggests that although VUC encourages students to view more videos for multiple courses, there are other factors that can further affect the time that is spent viewing videos.

RQ2: As shown in Figure 4, approximately 90% of the students feel that VUC is easy to understand (Q1) and approximately 83% of the students feel that VUC is useful in promoting their course progress, while approximately 13% do not (Q2 and Q3). In the open-ended question, most students give positive comments on VUC, such as *"the chart is simple and intuitive"*, *"the calendar is very helpful*

Table 2: Statistics on three metrics for two groups

Metric	Control Group Median(Mean, SD)	Treatment Group Median(Mean, SD)	MWW Test
Semester AR	0.049 (0.112, 0.135)	**0.094** (0.137, 0.152)	<0.05
Semester UR	0.035 (0.132, 0.224)	**0.061** (0.134, 0.205)	0.152
Active Days	6.0 (10.4, 10.7)	**10.0** (13.4, 14.3)	<0.01

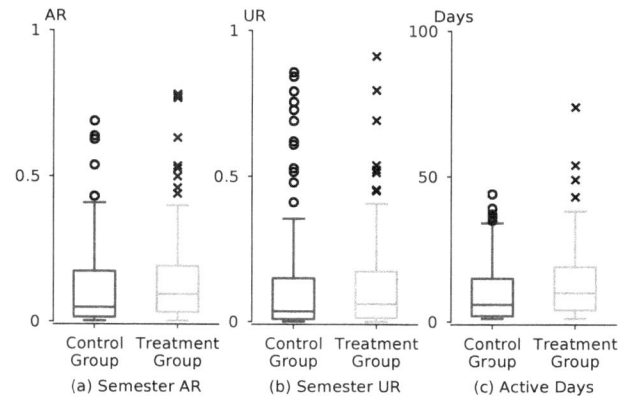

Figure 3: Box plot of the distribution of each metric in two groups. (a) Semester AR. (b) Semester UR. (c) Active Days.

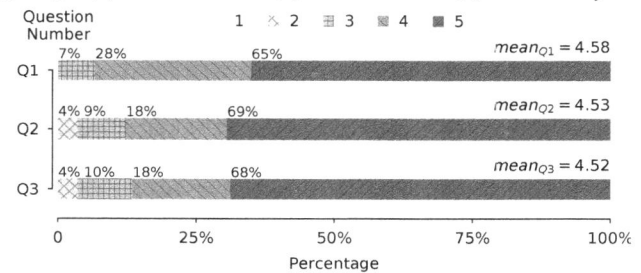

Figure 4: Results of Q1-Q3 (N=131).

for me to arrange study time", and *"it is easy to find out which videos I have not watched"*. In addition, students also describe the issues that are encountered when using VUC. We summarize these comments as follows:

- *The video I just watched doesn't appear*: Some students want to check the videos they just viewed; however, VUC doesn't behave as expected. We will improve this in the future.
- *I don't know which video to watch next*: These students have difficulty choosing the videos to watch when they schedule a study plan according to the viewing calendar. They expect VUC to provide suggestions about when and which videos to watch. We plan to add more interactive tips for the interface and send direct notifications by instant massager to guide students through the videos.
- *There are too many unwatched videos, I give up*: These students no longer watch any videos due to limited study time when they find that there are many unwatched videos in VUC. They suggest that VUC should mark the videos that involve key points in the exam to reduce the number of videos that must be watched.

The results indicate that VUC is helpful for promoting video utilization for ODE students, but there is still a gap between the present functionality and the students' expectations. Since most ODE students have jobs on weekdays, their study time is very limited. The existing features of VUC can only help them understand the past viewing status and do not provide further assistance. The results also demonstrate that students may need more guidance or recommendations (e.g., a weekly video viewing plan and an important video list) from the LMS to help them manage their video viewing. Especially when their viewing progress falls behind relative to the plan, they may benefit from the help of the LMS.

5.2 Engagement Pattern Analysis

To further evaluate VUC, we collaborated with two course instructors (IA and IB) during the experiment. Both of them are from the ODE school and have prior experience with VUC. At the end of the semester, we collected the VUC screenshots of all students in this study, and then performed interviews with IA and IB. During the interview, the screenshots were shown in ascending order of active days to them for analysis of the engagement pattern throughout the semester. We collected their feedback and discussion as follows.

First, they found that the overall video utilization was lower than expected for the ODE school. As shown in Figure 3, both the semester AR and the semester UR of most students were less than 50%, which means that more than 50% of the course videos were not viewed. IA explained that although students had a variety of factors that affect learning, they should view at least a third of the videos. In addition, the content of these videos may exceed the examination requirements; thus, viewing a few videos is sufficient for passing the exams and earning credit. Hence, there may be a mismatch between the current videos and the needs of the students. Therefore, IA and IB considered providing these results to ODE managers as a reference for improving the course design.

Second, as shown in Figure 5(a), for most students, no pattern is identified since they spent only a few days online. However, for students with more active days, two interesting patterns are identified: (1) the "cram session" pattern: these students begin viewing videos almost every day approximately a month before the exam (Figure 5(b)) and (2) the "long-term learning" pattern: as shown in Figure 2(b) and Figure 5(c), these students view videos for most weeks throughout the semester. IA commented that these utilization patterns may reflect different learning motivations and habits, which can be used for recommending learning materials.

5.3 Limitations

The following internal and external validity concerns are raised: Although all the students in this study have the same academic background and major, their motivation, learning ability, work experiences and learning environments vary. For example, some students have been working for many years, while others have just graduated from high school. The experienced students may perform better in these self-paced courses. In addition, it is possible that some students are in an environment with a poor network connection, which would affect their online learning.

The results may depend on course arrangement, course content, and the ODE school's requirement. Other majors may have fewer

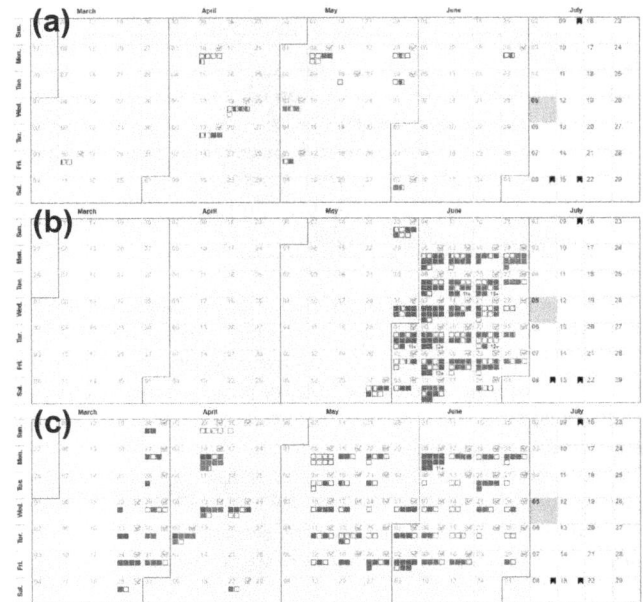

Figure 5: Different patterns of viewing history. (a) An example of s student spent a few days online. (b) "cram session" pattern. (c) "long-term learning" pattern .

courses and videos each semester and the content may be more suitable for students' needs. In some ODE schools, the number of viewed videos or the time that is spent viewing videos is counted as part of the students' grades, in which case students are incentivized to open many videos, even if they are not watching them.

6 CONCLUSION AND FUTURE WORK

In this paper, we presented a visualization tool called VUC for visualizing the video utilization of multiple online courses to help students improve their viewing progress. We conducted a randomized controlled trial and a survey to evaluate VUC. The results demonstrated that VUC was helpful for students in terms of viewing more videos and spending more days online, while the viewing time was not affected. In addition, two patterns were identified by course instructors with the support of VUC; hence, VUC may be of assistance to instructors in determining how students schedule their video viewing throughout the semester.

In the future, we will continue to improve VUC by implementing a real-time viewing progress functionality to help students check their current video viewing times. Moreover, we plan to recommend video lectures in VUC and send notifications by instant massager to help students schedule their online learning.

ACKNOWLEDGMENTS

This research was partially supported by "The Fundamental Theory and Applications of Big Data with Knowledge Engineering" under the National Key Research and Development Program of China with Grant No. 2018YFB1004500, the MOE Innovation Research Team No. IRT17R86, the National Science Foundation of China under Grant Nos. 61721002, 61532015, and Project of China Knowledge Center for Engineering Science and Technology.

REFERENCES

[1] Ashton Anderson, Daniel Huttenlocher, Jon Kleinberg, and Jure Leskovec. 2014. Engaging with Massive Online Courses. In *Proceedings of the 23rd International Conference on World Wide Web (WWW '14)*. ACM, New York, NY, USA, 687–698. https://doi.org/10.1145/2566486.2568042

[2] T. Auvinen, L. Hakulinen, and L. Malmi. 2015. Increasing Students' Awareness of Their Behavior in Online Learning Environments with Visualizations and Achievement Badges. *IEEE Transactions on Learning Technologies* 8, 3 (July 2015), 261–273. https://doi.org/10.1109/TLT.2015.2441718

[3] Jiye Baek and Jesse Shore. 2016. Promoting Student Engagement in MOOCs. In *Proceedings of the Third (2016) ACM Conference on Learning @ Scale (L@S '16)*. ACM, New York, NY, USA, 293–296. https://doi.org/10.1145/2876034.2893437

[4] Miguel L. Bote-Lorenzo and Eduardo Gómez-Sánchez. 2017. Predicting the Decrease of Engagement Indicators in a MOOC. In *Proceedings of the Seventh International Learning Analytics & Knowledge Conference (LAK '17)*. ACM, New York, NY, USA, 143–147. https://doi.org/10.1145/3027385.3027387

[5] Emma Brunskill, Dawn Zimmaro, and Candace Thille. 2018. Exploring the Impact of the Default Option on Student Engagement and Performance in a Statistics MOOC. In *Proceedings of the Fifth Annual ACM Conference on Learning at Scale (L@S '18)*. ACM, New York, NY, USA, 34:1–34:4. https://doi.org/10.1145/3231644.3231692

[6] Qing Chen, Yuanzhe Chen, Dongyu Liu, Conglei Shi, Yingcai Wu, and Huamin Qu. 2016. PeakVizor: Visual Analytics of Peaks in Video Clickstreams from Massive Open Online Courses. *IEEE Transactions on Visualization and Computer Graphics* 22, 10 (Oct. 2016), 2315–2330. https://doi.org/10.1109/TVCG.2015.2505305

[7] Carleton Coffrin, Linda Corrin, Paula de Barba, and Gregor Kennedy. 2014. Visualizing Patterns of Student Engagement and Performance in MOOCs. In *Proceedings of the Fourth International Conference on Learning Analytics And Knowledge (LAK '14)*. ACM, New York, NY, USA, 83–92. https://doi.org/10.1145/2567574.2567586

[8] R. Wes Crues, Nigel Bosch, Michelle Perry, Lawrence Angrave, Najmuddin Shaik, and Suma Bhat. 2018. Refocusing the Lens on Engagement in MOOCs. In *Proceedings of the Fifth Annual ACM Conference on Learning at Scale (L@S '18)*. ACM, New York, NY, USA, 11:1–11:10. https://doi.org/10.1145/3231644.3231658

[9] Paul Denny. 2013. The Effect of Virtual Achievements on Student Engagement. In *Proceedings of the SIGCHI Conference on Human Factors in Computing Systems (CHI '13)*. ACM, New York, NY, USA, 763–772. https://doi.org/10.1145/2470654.2470763

[10] Jennifer A Fredricks, Phyllis C Blumenfeld, and Alison H Paris. 2004. School Engagement: Potential of the Concept, State of the Evidence. *Review of Educational Research* 74, 1 (March 2004), 59–109. https://doi.org/10.3102/00346543074001059

[11] Philip J. Guo, Juho Kim, and Rob Rubin. 2014. How video production affects student engagement: an empirical study of MOOC videos. In *Proceedings of the First (2014) ACM Conference on Learning @ Scale*. ACM Press, 41–50. https://doi.org/10.1145/2556325.2566239

[12] Curtis R. Henrie, Lisa R. Halverson, and Charles R. Graham. 2015. Measuring student engagement in technology-mediated learning: A review. *Computers & Education* 90 (Dec. 2015), 36–53. https://doi.org/10.1016/j.compedu.2015.09.005

[13] Khe Foon Hew. 2015. Promoting engagement in online courses: What strategies can we learn from three highly rated MOOCS. *British Journal of Educational Technology* (2015), n/a–n/a. https://doi.org/10.1111/bjet.12235

[14] Kalle Ilves, Juho Leinonen, and Arto Hellas. 2018. Supporting Self-Regulated Learning with Visualizations in Online Learning Environments. In *Proceedings of the 49th ACM Technical Symposium on Computer Science Education (SIGCSE '18)*. ACM, New York, NY, USA, 257–262. https://doi.org/10.1145/3159450.3159509

[15] Ryosuke Ishizue, Kazunori Sakamoto, Hironori Washizaki, and Yoshiaki Fukazawa. 2018. PVC: Visualizing C Programs on Web Browsers for Novices. In *Proceedings of the 49th ACM Technical Symposium on Computer Science Education (SIGCSE '18)*. ACM, New York, NY, USA, 245–250. https://doi.org/10.1145/3159450.3159566

[16] Yeonji Jung and Jeongmin Lee. 2018. Learning engagement and persistence in massive open online courses (MOOCS). *Computers & Education* (Feb. 2018). https://doi.org/10.1016/j.compedu.2018.02.013

[17] Geza Kovacs. 2016. Effects of In-Video Quizzes on MOOC Lecture Viewing. In *Proceedings of the Third (2016) ACM Conference on Learning @ Scale (L@S '16)*. ACM, New York, NY, USA, 31–40. https://doi.org/10.1145/2876034.2876041

[18] Kyungmee Lee. 2017. Rethinking the accessibility of online higher education: A historical review. *The Internet and Higher Education* 33 (April 2017), 15–23. https://doi.org/10.1016/j.iheduc.2017.01.001

[19] Deqing Li, Honghui Mei, Yi Shen, Shuang Su, Wenli Zhang, Junting Wang, Ming Zu, and Wei Chen. 2018. ECharts: A declarative framework for rapid construction of web-based visualization. *Visual Informatics* 2, 2 (June 2018), 136–146. https://doi.org/10.1016/j.visinf.2018.04.011

[20] M. Liu, R. A. Calvo, A. Pardo, and A. Martin. 2015. Measuring and Visualizing Students' Behavioral Engagement in Writing Activities. *IEEE Transactions on Learning Technologies* 8, 2 (April 2015), 215–224. https://doi.org/10.1109/TLT.2014.2378786

[21] Jing Ma, Xibin Han, Juan Yang, and Jiangang Cheng. 2015. Examining the necessary condition for engagement in an online learning environment based on learning analytics approach: The role of the instructor. *The Internet and Higher Education* 24 (2015), 26–34. https://doi.org/10.1016/j.iheduc.2014.09.005

[22] Trang Phan, Sara G. McNeil, and Bernard R. Robin. 2015. Students' Patterns of Engagement and Course Performance in a Massive Open Online Course. *Computers & Education* (Dec. 2015). https://doi.org/10.1016/j.compedu.2015.11.015

[23] Vivek Singh, Balaji Padmanabhan, Triparna de Vreede, Gert-Jan de Vreede, Stephanie Andel, Paul E. Spector, Steve Benfield, and Ahmad Aslami. 2018. A Content Engagement Score for Online Learning Platforms. In *Proceedings of the Fifth Annual ACM Conference on Learning at Scale (L@S '18)*. ACM, New York, NY, USA, 25:1–25:4. https://doi.org/10.1145/3231644.3231683

[24] Frans Van der Sluis, Jasper Ginn, and Tim Van der Zee. 2016. Explaining Student Behavior at Scale: The Influence of Video Complexity on Student Dwelling Time. In *Proceedings of the Third (2016) ACM Conference on Learning @ Scale (L@S '16)*. ACM, New York, NY, USA, 51–60. https://doi.org/10.1145/2876034.2876051

[25] Jinyue Xia and David C. Wilson. 2018. Instructor Perspectives on Comparative Heatmap Visualizations of Student Engagement with Lecture Video. In *Proceedings of the 49th ACM Technical Symposium on Computer Science Education (SIGCSE '18)*. ACM, New York, NY, USA, 251–256. https://doi.org/10.1145/3159450.3159487

[26] Qian Zhao, Sashank Varma, and Joseph A. Konstan. 2017. In-Video Reuse of Discussion Threads in MOOCs. In *Proceedings of the Fourth (2017) ACM Conference on Learning @ Scale (L@S '17)*. ACM, New York, NY, USA, 153–156. https://doi.org/10.1145/3051457.3053972

Does Creating Programming Assignments with Tests Lead to Improved Performance in Writing Unit Tests?

Vilma Kangas
University of Helsinki
Helsinki, Finland
vilma.l.kangas@helsinki.fi

Nea Pirttinen
University of Helsinki
Helsinki, Finland
nea.pirttinen@helsinki.fi

Henrik Nygren
University of Helsinki
Helsinki, Finland
henrik.nygren@helsinki.fi

Juho Leinonen
University of Helsinki
Helsinki, Finland
juho.leinonen@helsinki.fi

Arto Hellas
University of Helsinki
Helsinki, Finland
arto.hellas@helsinki.fi

ABSTRACT

We have constructed a tool, CrowdSorcerer, in which students create programming assignments, their model solutions and associated test cases using a simple input-output format. We have used the tool as a part of an introductory programming course with normal course activities such as programming assignments and a final exam.

In our work, we focus on whether creating programming assignments and associated tests correlate with students' performance in a testing-related exam question. We study this through an analysis of the quality of student-written tests within the tool, measured using the number of test cases, line coverage and mutation coverage, and students' performance in testing related exam question, measured using exam points. Finally, we study whether previous programming experience correlates with how students act within the tool and within the testing related exam question.

CCS CONCEPTS

• **Software and its engineering** → **Software testing and debugging**; • **Information systems** → **Crowdsourcing**; • **Human-centered computing** → *Collaborative content creation*; • **Social and professional topics** → *Computing education*;

KEYWORDS

testing, crowdsourcing, assignment creation, educational data mining

ACM Reference Format:
Vilma Kangas, Nea Pirttinen, Henrik Nygren, Juho Leinonen, and Arto Hellas. 2019. Does Creating Programming Assignments with Tests Lead to Improved Performance in Writing Unit Tests?. In *ACM Global Computing Education Conference 2019 (CompEd '19), May 17–19, 2019, Chengdu, Sichuan, China.* ACM, New York, NY, USA, 7 pages. https://doi.org/10.1145/3300115.3309516

1 INTRODUCTION

Testing "is not a glamorous topic within software engineering" [7]. There seems to be a consensus on this in the field – testing is traditionally treated as the boring and unpleasant part of a software project, and there are often not enough time nor resources provided to do it well, let alone comprehensively [3, 18]. There is no general agreement in software engineering education and computer science education on to what extent one should integrate testing into introductory programming courses, even though the topic is considered important.

For example, Lappalainen et al. [14] suggest writing input-output test cases into method comments, Edwards [10] suggests having students write unit tests and providing students' feedback on the tests that they wrote, including test coverage, and Pirttinen et al. [19] suggest having students create problems with input-output test cases. At the same time, successful integration of testing practices into introductory programming courses is not trivial. For example, when integrating unit testing into first-semester programming classes, Barriocanal et al. found that only approximately 10% of the students actually wrote unit tests [1]. Interest and motivation also plays a role – Carrington suggests that students find writing tests for programs developed by other people more constructive than finding faults in their own programs [4].

In this study, we look at an approach where software testing – without mentioning software testing – is introduced to students in a first-semester introductory programming course through the use of CrowdSorcerer, a tool in which students come up with programming assignments and their associated tests. Using the tool, first described by Pirttinen et al. [19], we ask the students to create programming assignments to other students in the class and to generate simple input-output test cases for the assignments that they are creating. While the course does not initially discuss testing at all, the final course week provides a worked example on unit testing, and refers students back to the programming assignments and test cases that the students themselves have written.

We are interested if the use of the simple assignment generation tool in which students both write the assignment and the tests helps students learn testing. That is, whether experience gained from assignment and test generation transfers to other testing related activities. To evaluate this, we study students' performance in a computer-based exam where students are expected to implement unit tests for a given class, measured using manually graded exam points. We study how automatically extractable metrics such as test count, line coverage and mutation coverage correlate with students' performance in the testing related exam question, and also study whether students' previous programming background contributes to their behavior in the tool and the exam.

This article is organized as follows. First, in Section 2, we discuss related work. Then, in Section 3, we introduce the research questions and describe the methodology of the study. We present the results in Section 4 and discuss their implications and the limitations of the study in Section 5. Finally, conclusions and future work are presented in Section 6.

2 BACKGROUND

We first discuss research on ways of teaching testing and how to assess the quality of students' tests. Then, we briefly discuss how testing could be incorporated into introductory programming courses. Finally, we discuss research on influence of previous programming experience on performance in programming courses.

Testing is an important concept to teach, even if students do not like the increased workload and time spent on creating test cases. One way to make the learning process more fun and engaging is using tools or games for teaching testing. Mutation testing game Code Defenders by Clegg et al. [6] teaches software testing concepts such as statement or branch coverage through gameplay. CodeWrite [9] teaches students testing by first letting them write their own programming exercises and then a set of test cases for those exercises. Similarly, CrowdSorcerer [19] can be used to crowd-source programming assignments while teaching testing practices and encouraging students to read each others' code through a peer review functionality. Studies have shown that these kinds of exercise generation activities in programming courses can improve exam performance and help learning programming [8, 15, 16].

When investigating ways to teach testing, a question of how to evaluate the quality of student-written tests arises. CodeWrite and CrowdSorcerer both rely on peer-assessment [9, 19], but automated measures also exist. Edwards et al. [11] conducted an experiment with three test quality measures for assessing programs written by students in a data structures course: composite code coverage (counts how many of the methods, statements and branches of the code are executed), all-pairs scores (students' tests are run against the programs of others) and mutant kill ratios (creates mutants, where artificial defects are inserted into the program, and then runs student's test suite to see if it can distinguish the mutated version from the original program). The all-pairs score correlated the best with how well students' tests could reveal a bug.

A study by Marrero and Settle [17] investigated benefits of placing greater emphasis on testing in programming assignments in introductory programming courses. Their study did not find any uniform improvement in student performance, and concluded that especially novice programmers can struggle with the idea of handling assignments in several parts (program itself and its tests). Students in the group with more emphasis on testing seemed to struggle less with the abstraction that involved designing and implementing classes. Emphasis on testing also forced the students to concentrate on good software engineering practices even beyond

testing, such as interaction with colleagues and peers, and appreciation of clear requirements. Jansen and Saiedian [13] concluded their study with similarly inconclusive results, stating that while test-driven learning in introductory programming courses does have its benefits in adopting good testing practices early on, especially student responses highly favoured test-last approach because of apparent increased workload of test-first approach.

Teachers often integrate at least some testing practices into introductory programming, though the level of emphasis varies greatly. At best, students can be very accepting to including for example unit testing practices to programming assignments, and think that the effort spent on them is worthwhile and has a positive impact on the quality of their code [1]. A study by Edwards [10] suggests that teaching test-driven development in introductory programming courses can improve both the programming and testing skills of the students. Whether one should start with test-driven development or gradually increase testing remains an open question.

Prior programming experience seems to have a positive impact on students' learning and performance in programming courses [12]. The more programming languages a student has learned before taking an introductory programming course, the greater the effect. These observations on the impact of prior experience are supported by several researchers, for example Wiedenbeck et al. [22] noted that factors related to programming experience had a weak but significant correlation with introductory programming course scores. The experience does not necessarily need to be even related to programming, but to computer use in general. For example, Wilson and Shrock [23] note that even factors such as the use of internet, time spent on gaming, and the use of productivity software explain some of the variance in the score of an introductory programming exam [23]; this suggests that mere experience from the use of a computer can be beneficial for learning programming.

However, some studies have noted contradicting results. For example, Watson et al. [21] found that while previous programming experience had significant positive impact on introductory programming course scores when compared to those with no experience at all, there was a weak but statistically insignificant negative correlation with course points and programming years – that is, prior experience may contribute negatively to students' effort. Similarly, Bergin and Reilly [2] found no statistically significant difference between students with or without previous programming experience, and that students with no previous experience had marginally higher mean overall score on an introductory programming course.

3 METHODOLOGY

3.1 Context and tool description

Our study was conducted in spring 2018 in an introductory programming course organized in Java at University of Helsinki. The course offered help in walk-in laboratories with the option of doing the course fully online. The material consists of 7 weeks of content and programming exercises that go through the basics of Java programming, starting from basic procedural programming and ending with building programs that use several classes with different responsibilities ranging from a textual user interface to methods for storing data.

The course also lets the students write their own programming assignments using CrowdSorcerer [19]. Within CrowdSorcerer, students are instructed to create programming assignments in the following manner: First, create an assignment handout that is related to the given topic, for example if-else-statements. Then, write a model solution for the assignment and adjust it to create a code template that can be given to others. Finally, write a set of test cases for the assignment. The test cases are written as pairs of inputs and outputs: for a given input, the output of the program is expected to be the given output or to contain parts of the given output. The students were required to write at least one test case for each programming assignment they created. In our context, creating assignments with the tool was voluntary. The assignments created by students were peer reviewed by other students on the course in subsequent weeks of the course (see [20] for more details); students had three opportunities to create new assignments, during week 2, week 4 and week 6 of the 7 week course.

Creating assignments with CrowdSorcerer has many potential benefits in addition to having the students think about how their program needs to be tested. When students peer review other students' assignments, they get to look at source code written by others. This can have benefits such as students possibly understanding why clean code is important for code maintenance, as well as learning alternative ways to approach a programming problem. Additionally, some of the assignments created by students can be integrated into subsequent course iterations.

The last week of the course material discussed testing and provided a worked example of creating a set of unit tests, which the students were expected to follow. The material referred back to the assignment generation problems with CrowdSorcerer.

3.2 Research questions

We study whether the tool has benefit to students' skills in testing their programs. The research questions for this study are as follows:

RQ1. Are students who use the tool more likely to answer testing-related exam questions?

RQ2. Does the quality of the tests the students create with the tool predict the quality of their answer to testing-related exam questions?

RQ3. How does students' previous programming experience influence their willingness to use the tool?

RQ4. Does students' previous programming experience contribute to the quality of written tests?

The first research question is answered through a statistical analysis of the usage of the tool and students' performance in a testing-related question in our course exam. The second question is answered through an analysis of student-generated test quantity, line coverage, and mutation coverage, and their correlation with the test-related exam question. The third and fourth research questions look into whether students' previous programming background contribute to students' tool usage or the quality of the written tests.

3.3 Data

CrowdSorcerer collects student identifiers, created programming assignments and tests, and time stamps of events within the tool. Besides this data, we use exam results, focusing on a question

# Assignments	# Students	% Answered	Avg. points (sd)
None	168	97.6%	2.78 (1.54)
1-2	80	97.5%	2.92 (1.54)
3	22	100%	3.47 (1.08)

Table 1: Testing exam question performance categorized based on the number of generated programming assignments. # Assignments column indicates the number of generated assignments, # Students column the number of students in that category, % Answered the percentage of students in that category who answered to the exam question on testing, and Avg. points (sd) represents the average points and standard deviation from the testing-related exam question (on a scale from 0 to 4).

where the students were expected to implement unit tests for a given program. The exam question is provided in Appendix A.

The data consists of students who participated in the exam and gave a permission to use their data for research purposes ($n = 270$). When calculating particular values, for example the average points received from the testing-related exam question, only students who answered the question were included. If a student retook the exam, for example to raise their course grade, only the first exam attempt was investigated. Finally, when calculating correlations between performance of the tests written in the tool and the points received from the testing-related exam question, only those who had created at least one assignment and answered the testing-related exam question were studied.

4 RESULTS

4.1 Usage and exam question performance

In total, 270 students gave permission for the collection and usage of their data. From these students, 22 used CrowdSorcerer to create assignments every time it was visible in the material, 80 used it 1 to 2 times, and 168 did not use it at any point of the course. When calculating usage, we count only the times when a student created a new programming assignment for a different problem – repeated returns for the same problem are excluded from analysis. From the 270 students, 264 answered the testing-related exam question, 100 of whom had used the tool to create an assignment and 164 had not. 97.5% of the students who used the tool 1 to 2 times attempted the testing exercise in the exam, whereas 97.6% of those who did not use the tool answered to the testing exercise.

On average, those who did not use CrowdSorcerer received 2.78 points from the testing-related exercise. Those who used the tool once or twice received an average of 2.92 points, and the average was 3.47 points for those who used it every time. The standard deviations were 1.54, 1.54 and 1.08 for these groups respectively. These results can also be seen in Table 1.

We studied if the number of assignments created using CrowdSorcerer correlated with the points that the student received from the testing-related exam question. Using Kolmogorov–Smirnov test, we compared the exam results of the groups: no assignments created; 1–2 assignments created; and 3 assignments created. The test, when corrected for multiple comparisons using Bonferroni correction, showed no statistically significant difference between the groups.

4.2 Time and exam performance

Time spent using CrowdSorcerer was estimated based on the time stamps collected by the tool. The students were divided into three groups of approximately equal sizes based on the time spent with the tool. The first group contains those who used the tool for less than half a minute, since most students did not use the tool at all. The rest were divided into two groups based on the median of the usage times, which was around 17 minutes, so that the first group contains the students who spent 0.5 to 17 minutes using the tool, and the students in the last group spent more than 17 minutes.

In the first group, 95.1% had answered the testing-related exam question. In the second group, the response rate was 100%, and in the last group, it was 99%. The average points received from the question were 2.68 for the first group, 2.81 for the second group, and 3.12 for the last group, with the standard deviations 1.52, 1.58 and 1.44, respectively. These results can be seen in Table 2.

Time	# Students	% Answered	Avg. points (sd)
< 0.5 minutes	102	95.10%	2.68 (1.52)
0.5 - 17 minutes	68	100%	2.81 (1.58)
> 17 minutes	100	99%	3.12 (1.44)

Table 2: Testing exam question performance categorized based on the amount of time spent in the tool. Time column indicates the time spent on generating the assignments, # Students column the number of students in that category, % Answered the percentage of students in that category who answered to the exam question on testing, and Avg. points (sd) represents the average points and standard deviation from the testing-related exercise (on a scale from 0 to 4).

We studied whether the time spent on CrowdSorcerer correlated with the points that the student received from the testing-related exam question. Using Kolmogorov–Smirnov test, we compared the exam results of the groups: less than 0.5 minutes in the tool; 0.5–17 minutes in the tool; and over 17 minutes in the tool. Kolmogorov–Smirnov test, when corrected for multiple comparisons using Bonferroni correction, showed no statistically significant difference between the groups – the test comparing the less than 0.5 minutes in the tool and the over 17 minutes in the tool groups had $p = 0.017$.

4.3 Testing effort and exam performance

Next, we calculated the correlations between the points received from the testing-related question in the exam and the test performance when using the tool. Three metrics were used to evaluate the testing effort: (1) number of test cases, (2) line coverage, and (3) mutation coverage.

We used Spearman's rank correlations, as the relationship between test performance and exam question points is not necessarily linear. For example, it could be that the increase from 0% coverage to 50% is more meaningful than the increase from 50% coverage to 100% coverage. The correlations and p-values can be seen in Table 3. All of the correlations are weak and not statistically significant.

4.4 Influence of programming experience

At the beginning of the course, students were asked about their previous programming experience. Out of the 270 students who had

	Course exam points
# Test cases	$r = 0.093, p = 0.372$
Line coverage (pct)	$r = -0.086, p = 0.400$
Mutation coverage (pct)	$r = 0.143, p = 0.162$
Time spent on the tool	$r = 0.184, p = 0.072$

Table 3: Spearman correlations and p-values between the testing effort – measured using the number of test cases, line coverage, mutation coverage and time spent – and points received from the testing-related question in the exam.

given consent for the study, 141 provided details on their programming background. From these 141 students, 28 had no previous experience at all, 50 had programmed for 6 to 49 hours, and 63 for over 50 hours. We organized these students into four groups: "did not report programming experience", "no programming experience", "some programming experience" and "a lot of programming experience", respectively.

From those who did not report programming experience, 40.6% completed at least one assignment with CrowdSorcerer. The rates were 39.3% (novices), 36.0% (some programming experience) and 33.3% (a lot of programming experience). The average time spent on the tool was 23.2 minutes with a standard deviation of 42.8 (did not report programming experience), 20.8 minutes with the standard deviation of 37.2 (novices), 38.5 minutes with the standard deviation of 114.1 (some experience), and 25.9 minutes with the standard deviation of 50.1 (a lot of programming experience).

The average amounts of completed assignments were: 1.60 (no reported programming experience), 1.27 (no experience), 1.39 (some experience), and 1.86 (a lot of experience). Standard deviations were 1.79, 1.41, 1.55 and 2.08, respectively.

100% of those with at least some programming experience had answered the testing-related question in the course exam, whereas 96.4% of those with no experience and 96.9% of those who did not report programming experience answered the question. Averages of points received from the question were 2.55 (did not report programming experience), 2.93 (no experience), 2.86 (some experience), and 3.05 (a lot of experience), and the standard deviations were 3.12, 3.37, 3.28 and 3.45, respectively. The difference between these populations is shown in Table 4.

We studied whether those with more programming experience were more likely to use the tool. Using Kolmogorov–Smirnov test, we compared the time spent on the tool as well as the number of created assignments with it for the three groups: those who had no programming experience, those with some experience, and those with a lot of experience. The test showed no statistically significant difference between the groups.

5 DISCUSSION

5.1 Tool usage and student performance

When analyzing the usage of the tool, most of the participants (62%) chose not to use the tool at all, while only 8% of the population used it every time it was in the material. This reflects previous results in teaching testing to novices, for example Borriocanal et al. [1] observed that only 10% of their students wrote unit tests.

	Did not report programming experience	No programming experience	Some programming experience	A lot of programming experience
Participated in the course exam	129	28	50	63
Created at least one assignment with the tool	40.6%	39.3%	36.0%	33.3%
Average and SD of time spent on the tool (in minutes)	Average: 23.2 SD: 42.8	Average: 20.8 SD: 37.2	Average: 38.5 SD: 114.1	Average: 25.9 SD: 50.1
Average and SD of the number of completed assignments with the tool	Average: 1.60 SD: 1.79	Average: 1.27 SD: 1.41	Average: 1.39 SD: 1.55	Average: 1.86 SD: 2.08
Answered the testing-related exam question	96.9%	96.4%	100%	100%
Average and SD of the points from the testing-related exam question	Average: 2.55 SD: 3.12	Average: 2.93 SD: 3.37	Average: 2.86 SD: 3.28	Average: 3.05 SD: 3.45

Table 4: Influence of previous programming experience for those who participated in the course exam. Points from the testing-related question are scaled from 0 to 4. In the columns, "no programming experience" means that the student reported less than five hours of previous programming experience, "some" means 6-49 hours of experience, and "a lot" more than 50 hours. Usage of the tool is counted on separate occurrences, not from repeated attempts of the same task. The average time is calculated based on all students in the group, not only those who used the tool. SD means standard deviation.

Our results do not indicate that students who use the tool more would be more likely to correctly answer the testing-related question in the course exam. However, it still seems that the more time the students spend using CrowdSorcerer and the more assignments they created, the better they performed in the testing-related exam question. Not creating assignments led to an average of 2.78 points from the exam question, while always using the tool to create an assignment led to an average of 3.47 points. Similarly, those who used the tool for less than half a minute got an average of 2.68 points from the exam question, while those who spent more than 17 minutes using it received an average of 3.12 points. None of the differences were statistically significant after adjusting the statistical significance level using the Bonferroni correction. This was done in order to avoid the problem of multiple comparisons.

When contrasting the time spent on creating the assignments, we notice that the population that did not spend almost any time on the task is smaller than the population that did not complete any assignments. Thus, there is a population who have attempted to use the tool, but have not completed an assignment due to reasons currently unknown to us. Approximately one third of the population spent more than 17 minutes on creating the assignments.

Similarly, when analyzing the student-written tests for the assignments in more detail, no statistically significant correlation between the exam points from the testing-related exam question and test cases, line coverage, and mutation coverage was identified. This suggests that the quantity or the quality of the test cases that the students implement do not tell much about their exam performance, which also means that the studied context should consider the use of the tool further. It is possible, for example, that the generation of an assignment takes too much focus, and the tests that students create are rather simple. On the other hand, as the testing question in the exam also expects syntactically correct unit tests, which the students do not practice in the tool, it is possible

that the exam performance and the tool usage measure different underlying constructs.

5.2 Course material and previous programming experience

The course material also included a worked example on unit testing that the students were expected to follow. It is possible that, as worked examples are a good way for teaching a topic [5], the direct instruction – in a single worked example – worked better than teaching testing with CrowdSorcerer. We must note, however, that in a preliminary investigation in which the tool was isolated from the programming course and shown to a handful of students, our observations indicated that the use of the tool could be a viable approach for easing students into learning testing.

Finally, when analyzing previous programming experience, we note that programming experience has more to do with answering the testing-related exam question than the number of programming assignments created with the tool. On the other hand, creating assignments with the tool might have helped those with no experience in programming to learn testing more than those with some experience. As stated in Table 4, the average score received by the novices is marginally higher than that of those with some programming experience, but the difference is not statistically significant. Interestingly, while novices may be more likely to create an assignment with CrowdSorcerer, they use less time in the tool on average when compared to more experienced programmers. This means that when the more experienced programmers use CrowdSorcerer, they spend more time, possibly creating more thorough or complex assignments.

5.3 Limitations of work

This study comes with a number of limitations, which we address next. First, measuring performance is always hard, and it is possible that the proxies that we chose (exam performance, tool usage, test quality) are poor approximations of the students' knowledge. Second, the studied exam question was the last question on the exam. While almost everybody answered the exam question, it is possible that some did not have sufficient time to answer the question properly. It is also possible that if students are uncertain of their testing-related skill set, as it is a topic that is not as widely studied on the course, they focus on other exam questions first and try to scramble together an answer at the very end of the exam, which results in lower score. On the other hand, the overall average score from the exam question was 72%, which was close to the average score from the exam overall; it is possible that some of the results are also influenced by a ceiling effect. Third, as we limited our analysis to the population who had attended the exam, there is bound to be selection bias in the data. This is visible also in those who used CrowdSorcerer; the students used the tool voluntarily, and it is possible that we have solely captured the more active population and consequently the use of the tool is secondary. It is possible that this more active population would have performed better regardless. Finally, the way CrowdSorcerer was introduced into the course may have influenced outcomes: the tool was not advertised as a testing learning tool, but it emphasized the benefit of creating a programming assignment and thinking about the process of programming from another perspective, and the students also had a worked example emphasizing unit testing in the material. It is possible that a different kind of focus in the material could have influenced students' focus when working with the tool.

6 CONCLUSIONS

We studied the use of CrowdSorcerer, a tool that can be used for creating and programming assignments with tests. When using it, students first create the problem description, then the model solution, and then the tests for the problem. The tests are written using a simple input-output format, where each input-output test pair provides the input and the expected output. Our hypothesis was that the use of the tool would contribute to students ability to test programs.

The hypothesis was studied using statistical tests between the usage of the tool and a testing-related question in a course exam. We studied whether the number of tests written, the line coverage or the mutation coverage of the students' tests in the student-generated assignments explain students' performance in the testing-related exam question.

To summarize, our answers to the research questions are:

RQ1. Are students who use the tool more likely to answer testing-related exam questions? **Answer:** When analyzing the tool usage and the tendency to answer the testing-related exam question, we found no statistically significant differences between the populations (see Tables 1 and 2).

RQ2. Does the quality of the tests the students create with the tool predict the quality of their answer to testing-related exam questions? **Answer:** None of the correlations (Table 3) between the quality metrics for student-generated assignment tests and exam performance were statistically significant.

RQ3. How does students' previous programming experience influence their willingness to use the tool? **Answer:** Those with no programming experience used the tool marginally more than

those with some or a lot of experience (see Table 4). Students with no programming experience also got marginally more points on average in the testing-related question of the course exam than those with at least some experience, but the difference is not statistically significant.

RQ4. Does students' previous programming experience contribute to the quality of written tests? **Answer:** Students with no programming experience got marginally more points on average in the testing-related question of the course exam than those with at least some experience, but the difference is not statistically significant.

Our analysis showed that there was no statistically significant connection between the used metrics and the course outcomes. This highlights a number of issues with learning to write tests, some of which generalize to the broader domain of learning programming. First, it is possible that asking students to generate a full programming assignment is too complex for learning testing, and as such, the methodology should be changed to focus more specifically on tests. It is also possible that the performance metrics chosen here are not optimal, as students were supposed to write syntactically correct tests in the exam, while the tool provided students scaffolding in the form of being able to limit to input-output tests. Similarly, as students were also given a focused worked example on unit testing in the course material, it is possible that it influenced students' behavior and thus reduced the visible effect of the tool.

As a part of our future work, we are looking into elaborating the influence of creating the problem statement and the model solution on students' learning. Do they move students' focus away from the testing task, or do they help students write the tests as they have designed the assignment as well? We are also looking into gamifying the system, as well as diversifying the ways how testing is taught with the tool, for example asking students to create test cases for assignments instead of creating the full assignments.

A APPENDIX - QUESTION: TESTING

You have been given a class **Grading** that reportedly offers the possibility to add course grades, to search for a grade by entering a student ID, and to search for all students who have received a certain grade.

Add a test class **GradingTest** to the code template and write the following unit tests.

- Check that a student with a grade added to the Grading object can be found using the object's **getGrade** method.
- Check that when calling the **getGrade** method for a student ID that has not been added, −1 is returned.
- Check that adds a student with a grade to the Grading object and then verifies that that student is found using the **getStudentsWithGrade** method.
- Check that when there are no students, the method **getStudentsWithGrade** returns an empty list.

Note: Each of the items were graded manually and for each fully working test case, students received 1 point. Deductions were made based on unnecessarily complex code, bad naming of variables and so on.

REFERENCES

[1] Elena García Barriocanal, Miguel-Ángel Sicilia Urbán, Ignacio Aedo Cuevas, and Paloma Díaz Pérez. 2002. An experience in integrating automated unit testing practices in an introductory programming course. *ACM SIGCSE Bulletin* 34, 4 (2002), 125–128.

[2] Susan Bergin and Ronan Reilly. 2005. Programming: Factors that Influence Success. In *SIGCSE '05 Proceedings of the 36th SIGCSE technical symposium on Computer science education*. ACM, 411–415. http://eprints.maynoothuniversity.ie/8209/

[3] Barry W. Boehm. 1984. Software Engineering Economics. *IEEE Trans. Softw. Eng.* 10, 1 (Jan. 1984), 4–21. https://doi.org/10.1109/TSE.1984.5010193

[4] David Carrington. 1996. Teaching Software Testing. In *Proceedings of the 2Nd Australasian Conference on Computer Science Education (ACSE '97)*. ACM, New York, NY, USA, 59–64. https://doi.org/10.1145/299359.299369

[5] Ruth C Clark, Frank Nguyen, and John Sweller. 2006. *Efficiency in learning: Evidence-based guidelines to manage cognitive load*. Pfeiffer, John Wiley & Sons.

[6] Benjamin S. Clegg, José Miguel Rojas, and Gordon Fraser. 2017. Teaching Software Testing Concepts Using a Mutation Testing Game. In *Proceedings of the 39th International Conference on Software Engineering: Software Engineering and Education Track (ICSE-SEET '17)*. IEEE Press, Piscataway, NJ, USA, 33–36. https://doi.org/10.1109/ICSE-SEET.2017.1

[7] T. Cowling. 2012. Stages in teaching software testing. In *2012 34th International Conference on Software Engineering (ICSE)*. 1185–1194. https://doi.org/10.1109/ICSE.2012.6227024

[8] Paul Denny, Diana Cukierman, and Jonathan Bhaskar. 2015. Measuring the Effect of Inventing Practice Exercises on Learning in an Introductory Programming Course. In *Proceedings of the 15th Koli Calling Conference on Computing Education Research (Koli Calling '15)*. ACM, New York, NY, USA, 13–22. https://doi.org/10.1145/2828959.2828967

[9] Paul Denny, Andrew Luxton-Reilly, Ewan Tempero, and Jacob Hendrickx. 2011. CodeWrite: Supporting Student-driven Practice of Java. In *Proceedings of the 42Nd ACM Technical Symposium on Computer Science Education (SIGCSE '11)*. ACM, New York, NY, USA, 471–476. https://doi.org/10.1145/1953163.1953299

[10] Stephen H. Edwards. 2003. Improving Student Performance by Evaluating How Well Students Test Their Own Programs. *J. Educ. Resour. Comput.* 3, 3, Article 1 (Sept. 2003). https://doi.org/10.1145/1029994.1029995

[11] Stephen H. Edwards and Zalia Shams. 2014. Comparing Test Quality Measures for Assessing Student-written Tests. In *Companion Proceedings of the 36th International Conference on Software Engineering (ICSE Companion 2014)*. ACM, New York, NY, USA, 354–363. https://doi.org/10.1145/2591062.2591164

[12] Dianne Hagan and Selby Markham. 2000. Does It Help to Have Some Programming Experience Before Beginning a Computing Degree Program?. In *Proceedings of the 5th Annual SIGCSE/SIGCUE ITiCSE conference on Innovation and Technology in Computer Science Education (ITiCSE '00)*. ACM, New York, NY, USA, 25–28. https://doi.org/10.1145/343048.343063

[13] David Janzen and Hossein Saiedian. 2008. Test-driven Learning in Early Programming Courses. In *Proceedings of the 39th SIGCSE Technical Symposium on Computer Science Education (SIGCSE '08)*. ACM, New York, NY, USA, 532–536. https://doi.org/10.1145/1352135.1352315

[14] Vesa Lappalainen, Jonne Itkonen, Ville Isomöttönen, and Sami Kollanus. 2010. ComTest: a tool to impart TDD and unit testing to introductory level programming. In *Proceedings of the fifteenth annual conference on Innovation and technology in computer science education*. ACM, 63–67.

[15] Andrew Luxton-Reilly, Daniel Bertinshaw, Paul Denny, Beryl Plimmer, and Robert Sheehan. 2012. The Impact of Question Generation Activities on Performance. In *Proceedings of the 43rd ACM Technical Symposium on Computer Science Education (SIGCSE '12)*. ACM, New York, NY, USA, 391–396. https://doi.org/10.1145/2157136.2157250

[16] Andrew Luxton-Reilly, Paul Denny, Beryl Plimmer, and Robert Sheehan. 2012. Activities, Affordances and Attitude: How Student-generated Questions Assist Learning. In *Proceedings of the 17th ACM Annual Conference on Innovation and Technology in Computer Science Education (ITiCSE '12)*. ACM, New York, NY, USA, 4–9. https://doi.org/10.1145/2325296.2325302

[17] Will Marrero and Amber Settle. 2005. Testing First: Emphasizing Testing in Early Programming Courses. In *Proceedings of the 10th Annual SIGCSE Conference on Innovation and Technology in Computer Science Education (ITiCSE '05)*. ACM, New York, NY, USA, 4–8. https://doi.org/10.1145/1067445.1067451

[18] Glenford J. Myers. 1979. *Art of Software Testing*. John Wiley & Sons, Inc., New York, NY, USA.

[19] Nea Pirttinen, Vilma Kangas, Irene Nikkarinen, Henrik Nygren, Juho Leinonen, and Arto Hellas. 2018. Crowdsourcing Programming Assignments with Crowd-Sorcerer. In *Proceedings of the 23rd Annual ACM Conference on Innovation and Technology in Computer Science Education (ITiCSE 2018)*. ACM, New York, NY, USA, 326–331. https://doi.org/10.1145/3197091.3197117

[20] Nea Pirttinen, Vilma Kangas, Henrik Nygren, Juho Leinonen, and Arto Hellas. 2018. Analysis of Students' Peer Reviews to Crowdsourced Programming Assignments. In *Proceedings of the 18th Koli Calling International Conference on Computing Education Research*. ACM.

[21] Christopher Watson, Frederick W.B. Li, and Jamie L. Godwin. 2014. No Tests Required: Comparing Traditional and Dynamic Predictors of Programming Success. In *Proceedings of the 45th ACM Technical Symposium on Computer Science Education (SIGCSE '14)*. ACM, New York, NY, USA, 469–474. https://doi.org/10.1145/2538862.2538930

[22] Susan Wiedenbeck, Deborah Labelle, and Vennila N. R. Kain. 2004. Factors Affecting Course Outcomes in Introductory Programming. (05 2004), 97–110.

[23] Brenda Cantwell Wilson and Sharon Shrock. 2001. Contributing to Success in an Introductory Computer Science Course: A Study of Twelve Factors. In *Proceedings of the Thirty-second SIGCSE Technical Symposium on Computer Science Education (SIGCSE '01)*. ACM, New York, NY, USA, 184–188. https://doi.org/10.1145/364447.364581

The Relationship Between Voluntary Practice of Short Programming Exercises and Exam Performance

Stephen H. Edwards, Krishnan P. Murali, and Ayaan M. Kazerouni
Virginia Tech, Department of Computer Science
Blacksburg, VA
edwards@cs.vt.edu,metarus208@gmail.com,ayaan@vt.edu

ABSTRACT

Learning to program can be challenging. Many instructors use drill-and-practice strategies to help students develop basic programming techniques and improve their confidence. Online systems that provide short programming exercises with immediate, automated feedback are seeing more frequent use in this regard. However, the relationship between practicing with short programming exercises and performance on larger programming assignments or exams are unclear. This paper describes an evaluation of short programming questions in the context of a CS1 course where they were used on both homework assignments, for practice and learning, and on exams, for assessing individual performance. The open-source drill-and-practice system used here provides for full feedback during practice exercises. During exams, it allows limiting feedback to compiler errors and to a very small number of example inputs shown in the question, instead of the more complete feedback received during practice. Using data collected from 200 students in a CS1 course, we examine the relationship between voluntary practice on short exercises and subsequent performance on exams, while using an early exam as a control for individual differences including ability level. Results indicate that, after controlling for ability, voluntary practice does contribute to improved performance on exams, but that motivation to improve may also be important.

CCS CONCEPTS

• **Social and professional topics** → **Computer science education**; **CS1**; **Student assessment**; • **Applied computing** → **Interactive learning environments**; *Computer-managed instruction*.

KEYWORDS

programming exercises; homework; coding; skill development; practice; exam

ACM Reference Format:
Stephen H. Edwards, Krishnan P. Murali, and Ayaan M. Kazerouni. 2019. The Relationship Between Voluntary Practice of Short Programming Exercises and Exam Performance. In *ACM Global Computing Education Conference 2019 (CompEd '19), May 17–19, 2019, Chengdu,Sichuan, China*. ACM, New York, NY, USA, 7 pages. https://doi.org/10.1145/3300115.3309525

1 INTRODUCTION

A number of drill-and-practice tools have been developed to help students build their skills with basic programming techniques while improving their programming confidence. Despite the presence of some experimental research on the impact of small programming exercises [10, 15], many tools have not been evaluated for impact, particularly in the face of the various choices instructors can make about how to employ them in class. This paper explores the question of whether *voluntary practice* on small programming questions affects student performance, as measured by summative exam scores. While it seems obvious that practice would help, one significant issue is that in a voluntary practice situation, the students who choose to practice are completely self-selected. Thus, it is difficult to separate out any potential gains due to practice from other individual traits that may lead them to choose to practice, and that might also lead to improved performance.

This research was conducted using CodeWorkout [6], an online drill-and-practice system designed to provide small-scale practice assignments in the contexts of both individual learning, and learning in the CS classroom. It is a completely online and open system and is not limited to short single-method programming questions but is capable of supporting different kinds of questions, including multiple choice (both forced choice and multiple answer), coding by filling in the blanks, using arbitrary objects (lists, maps, or even instructor-defined classes) instead of only primitives, writing collections of methods or an entire class (instead of just single functions), multi-part questions that include multiple prompts, and "find and fix the bug" style questions where students are given a code implementation containing one or more errors to repair.

In this paper we build on the work presented in [6] by reporting on a study of the use of short programming exercises in a CS1 course, including both required exercises completed for credit, and optional ungraded practice exercises. Using one course exam to estimate student academic ability before practice is available, and a second to assess performance afterward, we find that opting to practice non-graded exercises is associated with a statistically significant increase in performance, independently of student ability. In contrast, scores on the first exam were not a strong predictor of the choice to practice, indicating that this is not simply an issue of "strong students" performing better on multiple tasks, and choosing to practice simply because they are higher performers.

Section 2 discusses related work and Section 3 gives a brief summary of CodeWorkout. Section 4 describes the study's subjects, method, data, and analysis used to explore student practice.

2 RELATED WORK

Coding systems have begun to emerge specifically to support practice at programming. Instead of questions, these systems ask students to solve problem descriptions through code. CodingBat [14] (formerly JavaBat) offers a collection of small programming problems and now also supports instructor-contributed problems. CodingBat takes advantage of test cases to evaluate the correctness of students' code. CodeWrite [5] similarly evaluates student code, but specifically holds students responsible for writing exercises and their respective test cases.

When students practice the exercises in either system, the only feedback they receive is whether each test case passed or failed. Identifying the failed test cases help students revise their solutions. However, by exposing the test cases, the systems no longer require students to think critically about what situations their code needs to consider. Instead, the feedback of failed/passed test cases isolates a path-of-least-resistance to the solution. The purpose of drill-and-practice is to learn problem solving. Therefore, it would be more beneficial to provide students with guidance rather than just making the solution easier to recognize.

Estey et al. developed BitFit [11] to provide a platform for CS 1 students to engage in voluntary programming practice. The practice was voluntary because usage of the system did not contribute to course grades. Using log data from the system, Estey et al. were able to explore the relationship between this voluntary practice and final exam performance [10]. Analysis showed negative correlations between the number of hints requested and final exam performance: low-scoring students requested more hints than mid-scoring students, who requested more hints than high-scoring students. There was no relationship observed between time spent practicing and final exam performance.

Spacco et. al developed the online coding practice tool Cloud-Coder [13], which was part of the inspiration for CodeWorkout. Using usage data from several universities [15], analysis showed that the number of programming sessions in CloudCoder was associated with higher performance on exercises. The study also found that the number of exercises completed and attempted, and the percentage of exercises completed were weakly correlated with final exam performance. Correlations with exam performance were even weaker when practice was optional (R^2 = 0.060–0.138) compared to required (R^2 = 0.149–0.295).

Neither [10] nor [15] describe the use of controls for individual differences, or any analytical approach to differentiate between "strong" and "weak" students in their analyses. As a result, correlations might be explained by an uncontrolled individual trait (such as academic strength, prior experience, good study habits, etc.). For example, stronger students who perform well on exams might simply be choosing to practice more because they are higher performers (or might opt out of voluntary practice because they are confident in their abilities). That is, students' tendency to practice and their exam performance might *both* be results of some other unaccounted for effect related to their ability. This makes the reported correlations harder to interpret. To account for this in our analysis (Section 4), we use an early exam as a proxy for student ability, and then investigate the effect of voluntary code writing practice on later exam performance.

Related to code writing exercises, researchers have studied the effectiveness of using Parsons problems for novice programming practice [7, 8]. In [8], Ericson et al. compared students who practiced code-writing, code-fixing, and Parsons problems, and found no differences among the groups in terms of learning performance or cognitive load. A subsequent study used a system with adaptive Parsons problems [7] – problems provided implicit hints when asked for, and had their difficulties adjusted based on the student's performance on the previous problem. The study confirmed that Parsons problems (adaptive and non-adaptive) are just as effective as code-writing exercises in terms of learning gains based on a pre- and post-test. Both studies found that Parsons problems (adaptive and non-adaptive) took less time than code-writing exercises. In our study, we consider a mixture of code-writing and multiple-choice questions, and we do not consider the time taken to complete exercises for reasons described in Section 4.

Perhaps the most common and versatile types of practice systems are those that support free response (FR) and multiple-choice questions (MCQ). Since neither question format is domain-specific, these systems have been adapted in a variety of different fields. However, the versatility of this format also introduces limitations. The developers of StudySieve confirmed that FR answers are difficult to evaluate automatically and consequently had to rely on students to provide feedback [12]. MCQs suffer from the opposite problem: answers are constrained to only a few options so instead it is a challenge to write questions that will evaluate non-trivial knowledge [1]. Furthermore, this broad approach does not lend itself well to providing assistance to support learning specific skills. Despite the shortcomings with its MCQ format, PeerWise takes a novel approach to developing content [2]. PeerWise concentrates on the benefits of peer assessment by allowing students to write questions [3]. Additionally, students review each others' questions and write evaluative feedback. However, Denny identifies a need for external motivators for students to contribute content [4]. While writing and evaluating questions can activate higher order thinking skills, the degree to which these activities constructively contribute to the drill-and-practice environment itself is unknown.

3 CODEWORKOUT

CodeWorkout is a completely online and open drill-and-practice system for all those who are interested in teaching programming to their students. For a complete description of its design and features, refer to [6]. CodeWorkout is not limited to short single-method programming questions but is capable of supporting different kinds of questions, including multiple choice (both forced choice and multiple answer) and coding by filling in the blanks. Exercises are available to be either directly used in the public practice area or to be organized into an assignment. The exercise model is polymorphic: an exercise can be of different types like multiple-choice or coding; they can also consist of multiple parts, allowing for a richer variety of questions.

In addition to programming homework assignments, CodeWorkout is designed to fully support classroom use by instructors who wish to use graded assignments in exam-like situations. In these situations, instructors may choose to impose time limits and limit feedback hints from failed test cases. For example, they may limit feedback to compiler errors, or provide hints about only a few situations under test.

At the same time, it also provides a completely open "free practice" area where anyone, whether enrolled in a course or not (or even signed in or not), can browse and practice a large collection of publicly available exercises–a concept successfully pioneered by CodingBat. CodeWorkout provides full support for both uses. The analysis in this paper focuses on the second use case, i.e., *voluntary* practice by students in a CS 1 course over two semesters at our university.

4 EFFECTS OF PRACTICE

While most educators already acknowledge the value of practice, it is important to examine the impact of such practice on student performance, as well as to capture experiences in using tools that contribute to this impact. Here, we describe out experiences using CodeWorkout in class, together with a study of how it affects student performance as measured by exam scores.

Ericsson [9] summarizes much of the historical research on practice to improve performance and states the critical aspects necessary for practice to be effective:

> The most cited condition concerns the subjects' motivation to attend to the task and exert effort to improve their performance. In addition, the design of the task should take into account the preexisting knowledge of the learners so that the task can be correctly understood after a brief period of instruction. The subjects should receive immediate informative feedback and knowledge of results of their performance. The subjects should repeatedly perform the same or similar tasks.
>
> When these conditions are met, practice improves accuracy and speed of performance on cognitive, perceptual, and motor tasks.

CodeWorkout has been designed to provide immediate feedback to students as they practice, and to allow them to practice on a series of similar tasks. It also provides instructors with the ability to design specific tasks and arrange them into assignments that guide the students' practice activities. This fits directly into Ericsson's definition of *deliberate practice*, where: "the teacher designs practice activities that the individual can engage in between meetings with the teacher," where the activities are chosen by the teacher with the aim of maximizing improvement [9].

Here, our primary question is whether optional (voluntary) practice has measurable impact on student performance, independent of ability level. In the context of deliberate practice, the exercises are still provided by a teacher with the aim of improving performance. However, the "voluntary" choice by the student directly relates to the student's "motivation to attend to the task and exert effort to improve." We hypothesize that students who have this motivation will opt to complete voluntary practice assignments and benefit more, while students who do not opt to participate in voluntary practice will not see the same benefits.

4.1 Population

CodeWorkout has been used in two courses each semester at Virginia Tech during the 2015-2016 academic year, including use by 372 students in a CS1 course during Fall 2015, and 378 students in the same course in Spring 2016. The study reported here focuses on the Spring 2016 semester, where 200 students in CS1 consented to allowing their data to be used for research purposes. During that semester, CodeWorkout was used for graded homework assignments, for optional practice assignments, and for coding questions on in-class proctored and timed examinations. Students also had larger program assignments as well as homework assignments that did not involve programming in this course.

4.2 Method

The study encompassed four separate phases. First, students began working with automatically graded short practice exercises in required homework assignments during a *training* phase. Next, one third of the way through the course an exam was given that was used as a form of *pretest* to control for individual factors differing between students. Then students engaged in a *practice* phase where they participated in both required and optional practice. Finally, two thirds of the way through the course students took a second exam as a *post-test* where effects from practice were demonstrated.

4.2.1 Training. During the first 5 weeks of the course, CodeWorkout was used by students during homework assignments to practice skills solving basic programming problems. Students were required to complete 20 graded exercises. This arrangement ensures that prior to any exams, students already had exposure to CodeWorkout and were familiar with its interface and how to complete questions online. During graded homework assignments, students had unlimited attempts and unlimited time to practice, and were shown the maximum amount of feedback on each exercise–that is, they saw the results of all software tests applied to their answers, and for nearly all software tests, they also saw the full details of test values and expected results. Only a small number of software tests did not expose the details of what was being tested.

In this situation, most students worked on their solutions until they received a perfect score on an exercise. No penalty was associated with this approach to practicing. Average scores for graded homework were extremely high (96–100%), since most students received full marks on every exercise after sufficient effort. This raises a problem, however, in that scores on such an assignment may be poor predictors, since nearly all students received the same final score, regardless of ability. Only students who allowed themselves insufficient time, or who gave up on exercises without seeking coaching or assistance from the course staff, or who opted not to participate in the assignment at all, received less than perfect scores.

4.2.2 Pretest. One third of the way through the academic term, students took a regularly scheduled exam covering the material learned so far. The exam was held in class and limited to 50 minutes. The test consisted of a number of multiple choice or short answer questions given as an online quiz through the course's learning management system (worth 72% of the exam grade), together with a pair of code writing exercises given using CodeWorkout (worth 28%

Table 1: CodeWorkout assignments in CS1

Assignment	Exercises	Students	Avg. attempts per exercise	Avg. score
Training phase				
Required Homework A	10	197	1.4	100%
Required Homework B	10	176	6.7	98.6%
Pretest phase				
Exam 1	2	198	7.7	84.8%
Practice phase				
Required Homework C	5	195	9.9	96.0%
Required Homework D	10	195	9.0	93.3%
Voluntary Assignment	10	155	7.0	64.9%
Post-test phase				
Exam 2	2	190	11.3	63.7%

of the exam grade). Students saw the online test as a single online activity, with direct links to the CodeWorkout exercises embedded among the other questions of the exam.

During the exam, however, students completed code writing questions under different constraints than during homework. Students had hard time limits and were expected to complete their code writing exercises along with all of the non-coding questions that were also on the exam. In addition, CodeWorkout did *not* give full feedback to students during the exam. Instead, exercises showed compilation errors and limited test results to only three provided examples that were part of the question prompt, keeping all other testing results hidden. Students were expected to judge for themselves whether their answers behaved as intended. Although exercises included an extensive set of tests to assess the correctness of student answers, they could not see the results for these tests or the numeric scores for individual exercises during the exam. Since student work is automatically saved on CodeWorkout each time they check their work, students were free to work on other parts of the exam and come back to review their work, complete with the most recent results on the limited set of examples, whenever necessary until the exam ended.

One critical question of concern is whether optional practice has measurable impact on student performance, independent of ability level. One would expect that practice does have benefits, but one would also expect that more capable students who are already operating at a high level of skill may also be more likely to opt to practice. To address this issue, we used Exam 1 scores as a proxy measure for student ability. It served as a form of pretest to capture individual factors that affect performance on an exam, rather than as a pretest measuring specific knowledge content. Since Exam 1 covered different content (from the first one third of the course) than Exam 2 (the post-test, which covered content from the second third), we could not directly use differences between the two exam scores as a measure of learning gains. However, by using Exam 1 as a proxy for ability (or other individual differences that significantly affect exam performance), we could employ it as an independent variable in testing hypotheses about impacts on Exam 2 scores.

4.2.3 Practice.
During the middle third of the course, students completed two more required assignments consisting of short programming questions on CodeWorkout. These covered the basic

knowledge content tested on the second exam that serves as the post-test. The two required assignments contained 15 problems.

In addition, prior to the second exam, students were given a purely optional, ungraded practice assignment (the *Voluntary Assignment*) on CodeWorkout consisting of 10 practice problems. This optional practice assignment is the primary focus of this study. The *Voluntary Assignment* occurred after Exam 1, but prior to Exam 2. Because it was optional, only some of the students elected to attempt it—81.6% of students taking Exam 2 opted to attempt at least one exercise on the practice assignment, while just 35.3% percent attempted every exercise in the practice assignment at least once.

Another important issue is how best to characterize participation in the optional *Voluntary Assignment* that occurred between the two tests. Since students were able to continue working on exercises until they mastered them, absolute scores on exercises have questionable value as predictors of outcomes. While other researchers have used time needed to complete an exercise, that measure is also suspect. While some students may successfully complete an exercise in a small amount of time, what does it mean when a different student takes a longer amount of time to achieve the same result? Are longer times indicative of lower skill, if both students achieve full marks on the same exercise? Or are longer times indicative of more time on task and more effort practicing? A more extensive discussion of time effects appears in [15].

Here, because we are interested in the effects of voluntary practice, we divided the subjects into three groups: the *No-Practice* group (18.4% of students) included all students who did not attempt any exercises on the *Voluntary Assignment* at all; the *Some-Practice* group (46.3%) attempted some but not all *Voluntary Assignment* exercises; and the *Full-Practice* group (35.3% of students) attempted every exercise in the *Voluntary Assignment* at least once. This partitioning is based on Ericsson's [9] observation of the importance of the student's motivation to "exert effort to improve" through practice. The student's actions regarding how much of the optional practice assignment to complete is the direct measure that is most closely associated with their motivation to invest in practice.

4.2.4 Post-test.
Finally, students took Exam 2 two-thirds of the way through the semester, following the same structure as Exam 1 with both multiple-choice and code-writing questions. Measures of both the multiple-choice question performance and the code-writing

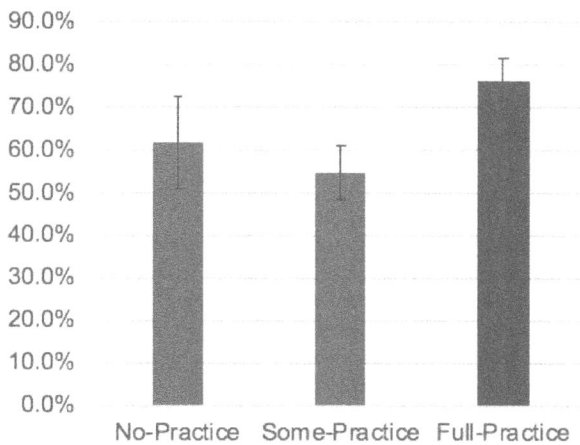

Figure 1: Code writing scores on Exam 2 by group (Full-Practice is significantly different from other groups).

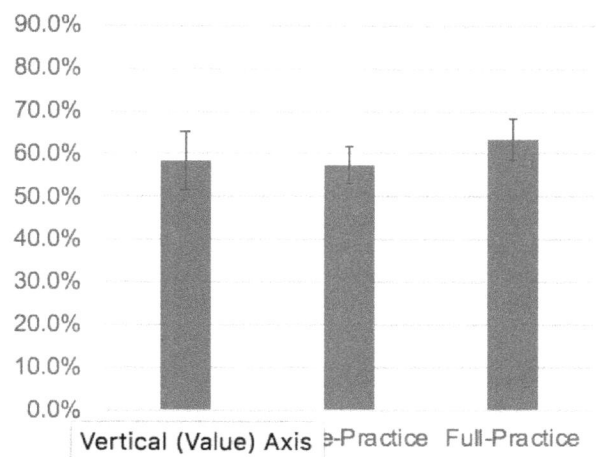

Figure 2: Multiple choice scores on Exam 2 by group (no significant difference).

question performance were analyzed independently to determine if optional practice effects were present. Table 1 shows that Exam 2 scores were lower than Exam 1, which is typical for the course and is due to the larger amount of content knowledge and skills expected two-thirds of the way through the course.

5 RESULTS

Table 1 summarizes CodeWorkout's usage across the four phases of this study. The training phase includes required assignments that ensure a basic level of familiarity with the tool and the style of questions; the first exam serves as a baseline for assessing individual ability; the practice phase includes the *Voluntary Assignment* that is the focus of the study; and the second exam serves as the observation of effects of practice.

5.1 Effects on Exam Code Writing Questions

Since both exams included code writing questions, which presumably require skills similar to those appearing in the practice exercises, as well as other styles of questions that may test other knowledge or skills covered in the course, we can consider the two types of questions separately. On code writing questions answered on CodeWorkout, *Full-Practice* students earned a mean score of 76.5%, compared to 61.5% for *No-Practice* students (s.d. = 31.8%) and 54.7% for *Some-Practice* students (s.d. = 29.7%). Figure 1 illustrates the differences and 95% confidence intervals.

By considering both Exam 1 scores and practice group as independent variables, as well as the cross interaction between them, an analysis of variance indicates a significant effect on the code writing scores in Exam 2 ($df = 189, F = 20.0, p < 0.0001$). Separate effect tests for the two variables indicate both Exam 1 scores (F = 21.3, p < 0.0001) and practice group (F = 8.7, p = 0.0002) are significant, but there is no significant interaction between them (F = 0.4, p = 0.69). The differences in least-squares means indicate that *Full-Practice* is significantly different than the other two groups ($t = 1.97, p = 0.049$), but *No-Practice* and *Some-Practice* were not significantly different.

From this analysis, it seems that students who elected to practice some, but not all, of the practice exercises did not perform significantly differently than those who opted not to practice at all. If anything, their scores were lower on all measures (but not significantly). Instead, only students who at least *attempted* all of the practice problems saw significant performance improvements. Most importantly, this improvement is associated with choosing to practice voluntarily, independent of student ability (as measured on Test 1).

To determine effect sizes on code writing scores, partial η^2 values were computed for both the Exam 1 effect and the practice group effect. The effect size for Exam 1 scores is $\eta^2 = 0.264$, indicating that approximately 26.4% of the variance in Exam 2 code writing performance is accounted for by the student's earlier Exam 1 score, which is considered a large effect size. This suggests that some individual traits (such as student ability, prior experience, enjoyment of coding, etc.) may play a role in increasing exam scores independently of voluntary practice. The effect size for the practice group is $\eta^2 = 0.143$, indicating that approximately 14.3% of the variance in Exam 2 code writing performance is associated with whether or not the student chooses to practice all practice problems on the *Voluntary Assignment*, which is also considered a large effect size. As can be seen from the means, Cohen's d for the *Full-Practice* group on code writing exercises in Exam 2 is 0.69.

5.2 Effects on Exam Multiple Choice Questions

On multiple choice and short answer questions, *Full-Practice* students earned 63.6%, compared to *No-Practice* students at 58.6% and *Some-Practice* students at 57.6% (s.d. = 20.5%).

We can also consider the effect on the multiple-choice portion of Exam 2, which does not involve code writing skills directly. Again by considering both Exam 1 scores and practice group as independent variables, as well as the cross interaction between them, an analysis of variance indicates a significant effect on the multiple-choice scores in Exam 2 ($df = 190, F = 14.3, p < 0.0001$). Separate effect tests for the two variables indicate that Exam 1 score (F = 18.2, p < 0.0001) is significant while practice group (F = 0.12, p = 0.89) is not. There is no significant interaction between them (F = 0.10, p = 0.90).

To determine effect sizes on multiple-choice scores, partial η^2 values were computed for the Exam 1 effect. The effect size for Exam 1 scores is $\eta^2 = 0.265$, which is considered a large effect size. Cohen's d for *Full-Practice* on the non-code-writing portion of Exam 2 is 0.28. In addition to being much smaller than the difference on code writing exercises, there is no significant evidence of differences on code writing questions between the practice groups on the multiple-choice and short answer portion of Exam 2.

5.3 Threats to Validity

One major consideration in this study is the potential threat due to individual traits that may affect the choice to opt for voluntary practice. Such individual traits may introduce a form of selection bias that can affect the inferences drawn from correlations between voluntary practice and exam performance. In this study, we used Exam 1 as an indirect measure of individual differences that affect exam performance that could be included in the analysis to see whether the choice to perform additional practice shows an independent effect on exam performance. Greater explanatory power would come from explicitly measuring the most likely individual differences so they could be independently analyzed, but that is beyond the scope of this paper. Still, controlling for individual differences is an important step in establishing whether voluntary practice itself has an independent effect.

At the same time, while the gains experienced by *Full-Practice* students are associated with practice, this study does not provide evidence for the cause of the improvement. Instead, it is clear that the practice alone is insufficient, since students who practiced some, but not all, exercises did not perform significantly differently on any measure from students who participated in no voluntary practice at all. Instead, it appears that the motivation that students have to engage in deliberate practice is also critical, as noted by other researchers and summarized by Ericsson.

Further, this study includes both required and voluntary practice. As shown using CloudCoder [15], requiring short programming exercises is more strongly associated with improvements in exam performance than voluntary practice. While lack of controls on individual differences in that study requires caution, its results suggest that examining the effects of required practice vs. optional practice is warranted. In addition, the CloudCoder study suggests that larger numbers of practice exercises offered in more assignments may offer more impact. The results shown here are likely to be different if more (or fewer) required assignments using more (or fewer) exercises were included, or if a larger number of voluntary exercises were offered, perhaps at more points throughout the course. Additional research is needed to understand the effects of required vs. optional assignments and choices about number of practice opportunities designed by the instructor.

Finally, throughout the short programming exercise community, quality of exercises is a known issue that constantly requires attention. This study tacitly assumes that the exercises employed on practice assignments and on exams are effective. However, given the 50 or so exercises used in this study, some degree of variation is quality is unavoidable. According to the theory of deliberate practice, exercises need to be carefully designed by an expert teacher or coach, and ideally are tailored to the ability level of the student. Potentially, different gains could be achieved with a different set of practice exercises, which is not taken into account in this study.

6 CONCLUSION

CodeWorkout is a new drill-and-practice system designed to provide a larger range of opportunities for students to practice basic coding skills. Inspired by predecessors, it design aims to combine the best strengths of prior work with new strategies for enhancing classroom support and supporting student practice. In the experiences reported in this paper, CodeWorkout was used quite successfully in an introductory course with a large number of students. Students reacted positively and appear to see clear benefits to using this style of exercise practice to develop their skills.

We also conducted an evaluation of how voluntary practice affects student performance, as measured by exam scores. Nevertheless, there are still many research questions needing further exploration. In the future, we plan to continue refining CodeWorkout to support such investigations. An important part of this effort is the use of item response theory to characterize the performance of questions and the identification of questions that may need revision or editorial attention. At the same time, IRT offers a deeper, more data-driven way of estimating student ability. By modeling both student ability and question performance, it is possible to intelligently recommend new problems for practice that are closer to the student's zone of proximal development. The addition of social features and Stack Overflow-inspired Q&A discussions for questions offers a unique strategy to try to help students who get stuck. Similarly, prompting successful students to offer hints on how to tackle questions they have completed, together with analysis of when those hints help later students get unstuck, offer new strategies for engaging students in the community of users, instead of encouraging them to pursue individual practice in isolation. A consolidated approach to these issues is more likely to meet the needs of current and future educators.

Still, the current evaluation does provide some evidence for how voluntary practice affects student exam performance. By using an exam earlier in the course as a proxy for student ability level, we compared how students who practiced all practice problems in an optional practice assignment performed compared to students who did not, while accounting for ability level. While ability level explained a larger amount of variance in Exam 2 scores, improved performance on Exam 2 code writing questions was significantly associated with optional practice, independently of student ability. Further, it is clear that practicing *all* of the optional exercises instead of just some was also important—a behavior we hypothesize as being associated with a student's intrinsic motivation to exert effort to improve, which is a critical component for deliberate practice to be effective. This gives some evidence that the basic intuition of educators—that practice helps, when students engage in it—is associated with better performance, at least with the skills that were practiced, and that this affect may be distinguishable from that of performance gains driven by simple ideas of student ability or pre-existing skill level.

ACKNOWLEDGMENTS

This work is supported in part by the National Science Foundation under grant DRL-1740765. Any opinions, findings, conclusions, or recommendations expressed in this material are those of the authors and do not necessarily reflect the views of the National Science Foundation.

REFERENCES

[1] Albert Corbett, John Anderson, Art Graesser, Ken Koedinger, and Kurt VanLehn. 1999. Third Generation Computer Tutors: Learn from or Ignore Human Tutors?. In *CHI '99 Extended Abstracts on Human Factors in Computing Systems (CHI EA '99)*. ACM, New York, NY, USA, 85–86. https://doi.org/10.1145/632716.632769

[2] Paul Denny, John Hamer, Andrew Luxton-Reilly, and Helen Purchase. 2008. PeerWise: Students Sharing Their Multiple Choice Questions. In *Proceedings of the Fourth International Workshop on Computing Education Research (ICER '08)*. ACM, New York, NY, USA, 51–58. https://doi.org/10.1145/1404520.1404526

[3] Paul Denny, Andrew Luxton-Reilly, and John Hamer. 2008. The PeerWise System of Student Contributed Assessment Questions. In *Proceedings of the Tenth Conference on Australasian Computing Education - Volume 78 (ACE '08)*. Australian Computer Society, Inc., Darlinghurst, Australia, Australia, 69–74. http://dl.acm.org/citation.cfm?id=1379249.1379255

[4] Paul Denny, Andrew Luxton-Reilly, and John Hamer. 2008. Student Use of the PeerWise System. In *Proceedings of the 13th Annual Conference on Innovation and Technology in Computer Science Education (ITiCSE '08)*. ACM, New York, NY, USA, 73–77. https://doi.org/10.1145/1384271.1384293

[5] Paul Denny, Andrew Luxton-Reilly, Ewan Tempero, and Jacob Hendrickx. 2011. CodeWrite: Supporting Student-driven Practice of Java. In *Proceedings of the 42Nd ACM Technical Symposium on Computer Science Education (SIGCSE '11)*. ACM, New York, NY, USA, 471–476. https://doi.org/10.1145/1953163.1953299

[6] Stephen H. Edwards and Krishnan Panamalai Murali. 2017. CodeWorkout: Short Programming Exercises with Built-in Data Collection. In *Proceedings of the 2017 ACM Conference on Innovation and Technology in Computer Science Education (ITiCSE '17)*. ACM, New York, NY, USA, 188–193. https://doi.org/10.1145/3059009.

3059055

[7] Barbara J. Ericson, James D. Foley, and Jochen Rick. 2018. Evaluating the Efficiency and Effectiveness of Adaptive Parsons Problems. In *Proceedings of the 2018 ACM Conference on International Computing Education Research (ICER '18)*. ACM, New York, NY, USA, 60–68. https://doi.org/10.1145/3230977.3231000

[8] Barbara J. Ericson, Lauren E. Margulieux, and Jochen Rick. 2017. Solving Parsons Problems Versus Fixing and Writing Code. In *Proceedings of the 17th Koli Calling International Conference on Computing Education Research (Koli Calling '17)*. ACM, New York, NY, USA, 20–29. https://doi.org/10.1145/3141880.3141895

[9] K. Anders Ericsson, Ralf T. Krampe, and Clemens Tesch-RÃ¼mer. 1993. The Role of Deliberate Practice in the Acquisition of Expert Performance. *Psychological Review* 100, 3 (July 1993), 363–406.

[10] Anthony Estey and Yvonne Coady. 2017. Study Habits, Exam Performance, and Confidence: How Do Workflow Practices and Self-Efficacy Ratings Align?. In *Proceedings of the 2017 ACM Conference on Innovation and Technology in Computer Science Education (ITiCSE '17)*. ACM, New York, NY, USA, 158–163. https://doi.org/10.1145/3059009.3059056

[11] Anthony Estey, Anna Russo Kennedy, and Yvonne Coady. 2016. BitFit: If You Build It, They Will Come!. In *Proceedings of the 21st Western Canadian Conference on Computing Education (WCCCE '16)*. ACM, New York, NY, USA, Article 3, 6 pages. https://doi.org/10.1145/2910925.2910944

[12] Andrew Luxton-Reilly, Paul Denny, Beryl Plimmer, and Daniel Bertinshaw. 2011. Supporting Student-generated Free-response Questions. In *Proceedings of the 16th Annual Joint Conference on Innovation and Technology in Computer Science Education (ITiCSE '11)*. ACM, New York, NY, USA, 153–157. https://doi.org/10.1145/1999747.1999792

[13] Andrei Papancea, Jaime Spacco, and David Hovemeyer. 2013. An Open Platform for Managing Short Programming Exercises. In *Proceedings of the Ninth Annual International ACM Conference on International Computing Education Research (ICER '13)*. ACM, New York, NY, USA, 47–52. https://doi.org/10.1145/2493394.2493401

[14] Nick Parlante. [n. d.]. CodingBat. http://codingbat.com/. last accessed 04-06-2016.

[15] Jaime Spacco, Paul Denny, Brad Richards, David Babcock, David Hovemeyer, James Moscola, and Robert Duvall. 2015. Analyzing Student Work Patterns Using Programming Exercise Data. In *Proceedings of the 46th ACM Technical Symposium on Computer Science Education (SIGCSE '15)*. ACM, New York, NY, USA, 18–23. https://doi.org/10.1145/2676723.2677297

Mnemonic Variable Names in Parsons Puzzles

Amruth N. Kumar
Computer Science
Ramapo College of New Jersey
Mahwah, NJ, USA
amruth@ramapo.edu

ABSTRACT

In Parsons Puzzles, students are asked to arrange the lines of a program in their correct order. We investigated the effect of using mnemonic variable names in the program on the ease with which students solved the puzzles – whether students were able to solve puzzles containing mnemonic variable names with fewer actions or in less time than single-character variable names. We conducted a controlled study with cross-over design over four semesters. Much to our surprise, we found no statistically significant difference between students solving puzzles with mnemonic variable names versus single-character variable names – either in terms of the number of actions taken, the grade earned or the time spent per puzzle. In this paper, we will describe the experimental setup and data analysis and present the results of the study. We will discuss some hypotheses as to why the readability of the variable names did not impact students' ability to solve Parsons puzzles.

KEYWORDS

Parsons puzzles; Mnemonic variable names; Controlled study

ACM Reference format:
Amruth N. Kumar. 2019. Mnemonic Variable Names in Parsons Puzzles. In *Proceedings of ACM Global Computing Education conference (CompEd'19), May 17–19, 2019, Chengdu, Sichuan, China. ACM, New York, NY, USA, 7 pages.*
https://doi.org/10.1145/3300115.3309509

1 Introduction

Parsons puzzles have gained a lot of popularity since their introduction [17]. In a Parsons puzzle, the student is presented a program for a problem, but the lines in the program are scrambled. The student must reassemble the lines in their correct order. The puzzles were designed to be an engaging way to learn programming.

Parsons puzzles have since been proposed for use in exams [4], since they are easier to grade than code-writing exercises. At the same time, scores on Parsons puzzles have been found to correlate with scores on code-writing exercises [4]. Researchers have found solving Parsons puzzles to be part of a hierarchy of programming skills alongside code-tracing [15]. In electronic books, students have been found to prefer solving Parsons puzzles more than other low-cognitive-load activities such as answering multiple choice questions and high-cognitive-load activities such as writing code [6]. Solving Parsons puzzles was found to take significantly less time than fixing errors in code or writing equivalent code, but resulted in the same learning performance and retention [7]. Software to administer Parsons puzzles have been developed for Turbo Pascal [17], Python (e.g., [3,10]) and C++/Java/C# [12].

Lately, there has been interest in finding patterns in how students go about solving the puzzles [9,11]. Researchers have also looked into what helps students solve the puzzles better, e.g., sub-goal labels help students solve puzzles significantly better [16]; adaptive practice of Parsons puzzles is more efficient while being just as effective as writing code [5]; but motivational supports did not seem to help students while solving puzzles [13]. In this vein, we investigated whether the use of mnemonic variable names in the code had any effect on solving Parsons puzzles. We report the results of our study and discuss their implications.

2 The Study

2.1 Hypothesis

Our research hypothesis was that students would find Parsons puzzles easier to solve when the code in the puzzles used mnemonic variable names rather than single-character variables names (e.g., i, j, k).

Several researchers have documented the importance of mnemonic variable names in programs (e.g., [2,18]): mnemonic variable names improve the readability of a program whereas non-mnemonic single-character variable names make a program harder to read. Mnemonic variable names may lead to better comprehension than single-character variable names [14]. So, we expected that students would be able to solve Parsons puzzles with mnemonic variables faster and with fewer missteps than puzzles with single-character variables. We presented two versions of the same program: one with mnemonic variable names to experimental group and the other, with non-mnemonic single-character variable names to control group, while keeping all the other factors such as indentation, commenting and structure the same between the two versions.

2.2 Tools

For this study, we used epplets (epplets.org), a Parsons puzzle tool [12]. The tool presents the scrambled lines of code in the left panel, called Problem panel, and has the student reassemble the lines of code in their correct order in the right panel, called Solution Panel using drag-and-drop action. Students can also delete a line of code by dragging it into Trash panel (Please see [12] for a figure of the user interface). The student is required to solve a puzzle completely and correctly before going on to the next puzzle. The tool provides feedback to help the student fix an incorrect solution. The tool also allows the student to bail out of solving a puzzle when hopelessly lost.

The tool requires that the student reassemble the code one line at a time, instead of one program fragment at a time [17]. So, given a program with n lines of code, a student can solve the puzzle with n drag-and-drop actions. The tool presents comments in the code *in situ* in the solution panel. Students are expected to drag and drop lines of code under appropriate comments.

For this study, we had the students solve Parsons puzzles on two topics: `while` loops and `for` loops.

2.2.1 `while` Loop Puzzle

We had students solve two puzzles on `while` loops. The first puzzle was used to get students accustomed to the user interface of the tool. So, all the students were presented code with mnemonic variable names on the first puzzle. The puzzle presented code for the problem: "Read numbers till the same number appears back to back. Print the first number to appear back to back (e.g., 4 appears back to back in 3,7,5,7,4,4,5 and is printed)."

The second puzzle presented on `while` loops was used to conduct this study. It was for the problem: "Input the face of a card. Next, read a deck of cards and print how many cards into the deck the input card is found, followed by its successor. For example, if the input card is 6, in a deck that starts with the cards 1,8,6,10,7,9,13, the 6 card is in 3rd place and 7 card is in 5th place."

The single-character variable code provided to control group on the second puzzle was as follows (in C++):

```
#include <iostream>
using namespace std;
int main()
{
  // Declare y
  long y;
  // Declare r
  long r;
  // Declare b
  long b = 1;
  // Read into y the face of the card to look for in the deck
  cout << "Enter the face of the card to look for in the deck (1-13)";
```

```
cin >> y;
// Find the card and its successor in a deck of cards
cout << "Enter the cards in the deck one at a time";
cin >> r;
while( r != y )
{
  cin >> r;
  b = b + 1;
} // End of while loop from line 24
cout << "Card " << y
    << " found in deck at position " << b;
y = y + 1;
cin >> r;
b = b + 1;
while( r != y )
{
  cin >> r;
  b = b + 1;
} // End of while loop from line 33
cout << "Card " << y
    << " found in deck at position " << b;
} // End of function main
```

Note that the code used single-character variable names, with the characters having no mnemonic association with the purposes they served. The corresponding mnemonic variable code presented to experimental group was as follows (in C++):

```
#include <iostream>
using namespace std;
int main()
{
  // Declare selectCard
  int selectCard;
  // Declare cardDeck
  int cardDeck;
  // Declare counter
  int counter = 1;
  // Read into selectCard the face of the card to look for in the deck
  cout << "Enter the face of the card to look for in the deck (1-13)";
  cin >> selectCard;
  // Find the card and its successor in a deck of cards
  cout << "Enter the cards in the deck one at a time";
  cin >> cardDeck;
  while( cardDeck != selectCard )
  {
    cin >> cardDeck;
    counter = counter + 1;
  } // End of while loop from line 24
  cout << "Card " << selectCard
      << " found in deck at position " << counter;
  selectCard = selectCard + 1;
  cin >> cardDeck;
  counter = counter + 1;
  while( cardDeck != selectCard )
  {
```

```
    cin >> cardDeck;
    counter = counter + 1;
  } // End of while loop from line 33
  cout << "Card " << selectCard
        << " found in deck at position " << counter;
} // End of function main
```

In the two versions of the code presented before, the longest stretch of code re-assembled by students without the benefit of any comments is highlighted in bold.

2.2.2 `for` Loop Puzzle

Once again., we had students solve two puzzles on `for` loops. The first puzzle was used to get students accustomed to the user interface of the tool. So, all the students were presented mnemonic variable code on the first puzzle. The puzzle presented code for the problem: "Read two numbers. Calculate the sum of all the numbers between the two and print it, e.g., if 4 and 7 are read, print 22, which is the sum of 4,5,6 and 7."

The second puzzle presented on `for` loops was used to conduct this study. It was for the problem: "Read the monthly income for a year. Print its sum. Read the monthly expenses for the year. Print money left over after expenses."

The single-character variable code provided to control group on the second puzzle was as follows (in C++):

```
#include <iostream>
using namespace std;
int main()
{
  // Declare x
  long double x;
  // Declare r
  long double r;
  // Declare a
  unsigned long a;
  // Read monthly income into x, print sum in r
  r = 0;
  for( a = 1; a <= 12; a ++ )
  {
    cout << "Please enter the income for month " << a;
    cin >> x;
    r = r + x;
  } // End of for loop from line 19
  cout << "Sum of monthly income is $ " << r;
  // Read monthly expenses into x, print balance in r after
expenses
  for( a = 1; a <= 12; a ++ )
  {
    cout << "Please enter the expenses for month " << a;
    cin >> x;
    r = r - x;
  } // End of for loop from line 30
  cout << "Balance after expenses is $ " << r;
} // End of function main
```

The corresponding mnemonic variable code presented to experimental group was as follows, wherein, the longest stretch of code re-assembled by students without the benefit of comments is highlighted in bold:

```
using namespace std;
int main()
{
  // Declare amount
  float amount;
  // Declare balance
  float balance;
  // Declare counter
  unsigned short counter;
  // Read monthly income into amount, print sum in
balance
  balance = 0;
  for( counter = 1; counter <= 12; counter ++ )
  {
    cout << "Please enter the income for month "
        << counter;
    cin >> amount;
    balance = balance + amount;
  } // End of for loop from line 19
  cout << "Sum of monthly income is $ " << balance;
  // Read monthly expenses into amount, print balance in
balance after expenses
  for( counter = 1; counter <= 12; counter ++ )
  {
    cout << "Please enter the expenses for month " <<
counter;
    cin >> amount;
    balance = balance - amount;
  } // End of for loop from line 30
  cout << "Balance after expenses is $ " << balance;
} // End of function main
```

2.3 Protocol

We conducted a crossover study. We divided students into two groups: A and Z. Their treatments on `while` and `for` loop puzzles were as shown in Table 1.

Table 1: Treatment for Groups A and Z on `while` loop and `for` loop Parsons puzzles

Group	while loop	for loop
A	Single-Character	Mnemonic
Z	Mnemonic	Single-Character

The puzzles used in this study were the second puzzles students solved on `while` and `for` loops. This ensured that students would have overcome any user interface issues by the time they solved these puzzles.

2.4 Variables

Students were required to completely and correctly solve each puzzle. The independent variable in the study was the variable naming scheme in the puzzle presented to the student: mnemonic versus single-character.

We used four dependent variables:

- The number of steps taken by the student to solve the puzzle. The steps included moving a line of code from the problem panel to the solution panel, reordering a line within the solution panel, and deleting a line from the problem or solution panel to the trash panel.

- The grade on the puzzle, calculated as 100% if the student solved the puzzle with as many steps as the number of lines in the code. If the student took more steps than the number of lines in the code, each superfluous step was penalized against one correct step, e.g., if the program contained 20 lines and the student took 30 steps to solve the puzzle completely and correctly, the student got credit for 10 steps out of 20. So, the normalized score awarded to the student was 10 / 20 = 0.5. The normalized score was bound to the range 0 → 1.0. This negative grading scheme meant that a student could score 0 on a puzzle even after having solved it correctly.

- The time taken by the student to solve the puzzle completely and correctly, in seconds.

- The time taken per step by the student to solve the puzzle completely and correctly, calculated as time / number of steps taken.

2.5 Data Collection

We collected data over four semesters: Fall 2016 – Spring 2018. The subjects were students in the introductory programming course, both majors and non-majors. The puzzles were provided as two of a dozen after-class assignments. The number of students who solved Parsons puzzles on `while` and `for` loops in each treatment over the four semesters is listed in Table 2. Group A consisted of students from 5 baccalaureate institutions, 2 community colleges and 2 high schools and Group Z from 6 baccalaureate institutions and one community college.

Students had the option to solve the puzzles on the two topics as many times as they wanted. For our analysis, we considered data from only the first time a student solved puzzles on either topic. Since this was a crossover study, we considered only the students who had served as both control and experimental subjects, i.e., we eliminated students who had not solved all four puzzles: two each on `while` and `for` loops. For the same reason, we also eliminated students who had bailed out of solving any of the four puzzles. After these eliminations, group A consisted of 34 students and Group Z consisted of 40 students.

Table 2: Number of students who solved Parsons puzzles in each condition over four semesters

	Single-Character	Mnemonic
while	67	82
for	75	65

2.6 Data Analysis

On each topic (`while` and `for` loop), we compared the control and experimental group performance on the first puzzle to check if the two groups were comparable – both the groups were presented the same code with mnemonic variables for the first puzzle. We used data from the second puzzle to compare mnemonic versus single-character variable treatments: control group was presented single-character variable code and experimental group was presented mnemonic code.

Table 3 lists the mean and 95% confidence interval of the number of steps taken, the normalized score, the time in seconds, and the time taken per step by the two treatment subjects on the first `while` loop puzzle. ANOVA analysis yielded no significant difference between the two groups for steps [F91,73) = 0.6, p = 0.44], grade [F(1,71) = 1.05, p = 0.31], time [F(1,73) = 1.84, p = 0.18] or time per step [F(1,73) = 1.66, p = 0.20]. *So, the two treatment groups, when provided the same treatment, were comparable.*

Table 3: Comparison of the two groups on the first `while` loop puzzle with the same treatment

while loop	Single-Character (Group A, N = 34)	Mnemonic (Group Z, N=40)
Steps	24.65 ± 3.68	22.70 ± 3.40
Grade	0.62 ± 0.13	0.71 ± 0.12
Time	352.92 ± 65.24	292.55 ± 60.15
Time/Step	14.27 ± 1.88	12.61 ± 1.73

Table 4 lists the same figures for the two groups on the second puzzle on `while` loops, wherein, control group (A) was presented single-character code and experimental group (Z) was presented mnemonic variable code. ANOVA analysis yielded no significant difference between the two groups for steps [F(1,73) = 0.03, p = 0.86], grade [F(1,73) = 0.02, p = 0.88], time [F(1,73) = 0.10, p = 0.75] or time per step [F(1,73) = 0.17, p = 0.68]. In other words, *the use of mnemonic variable names had no impact on the number of steps taken to solve the puzzle, the score earned on the puzzle or the time taken to solve the puzzle.*

Table 4: Comparison of the two groups on the second `while` loop puzzle with differential treatments.

while loop	Single-Character (Group A, N = 34)	Mnemonic (Group Z, N = 40)
Steps	46.29 ± 7.65	47.23 ± 7.05
Grade	0.42 ± 0.13	0.41 ± 0.12
Time	690.38 ± 103.1	667.75 ± 95.05
Time/Step	15.76 ± 2.28	15.12 ± 2.10

Table 5 lists the performance of control (Z) and experimental (A) groups on the first `for` loop puzzle, where both were provided the same treatment, viz., mnemonic variable code. Once again, ANOVA analysis yielded no statistically significant difference between the two treatments on the steps [F(1,73) = 0.11, p = 0.74], grade [F(1,73) = 2.18, p = 0.14], time [F(1,73) = 0.28, p = 0.60] or time taken per step [F(1,73) = 0.67, p = 0.42]. So, once again, the two groups were comparable in their performance when provided the same treatment, viz., mnemonic variable code.

Table 5: Comparison of the two groups on the first `for` loop puzzle with the same treatment

`for` loop	Single-Character (Group Z, N= 40)	Mnemonic (Group A, N = 34)
Steps	22.98 ± 1.90	22.50 ± 2.06
Grade	0.82 ± 0.07	0.89 ± 0.08
Time	237.25 ± 42.57	253.79 ± 46.17
Time/Step	10.38 ± 1.95	11.57 ± 2.12

Finally, Table 6 lists the figures for the second `for` loop puzzle, wherein, control group (Z) was presented single-character variable code and experimental group (A) was provided mnemonic variable code. ANOVA analysis yielded no statistically significant difference between the treatments on steps [$F(1,73) < 0.01$, p = 0.94], grade [$F(1,73) < 0.01$, p = 0.93], time [$F(1,73) = 1.01$, p + 0.32] or time taken per step [$F(1,73) = 1.28$, p = 0.26]. So, mnemonic variables in *the code had no impact on the performance of the students.*

Table 6: Comparison of the two groups on the second `for` loop puzzle with differential treatments

`for` loop	Single-Character (Group Z, N= 40)	Mnemonic (Group A, N = 34)
Steps	37.20 ± 3.46	37.38 ± 3.76
Grade	0.59 ± 0.11	0.58 ± 0.12
Time	443.0 ± 56.0	484.68 ± 60.73
Time/Step	12.17 ± 1.37	13.32 ± 1.49

Next, we conducted ANCOVA analysis of the grade on the second puzzle, with treatment as the fixed factor and grade on the first problem as a covariate. For this analysis, we combined the data from both the loops. We found no main effect for treatment [$F(1,145) = 0.51$, p = 0.48]: the grade with single-character variable version was 0.53 ± 0.08 compared to 0.49 ± 0.08 with mnemonic variable version. Similarly, ANCOVA analysis of the time taken per step on the second puzzle with the time taken per step on the first puzzle as covariate yielded no significant effect for treatment [$F(1,147) = 0.28$, p = 0.60]: subjects spent 13.82 ± 1.27 seconds per step with single-character variable version compared to 14.30 ± 1.27 seconds with mnemonic variable version. *So, even after accounting for variations in student performance on the first puzzle, we found no effect of treatment on their performance on the second puzzle.*

We compared the performance on the first puzzle with that on the second puzzle on each topic. On each topic, everyone was presented mnemonic variable version on the first puzzle, but only one of the two groups (A/Z) was presented mnemonic version on the second puzzle while the other group was presented single-character version. Since the puzzles were different, and involved different numbers of lines of code, we compared only the time taken per step. If mnemonic variables decreased puzzle-solving

time, the group that was presented single-character version on the second puzzle would have spent significantly more time on the second puzzle compared to the first puzzle than the mnemonic variable group. The time spent per step for the two groups on the two puzzles in the two topics are listed in Table 7. Repeated measures ANOVA analysis yielded no significant interaction between the puzzle and treatment on `while` loops [$F(1,72) = 1.07$, p = 0.30] or `for` loops [$F(1,72) = 1.31$, p = 0.26]. *So, working with mnemonic variable code on one puzzle did not influence the performance of students on a subsequent puzzle.*

Table 7: Repeated measures comparison of the time taken per step on the first and second puzzles for the two groups

`while` loop	Single-Character (Group A, N = 34)	Mnemonic (Group Z, N=40)
Puzzle 1	14.27 ± 1.88	12.61 ± 1.73
Puzzle 2	15.76 ± 2.28	15.12 ± 2.10
`for` loop	Single-Character (Group Z, N= 40)	Mnemonic (Group A, N = 34)
Puzzle 1	10.38 ± 1.95	11.57 ± 2.12
Puzzle 2	12.17 ± 1.37	13.32 ± 1.49

We computed the average grade on the first puzzle on each topic and used it to group students into two: less-prepared students who scored below average and better-prepared students who scored average or above. One-way ANOVA of the grade on the second puzzle with treatment and preparedness as fixed factors yielded interaction between the two factors as shown in Table 8, but it was not statistically significant. Similar analysis of the time taken per step yielded a significant interaction between the two factors [$F(1,147) = 7.475$, p = 0.007]: less-prepared students spent more time with mnemonic treatment than single-character treatment whereas better-prepared students spent more time with single-character treatment than mnemonic treatment. This was not an artifact of the puzzle topic (`while` versus `for`) because the interaction with topic was not significant. So *mnemonic variables in Parsons puzzle code may differentially affect students based on their level of preparation.*

Table 8: The effect of treatment on the grade and time taken per step on the second puzzle by less- versus better-prepared students

Grade	Single-Character	Mnemonic
Less	0.40 ± 0.13 (33)	0.46 ± 0.16 (22)
Better	0.60 ± 0.11 (41)	0.50 ± 0.10 (52)
Time per step	Single-Character	Mnemonic
Less	11.81 ± 1.94 (33)	15.49 ± 2.38 (22)
Better	15.44 ± 1.74 (41)	13.79 ± 1.55 (52)

2 Results and Discussion

We expected that students would be able to solve Parsons puzzles faster and with fewer steps when the puzzles contained mnemonic variables instead of single-character variables. But, the results of the study did not support this hypothesis, much to our surprise. We considered various explanations for this outcome.

The puzzles used in the study involved 3 variables each. It could be argued that the readability of a program is not impaired if it contains only three variables that are poorly named. But, poorly named variables make it harder to track the flow of data in the program, especially in the section of the code that involves back-to-back loops – the section boldfaced in the listings presented earlier. This is true even for experienced programmers, not just novices. Nevertheless, we plan to repeat the study with puzzle programs involving many more than 3 variables.

It could be argued that the programs presented in the puzzles are short: 19-24 lines long. But, they are complicated enough for beginning programmers. It could be argued that the comments provided by the tool in the solution panel make it easy to assemble some of the lines of code such as variable declarations and input statements. But, some comments in the program are followed by 9 – 19 lines of back-to-back code, wherein, students had to reassemble code without any assistance from comments. Since these uncommented lines carry out the actual computations in the program, assembling them is the hardest part of each puzzle.

A third possible explanation is that mnemonic variables indeed facilitate solving Parsons puzzles, but the effect size is so small that we need much larger sample sizes to evaluate the hypothesis - power analysis yielded observed power of 5% to 14% for many of the analyses. We plan to repeat the controlled experiment every semester, and plan to revisit this study with additional data in the future.

In a recent study, professional developers were presented two versions of six library code segments: one with mnemonic variables and the other with meaningless single-character variable names. In three of the code segments, no statistically significant difference was observed between the two treatments in terms of code comprehension [1]. Authors of the study attributed this surprising result to the use of poorly chosen mnemonic names. It turns out, choosing mnemonic names is not as objective an exercise as one might like – the probability that two people choose the same name for a variable was found to be less than 20% in one study [8]. Even if universally acceptable mnemonic names are used, they may hinder program comprehension by serving as misleading "beacons" (code elements that illuminate the code's function) when novices hold an incorrect model of the purpose of the program [1].

The counter-arguments to these issues that confound the utility of mnemonic names are: 1) we chose mnemonic names from the problem statement provided for each puzzle (e.g., `cardDeck`) or listed them in the comments preceding each section (e.g., `amount`); and 2) unlike in the earlier study [1] wherein, programmers had to guess the purpose of each code segment, we described the purpose of each Parsons puzzle program in the accompanying problem statement. So, even though we found mnemonic variable names did not seem to provide any benefits and this result concurs with some of the results found in the previous study [1], the reasons why are not the same. Given the counter-intuitive nature of our result, this study should be reproduced in different settings before any definitive conclusions are drawn.

We expect students to build a mental model of the semantics of the program as they solve a Parsons puzzle: tracing each variable through its lifecycle, tracing the flow of data and control through the program, and thereby, understanding how each line of code fits into the overall program. If so, mnemonic variables would make it easier to build such a model by making it easier to trace each variable through its lifecycle and trace the flow of data through the program. Single-character variables on the other hand force the reader to scan the program repeatedly to re-establish the purpose of each unhelpfully named variable.

May be students resort to techniques other than constructing a complete mental model of the program to solve Parsons puzzles. So, the use of mnemonic variables neither helps nor hurts their ability to solve the puzzles. If a student can solve a Parsons puzzle without building a mental model of the underlying program first, it is essential for researchers to isolate and identify the alternative puzzle-solving techniques, and see whether and how those techniques contribute to the learning of programming. In the future, we plan to test whether students re-assemble the lines of code in a puzzle in random order, or in an order influenced by the semantics of the lines of code.

ACKNOWLEDGMENTS

Partial support for this work was provided by the National Science Foundation under grants DUE 1502564 and DUE-1432190.

REFERENCES

[1] Eran Avidan and Dror G. Feitelson. 2017. Effects of variable names on comprehension an empirical study. In *Proceedings of the 25th International Conference on Program Comprehension (ICPC '17)*. IEEE Press, Piscataway, NJ, USA, 55-65. DOI: https://doi.org/10.1109/ICPC.2017.27.

[2] Scott Blinman and Andy Cockburn. 2005. Program comprehension: investigating the effects of naming style and documentation. In Proceedings of the Sixth Australasian conference on User interface - Volume 40 (AUIC '05), Mark Billinghurst and Andy Cockburn (Eds.), Vol. 40. Australian Computer Society, Inc., Darlinghurst, Australia, Australia, 73-78.

[3] Nick Cheng and Brian Harrington. 2017. The Code Mangler: Evaluating Coding Ability Without Writing any Code. In *Proceedings of the 2017 ACM SIGCSE Technical Symposium on Computer Science Education (SIGCSE '17)*. ACM, New York, NY, USA, 123-128. DOI: https://doi.org/10.1145/3017680.3017704.

[4] Paul Denny, Andrew Luxton-Reilly, and Beth Simon. 2008. Evaluating a new exam question: Parsons problems. In *Proceedings of the Fourth International Workshop on Computing Education Research (ICER '08)*. ACM, New York, NY, USA, 113-124. DOI=http://dx.doi.org/10.1145/1404520.1404532.

[5] Barbara J. Ericson, James D. Foley, and Jochen Rick. 2018. Evaluating the Efficiency and Effectiveness of Adaptive Parsons Problems. In *Proceedings of the 2018 ACM Conference on International Computing Education Research (ICER '18)*. ACM, New York, NY, USA, 60-68. DOI: https://doi.org/10.1145/3230977.3231000

[6] Barbara J. Ericson, Mark J. Guzdial, and Briana B. Morrison. 2015. Analysis of Interactive Features Designed to Enhance Learning in an Ebook. In *Proceedings of the eleventh annual International Conference on International Computing Education Research (ICER '15)*. ACM, New York, NY, USA, 169-178. DOI: https://doi.org/10.1145/2787622.2787731.

[7] Barbara J. Ericson, Lauren E. Margulieux, and Jochen Rick. 2017. Solving Parsons problems versus fixing and writing code. In *Proceedings of the 17th Koli Calling International Conference on Computing Education Research (Koli Calling '17)*. ACM, New York, NY, USA, 20-29. DOI: https://doi.org/10.1145/3141880.3141895.

[8] G. W. Furnas, T. K. Landauer, L. M. Gomez, and S. T. Dumais. 1987. The vocabulary problem in human-system communication. Communications of the.ACM 30,(November 1987), 964-971 DOI= https://doi.org/10.1145/32206.32212

[9] Juha Helminen, Petri Ihantola, Ville Karavirta, and Lauri Malmi. 2012. How do students solve parsons programming problems?: an analysis of interaction traces. In *Proceedings of the ninth annual international conference on International computing education research (ICER '12)*. ACM, New York, NY, USA, 119-126. DOI: https://doi.org/10.1145/2361276.2361300.

[10] Petri Ihantola and Ville Karavirta. 2010. Open source widget for parson's puzzles. In *Proceedings of the fifteenth annual conference on Innovation and technology in computer science education (ITiCSE '10)*. ACM, New York, NY, USA, 302-302. DOI: https://doi.org/10.1145/1822090.1822178

[11] Petri Ihantola and Ville Karavirta. 2011.Two-Dimensional Parson's Puzzles: The Conceot, Tools, and First Observations. *Journal of Information Technology Education: Innovations in Practice*. Vol 10. 2011. 119-132. DOI= https://doi.org/10.28945/1394

[12] Amruth N. Kumar. 2018. Epplets: A Tool for Solving Parsons Puzzles. In *Proceedings of the 49th ACM Technical Symposium on Computer Science Education (SIGCSE '18)*. ACM, New York, NY, USA, 527-532. DOI: https://doi.org/10.1145/3159450.3159576.

[13] Amruth N. Kumar. 2017. The Effect of Providing Motivational Support in Parsons Puzzle Tutors. In *Proceedings of Artificial Intelligence in Education. (AI-ED 2017)*, Wuhan, China, June 2017, 528-531. DOI= https://doi.org/10.1007/978-3-319-61425-0_56

[14] Dawn Lawrie, Christopher Morrell, Henry Feild, and David Binkley. 2006. What's in a Name? A Study of Identifiers. In Proceedings of the 14th IEEE International Conference on Program Comprehension (ICPC '06). IEEE Computer Society, Washington, DC, USA, 3-12. DOI: https://doi.org/10.1109/ICPC.2006.51

[15] Mike Lopez, Jacqueline Whalley, Phil Robbins, and Raymond Lister. 2008. Relationships between reading, tracing and writing skills in introductory programming. In *Proceedings of the Fourth International Workshop on Computing Education Research (ICER '08)*. ACM, New York, NY, USA, 101-112. DOI=http://dx.doi.org/10.1145/1404520.1404531.

[16] Briana B. Morrison, Lauren E. Margulieux, Barbara Ericson, and Mark Guzdial. 2016. Subgoals Help Students Solve Parsons Problems. In Proceedings of the 47th ACM Technical Symposium on Computing Science Education (SIGCSE '16). ACM, New York, NY, USA, 42-47. DOI: https://doi.org/10.1145/2839509.2844617.

[17] Dale Parsons and Patricia Haden. 2006. Parson's programming puzzles: a fun and effective learning tool for first programming courses. In Proceedings of the 8th Australasian Conference on Computing Education - Volume 52 (ACE '06), Denise Tolhurst and Samuel Mann (Eds.), Vol. 52. Australian Computer Society, Inc., Darlinghurst, Australia, Australia, 157-163.

[18] Felice Salviulo and Giuseppe Scanniello. 2014. Dealing with identifiers and comments in source code comprehension and maintenance: results from an ethnographically-informed study with students and professionals. In Proceedings of the 18th International Conference on Evaluation and Assessment in Software Engineering (EASE '14). ACM, New York, NY, USA, , Article 48 , 10 pages. DOI: http://dx.doi.org/10.1145/2601248.2601251

Perspectives on Global Bachelor Computing Education

John Impagliazzo
(Moderator) Hofstra University
Hempstead, New York, USA
+1 631-513-2833
john.impagliazzo@hofstra.edu

Brett A. Becker
University College Dublin &
Beijing-Dublin International College
Dublin, Ireland & Beijing, China
+353 1 716 2933
brett.becker@ucd.ie

Alison Clear
Eastern Institute of Technology
Auckland, New Zealand
+64 21-955-495
AClear@eit.ac.nz

Ernesto Cuadros-Vargas
Universidad de Ingeniería y Tecnología
Lima, Peru
+51 1 230-5000
ecuadros@utec.edu.pe

Xiaoyong Du
Renmin University of China
Beijing, China
+86 10-62515259
duyong@ruc.edu.cn

Abhijat Vichare
ACM India
Pune, India
+91 9960355169
abhijatv@acm.org

ABSTRACT

The update of the broadly influential document Computing Curricula 2005 (CC2005), is underway with a project called Computing Curricula 2020 (CC2020). The project consists of a task force of more than forty academic, industry, and government professionals representing seventeen countries from six continents. The CC2020 project plans to provide a vision for the future of computing, to produce a comprehensive report that contrasts curricular guidelines, and to contextualize those guidelines within a landscape of computing education based on a framework of competency-based educational principles. As part of the CC2020 project and as the worldwide demand for competent computing professionals grows, it is increasingly important to understand the attributes and challenges of computing programs from different global perspectives. The panelists plan to present different viewpoints on ways their countries structure computing programs. Audience involvement and panelist interactions promise to explore additional points of view on computing programs toward developing a shared understanding of undergraduate computing programs as they currently exist.

CCS CONCEPTS

Social and professional topics → Professional topics → Computing Education → Model Curricula

KEYWORDS

Computing curricula, CC2020, global perspectives

ACM Reference format:
John Impagliazzo, Brett A. Becker, Alison Clear, Ernesto Cuadros-Vargas, Xiaoyong Du and Abhijat Vichare. 2018. Perspectives on Global Bachelor Computing Education. In *Proceedings of the 2019 ACM Global Computing Education Conference (CompEd'19), May 17-19, 2019, Chengdu, Sichuan, China.* ACM, New York, NY, USA, 2 pages. https://doi.org/10.1145/3300115.3310367

1 INTRODUCTION

ACM began exploring the possible update of the broadly influential document, Computing Curricula 2005 (CC2005) [1] and in 2016, ACM decided to initiate a new project called Computing Curricula 2020 (CC2020). ACM and IEEE-CS became the principal sponsors of the CC2020 project, which supports a task force of more than forty academic, industry, and government professionals worldwide. A subset of this task force forms a steering committee of up to fifteen members. Currently, the task force represents seventeen countries from six continents. The CC2020 project plans to examine the current state of curricular guidelines for academic programs granting bachelor degrees in computing. The project also provides a vision for the future of computing. It intends to produce a comprehensive report that contrasts curricular guidelines and to contextualize these guidelines in the landscape of a competency-based educational framework for computing education.

This panel complements the CC2020 project. It plans to address commonalities and differences in describing computing programs from different global perspectives. The presentations from the panelists sets the stage to highlight different viewpoints on computing education at the university level. Audience engagement promises to generate other perspectives from a global scale. The overall intention is to develop a shared understanding on the structure of undergraduate computing programs worldwide and, their similarities and differences.

2 PANEL GOALS

The primary goals of this panel session are to (a) present diverse perspectives on curricular models for baccalaureate undergraduate computing degree programs, (b) discuss the challenges that exist in developing strong computing programs globally, and (c) garner audience perspectives on the ideas presented by the panelists. The panelists welcome a highly active discourse surrounding worldwide computing education degree programs.

3 PANEL DESCRIPTION

This panel focuses on presenting the views of the panelists as they relate to computing curricula from a global perspective. The presentations and audience discussion aim to contrast similarities and differences. The structure of the panel presentation assumes a total session of seventy-five minutes with panelist presentations limited to six minutes approximately. This allows thirty minutes for debate and discussion between the panelists themselves and between the panelists and the audience. The allotted time allows a few minutes for introductions and for closing remarks.

4 PANEL MEMBERS

The members for this panel are computing academicians currently based in China, India, Ireland, New Zealand, Peru, and the United States. Their brief presentations provide a basis for greater understanding on the dynamics that produce meaningful computing programs for the future.

John Impagliazzo – John Impagliazzo, professor emeritus from Hofstra University, is a steering committee member of the CC2020 project. He was chair of the committee that produced the computer engineering curricular report (CE2016) [2], was an active member of the CC2005 project, and a member of the executive committee of a parallel project for information technology (IT2017) [3]. Impagliazzo is an IEEE Fellow, an IEEE Life Member, an ACM Distinguished Educator, and a CSAB Fellow. John presents computing education as it currently exists in the United States and his concerns for the future.

Brett A. Becker – Brett A. Becker is faculty member at the University College Dublin and has been teaching computer science at the undergraduate level for twelve years. He currently teaches in Ireland as well as in China at the Beijing-Dublin International College, an Irish-Chinese partnership at the Beijing University of Technology. He has experienced computing programs as a student and/or lecturer in the United States, Ireland, and China, at public and private institutions. He has been on several program design committees and is particularly interested in the interface between second-level and undergraduate curricula. Brett believes country-specific differences in university structure and he also warns that the world may have to change undergraduate program structures more rapidly than before as the profile of incoming students become more adept at computing as they were in the past.

Alison Clear – Alison Clear from Eastern Institute of Technology is a steering committee member and co-chair of the CC2020 project. She has also been either conference chair or program chair of dozens of international conferences in computing education. She is a past vice chair and member of the SIGCSE board and a life member of the New Zealand Institute of IT Professionals and the Computing and Information Technology Research and Education of New Zealand. Alison plans to contrast computing education as it exists in Australasia compared to other global regions.

Ernesto Cuadros-Vargas – Ernesto Cuadros-Vargas received his PhD in computer science from the University of Sao Paulo-Brazil (2004). He is a founder member of Peruvian Computer Society (SPC), served as its president, and served as executive secretary of Peru for the Latin American Computing Conference (CLEI). He was a member of the IEEE-Educational Activities Board, served on the steering committee of the ACM/IEEE-CS computing curricula for computer science (CS2013), and is currently a member of the steering committee member of the CC2020 project. Ernesto presents the landscape of undergraduate computing education as it exists throughout Latin America.

Xiaoyong Du – Xiaoyong Du is a full professor of computer science at Renmin University of China. He is a fellow of the Chinese Computer Federation (CCF) and an executive member of CCF Board. He is Director of the CCF Committee of Higher Education, Chair of CCF Technical Committee of Databases, and a board member of the IEEE Technical Committee on Data Engineering. Xiaoyong discusses the higher education structure as it exists in China and the way bachelor computing education has transformed at universities over the past two decades in the country.

Abhijat Vichare – Abhijat Vichare has been teaching computer science in India for more than twenty years. Within ACM India he has been involved with curriculum design problems in India. He serves on academic boards of study at various educational institutions and tries to bring in ACM-IEEE CS2013 approaches into their curricula. He is currently a member of the steering committee of the CC2020 project. Abhijat plans to convey his perspectives on the state of computing education in India and various contrasts within regions and institutions.

5 RATIONALE

The panelists have diverse expertise in computing curricula and education. They can both inform the audience and solicit advice from them. The session provides ample time for direct audience interaction to provide an engagement with the panelists from the computing and engineering education communities. The discussions should generate multiple perspectives on computing education from different parts of the world and enhance the knowledge and understanding of both participants and panelists.

6 AUDIENCE DESCRIPTION

The panel targets university faculty members and administrators interested in the global landscape of computing curricular content. Information gathered is useful toward developing their own programs, developing new programs, or modifying existing programs in computing. Audience participation is important for the success of this panel.

REFERENCES

[1] ACM, et al., Computing Curricula 2005: The Overview Report covering undergraduate degree programs in Computer Engineering, Computer Science, Information Systems, Information Technology, and Software Engineering (CC2005). https://www.acm.org/binaries/content/assets/education/curricula-recommendations/cc2005-march06final.pdf. Accessed 2019 Jan 30.

[2] ACM et al., Computer Engineering Curricula 2016: Curriculum Guidelines for Undergraduate Degree Programs in Computer Engineering (CE2016); https://www.acm.org/binaries/content/assets/education/ce2016-final-report.pdf. Accessed 2019 Jan 30.

[3] ACM et al., Information Technology Curricula 2017: Curriculum Guidelines for Undergraduate Degree Programs in Information Technology (IT2017); https://www.acm.org/binaries/content/assets/education/curricula-recommendations/it2017.pdf. Accessed 2019 Jan 30.

Teaching AI Algorithms with Games Including Mahjong and FightTheLandlord on the Botzone Online Platform

Wenxin Li
Peking University
Department of Computer Science
Beijing, China
lwx@pku.edu.cn

Haoyu Zhou
Peking University
Department of Computer Science
Beijing, China
sohu@pku.edu.cn

Chris Wang
Peking University
Department of Computer Science
Beijing, China
chris_wang@pku.edu.cn

Haifeng Zhang
Peking University
Department of Computer Science
Beijing, China
pkuzhf@pku.edu.cn

Xingxing Hong
Peking University
Department of Computer Science
Beijing, China
jwbhxx@pku.edu.cn

Yushan Zhou
Peking University
Department of Computer Science
Beijing, China
zysls@pku.edu.cn

Qinjian Zhang
Peking University
Department of Computer Science
Beijing, China
zqj@pku.edu.cn

ABSTRACT

This paper presents a course design, named Algorithms in Game AI, as an undergraduate elective course. The course mainly focuses on common and state-of-the-art algorithms in the game AI area, including game tree based algorithms and reinforcement learning. Powered by Botzone, our game AI platform, we designed different types of assignments for this course to bring a rich and fun learning experience. We chose several games including two popular Chinese classic ones, namely Mahjong and FightTheLandlord, which are both collaborative, stochastic and partially observable. To our best knowledge, it is the first time to adopt these games in AI courses, thus providing a new benchmark for game AI education. To encourage participation and reduce frustration, milestone-based competitions and bonus tasks were adopted. In this paper, we present the structure, teaching tools, techniques, performance and findings of this course. By reviewing students' performance and feedback, we found that students enjoyed the games we provided. We also found that reinforcement learning algorithms did not perform as well as other algorithms in limited time and resources.

KEYWORDS

AI Education, Reinforcement Learning, Game AI

ACM Reference Format:
Wenxin Li, Haoyu Zhou, Chris Wang, Haifeng Zhang, Xingxing Hong, Yushan Zhou, and Qinjian Zhang. 2019. Teaching AI Algorithms with Games Including Mahjong and FightTheLandlord on the Botzone Online Platform. In *ACM Global Computing Education Conference 2019 (CompEd '19), May 17–19, 2019, Chengdu,Sichuan, China.* ACM, New York, NY, USA, 7 pages. https://doi.org/10.1145/3300115.3309510

1 INTRODUCTION

Artificial Intelligence is a rapidly developing field, attracting an increasing number of researchers and learners in the past few years. As is stated in [1], games have long been seen as the perfect test-bed (e.g. the game of Go used by AlphaGo [2]) for artificial intelligence methods, and are also becoming an increasingly important application area. Needless to say, such a course with the topic of game AI is meaningful and helpful for students to develop interest and skill in the AI field.

1.1 The course

We are aware of existing courses adopting this idea, for example Berkeley CS188 [1] and Stanford CS221 [2], covering a large number of topics in the AI field, including Bayes' Nets, robotics, perceptron, hidden markov model (HMM), natural language processing (NLP) and more. We would like provide a different perspective to AI education, by focusing on the common and state-of-the-art algorithms related to game playing, for example, game tree based search, reinforcement learning (RL) and neural networks. Concentrating on this scope, we will be able to reduce the prerequisites of the course, and provide a narrower yet deeper perspective of algorithms playing games, and hopefully equip students with the ability to understand and replicate the outstanding AlphaGo [2] or AlphaGo Zero [3]

---

[1] http://ai.berkeley.edu/home.html
[2] http://web.stanford.edu/class/cs221/

Table 1: Examples of interactive platforms in computing education

Task	Examples
Computer Architecture and OS	Autolab [5]
Programming Basics	Codeacademy [5]
Algorithms	POJ [6], Code Hunt [7]
Game AI topics	OpenAI Gym [8], Botzone [9, 10], The AI Games [6]

on their own. In addition, we provided two more classical Chinese games, Mahjong [3] (a tile-based game that was developed in China during the Qing dynasty and has spread throughout the world since the early 20th century) and FightTheLandlord [4] (a 3-player card game in the genre of shedding and gambling), for students to challenge, which are different from other games in being collaborative, stochastic and partially observable.

1.2 Assessment tool for this course

In computing education, assessment is a unavoidable topic. Assessment can be the core content in performance-based learning, which allows students to learn through practice in the process. However, traditional human-based assessment methods need many course staff for evaluation, and cannot give responses to students quick enough. To get over the shortcomings, computer-based assessment tools come to rescue. These tools can create feedback for students instantly and automatically, therefore shorten the cycle of learning and self-improvement, as mentioned in [4].

Some of the tools are home-brew program and grading script provided by course staff, which make up lab assignments. These tools are often one-time use or specialized for this course. Preparing these assets repeatedly can be a waste of time. Therefore, there rises a need to categorize, serve and share the assets of similar tasks and purposes. In this paper, we call the kind of tools fulfilling the said need interactive platforms.

Table 1 shows examples of platforms for computer science education, classified by their task.

For game AI education, we are especially interested in the last row of Table 1. The platforms listed here share the same purpose to let users to write AI programs for game agents. We have already developed an interactive platform named Botzone [9, 10] specifically for game AI related coursework which has been continuously improving in the past few years. Details of how we design and teach the course with the Botzone platform are being discussed in the section 3.1 of this paper.

2 COURSE DESIGN

We designed the algorithms in game AI course where students learn mainstream algorithms in game AI, including basic concepts, planning on game tree and reinforcement learning, with the help of an interactive game playing platform (Botzone). This course is an undergraduate elective course for students majoring in computer

science. Students enrolled are expected to have basic knowledge and experience in at least one programming language.

2.1 Outline

The outline of this course is shown in Table 2.

We briefly divided the course into two parts - planning algorithms and learning algorithms. Planning algorithms are classic methods in the model of searching on a game tree, while learning algorithms are mostly reinforcement learning methods. We referred to [14] when structuring the second part. Implementations of well-played AI examples were also provided as case studies, with the expectation that students are able to implement an AlphaGo-like AI on their own in the end.

2.2 Assignments

As is shown in the outline, there are several exercise classes in the course, where we teach students practical skills and provide detailed tutorial of taught algorithms in the course. Some of the exercises are warm-ups for the subsequent assignment to explain a sample solution to students. The final project (game contest) requires students to team up and finish in one month. The subjects of these assignments are listed as follows:

(1) **Play a Game**: Play the Mahjong game in class with classmates on our interactive game AI platform (Botzone). No score assigned.
(2) **Renju Challenge**: Write AI program based on game tree to play Renju, and challenge the "Bosses" (staff provided AI programs) on Botzone.
(3) **Q-learning Lab**: Adopt the q-learning method taught in class to play the CartPole game and score an average reward of 500.
(4) **Policy Gradient Lab**: Adopt the policy gradient method taught in class to play the Pong game and score over 16 points.
(5) **Final Contest**: Choose one from the 3 provided games (Go, Mahjong and FightTheLandlord) and team up for a game contest with each other.

Some of the design choices regarding these assignments are being explained later in section 3.2.

For the games we adopted in this course, the comparison to other AI courses is shown in Table 3. We tried to cover many game properties with many games to better address the topics in class, and arouse interest from students of different taste of games.

2.3 The games of Mahjong and FightTheLandlord

For the final contest, we not only provided the game of Go, but also introduced the newly implemented games Mahjong and FightTheLandlord.

---

[3]https://en.wikipedia.org/wiki/Mahjong
[4]https://en.wikipedia.org/wiki/Dou_dizhu
[5]Renju is the professional variant of Gomoku. https://en.wikipedia.org/wiki/Renju
[6]https://gym.openai.com/envs/CartPole-v0
[7]https://gym.openai.com/envs/Pong-v0/
[8]StarCraft is a military science fiction media franchise, created by Chris Metzen and James Phinney and owned by Blizzard Entertainment. https://en.wikipedia.org/wiki/StarCraft

Table 2: Outline of the course

Subject	Topics
Introduction: Evolution of Game AI	History of game AI, Current Frontier in Research Field
Exercise: Play games with classmates	Get familiar with the interactive game playing platform (Botzone)
Definition and Classification of Games	Markov Decision Process, Game Theory, Game Description Language
Complexity Analysis of Games	State Complexity, Game Tree Complexity
Planning Algorithms - Alpha-beta Pruning	A* Algorithm, Minimax Search, Alpha-beta Pruning [11]
Exercise: Introduction to Python and AI frameworks	Language basics, Numpy, Tensorflow
Planning Algorithms - Monte-Carlo Tree Search [12] (MCTS)	Monte-Carlo Tree Search, Upper Confidence Bounds [13]
Exercise: Alpha-beta Pruning and MCTS in Renju [7] Game	Empirical evaluation function and optimizations
Planning Algorithms - Dynamic Programming	Reinforcement Learning (RL), Policy Iteration, Value Iteration
Learning Algorithms - Monte-Carlo Learning	Prediction and Control, On-policy and Off-policy
Learning Algorithms - Temporal Difference Learning	Prediction and Control, Q-learning, SARSA, $TD(\lambda)$
Exercise: Implementation of Q-learning	Tabular methods, CartPole [8] game
Learning Algorithms - On-Policy Learning with Approximation	Approximation Function Semi-gradient Control, Deep Q Network
Learning Algorithms - Policy Gradient	Policy Gradient Theorem, Monte-Carlo Policy Gradient, Actor-Critic
Exercise: Implementation of Policy Gradient	Training agent to play Pong [9] game
Learning Algorithms - Combination of Planning and Learning	Model-Based RL, Model-Free RL, Dyna
Case Studies - Planning and Learning in Games	AI Examples, AlphaGo, StarCraft [10], Mahjong, FightTheLandlord
Final Project: Game Contest	Go (8x8) / Mahjong / FightTheLandlord

Figure 1: The Mahjong Game.

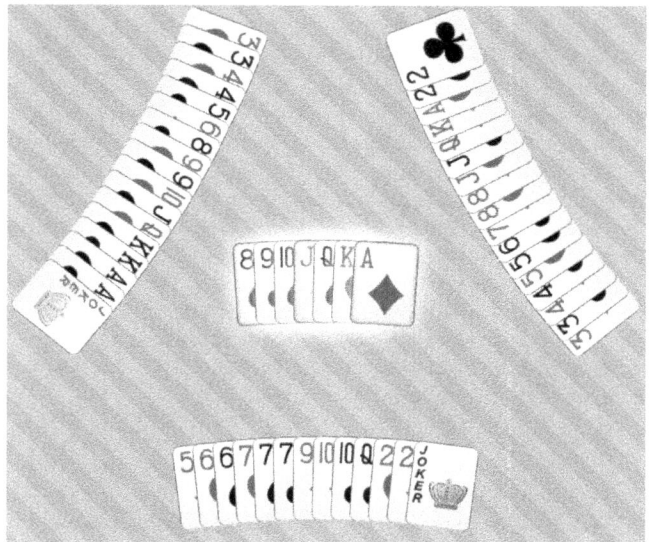

Figure 2: The FightTheLandlord Game.

Mahjong is partially observable, stochastic, episodic, static, discrete and multi-agent. (Shown in Figure 1) The four players compete with each other most of the time, but sometimes one may collaborate with others for a common interest. For example, three players can work together to prevent a player from winning (called Hu), thus making the game complex.

Fight the Landlord is also partially observable, stochastic, episodic, static, discrete and multi-agent. (Shown in Figure 2) However, in this 3-player card game, two of them (called peasants) have to team up to fight against the other player (called landlord). Player who finishes their card wins the game, and if one of the peasants wins, they both win. The game is described as easy to learn but hard to

master, requiring mathematical and strategic thinking as well as carefully planned execution.

Most Chinese students are already familiar with these games as the games are very popular and classic, therefore providing them smoother experience to learn AI this way. These games are also challenging due to their nature of being partially observable and stochastic, which is different from most games used in AI courses. With our newly implemented games, the course can cover more aspects of game AI, especially Bayesian game (imperfect information game).

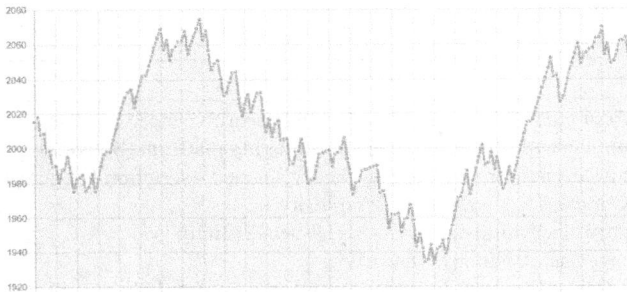

Figure 3: Score variation of a top-ranked AI algorithm on the ranking. The score changes due to winning or losing to others.

3 TEACHING ON BOTZONE

To improve students' learning experience, let every student see their progress and offer them the sense of achievement, we made use of Botzone, an interactive game playing platform that we had developed in the past few years [10], and also adopted various teaching techniques in this course.

3.1 Brief introduction to the Botzone platform

Botzone is a graphical online game playing platform, designed in aid of the application of game in AI education. Either human or AI programs are able to control the players in various multi-agent games. Students are allowed to code, test and improve their AI programs against other AI programs or human players easily on Botzone, practicing their coding skills and various AI algorithms in the process. We also equipped Botzone with various functionalities, for instance, a dynamic ranking for all existing AI algorithms, to encourage students to compete with and learn from each other. Moreover, we collected data from all the matches to create a public dataset for students to train their AI algorithms.

Some of the highlights of Botzone is listed below:

- **Interactive match display**: Real-time HTML5 players for all the games, with decent graphical effect and human interaction ability.
- **ELO [15] based dynamic ranking**: A global ranking for each game based on the ELO rating algorithm, updated every 5 minutes by automatic ranked matches, providing students the trending of their AI algorithms and mainstream algorithms. Figure 3 shows the graph of an AI algorithm on the ranking.
- **Multiple programming language and machine learning support**: C/C++, Java, C#, JavaScript (Node.js) and Python (2 and 3) are all supported, as well as machine learning libraries such as tensorflow, pytorch and mxnet.
- **Contest system addressing fairness**: For courses or competitions, customizable contest systems are available on Botzone, including Swiss-system and Single-elimination. As some of the games are stochastic, option to use a same random seed in each round is provided, making sure the contest is fair.

The Botzone platform itself (without the games) contains many game-like elements, as is shown above. Therefore, it may also benefit from gamification [16].

3.2 How the course made use of Botzone

In a course teaching AI algorithms, it is better to provide a challenging yet fun programming experience for students. Botzone aims to arouse the interests and motivation of students, and has the nature to be fun and interactive.

Students can get immediate response (match results) after submitting their programs. They are easily committed to improve their algorithms a lot on their own and keep on trying to achieve higher ranks. Moreover, after their experience in programming AI agents, they are likely to have developed interest and skill in the AI field.

We used Botzone for the first two assignments as well as the final project, and the details are discussed below.

3.2.1 Assignment 1: Play a Game. This assignment was designed to arouse students' interest at the beginning of the course through playing the games, and make them familiar with the usage of Botzone. Students would either host a game table or join others on Botzone to play the classic Mahjong game. They would share how they learned to play the game from a human being's perspective, which can be meaningful after they have learned how to teach AI to play games.

Students participating this assignment would gain a bonus score regardless of their performance.

3.2.2 Assignment 2: Renju Challenge. After students have learned Alpha-beta pruning algorithm and Monte-Carlo Tree Search for the first time, students should be able to try these methods in a real world board game. We chose Renju for this assignment as it is well-known and its rules are easy to understand.

To prevent fierce competition from occurring too early in this course, and to reduce amount of effort tuning their AI, we did not make them compete with each other at this point. Instead, we selected three AI program from the ranking of different level on Botzone to act as "bosses". Students need to write AI program to defeat them one by one for this assignment on Botzone. Their winning rate would be converted to their score in this assignment.

3.2.3 Final Project: Game Contest. The final projects are three contests held on Botzone of different games, namely Go (8x8), Mahjong, and FightTheLandlord. Students would choose one from these three games, and then team up with their classmates. Each team consists of at most three students. They would code an AI program against one game collaboratively for the competition using all of the knowledge from both inside the course and outside the course.

We expected the students to gain a deeper understanding of what we taught by trying out different algorithms, comparing their performances and finding out themselves which algorithm fits the game well.

The final contests would run on Botzone automatically. For the stochastic games (Mahjong and FightTheLandlord), we made sure that for each round, the random seed of matches stayed the same, to address the fairness in contests. The final grades would be the percentages of their contest scores proportionally to the highest score.

Table 3: Comparison of games between this course and other courses

Game Property	Algorithms in Game AI	Berkeley CS188	Stanford CS221	University of Oklahoma [17]	Lafayette College CS414 [18]
Single Agent	Cartpole, Pong	Pacman, Ghostbuster	Pacman, Car-tracking	Pacman	Mario
Multi Agent, Fully Observable	Renju, Go	N/A	N/A	Spacewar, Mancala	N/A
Multi Agent, Partially Observable	FightTheLandlord, Mahjong	N/A	Blackjack	Roborally	N/A

To ease the pressure and frustration, we would hold several invited talks from other researchers expert in one of these games. Students would get a higher level overview of the mainstream methods for the games and gain confidence to make their own.

3.3 Encouraging students and mitigating frustration

As a course with topics of intermediate difficulty, students may need to make efforts to learn it well. Therefore, we were interested in promoting student retention and would like to make their learning experience smooth and comfortable.

Throughout the course, we tried to make the class as lively as possible by offering bonus open questions and chances to challenge their own AI algorithm in front of the class. Students would explain their algorithms while playing with their own AI, which eases their stress because either winning or losing is acceptable.

We designed the first assignment to encourage students to try the games on Botzone, by giving extra points to those who have participated regardless of how well they played. They would play the games with classmates just like playing computer games after-class with their friends. While they play, we would also make them notice how they learned to play new games with little knowledge, which is related to what we are going to teach soon.

As for the second Renju Challenge assignment, we tried not to frustrate students by setting fixed goals - the three "bosses" for them to challenge. These bosses are labeled as novice, easy and medium difficulties, respectively. Even beginner level student can defeat the novice boss easily by slightly optimizing the sample algorithm provided by the course staff. Therefore, we can give them a sense of achievement rather than let them down, thus reducing their frustration.

As the final project, the game contest was unavoidably competitive due to the nature of the assignment. If there was someone scoring high, then someone else would score relatively lower meanwhile. To narrow the gaps between them, we modified how the final grades are calculated - their grades would be the percentages of their original contest scores proportionally to the highest score. Moreover, some AI programs disguised as their classmates' ones would be added to the contest, which were of easier levels, and beating them is not as hard as defeating other students. The disguised programs would hopefully increase the base score of all participants. In fact, they represented our minimum requirements for this course.

4 PERFORMANCE AND ANALYSIS

Algorithms in game AI was a newly designed course and it began in March, 2018 for the first time. We had 51 students enrolled in the course, and 10 auditing. In this section, we firstly provide an analysis of their final projects, and then compare the learning trace collected from Botzone with other students participating in the final contest without taking this course. The voices from students in this course are also discussed later.

4.1 Analysis of final projects

Though the teams participating in the final game contests only selected one AI program as the contestant on Botzone, they had experimented with a variety of other algorithms in the process, as is seen from their learning trace on Botzone and their submitted reports.

The summary of their final projects are shown in Table 4. The table includes the algorithms they experimented on and the average score of each type of algorithm for each game. Please note that the disguised AI programs, as is described in section 3.3, is not included in the scores shown here - the average scores are "raw" performance.

The outcome is not quite satisfactory - there is a gap between the methods being taught and methods being effective. Students did not adopt the reinforcement learning methods in the end, contrast to what we expected, especially in the game of Go. From what they said in their reports, they had all tried to replicate the structure of AlphaGo [2] or AlphaGo Zero [3], but had a hard time training and improving their AI. We inspected their implementations and summarized the reasons as follows:

- **Limited computation power**: Even though we had simplified the game of Go to a 8x8 field, it seemed not enough for students to train the neural network described in AlphaGo Zero on their own computer within reasonable time. Students needed more CPU, memory and GPU to improve their model, at least comparable to the amount AlphaGo Zero used (64 GPU and 19 CPU), which were not available to most of them.
- **Limited Project Time**: Training and fine-tuning a model is quite time-consuming, especially for beginners and limited hardware. Most teams only tried one or two methods taught in class due to the fear of unable to produce a good version of AI program on time. It may seemed enough at first to allocate one month for the final project, but it turned out not sufficient.

Table 4: Summary of final projects. Each team may experiment with and finally adopt more than one type of algorithm. The scores in this table are the percentages of their original contest scores proportionally to the highest score of that game.

Game	Teams (Students)	Results Type	Expert System	Game Tree Based Search	MCTS	RL
		Teams Experimented	2	3	7	8
Go (8x8)	8 (22)	Teams Adopted	2	2	5	0
		Average Score (out of 100)	42.35	22.45	70.82	N/A
		Teams Experimented	10	4	3	5
FightTheLandlord	12 (24)	Teams Adopted	9	4	1	2
		Average Score (out of 100)	75.46	78.61	50.26	72.52
		Teams Experimented	2	3	0	1
Mahjong	3 (5)	Teams Adopted	2	3	0	1
		Average Score (out of 100)	46.02	64.02	N/A	45.58

Table 5: Survey result of the course. Each statement has a maximum of 100 points, representing how student agrees with the statement.

Statement	Course Average	Department Average
This course has a clear goal and is well-organized	96.24	91.53
This course is challenging enough to encourage active learning	97.73	91.90
The assessment system is reasonable and fair	94.32	90.71
I have improved my knowledge structure and skills	97.08	91.78
My passion and interest to go deeper are aroused	96.91	89.98
I will recommend this course to friends	95.45	86.77

- **Insufficient high-quality training data**: When students abandon the structure of AlphaGo Zero where the AI program play the game itself, and let the model be trained from existing match data (i.e. supervised learning), they complained about their lack of training data. It was not trivial for the students to generate high-quality Go matches.

4.2 Voices from students

At the end of each semester, the office of educational administration will carry out mandatory anonymous university-wide surveys on students' feedback of all courses. The results of the latest one are shown in Table 5. Students responded positive to this course overall.

Some students said they enjoyed the Mahjong and FightTheLandlord games because these games were fun as well as challenging involving the concepts of imperfect information game and multi-agent collaboration. The students pointed out that they had a hard time playing with their own AI programs - the AI programs would beat human easily after improving, bringing them great senses of achievement.

We also observed a number of students still play games with their bots occasionally on Botzone even after their course session. As seen on the social networks, students finishing this course are impressed by the methods from each other, and often talks about the AI algorithms they implemented. We found students expressing their addiction to playing games on Botzone, which might indicate improvement of engagement.

5 CONCLUSION AND FUTURE WORKS

In this paper, we presented the course design of algorithms in game AI, to which we applied different tools and techniques. We also presented an interactive game playing platform (Botzone) for AI education, and described how we teach this course on the platform. We adopted various games in this course, including Mahjong and FightTheLandlord, resulting in a new benchmark for game AI education.

We also formed a performance analysis on the first session of this course in 2018, and had several findings. As is stated in section 4.1, students could not get their reinforcement learning based methods performing well within the limited time and resources. More machines with GPU and more time for experimenting may be needed for future projects. Though the effectiveness of this course is hard to assess due to the lack of baseline, practitioners can still benefit from this research and employ similar interventions.

What is more, the presented platform is not intelligent enough to truly "tutor" the students. They sometimes feel lost if they do not know how to improve their AI algorithms. To reduce the burden of the course staff and instruct students when they are lost, we are going to investigate how to incorporate a smart tutor into the existing platform. Imitating existing AI program on the platform may also be useful to provide learning information to the smart tutor.

ACKNOWLEDGMENTS

The paper is partially supported by The National Key Research and Development Program of Chinander Grant No.: 2018YFB0204100 as well as the key program of Online Education Foundation (Quantong Education) of MOE Research Center for Online Education of China under Grant No.: 2017ZD102.

REFERENCES

[1] Georgios N Yannakakis and Julian Togelius. *Artificial Intelligence and Games*. Springer, 2018.

[2] David Silver, Aja Huang, Chris J Maddison, Arthur Guez, Laurent Sifre, George Van Den Driessche, Julian Schrittwieser, Ioannis Antonoglou, Veda Panneershelvam, Marc Lanctot, et al. Mastering the game of go with deep neural networks and tree search. *nature*, 529(7587):484, 2016.

[3] David Silver, Julian Schrittwieser, Karen Simonyan, Ioannis Antonoglou, Aja Huang, Arthur Guez, Thomas Hubert, Lucas Baker, Matthew Lai, Adrian Bolton, et al. Mastering the game of go without human knowledge. *Nature*, 550(7676):354, 2017.

[4] Chris Ricketts and SJ Wilks. Improving student performance through computer-based assessment: Insights from recent research. *Assessment & evaluation in higher education*, 27(5):475–479, 2002.

[5] Dejan Milojicic. Autograding in the cloud: interview with david o'hallaron. *IEEE Internet Computing*, 15(1):9–12, 2011.

[6] Li Wen-xin and GUO Wei. Peking university oneline judge and its applications [j]. *Journal of Changchun Post and Telecommunication Institute S*, 2, 2005.

[7] Nikolai Tillmann, Jonathan De Halleux, Tao Xie, and Judith Bishop. Code hunt: Gamifying teaching and learning of computer science at scale. In *Proceedings of the first ACM conference on Learning@ scale conference*, pages 221–222. ACM, 2014.

[8] Greg Brockman, Vicki Cheung, Ludwig Pettersson, Jonas Schneider, John Schulman, Jie Tang, and Wojciech Zaremba. Openai gym. *arXiv preprint arXiv:1606.01540*, 2016.

[9] Haoyu Zhou, Yushan Zhou, Haifeng Zhang, Houjun Huang, and Wenxin Li. Botzone: a competitive and interactive platform for game ai education. In *Proceedings of the ACM Turing 50th Celebration Conference-China*, page 6. ACM, 2017.

[10] Haoyu Zhou, Haifeng Zhang, Yushan Zhou, Xinchao Wang, and Wenxin Li. Botzone: an online multi-agent competitive platform for ai education. In *Proceedings of the 23rd Annual ACM Conference on Innovation and Technology in Computer Science Education*, pages 33–38. ACM, 2018.

[11] Donald E Knuth and Ronald W Moore. An analysis of alpha-beta pruning. *Artificial intelligence*, 6(4):293–326, 1975.

[12] Rémi Coulom. Efficient selectivity and backup operators in monte-carlo tree search. In *International conference on computers and games*, pages 72–83. Springer, 2006.

[13] Levente Kocsis and Csaba Szepesvári. Bandit based monte-carlo planning. In *European conference on machine learning*, pages 282–293. Springer, 2006.

[14] Richard S Sutton and Andrew G Barto. *Reinforcement learning: An introduction*, volume 1. MIT press Cambridge, 1998.

[15] Arpad E Elo. *The rating of chessplayers, past and present*. Arco Pub., 1978.

[16] Thomas M Connolly, Elizabeth A Boyle, Ewan MacArthur, Thomas Hainey, and James M Boyle. A systematic literature review of empirical evidence on computer games and serious games. *Computers & Education*, 59(2):661–686, 2012.

[17] Amy McGovern, Zachery Tidwell, and Derek Rushing. Teaching introductory artificial intelligence through java-based games. In *AAAI Symposium on Educational Advances in Artificial Intelligence, North America*, 2011.

[18] Matthew E Taylor. Teaching reinforcement learning with mario: An argument and case study. In *Proceedings of the Second Symposium on Educational Advances in Artifical Intelligence*, pages 1737–1742, 2011.

A Project-based Learning Experience in a Compilers Course

Adrian Lara and Luis Quesada
University of Costa Rica
Montes de Oca, San Jose
{adrian.lara,luis.quesada}@ucr.ac.cr

ABSTRACT

This paper describes a project-based learning (PBL) experience in a compilers course. In PBL, students play an active goal in learning and professors act like facilitators of knowledge. In PBL, students face authentic and motivating problems that require them to answer to complex questions and develop success skills. We first explain why the majority of projects used in the compilers course are not fit for this teaching strategy. Based on this problem, we propose a project that enables student motivation and sustained inquiry. We describe a one-semester experience with two professors and 40 students. In the experience described, students were asked to work in groups to build a complete compiler for a language designed on their own. Furthermore, we designed different types of classes, such as traditional lectures, time in the lab, group meetings and design discussions to enable student voice, reflection, critical thinking and critique, essential elements of PBL that are commonly not sufficiently addressed in traditional course organizations. The results show that students were highly motivated and capable of identifying which success skills needed improvement.

KEYWORDS

project-based learning, compilers

ACM Reference Format:
Adrian Lara and Luis Quesada. 2019. A Project-based Learning Experience in a Compilers Course. In *ACM Global Computing Education Conference 2019 (CompEd '19), May 17–19, 2019, Chengdu,Sichuan, China.* ACM, New York, NY, USA, 7 pages. https://doi.org/10.1145/3300115.3309502

1 INTRODUCTION

Several studies have identified a gap between the skills needed in industry and those supplied by education in Science, Technology, Engineering, and Mathematics (STEM) academic disciplines [6, 14]. Studies identify different solutions to bridge the gap, such as supporting research groups, developing curricula at universities, supporting students competitions, implementing project-based learning (PBL) and others [7].

One of the goals of the new curricula of the Computer Science department of the University of Costa Rica is to incorporate PBL [4, 5]. A successful implementation of this pedagogical technique engages students in learning that is deep and long-lasting [7]. Some

key aspects of PBL include enabling critical thinking by the students and using challenging, real-world and motivating problems. Likewise, projects should promote sustained inquiry, allow students to make some decisions on their projects and enable students to reflect on their learning and their ability to overcome obstacles. Finally, students should give and receive feedback and should display their products publicly [7].

In this paper, we share our experience of implementing PBL in the compilers course taught for third year undergraduate students. Existing course projects for the compilers class often face the following problems regarding PBL. First, the traditional teaching method is to teach all the content during lectures and then ask students to work on a project [19, 20]. This is a problem because students do not create their own knowledge, they simply apply what they know to solve a specific problem. By doing this, they become passive students. Instead, PBL seeks for active learning.

Second, the majority of projects work on either a subset of a widely used programming language, or a new language designed specifically for the compilers course [2, 11, 23]. The motivation to do this is clear: it limits the scope of the project and allows students to focus on the relevant aspects of building a compiler. However, this approach also faces some limitations. First, it is less motivating for the student, because they do not feel attached to the programming language. Second, the students miss the opportunity of being creative and designing their own language. Third, pre-designed languages are usually conflict-free and in some cases the grammar is given. Thus, the students do not face the problem of building a grammar from scratch.

Third, some existing projects have only four or five stages with a significant amount of knowledge involved in each stage [19, 20]. This requires students to write code that they do not fully understand. For example, a lexer is usually connected to a parser through programming statements that are not understandable if the student is only discovering lexical analysis. Likewise, when building a grammar, the grammar itself is a separate problem from the actions within the grammar. The earlier is needed to enforce the syntax, while the latter usually involves building an abstract syntax tree (AST).

In this paper we attempted to design a PBL project for the compilers course that overcomes the problems described above. In particular, we designed a project that would enable us to accomplish the following. First, instead of "pushing" knowledge to the students via lectures, the goal was to design a project that would make students ask for knowledge, thus achieving sustained inquiry. Second, instead of having few assignments in the project, each of them requiring a large amount of knowledge, the goal was to split the project in eight stages with a smaller amount of knowledge needed for each stage. Third, instead of forcing students to adhere to a specific input programming language, the goal was to enable innovation and increase motivation by allowing students to design their own programming language. This would allow students to be creative about their programming language and hopefully motivate them. Fourth, to enable giving and receiving feedback, we asked students to work in groups of four and discuss with each other the contributions of each team member after every project stage.

We describe a one-semester experience in which we created a project for the compilers course that followed the design requirements described above. The experience described involves two professors teaching separate groups of a 16-weeks automata and compilers course. None of the students had previous experience using PBL. This course focuses both on writing a compiler as well as teaching the theoretical contents of regular and context-free languages. Both professors organized lectures in the same way and each class had 20 students. The course includes four hours of lectures per week. Our results show that students found the project motivating. Likewise, the results show that the students appreciated having different types of classes besides lectures. Furthermore, students found value in the PBL teaching method and were satisfied with the course.

The rest of this paper is organized as follows. First, survey the related work in Section 2. After that, we describe the course organization and project in Section 3. Next, we show the results of a student survey in Section 4. After that, we discuss what went well in this experience and what could be improved in the future in Section 5. Finally, we draw our conclusions in Section 6.

2 RELATED WORK

We begin by citing previous studies that motivated our work. First, the Cool project was our first experience in which students developed a complete compiler [2]. Experiencing with Cool was instrumental to convince us that building a full compiler was possible. In Cool, the language, the grammar and a large code skeleton are given to the students. When using Cool, we noticed that students faced the problem of not fully understanding what was going on in the code. They were able to complete the lexer and the parser, but struggled to understand why each bit of code was needed. When they reached semantic analysis, they struggled significantly to understand the structure of the given AST. Therefore, we decided to try a different approach in our experience where students could build the grammar and the AST, thus simplifying the semantic analysis stage.

There are other studies on teaching compilers that have also focused on student motivation. For instance, Sag et al. [17] proposed a course named Defense against the dark arts and Adams et al. [1] proposed using XML to allow students to design their own input language. Similarly, Xu describes an experience where students wrote a compiler for the Scribbler robot. Finally, Larkins et al. [12] proposed targeting FPGA processors.

Finally, other studies have proposed tools that enable student learning. Instead of being complete projects, these tools target specific stages of the compiler construction such as visualizing LL(1) tables [16], code generation [18] and visualizing the symbols table [21]. Haynes et al. [10] proposed a project focused on semantic analysis [10], Lorenzo et al. [13] proposed an automated testing

tool and Fossum et al. [8] proposed a PLCC, a programing language compiler-compiler tool that simplifies how students specify the tokens and grammar of a compiler. Chakraborty et al. [3] described an experience where complete compilers were distributed among students for experimentation. All these techniques can be incorporated in a semester-long experience like the one we describe in this paper. We will consider this in future work, as well as including object orientation [9].

All of the project ideas cited above are interesting and novel. The contribution of this paper is to provide some guidance on how to modify these projects to better fit the PBL teaching method.

3 PROJECT DESIGN

We designed the course project so that it would enable some of the essential PBL components: success skills, challenging problem, sustained inquiry, authenticity, student voice, reflection, critique and revision and public product.

3.1 Student motivation

A novel aspect of our project was to allow students to design their own programming language. To guide them, we requested in stage 1 that each group should design a programming language capable of solving three programming problems: recursive Fibonacci, Sieve of Eratosthenes and drawing triangles with n rows, where n was input by the user. The ultimate goal was to generate MIPS code that would run on at least one simulator.

By allowing students to design their own language, we expected to increase their motivation. This was successful because several groups designed language that would help teaching programming to new spanish-speaking students. Also, we asked them to name their groups and language so that they would feel part of an important project. Existing works support the idea of fostering group belonging ([15, 22]) so we made sure that group work was a significant aspect of the project.

3.2 Course organization

In PBL, students become active learners and the professor responds to the students' needs and becomes a facilitator. This is not possible to achieve with traditional lectures where the professor gives an explanation of a topic with all the details and then asks the students to put in practice what they learned via a programming assignment. While lectures like these can be very entertaining, they reduce the students' ability to become active learners.

To overcome this challenge, we designed four different types of classes. First, we kept traditional lectures to teach automata theory and also have group discussions of the project when needed. Second, we had 30 minutes-long meetings with groups to address their specific questions. Third, we had lab classes where groups could work on their specific needs. Finally, we had classes where each group presented their design of some artifact (AST, symbols table) and other students could listen and provide feedback.

By the second half of the semester, students decided what they needed most and we did different things with each group. This is also important in PBL because, as we described in the introduction, it allow students to make some decisions on their project.

Table 1: List of deliverables per stage

Stage	Deliverable
1	Source code of new programming language
2	Print tokens from the lexer
3	Print tokens from the parser
4	Enforce syntax
5	Design AST
6	Create AST from the grammar
7	Semantic analysis
8	Code generation

```
<YYINITIAL>t(R|r)(U|u)(E|e) {
    return new Symbol(TokenConstants.BOOL_CONST,new Boolean(true));
}

<YYINITIAL>f(A|a)(L|l)(S|s)(E|e) {
    return new Symbol(TokenConstants.BOOL_CONST,new Boolean(false));
}
```

Figure 1: Screenshot of part of the solution to the lexer stage of Cool.

```
feature:
OBJECTID'(' formal_list ')' ':' TYPEID '{' expr '}'
{ $$ = method($1, $3, $6, $8); }
| OBJECTID ':' TYPEID
{ $$ = attr($1, $3, no_expr()); }
| OBJECTID ':' TYPEID ASSIGN expr
{ $$ = attr($1, $3, $5); }
;
```

Figure 2: Screenshot of part of the solution to the parser stage of Cool.

3.3 Project stages

A standard way of organizing a compilers course project is to have four stages: lexical analysis, syntactic analysis, semantical analysis and code generation. This is how the Cool project is organized. As we described earlier, a smaller amount of deliverables means that each stage is more complex. Students need a significant amount of knowledge to solve stages that involve several phases of a compiler. We argue that shorter deliverables allow students to figure out on their own how to solve them. This is a crucial step of PBL: we wanted students to have a clear goal in mind when tackling each stage. Fig. 1 shows a screenshot of the lexer code in the Cool project. This piece of code requires the following knowledge. First, the student must create regular expressions. Second, the student must understand that the compilation process is lead by the parser, which means that the lexer is only asked to return objects. Third, the student must understand that identified tokens will be added to a symbols table. Thus, the knowledge in the screenshot is quite broad. In our opinion, the students struggle to grasp all this knowledge at once.

A second example of this problem is shown in Fig. 2. This time, there is a separation between the grammar itself and the action of each production of the grammar. In Cool, students are given the grammar and are asked to complete the actions. In our project, students are also responsible for building the grammar. Therefore, combining the grammar with the action is, in our opinion, too complex for a single stage.

For these reasons, we decided to split the project in eight stages as shown in Table 1. With this separation, we hoped to narrow the scope of each deliverable so that students could easily understand

the requirement. Coming back to our previous example in Fig. 1, stage 2 required them to create regular expressions and print each token. This left enough room in the stage for students to discover on their own which lexer tool they wanted to use and focus only on how to add regular expressions to the tool and print output when tokens where found.

Next, linking the lexer to the parser was left to stage 3. Thus, the deliverable of stage 3 is a program that outputs the same results as stage 2, but that is driven by a parser instead of a lexer. As a result, students tackled in stage 3 all the complexity related to making a lexer (such as flex) and a parser (such as bison). One advantage of this setup was that students understood what was expected from them because the output was the same as the previous stage. Once again, the stage focused on allowing the students to pick a parser tool and learn how to write a simple grammar that recognizes any combination of valid tokens.

After that, in stage 4 students were asked to write the grammar of their programming language. The deliverable was simply "to show error messages if the input code is not recognizable by the grammar". If the code is grammatically correct, the program does nothing. The goal of this stage was to allow students to focus on the grammar only without worrying about the actions. Once again, students only need to know how to write a grammar to start with the stage.

A key motivation of this stage was to see how students would deal with reduce-reduce and shift-reduce conflicts. We did not cover these topics in any lecture. Instead, we let each group face the problem on their own and helped them during the 30-minutes sessions. This approach is significantly different from the usual lecture where all parsing algorithms are explained. We leave the discussion of this trade-off for Section 5.

After the first four stages, all groups had a working grammar. The rest of the project focused on semantic analysis and code generation. First, we asked students to design the AST in stage five. We discussed in class the need for an AST and how the parser was responsible for creating the structure. For this stage, we asked students to present their design during class time. The deliverable of stage 5 was a diagram of the classes needed for the AST. This stage required class presentations by students and 30-minutes individual meetings because all groups had different needs depending on their language.

Once the AST was designed, we asked students to create all the code needed for the AST classes and to complete the grammar actions to create the AST dynamically. In other words, students had to include lines as shown in Fig. 1 to create methods, classes, attributes and so on. The deliverable of this stage was a program that would output elements in the source code in a sorted way. For instance, the output could indicate that there is a class, which contains two methods. One method contains an int declaration and an if statement, and so on. Imagine a nicely tabulated output that allows a reader to clearly see the structure of the code.

We expected this stage to be quite simple. However, it proved to be one of the most challenging tasks for the students. On the one hand, groups struggled to understand how to create objects based on the grammar. Second, students discovered during this stage some problems in their grammar design. Some groups reported having to build a mostly new grammar. We discuss this further in Section 5.

Table 2: Course evaluation items

Item	Description	Percentage
Midterm	Automata theory written exam	20
Final exam	Build a small compiler	20
Project	Build a compiler	50
Class activities	Presentations and quizzes	10

In stage 7, students had to implement semantic analysis. We asked them to check for appropriate declaration of variables, type checking, correct usage of conditional and loop structures and adequate invocation of methods. No lectures were needed for this stage. We simply explained students what was expected from them and all other classes were 30-minutes meetings with groups. We expected this stage to be fairly complicated but all groups managed to finish it on time.

Finally, in stage 8 students were asked to generate code for their language. Based on our previous (successful) experience with Cool, we decided to ask students to generate code for the Microprocessor without Interlocked Pipeline Stages (MIPS) architecture. For this stage, we first asked students to solve simple problems using MIPS instructions to refresh their knowledge in assembly language. Next, we used one lecture to explain the need for a registry manager and a label manager. After that, students were left on their own to solve the problem.

The aspects of the project that we've described so far were meant to increase motivation and enable sustained inquiry by the students. Next, we also need to describe how we changed the organization of lectures to ensure that students were seeking knowledge, instead of us pushing information to them.

3.4 Course evaluation

The main difficulty of this teaching experience was how to evaluate progress given that students were working in groups of four. We used percentages as shown in Table 2.

The project was worth half of the grade. The project score was mainly a group score (we introduced student-to-student feedback, but we leave this discussion for later). Therefore, we included a final exam which consisted of building a small compiler over a period of three days. Students needed to complete this exam individually. We also included a written midterm with traditional questions on regular and context free languages (recall that this course is also about automata theory and not only about compilers).

The course described in this section was taught during the first semester of 2018. In the following section we describe the results of a student satisfaction survey that was completed by the students of both groups.

4 RESULTS

We designed the project proposed in this paper to support the following goals of PBL: student motivation, active learning and sustained inquiry. Next, we first show the results of a survey to evaluate the success of our teaching experience. After that, we show the project completion rate.

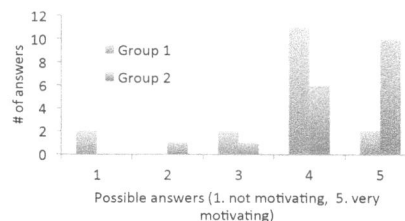

Figure 3: How motivating was this project?

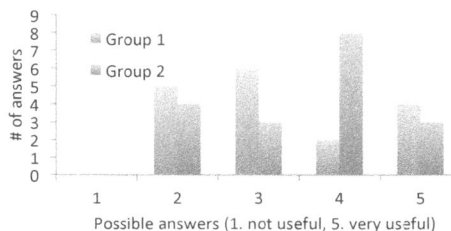

Figure 4: How useful was it to replace lectures with groups working in the lab?

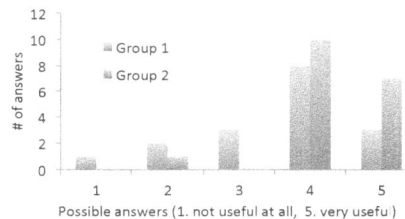

Figure 5: How useful was it to replace lectures with 30-minutess meeting per group?

4.1 Student survey

The survey was completed by 37 students in total: 18 in one class and 19 in the other.

First, we asked students how motivating was the project of our course. Fig. 3 shows that a majority of students found the project motivating. Furthermore, 10 students found the project very motivating. When asked, several students indicated orally that this project was more motivating than projects in other courses. In another open question of the survey, the most common for this extra motivation was the fact that students were able to design their own programming language. To illustrate this motivation, one student told us that he would add to his CV that he had invented a programming language to teach kids how to code. Further, he would add that he had built a compiler from scratch for his language. This is the type of motivation and project belonging that we are looking for using PBL.

Second, we were interested in learning which type of class was more beneficial for students. Recall that the course organization included lectures, 30-minutes meetings, laboratory sessions and classes where students presented some part of their design or progress in the project. One interesting result is that lab sessions

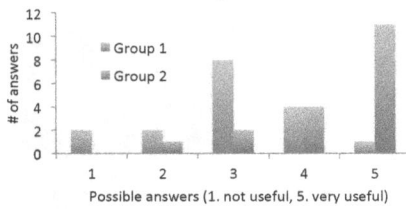

Figure 6: How useful was it to replace lectures with group presentations?

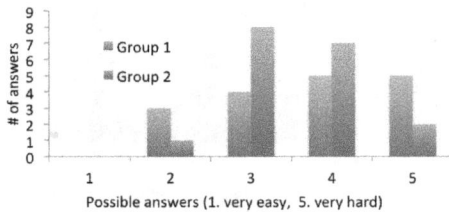

Figure 7: How difficult was this course in comparison to other courses?

Table 3: Project completion rate

# of groups	Fibonacci	Sieve	Triangles
2	✓	✓	✓
3	✓	✗	✓
1	✗	✗	✓
1	✗	✗	✗

were not as appreciated as we expected (see Fig. 4. This is a common practice in our program and we expected students to be more motivated by this type of class. Another finding is that 30-minutes were appreciated by the majority of students (see Fig. 5). One advantage of these meetings is that all the discussion is focused on the problems of each group. Therefore, they consider this time to be very productive. Lastly, the students also found group presentations useful (see Fig. 6). One crucial finding here, in our opinion, is that we found a way to motivate students to pay attention to presentations made by others. This is traditionally complicated in our program because students are only worried about their own presentations. In this scenario, other groups were very interested in others' designs. For each presentation, at least one student asked questions on why or how something was done. For example, when groups were asked to present the design of the AST, one group explained their design of the symbols table too. As soon as the class ended, one group went to office hours to ask what was a symbols table so that they could start working on it. This is a an excellent result for us, because students came to the professor to ask for knowledge instead of us giving a lecture on how a symbols table works.

Finally, we were interested in knowing how hard was this course in comparison to other courses in the program. PBL requires more work from the students and we wanted to evaluate if this course was harder than others. The results (see Fig. 7) show that there is

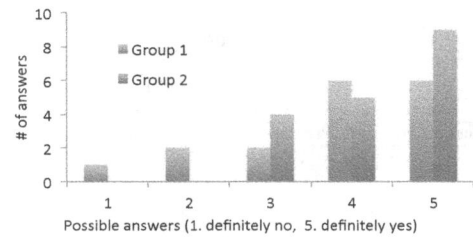

Figure 8: Would you enroll in another course using the teaching methods used in this course?

no clear tendency towards one answer or the other. We confirmed verbally that this answer varied based on groups. Some of them considered that the course was very time consuming, while others considered that it was the same as other courses. Therefore, we cannot conclude whether or not this course was harder than others. However, Fig. 8 shows that a majority of students would enroll in a course that uses PBL in the future. The survey included open questions on how PBL had helped students learn the material and the responses were positive. Students appreciate learning on their own, being independent and managing their own time.

4.2 Success rate

Another way to evaluate the success of this teaching experience is to look at the completion rate of the projects. First, all groups were able to successfully complete the lexical, syntactical and semantic stages of the project. The majority of difficulties occurred in the code generation stage. Table 3 shows whether or not groups were able to run the three products on a MIPS simulator: recursive Fibonacci, Sieve of Eratosthenes and drawing triangles with n rows. Results show that at least two groups were capable of finishing the project. All other groups were successful at all stages except for code generation. Within each group, some students were more engaged than others but the results in the final exam indicate that no subgroup was left behind.

In the following section we discuss the trade-offs of this experience, as well as the lessons learned.

5 DISCUSSION

5.1 Trade-offs

First, we want to analyze the advantages and disadvantages of asking students to design their own language. We argued several times that this was a key change to increase student motivation and our results show that it worked. However, this decision also has downsides. The main problem of this approach is that no support code can be given to the students and they need to build everything from scratch. One could argue that there is a lot of work in this approach that is not useful. Also, students are on their own in terms of project success because they cannot come back to a working base during the semester. We thought this would be a major problem and prepared a compiler for students to use if necessary. However, this was not necessary because all groups were able to make progress during the entire semester.

Table 4: Discussion by PBL essential element.

Success skills: ★ ★ ★ ★ ★ Students practiced group work, self-management, collaboration and had several discussions on how to design the language and the compiler.	**Challenging problem:** ★ ★ ★★ At the beginning of the semester, students did not believe they would be capable of building a complete compiler. Missing: adding additional complexity such as optimized code.
Sustained inquiry: ★ ★ ★ ★ Students requested the topics of some classes. They had to investigate the software tools, and how to use them. In addition, they had to learn the MIPS language (language generated by the compiler)	**Authenticity:** ★★ Although the development of a unique programming language was encouraged, it does not necessarily have an impact in the real world.
Student voice and choice: ★ ★ ★ ★ ★ Students chose: project language, programming language (to implement the project), software tools (such as Flex, Bison, Ply, Coco/R, SPIM and MARS), and how some classes were taught (meetings, presentations, lectures, etc.).	**Reflection:** ★ ★ ★★ Students identified that they needed to work on self learning, time organization and team work. Missing: adding some discussion on how to improve the construction of the compiler if they could start over.
Critique and Revision: ★ ★ ★★ Students received feedback from their classmates and professors at every stage. Missing: we still need to solve how to allocate more evaluation points to peer-to-peer evaluation.	**Public product:** There was no public presentation of the project's product.

Second, we discuss the trade-off between having students build their own grammar and giving them one. Clearly, if students must design their own language, they will have to create the grammar from scratch. Once again, one could argue that this work is very repetitive and unnecessary. However, we would like to make a strong point on how building a grammar from scratch forces students to face and solve shift-reduce and reduce-reduce conflicts. In our opinion, this was a major change in the semester. Instead of giving lectures on how to run manually all the algorithms, we helped students modify their grammars so that they would be conflict-free.

As a result, our students are not capable of building canonical tables or finding the first or follow sets. But they are capable of constructing a fully-working, conflict-free grammar. From a PBL perspective, this is a success because students came to us asking for knowledge that would allow them to solve a real-life problem. When explaining this, we did explain some basic concepts of parsing algorithms. However, their goal was not building canonical tables manually, but creating a grammar for their parser.

5.2 Lessons learned

5.2.1 Feedback from students in group one. First, students asked for guidance on errors that can be expected during a stage. For example, when building their grammar, they faced conflicts and thought that they were heading in the wrong track. Thus, it might be a good idea to warn students, at each stage, about the possible problems they might face. This does not mean giving them the solution, simply a heads-up so that they know that what they are facing is expected.

Second, students would have appreciated group discussions after each research iteration. Group discussions started late in the semester and students from other groups wished they had known what others have discovered. For example, some lexers, parsers or MIPS simulators were more user-friendly than others. In the survey, students indicated that they would have benefited from a wrap-up discussion after each stage so that they could learn what others knew, as well as fully understand concepts. Thus, we plan to add group discussions more often in following iterations.

5.2.2 Feedback from students in group two. In the second group, students also suggested that group discussions should be started earlier in the semester. This leads us to a third lesson learned.

In this group, students would have appreciated having more insight on how to pick one lexer or parser over the other. In general, their first choice was based on the programming language of their preference. In retrospective, they realized later that other tools were better but they did not know it when they chose them.

Fifth, the fourth lesson learned was that students had no clear idea of the path that leads to building a compiler. While they understood what they needed to deliver at each stage, they still did not know what would happen after that. For example, they would have appreciated to know that the grammar was later used to dynamically build a data structure. They argue that they would have designed the grammar differently. Thus, we suggest for future iterations to first give an overview of all the steps before going into the details of each project stage. Finally, we also need to improve how to help groups to work together. In several groups, students were not satisfied and ended up working in couples. Ideally, groups should stay together during the entire project.

5.2.3 Other lessons learned. Third, we believe that more individual evaluation is needed within the project. This semester, the project was worth 50% of the total grade. The only individual item within that 50% was that each group could allocate points individually based on their effort for each stage. However, we believe that we should implement individual oral examinations after each stage, to make sure that all students are capable of building a compiler.

Table 4 summarizes our self evaluation for each of the elemental components of PBL according to the Buck Institute for Education.

6 CONCLUSION

In this paper, we described a successful experience using PBL in a compilers course. We listed the limitations of existing projects for this course and we explained how some modifications can make the project better fit for PBL. The most important conclusion of this experience is that students were more motivated by this project compared to other courses. Likewise, the experience was successful at teaching students success skills such as self-organization and group work. In future work, we would like to evaluate how effective is PBL in terms of student learning outcomes. The results in this paper are promising, but more work is needed to measure the effectiveness of PBL compared to other teaching techniques.

REFERENCES

[1] D. Robert Adams and Christian Trefftz. 2004. Using XML in a compiler course. *ACM SIGCSE Bulletin* 36, 3 (2004), 4. https://doi.org/10.1145/1026487.1008001

[2] Alexander Aiken. 1996. Cool: A Portable Project for Teaching Compiler Construction. *ACM SIGPLAN Notices* 31, 7 (1996), 19–24. https://doi.org/10.1145/381841.381847

[3] Pinaki Chakraborty. 2011. Teaching Purpose Compilers : An Exercise and Its Feedback. 2, 2 (2011), 47–51.

[4] University of Costa Rica Computer Science Department. [n. d.]. Communication Networks and Operating Systems Integrated Project: course description. https://www.ecci.ucr.ac.cr/cursos/ci-0123.

[5] University of Costa Rica Computer Science Department. [n. d.]. Software Engineering and Databases Integrated Project: course description. https://www.ecci.ucr.ac.cr/cursos/ci-0128.

[6] Rebecca Ellis. [n. d.]. Bridging the STEM Skills Gap Involves Both Education and Industry Commitments. https://www.usnews.com/news/stem-solutions/articles/2018-07-09/commentary-industry-education-needed-to-bridge-stem-skills-gap.

[7] Buck Institute for Education. [n. d.]. What is Project-based learning. https://www.bie.org/about/what_pbl.

[8] Timothy Fossum. 2014. PLCC : A Programming Language Compiler Compiler. *Proceedings of the 45th ACM Technical Symposium on Computer Science Education (SIGCSE '14)* 1 (2014), 561–566. https://doi.org/10.1145/2538862.2538922

[9] José de Oliveira Guimarães. 2003. Experiences in Building a Compiler for an Object-oriented Language. *SIGPLAN Not.* 38, 4 (April 2003), 25–33. https://doi.org/10.1145/844091.844098

[10] Christopher T Haynes. 1996. Compiling : A High-level Introduction Using Scheme *. (1996), 253–257. https://doi.org/10.1145/268085.268181

[11] Tyson R. Henry. 2005. Teaching compiler construction using a domain specific language. *ACM SIGCSE Bulletin* 37, 1 (2005), 7. https://doi.org/10.1145/1047124.1047364

[12] D. Brian Larkins and William M. Jones. 2011. Targeting FPGA-based processors for an implementation-driven compiler construction course. *Proceedings of the 49th Annual Southeast Regional Conference on - ACM-SE '11* (2011), 31. https://doi.org/10.1145/2016039.2016056

[13] Emilio Julio Lorenzo, Javier Velez, and Anselmo Peñas. 2011. A proposal for automatic evaluation in a compiler construction course. *Proceedings of the 16th annual joint conference on Innovation and technology in computer science education - ITiCSE '11* (2011), 308. https://doi.org/10.1145/1999747.1999833

[14] Mohtadi. 2014. Bridging the Skills Gap in STEM Industries. *J Academic Technical Specialist* April 2016 (2014). https://doi.org/10.13140/RG.2.1.1704.3606

[15] Catherine Mooney, Brett A. Becker, Lana Salmon, and Eleni Mangina. 2018. Computer Science Identity and Sense of Belonging: A Case Study in Ireland. In *Proceedings of the 1st International Workshop on Gender Equality in Software Engineering (GE '18)*. ACM, New York, NY, USA, 1–4. https://doi.org/10.1145/3195570.3195575

[16] R. Daniel Resler and Dean M. Deaver. 1998. VCOCO: a visualisation tool for teaching compilers. *ACM SIGCSE Bulletin* 30, 3 (1998), 199–202. https://doi.org/10.1145/290320.283123

[17] Matthew Sag and Jake Haskell. 2018. Defense against the dark arts of copyright trolling. *Iowa Law Review* 103, 2 (2018), 571–661. https://doi.org/10.1145/1352322.1352245

[18] Tyler Sondag, Kian L. Pokorny, and Hridesh Rajan. 2010. Frances: A Tool for Understanding Code Generation. *ACM Technical Symposium on Computer Science Education (SIGCSE)* (2010), 12–16. https://doi.org/10.1145/1734263.1734269

[19] Rice University. [n. d.]. COMP 412: Compiler Construction for Undergraduates. https://www.clear.rice.edu/comp412/Lectures/.

[20] Stanford University. [n. d.]. CS143-Compilers, Stanford University. http://web.stanford.edu/class/cs143/syllabus.html.

[21] Jaime Urquiza-Fuentes, Micael Gallego-Carrillo, Francisco Gortázar-Bellas, and J Ángel Velázquez-Iturbide. 2006. Visualizing the Symbol Table. *Proceedings of the 11th Annual SIGCSE Conference on Innovation and Technology in Computer Science Education* 3 (2006), 341. https://doi.org/10.1145/1140124.1140249

[22] Nanette Veilleux, Rebecca Bates, Cheryl Allendoerfer, Diane Jones, Joyous Crawford, and Tamara Floyd Smith. 2013. The Relationship Between Belonging and Ability in Computer Science. In *Proceeding of the 44th ACM Technical Symposium on Computer Science Education (SIGCSE '13)*. ACM, New York, NY, USA, 65–70. https://doi.org/10.1145/2445196.2445220

[23] Li Xu. 2008. Language engineering in the context of a popular, inexpensive robot platform. *ACM SIGCSE Bulletin* 40, 1 (2008), 43. https://doi.org/10.1145/1352322.1352154

Adopting Git/Github within Teaching: A Survey of Tool Support

Richard Glassey

KTH: Royal Institute of Technology

Stockholm, Sweden

glassey@kth.se

ABSTRACT

The adoption and use of Git and Github within computer science education is growing in popularity. The motivation for this shift is strong: it combines a robust system for managing student coursework, sophisticated collaboration and communication tools for students and teaching staff, and an authentic experience of an important software engineering skill. Whilst previous literature has reported upon experience and benefits, there still exists a technical barrier to overcome in adopting Git and Github within an educational context. In response, both the community of teachers using Git/Github and the Github organisation itself have developed tool support to help solve the challenge of adoption, however these efforts are somewhat isolated and relatively unstudied. This work aims to provide an overview of these tools, identify the commonalities and differences, and develop a framework for comparison to assist teachers when looking for solutions for their own courses.

CCS CONCEPTS

• Social and professional topics → Computing education;

KEYWORDS

Version Control System, Git/Github, Computing Education

ACM Reference Format:

Richard Glassey. 2019. Adopting Git/Github within Teaching: A Survey of Tool Support. In *ACM Global Computing Education Conference 2019 (CompEd '19), May 17–19, 2019, Chengdu, Sichuan, China.* ACM, New York, NY, USA, 7 pages. https://doi.org/10.1145/3300115.3309518

1 INTRODUCTION

Version control systems (VCS) have become a vital component of managing resources and teamwork in modern software engineering [23]. This has led to an increasing demand upon teachers to prepare computing students for this future working environment by incorporating VCS into their courses. Software project courses that organise teams of students working together on a single project specification have been an initial point of adoption. However, use of VCS has spread further, for managing assignments, assessment and feedback within entry level CS1 courses and beyond.

There is a growing thread of literature within computing education that reports upon the benefits, challenges and experiences of adopting VCS into the learning environment. Examples can be found from the older centralised systems, such as CVS and Subversion [2, 21], to the more modern distributed and hosted systems, such as Mercurial and Git [17, 22]. In particular, Git combined with the hosting service Github has become the most popular approach, according to the literature [5, 9, 12, 15, 18]. Whilst this thread makes a convincing case for VCS in teaching, the problem still exists that this is not a system designed with education in mind. Barriers to adoption include (1) concerns about privacy and access control between students' work, (2) additional time it takes to investigate how VCS might work within a course, (3) complexity of using a system that is not designed to support teachers, (4) the uncertainty of how best to use VCS effectively for both students and teachers. As such, teachers have attempted to reduce these barriers by developing tools that integrate the common teaching tasks of distributing assignments and projects, managing and automating assessment, and providing feedback to students on their efforts. However, these efforts have been somewhat independent, isolated, and there has not been an effort to study their similarities and differences.

This paper has two main contributions. First, it provides a brief literature survey that charts the development of VCS usage within an educational context via different VCSs, with a focus on the use of Git/Github. Second, it surveys the open source solutions that teachers (and Github Inc.) have developed. The survey is structured according to the general aspects of each tool, their technical aspects, and most importantly their pedagogical features for supporting grouping of students, distribution of assignments, and support for assessment and feedback. Despite aiming at a similar problem, each of the tools have interesting differences, and bringing them together in this survey provides a useful reference for teachers who may wish to adopt such tools, or find inspiration for developing future tools that better meet the needs of teachers and students.

2 RELATED WORK

The use of VCSs in teaching has a history almost as long the systems themselves. One of the earliest mentions came in 1989, where students tasked with maintaining a Pascal compiler were disappointed *not to be able to use* the revison control system [3]. The importance of these change management and collaboration tools to software engineering is well established by now and is a defacto skill for all developers. This importance has motivated the adoption of such systems into teaching, either as a topic, or a means to manage the materials of a project-related course. As Git/Github continues to grow in popularity, more use cases in teaching are being revealed by practitioners and researchers. This section first develops the timeline of academic works that have reported the adoption and experience of VCS, and then focuses specifically upon work that reports the adoption and experience of Git/Github.

2.1 Use of Version Control Systems in Teaching

Within software engineering courses, especially those oriented towards team projects, there is a strong desire to ensure that students make use of authentic tools in order to give them practical experience with the *training wheels removed*. Typically this implies the use of a serious integrated development environment (IDE) and a VCS. A series of articles proposed the potential value of using CVS within an educational context, however they did not report upon actual interventions with students [10, 19, 24].

In May 2003, teachers for a software engineering group project course at the University of Toronto adopted Concurrent Versions System (CVS) to manage the shared resources that students developed together for their coursework submissions [21]. Besides simplifying the coordination aspects between students (who had used email to share code previously), it was also reported as an effective way to teach version control principles in real time as the students used the tools on their own work. Teaching staff also benefited by being able to more easily share starter code in an immediately usable form (not zipped, archived or hosted on a web page), manage a student body spread over multiple campuses, and deliver feedback to students directly within the repository. Disadvantages included the risks of students damaging their repositories as well as preventing authorised access to the students' repositories.

As version control software evolved, from CVS to Subversion as the dominant choice amongst software engineers, teachers also moved with the changes in technology [2, 7]. In the Fall of 2005, teachers at the Rose-Hulman Institute of Technology (RHIT) adopted Subversion as a means to more effectively share the high volume of course resources between distributed staff, as well as also distributing and collecting student assignments [2]. The authors noted that this simplified the interaction with students, and allowed the direct and timely delivery of feedback, which was much faster than previous methods. From the teachers' perspective, this method also allowed them to spot-check students' work without having to explicitly request a submission, check the balance between group projects in terms of interaction counts, and detect when students were effectively (or not) distributing their work over time, and procrastinating before the deadline. The authors concluded that such an approach opened up a whole range of insights that were previously unavailable to them. By this stage, it was clear that version control, irrespective of tool, could find a useful place in support of teaching and learning, and general patterns for usage were suggested in the literature [20].

The centralised mode of revision control that CVS and Subversion used eventually became superseded by more flexible distributed version control systems (DVCS), such as Git and Mercurial. At the University of West Georgia, Mercurial was adopted as a DVCS for managing their CS1 course in Fall 2009 [22]. The authors noted that the complexity involved in using Mercurial was greatly reduced, compared to older centralised systems, like CVS and Subversion. This simplification encouraged the use of version control amongst students, and to such an extent that it was usable with entry level students in a CS1 course. They further identified that the

administrative burden was also reduced when using DVCS, there was less chance of repositories being damaged by students, and there was better control over administrative access control to avoid students seeing other student's work. Most encouragingly, there was anecdotal evidence of students using Mercurial in courses that did not mandate its usage, indicating transfer of the skills.

2.2 Use of Git/Github in Teaching

Git was released in 2005, and is an example of a DVCS, which supports distributed and non-linear workflows. Github is both the organisation and the name of the web hosting service for Git repositories. Typically the two terms are rolled together or exchanged in common parlance. Whilst the previous section highlighted how CVS, Subversion and Mercurial have been used within educational contexts, there appears to be much more activity using Git and Github within educational contexts, as evidenced by the number of articles within the literature. There are two explanations for this: (1) Git/Github are the defacto VCS tool/platform for open source projects, and (2) Github Inc. have embraced the educational community by creating educational resources/training, hosting an online community, and providing free repository hosting for teachers.

One of the first reported uses of Git in a teaching context can be found in [17], as part of an operating systems course that made use of virtualisation and version control to manage student work, where similar benefits were found as per previous literature. In [18], the authors went beyond the normal discourse of describing the virtues of version control and focused instead upon the administrative benefits of using Git in coordination with hosting services that were cloud-based, rather than teachers needing to overcome the complexities of setting up local servers. As far as the literature is concerned, they were the first to report on their experiences of using Git with CS1 students. Another work reported some of the disadvantages with having dependencies upon external hosting services [1]. They used GitLab, which mirrors many features of Github, however due to the rapid pace of development, there were many issues, which resulted in negative feedback from students, with only some understanding the vision the teachers were trying to achieve. Nevertheless, the hosting service enabled advanced features, such as automatically triggering evaluation whenever a student pushed their work.

After these initial examples, further work elaborated upon the benefits, challenges and experiences of using Git and Github within a teaching context [5, 9, 12, 15]. In [15], one of the first to report within the literature on the availability of unlimited free repositories available via Github Inc. for teachers, noted the key benefits as being: (1) secure submission, (2) underwriting provenance and derivation of submitted work, (3) better source file organisation, (4) integrated Issue Tracking, and (5) exposure to standard industry practice. In contrast, [12] reported some of the underlying challenges that students faced, in spite of the many benefits reported in previous articles. In particular they highlight how students (1) may have had a badly formed mental model of version control, confusing branches with files and folders, (2) faced challenges with the terminology like `origin master`, (3) replaced communication via the issue tracker with physical communication whenever collocated with their teammates, and (4) missed out on an authentic experience of VCS usage due to the changes required to manage distribution, assessment and feedback, which deviated from a regular software engineering project.

Despite the benefits and challenges that can be observed by teachers, the student voice has also been a source of insight into the experience of using Git/Github within courses. [9] reports that whilst the teachers were surprised by how overwhelming the student enthusiasm is for adopting VCS, they also discovered that they lacked understanding about the system or having confidence in their ability to use it effectively beyond the course. In [5], the benefits that students themselves reported were: (1) gaining and demonstrating industry relevant skills and practices, (2) enabling cross-team collaboration and contributions, (3) encouraging student contributions to course content, (4) breaking down the walled garden, and (5) version controlled assignments. Students also reported challenges that they encountered, including: (1) the perils of public projects, (2) unfamiliarity with Git and Github, (3) notification overload, and (4) Github is not designed for education.

More recently, attention has turned towards the value that can be derived from analysing the data that is generated when using a VCS. In particular, the Github API provides a wealth of information that can be used to generate input for learning analytics and educational data mining, as examples from software engineering projects have demonstrated [4, 8, 14]. In [13], the authors derived a range of indicators that could be used to more objectively and systematically determine the project quality and student behaviour in terms of individual and team contributions. These indicators then were found to be beneficial to encourage conformance within student teams to maintain quality both of their interactions as well as their behaviour within a software engineering course. A further example of possible indicators that teachers can use to improve their own courses was presented in [6], where the feedback captured in the issue tracker could be used to better understand individual assignments as well as differences in teaching assistant behaviour. In other works, automatic assessement has been added as a feature via the use of a continuous integration framework that runs testing automatically when students push their work, highlighting the extensibility of this platform[11, 16].

Despite the growth of interest in Git/Github by the academic community, one pressing issue is the technical barrier that must be overcome to make the most effective use of the technology. Besides the literature that has been presented here, various teachers and Github Inc. themselves have developed tools to support basic and advanced usage in terms of distribution of assignments, assessment and feedback. The next section surveys tools that have been shared as open source projects, with good documentation, which can support teachers who are interested in using this approach.

3 SURVEY OF OPEN SOURCE SOLUTIONS

The adoption of Git/Github introduces technical challenges to overcome. Besides the technical challenge in adopting Git/Github for teaching, there is a lack of information about solutions that may ease the burden, as well as no means to evaluate which may be the most suitable choice. Several teachers have shared their efforts online as open source projects, and Github Inc. has contributed to the community by providing official solutions as well. Undoubtedly,

many more solutions have been developed by teachers working in isolation, however the scope here is limited to the tools that are publicly available as open source projects.

This section presents an analysis of the open source tools that were found. The following method was adopted. First, candidates for analysis were selected via keyword searching (keywords: *git | github | education | student | teacher*) of academic literature in Google Scholar, Github itself, and the education community discussion forum that Github Inc. has created[1]. Second, inclusion criteria for analysis required that the tool should be (1) publicly available as an open source project, and (2) well documented so that it is clear to understand the basic usage, main features, and central ideas behind the tool in its support for teachers and students. Third, a framework for evaluation was developed and applied that allowed different tools to be compared according to common criteria. To help organise understanding of the different tools, the criteria are organised into three sections that cover the general, technical and pedagogical aspects of each tool analysed.

3.1 General Aspects

The first component of the survey establishes some general aspects about each of the identified tools. Table 1 lists eight tools[2]. As might be expected, six of these tools originated from an educational context within a university. The geographic distribution is mostly tilted towards North America, but also includes two Scandinavian efforts. Github Inc. itself has created two tools: Teacher's Pet and Classrooms. Teacher's Pet was the forerunner of Classrooms, and as the last activity criteria shows, core development appears to have ceased in 2016. Interestingly, when searching for Teacher's Pet, it is clear that several people have forked the project and continued their own development of it, however these will be assumed to indistinct from the original for the purposes of clarity within this survey. All of the tools are hosted on Github itself and are open source projects, containing the source code, tutorial and documentation within each respective repository. For presentation convenience, the official Github URL shortener was used on each project repository URL[3]. At the time of writing, four of the projects displayed evidence of recent activity (as of October 2018), whereas four other projects showed no recent activity. It is unclear whether they had reached a level of maturity that change was no longer required, or that another solution had been adopted.

3.2 Technical Aspects

The second component of the survey switches attention to the technical aspects about each of the identified tools. Table 2 shows each of the tools in terms of their interface, implementation, and extensibility. In terms of interface, the majority of tools rely upon command line usage. Given the nature of regular and advanced Git interaction, this is not surprising. The teachers who adopt Git into their teaching most likely were already using it in their own practice. Whilst this is the obvious path, in terms of power and control that a command line interface affords, it also raises a technical

---

[1]https://education.github.community
[2]The author was also part of the Repomate project development, and efforts have been take to avoid deliberate bias or favour in the survey
[3]See: https://git.io/

Table 1: General aspects for evaluation of open source Git/Github tools

Tool	Organisation	Homepage	Last Activity
ACAD	UC Santa Barbara, USA	https://git.io/fxwj9	May 2014
Classrooms	Github Inc.	https://git.io/vGVC2	October 2018
GHClass	Duke University, USA	https://git.io/fxwjb	October 2018
Repomate	KTH: Royal Institute of Technology, Sweden	https://git.io/fxwjx	October 2018
Rhomboid	University of British Columbia, Canada	https://git.io/fxwjh	September 2017
Submit50	Harvard University, USA	https://git.io/fxree	October 2018
Teacher's Pet	Github Inc.	https://git.io/PCz4Vg	October 2016
Virtual Classroom	Simula School of Research and Innovation, Norway	https://git.io/fxref	October 2017

Table 2: Technical aspects for evaluation of open source Git/Github tools

Tool	Interface	Implementation	Extensibility
ACAD	Command Line	Python	N/A
Classrooms	Web Interface	Ruby	N/A
GHClass	Command Line	R	N/A
Repomate	Command Line	Python	Plugin Architecture
Rhomboid	Command Line	Python	N/A
Submit50	Simplified Command Line	Python	Internationalisation
Teacher's Pet	Command Line	Ruby	N/A
Virtual Classroom	Command Line	Python	How-to Documentation

barrier for many that may not be as comfortable with this form of interaction with a pedagogical tool. Two tools, Classrooms and Submit50, have taken a different approach. Classrooms simplifies the effort in creating repositories and distributing to students by making use of a web interface. Submit50 takes a different approach and simplifies the command line effort for students, by creating an abstraction over the regular git commands require to `add`, `commit` and push into a single `submit` command.

In terms of implementation, Python is the most dominant programming language used for development, with five tools making use of it. Ruby is used in both of the Github Inc. solutions, due to Ocktokit, the official wrapper for the Github API being implemented in Ruby. Demonstrating the flexibility of developing against the Github API, one tool is implemented in R, due to the data science context of its usage. It is worth noting that wrappers for the Github API have been developed and a list is maintained by Github[4].

Each of the tools supports a range of basic features, as described in Sec. 1. However, as each educational context may have different requirements beyond the basic use cases, the final criteria considers the support for custom extensions. Only three projects included explicit support for extensibility. To be clear, all of the projects are open source and by default can be forked and extended endlessly, but here we are most interested in tools that have the potential to adapt to new use cases with minimal effort or grow through

---

[4]https://developer.github.com/v3/libraries/

3rd party contributions. Therefore, tools that did not make explicit mention of how to extend their work are marked with N/A.

Repomate was the only project to anticipate this need, and has a plugin architecture that allows teachers to develop extensions depending on their use cases. For example, three core plugins included as exemplars integrate the actions of compiling code (via `javac`), running unit tests (via `junit`), and linting code via static analysis (using `pylint`). Submit50, whilst not providing explicit documentation on adding new features, takes a different approach to extensibility and includes the ability to internationalise the tool. This is a nice addition that allows reuse in many different geographic contexts. Finally, Virtual Classrooms includes guides within their documentation that shows where in the source code that extension can be made, in order to alter the behaviour of the tool.

3.3 Pedagogical Aspects

The third and final component of the survey considers the pedagogical aspects of each of the tools. This is by far the most important aspect of this analysis, and the findings are shown in Table 3. The first two survey aspects contribute which tools exist, as well as establishing some relevant technical information. The pedagogical aspect attempts to dive into the ways that Git/Github have been used to support education, and then use these as a means of differentiation between the tools presented here. Four key criteria are considered: which grouping of students is supported, the model

Table 3: Pedagogical aspects for evaluation of open source Git/Github tools. *ORpSpA* stands for one repository per student per assignment. *OBpP* stands for one branch per problem, which uses a single repository with multiple branches.

Tool	Grouping	Distribution	Assessment	Feedback
ACAD	Solo & Pair	ORpSpA	Batch clone	N/A
Classrooms	Solo & Team	ORpSpA	Batch clone — requires additional application	Travis CI Support
GHClass	Solo & Team	ORpSpA	N/A	Wercker Badge Support
Repomate	Solo	ORpSpA	Batch clone, Plugins, Peer Assessment	Batch open/close issues
Rhomboid	Solo	ORpSpA	Grading & Peer Assessment	Integrated Rubric Feedback
Submit50	Solo	OBpP	Grading — requires Check50 tool	N/A — requires Check50 tool
Teacher's Pet	Solo	ORpSpA	N/A	N/A
Virtual Classroom	Solo	ORpSpA	Peer Assessment	N/A

of repository distribution, support for assessment, and support for feedback to students.

3.3.1 Grouping. Git/Github was not designed as a learning management system (LMS), but this has not stopped inspired teachers from finding ways to retrofit important aspects that a traditional LMS would support. Key amongst these is how to arrange students and their assessments, answering the question of whether this should be solo work or team work.

All tools supported solo work, where an individual student works in isolation, and others cannot view their work. At first glance, an open source platform may seem to be at odds with this use case. Whilst students could create their own private repositories, this does not help as most often each tool is trying to help a teacher distribute an assignment to students, and relieve them of the burden of creating a repository correctly that can then be accessed and assessed by a teacher at a later date. The common solution adopted by the tools considered here is to create an organisation on Github to establish ownership rights of all repositories, then, to prevent students from seeing other students work, create teams that only contain a single student.

With this model of creating teams, it is then a matter of adding new members to support groups of students, whether for group project work (e.g. Classrooms and GHClass), or for peer assessment (e.g. Rhomboid). ACAD was the only project that differed in that grouping could be either solo or pairs, but none of the documentation indicated that it was flexible in raising the size of group. Classrooms differed from GHClass in that students were expected to find their way to the correct team via the web interface. GHClass notes in their documentation that most educators would prefer to have this control themselves and create predefined teams rather than rely on students to get it right.

3.3.2 Distribution Model. One of the driving motivations to create these tools in the first place is to generate and distribute assignments to a class of students. As classes can become large, achieving this manually is not realistically possible. However, each tool at a basic level works on the notion of taking as input a roster of students, and then as output, assignments that students can work on within the Git/Github environment. Two models of how to manage this have emerged from the analysis of these tools. The dominant model

is *one repository per student per assignment* (ORpSpA), noting that we can substitute student for team depending upon the desired grouping. The alternative model that is employed in only one tool considered here is *one branch per problem* (OBpP).

For ORpSpA, this is the most simple solution to implement. For every given student, create a repository with identical contents to a master repository containing the assignment materials for a specific assignment. Whilst seven of the tools considered here use this model, they implement it in different ways, but the result is the same. Typically the student will see a repository in their Github account that is named with the following pattern, or similar derivation: <student-name>-<assignment-number/name>.

On the other hand OBpP uses an alternative model, where the student has one repository, but many branches within that repository to store the solutions for their assignments. Whilst this is slightly more complex to implement, requiring a deeper understanding of Git branching, it does create some nice advantages. First, the student is not overwhelmed by having many repositories. Second, teaching staff are not overwhelmed by having N students × M assignments to keep track of. Finally, students are exposed to branching early (although perhaps not quite how it is supposed to be used) and get to make use of pull requests to signal that they are ready to have this particular branch/problem assessed.

3.3.3 Assessment. In terms of support for assessment, differences emerge in the level of sophistication used by each of the tools, influenced by the workflow that each tool follows. In some tools, there is no support for assessment, and they only help with the task of distributing assignments to students. Others provide limited support to help with the task of gathering student assignments for assessment via batch cloning. Finally, some tools provide a much more automated workflow with integrated support for assessment.

Teacher's Pet and GHClass do not explicitly mention support for assessment. ACAD, Classrooms and Repomate all provide different solutions for the task of batch-cloning student repositories to a local file-system in order to conduct assessment. Batching cloning gives the teacher the ability to clone all repositories for a particular assignment (Repomate also supports sub-groups of students for multiple teaching assistant use case). Classrooms differs the most because it makes use of a stand-alone desktop application to handle the bulk cloning of repositories, whereas both ACAD and Repomate use the command line interface consistently for all operations. Repomate also integrates the use of plugins that execute third party tools (e.g. `javac`, `junit`, `pylint`) once a batch of repositories has been cloned. A typical use case of this would be to clone all repositories for a group of students, locate and run all unit tests in each repository, and generate a report of the outcome.

Submit50 can be combined with a separate tool, Check50, that allows both student and teacher to run assessment operations automatically upon work that has been committed to a repository. This creates a more symmetric level of access and heightened interactivity with the system for students, which is in contrast to other approaches that are asymmetric in the sense that students submit and then are forced to wait until teachers have assessed their work and communicated the results.

Rhomboid has the most sophisticated assessment system that is entirely integrated into Git/Github. First, it supports the notion of open and closing assignments, which alters the visibility for students. Second, it connects teaching assistants with the students' work they have to assess, and integrates the grading rubric and results into special repositories for tracking results. Third, once teaching assistants have graded students, the students can then update their own repository and see their results. Fourth, this builds up over all assignments and can deliver a grade profile and final result for the course. By far this was the most advanced system used that only depends upon the tool and Github itself.

Finally, Repomate and Virtual Classroom both support peer assessment. This takes advantage of the underlying team model for organising repositories for individuals, then this allows additional students to be added at a later date, with the intention that they will perform a peer review of the individual work.

3.3.4 Feedback. As Github has good support for communication and coordination between developers in terms of the issue tracker and the pull request mechanisms, a rich opportunity for student feedback presents itself. Once more, each of the tools adopted different strategies. ACAD and Teacher's Pet did not have explicit support for feedback. Virtual Classrooms does not have built in support for feedback, but presumably the peer assessment relies upon the use of issue tracking to capture the peer feedback. Submit50 itself does not have explicit support for feedback, but as mentioned in the previous section, Check50 will assess the student work automatically and will also generate feedback, however this is received via the command line, rather than via the issue tracker. Rhomboid is similar, but updates the readme file that sits at the root of the repository. Repomate differs by supporting the bulk opening and closing of issues on the issue tracker. Here the two main use cases were to take the output of the plugins (e.g. `junit`) and post this to the issue tracker for a specific student, or to post course wide updates and grading criteria in the form of an issue.

Finally, both Classrooms and GHClass connect with continuous integration (CI) services in order to generate feedback for student assignments whenever they push their attempts. In the case of Classrooms, Github Inc. has an agreement with Travis CI that allows educational users to have their repositories connected to a CI Server, as long as a simple configuration file is included within the student repository. The typical use case for a teacher would be to have a

unit test suite setup that the student must pass before receiving their final grade. For GHClass, another CI service, Werker is used. It was not clear in the documentation quite how this was meant to be used, but there was evidence of using status badges on a repository in order to convey some status that may be helpful for the student. Typically these badges are found on open source projects to indicate whether tests are passing and so on.

3.4 Limitations of Survey

This survey was a first attempt to bring together work that has focused on a common problem. Part of the value is formulating a basis for comparison, then stimulating further discussion of these ideas so more teachers can benefit. However, there are some important limitations to report on this effort:

(1) Data was sourced from public material — Features may have been missed or used alternative terminology. Future work will survey teachers that have created similar tools.
(2) Other languages have not been considered - As reflected in the North American bias, other international tools might have been missed.
(3) Forked versions of projects (e.g. Teacher's Pet) not considered — Extensive modifications could have been made to projects that could reveal solutions to criteria deemed N/A. The main justification here was that documentation was not available to make an informed decision.

4 CONCLUSION

There is a growing thread of research on the use of VCS in educational contexts. The benefits, challenges and experiences have been shared across the computing education community. Whilst promising, this work has been somewhat independent and isolated, and there is an ongoing need to keep track of developments and ensure that knowledge is gathered and shared effectively.

The survey of eight tools presented here considered their general, technical and pedagogical aspects. This is only scratching the surface, constrained by what is publicly discoverable — many other teachers may have created solutions to the tasks of grouping students, distributing assignments, and managing assessment and feedback, but not shared them publically. However, as this survey has illustrated, there are commonalities and differences in the approach to supporitng these tasks. By bringing these tools together in this survey, it is hoped that (1) teachers will not waste time by starting from scratch, and (2) new tools and innovative features can build upon the knowledge gathered.

What is most promising is the ongoing development in this area. Half of of the tools surveyed are still active at the time of writing, and furthermore, Github Inc. has devoted resources towards supporting teachers in their exploration of using VCS by both providing free resources, tools, and a community for teachers with similar interest to share their knowledge. In terms of what comes next, the future seems bright. The literature review and tools surveyed provide evidence that this area is growing. Whether Git/Github remains the defacto approach remains to be seen. However, the integration into modern teaching environments for both students and teachers have had a clear impact already and will continue to do so within computing education.

REFERENCES

[1] Miroslav Biňas. 2013. Version Control System in CS1 Course: Practical Experience. In *IEEE 11th International Conference on Emerging eLearning Technologies and Applications (ICETA'13)*. pp. 23–28. https://doi.org/10.1109/ICETA.2013.6674398

[2] Curtis Clifton, Lisa C Kaczmarczyk, and Michael Mrozek. 2007. Subverting the Fundamentals Sequence: Using Version Control to Enhance Course Management. In *Proceedings of the 38th ACM Technical Symposium on Computer Science Education (SIGCSE'07)*. ACM New York, NY, USA, pp. 86–90. https://doi.org/10.1145/1227310.1227344

[3] B J Cornelius, M Munro, and D J Robson. 1989. An approach to software maintenance education. *Software Engineering Journal* 4, July (1989), pp. 233–236. https://doi.org/10.1049/sej.1989.0030

[4] Valerio Cosentino, Javier Luis, and Jordi Cabot. 2016. Findings from GitHub: Methods, Datasets and Limitations. In *Proceedings of the 13th International Workshop on Mining Software Repositories (MSR'16)*. ACM New York, NY, pp. 137–141. https://doi.org/10.1145/2901739.2901776

[5] Joseph Feliciano, Margaret-Anne Storey, and Alexey Zagalsky. 2016. Student experiences using GitHub in software engineering courses: a case study. In *Proceedings of the 38th International Conference on Software Engineering Companion (ICSE'16)*. 422–431. https://doi.org/10.1145/2889160.2889195

[6] Richard Glassey. 2018. Managing assignment feedback via issue tracking. In *Proceedings of the 23rd Annual ACM Conference on Innovation and Technology in Computer Science Education (ITiCSE 2018)*. ACM New York, NY, USA, p. 382. https://doi.org/10.1145/3197091.3205819

[7] Louis Glassy. 2006. Using version control to observe student software development processes. *Journal of Computing Sciences in Colleges* 21, 3 (2006), pp. 99–106.

[8] Georgios Gousios and Diomidis Spinellis. 2017. Mining Software Engineering Data from GitHub. In *Proceedings of the 39th International Conference on Software Engineering Companion (ICSE-C '17)*. IEEE Press, Piscataway, NJ, USA, 501–502. https://doi.org/10.1109/ICSE-C.2017.164

[9] Lassi Haaranen and Teemu Lehtinen. 2015. Teaching Git on the Side. In *Proceedings of the 20th Annual ACM Conference on Innovation and Technology in Computer Science Education (ITiCSE'15)*. ACM New York, USA, 87–92. https://doi.org/10.1145/2729094.2742608

[10] Ken T. N. Hartness. 2006. Eclipse and CVS for Group Projects. *Journal of Computing Sciences in Colleges* 21, 4 (2006), pp. 217–222.

[11] Sarah Heckman and Jason King. 2018. Developing Software Engineering Skills using Real Tools for Automated Grading. In *Proceedings of the 49th ACM Technical Symposium on Computer Science Education*. ACM, 794–799. https://doi.org/10.1145/3159450.3159595

[12] Ville Isomöttönen and Michael Cochez. 2014. Challenges and Confusions in Learning Version Control with Git. In *Communications in Computer and Information Science*, Zholtkevych G. (eds) Ermolayev V., Mayr H., Nikitchenko M., Spivakovsky A. (Ed.). Vol. 469. 178–193. https://doi.org/10.1007/978-3-319-13206-8_9

[13] An Ju and Armando Fox. 2018. TEAMSCOPE: Measuring Software Engineering Processes with Teamwork Telemetry. In *Proceedings of the 23rd Annual ACM Conference on Innovation and Technology in Computer Science Education (ITiCSE'18)*. ACM New York, NY, USA, pp. 123–128. https://doi.org/10.1145/3197091.3197107

[14] Eirini Kalliamvakou, Georgios Gousios, Kelly Blincoe, Leif Singer, Daniel M. German, and Daniela Damian. 2016. An in-depth study of the promises and perils of mining GitHub. *Empirical Software Engineering* 21, 5 (2016), pp. 2035–2071. https://doi.org/10.1007/s10664-015-9393-5

[15] John Kelleher. 2014. Employing git in the classroom. In *World Congress on Computer Applications and Information Systems (WCCAIS'14)*. IEEE, pp. 1–4. https://doi.org/10.1109/WCCAIS.2014.6916568

[16] Stephan Krusche and Andreas Seitz. 2018. ArTEMiS: An Automatic Assessment Management System for Interactive Learning. In *Proceedings of the 49th ACM Technical Symposium on Computer Science Education*. ACM, 284–289. https://doi.org/10.1145/3159450.3159602

[17] Oren Laadan, Jason Nieh, and Nicolas Viennot. 2010. Teaching Operating Systems Using Virtual Appliances and Distributed Version Control. In *Proceedings of the 41st ACM technical symposium on Computer Science Education (SIGCSE'10)*. ACM New York, NY, USA, pp. 480–484. https://doi.org/10.1145/1734263.1734427

[18] Joseph Lawrance, S Jung, and Charles Wiseman. 2013. Git on the cloud in the classroom. In *Proceeding of the 44th ACM technical symposium on Computer science education (SIGCSE'13)*. pp. 639–644. https://doi.org/10.1145/2445196.2445386

[19] Stephen Paul Linder, David Abbott, and Michael J. Fromberger. 2006. An instructional scaffolding approach to teaching software design. *Journal of Computing Sciences in Colleges* 21, 6 (2006), pp. 238–250.

[20] Ivan Milentijevic, Vladimir Ciric, and Oliver Vojinovic. 2008. Version control in project-based learning. *Computers and Education* 50, 4 (2008), pp. 1331–1338. https://doi.org/10.1016/j.compedu.2006.12.010

[21] Karen L. Reid and Gregory V. Wilson. 2005. Learning by Doing : Introducing Version Control as a Way to Manage Student Assignments. In *Proceedings of the 36th ACM technical symposium on Computer Science Education (SIGCSE'05)*. ACM New York, NY, USA, pp. 272–276. https://doi.org/10.1145/1047124.1047441

[22] Daniel Rocco and Will Lloyd. 2011. Distributed version control in the classroom. In *Proceedings of the 42nd ACM technical symposium on Computer Science Education (SIGCSE'11)*. pp. 637–642. https://doi.org/10.1145/1953163.1953342

[23] Ian Sommerville. 2015. *Software Engineering* (10th ed.). Addison-Wesley.

[24] Ying Liu. 2004. CVS historical information to understand how students develop software. In *International Workshop on Mining Software Repositories (MSR'04)*. In proceedings of the 26th International Conference on Software Engineering (ICSE'04). ACM Press, pp. 32–36. https://doi.org/10.1049/ic:20040472

Integrating Drawing Tablet and Video Capturing/Sharing to Facilitate Student Learning

Chen-Wei Wang

EECS Department, Lassonde School of Engineering, York University, Toronto, Canada

jackie@eecs.yorku.ca

ABSTRACT

We report the experience of adopting an innovative technique for in-class instruction. The technique relies on: **1)** replacing the blackboard/whiteboard by a portable drawing tablet; **2)** preparing starter pages consisting of code fragments or writings/figures on the drawing tablet for in-class illustrations on complex ideas; **3)** recording the in-class illustrations on the drawing tablet for students to review the thinking process after class. This technique has been adopted in three Computer Science and Software Engineering courses, ranging from freshman to junior years, and the student evaluation results indicate that this technique is effective and helps students achieve the course learning outcomes. Comparison of student performance on complex ideas also indicates a positive impact of our approach.

KEYWORDS

Communication Skills; Computational Thinking; Instructional Technologies; Learning Environment; Undergraduate Instruction

ACM Reference Format:
Chen-Wei Wang. 2019. Integrating Drawing Tablet and Video Capturing/Sharing to Facilitate Student Learning. In *ACM Global Computing Education Conference 2019 (CompEd '19), May 17–19, 2019, Chengdu,Sichuan, China.* ACM, New York, NY, USA, 7 pages. https://doi.org/10.1145/3300115.3309530

1 INTRODUCTION

It is challenging to teach complex computational thinking [2, 5, 6, 14] (e.g., nested loops on 2D arrays, recursion) and design principles (e.g., design by contract, object-oriented design patterns leveraging polymorphism and dynamic binding) in undergraduate courses, when the students have limited prior exposure to the course content. The class size of these courses is typically large (e.g., 400+ for freshman courses, 150+ for sophomore courses, and 100+ for junior courses in our department). Many students encounter obstacles to full comprehension of course content because: **1)** the class size restricts the instructor's intentional pauses and student interactions; and **2)** students are occupied by copying (often blindly) the instructor's remarks and board notes. For **2)**, such remarks and notes reflect the instructor's insights into the taught subjects, and are thus a valuable aid for student learning.

How can we make the in-depth and detailed illustrations in class accessible to students for their self-paced study outside the classroom? To address this question, we support student learning by allowing them, outside the classroom, to review contents taught in class (presented verbally and in written form). To achieve this, we have adopted, in three undergraduate Computer Science (CS) courses, the integrated use of: **1)** a drawing tablet (replacing the blackboard/whiteboard) for illustrating concepts and code examples; **2)** a program for recording all desktop activities, such as the slide presentation as well as illustrations on the tablet and programming IDEs; **3)** a wireless microphone allowing the instructor to move around the classroom without compromising the recorded sound quality; and **4)** online access to recordings and notes for students to review the class.

Our proposed teaching technique is novel in that it replaces a conventional blackboard/whiteboard with a *portable* drawing tablet, and it relies on recording the process of building up complex examples (e.g., static software architecture, dynamic runtime execution) from scratch. Such illustrations and examples represent the insight into the taught subjects and thinking process which, due to the recording, students can review as needed and thereby learn from. We maintain a website for students to access the recordings and illustration notes after class, and even after completing the courses: https://www.eecs.yorku.ca/~jackie/teaching/lectures/index.html. As an example, Figure 2b (p4) shows an annotated fragment of code at the end of our illustration on a 2D array. The reasoning process of moving from Figure 2a to Figure 2b, through recording, can be reviewed by students whenever they need.

Nonetheless, our proposed teaching technique cannot be implemented via a smart board (e.g., [11]). First, the installation of a smart board, similar to that of a conventional blackboard/whiteboard, has limited visibility due to the size of classroom and the position of students' seats. Second, it is not effective for the instructor to build up illustrations on complex examples, requiring a large amount of hand writing, on the touch screen of a smart board. Third, it is not yet the standard practice for a classroom to be equipped with a smart board: our technique with a portable drawing tablet can be adopted in any classroom with a standard projector.

The main contribution of this paper is a technique (as exemplified in Section 4) for setting up in-class illustrations on complex ideas. Our proposed technique is much more than the occasional and lightweight annotations on an in-class slide show using a tablet computer. Instead, our technique requires the instructor to prepare starter artifacts (e.g., code fragments, figures, an enumeration of theorems) on the drawing tablet prior to each class, so as to save time on setting up these artifacts on a conventional in-class blackboard/whiteboard "on the fly". Such carefully prepared starter artifacts provide the basis for building up the illustrations in class.

The rest of the paper is organized as follows. Section 2 summarizes the topics and learning outcomes of the three undergraduate CS courses, in which we adopted the proposed approach. Section 3 discusses our proposed approach. Section 4 describes an example of adopting our approach. Section 5 presents results of course evaluations and performance comparison. Section 6 outlines the equipment requirements. Section 7 reflects on our experience. Section 8 discussed the related works. Section 9 concludes the paper.

2 TEACHING CONTEXT

The proposed approach is meant for effective teaching (for instructors) and learning (for students) of courses involving complex computational thinking or abstract theories. For example, in the academic year of 2017 – 2018, we adopted this approach in three undergraduate, computer science courses. Examples of some of the course topics and course learning outcomes (CLOs) are summarized below.

2.1 First-Year Course: Introductory OOP

CS1 Mobile Computing (with 400+ students) is the second-semester course for CS[1] students at the first year. Students learn about basic computational thinking and object orientation through developing Android mobile apps using the Android Studio IDE (Integrated Development Environment), and visualizing the effects of their Java programs on physical tablets. Example topics covered in CS1 are: **1)** elementary programming (variables, data types, assignments); **2)** conditionals; **3)** loops; **4)** primitive 1D and 2D arrays; and **5)** object orientation (attributes, methods, classes, and class associations).

Some CLOs of CS1 are: **CLO1)** Understand software development within an object-oriented framework using a modern programming language and tool set; and **CLO2)** Use a set of computing skills such as reasoning about algorithms, tracing programs, test-driven development, and diagnosing faults.

2.2 Second-Year Course: More Advanced OOP

CS2 Advanced Object Oriented Programming (with 150+ students) is the first-semester course for both CS and engineering students at the second year. Students in CS2 are required to develop, test, and debug their Java programs in the Eclipse IDE. Example topics covered in CS2 are: **1)** unit testing (using JUnit); **2)** code reuse and subtyping via inheritance; **3)** polymorphic assignments and dynamic binding; **4)** recursion; **5)** asymptotic upper bounds (i.e., the big-o notation) of programs; and **6)** implementations of simple data structures such as singly-linked lists, stacks and queues, and binary trees.

Some CLOs of CS2 are: **CLO1)** Implement aggregations and compositions; **CLO2)** Implement inheritance; **CLO3)** Use recursion; and **CLO4)** Implement linked lists.

2.3 Third-Year Course: Software Design

CS3 Software Design (with 100+ students) is a required course for third-year CS and software engineering students. Example topics covered in CS3 are: **1)** the Design-by-Contract (DbC) method for constructing object-oriented software [7] (using loop invariants and

variants, method preconditions and postconditions, and class invariants); **2)** the information hiding design principle [9] (exemplified by the Iterator design pattern); **3)** object-oriented design patterns leveraging polymorphism and dynamic binding (e.g., composite, visitor, observer); and **4)** introduction to program verification using Hoare Triples [4].

Some CLOs of CS3 are: **CLO1)** Describe software specifications via Design by Contract; **CLO2)** Implement specifications with designs that are correct, efficient and maintainable; and **CLO3)** Design software using appropriate abstractions, modularity, information hiding, and design patterns.

3 THE PROPOSED APPROACH

This paper proposes an approach visualized in Figure 1 to both effective teaching (for instructors) and learning (for students) of complex ideas (e.g., computational, design, abstract). We discuss the proposed approach from two perspectives.

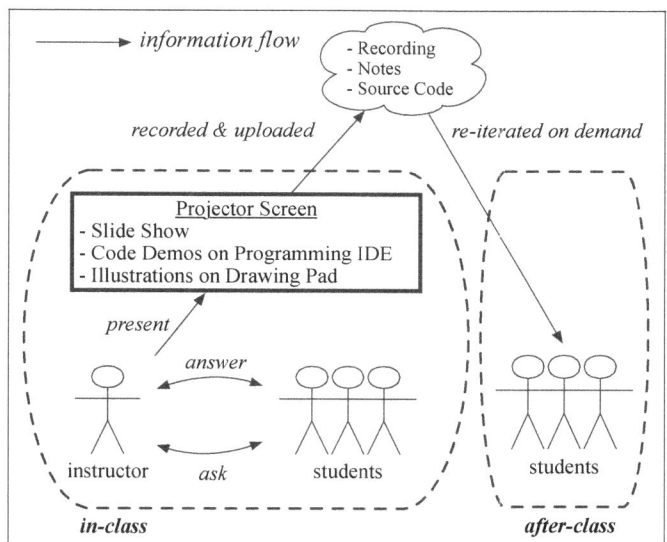

Figure 1: Proposed Approach: Effective After-Class Learning

The *instructor* presents course materials on a personal computer. The entire presentation, as desktop activities of the instructor's computer, is not only projected to the projector screen for students to follow in class, but also recorded (and later uploaded and made accessible) for students to review after class. Formats of presentation include the conventional slide show and code demonstrations on some programming IDE. Furthermore, a drawing tablet connected to the instructor's computer replaces the conventional whiteboard or blackboard (See Section 6 for its configuration). Given that illustrations on the connected drawing tablet become part of the desktop activities, the instructor is able to record: **1)** discussion of pre-selected topics (e.g., a code fragment, an example to be solved from scratch) using coloured annotations; and **2)** answers to students' questions that require detailed illustrations.

The *students* follow the tablet-based presentation via the same projector screen as the slideshow meaning that visibility is ensured

---

[1]The corresponding Java course for engineering students uses fidget boards connected with hardware equipment such as LED light bulbs.

(as opposed to the case of a whiteboard or blackboard which may have limited visibility due to the size of classroom, the position of students' seats). With the understanding that the entire presentation is recorded and will later be made accessible for review at their own pace, students may focus more on thinking through the contents and asking questions accordingly, without being distracted by copying (often blindly) the instructor's written or verbal notes.

4 EXAMPLE: TEACHING 2D ARRAYS

In this section, we illustrate how the proposed technique was adopted to teach the topic of two-dimensional arrays in CS1 (see Section 2 for examples of the topics and learning outcomes of the course). The same approach was also adopted for teaching CS2 and CS3.

Consider the following problem: Given a two-dimensional table specifying the distances between cities (where rows and columns denote, respectively, departure and destination cities), and given an itinerary of an array of cities, calculate the total distance. How would you teach students about solving this problem programatically (using a 2D array)?

Recording of how we taught concepts involved in the solution to this problem can be found here: https://youtu.be/Vrukh2LKvbE (from 00:00 to 43:48). The assumption is that the previous lectures already covered the basics of manipulating 2D arrays. This lecture is composed of various forms of illustrations:

- Using a slide show, review the problem at a high level without mentioning any code. (00:00 – 01:44)
- Using the tablet, illustrate how program variables are declared and manipulated. (1:44 – 6:47)
- Using the Android Studio IDE, illustrate a use-case for the calculator (with no errors). (6:47 – 10:06)
- Using a first starter page on the tablet, containing the main code of calculation, illustrate for the given use-case and how each line of code is executed, by visualizing how variables are initialized and manipulated. (10:06 – 27:03)
  Figure 2 (p4) compares the "clean" starter page and the annotated page at the end of this illustration.
- Using a second starter page on the tablet containing code handling errors, illustrate how the flow execution would branch differently, again by visualizing how variables are manipulated accordingly. (27:03 – 37:57)
- Starting with a blank page on the tablet, respond to a student's confusion as to how the two parts of the code work. Here the illustration is meant for reviewing the critical control structure from scratch. (37:57 – 43:48)

Remark. The above teaching pattern—choreographing slide show, code demo on a programming IDE, tablet illustration with a starter page, and answering questions or making additional remarks using tablet illustration with a blank page—is sufficiently general and may thus be applied to teaching many other topics.

In order for students from CS1, CS2, and CS3 to access recorded illustrations and notes for their self-study, even after the completion of the courses, we have maintained a public site of recorded lectures organized by topics, and containing hyperlinks to the recording on YouTube, PDF notes of tablet illustrations, example source code, and slides. Examples on teaching other complicated topics in all

three courses can be found on this lectures page: https://www.eecs.yorku.ca/~jackie/teaching/lectures/index.html.

5 EVALUATIONS

5.1 Improvement on Performance

Table 1 (p3) presents data on students' performance on questions related to the various complex ideas:

(1) Subcontracting (Inheritance of Contracts in Descendant Classes)
(2) The Visitor Design Pattern
(3) Genericity
(4) Formal Verification of Software (Proofs of Loop Correctness and Termination)
(5) Object-Oriented Programming (Inferring Classes, Attributes, and Methods from a Given API Tester)

Topics (1) to (4) were taught in CS3[2] by the author in both Summer 2015 (where the proposed technique was not adopted) and Fall 2017 (where the proposed technique was adopted), and we compare the percentage values of students' scores on the same set of final exam questions. Topic (5) was taught in CS1 by the author in both Spring 2017[3] (where the proposed technique was not adopted) and Winter 2018[4] (where the proposed technique was adopted), and we compare the percentage values of students' scores on the same set of computer test questions.

COURSE	CS3 (SU15)	CS3 (F17)
PROPOSED TECHNIQUE ADOPTED?	No	Yes
CLASS SIZE	49	80
TOPIC	STUDENT AVERAGE SCORES	
Subcontracting	51.63%	54.81%
Visitor Pattern	51.33%	58.33%
Genericity	63.27%	67.00%
Formal Verification of Software	63.62%	63.17%
COURSE	CS1 (SP17)	CS1 (W18)
PROPOSED TECHNIQUE ADOPTED?	No	Yes
CLASS SIZE	38	190
TOPIC	STUDENT AVERAGE SCORES	
Object-Oriented Programming	42.97%	56.4%

Table 1: Comparison of Student Performance

Table 1 (p3) indicates that our proposed teaching technique has a positive impact[5] upon students' performance on complex topics, particularly the visitor design pattern (a 16.64% improvement from 51.33% to 58.33%) and programming with classes and objects (a 30% improvement from 42.97% to 56.4%).

---

[2]Both instances had a large project. Before the project, the earlier instance of CS3 in 2015 had a single assignment, whereas the one in 2017 had six.
[3]This topic was taught at the author's previous institution, in a course whose curriculum overlaps with that of CS1.
[4]Due to a labour disruption at our institution in Winter 2018, this test occurred during the remediation period, where only a subset of the students participated.
[5]Although the results of an independent t-test showed that there was no significant difference between the two groups, in Subcontracting ($t(127) = .77, p > .05$), Visitor Pattern ($t(127) = 1.81, p > .05$), Genericity ($t(127) = .72, p > .05$), and Formal Verification of Software ($t(127) = .13, p > .05$), there was a significant difference between the two groups in Object-Oriented Programming ($t(226) = 2.29, p < .05$).

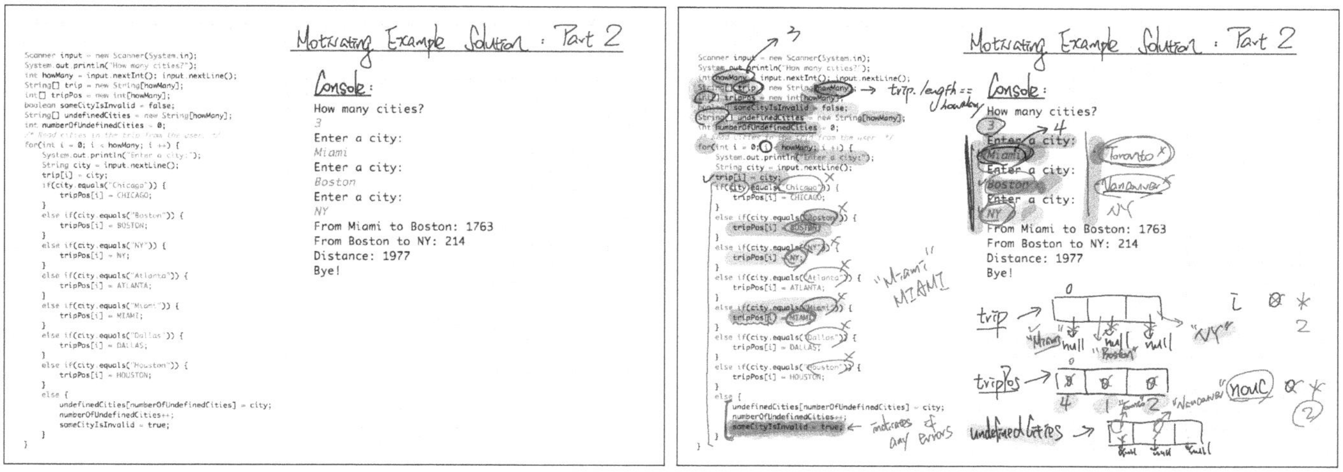

(a) Before Annotations Began (11:02)

(b) After Annotations Ended (27:03)

Figure 2: Illustrating a Code Fragment on a Drawing Tablet (11:02 – 27:03 of https://youtu.be/Vrukh2LKvbE)

5.2 Student Evaluations

The anonymized online course evaluations of the three context courses, which contain both numerical ratings and student comments[6], indicate that the in-class instruction, which relies on the proposed technique of this report, is effective. The data are representative due to the high response rates:

Course	CS1	CS2	CS3
Response	58.09% (219/377)	58.42% (59/101)	85.73% (70/82)

In this section, we present the numerical results (on a 7-point scale[7]) for those questions that are relevant to the effectiveness of teaching and learning:

Q1: The course helped me grow intellectually.

Q2: The course learning outcomes were clearly stated and achieved in the course.

Q3: The instructor conveyed the subject matter in a clear and well-organized manner.

Q4: The instructor helped me understand the importance and significance of the course content.

Q5: Overall, the instructor was an effective teacher in this course.

Table 2 (p4) summarizes the responses grouped as: Agree (denoting the percentage of responses > 4), Disagree (denoting the percentage of responses < 4), and Neutral (denoting the percentage of responses = 4). Table 2 clearly indicates that students value the instructor's method of teaching as proposed in this paper. Questions 1, 2, and 4 explicitly address students' views on their learning outcomes and indicate that the approach is highly effective in helping them achieve the course learning outcomes and grow intellectually. Although the evaluation results for **Q3** – **Q5** are not available for

CS1[8], their results may be anticipated as similar to those of CS2 and CS3, extrapolated from observing that the majority of essay results of the three courses are positive about the teaching instructions.

		Q1	Q2	Q3	Q4	Q5
CS1	agree	82.33	90.6	not available		
	neutral	9.02	4.51	not available		
	disagree	7.15	4.14	not available		
CS2	agree	91.53	98.3	100	98.3	96.61
	neutral	6.78	0	0	0	1.69
	disagree	1.69	1.69	0	1.69	1.69
CS3	agree	80	80	94.28	98.3	90
	neutral	1.43	11.43	2.86	0	2.86
	disagree	18.57	8.58	2.86	10.0	7.25

Table 2: Numerical Evaluation Results: Distribution

Furthermore, Table 3 (p5) suggests that answers to all questions have a high median value, and have a mean value that is consistently[9] higher than that of the department and faculty.

6 ADOPTING THE APPROACH

Figure 3 summarizes how to assemble the various equipment to implement the proposed approach. Here we described what we used, but the interested reader may choose other equipment with the same functionality.

Install the following software programs on your teaching computer (e.g., a MacBook): **1)** a presentation program (e.g., any PDF reader, PowerPoint reader) for your slides; **2)** a programming IDE

---

[6]Some student comments are quoted in Section 7.

[7]**7** for "Strongly Agree", **6** for "Agree", **5** for "Somewhat Agree", **4** for "Neither Agree nor Disagree", **3** for "Somewhat Disagree", **2** for "Disagree", and **1** for "Srongly Disagree".

[8]Due to a recent labour disruption at our institution, **Q3** – **Q5** were excluded from the course evaluation, preventing instructors supporting it by not continuing with classes.

[9]The only exceptions are the mean values of **Q1** and **Q2** for CS3, which may be explained by the essay results, where a good number of students do not appreciate the chosen language for teaching design that is not at the same time a popular implementation language in the industry.

		Q1	Q2	Q3	Q4	Q5
CS1	mean	5.76	5.97	not available		
	median	6.0	6.0	not available		
	std. dev.	1.41	1.13	not available		
	dep. mean	5.3	5.48	not available		
	fac. mean	5.48	5.65	not available		
CS2	mean	6.32	6.34	6.74	6.59	6.51
	median	7.0	7.0	7.0	7.0	7.0
	std. dev.	1.11	0.99	0.55	0.65	0.86
	dep. mean	5.63	5.74	5.89	5.78	5.89
	fac. mean	5.66	5.8	5.87	5.82	5.88
CS3	mean	5.41	5.67	6.39	6.10	6.23
	median	6.0	6.0	7.0	7.0	7.0
	std. dev.	1.97	1.53	1.07	1.70	1.33
	dep. mean	5.63	5.74	5.89	5.78	5.89
	fac. mean	5.66	5.8	5.87	5.82	5.88

Table 3: Numerical Evaluation Results: Mean and Median

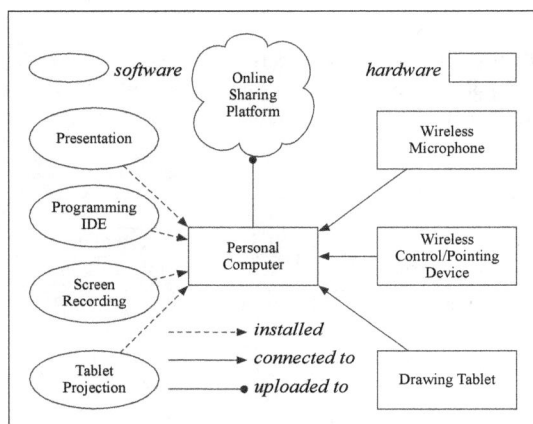

Figure 3: Adopting the Approach: Schematic View

as applicable to your course (e.g., Android Studio, Eclipse); **3)** a screen recording program (e.g., the free Active Presenter [10][10]) for recording all desktop activities on the computer; and **4)** a program for projecting the screen of your drawing tablet (e.g., the free QuickTime Player).

Upon arriving in the classroom, connect the following hardware to your teaching computer: **1)** a wireless microphone (e.g., Revolabs xTag [15]) using a USB cable; **2)** a wireless control or pointing device (e.g., a wireless or bluetooth mouse, trackpad, keyboard, laser pointing device) for showing slides, typing code in an IDE, or switching between programs; and **3)** a drawing tablet (e.g., iPad Pro) installed with an app for annotations (e.g., GoodNotes, Notability). For **3)**, a wire connection to the USB port is recommended for a stable connection throughout the class. To project the screen of the drawing tablet to your computer desktop, if you use the QuickTime player and an iPad Pro, start a "New Movie Recording" and select your iPad as the camera.

[10]Another lecture capturing system such as Panopto and TechSmith may also work.

When ready to start your lecture: **1)** wear the wireless microphone connected to your teaching computer (and optionally another microphone connected to the classroom speaker); and **2)** start the screen recording program and choose the connected wireless microphone as the input device.

When the lecture is finished, stop the screen recording, export it to an acceptable form (e.g., MP4), upload it to an online video sharing platform (e.g., YouTube), and publish the link to students. The annotation app on your drawing tablet should allow you to export the annotated notes (e.g., Figure 2a, p4) as an PDF file.

7 REFLECTION

In this section we share our reflections on the proposed approach, after adopting it for teaching the three courses (Section 2).

Drawing Tablet vs. Blackboard/Whiteboard. Often students sitting at the rear or sides of a class room find it difficult to copy contents of the front blackboard/whiteboard into their notes, let alone comprehend the concepts and processes being illustrated. Instead, projecting contents to a high, centred screen allows students not to miss any parts of the instructor's presentation. More importantly, the use of an annotation app allows the instructor to save time on copying, e.g., code fragments, in order to start a new discussion. Instead, a starter page on the tablet can be preset and launched at the appropriate time. Furthermore, the ability to draw and annotate with the various colours (e.g., red-underline a line of code, colour a portion of drawing) helps the instructor communicate key points to students.

Essay results of student evaluations from all three context courses confirm the effectiveness of using a drawing tablet: e.g.,

- "Lectures are well planned and use of iPad with slides is a great way to explain things." [CS1]
- "[Best things about the course are] Using iPad notes to explain the logic and to trace the certain parts of code." [CS1]
- "the teaching style of instructor is awesome, he uses an Ipad instead of black board and record every lecture, which is very helpful. if this kind teaching style is used by other instructor then student will pay more attention to teacher then copying notes from blackboard and doing multitasking." [CS2]
- "Great supplementary materials (recordings, lecture notes, ipad notes, etc..)" [CS3]

Drawing Tablet vs. Slide Animations. Animated slides have the great advantage that information can be revealed at a planned time. However, when teaching complicated ideas, it is often not effective to encode all details in animations, since the order of animations is *static*, and the instructor may not be able to account for how students actually understand the concepts dynamically in class. Instead, with the use of a drawing tablet, the instructor can teach more effectively by creating a starter page, and then gradually adding annotations as illustrated in Section 4. This is essentially a *dynamic* way to control the pace and level of details that the instructor judges appropriate for how the current class is understanding the materials.

Review of Lectures. We strongly believe that the most valuable component of in-class instruction is the *dynamic* illustrations of difficult concepts. Despite how effective such illustrations are, we would never expect students to fully comprehend the concepts from in-class presentation alone simply because they are hard and naturally require repetitions. As a result, being able to record all transitions among the slide show, code demos, and tablet illustrations is invaluable for students to review the concepts after class. Such review[11] also helps them reflect on the materials and ask thoughtful questions. Furthermore, the proposed approach also allows students who miss classes for legitimate reasons (e.g., medical, family) to catch up with the course content at their own pace. To facilitate students' selection of parts of a lecture recording which they are interested in reviewing, we may add links to the various timings of starting critical examples or concepts.

A Suitable, Transferrable Teaching Pattern. How would the teaching and learning experience be different if the proposed approach, particularly the interactive experience of tablet illustrations, was not adopted for teaching the 2D array solution (Section 4)? Our previous experience of teaching concepts with a similar or higher level of difficulty, without using the proposed approach, was that we had to rush through parts that really need the most detailed, in-depth illustrations, primarily because it was time consuming to copy the starting code fragments onto the board. Even if such illustrations were performed, students would not be able to review them after class. Therefore, with the ability to record illustrations on a drawing tablet, the teaching pattern as observed in Section 4 may be generalized as follows:

- Use slide show to present the general problem to be solved.
- Use a programming IDE to demonstrate what is ultimately expected from the final (e.g,. software) product.
- Pre-set a list of starter pages on the drawing tablet, each containing selected code fragments or formulas, then annotate them to gradually build towards the solutions or conclusions.
- Answer students' questions by starting a blank page on the drawing tablet, and build up the answers there from scratch.

Some items (except tablet illustrations) may be omitted, and the order of choreographing these components may be adjusted according to the subject being taught.

Required Preparation. The instructor should determine what concepts/examples they will illustrate in class, and then create the starter pages on the drawing tablet accordingly. Compared with simply writing them "on they fly" in class, the instructor may take more time carefully planning the layout of each page. But most valuably, these starter pages, once created, may be *elaborated* over time and later *reused* for teaching the same or similar subjects.

Complexity of Integration. The current practice of the proposed approach requires us to manually assemble an array of equipment (Section 6). A better solution is to have the classroom podium computer being setup according to the schematics (Figure 3, p5).

8 RELATED WORKS

Our proposed teaching technique requires the careful setup of starter artifacts (e.g., code fragments, figures, writings) on a drawing tablet for in-class illustrations, which are recorded for students to review after class. Our technique is suitable for teaching complex

computational thinking [2, 5, 6, 14] through carefully planned illustrations on a drawing tablet which, based on our experience, are perceived as less difficult and boring by students compared with in-class instruction that heavily relies on slide shows. Although there are other systems allowing the instructor to handwrite on slides projected from a tablet PC (e.g., [1]), our approach also allows other desktop activities (such as demonstrating on a programming IDE) to be integrated into the lecture instruction and recording.

The platform offering the most similar support is the MIT Open Course [8], but the posted contents there are limited to filming of instructors and the projector screen (as opposed to desktop activities of the instructor's computer) and in-class illustrations on a blackboard. Setting up the starting ground for such illustrations on a conventional in-class blackboard "on the fly" takes up class time, whereas in our proposed approach, the instructor can carefully set up the starter artifacts (e.g., code fragments, figures, writings) on the drawing tablet and plan their lectures accordingly.

Also relevant is the Stanford Online [13], which is designed for online distance learning. The use of a drawing tablets for intensive illustrations, as well as constant switches between the various desktop activities, is not typical for courses there. On the other hand, we have also adopted the proposed technique to prepare tutorial videos as detailed pre-study materials for lab assignments. Our students expressed in their written comments that these tutorial videos, with detailed and in-depth illustrations on a drawing tablet, are valuable study materials for completing lab assignments and preparing for tests. For example, for *CS1*, a tutorial series (21 videos, 6 hours) is made available on day one of the course on developing, from scratch, an Android Mobile app for calculating the BMI (Body Mess Index), with a clear separation among the model, the view, and the controller. Similar to Stanford Online are the online course repositories such as Coursera [3] and Udemy [12], but these are meant to be commercial, unlike the proposed approach as well as MIT Open Course and Stanford Online. Moreover, the use of intensive tablet illustrations is also not typical in these commercial courses (e.g., an introduction to Android app development).

9 CONCLUSION

We describe the use of a drawing tablet to conduct in-depth and detailed illustrations of complex ideas, and to record all in-class desktop activities on the instructor's computer (including slide show, code demonstrations, tablet illustrations). Comparison of student performance on complex topics indicates a positive impact of our approach. Student evaluation results also indicate that this approach is effective for helping students achieve the expected course learning outcomes.

The proposed approach was only adopted in three undergraduate CS courses so far. Nonetheless, given that **1)** the total number (344) of students participating in the online course evaluation; **2)** the vast majority of (numerical and essay) evaluation results concerning the effectiveness of the instruction being positive; and **3)** the wide range of topics being covered in these courses, we believe that this experience report would benefit colleagues who wish to improve their teaching of complex (programming, design, or abstract) ideas.

To reaffirm the effectiveness of the approach, we will adopt it in teaching courses involving more abstract theories of computation.

---

[11] According to the YouTube statistics, students in all three courses spent a decent amount of time reviewing the recorded lectures: each student in CS1 spent an average time of 213 minutes, 740 minutes for CS2 students, and 871 minutes for CS3 students.

REFERENCES

[1] Richard Anderson, Ruth Anderson, Beth Simon, Steven A. Wolfman, Tammy VanDeGrift, and Ken Yasuhara. 2004. Experiences with a Tablet PC Based Lecture Presentation System in Computer Science Courses. *SIGCSE Bull.* 36, 1 (March 2004), 56–60. https://doi.org/10.1145/1028174.971323

[2] Jens Bennedsen, Michael E. Caspersen, and Michael Klling. 2008. *Reflections on the Teaching of Programming: Methods and Implementations* (1 ed.). Springer Publishing Company, Incorporated.

[3] Coursera. [n. d.]. https://www.coursera.org/

[4] C. A. R. Hoare. 1969. An Axiomatic Basis for Computer Programming. *Commun. ACM* 12, 10 (Oct. 1969), 576–580. https://doi.org/10.1145/363235.363259

[5] Anna Lamprou and Alexander Repenning. 2018. Teaching How to Teach Computational Thinking. In *Proceedings of the 23rd Annual ACM Conference on Innovation and Technology in Computer Science Education (ITiCSE 2018)*. ACM, New York, NY, USA, 69–74. https://doi.org/10.1145/3197091.3197120

[6] James Lockwood and Aidan Mooney. 2017. Computational Thinking in Education: Where does it Fit? A systematic literary review. *CoRR* abs/1703.07659 (2017). arXiv:1703.07659 http://arxiv.org/abs/1703.07659

[7] Bertrand Meyer. 1997. *Object-oriented Software Construction (2Nd Ed.).* Prentice-Hall, Inc., Upper Saddle River, NJ, USA.

[8] Masschusetts Institute of Technology. [n. d.]. MIT Open Courseware. https://ocw.mit.edu/index.htm

[9] D. L. Parnas. 1972. On the Criteria to Be Used in Decomposing Systems into Modules. *Commun. ACM* 15, 12 (Dec. 1972), 1053–1058. https://doi.org/10.1145/361598.361623

[10] Active Presenter. Version 7. All-in-one Screen Recorder, Video Editor & eLearning Authoring Software. https://atomisystems.com/activepresenter/

[11] SMART. [n. d.]. SMART Board for Education. https://smarttech.com/

[12] Udemy. [n. d.]. https://www.udemy.com/

[13] Stanford University. [n. d.]. Stanford Online. https://online.stanford.edu/courses

[14] Jeannette M. Wing. 2006. Computational thinking. *Commun. ACM* 49, 3 (2006), 33–35. https://doi.org/10.1145/1118178.1118215

[15] Revolabs xTag. 2007. Wireless Microphone System. Model 02-DSKMAN-DPP-11.

Replicating and Unraveling Performance and Behavioral Differences between an Online and a Traditional CS Course

David Joyner
College of Computing
Georgia Institute of Technology
Atlanta, GA USA
david.joyner@gatech.edu

Melinda McDaniel
College of Computing
Georgia Institute of Technology
Atlanta, GA USA
mcdaniel@cc.gatech.edu

ABSTRACT

In January 2017, a major public research university launched an online version of CS1 targeted at on-campus students to address rising enrollments and provide students with flexibility in their schedules. Prior research on this class has found positive outcomes: students in the course achieve the same learning outcomes as those in a traditional course, while reporting a lower time investment to reach those outcomes and a high level of student satisfaction. This research builds on that prior work in two ways. First, it replicates the findings from that earlier semester with an entirely new semester of students. Second, it delves deeper into the student experience within the online course and its traditional counterpart. This deeper analysis focuses specifically on the differing ways in which students in each section allocated their time, whether or not students in either section accessed the opposite section's material, and their future preferences in online vs. residential CS classes.

CCS CONCEPTS

• **Social and professional topics~CS1** • **Applied computing~ Distance learning** • **Applied computing~E-learning**

1 Introduction

Over the past several years, universities have seen a dramatic rise in enrollments in computer science classes. Part of this is due to the rising number of entering computer science majors [16], but it is also because of the rising number of universities requiring computer science for all students, regardless of major [17]. This trend has run into the difficulty many schools and universities have in attracting computer science teachers, a trend well documented in the K-12 space [1] but persistent in higher education as well.

CompEd '19, May 17–19, 2019, Chengdu,Sichuan, China
© 2019 Copyright is held by the owner/author(s). Publication rights licensed to ACM.
ACM ISBN 978-1-4503-6259-7/19/05...$15.00
https://doi.org/10.1145/3300115.3309533

To address these rising enrollments, one major public research university in the United States launched an online version of one of its CS1 classes in January 2017. By offering the class online, the university aimed to bypass many of the constraints on course capacity, particularly lecture hall capacity and scheduling. However, online classes have been met with deserved skepticism: some studies have shown negative outcomes from online courses relative to their traditional counterparts [6][15], while others have found comparable or even advantageous outcomes [3][5].

To investigate this skepticism, significant research has been devoted to this online CS1 class to ensure that student learning outcomes and the student experience are both commensurate to traditional delivery mechanisms. An online section can only be considered to successfully raise capacity to teach CS1 if the product remains comparable. Thus far, that research has found positive outcomes: students in the online section learn at least as much as students in a parallel traditional offering, both overall [8][10] and when subdivided by prior CS experience, with some tentative evidence suggesting the online course may be specifically advantageous for students with prior negative CS experiences [9]. Students also report more positive perceptions of the online experience, and report spending less time per week on the course despite the comparable learning outcomes [8].

This prior research, as well as trends in online learning research, has led to additional questions. First, there is the question of replication: prior research has focused on the initial class two semesters, Spring and Fall 2017, each of which may have had confounding issues affecting the results. Do the results seen in these semesters replicate in a new term? Additionally, not all offerings are equal; changes are made between semesters. Do the results replicate in despite the changes made?

Second, the results themselves raise interesting questions. If students in the online section achieve the same learning outcomes in less time, what specific tasks are requiring less time? Are they using shared supporting infrastructure in the same way? How do they rate the perceived value of components accessible to both course sections?

This research addresses these questions. First, we will perform the same analysis from previous semesters on a new semester's data to identify what trends replicate. Then, using new questions added to the courses' surveys, we will investigate the behavioral differences among students in the two sections. Finally, we will also replicate the analysis of students' perceptions of the course to see if perceptions have changed with the modifications made for the Spring 2018 semester.

2 Course Background

The university's CS1 class teaches introductory Python, covering variables, operators, conditionals, loops, functions, error handing, strings, lists, dictionaries, files, objects, and algorithms. The online class mirrors the traditional version's learning goals but uses its own assessments and instructional materials to leverage the online medium.

The major differences between the courses flow from the affordances of teaching online. While the traditional version has three lecture periods per week and take-home homework assignments, the online version has short 5-10 minute pre-recorded videos with smaller problems interspersed for frequent practice. The traditional version includes human evaluation, while the online version exclusively uses automated evaluation; the feedback and results are returned to students immediately. The two versions have similar supporting infrastructure (a course forum, a help desk, and a recitation), use the same pre-test, post-test, and course surveys to compare between the delivery methods, and are taught by different instructors.

2.1 Online Course Design

A full background of the design of the online course is available in prior work [8]. At a high level, the online course is comprised of 455 videos averaging 2 minutes in length, in line with best practices identified by researchers studying MOOC engagement [4]. Students also use an adaptive textbook written for the class on McGraw-Hill's SmartBook platform, following an identical organizational structure to the course lecture videos.

Lecture videos are rapidly interspersed with exercises. Some exercises are multiple choice or fill-in-the-blank, while others require live coding to pass an automated grader. The textbook, similarly, has embedded multiple choice and fill-in-the-blank questions. These questions are completed for course credit, with unlimited attempts and feedback given on incorrect answers.

After each major chapter of the course, students complete a problem set comprised of additional multiple choice, fill in the blank, and live coding problems. After each major unit of the course, students complete a timed and proctored exam featuring more of the same structure of problems, including live evaluation. Altogether, students complete over 1,000 multiple choice and fill-in-the-blank problems and 450 coding problems.

2.2 Semester Details

This analysis takes place during a standard 17-week semester. Students in the online course are given a recommended calendar to follow, although significant flexibility is built in. The major deadlines are the four course tests, at which point students are required to have all prior work completed; outside of these deadlines, however, students have flexibility.

As part of the semester, students have access to three additional resources: a course forum, a help desk, and recitation. The forum is the recommended place to ask questions and receive help from classmates or the teaching team. The help desk allows students to come for in-person help with one of the teaching assistants. Recitations are optional meeting times, during which the teaching assistants deliver supplemental lectures, provide practice materials, and answer questions.

3.2.1 Semester Changes. Although we consider this a replication study to test the same pair of courses during a new semester, there are always changes that occur between terms. During this semester, the online section introduced two new features: students are now required to complete four 30-minute check-ins with teaching assistants during which they receive additional feedback, and students are now required to complete approximately 75 additional "advanced" problems specifically constructed to test their knowledge on more advanced concepts. Differences observed this semester in outcomes, time invested, or attitudes may be due in part to these differences.

3.2.2 Semester Demographics. During this semester, we observed similar trends to prior semesters in enrollment patterns: the online section drew fewer students with no prior experience (51.2% vs. 64.2%) with statistical significance (X^2 = 8.462, p = 0.0036). However, there was no statistically significant difference in the number of students who had previously *completed* a CS course; online students were more likely to have previously failed or withdrawn, while traditional students were more likely to have never enrolled in a CS class before Significant differences were also seen in employment, major, and age: online students were more likely to be older, employed, or business majors, while traditional students were more likely to be younger, unemployed, or engineering majors. A more thorough breakdown of the differences in student demographics between the sections is available in [12].

3 Performance Differences

To assess performance differences, students in both the online and the traditional version of the class complete the SCS1 inventory, a standardized and validated instrument for assessing introductory CS knowledge [14], at the beginning and end of the semester. Students in both sections receive course credit for completing the inventory regardless of their performance on it.

3.1 Overall Differences

Table 1 shows the pre-test, post-test, and change in scores for students in the online and traditional sections in Spring 2018. Change scores are calculated by subtracting the pre-test score from the post-test score for students who completed both tests.

Notably, while previous semesters have seen no overall statistically significant difference in performance [8], this semester was different: while there was no statistically significant difference between traditional and online students on the pre-test, statistically significant differences were present on both the post-test and in the change in test scores. Students in the online section improved their scores more and ultimately performed better than students in the traditional section.

Table 1. Pre-Test, Post-Test, and Change (Post-Test – Pre-Test) scores for students in the traditional and online sections. A Student's t-test is used to check for statistically significant differences among these scores.

	Pre-Test		Post-Test		Change	
	Trad.	Online	Trad.	Online	Trad.	Online
Mean	6.25	6.75	8.37	9.81	+2.26	+3.58
SD	3.72	4.29	3.90	4.65	4.70	4.58
N	286	204	171	158	168	158
t	1.3946		3.0416		2.5646	
p	0.1638		0.0025		0.0108	

3.2 Differences by Prior Experience

Previous analyses have also segmented students by their prior experience to investigate for more fine-grained differences in performance. Specifically, it was hypothesized—and later observed [9]—that students who had previously failed or withdrawn from a CS course may be more advantaged by taking the online section. Weak evidence was observed that students with prior expertise or informal experience might be advantaged by the online section as well.

Table 2 to the right shows the segmented scores based on prior experience for this semester's data. Students were asked to report their level of prior CS experience on the start-of-course surveys in both sections. Students who reported previously withdrawing from or failing a CS class are classified as "Prior Experience". Students who reported previously completing a CS class are classified as "Prior Expertise/Success". Students who reported informal or self-taught ways of learning CS are classified as "Informal Experience". In most cases, students selected these options from a multiple-choice question; 21 students reported "other" experiences, but their responses were ultimately coded as one of these four categories (e.g. "I took APCS in high school" was coded as "Prior Expertise/Success").

In this term, too few students classified as Prior Experience were present in the traditional class for a meaningful comparison. Additional evidence emerged supporting the suggestions of prior work [9] that students in the online section classified as Prior Expertise and Informal Expertise improved more or performed better at the end than their traditional counterparts. However, the number of t-tests and the lack of corroborating results from the post-test (for Informal Experience) or change scores (for Prior Expertise) weakens this potential conclusion.

4 Behavioral Differences

These results suggest that students in the online section are improving more and ending the class with higher post-test scores. That alone may have multiple explanations that may or may not be related to the online delivery mechanism. For example, it may be the case that students in the online section also attend the traditional lectures, make heavier use of supporting infrastructure, or simply are required to spend more

time on the class. To investigate these, the post-course survey in both sections asked students to reflect on several of their behaviors during the semester.

Table 2. Pre-Test, Post-Test, and Change scores for students in the traditional and online sections, segmented by prior CS experience. A Student's t-test is used to check for statistically significant differences among these scores.

No Prior Experience

	Pre-Test		Post-Test		Change	
	Trad.	Online	Trad.	Online	Trad.	Online
Mean	5.19	9.45	8.19	8.84	+3.28	+3.91
SD	2.50	4.92	3.93	3.79	4.21	4.38
N	183	105	118	95	115	95
t	0.6950		1.1238		1.0554	
p	0.4876		0.2262		0.2925	

Prior Experience

	Pre-Test		Post-Test		Change	
	Trad.	Online	Trad.	Online	Trad.	Online
Mean	6.76	7.20	8.00	8.93	+0.83	+2.29
SD	3.25	4.92	2.53	3.22	2.86	4.38
N	17	20	6	14	6	14
t	0.4245		0.6249		0.7419	
p	0.6738		0.5399		0.4677	

Prior Expertise/Success

	Pre-Test		Post-Test		Change	
	Trad.	Online	Trad.	Online	Trad.	Online
Mean	8.19	9.45	8.89	12.73	+0.34	+2.91
SD	4.59	4.92	3.68	5.91	5.34	5.38
N	64	55	35	33	35	33
t	0.1493		3.2358		1.9729	
p	1.4514		**0.0019**		0.0527	

Informal Experience

	Pre-Test		Post-Test		Change	
	Trad.	Online	Trad.	Online	Trad.	Online
Mean	9.05	7.96	8.83	10.31	-1.25	+4.13
SD	5.71	6.45	4.91	5.25	4.81	4.22
N	22	24	12	16	12	16
t	0.6029		0.7579		3.1412	
p	0.5497		0.4553		**0.0042**	

4.1 Cross-Attendance

One prior hypothesis was that students in the online section might be attending the traditional lectures as well. It has also been noted that students in the traditional section can access the online course material through its parallel publicly available Massive Open Online Course (MOOC). Thus, the post-course survey asked students to report how frequently they consumed the other version's materials.

Throughout the rest of this research, we use a X^2 test to check for significant differences in proportions of students between the sections. Here, both sections used the other's materials at comparably low rates: 87.4% of students in the traditional section reported "never" using the online section's course materials, and 89.6% of online students reported that they "never" attended in-person lectures ($X^2 = 0.444$, $p = 0.5053$).

4.2 Use of Supporting Infrastructure

Both the traditional and the online sections take advantage of three pieces of supporting infrastructure: a help desk, a scheduled recitation, and a course forum. These three environments are described under section 3.2.

A possible explanation for the differences in performance noted above is that students in the online section, liberated from the time commitment of weekly lecture attendance, may use the supporting infrastructure more heavily. Thus, our post-course survey asked students in both sections to report how frequently they used each environment, and how useful they assessed each to be. For frequency, students were given ranges (e.g. 1-2 times, 3-5 times), which were distilled into two categories for analysis. For recitation attendance and help desk visits, students were divided between those who reported attending two times or fewer and those who reported attending three times or more. For course forum usage, students were divided between those who reported using the forum three times or fewer and those who reported using it four times or more. Table 3, below, shows these usage patterns and student evaluations of each environment's usefulness.

Table 3. Frequency with which students in each section reported using the help desk, recitations, and forum.

		Traditional	Online
Help Desk Visits	% <= 2 visits	52.9%	74.9%
	N	208	175
	X^2, p	19.672, **< 0.0001**	
Recitation Visits	% <= 2 visits	18.8%	85.1%
	N	208	175
	X^2, p	166.724, **< 0.0001**	
Course Forum Usages	% <= 3 uses	76.9%	67.5%
	N	208	175
	X^2, p	4.211, **0.0402**	

Based on the reported usage patterns, online students use the help desk and recitations far less often than their traditional counterparts. The most pronounced difference is in recitation attendance: only 14.9% of online students reported attending 3 or more recitation sessions, while 81.2% of traditional students reported attending 3 or more recitation sessions.

A smaller, but still statistically significant, difference is observed on the course forum. Online students make heavier use of the course forum than on-campus students. This may be due to the apparent parallelism: the traditional class, help desk, and recitations are all in person, while the online class and course forum are online. However, this may also be unrelated to the medium and more related to the teaching teams' respective involvement in the forum: students were asked who responded to most of their questions on the forum; 55.2% of students in the

online section reported that the instructor responded, compared to 9.8% of students in the traditional section ($X^2 = 90.385$, $p < 0.0001$). 42.2% of traditional students reported a teaching assistant answered, and 20.1% reported another student answered, compared to 2.9% and 15.7% respectively for the online section. Therefore, online students may have gravitated toward the course forum as a place where the instructor was visible and active in answer questions.

Regardless of their cause, these differing usage patterns are reflected in the reported rating of the usefulness of the help desk and recitations. Students were asked to rate the usefulness of each on a 7-point Likert scale. These results are reported in Table 4 below. A Mann-Whitney U Test was used to compare for differences here and in all comparisons of Likert-scale responses due to the nonparametric nature of Likert scale data. Scores are shown as numeric averages of the reported values.

Table 4. Average 7-point Likert-scale ratings of the usefulness of the help desk, recitation, and course forums, and results of a Mann-Whitney U Test comparing them.

		Traditional	Online
Help Desk	Mean	4.94	4.32
	Z, p	4.5868, **< 0.0001**	
Recitation	Mean	5.05	4.06
	Z, p	7.8772, **< 0.0001**	
Course Forum	Mean	4.65	5.73
	Z, p	-6.7937, **< 0.0001**	

As expected, perceptions of usefulness followed the usage patterns: traditional students rated the help desk and recitations as more useful with statistical significance, and online students rated the course forum as more useful with statistical significance. It is interesting that even though 2/3rds of the online class used the forum 3 or fewer times, the vast majority rated it as positively helpful.

4.3 Allocation of Time

Given that the two courses have different assessments, it may be the case that students in the online section learn more solely because the assessments demand more practice time. Discussions with teaching assistants who have worked on both courses reflect this: they note that the frequently interspersed practice means that online students tend to do more actual coding in the class. Thus, we ask students to report two details regarding their time investment: the total time they spent on the class, and how that time was allocated. While it is known from multiple fields that self-report is not accurate to reality [18], we hypothesize that there is no systematic under- or over-reporting bias specific to one section against the other; this assumption, however, ought to be tested in future research.

For total time, students were offered a few categories: fewer than 5 hours per week, 5 to 7 hours per week, 8 to 10, 11 to 13, or 14 or more. Analysis divided students into two groups: those reporting 7 or fewer hours, and those reporting 8 or more hours spent. 41.0% of 210 traditional students reported spending 7 or fewer hours per week on the course; 71.1% of online students reported spending 7 or fewer hours per week on the course. This difference is statistically significant (X^2 = 35.0.36, p < 0.0001). Thus, it is not the case that online students—based at least on their self-reported time investment—are simply spending more time; in fact, it appears they are spending significantly less time.

This result was observed in previous semesters [8], but it was noted that we are unsure of what activities students include in their reported time investment. For example, as an online course, students do not walk to and from class. Are traditional students including this in their calculation? This alone could account for the difference in time investment. So, in Spring 2018, we asked students to self-assess what percentage of their total time spent on the class was allocated to different activities. As above, we note that these numbers may not closely resemble reality, but we hypothesize that they are useful as a point of comparison.

Activities are grouped into the following categories: lectures, support (help desk, recitation, forums), active work (homework, labs, assignments, tests), studying, and other. When selecting other, students could report what behaviors were not captured under other categories. Students whose total percentages added to below 95% or above 105% were excluded from the analysis. Table 5 below reports the average percent allocation to each of these categories in the Spring 2018 sections.

Table 5. Self-reported average time allocation to five categories of class-related activities in the traditional and online sections.

	Traditional	Online
Lectures	28.5%	17.4%
Support	15.3%	4.3%
Active Work	47.9%	75.2%
Studying	9.6%	3.0%
Other	1.8%	1.6%

This report significantly unraveled the behavioral and performance differences observed previously. Online students report allocating their time significantly differently: over 75% of their time invested in the course is spent on active work, while less time is spent consuming lecture material, pursuing support opportunities, or studying in general. This difference in active learning time is statistically significant (X^2 = 25.405, p < 0.0001). Therefore, while online students spend less time on the class overall, they may spend more time actively engaged in practice.

An option to list "Other" activities intended to capture whether students included unanticipated activities in their time reported. Although "Other" time comprised a small percentage of the reported time, there were a few trends observed: check-ins, review sessions, practice on third-party sites, helping others, reading the textbook, and seeking additional resources for aid.

There may be several reasons for this difference. First, as noted when describing the course design, exercises are frequently interleaved with the lecture material, meaning that opportunities for practice are not relegated to homework or set-aside lab activities. Second, because the course assessments are automatically evaluated, grader time is not a concern: the number of assessments can be increased without demanding additional staff. Third, it has been observed that with pre-planning, pre-visualization, and video editing, recorded videos deliver the same content more efficiently [13]. Fourth, students have reported that because the course material is persistently available, they do not have as strong a need to visit the help desk or attend recitations: if they need additional instruction, the material itself is available. We hypothesize this builds on a perceived greater connectedness between instructional material and assessment in the online course: students in a traditional course may feel the need to consume as much instructional material as possible "just in case"; online, the material is persistently available; if they need it, they may revisit it.

4.4 Summary of Behavioral Differences

To summarize the observed differences, students in the online section are observed more heavily using the course forum, less heavily using the course help desk or recitations. They report spending less time on the course overall, but they report spending a much greater percentage of that time on active learning activities, and significantly less watching lecture videos, using supporting infrastructure, and studying in general.

5 Perceptual Differences

Prior research also noted different student perceptions of the value of certain course components, as well as the overall pace, rigor, and quality of the courses themselves [8][10]. To replicate as much of these previous studies as possible, we performed these analyses on this semester's data as well.

First, students completed 7-item Likert-scale items on the value of seven course components present in some form in both sections: lectures, a textbook, assignments, tests, recitations, the help desk, and the course forum. Results for the last three of these are presented in the previous section; results for the remaining four are in Table 6 below.

Table 6. Student perceptions of the value of four course elements on a 7-point Likert-scale. A Mann-Whitney U Test is used to test significant differences.

		Traditional	Online
Lectures	Mean	5.45	5.95
	Z, p	-3.9033, **< 0.0001**	
Textbook	Mean	4.06	4.09
	Z, p	-0.0698, 0.9442	
Assignments	Mean	6.02	6.45
	Z, p	-3.5154, **0.0004**	
Tests	Mean	4.86	5.35
	Z, p	-2.8416, **0.0045**	

In line with previous terms' results, lectures, assignments, and tests were rated as more valuable by students in the online section with statistical significance. Interestingly, while the textbook has been rated as more valuable by traditional students in the past, no difference was observed during this semester.

Secondly, students rated the perceived quality, quality compared to other college courses, pace, and rigor each on a 7-point Likert scale. Pace and rigor were both rated on scales of Way Too Slow/Easy (1) to Way Too Difficult/Fast (7), with About Right in the middle (4). Quality was rated on a scale of Bad (1) to Excellent (7). Quality compared to other classes was rated on a scale of Far Worst than Other Classes (1) to Far Better than Other Classes (7), with About the Same in the middle (4). The results of these questions are shown in Table 7 below.

Table 7. Student assessments of the pace, rigor, and quality of the two courses.

		Traditional	Online
Pace	Mean	4.17	4.06
	Z, p	0.9984, 0.3173	
Rigor	Mean	4.36	3.99
	Z, p	3.7624, **0.0002**	
Quality	Mean	5.47	5.98
	Z, p	-4.2195, **< 0.0001**	
Quality Compared	Mean	5.05	5.58
	Z, p	-5.2081, **< 0.0001**	

These results generally match prior semesters: pace and rigor in the online course have been reported as closer to "about right", and quality both on its own and compared to other courses has been rated higher in the online section. Altogether, 66.5% of 203 students in the traditional section and 85.1% of 175 students in the online section rate their class as better (5 or above) than other courses, a statistically significant difference (X^2 = 17.346, p < 0.0001). Moreover, 88.2% of those traditional students and 98.3% of those online students rate their class as at least as good (4 or above) as other college classes, another statistically significant difference (X^2 = 14.451, p < 0.0001).

6 Conclusion

This study has aimed to simultaneously replicate and unravel observed differences between students in parallel online and traditional versions of CS1. Prior work noted that students in the online and traditional versions of this university's CS1 course performed similarly, while this research found that instead, the online students actually achieved superior learning outcomes despite spending less time. In both cases, however, the implicit question exists: how were the online students able to learn as much or more in less time? Delving into this further, this research finds that the online students allocate their time differently, spending more time on active practice. Despite spending fewer total hours on the course material, they spend a greater amount of time on actively practicing.

Given that the courses are taught by different instructors, this could be a product of teacher differences. However, we note that there are several characteristics of the online medium that afford this altered behavior. First, prior research has suggested that video presents a more efficient medium for presenting content than live lecture [4][13], reducing the time students must spend on lecture-viewing. Second, the persistent availability of online

lectures means that students need not over-consume "just in case"; they may wait and consume lecture material as needed, further reducing their passive learning time. Third, the deep compatibility between online delivery and online automation means additional practice may be required without hiring additional human support to evaluate student work.

We thus hypothesize that a well-designed online course can achieve comparable or superior outcomes to a traditional course by taking advantage of the online delivery medium's ability to decrease time spent on passive learning and emphasize active practice. We do not hypothesize this to be inherent in online learning, but rather to be an opportunity that must be leveraged.

6.1 Limitations

Although many of these differences have now replicated across semesters, there remain two major limitations to this study. First, the instructors for the two sections are different. It is difficult to isolate the difference between online and traditional sections in general from the difference between these two instructors' classes. Both are award-winning instructors and specialists at their respective mediums, and so this study in many ways compares the ideal circumstances for an online class; it should be taken as evidence of the high potential of online delivery, not a guarantee that online delivery will be effective.

Second, given the generally universal high ratings given to the online section, there is the potential for a Halo effect [2]. Under this effect, students appreciate the course in general, and therefore give positive ratings to each individual component, regardless of whether they appreciate that component. Further research ought to elucidate how students leverage individual course components course without relying on self-report.

6.2 Future Work

This analysis has focused largely on reporting broad trends in the two classes rather than more specific relationships among the variables observed. Significant questions remain regarding many of these relationships. We know from prior research that there are relationships between which section is selected and factors like college major, race or ethnic identity, and level of employment; we do not yet know, however, if there are certain such sections that perform better in one section, and moreover whether students are likely to choose the section in which they are more likely to perform well. These questions have particular relevance given data that suggests that the types of students who choose online courses are often those less likely to succeed in them than in comparable traditional courses [7]. Similarly, future work may also look at how fine-grained behaviors correspond to student success, and whether we can automatically intervene with students demonstrating behaviors known to correlate to an increased likelihood of failure. Automated evaluation also provides rich opportunity for systematic evaluation of student answer patterns for tailoring individualized feedback or informing large-scale course revision. Work is underway to use automated clustering to examine patterns in student work [11].

REFERENCES

[1] Gail Chapman (2017, March). Inspire, Innovate, Improve!: What does this mean for CS for All? In *Proceedings of the 2017 ACM SIGCSE Technical Symposium on Computer Science Education,* 1-1. ACM Press.

[2] W. Timothy Coombs & Sherry J. Holladay (2006). Unpacking the halo effect: Reputation and crisis management. Journal of Communication Management, 10(2), 123-137.

[3] Ashok Goel & David A. Joyner (2016). An Experiment in Teaching Cognitive Systems Online. In Haynes, D. (Ed.) *International Journal for Scholarship of Technology-Enhanced Learning 1*(1).

[4] Philip J. Guo, Juho Kim, and Rob Rubin (2014, March). How video production affects student engagement: an empirical study of MOOC videos. In *Proceedings of the First ACM Conference on Learning @ Scale*, 41-50. ACM.

[5] Kimberly Colvin, John Champaign, Alwina Liu, Qian Zhou, Colin Fredericks, and David Pritchard (2014). Learning in an Introductory Physics MOOC: All Cohorts Learn Equally, Including an Online Class. The International Review of Research in Open and Distributed Learning, 15(4).

[6] Susan Dynarski (2018, January 19). Online Courses Fail Those Who Need Help. The New York Times, BU3.

[7] Hans P. Johnson and Marisol Cuellar Mejia (2014). Online learning and student outcomes in California's community colleges. Public Policy Institute.

[8] David A. Joyner (2018). Toward CS1 at Scale: Building and Testing a MOOC-for-Credit Candidate. In *Proceedings of the Fifth Annual ACM Conference on Learning @ Scale*. London, United Kingdom. ACM Press.

[9] David A. Joyner (2018). Intelligent Evaluation and Feedback in Support of a Credit-Bearing MOOC. In *Proceedings of the 19th International Conference on Artificial Intelligence in Education*. London, United Kingdom. Springer.

[10] David A. Joyner (2019). Building Purposeful Online Learning: Outcomes from Blending CS1. In Madden, A., Margulieux, L., Kadel, R., & Goel, A. (Eds) *Blended Learning in Practice*. MIT Press.

[11] David A. Joyner, Ryan Arrison, Mehnaz Ruksana, Evi Salguero, Zida Wang, Ben Wellington & Kevin Yin. From Clusters to Content: Using Code Clustering for Course Improvement (2019). In *Proceedings of the 50th ACM Technical Symposium on Computer Science Education*. Minneapolis, Minnesota, USA. ACM.

[12] Melinda McDaniel & David A. Joyner (2019). Online or In Person? Student Motivations in the Choice of a CS1 Experience. In *Proceedings of the 50th ACM Technical Symposium on Computer Science Education*. Minneapolis, Minnesota, USA. ACM.

[13] Chaohua Ou, Ashok Goel, David A. Joyner & Daniel Haynes (2016). Designing Videos with Pedagogical Strategies: Online Students' Perceptions of Their Effectiveness. In *Proceedings of the Third Annual ACM Conference on Learning @ Scale*. Edinburgh, Scotland. ACM.

[14] Miranda C. Parker, Mark Guzdial, & Shelly Engleman. (2016). Replication, Validation, and Use of a Language Independent CS1 Knowledge Assessment. In *Proceedings of the 2016 ACM Conference on International Computing Education Research*. ACM Press.

[15] Ry Rivard (2013). Citing disappointing student outcomes, San Jose State pauses work with Udacity. Inside Higher Ed. Retrieved from http://bit.ly/2F3QvZ

[16] Eric S. Roberts (2011). Meeting the challenges of rising enrollments. *ACM Inroads, 2*(3), 4-6.

[17] Kelsey Sheehy. (2012, April). Computer Science Transitions From Elective to Requirement. *US News & World Report*. Retrieved from https://www.usnews.com/education/best-colleges/articles/2012/04/03/computer-science-transitions-from-elective-to-requirement-computer-science-transitions-from-elective-to-requirement

[18] Jostein Steene-Johannessen, Sigmund A. Anderssen, Ingrid JM Hendriksen, Alan E. Donnelly, Soren Brage& Ulf Ekelund. (2016). Are Self-report Measures Able to Define Individuals as Physically Active or Inactive? *Medicine and Science in Sports and Exercise, 48*(2), 235.

Automatic Clustering of Different Solutions to Programming Assignments in Computing Education

Lei Gao
School of Computer Science and
Technology, Xidian University
Xi'an, China
gaolei_oriana@163.com

Bo Wan
School of Computer Science and
Technology, Xidian University
Xi'an, China
wanbo@xidian.edu.cn

Cheng Fang
School of Computer Science and
Technology, Xidian University
Xi'an, China
alanfangmail@sina.com

Yangyang Li
School of Computer Science and
Technology, Xidian University
Xi'an, China
lyyzwift02@163.com

Chen Chen
School of Computer Science and
Technology, Xidian University
Xi'an, China
sunshinenanjiao@163.com

ABSTRACT

A computer programming assignment may have various solutions, and extracting them is of great significance for both teaching and learning. However, it could be challenging for instructors and students to identify the differences between those solutions if they are on a large scale. Since code similarity is of vital importance in identifying the differences between solutions, we review previous researches on code similarity and design a neural network-based algorithm for detecting the similarity between codes in a pair as well as identifying the features that have a big impact on code similarity. Then we develop a clustering algorithm based on code similarity that can automatically generate clusters for all correct solutions to a given programming assignment. Our experiment demonstrates that the clustering algorithm can successfully obtain distinctive clusters in our dataset. Our analysis of typical solutions can provide inspirations for instructors and students.

CCS CONCEPTS

• **Social and professional topics** → **Computing education**; • **Applied computing** → **Computer-assisted instruction**;

KEYWORDS

code clustering; code similarity; neural network; programming education

ACM Reference Format:
Lei Gao, Bo Wan, Cheng Fang, Yangyang Li, and Chen Chen. 2019. Automatic Clustering of Different Solutions to Programming Assignments in Computing Education. In *ACM Global Computing Education Conference 2019 (CompEd '19), May 17–19, 2019, Chengdu,Sichuan, China*. ACM, New York, NY, USA, 7 pages. https://doi.org/10.1145/3300115.3309515

1 INTRODUCTION

With the popularity of online teaching, more and more people have easy access to various courses, especially programming courses. In a programming course, students are usually given programming assignments. However, for one assignment they may submit a large number of solutions, many of which are similar and some, unique. Those with significant differences can be used as valuable teaching resources. Through these various solutions, teachers can have a good knowledge of students' learning process and offer more accurate and specific feedback. However, it would be a tedious job for the instructor to select useful solutions from a large number of solutions submitted.

And peer review is commonly adopted in the traditional classroom, which can help students learn from their peers [16]. In online programming courses, however, learning from others is hardly possible. Students may encounter difficulties in trying to revise and improve their codes or even their thoughts on solving problems. The only feedback they can receive is whether their submissions are failed or passed, which is done by a test suite of input-output pairs. Therefore, it is particularly necessary to expose students to different typical solutions, since students' programming competence can be improved after reading codes produced by others [9, 18].

Unfortunately, few studies on code clustering focus on identifying typical solutions among a variety of solutions submitted, which, however, can provide valuable feedback for instructors and students. To our knowledge, in the community of computing education, most researchers analyze students' solutions from a low level perspective (correctness, textual and structural difference, and so on) rather than from a high level perspective(method of solving problems). In this paper, we aim to identify different kinds of solutions and even pick out interesting solutions as our examples. As we all know, correct solutions to one assignment may vary in many dimensions. To specifically evaluate each type of solution, we have studied the main algorithms for computing code similarity, including attribute-based, grammar-based and semantic-based approaches [2, 7, 13, 14]. In our work, we used different kinds of similarities of code pairs as code features, and developed our code clustering algorithm on the basis of the clustering algorithm. This algorithm can provide different clusters.

In this paper, we introduced three classical algorithms for computing code similarity, and realized them in preparation for future work. Because each code pair has different kinds of similarities, which can be regarded as different features of each code pair, we took the neural network algorithm into consideration and employed these code similarities as our training data. Finally, with five kinds of precomputed similarities, we set up a neural network model that can identify the similarity between codes in a pair with an accuracy of 90.8%. We also built other neural network models through the five precomputed code similarities and identified the importance of different kinds of similarities. Based on those efforts, we designed our code clustering algorithm on the basis of the spectral clustering algorithm. Then we conducted experiments with the dataset of the online judge (OJ) system of our university. The experiment results suggest that our clustering algorithm can produce different clusters for different programming assignments. Our analysis of typical solutions can provide useful feedback for instructors and students.

The main contributions of our work are as follows:

First, we summarized and analyzed current code similarity detection algorithms and implemented them in our experiments, which had never been done in prior work.

We also proposed a novel similarity detection algorithm based on the neural network and identified the importance of each kind of similarity.

Finally, we proposed a clustering algorithm for clustering students' correct solutions based on the spectral algorithm and verified its effectiveness via solutions submitted to four program assignments.

2 RELATED WORK

2.1 Code Similarity

Researches on code similarity detection have been developed for about 40 years and all these detection approaches can be roughly classified into three categories, attribute-based, grammar-based and semantic-based.

The attribute-based approach mainly compute similarity by using attribute features of the source code, including code style, annotation style and statistical features. Parker [13] listed a general algorithm to measure similarity using attribute features. The advantage of this method is that it will not be affected by the programming language, and it is unnecessary to analyze the syntax structure of the code. Its disadvantage is also obvious in that it is a global code measurement pattern and cannot analyze the similarity of part of a code.

The grammar-based method mainly analyzes the lexical information of a program. The typical grammar-based method is to compare Token-sequence [7], which first puts the source code into a lexical analyzer and converts it into token-sequences, and then replaces the actual source code in the next process. Finally the matching algorithm is used to detect the similarity between the token-sequences of the program. Besides, the practice of comparing token-sequences is widely adopted in code similarity detection and proves efficient in large-scale clone detection [7].

The semantic-based algorithms mainly analyzes the structure information and execution process of a program, including AST (Abstract Syntax Tree) and PDG (Program Dependency Graph).

AST is an intermediate representation of the compiling process of a program, which can explicitly express the syntax structure and includes all the static information. This method detects the code similarity by calculating the similarity between sub-trees of different ASTs. Fu et al. [2] proposed an improved method called Abstract Syntax Tree Kernel for computing code similarity, which has good performance. PDG [1] can represent the data relationship and the control and dependency relationship of codes. It can analyze programs at the semantic level but causes a big waste of time in constructing and comparing the program dependency graphs. All the methods above are suitable for program plagiarism detection, which, however, is not the focus of this paper.

2.2 Code Clustering

There are some existing researches on code clustering, which use only one indicator as their clustering criterion. For example, [8, 15] employed SOLO taxonomy to categorize students' SOLO level by their ability to explain solutions. This method shows that students perform better in exams the higher SOLO level they can reach. Besides, Luxton-Reilly et al. [11] proposed that different solutions have different structural variations, which can be illustrated by control flow graphs, and that clustering can be done by grouping these graphs. That is, all the students' solutions that own the same structure are classified into a category. Overcode [3] is a visualized system that can rename variables that behave the same way, and group solutions whose variables take the same sequences of values when executed. The system uses the dynamic information (sequence of variable values) of each solution to cluster tasks. This is different from all other methods that use static information. However, it may cost more storage space. Mou et al. [12] proposed a tree-based convolutional neural network by training a program vector presentation based on ASTs to classify tasks. Their model can only identify low-level information, such as data reference, control flow and declarations.

What's more, Glassman et al. [4] used multi-features to cluster students' solutions. In their work, they selected 12 high-level and 48 low-level code features from 50 students' solutions, then they used k-means to achieve the final result. In fact, their work was supervised clustering, which requiresd manual clustering labels. This method was not suitable for large-scale sample clustering. Other literature [5, 6] focuses on clustering correct and incorrect solutions and providing feedbacks on incorrect solutions.

In contrast, our code clustering algorithm employed multiple indicators, which makes it more reliable, and can help automatically generate clusters for all correct solutions.

3 METHOD

From previous studies, we have summarized three different approaches which measure codes from different aspects to compute the similarity between two programs. To fully utilize this effort to help our clustering algorithm, we reproduced the attribute-based, grammar-based and semantic-based approaches.

The attribute-based approach regards the program as text, extracting such information as word frequency, sentence length and other static information from the code to form the metric element of the code. In our experiment, we chose 7 code style features and

4 annotation style features[1] (listed on the website in Section 4.2) to identify the program style. According to Parker [13], 5 features which occur with high frequency are selected as statistical features. Suppose the code set to be detected is P1, P2, ..., and Pn, and any piece of code Px in this set has three features, code style: CS=$\langle a_1x, a_2x, \ldots, a_7x \rangle$, annotation style: $AS = \langle b_1x, b_2x, \ldots, b_4x \rangle$ and statistical features: $SC = \langle c_1x, c_2x, \ldots, c_5x \rangle$. The Euclidean distance is used to detect the attribute feature similarity between Pi and Pj of any two codes in the code set.Take the calculation of the code style as an example:

$$D(P_i, P_j) = \sqrt{\frac{\sum_{u=1}^{7}(a_{ui} - a_{uj})^2}{7}} \quad (1)$$

The grammar-based approach refers mainly to the Token Sequences method, which can be divided into four parts [19]: preprocessing, lexical analysis, code block comparison and similarity calculation.

1) Preprocessing: this part deals mainly with the functionally independent parts of the code. Characters that do not affect the semantics are set to empty during preprocessing, such as macro definition, annotation, TAB, enter, white-space, etc.

2) Lexical analysis: input the preprocessed source code information, then achieve the code token according to certain lexical rules [19].

3) Code block comparison: to compare the token-sequences of two pieces of code, we use LCS (longest common subsequence) to compare and analyze them.

4) Similarity calculation: the formula for calculating the similarity between Code A and Code B is as follows:

$$Sim_\alpha = \frac{2 * LCS(A, B)}{Length_A + Length_B} \quad (2)$$

In our work, the sematic-based approach we applied is to compare the abstract syntax trees, which is an intermediate representation of a source program. In the process of compiling, a representation of the tree structure can be formed by lexical analysis and syntax analysis. We obtained AST by parsing the source code using the python's third-party library called "pycparser". Then, we used a tree kernel method [2] to compare the similarity of two ASTs generated by two pieces of code. This method can be applied in the field of natural language processing to calculate the similarity of two segments. The number of identical sub-trees of two ASTs can be calculated by the following formula:

$$K(T_1, T_2) = \sum_{S_1 \in S_{T_1}} \sum_{S_2 \in S_{T_2}} C(S_1, S_2) \quad (3)$$

where S_{T_1} and S_{T_2} denote the set of all sub-trees in T_1 and T_2. $C(S_1, S_2)$ is the number of all the identical sub-trees of the current rootsS_1, S_2, which is obtained through computation. After computing the kernel value $K(T_1, T_2)$ between T_1 and T_2, a normalization is needed to obtain the similarity between 0 and 1.

3.1 Neural network model for similarity detection

In recent years, deep neural networks have an excellent learning ability in image classification, speech recognition and natural language processing, etc. We hold that identifying whether a pair of

codes are similar can be considered as a binary classification task, which can be easily solved by deep neural networks [20]. And advance programming languages, having their own features and rules, are easily represented by numeric feature vectors. Thus, we proposed a neural network approach to detect the similarity between source codes.

In our work, each similarity obtained through computation is viewed as a feature of a compared code pair. Thus, we used 5 features computed by the above algorithms (3 attribute similarities, 1 token similarity, and 1 AST similarity) as our input feature vector. We built our neural network,which contains 5 input layer nodes and 1 output layer node. The ground-truth of the similarity of each code pair is jointly determined by two teaching assistants. We hold that similarity cannot be measured from a single perspective. For example, the code pairs may be similar in code structure but different in grammar. Therefore, we consider manual similarity a suitable golden standard. The teaching assistants generally ignore low-level features and follow a basic rule that solutions can be regarded as different if students' thoughts on solving problems are different. When their opinions are inconsistent, the third teaching assistant's opinion will be decisive.

In our experiment, we selected 200 solutions to Assignment 1,169 solutions to Assignment 2, 242 solutions to Assignment 3 and 189 solutions to Assignment 4 from the dataset. We chose TensorFlow as our training tool, which is an open-source software library used to do research on deep neural networks. The different similarity values of code pairs obtained were used as our input feature vectors. Continuous parameters adjustment and iterative training were implemented. Then our neural network model can determine whether two pieces of code are similar or not (the output node of 1 denoting similar and that of 0, not similar).The number of hidden-layer nodes is set to 10,and the training steps and the learning rate are set to 50000 and 0.1, respectively.

Table 1: Different models with different feature combination

Rank	Feature combination	Accuracy rate
1	TS&AST&SF&CS&AS	0.908333
2	TS & AST	0.858333
3	TS & AS & AST	0.85
4	TS & SF	0.85
5	TS & AS	0.85
6	TS & SF & AST	0.841667

CS: code style   AS: annotation style   SF: statistical feature
TS: token-sequence   AST: abstract syntax tree

In **Table 1**, we show the top 6 performances of different neural network models with different feature combinations as input vectors. We can draw a conclusion that the best performance can be achieved when all the features are trained in our model. Namely, the more features are used as input vectors, the higher accuracy is probably achieved. And it is found that the feature combinations with TS(token-sequence) and AST(Abstract Syntax Tree) as input vectors have better performance than other cases.

3.2 Code Clustering algorithm

According to the above work, we propose a novel code clustering algorithm based on spectral clustering to get exact clusters and typical program examples. The spectral clustering [19] is based on the spectral theory, its essence being to transform clustering into the optimal partitioning of graphs. It is a point-pair clustering algorithm which can be used to deal with similarity values between code pairs.

When constructing the similarity matrix W in the following steps, we fully utilized the conclusion we drew in the similarity detection research.We assigned different weights to five kinds of similarities, producing our comprehensive similarity matrix W (Token-sequence-0.4, AST-0.3, code style-0.1, annotation style-0.1, and statistic feature-0.1). The weights of five similarities were rounded by counting the rankings of all the neural network models with corresponding similarities. Specifically, the higher the models ranked in similarity detection, the higher scores were assigned to these models, and each kind of similarity used in these models could get corresponding scores. Then we accumulated scores for each similarity and the ratios of the score of each similarity to the total score were regarded as the weights of these similarities. Each element of the similarity matrix W can be calculated by the following formula:

$$W(i,j) = Sim_{(TS)} * 0.4 + Sim_{(AST)} * 0.3 + Sim_{(AS)} * 0.1$$
$$+ Sim_{(CS)} * 0.1 + Sim_{(SF)} * 0.1 \tag{4}$$

The algorithm steps [10, 17] are as follows:

Step1: Construct the similarity matrix W. The dimension of W depends on the number of solutions to be clustered. In this step, we consider the similarity between code pairs is analogous to the distance between two data points. Therefore, the similarity between code pairs is directly used as matrix elements, while in the original spectral clustering, it should be computed as the pairwise distance between data points.

Step2: Construct the degree matrix D and Laplacian matrix. Degree matrix D's main diagonal element is D(i,i), which is the sum of the elements of the i-th column in the similarity matrix W, and all other non-main diagonal elements are 0. Then, we get Laplacian matrix L=D-W.

Step3: Compute the first k eigenvectors v1, v2... and vk of Laplacian matrix L.

Step4: Let $v \in R^{n*k}$ be the matrix X which has the vectors v1, v2..., and vk as columns. After normalizing the row vector of matrix X, X is noted as Y.

Step5: See each row of Y as a sample in space R_k(the number of samples being n and the sample dimension, k), then use the K-means algorithm for clustering.

Step6:The i-th code is categorized into the j-th cluster if and only if the i-th row of matrix Y is categorized into the j-th cluster.

4 EXPERIMENT RESULTS

4.1 The Dataset

To evaluate our proposed method, we used the dataset of the pedagogical programming online judge (OJ) system, where students submit their solutions to certain problems and get feedback about their correctness. All the source codes are written in the C language, and correct solutions and the corresponding problems' IDs are downloaded as our dataset. To analyze the clustering results in the following part, Assignment 1 and Assignment 4 are described as follows:

- Assignment1: PM2.5

Please calculate the maximum fluctuation of PM2.5(particulate matter) in the past few days, or the maximum absolute value of the difference between the PM2.5 value of one day and the that of the previous day.

- Assignment4: Password Strength

Assume that the password consists of four types of characters: uppercase, lowercase, numeric and non-alphanumeric symbols. 0 point for null password, and 1 point for non-null password; 1 point for password whose length exceeds 8 bits; 1 point for password which includes two different characters, 2 points for password which includes three different characters, and 3 points for password which includes four different characters. The calculated password strength ranges from 0 to 5.

4.2 Clustering Results

The primary clustering results are shown in **Figure 1**.

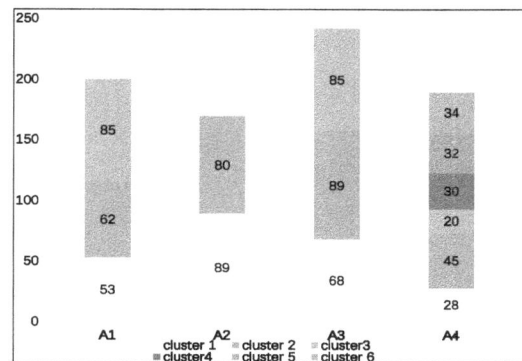

Figure 1: Solutions distribution of A1 ,A2,A3 and A4

We ultimately obtained 3 clusters for the programe code of PM2.5. The numbers of solutions included in each cluster is 53, 62, and 85 respectively. After analyzing those codes, we found that the logic structure of the solutions in C1, C2 and C3 are nearly the same. First, they get input values by a for statement, then compute the difference between adjacent values, and finally print the biggest difference. Interestingly, we found that the average length of solutions in C2 **(Figure 2a)** is shorter than that in C1 and C3, which may result from the use of concise statements to compute and compare the maximum differences. Additionally, the solutions in C3 **(Figure 2b)** usually use more complicated statements, more than 2 for statements, for example, to get the results even by declaring the custom functions such as Abs() and Max().

The clustering result of the password strength suggests that there are 28, 45, 20, 30, 32, 34 solutions respectively in each cluster. These solutions commonly have two parts, one part identifying whether the password contains uppercase, lowercase, numeric or

(a)   (b)

```
#include<stdio.h>
int main(){
  int a [50]={0};
  int n,i,max=0,c,k;
  scanf("%d",&n);
  for(i=0;i<n;i++){
    scanf("%d",&a[i]);
  }
  for(k=0;k<n-1;k++){
    c=a[k+1]-a[k];
    if(c<0) c=0-c;
    if(c>max) max=c;
  }
  printf("%d",max);
  return 0;

}
```

```
#include<stdio.h>
#include<math.h>
int  main()
{
  int n;
  scanf("%d",&n);
  int pi[n];
  int num[n-1];
  for(int i=0;i<n;i++)
  {
    scanf("%d",&pi[i]);
  }
  for(int j=0;j<n-1;j++)
  {
    num[j]=fabs(pi[j+1]-pi[j]);
  }
  int max=num[0];
  for(int h=1;h<n-1;h++)
  {
    if(max<num[h])
    {
      max=num[h];
    }
  }
  printf("%d",max);
  return 0;
}
```

Figure 2: Example solution in C2 and C3 to PM2.5

(a)   (b)

```
#include<stdio.h>
#include<string.h>
int main()
{
  char code[100];
  gets(code);
  int len,grade=0;
  len=strlen(code);
  if(len==0)  grade=0;
  else grade++;
  if(len>8) grade++;
  int i;
  int level1=0,level2=0,level3=0,level4=0;
  int temp=0,;
  for(i=0;i<len;i++)
  {
    if(code[i]<='9'&&code[i]>='0')
    {
      level1=1; temp=1;}
    if(code[i]<='z'&&code[i]>='a')
    {
      level2=1;  temp=1;}
    if(code[i]<='Z'&&code[i]>='A')
      level3=1; temp=1;}
    if(temp==0) level4=1;
      temp=0;
  }
  int sum;  sum=level1+level2+level3+level4;
  if(sum==2) grade=grade+1;
  if(sum==3) grade=grade+2;
  if(sum==4) grade=grade+3;

  printf("%d",grade);
}
```

```
#include<stdio.h>
#include<string.h>
int main(){
  int score=0,t=0;
  char a [50]={0};
  gets(a);
  if(strlen(a)>0)
    score++;
  else    goto label;
  if(strlen(a)>8)
    score++;
  for(int i=0;i<strlen(a)&&a[i ]!='\0'; i++){
    if(a[i]>='0'&&a[i ]<='9') {
      t++;
      break;
    }
  }
  for(int i=0;i<strlen(a)&&a[i ]!='\0'; i++){
    if(a[i]>='a'&&a[i]<='z') {
      t++;
      break;
    }
  }
  for(int i=0;i<strlen(a)&&a[i ]!='\0'; i++){
    if(a[i]>='A'&&a[i]<='Z'){
      t++;
      break;
    }
  }
  for(int i=0;i<strlen(a)&&a[i ]!='\0'; i++){
    if((a[i]>='a'&&a[i]<='z') ||( a[i]>='A'&&
       a[i]<='Z') ||( a[i]>='0'&&a[i
       ]<='9') ) ;
    else         {
      t++;
      break;
    }
  }
  score+=t-1;
label: printf("%d",score);
  return 0;
}
```

Figure 3: Example solution in C1 and C6 to Password Strength

(a)   (b)

```
#include<stdio.h>
int A(char s);
int B(int a,int c,int d,int e);
int main(){
  char s [51];
  int dzm=0,xzm=0,sz=0,ot=0,i,num=0,aLL=0;

  for(i=1;i<=51;i++)
  s[i]=0;
  i=0;
  while((s[i]=getchar()) !='\n')
  {
    switch(A(s[i++]))
    {
      case  0:sz=1;break;
      case  1:xzm=1;break;
      case  2:dzm=1;break;
      case  3:ot=1;break;
    }
    num++;
  }
  aLL=B(sz,xzm,dzm,ot,num);
  printf("%d",aLL);
  return 0;
}
int A(char s)
{
  if (s>='0'&&s <='9')
  return 0;
  else if (s>='a'&&s<='z')
  return 1;
  else  if (s>='A'&&s<='Z')
  return 2;
  else
  return 3;
}
int B(int a,int b,int c,int d,int e)
{
  int num=0,sum;
  sum=a+b+c+d;

  if (sum==2)
    num++;
  else  if (sum==3)
    num+=2;
  else  if (sum==4)
    num+=3;
  if(e!=0)
    num++;
  if(e>=8)
    num++;
  return num;
}
```

```
#include <stdio.h>
#include <string.h>
int main(){
  char a [100]={'\0'};
  int power=0;
  int i ;
  int w=0,x=0,y=0,z=0;
  gets(a);
  if (strlen(a)!=0){
    power++;
  }
  if (strlen(a)>8){
    power++;
  }
  for(i=0;a[i ]!='\0'; i++){

    if(a[i]>='0'&&a[i ]<='9') {
      w++;
    }
    else  if(a[i]>='a'&&a[i]<='z' ) {
      x++;
    }
    else  if(a[i]>='A'&&a[i]<='z'){
      y++;
    }
    else{
      z++;
    }
  }
  if (w!=0&&x!=0&&y!=0&&z!=0){
    power+=3;
  }
  else  if (( w==0&&x!=0&&y!=0&&z!=0)||(w!=0&&x
    ==0&&y!=0&&z!=0)||(w!=0&&x!=0&&y
    ==0&&z!=0)||(w!=0&&x!=0&&y!=0&&z
    ==0)){
    power+=2;
  }
  else  if (( w==0&&x==0&&y!=0&&z!=0)||(w==0&&x
    !=0&&y==0&&z!=0)||(w==0&&x!=0&&y
    !=0&&z==0)||(w!=0&&x==0&&y==0&&z
    !=0)||(w!=0&&x==0&&y!=0&&z==0)||(w
    !=0&&x!=0&&y==0&&z==0)){
    power+=1;
  }
  else  if (w==0&&x==0&&y==0&&z==0){
    power+=0;
  }
  else {
    power+=0;
  }
  printf("%d",power);

  return 0;
}
```

Figure 4: Example solution in C2 and C3 to Password Strength

non-alphanumeric symbols, and the other part being about the calculation of password strength. It is found that most solutions in C1 only use one for statement and some if/else statements to identify different characters (**Figure 3a**). In contrast, solutions in C6 prefer to use several for statements to finish the same task (**Figure 3b**).

We also find that the solutions in C2 self-define diverse functions for different needs and then call them in the main function (**Figure 4a**). Specifically, the solutions in C3 seem to have a distinctive feature that they employ many **"&&"**('and' logical operators) when they identify whether the password includes different characters, which account for a significant portion of the code as is shown in **Figure 4b**. We also employed the systematic sampling method to select example solutions in the same cluster, which can be seen on this website.[1] The sampling method follows the basic rules: first, we divide the solutions in the same cluster into 10 categories according to the ending number of their submission ID, and then we randomly sample one solution in each category.

Our programs were run on a workstation Intel Xeon E5 2.1GHz with 128GB of RAM. Our clustering algorithm can get clustering results after running immediately. However, the time spent on precomputing similarity between code pairs could be different if assignments have different levels of difficulty and numbers of solutions.

---

[1] https://github.com/fclearner/Code-Clustering

4.3 Validation study

To further assess the effectiveness of our clustering method, we recruited 15 participants who had been engaged in programming education for more than 3 years for our test. Ten solutions were randomly selected from each cluster of different assignments (140 solutions in total), and the participants completed the evaluation questions upon finishing reading and comparing those solutions. Questions are listed below and the evaluation results use the 5-point Likert scale ranging from 1 (strongly disagree) to 5 (strongly agree).

•**Q1:** Do you think the clustering method is helpful in understanding students' programming proficiency?

•**Q2:** Do you think the clustering method is helpful in improving the programming education?

As we have expected, the result of Q1 indicates that approximately **92%** of the participants feel that the clustering method is helpful in understanding students' programming proficiency. That is, students' solutions in different clusters can basically represent the typical solutions to these assignments, and can provide feedback for instructors at a macro level. According to the results of Q2, approximately **85%** of the participants agree that our clustering method is helpful in improving the programming education.

According to participants' subjective feedback, most of them feel solutions in the same cluster are similar, while some think that some solutions are ambiguous and that they can not judge whether these solutions are reasonably grouped into the current cluster.

We also made a survey of students' feedback about clustering results. We selected 15 students who had once submitted the 4 assignments as our participants. For each assignment, every participant was provided with 10 solutions grouped in the same cluster as their own solutions and 5 solutions in each different cluster. Questions for students are listed below:

•**Q1:** Do you think your solution is similar to the solutions which are grouped into the same cluster as your code?

•**Q2:** Do you think you have been inspired by reading the code from other groups?

•**Q3:** Do you think you have been inspired by reading the code from other groups in terms of problem-solving methods?

The majority of the students (**86.7%**) believe that their solutions are similar to the solutions grouped into the same cluster as theirs. After they have read solutions from other different clusters, **78.3%** of the students think they can acquire inspiration from others' codes and roughly **60%** clearly agree that they can benefit in learning problem-solving methods. Besides, we also asked students some open questions. Some of them said they could have used some existing library functions rather than define similar functions, such as Abs(), which can make code simpler. In addition, a student who used a solution similar to C3 in Assignment4 realized that students could use some variables to present different conditions instead of listing all possible conditions with redundant logical operators. Another student whose solution was grouped in C6 in Assignment4 said it could use flags to judge different situations while traversing in the same for statement. On the other hand, a few students argued that most solutions have no obvious differences in terms of problem-solving method except for different ways of dealing with input data. We assume that these assignments may be introductory with fixed

steps of solving problems, thus failing to provide more inspirations for them.

5 DISCUSSION

The above findings indicate that our code clustering method has a positive effect on clustering solutions. Both teachers and students can benefit from the clustering results. Take the password strength assignment for example. Comparing example solutions in C1 and C6, we consider it better for students to use fewer for statements for similar tasks, which makes it easier to read and reduce the length of the code. In addition, although it is reasonable for many solutions in C3 to use a load of logical operators to identify different cases, this practice may not be the most preferable compared with other clusters. Last but not the least, in the four assignments, we find some clusters include self-defined functions, which can help teachers find valuable and unique methods from the submitted solutions.

A worthwhile further study would be to show students different types of solutions produced by others. As Zeller[18]proposed, students are likely to get inspirations from reading different codes, especially when they are provided with some targeted solutions that they have never thought of, so that they can make progress by self-teaching instead of being instructed by teachers.

Besides, the number of different solutions to one assignment could be limited. When the clustering method is applied for several rounds, we suppose that we can obtain some stable clusters which can be used as standard solutions and even employed in the automatic grading approach. Students can immediately get their own scores when their solutions are submitted and grouped into corresponding clusters.

Finally, we believe the neural network model we proposed for similarity detection has a potential application in plagiarism detection when combined with existing code comparison techniques. The model remains to be improved and can be compared with some plagiarism detection tools mentioned in[7, 14] in terms of accuracy.

6 CONCLUSION

In this work we exploited different kinds of code similarities as features of code pairs for similarity detection. We also developed a novel clustering algorithm based on similarity to analyze students' solutions to their programming assignments. Our experiments show that the clustering algorithm can automatically generate definite clusters for solutions to given programming assignments, which can provide insights into different kinds of solutions for both teachers and students. There remain some limitations in our study. Our method deals only with solutions written in the C Language. And there is no distinct difference between the solutions in a very few clusters and those in the majority. The minority of clusters still need to be described by some interpretable features.

In the future, we intend to validate our clustering algorithm with larger datasets and more challenging programming assignments. Besides, we may add the runtime of each solutions as a clustering indicator. Having identified different clusters of solutions, we hope to enhance the interpretability of each type of solutions. Finally, we plan to integrate our algorithms into the online judge system of our university and make some large-scale surveys of student feedback.

REFERENCES

[1] Jeanne Ferrante, Karl J Ottenstein, and Joe D Warren. 1987. The program dependence graph and its use in optimization. *ACM Trasactions on Programming Languages & Systems* 9, 3 (1987), 125–132.

[2] Deqiang Fu, Yanyan Xu, Haoran Yu, and Boyang Yang. 2017. WASTK: A Weighted Abstract Syntax Tree Kernel Method for Source Code Plagiarism Detection. *Scientific Programming,2017,(2017-02-13)* (2017).

[3] Elena L Glassman, Jeremy Scott, Rishabh Singh, Philip J Guo, and Robert C Miller. 2015. OverCode: Visualizing variation in student solutions to programming problems at scale. *ACM Transactions on Computer-Human Interaction (TOCHI)* 22, 2, 7.

[4] Elena L. Glassman, Rishabh Singh, and Robert C. Miller. 2014. Feature engineering for clustering student solutions. In *ACM Conference on Learning @ Scale Conference*. 171–172.

[5] Sumit Gulwani, Ivan Radiček, and Florian Zuleger. 2018. Automated Clustering and Program Repair for Introductory Programming Assignments. (2018), 465–480.

[6] Shalini Kaleeswaran, Anirudh Santhiar, Aditya Kanade, and Sumit Gulwani. 2016. Semi-supervised verified feedback generation. In *Proceedings of the 2016 24th ACM SIGSOFT International Symposium on Foundations of Software Engineering*. ACM, 739–750.

[7] Toshihiro Kamiya, Shinji Kusumoto, and Katsuro Inoue. 2002. CCFinder: A Multilinguistic Token-Based Code Clone Detection System for Large Scale Source Code. *IEEE Transactions on Software Engineering* 28, 7 (2002), 654–670.

[8] Raymond Lister, Tony Clear, Simon, Dennis J. Bouvier, Paul Carter, Anna Eckerdal, Mike Lopez, Robert Mccartney, and Phil Robbins. 2010. Naturally occurring data as research instrument:analyzing examination responses to study the novice programmer. *ACM SIGCSE Bulletin* 41, 4 (2010), 156–173.

[9] Mike Lopez, Jacqueline Whalley, Phil Robbins, and Raymond Lister. 2008. Relationships between reading, tracing and writing skills in introductory programming. In *International Workshop on Computing Education Research*. 101–112.

[10] Ulrike Luxburg. 2007. *A tutorial on spectral clustering*. Kluwer Academic Publishers. 395–416 pages.

[11] Andrew Luxton-Reilly, Paul Denny, Diana Kirk, Ewan Tempero, and Se Young Yu. 2013. On the differences between correct student solutions. In *ACM Conference on Innovation & Technology in Computer Science Education*.

[12] Lili Mou, Ge Li, Zhi Jin, Lu Zhang, and Tao Wang. 2014. TBCNN: A Tree-Based Convolutional Neural Network for Programming Language Processing. *Eprint Arxiv* (2014).

[13] Alan Parker and James O Hamblen. 1989. Computer algorithms for plagiarism detection. *IEEE Transactions on Education* 32, 2 (1989), 94–99.

[14] Chaiyong Ragkhitwetsagul, Jens Krinke, and David Clark. 2017. A comparison of code similarity analysers. *Empirical Software Engineering* 9 (2017), 1–56.

[15] Judy Sheard. 2008. Going SOLO to assess novice programmers. *ACM SIGCSE Bulletin* 40, 3 (2008), 209–213.

[16] Harald Sondergaard. 2009. Learning from and with peers:the different roles of student peer reviewing. *ACM SIGCSE Bulletin* 41, 3 (2009), 31–35.

[17] Serafeim Tsironis, Mauro Sozio, Michalis Vazirgiannis, and LE Poltechnique. 2013. Accurate spectral clustering for community detection in mapreduce. In *Advances in Neural Information Processing Systems (NIPS) Workshops*. Citeseer.

[18] Andreas Zeller. 2000. Making students read and review code. *ACM SIGCSE Bulletin* 32, 3 (2000), 89–92.

[19] Jiujie Zhang, Chunhui Wang, Liping Zhang, Min Hou, and Dongsheng Liu. 2015. Clone code detection based on Levenshtein distance of token. *Journal of Computer Applications* (2015).

[20] Jure Zupan. 1994. Introduction to artificial neural network (ANN) methods: what they are and how to use them. *Acta Chimica Slovenica* 41 (1994), 327–327.

Birds of a Feather

Introductory Concurrency and Parallelism Education

Nasser Giacaman, *University of Auckland*
Joel Adams, *Calvin College*
Contact: n.giacaman@auckland.ac.nz

Undergraduate or novice programmers are often challenged by higher-level and abstract concepts in programming courses. Compared to constructing a sequential program, parallel and concurrent programming requires a different and more complex mental model of control flow. Now that multi-core processors have become the norm for computers and mobile devices, the responsibility of developing software to take advantage of this extra computing power now rests with the modern software developer. In recognition of this new era, curricula guidelines have been proposed specifically targeting the complex world of parallel and distributed computing. CS2013 also recognizes this with a dedicated Parallel and Distributed Computing knowledge area with core hours, as well as dispersing parallelism concepts across other fundamental knowledge areas. Parallel programming was once considered an advanced area of computing, and only taught to students by experts in graduate-level elective courses. However, *it is now expected that all undergraduate computing students will become familiar with the fundamentals of parallelism.* Concurrency and parallelism concepts are undoubtedly difficult for students to learn. This can even be daunting for teachers that are inexperienced with all elements of the underlying parallelism concepts, but even more daunting is devising pedagogically-sound materials that will allow undergraduate students to grasp the concepts. This is especially challenging for early undergraduate courses where students are often novice programmers, barely confident in sequential programming let alone parallel programming. This session will provide an opportunity for instructors to discuss and share ideas and experiences in this area, as well as explore potential collaboration opportunities.

Keywords: Concurrency; Parallel Programming; Multi-Core; Multi-Threading

DOI: https://doi.org/10.1145/3300115.3312505

Evolution and Revolution of Computer Systems Courses with the Open RISC-V ISA

Ke Zhang,
Institute of Computing Technology of Chinese Academy of Sciences; University of Chinese Academy of Sciences
Contact: zhangke@ict.ac.cn

Computer systems courses, including computer organization, architecture, operating system, compiler, and other relevant courses, play an important role in cultivating students' computational thinking, especially the ability of viewing hardware and software in a computer system as a whole. In order to help learners to better understand principles and concepts taught in lectures of aforementioned courses, some visionary instructors have started to design lab projects for their courses with real-world instruction set architectures (ISAs), such as MIPS, ARM and x86, or even request students to conduct projects on these ISAs-based hardware platforms. Meanwhile, with the overwhelming trend towards AI, IoT and heterogeneous computing, RISC-V, an open and free ISA, has emerged and recently attracted a lot of attention from both academia and industry. Compared with proprietary ISAs, RISC-V is more simple, affordable, extensible and compatible. Given this context, several arising questions can be examined and discussed in this BoF session. For example, 1) whether the computer systems courses should integrate RISC-V, 2) do we need minor (evolutionary) or major (revolutionary) curriculum changes with the involvement of RISC-V for each course or the entire CS curriculum, 3) how to help the majority of students accommodate to these changes, 4) what kind of new course materials should be provided to instructors, TAs and students, 5) whether it's possible for some senior students to tape-out their own RISC-V chip designs and finally produce a cornucopia of workable computing systems with this revolutionary and open curriculum.

Keywords: Computer System; Lab Project; Open Source; Hardware-software co-design; RISC-V

DOI: https://doi.org/10.1145/3300115.3312506

Development and Validation of an Instrument for Measuring Digital Empowerment of Primary School Students

Siu-Cheung Kong
Department of Mathematics and
Information Technology
The Education University of Hong
Kong
Hong Kong
sckong@eduhk.hk

Yi-Qing Wang
Centre for Learning, Teaching and
Technology
The Education University of Hong
Kong
Hong Kong
yiqing@eduhk.hk

Ming Lai
Centre for Learning, Teaching and
Technology
The Education University of Hong
Kong
Hong Kong
mlai@eduhk.hk

ABSTRACT

It is essential to enhance young learners' digital competency skills in the hope of empowering them in the digital world. Although past studies have examined measurements of university learners' digital empowerment, the literature has lacked discussion of digital empowerment in the primary school context. This study aims to develop and validate an instrument on digital empowerment of primary school students. The sample consists of 328 local primary school students from grades 4 to 6. Exploratory factor analysis showed a multi-dimensional structure of digital empowerment composed of (1) meaningfulness, (2) impact, (3) creativity belief, and (4) competence belief. Confirmatory factor analysis further confirmed the validity and reliability of digital empowerment as a multi-dimensional construct. This digital empowerment scale can serve as a tool to evaluate young learners' perceived competence when using digital technologies from the technological world in the primary school context.

CCS CONCEPTS

· **General and reference ~Measurement** • **General and reference ~Validation**

KEYWORDS

Digital competency; digital empowerment; primary school students; scale development; scale validation

ACM Reference format:
Siu-Cheung Kong, Yi-Qing Wang and Ming Lai. 2019. Development and Validation of an Instrument for Measuring Digital Empowerment of Primary School Students. In *Proceedings of ACM Global Computing Education Conference (CompEd'19), 17-19 May, 2019, Chengdu, Sichuan, China*. ACM, New York, NY, USA, 6 pages.
https://doi.org/10.1145/3300115.3309523

1 INTRODUCTION

The rapid advancement of digital technologies has essentially changed every aspect of society [1]. People nowadays must have digital competency to compete through adaptive learning in the face of the fast-changing digital world. Digital empowerment has become increasingly valued and should be prioritized among the young generation [2]. Digital empowerment refers to a person's perceived capacity to use digital technologies and his or her view of his/her competency in the digital world [3]. We argue that it is necessary to elicit one's digital empowerment perception. Young learners, growing up in a world in which technologies play a predominant role, should be equipped with digital competency skills learned through education and demonstrate innovative practices by using them to solve daily life problems. In this way they can contribute to the betterment of society.

In the 21st century, many places, like Singapore, Hong Kong, Taiwan, and Beijing, have started to integrate digital competency into their formal curricula [4]. Most of the efforts have been directed at incorporating it into the primary school context. For example, since 1998, the Hong Kong government has proposed educational plans to empower teachers and students through digital competency. It has been suggested that acquiring digital competency should be one of the generic skills in Hong Kong's curriculum reform [4, 5]. Therefore, to evaluate the effectiveness of the digital competency curriculum already implemented, it is important to investigate learners' perceived competency in using digital technologies and their views of digital competency in the technological world.

Based on a review of the existing literature, only one instrument was found that measured digital empowerment [2], and its target group was university students. No prior research has explored how digital empowerment is measured in the primary school context. Although the existing instrument for university students has been proven valid, measuring the digital empowerment of university students differs significantly from young learners. This study aims to develop and validate an instrument to capture the beliefs and attitudes of young learners toward digital empowerment in the primary school context. It enriches the context of empowerment research by developing a digital empowerment scale for young learners. The scale can help curriculum designers evaluate young learners' perceived competence when using digital technologies in the digital world.

2 LITERATURE REVIEW

2.1 Digital Competency

Digital competency refers to a set of abilities learners should acquire in the digital world from understanding the principles of digital technologies. Studies have suggested that learners wanting to become digitally competent must possess information and data literacy and create digital content [6-8]. To acquire information and data literacy, learners must understand how to use technologies to search for data, evaluate and analyze the reliability of the data, and organize and manage the information [6-8]. In addition, it is essential for them to know how to create digital content to express themselves in the digitalized world [6-8]. They should be required to learn how to program a computer to solve problems in digital environments [6].

2.2 Empowerment

The concept of empowerment originated with the plan to liberate oppressed populations through education [9]. It is "a multi-dimensional social process that helps people gain control over their own lives" (p.24) [10]. Such a process not only aims to enhance people's ability to better their own lives, but allows them to participate in issues they consider important to their communities and society. It operates in a wide variety of dimensions, including, without limitation, psychological, sociological and political, at the individual, group and community levels. According to Thomas and Velthouse [11], empowerment is broadly defined as increasing intrinsic task motivation, which can be manifested in four cognitive traits: meaningfulness, competence, self-determination and impact. Meaningfulness refers to the value of a task's purpose based on a person's ideals or standards [12]. It is the perceived value of a task [13]. When a task has more meaning for a person, he or she will make more effort to finish it [14]. Competence refers to the belief that an individual has the necessary skills and abilities to perform a task well [14]. In other words, it is perceived as one's self-efficacy in completing a task [15]. Competence and empowerment are positively related. When an individual is more confident in his or her skills and ability to finish a task, his/her feeling of empowerment increases [14]. Self-determination refers to a person's power to choose how to start and regulate his or her actions and reflects his/her autonomy [16]. Impact refers to how a person makes a difference in the scheme of things by completing a task [14]. The more influential a person thinks he or she can be, the more internal motivation he or she will have. Those four elements have frequently appeared in empowerment measures in various contexts such as in companies and schools [13-14, 16].

2.2 Digital Empowerment

According to Makinen [3], digital empowerment refers to a person's ability to effectively use digital technologies to form life skills that reinforce his or her ability in the digital world. It is an enabling process in which people first acquire the prerequisites, such as the awareness and motivation to learn to use digital technologies, then improve their knowledge and skills, and eventually become empowered and influential within the community. It is also a multi-dimensional process that helps to increase a person's opportunities to network, communicate and cooperate. Meanwhile, it enhances both a person's competence belief and his or her community to positively influence digital society [3].

2.4 Digital Empowerment Scale

As discussed in the introduction, only one digital empowerment scale [2] has been validated in the existing literature. This scale has frequently been adopted by other researchers to measure the digital empowerment of university students [2, 17]. It has also been used in the teacher context to explore their digital empowerment attitudes toward the use of educational technology and information literacy self-efficacy [18]. However, this digital empowerment scale [2] may not be an appropriate measure for learners in the primary school context. It contains 45 items, and some of their content is difficult for primary school students to understand, especially the construct of awareness. For example, children are probably unable to express their feelings about items such as how digital technologies provide business opportunities and how digital technologies allow people to participate in political and public issues.

Considering the lack of an appropriate scale to measure the perceptions of young primary school learners, this study aims to establish a new digital empowerment scale. The new scale is based on the theoretical conceptualization of empowerment and the digital empowerment literature [2, 11, 12, 14, 17, 19, 20]. The proposed instrument contains four components: meaningfulness, impact, creativity belief, and competence belief. Unlike the previous empowerment literature [11, 12, 19, 20], this study did not include self-determination as a key component during scale construction. Frymier et al. [14] found that when measuring learners' empowerment, only three factors (meaningfulness, impact, and competence) were relevant. Self-determination was not among them. The authors explained that learners might have less power to determine the activities conducted in a classroom than their teachers do. Thus, instead of self-determination, we included creativity belief as one of the components in the new digital empowerment scale. The goal of digital empowerment is to enable learners to play a meaningful and contributive role in society by applying digital technology [3]. To constructively participate in the community requires a certain degree of creativity to bring about change. Therefore, creativity belief related to digital empowerment was included in this study [21].

Empowerment is a process of creating intrinsic task motivation [14]. Researchers have found that the correlation between intrinsic motivation and meaningfulness, impact and competency is very high [22]. It indicates that these are the crucial factors influencing a person's sense of empowerment. Learners should first become motivated to use digital technologies to enhance their digital empowerment. If they do not find the technologies meaningful and useful, they will not be motivated to carry out high quality tasks [14]. When learners believe that digital technologies have a positive impact on their lives, they will be motivated to use them [14]. Therefore, meaningfulness and impact are essential components of digital empowerment. Cohen-Meitar, Carmeli and Waldman [23] argued that employees' creativity belief is correlated with meaningfulness in the workplace. In other words, when activity is perceived as meaningful, people develop more creative ideas. Oldham and Silva [24] found that the impact of digital technologies helps to enhance employees' creativity belief. Thus, we argue that meaningfulness, impact and creativity belief are closely related to each other. In addition, competence belief is an indispensable component of digital empowerment. Akkoyunlu and Yilmaz [25] suggested that learners should be required to understand why and how they need digital technologies, and how the technologies are developed to cultivate their digital empowerment. Hence, we posit that digital empowerment is a multi-dimensional construct composed of four related and unique components that are all crucial to explaining the overall construct of digital empowerment. In this study, "meaningfulness" means one's perceived value of digital technologies. "Impact" means one's perception of the influence of digital technologies. "Creativity belief" refers to one's belief in one's ability to produce novel and useful ideas and artefacts by applying digital technologies. "Competence belief" refers to one's belief in one's ability to acquire the necessary digital competency skills and ability to perform a task well.

3 METHOD

3.1 Item Development and Validation

A survey instrument was developed for data collection. After a thorough discussion with the research team, with backgrounds in psychology, education, and computer sciences, the scale items for the four components were developed according to the literature on empowerment theories and digital empowerment [2, 11, 12, 14, 17, 19, 20] as discussed in Section 2. More specifically, these experts gathered to review the four components, with the related readings provided. They were then asked to brainstorm the potential items that could best measure each specific component. The most frequently proposed items were listed and modified until each expert reached a consensus. Finally, a pool of 16 items was developed to capture the four components of digital empowerment, (four items for each component). For example, for meaningfulness, the sample item was "Digital technologies are important to me"; for impact, the sample item was "Digital technologies improve our daily lives"; for creativity belief, the sample item was "I can create something new with digital technologies"; and for competence belief, the sample item was "I have confidence in my ability to use digital technologies."

Researchers and school teachers who had not been involved in developing the items were invited to discuss the content validity of the new digital empowerment scale, and they further modified the 16 items according to the primary school context. Specifically,

they examined the adequacy of the four components and their corresponding items by categorizing the randomly listed items into the four components under the topic of digital empowerment. As the items were correctly assigned to the corresponding components, a consensus was reached that the scale items had been appropriately developed. No further amendments to the items were made. The original items were developed in English. They were then back-translated into Chinese. Some discrepancies were discussed and corrected. Finally, the face validity of the new digital empowerment scale measuring primary school students was assessed. All of the questions were measured using a 5-point Likert scale with anchors from strongly disagree (scored as 1) to strongly agree (scored as 5).

3.2 Data Collection

Questionnaires were distributed among three local primary schools. Given that most schools in Hong Kong are financed through aid (70.4%), we chose them as our targeted participants. Two of the targeted schools were co-educational, and one was a boy's school. All of the targeted learners were studying in grades 4 to 6. All of the learners had attended digital competency programs for more than one year. The questionnaires were distributed in either a paper-based format or an online Google format, depending on the schools' request. For School A, paper-based questionnaires were administrated with the help of the teachers. For Schools B and C, online surveys were carried out. In total, 383 questionnaires were distributed, and 328 questionnaires were received. In this study, data from School A were used for exploratory factor analysis (EFA) and data from Schools B and C were used for confirmatory factor analysis (CFA). This is a standardized process for the cross-validation [26, 27] of factor analysis. EFA was used for preliminary understanding of the factor structure, and CFA was used to reconfirm the measurement structure.

4 EXPLORATORY FACTOR ANALYSIS

4.1 Demographics of the Participants

In total, 150 paper-based questionnaires were distributed among the primary school students at School A. Five classes in grade 5 at School A were targeted. With the help of the teachers, 125 questionnaires were collected on site. The response rate was 83.3%. Among them, 72 (57.6%) were male and 50 (40.0%) were female. Three participants (2.4%) did not reveal their gender.

4.2 EFA

EFA was carried out with SPSS 21 to gain an initial understanding of the factor structure of the digital empowerment scale. Maximum likelihood estimation with promax rotation and Kaiser normalization was used to measure the goodness of fit of the model. Four factors were extracted based on our hypothesized measurement structure of the digital empowerment construct. According to the EFA results, the Kaiser-Meyer-Olkin measure of sampling adequacy was .91, which is greatly above the common recommended value of .60. Bartlett's test of sphericity was significant ($\chi 2$ (120) = 1090.88, p < .001). The communalities were all above .40, confirming that each item shared some common variance. All of these indicators showed that factor analysis was suitable for all 16 items on the digital empowerment scale. Table 1 presents the factor loadings, Cronbach's alpha coefficients and survey results for each item on the digital empowerment scale.

Table 1: Exploratory factor analysis, Cronbach's alpha and survey results

Factors and Items	Factor loadings	Mean (SD)
Factor 1: meaningfulness, α= .89		**3.70 (.96)**
Digital technologies are useful to me.	.95	3.82 (1.09)
Digital technologies are important to me.	.83	3.70 (1.15)
Digital technologies will help me achieve my goals.	.36	3.59 (1.09)
I want to learn how to use digital technologies.	.67	3.65 (1.09)
Factor 2: impact, α= .84		**3.71 (.92)**
Digital technologies make the world better.	.91	3.60 (1.12)
Digital technologies bring benefits to our daily lives.	.69	3.69 (1.09)
Digital technologies improve our daily lives.	.78	3.74 (1.07)
Digital technologies make a difference in the world.	.57	3.76 (1.13)
Factor 3: creativity belief, α= .83		**3.42 (.91)**
I can creatively perform the job duties with digital technologies.	.54	3.29 (1.22)
I can express my ideas with digital technologies.	.70	3.37 (.99)
I can build new solutions to day-to-day problems with digital technologies.	.72	3.48 (1.07)
I can create something new with digital technologies.	.70	3.55 (1.12)
Factor 4: competence belief, α= .83		**3.50 (.93)**
I have enough knowledge and skills to use digital technologies.	.58	3.43 (1.16)
I have confidence in my ability to use digital technologies.	.84	3.48 (1.06)
I can solve problems with digital technologies.	.79	3.44 (1.10)
I can learn how to use new digital technologies.	.62	3.64 (1.17)

Factor 1 consists of four items with loadings ranging from .36 to .95. The items in this factor represent the meaningfulness of digital technologies. The third item in factor 1 was .36, which was evidently much lower than the other loadings. Despite the low loading, the third item remained in the scale for two reasons. First, it was above the critical value of .30 in SEM studies [28]. Second, because the EFA sample size was not large enough, this finding might be specific only to our EFA data set. Factor 2 was composed of four items with loadings from .57 to .91. This reflected the impact of digital technologies. Factor 3 had four items with loadings from .54 to .72. This reflected creativity belief. Factor 4 included four items with loadings ranging from .58 to .84. It reflected competence belief. The Cronbach's alpha coefficients for the four factors were all above .70, indicating that the subscales had good internal consistency. The intercorrelations between the four factors on the digital empowerment scale ranged from .56 to .70. This indicates adequate convergent validity among the four components of digital empowerment. Exploratory factor analysis (EFA) showed a multi-dimensional structure for digital empowerment, composed of (1) meaningfulness, (2) impact, (3) creativity belief, and (4) competence belief.

5 CONFIRMATORY FACTOR ANALYSIS

5.1 The Demographics of the Participants

Two hundred and thirty-three students from Schools B and C (C was a boy's school) were invited to participate in this study. In total, 203 students submitted the online survey before the end of their lesson. The response rate was 87.1%. Among them, 78.3% of the students were male. Eighty-three students (40.9%) were in grade 4, 68 (33.5%) in grade 5 and 51(25.1%) in grade 6. One participant (0.5%) did not disclose his/her grade.

5.2 CFA

Based on the preliminary results of EFA, CFA using Amos 24 was conducted to reconfirm the measurement structure. The maximum likelihood estimation was also used in CFA, so that the estimation method would be consistent with EFA. $\chi 2$ (df), CFI, TLI, RMSEA were used as the fit indices for the measurement model of digital empowerment. CFI and TLI that are greater than .90 suggest a good fit, and greater than .95 indicate an excellent fit [29]. For RMSEA, a cut-off value close to .06 [29] or the upper limit of .08 seem to be acceptable to most researchers. In this study, $\chi 2$ (98) = 204.79, p < .001, CFI = .97, TLI = .96, and RMSEA = .07. All of the indices suggested that the hypothesized measurement model as a multidimensional factor fitted well with the data collected to validate the new construct. The factor loadings, Cronbach's alpha coefficients and survey results of the digital empowerment scale are shown in Table 2.

Table 2: Confirmatory factor analysis, Cronbach's alpha, and survey results

Factors and Items	Factor loadings	Mean (SD)
Factor 1: meaningfulness, α= .93		**3.67 (1.12)**
Digital technologies are useful to me.	.90	3.75 (1.25)
Digital technologies are important to me.	.86	3.65 (1.24)
Digital technologies will help me achieve my goals.	.87	3.62 (1.20)
I want to learn how to use digital technologies.	.87	3.65 (1.26)
Factor 2: impact, α= .90		**3.84 (1.04)**
Digital technologies make the world better.	.85	3.73 (1.25)
Digital technologies bring benefits to our daily lives.	.83	3.87 (1.17)
Digital technologies improve our daily lives.	.84	3.81 (1.24)
Digital technologies make a difference in the world.	.78	3.97 (1.15)
Factor 3: creativity belief, α= .91		**3.54 (1.12)**
I can creatively perform the job duties with digital technologies.	.81	3.58 (1.29)
I can express my ideas with digital technologies.	.88	3.49 (1.26)
I can build new solutions to day-to-day problems with digital technologies.	.92	3.51 (1.25)
I can create something new with digital technologies.	.78	3.59 (1.27)
Factor 4: competence belief, α= .92		**3.61 (1.07)**
I have enough knowledge and skills to use digital technologies.	.86	3.63 (1.22)
I have confidence in my ability to use digital technologies.	.88	3.59 (1.21)
I can solve problems with digital technologies.	.87	3.52 (1.19)
I can learn how to use new digital technologies.	.84	3.68 (1.17)

All of the factor loadings ranged from .78 to .92, confirming the convergent validity of digital empowerment. The Cronbach's alpha coefficients for the four factors were .93, .90, .91 and .92, respectively, meaning that the internal consistency of the components was good. CFA further confirmed the validity and reliability of digital empowerment as a multi-dimensional construct.

6 DISCUSSION

6.1 Theoretical Contributions

The EFA results supported our theoretical measurement structure of digital empowerment as a multi-dimensional construct. Further, CFA indicated that the measurement structure achieved excellent fit according to the fit indices ($\chi2$ (98) = 204.79, p < .001, CFI = .97, TLI = .96, and RMSEA = .07). Thus, digital empowerment as a four-factor model was further confirmed.

In the existing literature, many of the empowerment studies have focused on empowering women and other marginalized populations in developing countries [30-32]. Topics related to the digital empowerment of young learners have rarely been discussed. Moreover, creativity belief has rarely been considered in measuring digital empowerment despite its importance to digital technologies and its complementary relationship with empowerment [33]. The new digital empowerment scale, which adds creativity belief to its composition, is a more comprehensive tool to investigate how young learners perceive themselves and their relationship to the digital world. In other words, this study enriches the context of empowerment research by developing this digital empowerment scale for young learners.

6.2 Practical Contributions

This digital empowerment scale serves as an effective measurement tool for educational practitioners. It can help them gain insight into the perceived digital competency of young learners in the technological world. Knowing the learners' beliefs and perceptions can help practitioners refine their existing educational programs. This can help young learners build stronger digital competency skills in the primary school context. Further, this scale can collect feedback from learners on the programs they have enrolled in. Teachers can refine their curriculum and pedagogy by attending programs on digital competency, with the goal of empowering their students. This scale can be applied in the countries and regions that have launched digital competency programs in their primary school curriculum. They can modify the items on the scale to suit their educational context.

6.3 Limitations

Like most other research, this study has limitations. The use of self-reporting in the survey might have caused common-method bias, which inflates relationships between study variables. To avoid this problem, it is recommended that ratings from various sources be used in future studies. In addition, studies with both qualitative and quantitative designs are desirable. For example,

qualitative results from interviews can help to cross-validate and further explain quantitative evidence from survey studies like this one. Further, this study only investigated digital empowerment. Developing a nomological network around digital empowerment could be one possible direction for future research. Nevertheless, digital empowerment is still at the initial stage of scale development in the primary school context. Thus, the priority of this study was to develop and validate a useful scale to measure the digital empowerment of primary school students.

7 CONCLUSION AND FUTURE WORK

Although previous studies have focused on digital empowerment in higher educational settings, there has been a lack of related literature in the primary school context. This study developed and validated a 16-item scale on the digital empowerment of primary school students. This deepens our understanding of these young learners' perceptions of their digital competence and their relationships with the digital world. The conceptualization and operational definition of digital empowerment were established in this study. Both the EFA and CFA results supported the multidimensional structure of the hypothesized digital empowerment construct, including meaningfulness, impact, creativity belief, and competence belief. The scale enables curriculum designers to evaluate digital competency curricula in the primary school context. It also allows them to gain insight into young students' perceived competence when using digital technologies and their perceptions of their relationship with the digital world.

In the future, studies should focus more on investigating the important antecedents and outcomes of young learners' digital empowerment. Researchers are also encouraged to investigate school teachers' digital empowerment in more depth. The widespread adoption of computer-supported learning and teaching in the school curriculum has triggered a need to understand how teachers perceive their competency using digital technologies in the classroom setting, and how their perceived competency influences their teaching motivation and behavior.

ACKNOWLEDGEMENTS

The authors would like to acknowledge the funding support of this Coolthink@JC project from the Hong Kong Jockey Club Charities Trust.

REFERENCES

[1] Barbara R. Jones-Kavalier and Suzanne L. Flannigan (2006). Connecting the Digital Dots: Literacy of the 21st Century. Educause Quarterly, 29(2), 8-10.

[2] Buket Akkoyunlu, Meryem Yilmaz Soylu, and Mehmet Çağlar (2010). A Study on Developing "Digital Empowerment Scale" for University Learners. Hacettepe University Journal of Education, 39, 10-19.

[3] Maarit Makinen (2006). Digital Empowerment as a Process for Enhancing Citizens' Participation. E-learning, 3(3), 381-395.

[4] Siu-Cheung Kong, Tak-Wai Chan, Ronghuai Huang, and Horn-Mun Cheah (2014). A Review of E-Learning Policy in School Education in Singapore, Hong Kong, Taiwan, and Beijing: Implications to Future Policy Planning. Journal of Computers in Education, 1(2-3), 187-212.

[5] Curriculum Development Council (2001). Learning to Learn—The Way Forward in Curriculum Development. Curriculum Development Council, Hong Kong.

[6] Riina Vuorikari, Yves Punie, Stephanie Carretero, and Lieve Van den Brande (2016). DigComp 2.0: The Digital Competence Framework for Citizens. Update

Phase 1: The Conceptual Reference Model. Luxembourg Publication Office of the European Union, Seville, Spain.

[7]   José Janssen, Slavi Stoyanov, Anusca Ferrari, Yves Punie, Kees Pannekeet, and Peter Sloep (2013). Experts' Views on Digital Competence: Commonalities and Differences. Computers & Education, 68, 473-481.

[8]   Ester Van Laar, Alexander J.A.M. Van Deursen, Jan A.G.M. Van Dijk, and Jos De Haan (2017). The Relation between 21st-century Skills and Digital Skills: A Systematic Literature Review. Computers in Human Behavior, 72, 577-588.

[9]   Paulo Freire (1973). *Education for Critical Consciousness.* Continuum Publishing Company, NY, New York.

[10] Nanette Page and Cheryl E. Czuba (1999). Empowerment: What is it? Journal of Extension, 37(5), 24-32.

[11] Kenneth W. Thomas and Betty A. Velthouse (1990). Cognitive Elements of Empowerment: An "Interpretive" Model of Intrinsic Task Motivation. The Academy of Management Review, 15(4), 666-681.

[12] Guangping Wang and Peggy D. Lee (2009). Psychological Empowerment and Job Satisfaction: An Analysis of Interactive Effects. Group & Organizational Management, 34(3), 271-296.

[13] Keith Weber, Matthew M. Martin, and Jacob L. Cayanus (2005). Student Interest: A Two-study Re-examination of the Concept. Communication Quarterly, 53(1), 71-86.

[14] Ann B. Frymier, Gary M. Shulman, and Marian L. Houser (1996). The Development of a Learner Empowerment Measure. Communication Education, 45(3), 181-199.

[15] Paul R. Pintrich, David A. F. Smith, Teresa Garcia, and Wilbert J. McKeachie (1991). A Manual for the Use of the Motivated Strategies for Learning Questionnaire (MSLQ). Mediterranean Journal of Social Sciences, 6(1), 156–164.

[16] Gretchen M. Spreitzer (1995). Psychological Empowerment in the Workplace: Dimensions, Measurement, and Validation. Academy of Management Journal, 38(5), 1442-1463.

[17] Baybars R. Eynur (2016). Digital Empowerment Level of Physical Education and Sports Students. Arch Budo Sci Martial Art Extreme Sport, 12, 45-56.

[18] Arif Sarycoban (2013). Prospective and Regular ELT Teachers' Digital Empowerment and Self-Efficiacy. Porta Linguarum, 20, 77-87.

[19] Maria L. Kraimer, Scott E. Seibert, and Robert C. Liden (1999). Psychological Empowerment as a Multidimensional Construct: A Test of Construct Validity. Educational and Psychological Measurement, 59(1), 127-142.

[20] Christine S. Koberg, R. Wayne Boss, and Jason C. Senjem (1999). Antecedents and Outcomes of Empowerment. Group & Organization Management, 24(1), 71-91.

[21] Siu-Cheung Kong, Ming-Ming Chiu, and Ming Lai (2018). A Study of Primary School Students' Interest, Collaboration Attitude, and Programming Empowerment in Computational Thinking Education. Computers & Education, 127, 178-189.

[22] Catherine F. Brooks and Stacy L. Young (2011). Are Choice-Making Opportunities Needed in the Classroom? Using Self-Determination Theory to Consider Student Motivation and Learner Empowerment. International Journal of Teaching and Learning in Higher Education, 23(1), 48-59.

[23] Ravit Cohen-Meitar, Abraham Carmeli, and David A. Waldman (2009). Linking Meaningfulness in the Workplace to Employee Creativity: The Intervening Role of Organizational Identification and Positive Psychological Experiences. Creativity Research Journal, 21(4), 361-375.

[24] Greg R. Oldham and Nancy D. Silva (2015). The Impact of Digital Technology on the Generation and Implementation of Creative Ideas in the Workplace. Computers in Human Behavior, 42, 1-7.

[25] Buket Akkoyunlu and Ayhan Yilmaz (2011). Prospective Teachers' Digital Empowerment and Their Information Literacy Self-efficacy. Egitim Arastirmalari-Eurasian Journal of Educational Research, 11(44), 33-50.

[26] Timothy A. Brown (2006). *Confirmatory Factor Analysis for Applied Research.* Guilford Press, NY, New York.

[27] Isabel Izquierdo, Julio Olea, and Francisco José Abad (2014). Exploratory Factor Analysis in Validation Studies: Uses and Recommendations. Psicothema, 26(3), 395-400.

[28] Josep F. Hair, Rolph E. Anderson, Ronald L. Tatham, and William C. Black (1995). *Multiariate Data Analysis* (3rd. ed.). Macmillan Publishing Company, NY, New York.

[29] Li-tzeu and Peter M. Bentler (1999). Cutoff Criteria for Fit Indexes in Covariance Stcture Analysis: Conventional Criteria versus New Alternatives. Structural Equation Modeling, 6(1), 1-55.

[30] Sylviaaier and Usha Nair-Reichert (2007). Empowering Women Through ICT-Based Business Initiatives: An Overview of Best Practices in E-Commerce/E-Retailing Projects. Information Technologies & International Development, 4(2), 43-60.

[31] Jerett H. Nord, Tzong-Ru Lee, Fatih Cetin, Özlem Atay, and Joanna Paliszkiewicz (2016). Examining the Impact of Social Technologies on Empowerment and Economic Development. International Journal of Information Management, 36(6), 1101-1110.

[32] Lal B. Suresh (2011). Impact of Information and Communication Technologies on Women Empowerment in India. Journal of Systemics, Cybernetics and Informatics, 9(4), 17-23.

[33] Betty A. Velthouse (1990). Creativity and Empowerment: A Complementary Relationship. Review of Business, 12(2), 13-18.

The Effect of Reading Code Aloud on Comprehension: An Empirical Study with School Students

Alaaeddin Swidan and Felienne Hermans
Delft University of Technology
Delft, The Netherlands
{alaaeddin.swidan,f.f.j.hermans}@tudelft.nl

ABSTRACT

In recent times, programming is increasingly taught to younger students in schools. While learning programming is known to be difficult, we can lighten the learning experience of this age group by adopting pedagogies that are common to them, but not as common in CS education. One of these pedagogies is Reading Aloud (RA), a familiar strategy when young children and beginners start learning how to read in their natural language. RA is linked with a better comprehension of text for beginner readers. We hypothesize that reading code aloud during introductory lessons will lead to better code comprehension. To this end, we design and execute a controlled experiment with the experimental group participants reading the code aloud during the lessons. The participants are 49 primary school students between 9 and 13 years old, who follow three lessons in programming in Python. The lessons are followed by a comprehension assessment based on Bloom's taxonomy. The results show that the students of the experimental group scored significantly higher in the Remembering-level questions compared to the ones in the control group. There is no significant difference between the two groups in their answers to the Understanding-level questions. Furthermore, the participants in both groups followed some of the instructed vocalizations more frequently such as the variable's assignment (is). Vocalizing the indentation spaces in a for-loop was among the least followed. Our paper suggests that using RA for teaching programming in schools will contribute to improving code comprehension with its effect on syntax remembering.

KEYWORDS

Reading Aloud (RA), Programming Education, Primary School, Bloom's Taxonomy

ACM Reference Format:
Alaaeddin Swidan and Felienne Hermans. 2019. The Effect of Reading Code Aloud on Comprehension: An Empirical Study with School Students. In *ACM Global Computing Education Conference 2019 (CompEd '19), May 17–19, 2019, Chengdu, Sichuan, China.* ACM, New York, NY, USA, 7 pages. https://doi.org/10.1145/3300115.3309504

1 INTRODUCTION

Programming is increasingly taught to younger students, in some countries as part of the curriculum of primary and secondary schools [19]. We know, however, that learning programming is difficult [8, 24, 41]. The question arises on how do we make learning programming less difficult for younger students? One way could be applying pedagogies we know work for this age group but are uncommon in programming education.

Young children start to learn how to read by learning the connection between symbols, one or more letters in this case, and sounds and then combining them into words and sentences. Reading text aloud is encouraged for beginners since it focuses thoughts, help memorization and improves comprehension of text [9, 12, 37]. Also in mathematics, the same approach to reading aloud can be noticed in vocalizing simple operations and equations, or when introducing a new symbol [14, 35].

Although in later development stages and adulthood silent reading becomes the norm, our brains seem to be always ready for reading aloud. Studies have shown that the brain sends signals to the primary motor cortex, controlling the lips and the mouth, during silent reading [28, 33]. This brain activity is called *subvocalization*, which is used in particular when learners face long and new words. In programming education, educators seem to spend little effort on reading code aloud to, or with the students. The lack of this *phonology* knowledge leaves students with an extra cognitive load when reading code to understand functionality. In this regard, one study measured the subvocalization of experienced developers during programming tasks and showed that the subvocalization signals could differentiate the difficulty of the programming task [28]. Therefore, we hypothesize that training students in reading code aloud will lead them to spend less cognitive effort on the reading mechanics and thus improve their comprehension of code.

Therefore, the purpose of this paper is a first quantification of the effect of reading code aloud during lessons on school students' comprehension of basic programming concepts. Furthermore, we investigate how students benefit from the practice of Reading Aloud (RA) by following it as a sort of a guideline later.

To this end, we design and execute a controlled experiment in which 49 primary school students receive three lessons of programming in Python. The students are divided into two groups which get the same teaching materials and times. The students in the experimental group, however, are asked to repeat reading the code aloud following the instructor. We assess students' learning based on Bloom's taxonomy. Since the participants are absolute beginners in programming, we focus our assessment on the first two levels of the taxonomy: the Remembering-level and the Understanding-level. In this paper, we answer the following research questions:

RQ1 What is the effect of reading code aloud on the performance of students in the Remembering-level questions?

RQ2 What is the effect of reading code aloud on the performance of students in the understanding-level questions?

RQ3 How do students follow the vocalization guideline when they read code later?

Results show that the students in the experimental group scored significantly higher in the Remembering-level questions compared to the students in the control group. There is no significant difference between the two groups in their answers to the Understanding-level questions. The analysis shows that particular code vocalizations, such as the variable's assignment, are common among the two groups. On the other hand, the participants in both groups least vocalize the spaces needed for indentation in a for loop and list brackets. The following sections contain the details of the experiment's design and results.

2 BACKGROUND AND RELATED WORK

We provide an overview of research related to Reading Aloud (RA), particularly, the RA role in reading education for young students (Section 2.1) and previous literature involving the use of voice in programming environments (Section 2.2). We also overview selected prior research on the use of Bloom's taxonomy in assessing programming comprehension (Section 2.3).

2.1 RA and Comprehension: Natural Language Perspective

Most psychologists nowadays believe that reading is a process of sounding out words mentally even for skilled readers [33]. Brain studies [28, 29, 33] show that the primary motor cortex is active during reading, "presumably because it is involved with mouth movements used in reading aloud" [33, p. 90]. Therefore, it becomes highly important for beginner readers to learn the connection between sounds and symbols, or phonics. Previous research found that systematic phonics instruction produces higher achievement for beginning readers, where they can read many more new words compared to students following other approaches. For these reasons, in the United States, phonics has been included in reading programs in schools nationwide [33]. As a verbal approach, reading aloud (RA) helps in focuses thoughts and transforming it in specific ways, causing changes in cognition [12]. Takeuchi et al. [37] highlight that RA is effective for children language development in *"phonological awareness, print concepts, comprehension, and vocabulary"* [37]. Bus et al. [9] reports that reading books aloud brings young children *"into touch with story structures and schemes and literacy conventions which are prerequisites for understanding texts"*. Several experiments related to comprehension report that students identified the sounding out of words, or loudly repeating text as a means to regulate their understanding while reading [22, 25]. When comparing RA to silent reading, research has found that students comprehend significantly more information when they read aloud versus reading silently [27, 31]. Although other studies showed opposite results [17], there seems a consensus exists among researchers that the effects of reading aloud may differ based on the reading proficiency of the students: beginning readers, regardless of age, benefited from reading aloud rather than silently [17, 31].

Finally, Santoro et al. [34] stress the importance of careful planning when reading aloud is aimed at improving the comprehension of students. RA activities, in this case, should be combined with *"explicit comprehension instruction"* and *"active, engaging in discussions about the text"*.

2.2 The Role of Voice in Programming and CS Education

One main use of code vocalization is as an assistive technology that helps programmers who suffer from specific disabilities or stress injuries (RSI) to program in an efficient matter [4, 13, 16, 36]. Another area where code vocalization is essentially practiced is the remote peer-programming [10]. Vocalizing code can also be an element in some teaching strategies especially the direct instruction, modeling and think-aloud [2, 38]. However, in all of these cases, the way in which people vocalize code is not systematic, standardized, or agreed upon. In addition, there is some ambiguity over what to vocalize and on what granularity level: tokens, blocks or compilation units [16]. These factors lead to challenges for professional programmers and learners alike [6]. For example, [4, 36] mention the problematic issue of how to vocalize symbols, and when to speak out or leave specific symbols. Price et al. [30] mention the effect of natural language's flexibility on the difficulty of vocalizing programming commands, as multiple words could be used to do the same thing (for example begin class or create a class). Another effect of natural language is the ambiguity of the meaning of some words in different contexts, for example, *add* value to a variable and *add* a method to a class. These challenges show that the use of natural language in programming needs more attention from programming designers and educators. Recent work of Hermans et al. [20] calls for the programming languages to have phonology guidelines that specify how a construct should be vocalized. Finally, related is the work of Parnin [28] who investigated the role of subvocalization on code comprehension. Subvocalization is the process of the brain sending electrical signals to the tongue, lips, or vocal cords when reading silently. Silent reading is a relatively new technique for humanity. Therefore, when reading, especially the complicated segments or even words, the brain instructs the lips and the tongue to perform the read-aloud but without a voice. Their experiment on code reading showed that measuring the subvocalization signals can be an indication of the difficulty of a programming task.

2.3 Bloom's Taxonomy in CS Education

When it comes to the assessment of learning processes, Bloom's taxonomy is one of the common frameworks educators follow [23, 39, 41]. In this framework [1, 7], Bloom identifies six levels of cognitive skills that educators should aim at fulfilling with their students. The levels are Remembering, Understanding, Applying, Analyzing, Evaluating, and Creating. These cognitive levels are ordered from low to high, simple to complex and concrete to abstract, and each is a prerequisite to the next. This classification is combined with a practical guideline that educators could use to evaluate the learning outcome of their students by forming questions with certain verbs. In this way, it stimulates the cognitive process of the required level of the taxonomy. In CS education there appear two main usages of the taxonomy. First, the use of Bloom's taxonomy as a tool to measure the learning progress of students and how they perform in introductory courses in particular. Some research chose to build the assessment from scratch depending on the taxonomy. This includes the work of Whalley et al. [41] who assessed the reading and comprehension skills of students in introductory programming courses, creating a set of questions that conform to Bloom's taxonomy. The results show that the students performed consistently with the cognitive difficulty levels indicated by the taxonomy. Similar is the work of Thompson et al. [39] who created another set of programming questions per the main categories of the taxonomy, discussing each item and showing educators how to interpret the results. Both works have been insightful to our research. Second, other researchers have applied the taxonomy to evaluate existing programming exams or courses. Lister [23] argues that the taxonomy should be used as a framework of assessment, not learning since it provides a reliable tool with a standard level of assessment. Despite its popularity among researchers, there seems a consensus that applying the taxonomy to programming questions is challenging since a programming problem consists of several building concepts which makes isolating the problem to one cognitive category a hard job to do [15, 39, 41]. Although the challenging task to map the assessment items to Bloom's cognitive levels will always depend on the interpretation of the educators, the taxonomy should still provide a valuable tool to explore the cognitive processes involved in any programming exercise.

3 METHODOLOGY

The goal of this study is to answer an overarching research question: how does reading code aloud during lessons affect the students' learning of programming concepts? To this end, we designed and ran a controlled experiment with primary school students. In this section, we describe the setup and design of the experiment in addition to the theoretical basis we use for the assessment.

3.1 Setup

We provided Python lessons to 49 primary school students in the Netherlands. We split the participants into a control and an experimental group. Both groups received the same lessons: three lessons of 1.5 hours each given by the authors of this paper, one lesson per week. We gave the lessons to the groups subsequently: first the experimental group, followed by a break, followed by the control group. The students knew they were going to learn programming during the lessons but they were not aware of the experiment's goal. We asked the consent of the parents to collect the anonymous data needed for the research.

3.2 Participants

Participants are 49 students of one primary school in Rotterdam, the Netherlands. The programming lessons are provided as part of extracurricular activities arranged by the school, taking place during school days in a computer lab at the school. As shown in Figure 1, a total of 49 school children between 9 and 13 years with an average age of 11.12 years participated in the study. Participants were 28 boys, 20 girls, and 1 participant who chose not to specify their gender. The control group consisted of 24 children (age average=11.167 years, 6 girls - 17 boys - 1 unspecified), while the experimental group consisted of 25 children (age average=11.08

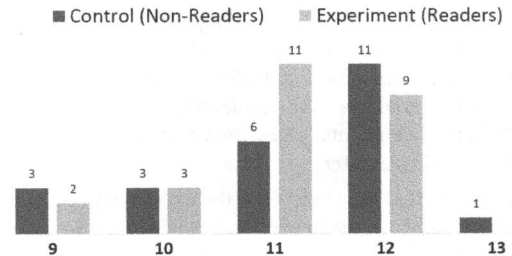

Figure 1: Age in years versus count of participants per group, mean=11.12 years. Both groups have equal age means

years, 14 girls, 11 boys). We could not control the split of groups since they are school classes hence the non-balance in gender.

3.3 Lesson Design and Materials

Each lesson starts by introducing a small working program. One teacher shows a program on the interactive white-board explaining the code per line and highlighting the concepts included. The lessons include the following concepts primarily:

Variables Setting and retrieving a variable's value
Lists Creating lists of integers and strings, accessing and modifying lists through built-in functions
For-Loops Using loops for repeating certain operations
Function use Calling built-in functions and using functions from packages.

During the program explanation, the teachers encourage the students to express their thoughts on what the code does via interactive questions, such as *What do you think happens if we change this value?* According to [34], reading text aloud aiming at improving the comprehension should be combined with *"active and engaging discussions about the text"*. Following, the students are instructed to work in pairs to carry out specific exercises according to the lessons' material. During the lessons, an online compiler for Python (Repl.it[1]) was used. The final assessment questions are on-line [2].

3.4 RA Design and Implementation

Understandably, there exists no guideline on how to read code. When reading code, however, people tend to find that there are ambiguous words, symbols, and even punctuation, and vocalizing them is both challenging and subjective [20]. Consider an example as simple as the variable assignment $a = 10$, is it vocalized as *"a is ten"*, *"a equals ten"*, *"a gets 10"* or *"set a to ten"*. In this experiment, we follow a similar approach to [5, 20] where the code is read as if the person is telling another beginner student what to type into a computer. For both the experimental and the control group, the instructor read the code aloud to the students during and following the explanation of a concept within the code, a for-loop for instance. Only the students in the experimental group, however, were asked to repeat the reading activity: all-together and aloud. We consistently read all keywords, symbols identifier names and punctuation marks that are essential to the working of a program, for example quotation marks, brackets, colons and white spaces necessary for

[1] https://repl.it/repls
[2] http://bit.ly/2EhAmB0

indentation. The full list of what and how we vocalized code during the lessons are presented in Table 1. We call this list the vocalization *guideline,* and we use it later to answer RQ3 which investigates the extent to which the students follow the taught guideline later during the assessment. We do this investigation for both groups since all the students in both groups listened to the teacher vocalizing the code during the lesson, but only the experimental group's participants performed it themselves.

3.5 Assessment

We choose to assess only the two basic levels of Bloom's taxonomy: Remembering and Understanding. According to Lister [23] the two categories are sufficient for beginners when we want to assess the effectiveness of their code reading. When relating these two categories to programming assessment, Thompson et al. [39] provide useful insights into how to interpret them into programming assessment terms. Remembering can be related to activities centered around identifying a programming construct or recalling the implementation of a concept in a piece of code. For example by *"recall the syntax rules for that construct and use those rules to recognize that construct in the provided code"*[39]. For the Understanding category, it includes translating an algorithm from one form to another, plus explaining or presenting an example of an algorithm or a design pattern. For example, tracing a piece of code into its expected output. Multiple choice questions are suitable to assess these two basic levels for beginners [23, 41]. We developed an 11-questions final assessment exam: 9 are multiple choice questions, one is of fill-in type in addition to vocalizing the code snippet, and one only requires the student to vocalize a code snippet. We aimed that the questions cover i) all of the programming concepts we taught (see section 3.3), and ii) for each concept to have a question assessing the two targeted levels of Bloom's taxonomy. Table 2 shows the questions and their mappings to Bloom's levels.

3.5.1 Following the Vocalization Guideline. We ask the students in both groups to answer two vocalization questions (Question 9 and 11). The students need to write down in words how they would vocalize a code snippet to another beginner student. Although the students in the control group did not read the code aloud themselves, they listened to the instructor performing the RA. Therefore, we ask both groups to answer these questions. We use the students' answers to address RQ3.

4 RESULTS

In this section, we provide the answers to our research questions.

4.1 RQ1: What is the effect of RA on the Remembering-level?

To answer this question, we investigate the answers to the questions in the Remembering-level (7 questions) (see Table 2). The control group has a mean of 3.58 while the experimental group has a mean of 4.56. To test the equality of means we use the Mann-Whitney U Test since the sample size is relatively small and the presence of some outliers. The results (Table 3) show that the difference between the control and experimental groups is significant (p =0.003). The effect size r= 0.42 which indicates a large effect [11, 18].

Age factor: There is no relationship between the student's age and the Remembering-level score across the two groups. All age groups have equal means in the two experimental groups.

4.2 RQ2: What is the effect of RA on the Understanding-level?

To answer this question, we investigate the answers to the questions in the Understanding-level (3 questions) (see Table 2). The control group has a mean of 0.92 while the experimental group has a mean of 0.90. Similar to RQ1, we use the Mann-Whitney U Test to check the equality of the means. The test results (Table 3) show that the difference between the control and experimental groups is not significant (p = 0.93).

4.3 RQ3: How do students follow the vocalization guideline when they read code later?

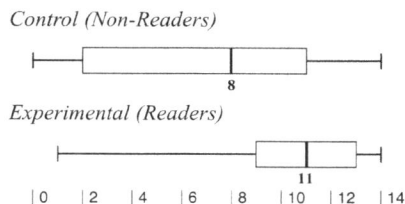

Figure 2: The vocalization score means by group

To answer this question we analyze students' answers to the vocalizing questions (Question 9 and 11 in Table 2), where we asked students to write down, in the answer paper, how would they vocalize two small code snippets.

The vocalization guideline is the way we chose to vocalize the code snippets provided during the lessons. It is summarized in Table 1. We grade the student's answers following the guideline; a point is given every time the guideline is followed, and the maximum possible is 14 points.

4.3.1 Following the Guideline: As expected there exists a significant difference between the two groups in following the vocalization guideline (see Figure 2). This is expected because of the intervention we did in the experimental group. The experimental group who read the code aloud themselves scored an average of 10.20, while the students in the control group, who only listened to the code being read, scored an average of 6.79. The Mann-Whitney test suggests the difference between the two means is significant (U=168.5, p= 0.009, r= 0.375 (a medium to large effect)).

4.3.2 Most and Least Followed Vocalizations. We analyzed the followed vocalization guidelines observed in both groups (Table 4. We notice that some vocalizations are frequent in both control and experimental groups especially the variable assignment (is), comma and single quotation mark. However, the colon in for-loop goes from one of the most frequent, in the experimental group, to the one of the least frequent in the control group. This difference can be linked to the intervention exercise making a lasting memory for the participants in the experimental group.

Table 1: The vocalization guideline used during the lessons

Vocalization Item	Description	Code	How Code was Vocalized
V1	Setting a variable value	temperature = 8	temperature **is eight**
V2	Function-calling with round brackets		for i in range **open round bracket** ten **close round bracket**
V3	For-loop colon	for i in range(10):	**colon**
V4	For-loop indentation space	temperature = temperature + 1	**space space**
V5	Plus sign in expressions		temperature is temperature **plus** one
V6	Symbols in identifiers (underscore)		healthy **underscore** food is
V7	List square bracket (open)		**open square bracket**
V8	Strings single quotation (begin)	healthy_food = ['apple', 'banana']	**single quotation** apple **single quotation**
V9	Comma separation between list items		**comma**
V8 (Repeated)	Strings single quotation (end)		**single quotation** banana **single quotation**
V7(Repeated)	List square bracket (close)		**close square bracket**
V10	Function use: calling from a package with dot	food = random.choice(healthy_food)	food is random **dot** choice **open round bracket** healthy underscore food **close round bracket**

Table 2: The list of questions and their corresponding Bloom's cognitive level

#	Concept(s)	Bloom's level	Prerequisite Knowledge	Student's Action(s) to Answer
1	List Create/Modify	Remembering	The syntax to create a list of string literals	Replace syntactically incorrect line by a correct option
2	Variables	Remembering	The syntax to increase an integer variable's value	Replace an empty line with a syntactically correct option
3	Function use	Remembering	The syntax to call a function with a variable parameter	Replace syntactically incorrect line by a correct option
4	Function use	Remembering	The syntax to call the print function with a string literal	
5	Function use & Variables	Remembering	The correct syntax to print a variable's value	
6	Sequential execution & Variables	Remembering	Same indentation for each line of a Python block	Identify/recognize/locate the cause of the error from choices
7	For-loop	Understanding	For-loop syntax. Indentation effect on lines being within/outside a loop	Trace and predict the outcome of a for-loop with a print statement within, followed by another print statement
8	For-loop	Remembering	For-loop syntax	Identify/recognize the syntactically correct for-loop to get a specific outcome
9	For-loop & Variables (with Vocalize)	Understanding	For-loop syntax. Indentation effect on lines being within/outside a loop	Trace and predict the outcome of a loop that increases the value of a variable. Then write in words how you would vocalize the code.
10	List Create/Modify & Function use	Understanding	The syntax of List creation, List access & modification using built-in functions	Trace code and interpret its use in one of low-, medium- or high natural language descriptions
11	Vocalize only	-	Vocalize code as if your are reading it to a friend	Write, in words, on the answer sheet how you would vocalize the code snippet

Table 3: The difference by group in the answer score means to each category of questions.

	Remembering-level Score 7 Questions		Understanding-level Score 3 Questions	
	Readers n=25	Non-Readers n=24	Readers n=25	Non-Readers n=24
Mean	4.56	3.58	0.90	0.92
Std. Dev.	1.00	1.28	0.76	0.75
Mann Whitney U	156.5	443.5	304.5	295.5
z-score	2.97		0.09	
(2-tailed) p	0.003		0.93	
Significant	Yes ($r = 0.42$)		No	

4.3.3 Effect of Following the Guideline: Within one group, we analyzed whether following the guideline affects the answers to either Remembering- or Understanding-level questions. Results so far showed that students in the experimental group are more likely to score higher in following the vocalization guideline, and at the same time are more likely to score higher in the Remembering-level score, than the students in the control group. However, comparing the students' score within the experimental group itself does not show a relationship between following the vocalization guideline

and the score in neither the Remembering- nor Understanding-level category. The control group, however, reveals a different behavior. Results show that students within the control group who followed the vocalization guidelines scored higher on the Understanding-level questions (see Figure 3). According to the ANOVA test, the vocalization varies across the quantiles of the Understanding-level score (F=8.232, p=0.002). We highlight again that students in this group were not instructed to repeat the reading of the code, they only listened to the instructor reading aloud the code snippets.

5 DISCUSSION

5.1 Reflection and explanation of the results

The main finding in this study is the significant effect RA has on remembering the syntax of the programming constructs taught to the students. We believe this result encourages teachers in primary schools to practice code vocalization as pedagogy in their programming classes. While learning how to program is unique and known to be difficult, it is still a learning process. We can, therefore, use pedagogies from other domains to help make programming easier to learn for younger students in particular. With that in mind, we can explain the effect of RA we observe in this study from two

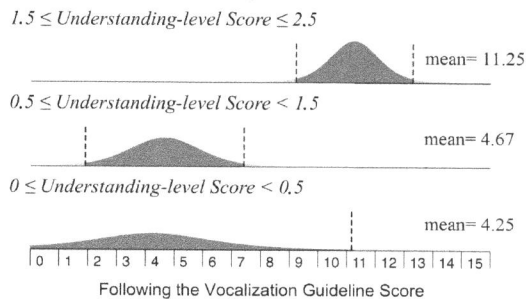

Figure 3: The variance of following the vocalization guideline among the participants in the control group and and the relation with the score on Understanding-level questions

Table 4: The most and least followed vocalizations following the guideline in Table 1

Most Followed		Least Followed	
The Experimental Group (n=25)			
V3 - Colon in for-loop (:)	22	V7 - List square brackets	11
V1 - Variable assignment (is)	21	V4 - Space indentation in for-loops	16
V9 - Comma (,)			
V8 - String single quotation (')	19	V5 - Plus sign	17
V10 - Dot in function call			
The Control Group (n=24)			
V1 - Variable assignment	14.25	V4 - Space indentation in for-loops	5
V6 - Underscore in variable names	14	V7 - List square brackets	6
		V3 - Colon in for-loop (:)	
V9 - Comma (,)		V2 - Round bracket for function call	
V8 - String single quotation (')	13	V10 - Dot in function call	11
		V5 - Plus sign	

angles. First, RA improves the learning environment by utilizing a familiar technique to young students. This subsequently raises focus and attention of the students. When attention is gained and sustained learning can happen as *"attention is a prerequisite for learning"* [21, p. 3]. Secondly, RA helps in automating the retrieval of basic knowledge required for cognitive development [3]. According to the neo-Piagetian theories of cognitive development [26], students in their initial phase of learning programming are at the sensorimotor stage. At that stage, students mostly struggle in interpreting the semantics of the code they read, which affects their performance in tracing tasks in particular [38, 40]. Practicing RA could potentially help in reducing the struggle because it automates the remembering of the language constructs, and helps the student moving faster to the next development phases.

5.2 RA and the granularity of the vocalization

There is currently no standard guideline specifying how constructs of Python, or other programming languages, should be vocalized. As presented in Section 2.2, there are various granularities and strategies one can read code with. In this study, however, we follow a specific technique to vocalization (Section 3.4) which can be considered of a low granularity, focusing on syntax rather than semantics or relations within the code. Nevertheless, when teaching young and novice students, the RA method we follow could help teachers create a benchmark where students know how to call

all the elements in their programming environment. We see from the answers of the control group students that there exist some variances in calling specific symbols. For example, calling the single (') a *"single quotation"*, *"apostrophe"*, or *"upper comma"*. This variance shows the challenges that beginners face to identify symbols in the first place. An extra cognitive effort is spent on remembering rather than on conceptual understanding. We hypothesize that higher granularities of vocalization of code structures or semantics can be integrated into the following phases. To determine the best vocalization method teachers start with, however, is out of this study's scope and is an opportunity for future research.

5.3 Threats to validity

Our study involves some threats to its validity. First, the split of the participants into the two groups might have influenced the results. The split was introduced by the school structure; i.e., per class. However, we randomly selected one class as the experimental group and the other as the control group. The second threat, the authors being the teachers at the same time could introduce a bias in favor of the experimental group. To reduce the effect of such bias we ensured that both groups studied the same materials over the same amount of time with the same teacher. The main teacher was accompanied by another teacher who among other things observed the teaching given to the two groups. By these steps, we ensured that the only difference between the two groups would be the reading-aloud method. Third threat, a wrongful assignment of a question to one of Bloom's cognitive levels by the authors. This is a common challenge for researchers in similar studies [39, 41], and future experiments will lead to refining this process. Finally, a threat to the external validity of our study is the difficulty to generalize its results. This is, however, an inherent issue in similar studies with small sample size [32]. To overcome this threat we should replicate the study across different participants in the future.

6 CONCLUSIONS AND FUTURE WORK

Our paper aims at measuring the effect of reading code aloud during programming lessons on comprehension. We perform a controlled experiment with 49 school students aged between 9 and 13. We assess the students' comprehension of basic programming concepts after three Python programming lessons. The assessment is based on Bloom's taxonomy and focused on the of remembering and understanding levels. The results show that the participants in the experimental group score significantly higher in remembering-level questions. However, the two groups perform similarly in understanding-level questions. Furthermore, we observe that the participants in both groups vocalize specific constructs more often than others. For example, the variable's assignment (is) and punctuation symbols (comma, underscore and quotation mark). Our paper suggests that using RA for teaching programming in schools will contribute to improving comprehension among young students. In particular, it will improve remembering the syntax, paving the way to spending more cognitive effort on the higher level understanding of the concepts. For future work, we aim at experimenting with different RA approaches with different code granularities to find the best approach to improve code comprehension at this age.

REFERENCES

[1] Lorin W Anderson and David Krathwohl. 2001. *A Taxonomy for Learning, Teaching, and Assessing*. New York.

[2] Richard Arends. 2012. *Learning to teach*. McGraw-Hill.

[3] Craig Barton. 2018. *How I wish I'd taught maths*. John Catt Educational Ltd.

[4] Andrew Begel. Programming By Voice: A Domain-specific Application of Speech Recognition. (????).

[5] A. Begel and S.L. Graham. Spoken Programs. *2005 IEEE Symposium on Visual Languages and Human-Centric Computing (VL/HCC'05)* (????). DOI : http://dx.doi.org/10.1109/vlhcc.2005.58

[6] A. Begel and S.L. Graham. 2006. An Assessment of a Speech-Based Programming Environment. *Visual Languages and Human-Centric Computing (VL/HCC'06)* (2006). DOI : http://dx.doi.org/10.1109/vlhcc.2006.9

[7] B.S. Bloom. 1956. *Taxonomy of Educational Objectives: The Classification of Educational Goals*. Number v. 1 in Taxonomy of Educational Objectives: The Classification of Educational Goals. D. McKay. https://books.google.nl/books?id=hos6AAAAIAAJ

[8] B. Du Boulay. 1986. Some Difficulties of Learning to Program. *Journal of Educational Computing Research* 2, 1 (1986), 57–73. DOI : http://dx.doi.org/10.2190/3LFX-9RRF-67T8-UVK9 arXiv:https://doi.org/10.2190/3LFX-9RRF-67T8-UVK9

[9] Adriana G. Bus, Marinus H. van IJzendoorn, and Anthony D. Pellegrini. 1995. Joint Book Reading Makes for Success in Learning to Read: A Meta-Analysis on Intergenerational Transmission of Literacy. *Review of Educational Research* 65, 1 (1995), 1–21. DOI : http://dx.doi.org/10.3102/00346543065001001

[10] G. Canfora, A. Cimitile, and C.A. Visaggio. Lessons learned about distributed pair programming: what are the knowledge needs to address? *WET ICE 2003. Proceedings. Twelfth IEEE International Workshops on Enabling Technologies: Infrastructure for Collaborative Enterprises, 2003.* (????). DOI : http://dx.doi.org/10.1109/enabl.2003.1231429

[11] Barry H Cohen. 2008. *Explaining Psychological Statistics* (3 ed.). John Wiley & Sons.

[12] Ryan Deschambault. 2011. Thinking-Aloud as Talking-in-Interaction: Reinterpreting How L2 Lexical Inferencing Gets Done. *Language Learning* 62, 1 (2011), 266–301. DOI : http://dx.doi.org/10.1111/j.1467-9922.2011.00653.x

[13] A. Desilets. 2001. VoiceGrip: A Tool for Programming-by-Voice. *International Journal of Speech Technology* 4, 2 (01 Jun 2001), 103–116. DOI : http://dx.doi.org/10.1023/A:1011323308477

[14] Richard Fateman. 1998. How can we speak math. *Journal of Symbolic Computation* (1998).

[15] Sue Fitzgerald, Beth Simon, and Lynda Thomas. 2005. Strategies that students use to trace code. *Proceedings of the 2005 international workshop on Computing education research - ICER '05* (2005). DOI : http://dx.doi.org/10.1145/1089786.1089793

[16] Joan M Francioni and Ann C Smith. 2002. Computer science accessibility for students with visual disabilities. In *ACM SIGCSE Bulletin*, Vol. 34. ACM, 91–95.

[17] Andrea D. Hale, Renee O. Hawkins, Wesley Sheeley, Jennifer R. Reynolds, Shonna Jenkins, Ara J. Schmitt, and Daniel A. Martin. 2010. An investigation of silent versus aloud reading comprehension of elementary students using Maze assessment procedures. *Psychology in the Schools* 48, 1 (2010), 4–13. DOI : http://dx.doi.org/10.1002/pits.20543

[18] John Hattie. 2009. *Visible learning*. Routledge.

[19] Felienne Hermans and Efthimia Aivaloglou. 2017. Teaching Software Engineering Principles to K-12 Students: A MOOC on Scratch. In *Proceedings of the 39th International Conference on Software Engineering: Software Engineering and Education Track (ICSE-SEET '17)*. IEEE Press, Piscataway, NJ, USA, 13–22. DOI : http://dx.doi.org/10.1109/ICSE-SEET.2017.13

[20] Felienne Hermans, Alaaeddin Swidan, and Efthimia Aivaloglou. 2018. Code phonology. *Proceedings of the 26th Conference on Program Comprehension - ICPC '18* (2018). DOI : http://dx.doi.org/10.1145/3196321.3196355

[21] John M. Keller. 1987. Development and use of the ARCS model of instructional design. *Journal of Instructional Development* 10, 3 (1987), 2–10. DOI : http://dx.doi.org/10.1007/bf02905780

[22] Sherry Kragler, Linda Martin, and Virginia Schreier. 2015. Investigating Young Children's Use of Reading Strategies: A Longitudinal Study. *Reading Psychology* 36, 5 (2015), 445–472. DOI : http://dx.doi.org/10.1080/02702711.2014.884031

[23] Raymond Lister. 2005. Computer Science Teachers as Amateurs, Students and Researchers. In *In Proceedings of the 5 th Baltic Sea Conference on Computing Education Research. (Koli*. 3–12.

[24] Raymond Lister, Elizabeth S. Adams, Sue Fitzgerald, William Fone, John Hamer, Morten Lindholm, Robert McCartney, Jan Erik Moström, Kate Sanders, Otto Seppälä, Beth Simon, and Lynda Thomas. 2004. A Multi-national Study of Reading and Tracing Skills in Novice Programmers. *SIGCSE Bull.* 36, 4 (June 2004), 119–150. DOI : http://dx.doi.org/10.1145/1041624.1041673

[25] Linda E. Martin and Sherry Kragler. 2011. Becoming a Self-Regulated Reader: A Study of Primary-Grade Students' Reading Strategies. *Literacy Research and Instruction* 50, 2 (2011), 89–104. DOI : http://dx.doi.org/10.1080/19388071003594697

[26] Michael F. Mascolo. 2015. Neo-Piagetian Theories of Cognitive Development. *International Encyclopedia of the Social & Behavioral Sciences* (2015), 501–510. DOI : http://dx.doi.org/10.1016/b978-0-08-097086-8.23097-3

[27] R. Steve McCallum, Shannon Sharp, Sherry Mee Bell, and Thomas George. 2004. Silent versus oral reading comprehension and efficiency. *Psychology in the Schools* 41, 2 (2004), 241–246. DOI : http://dx.doi.org/10.1002/pits.10152

[28] Chris Parnin. 2011. Subvocalization - Toward Hearing the Inner Thoughts of Developers. *2011 IEEE 19th International Conference on Program Comprehension* (2011). DOI : http://dx.doi.org/10.1109/icpc.2011.49

[29] M. Perrone-Bertolotti, L. Rapin, J.-P. Lachaux, M. Baciu, and H. Lœvenbruck. 2014. What is that little voice inside my head? Inner speech phenomenology, its role in cognitive performance, and its relation to self-monitoring. *Behavioural Brain Research* 261 (2014), 220–239. DOI : http://dx.doi.org/10.1016/j.bbr.2013.12.034

[30] David E Price, DA Dahlstrom, Ben Newton, and Joseph L Zachary. 2002. Off to See the Wizard: using a" Wizard of Oz" study to learn how to design a spoken language interface for programming. In *Frontiers in Education, 2002. FIE 2002. 32nd Annual*, Vol. 1. IEEE, T2G–T2G.

[31] Suzanne M Prior and Katherine A Welling. 2001. " Read in Your Head": A Vygotskian Analysis of the Transition from Oral to Silent Reading. *Reading Psychology* 22, 1 (2001), 1–15.

[32] Katherine E. Purswell and Dee C. Ray. 2014. Research With Small Samples. *Counseling Outcome Research and Evaluation* 5, 2 (2014), 116–126. DOI : http://dx.doi.org/10.1177/2150137814552474

[33] Keith Rayner, Barbara R. Foorman, Charles A. Perfetti, David Pesetsky, and Mark S. Seidenberg. 2002. How Should Reading be Taught? *Scientific American* 286, 3 (2002), 84–91. DOI : http://dx.doi.org/10.1038/scientificamerican0302-84

[34] Lana Edwards Santoro, David J. Chard, Lisa Howard, and Scott K. Baker. 2008. Making the Very Most of Classroom Read-Alouds to Promote Comprehension and Vocabulary. *The Reading Teacher* 61, 5 (2008), 396–408. DOI : http://dx.doi.org/10.1598/rt.61.5.4

[35] Marcel Schmeier and Ruud Bijman. 2017. *Effectief rekenonderwijs op de basisschool* (1st edition ed.). Uitgeverij Pica.

[36] Lindsey Snell and Mr Jim Cunningham. 2000. An investigation into programming by voice and development of a toolkit for writing voice-controlled applications. (2000).

[37] Osamu Takeuchi, Maiko Ikeda, and Atsushi Mizumoto. 2012. Reading Aloud Activity in L2 and Cerebral Activation. *RELC Journal* 43, 2 (2012), 151–167. DOI : http://dx.doi.org/10.1177/0033688212450496

[38] Donna Teague and Raymond Lister. 2014. Longitudinal Think Aloud Study of a Novice Programmer. In *Proceedings of the Sixteenth Australasian Computing Education Conference - Volume 148 (ACE '14)*. Australian Computer Society, Inc, Darlinghurst, Australia, Australia, 41–50. http://dl.acm.org/citation.cfm?id=2667490.2667495

[39] Errol Thompson, Andrew Luxton-Reilly, Jacqueline L. Whalley, Minjie Hu, and Phil Robbins. 2008. Bloom's Taxonomy for CS Assessment. In *Proceedings of the Tenth Conference on Australasian Computing Education - Volume 78 (ACE '08)*. Australian Computer Society, Inc., Darlinghurst, Australia, Australia, 155–161. http://dl.acm.org/citation.cfm?id=1379249.1379265

[40] Jacqueline Whalley and Nadia Kasto. 2014. A qualitative think-aloud study of novice programmers' code writing strategies. *Proceedings of the 2014 conference on Innovation & technology in computer science education - ITiCSE '14* (2014). DOI : http://dx.doi.org/10.1145/2591708.2591762

[41] Jacqueline L. Whalley, Raymond Lister, Errol Thompson, Tony Clear, Phil Robbins, P. K. Ajith Kumar, and Christine Prasad. 2006. An Australasian Study of Reading and Comprehension Skills in Novice Programmers, Using the Bloom and SOLO Taxonomies. In *Proceedings of the 8th Australasian Conference on Computing Education - Volume 52 (ACE '06)*. Australian Computer Society, Inc., Darlinghurst, Australia, Australia, 243–252. http://dl.acm.org/citation.cfm?id=1151869.1151901

Using Data to Understand Difficulties of Learning to Program: A Study with Chinese Middle School Students

Yizhou Qian
Dept. of Educational Technology
Jiangnan University
Wuxi, China
yqian@jiangnan.edu.cn

Peilin Yan
Wuxi Shanbei Middle School
Wuxi, China
plyan_wx@163.com

Mingke Zhou
Wuxi Shanbei Middle School
Wuxi, China
zmk.wx@163.com

ABSTRACT

Computing education has been expanding into K-12 schools in many countries. The new national curriculum standards in China are going to include computational thinking as a core literacy for every student and make computer programming as a required module in the information technology course. Hence, it is imperative to understand the difficulties Chinese students may face when learning to program. This study investigated Chinese middle students' difficulties in learning to program in Python using the student data in an automated assessment system. Our results showed that the students struggled with fundamental Python syntax and programming rules. We also found that Chinese students faced a special difficulty, which was using correct punctuation symbols in code. We noted that many syntax errors students made were due to the use of Chinese punctuation symbols, which look almost identical to the English equivalents but are invalid to the Python interpreter. Our results suggest that when teaching a programming course to Chinese middle school students, teachers should first help students develop certain typing skills (e.g., switching input methods, distinguishing Chinese and English punctuation symbols, etc.). Such preparation may reduce students' mistakes in code. Finally, future research directions are discussed, including examining the effects of the typing skill training, designing feedback components for the automated assessment system, and so forth.

CCS CONCEPTS

• **Social and professional topics~K-12 education** • Social and professional topics~Student assessment • Applied computing~Interactive learning environments

KEYWORDS

computing education; difficulties; misconceptions; novice programming; Chinese middle school students

ACM Reference format:

Yizhou Qian, Peilin Yan and Mingke Zhou. 2019. Using data to understand difficulties of learning to program: A study with Chinese middle school students. In *Proceedings of ACM Global Computing Education Conference 2019 (CompEd'19). ACM, New York, NY, USA, 7 pages.* https://doi.org/10.1145/3300115.3309521

1. Introduction

With the rapid development of computing technology, computing education is getting more important and popular. It has been expanding into K-12 schools in many countries, including the U.S. [13], the U.K. [6], New Zealand [4], and so forth. One key component of computing education is to teach students computer programming. However, learning to program is difficult for K-12 students, because a variety of difficulties including misconceptions may impede novices' learning of programming knowledge [12, 16, 20, 21, 25].

To understand and resolve learners' difficulties in introductory programming, researchers and educators have developed various instructional tools and approaches [1, 2, 7, 18, 21]. A common method is to integrate an automated assessment system into instruction and utilize the student data in it to identify and understand the difficulties students face when learning to program [3, 5, 21]. An automated assessment system is a tool that can automatically evaluate the correctness of students' programs [9, 17]. The student data in an automated assessment system, especially students' erroneous programs, are a good source for analyzing students' common errors and relevant difficulties. By using such a data-driven approach, previous studies have identified the most frequent errors CS1 students made in Java programming [1, 2, 7, 14]. However, this approach has not been widely applied to other programming languages (e.g., Python) and instructional settings (e.g. pre-college students).

This study investigated Chinese middle students' difficulties in learning to program in Python using the student data in an automated assessment system. In China, the new national curriculum standards are going to include computational thinking as a core literacy for every student and make computer programming as a required module in the information technology course. Hence, it is imperative to understand the difficulties Chinese students face when learning to program. The following two research questions guided this study:

RQ1. What are the most common errors in students' programs?

RQ2. What are the underlying difficulties relevant to the common errors?

2. Related Work

In introductory programming, students often face a variety of difficulties, such as deficient knowledge of the syntax, misunderstandings of programming concepts, lack of programming strategies, and so forth [20]. To understand students' difficulties in learning to program, researchers have developed various tools to collect and analyze students' erroneous programs [2, 15, 20, 22]. A typical method is to use an automated assessment system to evaluate the correctness of students' programs and further analyze the data collected by the system to identify common errors and understand the difficulties that students encounter in learning [1, 3, 8, 14, 21].

Most previous studies using such a method focused on Java programming. For instance, Jadud [15] used the BlueJ pedagogic programming environment and its data to explore students' compilation behaviors and reported the common Java compilation errors, including *missing semicolons, unknown symbol: variable, bracket expected*, and so forth. Denny et al. [7] examined student data in CodeWrite and identified the most common Java syntax errors in students' code. They also found that students spent different time solving different errors. Altadmri and Brown [1] analyzed 37 million compilations of over 250, 000 students in the Blackbox data set and investigated the frequencies of 18 mistakes students often made in Java programming. Becker [2] compared prior studies on common Java compilation errors and found that the top 10 errors usually account for the majority of all student errors. He used the tool Decaf, which allowed adding enhanced error messages to common Java compilation errors, in instruction and found that students made fewer errors after receiving enhanced error messages for common errors.

Few studies on this topic investigated students' common errors and difficulties in learning a programming language other than Java. Sirkia and Sorva [22] integrated UUhistle, a visual program simulation (VPS) system, into instruction and explored common misconceptions CS1 students had when learning Python programming. Qian and Lehman [21] analyzed student data in SangTian Programming Learning Environment (SPLE) and identified common errors and misconceptions of a group of Chinese middle school students in a Pascal programming course.

Prior research has mainly focused on CS1 students' difficulties in Java programming. Few studies have paid attention to pre-college students' difficulties in learning another programming language. As computing education has been expanding into K-12 schools, it is imperative to understand K-12 students' difficulties in learning to program. Python is getting more and more popular as an introductory programming language [11] and is syntactically easier for learners [10, 23]. The new information technology curriculum in China will also include Python

programming modules. This exploratory study investigated Chinese middle school students' difficulties in learning Python programming using student data in an automated assessment system.

3. Methodology

3.1 Participants and Research Settings

The participants of this study were a group of 35 middle school students (21 boys and 14 girls) who took an information technology course. These students were in the 7th grade (the first year of a typical Chinese middle school) of an average public middle school from a city in East China. In this school, the information technology course is required for every student. Typically, the topics of this course include making PowerPoint, designing simple Flash animation, designing websites, and a brief introduction to computer programming. However, as the new national curriculum standards have a focus on developing students' computational thinking skill, this school redesigned the information technology course with a focus on Python programming and computational thinking in 2018. The participants of this study were the first group of students who took this new course. This exploratory study was based on students' performance during the first six weeks of this course.

Every week, students attended two consecutive classes (a 90-minute block) in a computer lab. The Python version used in this course was Python 3.7. The programming environment used was Python IDLE, the default integrated development environment installed with the standard Python toolset. The topics introduced during the six weeks included Input, Output, Variables, and Operators.

In addition, an automated assessment system, Mulberry, was integrated into the instruction (Figure 1 presents a screen shot of Mulberry). Mulberry has a pool of 54 programming problems organized using Quests (Figure 2 shows three translated example problems in Mulberry). A Quest in Mulberry is a collection of programming problems that are related to the same programming topic. For example, problems of Quest 1 in Mulberry are related to Python Input and Output, and Quest 2 focuses on Variables and Operators. To start Quest 1 in Mulberry, a student first has to create his or her own avatar. When he or she solves a programming problem, his or her avatar gains a certain number of experience points. Once a student solves adequate problems and accumulates enough experience points, his or her avatar will level up and unlock next Quest.

Each problem in Mulberry has one or more test cases. A test case is a pair of input data and expected output. To correctly solve a problem in Mulberry, a student had to write a Python program that could correctly read the input data of each test case and produce output matching the expected output. When a student submitted an erroneous solution, he or she was told that the solution was incorrect and could revise and resubmit the solution until the solution was correct.

Figure 1: Screen shot of Mulberry

Example Problem #1:
You see an injured rabbit in a forest. It is polite to say hello to the rabbit. Write a program to print "Hello, Rabbit!" on the screen.

Example Problem #2:
Only printing words sometimes is not enough. Let's add some interaction between you and me. Write a program to read a name from the user and say "Hello". For instance, if the user enters **Jim**, your program needs to print **Hello, Jim!**

The following are examples of input and output:
Input: **Jim**   Output: **Hello, Jim!**
Input: **Olivia**   Output: **Hello, Olivia!**

Example Problem #3:
Given two numbers a and b, write a program to calculate and print the sum of $a^2 + b^2$.

The following are examples of input and output:
 Input: **2   2.5**   Output: **10.25**
 Input: **2.1 3.14**   Output: **14.2696**

Figure 2: Three translated example problems in Mulberry

3.2 Data Analysis

Students' erroneous solutions in Mulberry during the first six weeks of the course were used to analyze students' common errors and difficulties in learning Python programming. According to Python official documents, there exist two types of errors: syntax errors and exceptions. A syntax error in Python indicates that the code has a syntactic error, which makes the parser fail to decide the true intention of the code. Exceptions refer to the errors that occur during the execution of a syntactically correct program, including type errors, name errors, and so forth. In this exploratory study, we limited our scope of

data analysis to students' erroneous solutions with syntax errors or exceptions. In other words, the programming errors in this study referred to only Python syntax errors and exceptions. Our data analysis did not include incorrect student solutions that did not lead a Python error message.

Both quantitative and qualitative data analyses were conducted to investigate students' common errors in Python programming and the underlying difficulties. First, quantitative analysis was conducted to identify the most common errors students made in their code to answer RQ1. The frequencies of each type of syntax errors and exceptions were collected and compared. Second, qualitative analysis of students' code was conducted to identify common patterns of erroneous code pieces and understand the underlying difficulties relevant to the errors to answer RQ2. During the qualitative analysis, students' submissions were first grouped by their error types. Next, two reviewers (the first author and the third author) reviewed students' erroneous programs of each type of error to identify common patterns. For the errors that occurred less than 10 times (see #9-13 in Table 1), all the erroneous programs with those errors were reviewed by both reviewers. For the other errors (see #1-8 in Table 1), two reviewers selected about 30 erroneous programs per error and examined the code together to find common patterns. When selecting the erroneous programs, reviewers tried their best to make sure the programs were from as many different students as possible.

Table 1: Frequency and percentage of student errors

#	Error	Category	n	%
1	invalid syntax	Syntax Error	339	28.5%
2	invalid character in identifier	Syntax Error	291	24.5%
3	NameError	Exception	149	12.5%
4	EOFError	Exception	105	8.8%
5	EOL while scanning string literal	Syntax Error	93	7.8%
6	TypeError	Exception	85	7.2%
7	ValueError	Exception	61	5.1%
8	IndentationError	Exception	48	4.0%
9	Missing parentheses in call to 'print'	Syntax Error	7	0.6%
10	EOF while scanning triple-quoted string literal	Syntax Error	3	0.3%
11	ImportError	Exception	3	0.3%
12	can't assign to operator	Syntax Error	2	0.2%
13	AttributeError	Exception	2	0.2%

4. Results

4.1 RQ1: What are the most common errors in students' programs?

During the first six weeks of the information technology course, students submitted 2,091 solutions to Mulberry in total. Among them, 268 solutions were correct; 735 had syntax errors;

453 had exceptions; 635 had other errors (e.g., logic errors). The number of errors (syntax errors and exceptions) analyzed in this study was 1,188 in total. Six different syntax errors and seven different exceptions were identified in students' code (see Table 1). The top five most frequent errors were *invalid syntax, invalid character in identifier, NameError, EOFError,* and *EOL while scanning string literal*. Five errors (#9-13 in Table 1) seldom occurred (<1%). The results indicate that in general students struggled with syntactic knowledge of Python programming. However, only using the error names given by Python and the frequency of the errors was not enough to understand the real difficulties students faced when learning to program. Hence, qualitative analysis of students' erroneous code related to each error was conducted. The next section presents the results of the qualitative analysis.

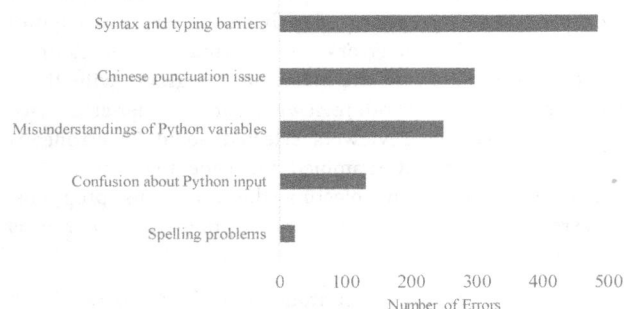

Figure 3: Number of errors related to each difficulty

4.2 RQ2: What are the underlying difficulties relevant to the common errors?

Our qualitative analysis of students' erroneous solutions identified five major difficulties: syntax and typing barriers, Chinese punctuation issue, misunderstandings of Python variables, confusion about Python input, and spelling problems. Figure 3 presents the numbers of errors related to each difficulty.

Difficulty 1: Syntax and typing barriers. According to the previous section, the most frequent error was *invalid syntax*. This error was usually due to students' unfamiliarity with Python syntax rules. Line 2 in Figure 4 was the code of a student that produced the *invalid syntax* error. He or she forgot to put the output message within quotation marks. Line 3 and 4 in Figure 4 also led to the *invalid syntax* error. However, it is hard to say whether they were due to the typos or inadequate knowledge of Python syntax. We also noted that some other errors had similar causes to an invalid syntax error but produced another error message. For example, line 7 in figure 4 actually had a similar mistake to line 2, but it produced the *EOL while scanning string literal* error. Thus, we grouped such errors together as syntax and typing barriers (see Figure 4 for example code). The *IndentationError* was put in this category, because students had not learned any Python statements that needed indentation, and the indentation errors here were mainly due to an unnecessary space at the beginning of a line (see line 18 in Figure 4). Probably

```
1    invalid syntax
2    print(Hello, Rabbit!)
3    b = round(a.2)
4    print('Hello,'+a+''!')
5
6    EOL while scanning string literal
7    print(Don't Worry! I can cure you.)
8    print('Hello,Rabbit!)
9
10   EOF while scanning triple-quoted string literal
11   print ('''Don't Worry!'')
12
13   can't assign to operator
14   a+b=print()
15   h=a+b=c
16
17   IndentationError
18     print("Hello,Rabbit!")
```

Figure 4: Code examples of syntax and typing barriers

```
1    invalid character in identifier
2    a=input ()
3    print( "Don't Worry!" )
4    print( 'I can cure you.' )
5
6    Missing parentheses in call to 'print'
7    print ( 'Hello, Rabbit' )
8    print ( 'Don't Worry!, I can cure you. ')
```

Figure 5: Code examples of using Chinese punctuation

these students did not notice such a space and had no idea why a space could lead to an error. Therefore, it was a mix of typos and insufficient syntactic knowledge. The total number of errors relevant to syntax and typing barriers was 485.

Difficulty 2: Chinese punctuation issue. The second most frequent error in this study was *invalid character in identifier*. This Python error message did not provide much information about what invalid characters existed in code. After analyzing students' code, we found that this error was due to the use of Chinese punctuation. For example, in line 2 of Figure 5, this student used a Chinese open parenthesis (, rather than the valid English one. In line 3 and 4, Chinese double and single quotation marks were used while the correct ones should look like " (the double quotation mark) and ' (the single quotation mark). These Chinese punctuation symbols look almost identical to the English equivalents but are invalid to the Python interpreter. Thus, when the Chinese punctuation was incorrectly used in the code, the Chinese middle school students might not be able to notice the issue. In addition, to type Chinese, students had to use Chinese input methods such as Google Pinyin software; to type English, students should switch the Chinese input method to the English mode or turn off the Chinese input method. However, these middle school students may not know how to do this and/or do not understand why they have to type in the English mode.

Interestingly, after examining students' code, we found that another error *Missing parentheses in call to 'print'* was also related to the Chinese punctuation issue. Line 7 and 8 in Figure 5 provide two examples of this error. The two students did not miss parentheses when calling the *print* function, but they used the Chinese open parenthesis, which made the Python interpreter unable to find the open parenthesis for the *print* function. In total, there were 298 errors related to the Chinese punctuation issue.

```
1    NameError
2    a=input()
3    n=int(n)
4
5    TypeError
6    a=input()
7    b=input()
8    c=a*a+b*b
9
10   ValueError
11   a=input()
12   a=int(a)
```

Figure 6: Code examples of misunderstandings of Python variables

```
1    EOFError
2    name=input()
3    print('Hello,Jim!')
4    name=input()
5    print('Hello,Olivia!')
6
7    TypeError 1
8    a=input
9    a=int(a)
10
11   TypeError 2
12   input(1,2)
```

Figure 7: Code examples of confusion about Python input

Difficulty 3: Misunderstandings of Python variables. Three errors were mainly related to students' misunderstandings of Python variables, including *NameError*, *TypeError*, and *ValueError*. Most *name errors* students made were caused by defining a variable with one name and using the variable with another name. For example, line 2 in Figure 6 read the input data and stored in variable *a*; however, when the student wanted to convert *a* (a string) into an integer, he or she used the name *n*, instead of *a*. While it seems to be a typo, more than 100 occurrences of this error suggest that it is more likely that students did not completely understand the concept variable and how Python variables work. There did exist 19 occurrences of *NameError*, which resulted from certain kinds of typos such as misspelling the word *print* (see Difficulty 5: Spelling problems). The majority of *type errors* in this study were related to failing to convert strings to numbers (see line 6-8 in Figure 6). In Python 3.x, the input function returns a *str* type. In the example above, this student forgot to convert the input data into numbers before doing

the calculation. Possibly these beginners did not fully understand that variables have types and certain operations can only be applied to certain types of variables. The *value errors* were also regarding variable types. Line 11 and 12 in Figure 6 seem to be correct. However, for that specific problem, the input data of the test case was a real number. Therefore, the correct way to convert variable *a* into a number was to use the *float* function, rather than the *int* function. Students might not understand the necessity of distinguishing types of variables in Python and the difference between the *float* type and *int* type, because numbers in math do not have types. In total, 250 errors were related to this difficulty.

Difficulty 4: Confusion about Python input. One important topic covered during the six weeks was the concept Input. In Python, the *input* function can be used to read input data. However, students often failed to use the *input* function correctly. For example, the *EOFError* occurred if no data was given when calling the *input* function. Many students did not understand how the *input* function works and put one or more extra *input* function calls in their code. For instance, in line 2-5 in Figure 7, there were two *input* function calls. However, the test cases of that programming problem only give a name as the input data, the correct solution should output a message like "Hello, XXX!", in which XXX is the input data. In the example above, this student might not understand how the program read input data and where the input data was stored. In addition, incorrect use of the input function also led to certain type errors (see line 7-12 in Figure 7). Errors related to this difficulty were 131 in total.

```
1    AttributeError
2    b=math.sprt(a)
3
4    ImportError
5    import match
6
7    NameError
8    a=flort(a)
9    n=imput()
10   m=imput()
```

Figure 8: Code examples of spelling problems

Difficulty 5: Spelling problems. Our qualitative analysis found that some errors were due to the English spelling problems. Figure 8 presents code examples related to this issue. As these Chinese middle school students had very limited English ability, the words like "float" and "input" may not be familiar to them. They probably did not know "square root", so mistakenly spelling "sqrt" as "sprt" is not surprising. Errors related to the spelling problems were 24 in total. The number was not large, but it is possible that the spelling problems increased students' cognitive load [24] when writing programs.

5. Discussion

Our results found that there were 13 different types of errors in students' code and the top five most frequent errors were *invalid syntax, invalid character in identifier, NameError, EOFError,* and *EOL while scanning string literal*. Five of the 13 errors (#9-13 in Table 1) seldom occurred (<1%). Based on these errors and the qualitative analysis of erroneous student code, five difficulties were identified, including syntax and typing barriers, Chinese punctuation issue, misunderstandings of Python variables, confusion about Python input, and spelling problems. Our results suggest that (1) certain programming knowledge seems to be basic and simple but is difficult for novices, and (2) Chinese students face special difficulties in learning to program (e.g., the Chinese punctuation issue, spelling issues, etc.), which may not be a problem to students whose native language is English.

While Python is considered a syntactically easier programming language than Java [23], our results indicate that the fundamental Python syntax and programming rules are not simple to novices. Three difficulties in this study were related to Python syntax and fundamental programming concepts such as Variables and Input. Previous research on Java learners' common errors also indicated that students struggled with Java syntactic knowledge, and top errors included *cannot resolve identifier, mismatching parentheses, braces, and quotation marks, missing semicolons*, and so on (see [1, 2, 7, 22]). While error names and types are different in Python and Java, the phenomenon is similar: beginners have difficulties with basic syntax of a programming language. However, knowing such a conclusion does not promise that teachers truly understand what difficulties their students face. To experts, programming knowledge about basic syntax, using variables, and reading input data is simple. Such a feeling may result from the "expert blind spot", which prevents programming experts accurately gauging the real difficulties faced by beginners [12]. Hence, computer science teachers' experience and feeling may not be able to help them correctly identify the difficulties their students encounter in learning to program [5, 21]. Using student data, especially erroneous code, to identify common student errors and difficulties can be an effective way to support instructional design and teaching. We recommend that computer science teachers integrate such tools into their instruction.

According to our results, two difficulties, the Chinese punctuation issue and spelling problems, can be special challenges of Chinese students, especially young middle school students who have limited typing skills and English ability. This finding is consistent with previous studies about Chinese middle school students' learning of programming [19, 21]. Qian and Lehman [21] also reported the Chinese punctuation issue in their study of a group of Chinese middle school students who learned Pascal programming. Possibly, this is due to middle school students' limited knowledge and skills of using a computer (e.g., switching between input methods). When students have to write Python programs and deal with the Chinese punctuation issue simultaneously, they may experience heavier cognitive load [24] than those who only have to write Python code. Similarly, because of their limited English ability, Chinese middle school students may have higher cognitive load when writing programs than students who are native English speakers. For example, Chinese middle school students may fail to type the "sqrt" function, because they probably do not know "sqrt" stands for "square root" and have no idea what "square root" means. Native English

speakers sometimes may also misspell certain programming commands, but possibly, they know the correct spelling and the meaning of the words.

Thus, we recommend that when teaching a programming course to Chinese middle school students, teachers should first help students develop certain typing skills. For example, teachers can teach students how to turn off/on the Chinese input method, how to use the English mode of the input method, and how to switch between input methods. They should also teach students to distinguish Chinese and English punctuation symbols. Such preparation may reduce students' errors relevant to Chinese punctuation issue. To address the spelling problems, we suggest that Chinese computer science teachers should teach their students the spelling and meaning of important statements and functions of a programming language before students learn to use the statements and functions in their code.

6. Limitations and Future Work

This study reports the preliminary results based on students' performance in the first six weeks of a programming course. The generalizability of the findings may be limited. When the course is completed, we will analyze all the data to see whether students exhibit different types of common errors. In addition, this study was based on a group of 35 middle school students, and the sample size was relatively small. In the future, we will expand our research to more Chinese schools to see whether the findings of this study can be generalized to other settings.

One major finding of this study was that these Chinese middle school students had a Chinese punctuation issue. We suggest that certain training of typing and spelling skills may reduce such errors. In the future, we will investigate the effectiveness of that kind of training. Second, we speculate that the Chinese punctuation issue may be specific to young Chinese students, and Chinese college students may not have this problem. Hence, we will examine Chinese college students' common errors when learning to program in Python. According to prior research on students' Java errors, adding a targeted feedback component by providing enhanced error messages can reduce students' mistakes [2]. Hence, one possible future research direction is to design and add a feedback component to Mulberry to examine whether enhanced error messages can reduce students' mistakes in Python.

7. Conclusion

This exploratory study investigated Chinese middle school students' difficulties in learning Python programming using student data in an automated assessment system. Using this data-driven approach, we found 13 different errors in students' code and identified five major difficulties. Our results indicate that Chinese middle school students struggle with the fundamental Python syntax and programming rules and face difficulties of using right punctuation symbols in their code and correctly spelling statements and functions. Based on the findings, we suggest that (1) using tools and student data to identify common student errors and difficulties, and (2) teaching Chinese students to correctly use input methods, distinguish Chinese and English punctuation symbols, and learn the spelling and meaning of important statements and functions.

REFERENCES

[1] Altadmri, A., & Brown, N. C. C. (2015). 37 million compilations: Investigating novice programming mistakes in large-scale student data. In *Proceedings of the 46th ACM Technical Symposium on Computer Science Education* (pp. 522–527). New York, New York, USA: ACM Press. https://doi.org/10.1145/2676723.2677258

[2] Becker, B. A. (2016). An effective approach to enhancing compiler error messages. In *Proceedings of the 47th ACM Technical Symposium on Computing Science Education - SIGCSE '16* (pp. 126–131). https://doi.org/10.1145/2839509.2844584

[3] Becker, B. A., Glanville, G., Iwashima, R., McDonnell, C., Goslin, K., & Mooney, C. (2016). Effective compiler error message enhancement for novice programming students. *Computer Science Education, 26*(2–3), 148–175. https://doi.org/10.1080/08993408.2016.1225464

[4] Bell, T., Andreae, P., & Robins, A. (2014). A case study of the introduction of computer science in NZ schools. *ACM Transactions on Computing Education, 14*(2), 1–31. https://doi.org/10.1145/2602485

[5] Brown, N. C. C., & Altadmri, A. (2017). Novice java programming mistakes: Large-scale data vs. educator beliefs. *ACM Transactions on Computing Education, 17*(2), 7:1–7:21. https://doi.org/10.1145/2994154

[6] Brown, N. C. C., Sentance, S., Crick, T., & Humphreys, S. (2014). Restart: The resurgence of computer science in uk schools. *ACM Transactions on Computing Education, 14*(2), 1–22. https://doi.org/10.1145/2602484

[7] Denny, P., Luxton-Reilly, A., & Tempero, E. (2012). All syntax errors are not equal. *Proceedings of the 17th ACM Annual Conference on Innovation and Technology in Computer Science Education - ITiCSE '12,* 75–80. https://doi.org/10.1145/2325296.2325318

[8] Denny, P., Luxton-Reilly, A., Tempero, E., & Hendrickx, J. (2011). Understanding the syntax barrier for novices. *Proceedings of the 16th Annual Joint Conference on Innovation and Technology in Computer Science Education - ITiCSE '11,* 208. https://doi.org/10.1145/1999747.1999807

[9] Douce, C., Livingstone, D., & Orwell, J. (2005). Automatic test-based assessment of programming. *Journal on Educational Resources in Computing, 5*(3), 4:1-13. https://doi.org/10.1145/1163405.1163409

[10] Grandell, L., Peltomäki, M., Back, R.-J., & Salakoski, T. (2006). Why Complicate Things?: Introducing Programming in High School Using Python. In *Proceedings of the 8th Australasian Conference on Computing Education - Volume 52* (pp. 71–80). Darlinghurst, Australia, Australia: Australian Computer Society, Inc. Retrieved from http://dl.acm.org/citation.cfm?id=1151869.1151880

[11] Guo, P. (2014). Python Is Now the Most Popular Introductory Teaching Language at Top U.S. Universities. Retrieved October 12, 2018, from https://cacm.acm.org/blogs/blog-cacm/176450-python-is-now-the-most-popular-introductory-teaching-language-at-top-u-s-universities/fulltext

[12] Guzdial, M. (2015). Learner-centered design of computing education: research on computing for everyone. *Synthesis Lectures on Human-Centered Informatics, 8*(6), 1–165. https://doi.org/10.2200/S00684ED1V01Y201511HCI033

[13] Guzdial, M. (2016). Bringing computer science to U.S. schools, state by state. *Communications of the ACM, 59*(5), 24–25. https://doi.org/10.1145/2898963

[14] Jackson, J., Cobb, M., & Carver, C. (2005). Identifying top Java errors for novice programmers. In *Proceedings Frontiers in Education 35th Annual Conference* (p. T4C–T4C). https://doi.org/10.1109/FIE.2005.1611967

[15] Jadud, M. C. (2005). A First Look at Novice Compilation Behaviour Using BlueJ. *Computer Science Education, 15*(1), 25–40. https://doi.org/10.1080/08993400500056530

[16] Kohn, T. (2017). Teaching Python Programming to Novices: Addressing Misconceptions and Creating a Development Environment. https://doi.org/10.3929/ETHZ-A-010871088

[17] Pettit, R. S., Homer, J., & Gee, R. (2017). Do enhanced compiler error messages help students? *Proceedings of the 2017 ACM SIGCSE Technical Symposium on Computer Science Education - SIGCSE '17,* 465–470. https://doi.org/10.1145/3017680.3017768

[18] Price, T. W., Dong, Y., & Lipovac, D. (2017). iSnap: Towards intelligent tutoring in novice programming environments. In *Proceedings of the 2017 ACM SIGCSE Technical Symposium on Computer Science Education - SIGCSE '17* (pp. 483–488). New York, NY, USA: ACM Press. https://doi.org/10.1145/3017680.3017762

[19] Qian, Y., & Lehman, J. D. (2016). Correlates of Success in Introductory Programming: A Study with Middle School Students. *Journal of Education and Learning, 5*(2), 73–83. https://doi.org/10.5539/jel.v5n2p73

[20] Qian, Y., & Lehman, J. (2017). Students' misconceptions and other difficulties in introductory programming: A literature review. *ACM Transactions on Computing Education, 18*(1), 1:1-24. https://doi.org/10.1145/3077618

[21] Qian, Y., & Lehman, J. (2018). Using technology to support teaching computer science: A study with middle school students. *Eurasia Journal of Mathematics, Science and Technology Education, 14*(12). https://doi.org/10.29333/ejmste/94227

[22] Sirkia, T., & Sorva, J. (2012). Exploring programming misconceptions: An analysis of student mistakes in visual program simulation exercises. In *12th Koli Calling International Conference on Computing Education Research* (pp. 19–28). https://doi.org/10.1145/2401796.2401799

[23] Stefik, A., & Siebert, S. (2013). An Empirical Investigation into Programming Language Syntax. *Trans. Comput. Educ., 13*(4), 19:1–19:40. https://doi.org/10.1145/2534973

[24] Sweller, J. (1988). Cognitive load during problem solving: Effects on learning. *Cognitive Science, 12*(2), 257–285. https://doi.org/10.1016/0364-0213(88)90023-7

[25] Swidan, A., Hermans, F., & Smit, M. (2018). Programming Misconceptions for School Students. In *Proceedings of the 2018 ACM Conference on International Computing Education Research* (pp. 151–159). New York, NY, USA: ACM. https://doi.org/10.1145/3230977.3230995

Panel: The Computing in Data Science

Lillian Cassel
Computing Sciences
Villanova University
Villanova PA 19085 USA
Lillian.cassel@villanova.edu

Wang Hongzhi
Computer Science and Technology
Harbin Institute of Technology
Harbin, Heilongjiang China
wangzh@hit.edu.cn

ABSTRACT

This panel brings the workings and results of the ACM Education Council Task Force on Data Science Education. The task force has gathered information on existing programs and has reviewed documents such as the result of the National Academies deliberations on data science. The task force is charged with exploring the role of computer science in data science education, understanding that data science is an inherently interdisciplinary field and not exclusively a computer science field. The panel will present a summary of the task force findings by two members of the task force and perspectives from leaders in data-intensive applications from China. The goal of the panel is to present the findings, but also to obtain perspectives from the attendees in order to enrich the task force's work.

CCS CONCEPTS

• Social and professional topics~Computing education programs

KEYWORDS

Data science, computing curriculum, computing for data science

ACM Reference format:

Lillian N. Cassel, Wang Hongzhi 2019. Computing for Data Science (Abstract Only). In Proceedings of the First ACM SIGCSE Global Computing Education Conference (CompEd 2019). ACM, NY, NY, USA, 2 pages, https://doi.org/10.1145/3300115.3312508

1 Background

In October of 2015, representatives of the ACM Education Council, with support from the U.S. National Science Foundation, convened a meeting of representatives of organizations with a demonstrated interest in Data Science. Attendees came from computer science and from statistics, from long-established programs and from new and innovative programs. All had deep interest and experience in education for

data science. The meeting participants discussed views of data science from a variety of perspectives. They concluded that it is extremely difficult to identify a clear core of the data science field. However, some things emerged as generally acknowledged significant elements.

Following that meeting, the ACM Education Council established a task force to identify the computing components of data science and to develop guidance for programs in data science. Data Science is an inherently interdisciplinary field. The need for education across multiple traditional disciplines greatly complicates the development of curricular guidelines. The task force has explored existing programs, looking for similarities and exceptions. The task force recognizes that data science is not an exclusively computer science field. Identifying the role of computer science and how it blends with statistics and with a wide variety of application domains presents a unique challenge in the history of ACM curriculum efforts.

This panel will discuss the current status of that work and will seek audience participation in identifying strengths and weaknesses in the task force output. The panel will make brief presentations, presenting the current thinking of the task force; but, the most important component of the session will be the interaction with the attendees. Much of the input into the current deliberations of the task force come from programs and organizations based in the United States and Western Europe. Expanding on that viewpoint is the reason for our interest in presenting and receiving input at CompEd 2019. The panel includes distinguished faculty from areas related to the management and use of large sets of data. Each has a perspective that will contribute to the conversation. Two members of the ACM Task Force, Dr. Lillian Cassel and Dr. Wang Hongzhi, will lead the discussion.

2 Panelists

Dr. Lillian N Cassel, Professor and chair of the Department of Computing Sciences, Villanova University. Dr. Cassel is a member of the ACM Task Force on Data Science and will represent the combined viewpoints of the members of the task force. This includes participants from the United States and also the United Kingdom. The United States participants include universities of several levels, a community college, and an industry representative from Intel. The task force has surveyed data science programs in the United States, Asia, and Europe.

Dr. Cassel has a particular interest in the breadth of data science. Although we recognize the importance of data science in the sciences and in business analytics, there are important application areas in less familiar domains. Historians, psychologists, political scientists, journalists, and many more have large troves of data and need the algorithms and techniques that data science brings to allow them to mine that data and discover the knowledge there. Dr. Cassel will co-lead the panel with Dr. Wang Hongzhi.

Dr. Wang Hongzhi is also a member of the ACM Task Force on Data Science, and is Professor School of Computer Science and Technology Harbin Institute of Technology. He is a senior member council of databases, computer application and communication member of CCF big data expert committee. He brings expertise in big data management, database, graph management and data quality – areas that transcend all areas depending on data science. As a task force member, he will co-lead the panel.

Dr. Jianzhong Li is a professor in the Department of Computer Science and Engineering, Harbin Institute of Technology, China. He worked in the Department of Computer Science, Lawrence Berkeley National Laboratory, as a scientist, from 1986 to 1987 and from 1992 to 1993. He was also a visiting professor with the University of Minnesota at Minneapolis, Minnesota, from 1991 to 1992 and from 1998 to 1999. His research interests include massive data intensive computing and wireless sensor networks. He has published more than 200 papers in refereed journals and conference proceedings, such as the VLDB Journal, Algorithmica, the IEEE Transactions on Knowledge and Data Engineering, the IEEE Transactions on Parallel and Distributed Systems, SIGMOD, SIGKDD, VLDB, ICDE, and INFOCOM. His papers have been cited more than 15,000 times. He has been involved in the program committees of major computer science and technology conferences including SIGMOD, VLDB, ICDE, INFOCOM, ICDCS, and WWW. He also served on the editorial boards for distinguished journals such as the IEEE Transactions on Knowledge and Data Engineering.

Dr. Aoying Zhou is a professor on computer science with East China Normal University (ECNU), where he is heading the School of Data Science & Engineering. Before joining ECNU in 2008, he worked for Fudan University at the Computer Science Department for 15 years. He is the winner of the National Science Fund for Distinguished Young Scholars supported by NSFC and the professorship appointment under Changjiang Scholars Program of Ministry of Education. He is now acting as a vice-director of ACM SIGMOD China and Database Technology Committee of China Computer Federation. He is serving as a member of the editorial boards the VLDB Journal , the WWW Journal, and etc. His research interests include data management, in-memory cluster computing, big data benchmarking, and performance optimization.

2 Position Statements

Prof. Lillian Cassel: Data Science is an inherently interdisciplinary field and requires careful balance of the components. Computer Science and Statistics are both essential elements and a meaningful experience for students also requires some area of use in order to put the theory into context. This panel considers the computing components of data science, but we can never neglect the other elements.

Prof. Hongzhi Wang: The data science major may be generated from computer science major by improving some core courses and adding some new courses including:
(1) Add data-centric techniques to system as well as algorithm courses including compilers, OS, data structure and algorithms and so on.
(2) Add some data-specific coursers including data govern, data-intensive super computing and data analysis
(3) Pay both attentions to both theory and practice.

Prof. Jianzhong Li: The data science education of difference types of university. Research universities should focus on the fundamental for further research job. While for application-oriented universities and collage, the focus should be tools and applications.

Prof. Aoying Zhou: The data science major has the following four concerns
(1) The core courses of computer science, statistics as well as information systems are combined.
(2) The courses of computer sciences are simplified by changing the existing encyclopedic course architecture of computer science.
(3) by abandoning DTP methodology and strengthening the training of algorithms with practice.
(4) The training process should be based on practice and problems.

3 Audience Participation

Each of the four panelists will speak briefly to present their perspective on the role of computing in data science. At least 30 of the 75 minutes will be reserved for audience feedback and discussion of the positions and of other perspectives on the topic. This feedback is a critical component of the session and will serve as input to the ACM Task Force on Data Science Curriculum.

ACKNOWLEDGMENTS

Initial work on developing computing elements of data science emerged from a workshop[1] funded by the United States National Science Foundation grant 1545135

REFERENCES

1.   Cassel, Lillian, Heikki Topi. Strengthening Data Science Education through Collaboration. Report on a Workshop on Data Science Education Funded by the National Science Foundation October 1-3, 2015
http://computingportal.org/sites/default/files/Data%20Science%20Education%20Workshop%20Report%201.0_0.pdf

Knowledge Graph based Learning Guidance for Cybersecurity Hands-on Labs

Yuli Deng, Duo Lu, Dijiang Huang, Chun-Jen Chung, Fanjie Lin

Arizona State University

Tempe, Arizona

{yuli.deng,duolu,dijiang,cchung20,flin11}@asu.edu

ABSTRACT

Hands-on practice is a critical component of cybersecurity education. Most of the existing hands-on exercises or labs materials are usually managed in a problem-centric fashion, while it lacks a coherent way to manage existing labs and provide productive lab exercising plans for cybersecurity learners. With the advantages of big data and natural language processing (NLP) technologies, constructing a large knowledge graph and mining concepts from unstructured text becomes possible, which motivated us to construct a machine learning based lab exercising plan for cybersecurity education. In the research presented by this paper, we have constructed a knowledge graph in the cybersecurity domain using NLP technologies including machine learning based word embedding and hyperlink-based concept mining. We then utilized the knowledge graph during the regular learning process based on the following approaches: 1. We constructed a web-based front-end to visualize the knowledge graph, which allows students to browse and search cybersecurity-related concepts and the corresponding interdependence relations; 2. We created a personalized knowledge graph for each student based on their learning progress and status; 3. We built a personalized lab recommendation system by suggesting more relevant labs based on students' past learning history to maximize their learning outcomes. To measure the effectiveness of the proposed solution, we have conducted a use case study and collected survey data from a graduate-level cybersecurity class. Our study shows that, by leveraging the knowledge graph for the cybersecurity area study, students tend to benefit more and show more interests in cybersecurity area.

CCS CONCEPTS

• **Information systems** → **Recommender systems**; • **Applied computing** → **E-learning**; *Interactive learning environments*;

KEYWORDS

Laboratory, Knowledge Graph, Cybersecurity

ACM Reference Format:

Yuli Deng, Duo Lu, Dijiang Huang, Chun-Jen Chung, Fanjie Lin. 2019. Knowledge Graph based Learning Guidance for Cybersecurity Hands-on Labs.

CompEd '19, May 17–19, 2019, Chengdu,Sichuan, China
© 2019 Association for Computing Machinery.
ACM ISBN 978-1-4503-6259-7/19/05. . . $15.00
https://doi.org/10.1145/3300115.3309531

In *ACM Global Computing Education Conference 2019 (CompEd '19), May 17–19, 2019, Chengdu,Sichuan, China.* ACM, New York, NY, USA, 7 pages. https://doi.org/10.1145/3300115.3309531

1 INTRODUCTION

Using hands-on labs is a critical learning approach for cybersecurity education. Existing lab materials are mainly managed in a problem-centric fashion, in which instructors arrange learning and corresponding lab materials based on a specific topic in security area. However, the inter-lab dependencies are usually complicated and unclear, which hinders both students and instructors to manage learning and teaching materials in a coherent way. It is challenging to build an effective and adaptive learning schedule for students according to their personal background and learning targets: First, efficient cybersecurity education heavily relies on hands-on labs since it focuses more on practical problem-solving skills instead of theory and models. In addition, it is more difficult to organize lab materials than textbooks, let alone manage a complicated experiment environment with multiple hosts, switches, routers, and cables. Second, due to inherent diversities in knowledge and skill sets in cybersecurity education, it is difficult to personalize the learning process and keep track of individual student's learning progress. Third, for instructors, the knowledge sets and instructing materials must be kept up-to-date to cope with the emerging new vulnerabilities, attacks and defense solutions. As a result, it is a continuing process to provide improved learning guidance and plan for students to keep up with the evolving of cybersecurity technologies. The cybersecurity education issues above inspired us to design a new learning solution that can provide a personalized knowledge graph (KG) and guidance to effectively organize, index, recommend reading materials and hands-on labs for learners.

To address the said challenges, we propose CyberKG, a cybersecurity knowledge graph for college-level cybersecurity education, which includes both learning-related and domain-specific knowledge. CyberKG is built on ThoTh Lab [2] [3], a web-based learning platform for cybersecurity hands-on labs by using publicly available hands-on labs, e.g., SEED Labs [19] . Our contribution in this paper is given as following:

1) We built a knowledge graph of concepts and terminologies of cybersecurity based on large amount of public cybersecurity contents, such as Wikipedia and public available cybersecurity lab descriptions. Nodes of the knowledge graph and their dependency relationship are obtained by mining the public cybersecurity contents and security concepts from many cybersecurity glossaries fine-tuned with reading materials and hands-on lab instructions used in our offered security courses.

2) We constructed a web-based front-end to visualize the knowledge graph and index all hands-on labs we surfed in the public domain.

3) We built a lab recommendation system for our hands-on lab environment. This system can make recommendations by exploiting the similarity relationship between nodes in the knowledge graph and the association between various knowledge graph nodes and lab instructions.

4) We personalized the knowledge graph for each student to help instructors and students to track individual learning progress.

The remainder of this paper is organized as follows. Section 2 describes related efforts in education area to construct Knowledge Graphs. Section 3 explains the system architecture and the approaches used to construct CyberKG and how we emphasize it as a learning guide for students. Section 4 reports a case study with our experience in teaching cybersecurity at a senior undergraduate level course and discusses various facets of this system. Finally, a short discussion and conclusion of the paper are given in Section 5 and Section 6, respectively.

2 RELATED WORKS

Building a KG is a challenging task though efforts have been done in this area in recent years. There are two major approaches to develop the knowledge bases in education: the first approach primarily relies on individual professional expert, which involves manual work to a certain degree to determine the discrepancies among different professionals and then generate a corresponding consolidated graph. There have been research efforts to describe and categorize knowledge and skills in cybersecurity area by a large board of professionals: Cybersecurity Curricular Guidelines [1], NIST NICE [14], NSA CAE Knowledge Units [13], etc. The outcome of these efforts are well-organized categories in tree structures, which provides clear guidance for human learners when exploring the area. However, it turns out to be significantly challenging for machine learning purposes as these structures contain very limited semantic data that is readable to a machine. The other approach is to automate the generation process by gathering data from web pages and books which is achievable by computers rather without human interaction, e.g., Wikimindmap [15]. There are various solutions been proposed in the last decade of research about building the KG: Mahdisoltani et al. [7] have shown how to construct a knowledge base from Wikipedia in multiple languages; Nickel et al. [12] gave a comprehensive review on training statistical models for large KG's, and further used them to predict new edges in the graph. Recently, attention has been drawn on word embedding for various learning tasks. While a word can be understood by a human being when it appears in the context, its numerical model has to be constructed based on the complex contexts using neural network. In 2013, Mikolov et al. [9], [8] proposed word2vec which included two models: CBOW (Continuous Bag of Words) and Skip-gram to minimize the complexity in computation of continuous vector representation. According to the previous work done by Milne et al. [11], two pages from Wikipedia are defined to be most similar when they have more common information being shared. As for other researches, e.g., Tsai et al. [20] showed that using the Anchor texts of Wikipedia led to better performance in learning the

phrase vectors. Grefenstette et al. [6] represented their work on constructing the specialized dictionary by using word2vec to train the Wikipedia data. Speer et al. [18] represented a knowledge graph - ConceptNet5.5, which combines several sources to acquire word embeddings by using distributional semantics, e.g. word2vec. All the related works described above focus on constructing KG for general knowledge. In this paper, we propose to construct a KG for cybersecurity area with an enhanced Word2Vec implementation.

3 SYSTEM DESIGN

Our proposed CyberKG system contains two-stage generation and utilization in its work-flow as shown in Figure 1. We first work out the process to generate the knowledge graph including text data processing, word embedding and the graph structure generation in sections 3.1 and 3.2. Then three applications closely related to personalized learning are built upon CyberKG, which includes lab material indexing and searching (Section 3.3), knowledge graph visualization (Section 3.4), and hands-on lab recommendation (Section 3.5).

3.1 Word Embedding and Similarity Calculation

For computer to understand natural language and the knowledge and concepts within, words need to be represented in a computer-readable manner. Traditionally, NLP systems treat words as discrete symbols which leads to data sparsity and usually means that we may need more data in order to successfully train statistical models. Word embedding is a set of language modeling techniques to represent word as a vector in a low dimensional space. Using vector representations makes natural language computer-readable, which allows us to perform powerful mathematical operations on words to detect their similarities. word2vec[8] is a two-layer neural network that embeds text. Its input is a text corpus and its output are a set of vectors, i.e., the feature vectors for words in that corpus. Our goal of using word2vec is to group the vectors of similar words together in a single vector space, which help us to connect highly related words (concepts) in our knowledge graph.

The main input of the word embedding module is Wikipedia pages. The English version of Wikipedia database dump on May 1st, 2018 from [4] has been used. We develop a toolkit using Python to scrape Wikipedia pages for the categories in computer security section to acquire more accurate related information. The tool that we developed iterates through categories and stores a list of the corresponding information. All main pages in computer security and their related pages in 10 levels of subcategories have been scrapped. There are 7,143 pages obtained under the criteria after removing duplicates. With the processed database dump, we design and develop several tool-kits to train our word embedding model. As a result, there are 4,724,129 unique word embeddings been acquired which are represented in a computer-readable vector space, of which 1,472,477 are Wikipedia pages titles (concepts). For each keyword, the most similar words can be calculated through the cosine similarity between two vectors. For example, for "DDoS", the top ten similar words generated by our word embedding model are shown in Table 1.

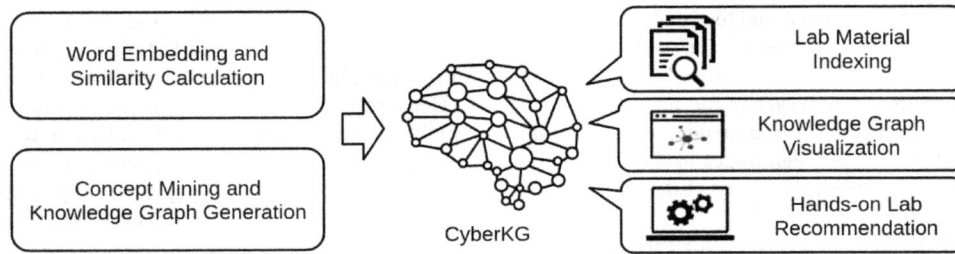

Figure 1: System architecture of CyberKG.

Table 1: Top ten similar words of "DDOS".

word	similarity	word	similarity
botnets	0.833809	honeypot	0.775258
phishing	0.767333	DDoS	0.751166
denial of service	0.708796	spoofing	0.641557
synflood	0.596164	malware	0.593467
attacks	0.584982	crimeware	0.549531

3.2 Knowledge Graph Generation

Knowledge graph, e.g., WordNet [10], is an abundant graph model, whose entity can be represented as a node and the link can be represented by the relationships between nodes. After gathering the word similarities from the previous section, we are able to generate a knowledge graph in our system.

Originally, the knowledge graph generation is handled by human experts. The first step is to do manual text analysis and get a list of concepts, represented as labeled points, and a list of links between these nodes. By combining the lists of concepts and links, a small knowledge graph from a single author is then generated, which is called an author graph. The next step is to combine graphs from various authors into one large graph by identifying common points with each other. When the texts of the nodes deal with the same subject, points with the same label are first identified. Then, human help is needed to identity synonyms for the same concept and connect these synonyms together. One way is to compare the neighborhoods of points. Computing the similarity between two concepts' neighborhood points help us to decide if these two concepts are identical. This method even helps us to detect homonyms, which means the same label but referring to different content.

In our case, each Wikipedia page represents a concept and its explanation (which contains knowledge). There are also hyperlinks within each Wikipedia page that links to other concepts. By analyzing the URL links within one Wikipedia page, we got a simple author graph. For example, on the DDoS page, there are hyperlinks that linked to Exploit, Trojan Horse, IDS, IPS, Computer Fraud, Botnet, Firewall and computer Virus. With 7,143 pages under computer security category in Wikipedia, we now have 7,143 single author graphs ready to be merged together. We utilize the similarities obtained during the word-embedding process described in section 3.1 to further connect these small graphs. Figure 2 showcases how we merge graph of 'Firewall' and 'DDoS' graph into one graph. Word pair like *Antivirus, Computer virus, Spyware, Trojan Horse* are connected together in Figure 2 as their similarity based on word embedding is high. We set the similarity lower limit to 0.8 (while

0 means no relationship and 1 means the two concepts share the same embedding) and connect all node pairs over this similarity threshold. After that, we get one unified and also highly connected knowledge graph ready for further utilization. The threshold 0.8 is used as the lower limit for the following reason according to our experiments: when 0.85 is applied, we get more than 2,000 unconnected nodes, which means these concepts under computer security category are not closely related compared to speaking language words, which is a sign for us to reduce the threshold. There still exist 673 disconnected nodes/small graphs that cannot be included in our main knowledge graph with a threshold as low as 0.7.

3.3 Lab Material Indexing

Within ThoTh Lab, our virtual lab platform, we create a cybersecurity lab repository that is available to instructors and students in our university. We implement our lab design and material from labs of computer science courses within our school and other high-quality open sources labs like SEED Labs from Syracuse University. Instructors are able to upload their own new lab materials into the lab repository at any time. All labs in our lab repository are tagged with keywords by matching the lab material with concepts available in our knowledge graph. For example, keywords our system identified in "Local DNS Attack Lab" from SEED lab include *DNS, bind9, cache, hostname, IP address, LAN, pharming, RFC, rndc, sudo, Ubuntu, Wireshark*. Some of these concepts, like *sudo, Ubuntu* are not directly related to DNS attack, but these are necessary knowledge for each student to finish this lab successfully. Instructors may also edit these concepts before adding them to our lab repository if they think some important concepts were skipped by our system.

We now get one lab to N concepts mapping in CyberKG, which allows us to index labs based on nodes in the knowledge graph, and vice versa. As each lab covers at least one node in the knowledge graph, given any two Lab material A and B, we may obtain their related knowledge graph nodes as the set S_A and S_B. A similarity of these two articles can be calculated as follows:

$$sim(A, B) = \frac{|S_A \cap S_B|}{|S_A \cup S_B|}.$$

General speaking, the more overlapping between two labs' knowledge graph coverage, the more similar these two labs are. This similarity will then be used as the input of the recommendation module described in Section 3.5. Learning material is another component in CyberKG. We currently linked each node in CyberKG to its Wikipedia page, which can serve as basic reading material for students. In order to expand the reading material repository, we

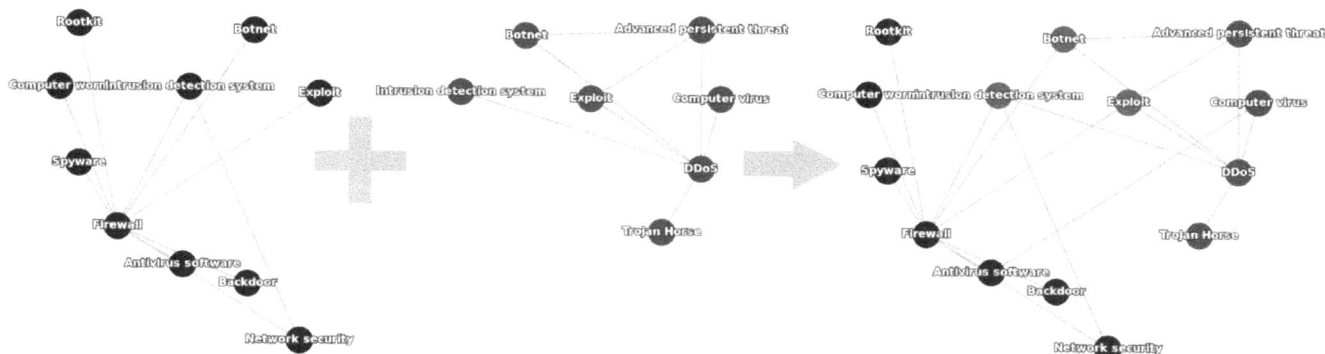

Figure 2: Merge two small graph together based on overlap and word embedding similarity. (Firewall Graph on the right, DDoS graph in the middle and merged result on the right.)

are working on indexing research papers available online with our knowledge graph.

3.4 Knowledge Graph Visualization

With the Knowledge Graph represents in a graph data structure, our next step is to represent the graph in an interactive GUI to empower instructor and students to use it. Since ThoTh Lab itself is a purely web-based lab environment [21], we want to integrate our CyberKG system into the Web UI seamlessly. In this project, we utilized *Echarts*, which is a web-based visualization library that features a plethora of APIs to creating interactive and dynamic content on the web. We first visualized our graph using three different ways. First, a full knowledge graph is presented to the user. As shown in Figure 3 (a). The user may zoom in and hang over nodes in the graph to highlight nodes' neighborhood and gray out unconnected nodes, as shown in Figure 3 (b). Furthermore, the user may click on one node to generate a tree graph using the selected node as root, as shown in Figure 3 (c), leaves in this graph can be further expanded. We also add the search function to help the user locate concept nodes and index function to show the related labs for each node. The color of the nodes represents the lab it belongs to.

We also develop a personalized knowledge graph according to a learner's knowledge gained through the lab experience. The personalized knowledge graph is represented as a subset of the cybersecurity knowledge map. When a learner accomplishes a lab, finish the assigned reading material, and get the pass from an exam or quiz, the personalized knowledge graph is automatically updated. The graphical UI allows the learner to view straightforwardly what has already been covered in his/her learning progress.

3.5 Recommendation of Hands-on Labs

Traditional education recommendation systems derive the user preferences from predefined features like user age, sex, educational background, previous grades and/or pre-course survey results and etc. Our system utilizes the concepts in CyberKG and in the lab materials to recommend labs that suit the needs for instructor or students.

There are two types of students who use our Lab system. The first type is those who are taking a course which uses our lab platform as an instructional tool. Instructors of such courses need

to create syllabus and lab planning for the class at the beginning of each semester. Our system provides instructors with adequate lab materials within our lab repository. An instructor may provide a list of concepts he/she wants to cover during the course run within CyberKG, and our system will return labs related to these concepts based on the concept-lab indexing generated in Section 3.3. During the course run, our system is also able to identify students at-risk or challenged based on their previous lab grades, quiz results, and lab activities to make extra lab practice suggestions. Such suggestions turns out to be simple and straightforward, that contains only one lab, which is either the lab with highest similarity (defined as $sim(A, B)$ in Section 3.3) to the lab which the student was not able to finish or a lab that covers concepts the student lost most points in their exam or quiz.

The second type of students is graduate students who use our virtual lab platform as a self-tutoring platform for cybersecurity study. They are the target audience of our recommendation module. For these students, we first create an entry-survey to check their background in the cybersecurity domain. Then, each student is asked to pick either a set of concepts/knowledge they want to cover or a lab within a lab repository they want to finish independently as their personal learning goal.

The CyberKG system first estimates the concept node coverage of a student based on his/her entry-survey results and update these concepts as mastered in his/her personal knowledge graph. We define the set of mastered concepts C_M and the concepts covered by the student's learning goal as C_G. After that, CyberKG is able to generate a set of paths P_{MG} between C_M and C_G using the knowledge graph. Each path P in P_{MG} contains a set of concepts C_p. Combine all C_p together we got C_P. It is assumed that C_P includes all the concepts a student needs to learn and practice in our lab system in order to achieve his/her learning goal. The last step is to find a set of labs L that covers all concepts in C_P. Currently, our system will generate L where each lab in L got high $sim(A, B)$ with another lab in L. This results in a set of labs that shares a lot of concepts between them. When students start working on such labs, they will have the chance to consolidate their current C_M while learning the new concepts. L becomes our recommendation to a user. Each time a lab is finished and graded, we update C_M and

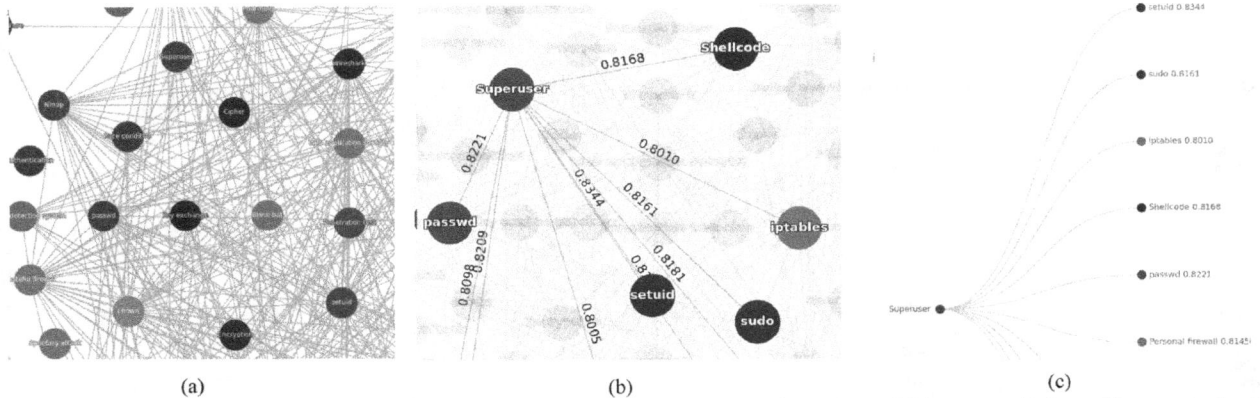

Figure 3: Web-UI for Knowledge Graph: (a)Part of KG; (b)Mouse hang-over 'Superuser';(c)Mouse click on 'Superuser', which generate a tree using 'Superuser' root;

regenerate L to see if there is an update needed in the suggested recommendation.

An example of the recommendation process for one user is shown below. At the beginning, our system estimates that his knowledge coverage C_M contains Linux command line, Linux Network and Firewall, and he picks the learning goal C_G containing only SSL Session Hijack. Then CyberKG generated C_P for him as shown in Figure 4. Based on C_P, a L of five labs were recommended to him: (1) Linux web service lab, which covers two concepts in C_P (blue squares), (2) Linux firewall lab, which covers two concepts in C_P (green squares), (3) Packet Sniffing lab, which covers three concepts in C_P (red squares), (4) IP and port scanning lab, which covers three concepts in C_P (purple squares), and (5) SSL Session Hijacking Lab, which covers four concepts in C_P (yellow squares).

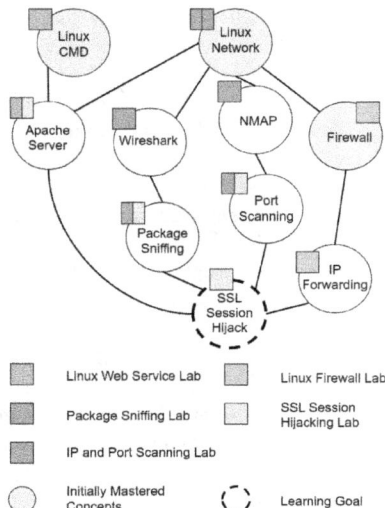

Figure 4: Lab Recommendation Process Example. Best viewed with color.

Another scenario is when a self-learning student uses CyberKG system without providing any personal data and goal. In such case, CyberKG will not give any recommendation at first. Instead, it will

obtain lab activity data when users start doing their first few labs and record their knowledge gained through the lab experience to generate C_M for the students. Once enough labs are completed and basic concepts are covered in the user's personalized knowledge graph, CyberKG system will start providing future lab recommendation based on lab similarity ranking calculated and sorted by $sim(A, B)$. By doing these recommended labs, the user will quickly consolidate the knowledge they have acquired and steadily expand their personalized knowledge graph.

4 CASE STUDY

An experiment using CyberKG was conducted in a graduate-level network security class during Fall 2017 at Arizona State University. This class involves three hands-on labs for computer networks security. 23 graduate students took the course, and all of them finished the pre-survey before the first lab to provide an estimation of their network knowledge backgrounds. During the semester, each student was asked to finish three labs in the virtual lab platform. They were also asked whether they wanted to volunteer in our research practice, and nine students participated. These nine students set their own learning goals on our knowledge graph and then got the recommendation of labs as a outcome of the CyberKG system. They continued to work on these labs, and 8 of them finished all recommended labs. All students' activities during the labs were recorded in the browser end and inside the virtual machine they used. At the end of the semester, all 23 students were asked to finish an exit survey, where those nine volunteers got extra questions to answer.

In the exit survey, the student satisfaction on our hands-on virtual lab platform has been analyzed and they were also asked about their opinion on CyberKG system. The following questions were asked in the exit survey: (Answer on a scale of 1 to 5, 1 being totally disagree, 5 being fully agree.)

Q1: The virtual lab platform is convenient to access.

Q2: Doing labs in virtual lab platform is easier compare to doing labs in a physical lab.

Q3: Personal knowledge graph in the virtual lab platform is accurate at the beginning of the class.

Q4: Personal knowledge graph is accurate at the end of the class.

Q5: I regularly check my personal knowledge graph.

The extra questions for research volunteers:

Q6: The recommendation a reasonable recommendation for me.

Q7: The connection/similarity between labs recommended to me is noticeable.

Q8: The recommendation system is easy to use.

Q9: Compare to labs required by the course, I find the labs recommended to me more interesting.

Q10: I want to keep on using the system as a self-guidance tool after this class.

Figure 5 shows the average score of each question in the exit survey. While the estimation of student knowledge coverage on the quiz is not accurate (Q3), it improved at the end of the class based on the user activity log (Q4). Among the 9 volunteers who utilized the CyberKG system for learning recommendation, 6 of them agreed that the recommendation is highly related to the topic they pick (in Q7). The survey results also show that majority of students confirmed the usefulness of the recommendation for hands-on labs (Q6), and students' personal preference on lab content have been satisfied by using our system during the semester (Q9).

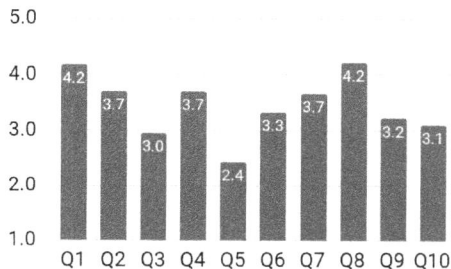

Figure 5: Average score of each question in the exit survey.

5 DISCUSSION

Our current knowledge graph generation module relies heavily on word2vec model to accurately represent words with vectors and calculate similarity among these vectors. However, there are known limitations in this task. For example, it is known that word frequency information in the embedding space affects cosine similarity greatly. As a result, we need to consider word frequency in the training process, especially for those cybersecurity terminologies that do not appear frequently. Another challenge we are facing is how to evaluate the generated knowledge graph. In English language domain, there are several datasets that contain similar word pairs defined by human experts, including Rubenstein and Goodenough dataset[17] and WordSim353 dataset[5]. These datasets can be used as an evaluation baseline for NLP processing modules in English language domain. But such dataset is absent in the cybersecurity domain. As a result, we can only rely on our own domain knowledge to check the results and fine-tune model parameters based on our own judgment. However, word embedding using unsupervised learning methods like word2vec is still the mainstream method on natural language dataset, as these datasets are way too large for human experts to supervise the learning process. One possible solution to these challenges is to construct an ontology with a group of experts in cybersecurity. A few examples of such ontology emerge in recent research works[16]. The difference between

ontology and our current knowledge graph is that the edge in the ontology is well defined during the construction, while the links in a knowledge graph may be meaningless. This makes the merging of ontology in the same domain simple and straightforward. Our next step is to add a human defined ontology module in our system to evaluate and trim the knowledge graph generated by CyberKG, then build a feedback loop and editing tool for users to give them the opportunity to help us improve CyberKG.

There are also several lessons we learned during the case study. First, students from all backgrounds take cybersecurity class. This is not surprising at all, but we were still shocked by the huge gap between students. At the beginning of the class, some students have no background on computer network, while some students already mastered most concepts we are going to cover in all labs. This makes the entry survey/quiz and estimation important as these students definitely need different kind of instruction from the very beginning. Second, it is extremely hard to stop students from cheating during online labs. Common cheats we found during the case study were searching answer online (as SEED Lab we used are widely used) and doing the labs together. Third, online support availability is important to keep students motivated. Students may do the lab any time anywhere, but when they encounter a problem that they struggle, they'll need help right away or they'll procrastinate. One solution to this is group lab, which enable students to help each other. Lastly, we want to further investigate CyperKG's impact on students' learning outcomes [22].

6 CONCLUSION AND FUTURE WORK

This paper describes our efforts towards creating a knowledge graph to represent concepts and their relationships in the cybersecurity domain. This work is intended to provide an organized knowledge that incorporates information from a large variety of data sources including Wikipedia pages and instruction materials, which includes all relevant concepts within the domain for educational usage. We then applied such knowledge graph into an e-learning virtual lab platform to test it. When using the knowledge graph as a recommendation/guidance tool for students, our case study proves that our prototyped system is able to meet students' expectation in making the desired recommendation.

In future work, we want to incorporate more unstructured data into our system, including but not limited to textbooks, internet web pages, and online video transcripts. We also plan to incorporate cybersecurity ontology which is intended to support our knowledge graph generation. We also need to come up with innovative solutions to the other challenges discussed in Section 5. Further experiments and in-class studies are necessary for system validation. Our ultimate goal is to build a knowledge graph that will serve as the backbone of the cybersecurity education domain, which would evolve and grow with additional cybersecurity lab sets as they become available, being fully adaptive to different learners who want to utilize it.

ACKNOWLEDGEMENT

All authors are gratefully thankful for research grants from NSF DGE-1723440, NSFC 61628201 and 61571375.

REFERENCES

[1] ACM. 2017. Cybersecurity Curricular Guidelines. https://cybered.hosting.acm.org/wp/

[2] Yuli Deng, Dijiang Huang, and Chun-Jen Chung. 2017. ThoTh Lab: A Personalized Learning Framework for CS Hands-on Projects. In *Proceedings of the 2017 ACM SIGCSE Technical Symposium on Computer Science Education*. ACM, 706–706.

[3] Yuli Deng, Duo Lu, Chun-Jen Cheng, Dijiang Huang, and Zhen Zeng. 2018. Personalized Learning in a Virtual Hands-on Lab Platform for Computer Science Education. In *2018 IEEE Frontiers in Education Conference (FIE)*.

[4] Wikimedia Foundation. 2018. Wikimedia Downloads. https://dumps.wikimedia.org/

[5] Evgeniy Gabrilovich. 2002. The WordSimilarity-353 Test Collection. http://www.cs.technion.ac.il/~gabr/resources/data/wordsim353/

[6] Gregory Grefenstette and Lawrence Muchemi. 2016. Determining the Characteristic Vocabulary for a Specialized Dictionary using Word2vec and a Directed Crawler. *arXiv preprint arXiv:1605.09564* (2016).

[7] Farzaneh Mahdisoltani, Joanna Biega, and Fabian M Suchanek. 2013. Yago3: A knowledge base from multilingual wikipedias. In *CIDR*.

[8] Tomas Mikolov, Kai Chen, Greg Corrado, and Jeffrey Dean. 2013. Efficient estimation of word representations in vector space. *arXiv preprint arXiv:1301.3781* (2013).

[9] Tomas Mikolov, Ilya Sutskever, Kai Chen, Greg S Corrado, and Jeff Dean. 2013. Distributed representations of words and phrases and their compositionality. In *Advances in neural information processing systems*. 3111–3119.

[10] George A. Miller. 1995. WordNet: A Lexical Database for English. *Commun. ACM* 38, 11 (Nov. 1995), 39–41. https://doi.org/10.1145/219717.219748

[11] David Milne and Ian H Witten. 2008. Learning to link with wikipedia. In *Proceedings of the 17th ACM conference on Information and knowledge management*. ACM, 509–518.

[12] Maximilian Nickel, Kevin Murphy, Volker Tresp, and Evgeniy Gabrilovich. 2016. A review of relational machine learning for knowledge graphs. *Proc. IEEE* 104, 1 (2016), 11–33.

[13] NIETP. 2018. CAE REQUIREMENTS AND RESOURCES. https://www.iad.gov/NIETP/CAERequirements.cfm

[14] NIST. 2018. NICE Cybersecurity Workforce Framework. https://www.nist.gov/itl/applied-cybersecurity/nice/

[15] F Nyffenegger. 2009. WikiMindMap.

[16] Leo Obrst, Penny Chase, and Richard Markeloff. 2012. Developing an Ontology of the Cyber Security Domain. In *STIDS*.

[17] Herbert Rubenstein and John B. Goodenough. 1965. Contextual Correlates of Synonymy. *Commun. ACM* 8, 10 (Oct. 1965), 627–633. https://doi.org/10.1145/365628.365657

[18] Robert Speer, Joshua Chin, and Catherine Havasi. 2017. ConceptNet 5.5: An Open Multilingual Graph of General Knowledge.. In *AAAI*. 4444–4451.

[19] Syracuse University. 2018. SEED Labs. http://www.cis.syr.edu/~wedu/seed/labs.html.

[20] Chen-Tse Tsai and Dan Roth. 2016. Cross-lingual wikification using multilingual embeddings. In *Proceedings of the 2016 Conference of the North American Chapter of the Association for Computational Linguistics: Human Language Technologies*. 589–598.

[21] L. Xu, D. Huang, and W. Tsai. 2014. Cloud-Based Virtual Laboratory for Network Security Education. *IEEE Transactions on Education* 57, 3 (Aug 2014), 145–150. https://doi.org/10.1109/TE.2013.2282285

[22] Zhen Zeng, Yuli Deng, I-Han Hsiao, and Dijiang Huang. 2018. Understanding StudentsâĂŹ Engagement behavior in Virtual Hands-on Lab: Findings from a Computer Network Security Course. In *2018 IEEE Frontiers in Education Conference (FIE)*.

Improve Student Performance
Using Moderated Two-Stage Projects

Juan Chen*
College of Computer, National
University of Defense Technology
Changsha, Hunan, China
juanchen@nudt.edu.cn

Yingjun Cao
University of California, San Diego
San Diego, California
yic242@eng.ucsd.edu

Linlin Du
College of Computer, National
University of Defense Technology
Changsha, Hunan, China
dulinlin17@nudt.edu.cn

Youwen Ouyang
Department of Computer Science and
Information Systems, California State
University, San Marcos
San Marcos, California
ouyang@csusm.edu

Li Shen
College of Computer, National
University of Defense Technology
Changsha, Hunan, China
lishen@nudt.edu.cn

ABSTRACT

Parallel programming skills are becoming more popular due to the unprecedented boom in artificial intelligent and high-performance computing. Programming assignments are widely used in parallel programming courses to measure student performance and expose students to constraints in real projects. However, due to the difficulty level of these assignments, many students struggle to write fully functional and adequately documented programs. To improve student performance, we implemented a moderated two-stage format for five course projects in a graduate-level introductory parallel programming class. Each project is divided into two stages where students complete the assignment individually without any collaboration in the first stage. Then students work in pairs to work on the same project in the second stage so they can review each other's work from the first stage and improve their programs collaboratively. For two of the five projects, a moderated meeting is conducted in between the two stages where the instructor moderated a group discussion on general issues raised by students. We found that students' performance improved from stage one to stage two. In addition, the two projects with a moderated meeting show better performance gains. This paper also examines students' perceptions of and experiences with the moderated two-stage projects. Students favor working on two-stage projects because they had a chance to discuss challenging concepts and the moderated discussion session tend to guide them to the correct path should they make mistakes in stage one.

CompEd '19, May 17–19, 2019, Chengdu,Sichuan, China
© 2019 Association for Computing Machinery
ACM ISBN 978-1-4503-6259-7/19/05...$15.00
https://doi.org/10.1145/3300115.3309524

KEYWORDS

Moderated Two-Stage Projects, Collaborative Project, Parallel Programming

ACM Reference Format:
Juan Chen*, Yingjun Cao, Linlin Du, Youwen Ouyang, and Li Shen. 2019. Improve Student Performance, Using Moderated Two-Stage Projects. In *ACM Global Computing Education Conference 2019 (CompEd '19), May 17–19, 2019, Chengdu,Sichuan, China*. ACM, New York, NY, USA, 7 pages. https://doi.org/10.1145/3300115.3309524

1 INTRODUCTION

Parallel programming is a challenging topic and instructors have used programming assignments to improve students' understanding of parallel programming knowledge and coding skills [9]. Feedbacks from programming assignments traditionally include a grade and some specific comments. Recently, researchers have adopted more collaborative approaches in CS classes such as the two-stage exams [2] and two-stage programming projects [1]. In particular, during two-stage projects, students submit their assignments individually in the first stage and are given an individual grade and feedback. They then resubmit a pair-coded version of the same project by collaborating with another student in the second stage. This two-stage approach has demonstrated effectiveness in helping students correct the issues in their assignments and also improve their final grades.

Not all projects are suitable for the two-stage format, however. For projects with standard answers and are relatively straightforward, instructor's feedback and pair programming can help students make further progress in the second stage. But for those tough projects with open answers, the instructor's feedback may not be sufficient for students to understand all the mistakes they made and determine if their problem-solving process is correct. Therefore, it is still very hard for them to continue the second stage based on the written feedback; hence limiting the impact of two-stage assignments on their learning. In fact, failures in both stages might severely impact students' confidence. Such an example is with a parallel programming class for college seniors prior to this study. The majority of students gave up participating in two-stage projects because of their lack of parallel programming skills and operational experience on real supercomputer systems. They lacked the confidence to finish the project even with a partner. All five two-stage projects were unfinished in that course.

Our approach to solving this problem is to add one moderated discussion session between the two stages. We call this project format *moderated two-stage project*, which consists of two stages and an additional discussion session in between the two stages. For the first stage, students work alone on the project and are given an individual grade with feedback. During the discussion session after the first stage, students proposed and discussed questions they have had in the first stage and strived to find possible solutions through peer discussion. The instructor plays the role of a guide in this discussion session. The instructor provided hints or guidance so as to make students better understand their individual feedback from stage one, and as a result, deepen their understanding for parallel programming. Therefore, students have three sources of feedback before moving on to the second stage: feedback from the instructor on their stage one work, peer feedback obtained from the moderated discussion, and self-reflection. The method and conclusion drawn from the discussion will become the impetus for improving students' performance in the second stage. For the second stage, all students must participate in the paired-code activities for the same project, address the feedback from stage one, and resubmit the assignment in pairs. As not all projects need the moderated discussion session between the two stages, we designed the following criteria to determine if the discussion session is necessary: if the number of questions and errors for the first stage is far beyond our expectations, a moderated discussion session will be added for the project. In particular, if one-third students raised questions on their stage one feedback or the average score for the first stage is lower than 60, the discussion session might be necessary. We required all students to participate in the discussion session if it is deemed necessary for a two-stage project.

Potential benefits of the moderated discussion session in the context of parallel programming may include the following. Our programming assignments focus on improving students' parallel programming ability as well as testing and problem-solving skills on a real platform. Based on multi-process and multi-thread parallel programming methods, students need to comprehensively consider parallelization methods, process/thread mapping, programming, and debugging skills, performance test and analysis, etc. These challenging assignments not only require solid parallel programming skills, but also other important high-performance computing concepts, such as parallel performance, computing precision, parallel scalability, etc. Students have to analyze the change of computing precision under the different computing scales, and then find out the reasons for computing precision reduction and parallel performance decrease as the computing scale increase. Test and analysis abilities on a real supercomputer system are challenging for students who have no parallel computing knowledge before.

In this study, we examine the effects of moderated two-stage programming projects in a parallel programming course. We focus on the following three research questions:

Q1: What are the impacts of two-stage programming projects on students' performance?

Q2: What are the effects of adding one moderated discussion session between two stages compared with the standard two-stage format?
Q3: What are the students' perceptions and experiences with moderated two-stage projects?

2 BACKGROUND

Pair Programming is a well-studied pedagogy in computer science as it has been shown to improve the quality of submitted programs [5, 13, 16]. Over the years, CS1/2 instructors who adopted pair programming have reported favorable student feedback, higher retention, and better quality codes [3, 14, 18]. As a peer collaboration pedagogy, pair programming [13, 16] provides students additional opportunities to code with peers and share their ideas by switching roles as the driver and navigator at regular intervals. Research on pair programming indicates that compatibility issues between the pairs may reduce its effectiveness [11] and researchers recently have started to examine and evaluate creative variations of pair programming to further improve its impact on learning [4].

Recently, educators in different fields have started to use two-stage exams to promote student learning [6, 8]. This exam format allows students to complete tests with two parts, one is a normal individual test and the other is a peer collaboration test where students work in small groups to solve the problems. It has been shown to improve students' knowledge on the topic so as to turn exams into a learning experience [2, 19]. Based on a similar two-stage idea, Battestilli et. al. [1] proposed and studied a variation of pair programming where students complete the same project twice. They complete the first stage individually and the second stage in pairs. The two-stage project format was shown to have a positive impact on student performance in AB tests, and student feedback was generally positive. However, student feedback [1] also showed that the limited feedback at the end of stage one is not productive, and this is especially true if both students in the pair are not able to fix their common mistakes in stage two. For upper division or graduate level classes, the lack of productive feedback might further reduce the benefit of two-stage projects. The moderated two-stage project format proposed in this paper addresses this issue by having a faculty-moderated discussion session between the two stages to provide timely and more targeted feedback to students. The learning benefit from the discussion session primarily results from peer instruction which has been shown to be effective [7].

Parallel Programming courses, in general, are upper division or graduate level courses and they tend to be demanding. However, some instructors argue that parallel programming topics should be covered in first or second-year undergraduate classes [9, 10, 12]. They reason that a solid understanding of parallel programming concepts will tremendously improve students' ability to write software that is able to effectively utilize the underlying parallel hardware architecture. For example, Yousun Ko et al. [12] disagreed that parallelism is an afterthought to writing single-threaded applications. They found if parallel programming concepts were introduced as a senior-level undergraduate or graduate elective, students had difficulty transition from sequential to parallel thinking. Lori Pollock et al. [15] also thought parallel programming required a very different thought process from traditional sequential programming, as the programmer must think of performing tasks in parallel, information communication, coordinating actions, and balancing workload between parallel processes. Making such a switch from sequential thinking to parallel thinking was a big step for many students. We also had a similar experience in our parallel programming classes. We did not have any undergraduate-level parallel programming course until Spring 2018. Undergraduate students learn some parallel programming knowledge by self-learning. Most of our graduate students who graduated from other universities had no parallel programming knowledge either. As a consequence, they struggle to produce functional and well-documented parallel programs.

Many education research on parallel programming focuses on pragmatic challenges of parallel programming on a real system. Pollock et al. [15] emphasized the importance of providing a more real-world context to the parallel programming course. They used cooperative learning to meet these practical challenges. Sadowski et al. [17] proposed that parallel and concurrent programming courses should emphasize high-level abstractions for performance and correctness. They presented a testing framework to help students effectively test their parallel programs. The authors also pointed out that parallel programming was about improving performance by making good use of the underlying parallel resources of a multicore machine or the set of machines in a cluster.

Learning parallel programming on a real supercomputer system is much more difficult as the debugging, testing, and analysis experience is very different from a multi-core system or a simulated environment. Process or thread mapping problems, computer node assignments, parallel debugging, scalability analysis, parallel performance bottleneck, and multi-node test problems will make the project more complicated and time-consuming Students also need to compete with other supercomputing center users for limited computing resources. Though the aforementioned issues may be unique to parallel programming classes, these realistic concerns may also be applicable to general upper-division or graduate-level CS classes. Therefore, we tested the moderated two-stage project format in a first-year graduate level course with a goal to increase student confidence and interest in parallel computing.

3 STUDY DESIGN

The study was carried out in a large research institution in Spring 2018. Fourteen graduate students enrolled in the "Parallel Programming" course, and all students participated in the study. Though all students held a bachelor's degree in computer science, most of them have no prior experience with parallel programming. The course learning objectives mainly include basic parallel programming interfaces and usage methods (parallel architecture, parallel programming model, MPI, OpenMP, Pthreads, parallel performance evaluation), parallel computing concepts (parallel efficiency, speedup), and parallel programming hardware platform usage. One of the authors is the lead instructor of this class.

The course has five parallel programming projects throughout a 9-week period, a comprehensive final exam and other low-weight formative assignments. In this study, we focus on the parallel programming projects which were graded primarily based on functionality and documentation. 2 students in the class were female

and the rest were male; 57% were first-year graduate students, 43% were second-year graduate students.

3.1 Moderated Two-Stage Project Format

All five projects follow the two-stage project format where students complete the assignment individually in the first stage and complete the same project again in the second stage with a partner using pair programming. To study the impact of the moderated discussion section on student performance, only projects 2 and 3 had the discussion section between the two stages. Project 2 is about Monte Carlo methods using randomness. Students need to write an MPI program that uses a Monte Carlo method to estimate π using randomness. In the first stage, many students cannot get an accurate π value because they incorrectly used the random number generator in the parallel environment. In project 3, students need to write an OpenMP program that uses a Monte Carlo method to estimate π. OpenMP directives and parallel random number generator make students confused in the first stage. Most of them cannot understand the relationship between the computing precision and parallel scales. The number of questions and errors in the first stage of projects 2 and 3 was far beyond our expectations. About one-third of students posed questions on the feedback they received for the first stage. And the average scores for the first stage of projects 2 and 3 were both lower than 60. For the reasons above, we added a moderated discussion session for projects 2 and 3 while keeping the original two-stage format for other projects. Figure 1 shows the structure of the five projects.

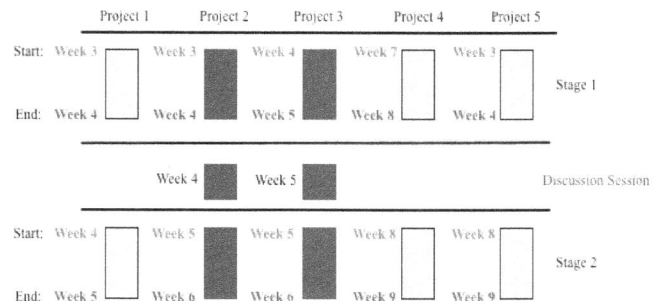

Figure 1: Structure of the five projects.

All programming projects were released between weeks 3 and 9 as Figure 1 shows. The first two weeks of the class were devoted to basic parallel programming introductions with no formal programming projects. Each stage of a project lasts about one week and the second stage usually follows stage one immediately except project 5 where there was a gap. A human scheduling error caused the gap between stages one and two for project 5.

Stage-1 (S1) - Individually-coded Project: In the first stage, students complete and submit the project individually. The first stage submissions were graded with feedback. Each student submission was graded based on programming&test and documentation, in which programming&test score is 70% of the grade and the remaining 30% is for documentation. Programming&test score reflects a student's programming and testing ability, which consists of compilation (45%), running (20%) and code specification (5%). We assigned a larger weight for compilation because most students have no prior experience writing parallel programs. Documentation score evaluates a student's project report, which consists of the completeness of reports (10%), the adequacy of experimental data (10%), and the correctness of experimental conclusion (10%). Project documentation requires students to provide a detailed experiment report including goals, steps, input data, results and analyses, and conclusions. Equation 1 shows how the grade for stage one was calculated.

$$Score_{stage} = S_{compilation} \times 45\% + S_{run} \times 20\% + S_{spec} \times 5\% \\ + S_{compl} \times 10\% + S_{adeq} \times 10\% + S_{concl} \times 10\% \quad (1)$$

Stage 1 project grade and feedback were returned to students before the moderated discussion session for projects 2 and 3 and before the second stage for projects 1, 4, and 5.

Moderated Discussion Session: For projects 2 and 3, an instructor-moderated discussion session was added between stages 1 and 2 where students present the issues they met in the first stage and discuss possible solutions. At the end of the discussion, students are expected to draw conclusions on what they can improve from the first stage and draft an experimental plan for the second stage. The preparatory work for the moderated discussion session has included a pre-compiled question list from the class forum and answers made by the instructor.

The discussion stage mainly consists of the following four components and lasts about 45 minutes.

- *Initial presentation (10 minutes).* Two or three students usually volunteer to present the problems they met in the first stage. These problems were usually posted and discussed, yet still unresolved, on our online forum before the discussion session. The presenters would sort out question/analysis/answer materials and prepare slides before the moderated discussion session.
- *Problem collection (10 minutes).* At this time, other students would start to add the problems they had met in the first stage. Sometimes, questions were raised to how the presenters analyze the problem. The purpose of this process is to guide students to expose as many problems as possible. The problem collection phase completes the pre-selected question list from the online forum.
- *Group discussion (15 minutes).* Students form groups of two to three to discuss all the collected questions and propose their solutions. The instructor guides students to classify their questions and when there was an impasse, the instructor would refine the question and provide some examples. No direct answers were allowed in group discussions.
- *Conclusion (10 minutes).* The instructor made conclusions on the proposed ideas to solve each problem. For students who were still lost, instructions were given for them to try one of the proposed ideas on the supercomputer.

Stage-2 (S2) - Pair-coded Project: In the second stage, students complete and submit again the same project using pair programming. The pairing is chosen at random. The second stage submission was graded using the same rubric as in stage one (Equation 1).

Reflections: Students were encouraged to complete an individual reflection about their experience at the end of stage 2. They were asked to reflect on where they had lost points during these two stages, how long they spent each stage, their levels of knowledge and skills for each project, and their evaluation for their partner during the second stage and discussion stage if there is a moderated discussion session. Most of the reflections are open-ended questions. 13 questions were included in the reflection questionnaire.

Overall Project Grade: The grade for each project was calculated by Equation 2). Here $Score_{stage1}$ and $Score_{stage2}$ represent the grade for Stages 1 and 2, respectively. A small weight was given for the reflections (RE) because we want to motivate more students to complete questionnaires.

$$Grade = Score_{stage1} * 0.45 + Score_{stage2} * 0.5 + RE * 0.05 \quad (2)$$

3.2 Programming Project Topics

The description of the five parallel programming projects are shown in Table 1. Projects 2 and 3 were chosen to add a moderated discussion session in between the two stages and projects 1, 4 and 5 follow the standard two-stage project format.

Table 1: Descriptions of the five parallel projects in the course.

Projects	Tasks
1	Write an MPI program that implements matrix-matrix multiplication by different data partitions
2	Write an MPI program that uses a Monte Carlo method to estimate π
3	Write an OpenMP program that uses a Monte Carlo method to estimate π
4	Test multi-node performance using HPLinpack benchmark
5	Write an MPI program that uses the ping-pong communication to test the delay for a point-to-point communication

For each project, students submitted source files and experimental documents. The project grading rubric took into account the correctness of code functions, input data completeness, the correctness of conclusions, etc. We encouraged students to list all the problems they have met and provided their assumptions and ideas.

3.3 End of Course Survey

At the end of the course, students were encouraged to complete a survey inquiring about their experiences with the programming projects. The survey also asked some questions about their confidence toward parallel programming projects.

Additionally, we also held an online discussion session at the end of the course to collect student feedback on the moderated two-stage projects. They were asked to evaluate if moderated two-stage projects improve their parallel programming ability compared with standard two-stage projects, and on how the moderated two-stage projects might have affected their attitude and confidence towards parallel programming.

4 RESULTS

4.1 Impact of Two-Stage Projects on Student Performance (RQ1)

We measure student performance using their project scores on both stages as shown in Figure 2. The average stage one score are all statistically lower than stage two for all 5 programming projects (Wilcoxon signed-rank test). We calculated the performance gain between the two stages as

$$gain = \frac{Score_{stage2} - Score_{stage1}}{Score_{stage1}} \times 100\% \qquad (3)$$

The performance gains for all the five projects from stage one to stage two are 25.3%, 45.7%, 28.9%, 5.1% and 21.4%, respectively. On average, students scored 62.50% on stage one across all five projects while having a 76.58% average for the second stage. This result confirms the finding by Battestilli et al. [1].

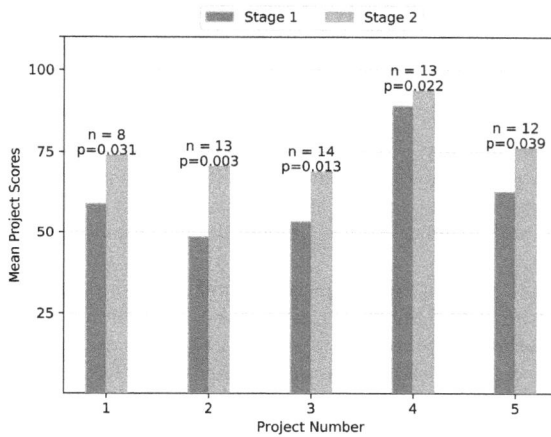

Figure 2: Mean project scores for stage one and stage two.

There are students who didn't submit work during stage one yet worked with a partner during stage two and was able to submit for stage two. These students' work is excluded from Figure 2 but we kept their partner's score. There was a cheating case for project 1 and that student's stage 1 and 2 scores are excluded from the analysis. In total, 10 aforementioned special cases that were dropped from our analysis shown in Figure 2. There is a 20% penalty for late submission and scores in Figure 2 reflect the score with the penalty already applied.

4.2 Impact of the Moderated Discussion on Two-Stage Projects (RQ2)

A moderated discussion session was inserted between stage one and two for projects 2 and 3. We calculated the performance gain for each student based on Equation 3.

As the score of each project is a composite of various factors (shown in Equation 1), the overall gain is broken down into gains on programming&test, and documentation. The performance gain of each project is shown in Figure 3. Projects 2 and 3 with a moderated

discussion session show the best gain compared to the other three projects. Figure 3 shows students' programming and testing ability improvement is much larger for projects 2 and 3. However, no statistical significance was observed.

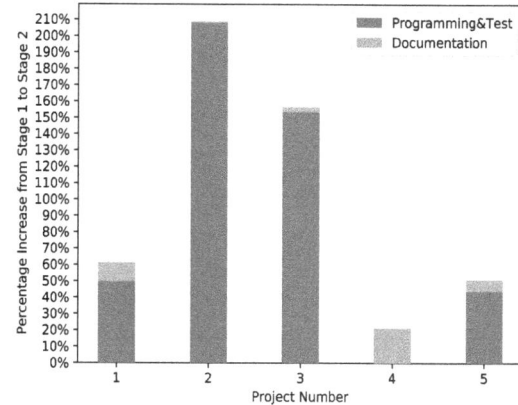

Figure 3: Learning gains for each project categorized into programming&test and documentation.

4.3 Students Experiences (RQ3)

At the end of the course, a multiple choice survey was sent to all 14 students and all of them responded. The survey was designed to examine students' experience with two-stage projects, and the impact of the moderated discussion session between the two stages. All questions in the survey are true/false questions and students can skip questions if they want to. The survey result is shown in Table 2. As can be seen, most students found the moderated two-stage project format to be beneficial for understanding their mistakes and basic concepts in parallel programming. No other significant pattern was found.

We also conducted a peer evaluation process to gauge the quality of collaborations during two-stage projects. Each student evaluated their second-stage partner for each project using a 5-point scale, with 5 being the highest score. All students participated in the peer evaluation process, and 70 evaluation scores were collected. 30 partners were rated at 5 points and 31 rated at 4 points. The rest of students considered they didn't get any help from their partners because they had no good communication with each other. Overall, students have high ratings for their partner which in turn reflecting good collaborations during two-stage projects.

As parallel programming projects can be challenging and time-consuming, we collected the number of hours student spent on each stage of a project. 36% students spent more than six hours on the first stage on average. About 29% students spent more than six hours on the second stage on average. As expected, the average time spent on stage two (5.5 hours) is less than that spent on stage one (8.0 hours).

Table 2: Survey results. The Counts column indicates the number of students who marked true for that question.

Question	Counts
Moderated two-stage projects showed me a different perspective	4
Moderated two-stage projects helped me understand my mistakes	14
Moderated two-stage projects helped me understand basic concepts for parallel programming	12
Moderated two-stage projects helped me grasp some operating methods on a real practice platform	7
Moderated two-stage projects helped me learn programming specification	8
Moderated two-stage projects helped me grasp some experiment design methods and test skills	3
Time was very limited	0
Moderated two-stage projects helped me a lot or some	14
Moderated two-stage projects didn't help me	0
Moderated two-stage projects helped the other person, but not me	0
My code didn't need any improvement	0
Moderated two-stage projects improve my collaboration skills	3

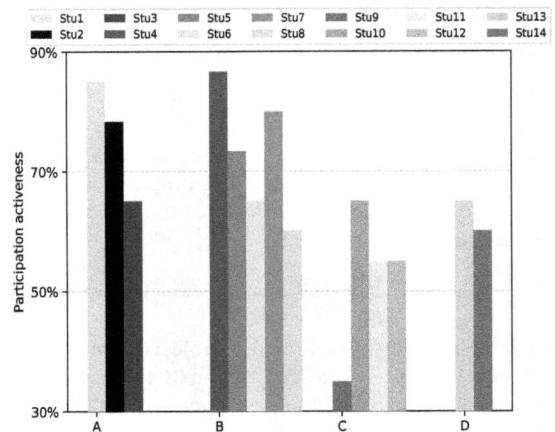

Figure 4: The distribution of participation activeness for each student against the their final grades. Students 1 to 14 are strictly ordered by their final course grades from high to low.

5 DISCUSSION

As shown in Figure 2, students' performance in stage two outperforms that of stage one. This finding is encouraging as it showed that two-stage projects not only improve student performance in CS1/2 [1], its effectiveness is also evident in upper division or graduate-level classes. The moderated discussion session seems to have a larger impact on students' coding and testing skills while having minimal effect on code documentation grades. We also examined the participation activeness of each student in each stage based on their final grades (Figure 4). We calculated the participation activeness for each student according to the following five categories: normal submission (1 point), late submission (0.5 point), unqualified submission (0.5 point), missing submission (0 point), code plagiarism (0 point). A weak positive correlation ($r = 0.49$) was observed between these two factors. For each student, her participation activeness for each submission is recorded, and a student's overall participation activeness is the average across the five projects. Students 9, 11 and 12 who got "C" had far lower participation activeness than all other students. That is because Student 9 had several missing submissions (0 point) and unqualified submissions (0.5 point). Student 11 had several late submissions and unqualified submissions (0.5 point). Student 12 had code plagiarism and several missing submissions (0 points).

The final course grade in Figure 4 is counted by the overall project grades (60%) and a final examination (40%). The overall project grade is counted by formula (2), which does not include participation activeness. The three students who received A (students 1, 2, and 3) have an average of 76.1% participation activeness, higher than those that got Bs (73.0%), Cs (52.5%) and Ds (62.5%). This might indicate that those students who actively participated in two-stage projects tend to master the subject better.

Threats to Validity

We identify the following threats to validity for this study:
–1. The sample size of this pilot study is small ($n = 14$). The research findings might need to be validated in other classes with varying sizes.
–2. Though we compared projects 1, 4, and 5 with projects 2 and 3 on the impact of the moderated discussion session, it isn't a strict experimental-control comparison. Though our results seem to favor a moderated discussion session, further studies in a controlled experimental setting are necessary.

6 CONCLUSIONS

This study proposed a moderated two-stage project format to help students improve their understanding of parallel programming and their confidence and interests for the subject. We found the project format was helpful for students to complete challenging parallel programming projects. Students showed progress in their learning and benefited from the moderated discussion session between the two stages. According to survey results, the majority of students liked two-stage projects and found the moderated discussion session helpful.

ACKNOWLEDGMENTS

This work was supported by the National Key Research and Development Program of China 2018YFB1003203, the Teaching Reform Research Project of Hunan Province under grant No.JG2017B004, the NUDT Teaching Reform Research Project under grant No.U2015013 and No.yjsy2016012.

REFERENCES

[1] Lina Battestilli, Apeksha Awasthi, and Yingjun Cao. 2018. Two-Stage Programming Projects: Individual Work Followed by Peer Collaboration. In *Proceedings of the 49th ACM Technical Symposium on Computer Science Education (SIGCSE '18)*. ACM, New York, NY, USA, 479–484. https://doi.org/10.1145/3159450.3159486

[2] Yingjun Cao and Leo Porter. 2017. Evaluating Student Learning from Collaborative Group Tests in Introductory Computing. In *Proceedings of the 2017 ACM SIGCSE Technical Symposium on Computer Science Education (SIGCSE '17)*. ACM, New York, NY, USA, 99–104. https://doi.org/10.1145/3017680.3017729

[3] J. C. Carver, L. Henderson, L. He, J. Hodges, and D. Reese. 2007. Increased Retention of Early Computer Science and Software Engineering Students Using Pair Programming. In *20th Conference on Software Engineering Education Training (CSEET'07)*. 115–122. https://doi.org/10.1109/CSEET.2007.29

[4] Mehmet Celepkolu and Kristy Elizabeth Boyer. 2018. The Importance of Producing Shared Code Through Pair Programming. In *Proceedings of the 49th ACM Technical Symposium on Computer Science Education (SIGCSE '18)*. ACM, New York, NY, USA, 765–770. https://doi.org/10.1145/3159450.3159506

[5] Alistair Cockburn and Laurie Williams. 2001. Extreme Programming Examined. Addison-Wesley Longman Publishing Co., Inc., Boston, MA, USA, Chapter The Costs and Benefits of Pair Programming, 223–243. http://dl.acm.org/citation.cfm?id=377517.377531

[6] D. Cohen and J. Henle. [n. d.]. The Pyramid Exam. *UME Trends* 10, 2 ([n. d.]).

[7] Scott Freeman, Sarah L Eddy, Miles McDonough, Michelle K Smith, Nnadozie Okoroafor, Hannah Jordt, and Mary Pat Wenderoth. 2014. Active learning increases student performance in science, engineering, and mathematics. *Proceedings of the National Academy of Sciences of the United States of America (PNAS)* 111, 23 (2014), 8410–8415.

[8] Brett Hollis Gilley and Bridgette Clarkston. 2014. Collaborative Testing: Evidence of Learning in a Controlled In-Class Study of Undergraduate Students. *Journal of College Science Teaching* 43, 3 (2014), 83–91.

[9] D. J. John. 1992. Integration of Parallel Computation into Introductory Computer Science. In *Proceedings of the Twenty-third SIGCSE Technical Symposium on Computer Science Education (SIGCSE '92)*. ACM, New York, NY, USA, 281–285. https://doi.org/10.1145/134510.134567

[10] Donald Johnson, David Kotz, and Fillia Makedon. [n. d.]. Teaching Parallel Computing to Freshmen. 1994. *Conference on Parallel Computing for Undergraduates* ([n. d.]).

[11] Neha Katira, Laurie Williams, Eric Wiebe, Carol Miller, Suzanne Balik, and Ed Gehringer. 2004. On Understanding Compatibility of Student Pair Programmers. In *Proceedings of the 35th SIGCSE Technical Symposium on Computer Science Education (SIGCSE '04)*. ACM, New York, NY, USA, 7–11. https://doi.org/10.1145/971300.971307

[12] Yousun Ko, Bernd Burgstaller, and Bernhard Scholz. 2013. Parallel from the Beginning: The Case for Multicore Programming in Thecomputer Science Undergraduate Curriculum. In *Proceeding of the 44th ACM Technical Symposium on Computer Science Education (SIGCSE '13)*. ACM, New York, NY, USA, 415–420. https://doi.org/10.1145/2445196.2445320

[13] Xiaosong Li. 2006. Using Peer Review to Assess Coding Standards - A Case Study. In *Proceedings of 36th Annual Conference in Frontiers in Education*. 9–14. https://doi.org/10.1109/FIE.2006.322572

[14] Charlie McDowell, Linda Werner, Heather Bullock, and Julian Fernald. 2002. The Effects of Pair-programming on Performance in an Introductory Programming Course. In *Proceedings of the 33rd SIGCSE Technical Symposium on Computer Science Education (SIGCSE '02)*. ACM, New York, NY, USA, 38–42. https://doi.org/10.1145/563340.563353

[15] Lori Pollock and Mike Jochen. 2001. Making Parallel Programming Accessible to Inexperienced Programmers Through Cooperative Learning. In *Proceedings of the Thirty-second SIGCSE Technical Symposium on Computer Science Education (SIGCSE '01)*. ACM, New York, NY, USA, 224–228. https://doi.org/10.1145/364447.364589

[16] Ken Reily, Pam Ludford Finnerty, and Loren Terveen. 2009. Two Peers Are Better Than One: Aggregating Peer Reviews for Computing Assignments is Surprisingly Accurate. In *Proceedings of the ACM 2009 International Conference on Supporting Group Work (GROUP '09)*. ACM, New York, NY, USA, 115–124. https://doi.org/10.1145/1531674.1531692

[17] Caitlin Sadowski, Thomas Ball, Judith Bishop, Sebastian Burckhardt, Ganesh Gopalakrishnan, Joseph Mayo, Madanlal Musuvathi, Shaz Qadeer, and Stephen Toub. 2011. Practical Parallel and Concurrent Programming. In *Proceedings of the 42Nd ACM Technical Symposium on Computer Science Education (SIGCSE '11)*. ACM, New York, NY, USA, 189–194. https://doi.org/10.1145/1953163.1953222

[18] Brenda Cantwell Wilson and Sharon Shrock. 2001. Contributing to Success in an Introductory Computer Science Course: A Study of Twelve Factors. In *Proceedings of the Thirty-second SIGCSE Technical Symposium on Computer Science Education (SIGCSE '01)*. ACM, New York, NY, USA, 184–188. https://doi.org/10.1145/364447.364581

[19] Benjamin Yu, George Tsiknis, and Meghan Allen. 2010. Turning Exams into a Learning Experience. In *Proceedings of the 41st ACM Technical Symposium on Computer Science Education (SIGCSE '10)*. ACM, New York, NY, USA, 336–340. https://doi.org/10.1145/1734263.1734380

Can Mobile Gaming Psychology Be Used to Improve Time Management on Programming Assignments?

Michael S. Irwin and Stephen H. Edwards
Department of Computer Science
Virginia Tech
Blacksburg, VA, USA
mikesir@vt.edu, edwards@cs.vt.edu

ABSTRACT

Students often procrastinate on assignments, sometimes to the extent that it negatively affects their work. Although many solutions have been researched, instructors continue searching for effective techniques that are easy to employ and require little faculty overhead. This paper describes experiences adapting techniques inspired by commercially successful mobile games. These games use structural features that limit the player's play time, and use reward systems to encourage students to cultivate game-based resources (like energy, gold, credits, etc.). This combination of limits plus incentives shapes the way players manage their play time: it deters "binge" play sessions and strongly promotes the use of a much larger number of play sessions spread over a longer period of time. By adapting this to the assignment self-checking and turn-in process, we hope to exert a similar effect on how students manage their time in completing assignments. The goal is to shift students to start earlier and spread their work time out over a longer period, engaging with the assignment more frequently. In addition to combating procrastination, this also offers a longer time frame to seek help from course staff when problems arise. We report on experiences using this strategy over a year and a half in CS 1, discuss the impact on student submission patterns, when students begin their work, how they spread their work out over time, and student perceptions of the technique.

Keywords

Time management; behavior modification; procrastination

ACM Reference Format:
Michael S. Irwin and Stephen H. Edwards. 2019. Can Mobile Gaming Psychology Be Used to Improve Time Management on Programming Assignments?. In ACM Global Computing Education Conference 2019 (CompEd '19), May 17–19, 2019, Chengdu, Sichuan, China. ACM, New York, NY, USA, 7 pages. https://doi.org/10.1145/3300115.3309517

1. INTRODUCTION

It is common for computer science students to procrastinate on classwork, and some instructors see this as a potential cause for poor performance. Indeed, past work in CS education has already shown a statistically significant correlation between when students start their work and the corresponding assignment grades, while controlling for individual differences [1]. Interest in addressing procrastination is grounded in the belief that by reducing procrastination, students will be able to use their time more appropriately to monitor their work, analyze their mistakes, learn from errors, and integrate this new information with their existing knowledge. Basically, they have more time to monitor themselves to determine what they do and do not understand [4].

In this paper, we present our experiences with techniques inspired by **commercially successful mobile games** that reshape the way players manage their time. We have adapted some of these time management reinforcement strategies from mobile games to the task of completing computer programming assignments. The two critical elements from mobile games that we aimed to leverage were limiting consumption and promoting frequent sessions.

Limiting consumption: Mobile games often use some form of resource management to limit the amount of time players engage with the game in one sitting. Whether the resource is energy, gold, food, karma, ammunition, or something else, one purpose of such resources is to limit the player's interaction by limiting the availability of the necessary resources. Limiting "binge playing" sessions helps prevent players from becoming oversaturated with the game, or desensitized to its fun elements.

Promoting frequent sessions: In many mobile games, players can naturally regenerate or "farm" resources over time. Effectively, this turns "wait time" between play sessions into resources, integrating time management as an implicit element of resource management. However, resource generators have limits, and once they reach those limits, they cannot generate more resources until the player "harvests". This naturally creates an incentive for players to return to the game regularly if they want to maximize resources—otherwise, too much intervening time means "wasted" time when resources are not being generated. This strategy, combined with limiting consumption, results in a strong incentive for a higher frequency of shorter sessions, and for players to pay attention to how frequently they visit the game.

In the context of students completing programming assignments, we aim to apply these strategies in the context of an electronic submission and feedback system, similar to systems used at many large universities. This approach will support a low effort intervention that can be applied by a wide variety of instructors in classrooms of any size with minimal investment.

Our goal is to apply gentle pressure that encourages students to avoid starting work late and avoid relying on long "binge" work sessions. By applying such game-inspired strategies, can we encourage students to use a larger number of work sessions spread out over time instead of pulling an all-nighter just before the due date (i.e., a "binge" session)? This paper describes the lessons learned from this experience, which suggest that employing such strategies does encourage students to start working earlier, increases the number of work sessions, increases the likelihood they finish work on time, and helps students earn higher scores on assignments.

2. RELATED WORK

2.1 Procrastination

Procrastination is delaying an action you intend to perform, despite the clear possibility of negative consequences [8]. Tuckman indicates that college students are particularly susceptible to procrastination [10]. Prior research in CS education summarizes research in other disciplines and describes a range of interventions that have been studied [2]. While a number of interventions intended to address student procrastination have been investigated, the most effective seems to be some form of supplementary course or workshop on motivation and time management strategies [6]. While this approach may be feasible for smaller, targeted populations of students at risk, it is not scalable to large classroom situations when 70-95% of students procrastinate [9]. In the context of this broader work on procrastination, the experiences described in this paper were inspired by efforts to devise lightweight interventions that are cheap or free for instructors to employ, to see if any impact might be observed.

2.2 Automated Grading Limits

While automated grading systems are employed at many universities, to our knowledge, none support mechanisms similar to the mobile game strategies described here. Instead, it is most common for grading tools to support simpler limits, such as a limit on the total number of submissions attempted by a student. Often, these limits are designed to prevent students from simply relying on the grading tool to perform all of the necessary testing, or to manage capacity issues. Among automated grading systems described in the literature Marmoset [7] provides features that are most similar to those described here. Marmoset is an automated grading system that provides two levels of feedback. Marmoset allows instructors to set up assignments with both a public set of tests—where students receive full feedback all the time on every submission—and a private set of tests—where students receive more limited feedback. When a student submits work to Marmoset, the student can choose whether to receive results only from the public tests, or from both. However, requesting results from both sets of tests uses a resource: one *token*. Students can hold up to three tokens, and once used, a token takes 24 hours to regenerate. This approach limits students in the amount of feedback they receive, and predates the current trends in mobile game applications. Our approach is different, however, in that the mechanisms in mobile games on which our approach is based have been honed through market pressures extensively. Here, we limit consumption by preventing submissions entirely, rather than limiting feedback, and are explicitly aiming for goals beyond limiting consumption, including changing time management behavior.

2.3 Time Management in Commercially Successful Mobile Games

While commercially successful mobile games are not primary targets for scholarly research or writing, the techniques they use have been honed through trial and error in the marketplace. The Game Theorists, a popular online video blog, provides a general summary along with the presumed psychology behind the most common techniques [3]. To be commercially successful, mobile games must attract players and encourage them to establish play patterns that eventually lead them to spend money on the game. While some games are successful in producing revenue through initial sales, many of the most successful mobile games make far more through in-app purchases. However, developing such an income stream requires games to encourage longer lasting relationships with players, which can be tricky. Developers of these games have tried and refined many mechanisms to encourage players to maintain and deepen longer term playing relationships with their games, and some of their techniques have been quite successful.

Candy Crush Saga, for example, gives players "lives" as a simple resource. A player has five lives, and when you fail to complete a level in the game, one life is used up. When all five lives are lost, the player must wait 30 minutes for a life to regenerate, forcing the player to limit the length of play sessions.

Puzzle & Dragons, another successful mobile game, uses a similar approach, where the resource that limits play is called *stamina*. Different levels (dungeons) in the game require different amounts of stamina, depending on their difficulty and rewards. Stamina regenerates at one unit each five minutes, but the longer a player plays, the more stamina is required for each new level. Other types of resources in *Puzzle & Dragons* are used to regulate other play features.

Dragons World is another example of a game with multiple types of in-game resources that each govern different aspects of play. Players who engage in tournament play in this game have a *battle energy* bar controlling their tournament challenges. The player starts with three units of battle energy, and each tournament challenge uses one unit. Once used, a unit of battle energy regenerates in one hour. During special events, energy regeneration speed doubles. Players also have the strategic option of using all three units of battle energy to significantly increase the strength of their attack in a tournament challenge.

In *Brave Frontier*, very similar rules govern player participation in the game's arena. The arena allows a player to place his or her squad in competition with another randomly selected player to win rewards. The player has a visible bar of three *arena orbs*, and each arena challenge consumes one orb. Orbs regenerate at the rate of one per hour. A similar system using a different type of resource appears in other parts of the game. *Brave Frontier* also uses an energy system similar to the stamina system in *Puzzle & Dragons* to regulate entry into regular game levels. Units of energy regenerate every three minutes, while entering a level consumes 3-25 units.

While the exact details of the resource mechanisms among games differ, the underlying idea is twofold: to limit the amount of time of any one play session, and to encourage a pattern of frequent, short play sessions spread out in a regular pattern over time. Limiting the length of play sessions has been theorized to reduce the likelihood that players will become oversaturated, desensitizing them to the enjoyment of the game [5][3]. Similarly, the use of time-based regeneration of critical resources, together with caps on how much regenerated resource can be held, encourages players to think of "time between play sessions" as roughly equivalent to "earning resources"—as long as they visit the game often enough to use the resources that are generated.

The result of combining these features is a carefully balanced arrangement of reinforcements that forces the player to spread play time out over a larger number of play sessions, instead of binge-playing in a few long sittings. However, this is exactly the same behavior we are trying to reinforce with students when they pursue programming assignments. We expect students to spend the same amount of time working on their assignments. But by encouraging students to spread their programming activities over a longer period of time, we can encourage the avoidance of procrastination and the adoption of time management strategies that are statistically associated with better student outcomes.

3. SUBMISSION ENERGY
3.1 Limiting Consumption
In adapting these techniques for use in programming assignments, it is necessary to devise a task appropriate resource model, determine how resources are consumed, and verify that this will limit consumption appropriately. The primary action that students perform using the assignment submission system is to submit their work in progress to receive feedback. When instructors require it, students also self-check their own work through software testing, and include those tests as part of their submission. The automated grading tool we use, Web-CAT, makes it easy to grade students on how well they test their own software, and feedback on the thoroughness of their tests is provided for each submission. As a result, students value the feedback they receive, and students average between 10-15 submissions on an assignment, depending on course level and assignment difficulty. In surveys, students indicate that they value the feedback they receive from the grading system and that it helps them improve their work.

As a result, we designed a **submission energy** system for assignment submissions, where students are limited to making submissions only when they have energy units available. Based on the most common features we observed in mobile games, we decided that students are able to carry a full charge of three submission energy units, where consumed units regenerate at the rate of one per hour. This capacity limit and recharge rate is common in many commercially successful mobile games. Different values could be chosen, and there is no scientific basis for the values chosen here—simply the fact that they have worked out in practice in another (unrelated) context, and appear intuitively to be a reasonable starting point for investigation.

Figure 1 shows how this appears in the user interface for the assignment submission system. This approach naturally limits

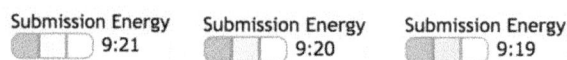

Figure 1: Submission energy bar, showing countdown and the animated fading of the next available unit being regenerated.

consumption of "assignment submission" resources by students, and discourages overly long work sessions, or last-minute "cramming" on the night an assignment is due. However, **judicious use of submissions would still allow students to perform multi-hour work sessions over an entire afternoon or evening without excessive restrictions**. For example, a student who begins working in the evening can easily make a total of 6 submissions in a three-hour work session.

However, when thinking of limiting a student's submission access, one must also ask whether students would be completely prohibited from making submissions on time, if there is time left before an assignment deadline but the student has no submission energy. Since the goal is to encourage students to explicitly manage their time differently, the answer is yes; students should be prevented from submitting without energy most of the time. However, we believe the energy system should provide one exception: if a student has used all of his or her submission energy, and the assignment deadline is close enough that no more energy units will be regenerated before the deadline, then the student is *not* prevented from submitting. We instead implemented a one-hour grace period immediately before the assignment deadline. Students who have exhausted all of their energy are still allowed to make submissions during this time instead of being prematurely cut off due to lack of energy. This approach balances the need for preserving a real world cost to using submission energy, while also preventing the lockout of students who make time management mistakes.

3.2 Promoting Frequent Sessions
As with the energy systems in many mobile games, submission energy regenerates after a fixed time. To encourage students to think carefully about their software changes, and to encourage them to self-check their own work before resubmitting, the regeneration time should not be too short. As a result, we chose a regeneration time of one hour, which is patterned after similarly limited resources in a number of mobile games, including both *Dragons World* and *Brave Frontier*. Similarly, capping the maximum number of energy units a student may hold at three is aimed at encouraging more frequent work sessions. If students wait until the last day to work on an assignment, the number of submissions they can make is physically limited—it would be difficult for a student to get 10-15 submissions in one such work session without working all day. Instead, the limited capacity of submission energy together with the choice for regeneration time strongly encourages students to divide their work into multiple work sessions spread out over a longer period of time.

In essence, this approach encourages students to think of *time* as a moderately liquid form of *submission energy*. Once a student makes a submission, time automatically begins to be converted into a replacement unit of submission energy. However, while the conversion is automatic, it is not instantaneous. Instead, to take advantage of energy regeneration, the student must plan out his or her use of submission energy to maximize the benefits of the time-to-energy conversion (to maximize the gains from regeneration). While we have implemented this strategy with our choices of a 3-unit capacity and one-hour regeneration time, we realize that there is no compelling reason to believe these choices are optimal. It would be interesting to study whether different choices might achieve better results.

3.3 Designing the Energy Bar Interface

The idea of an energy system exists in many mobile games, but is represented in as many ways as there are games. The next challenge was then to decide on a meaningful way to represent submission energy to students in Web-CAT. While preparing the design, we determined we wanted the user to be able to clearly determine:

1. The number of remaining/available submissions.
2. The number of possible submissions when "fully charged."
3. When the next unit of submission energy would be recharged.

To help meet these goals, we looked at the energy systems for various games. Two notable games were *Candy Crush* and *Sniper Arena*, games available for both the iOS and Android platforms.

In *Candy Crush*, energy is represented by hearts. The number of available hearts is presented simply as a number. A timer is also included to indicate when the next heart will be made available. When all hearts are available, the countdown timer is replaced with the text "Full".

In *Sniper Arena*, energy is represented as "Stamina." Numerous boxes are used to indicate the "fullness" of the energy bar; filled boxes indicate available energy, while empty boxes indicate consumed energy. This provides the player with an indication of not only their available energy, but also the maximum amount possible. In order to determine when the next unit of stamina will become available, the user must click on the stamina bar. A pop-up then displays the current countdown timer.

After a review of various implementations, we settled on the following concepts:

- Use the "box" approach to help the user know the available energy, as well as total possible energy.
- Place the countdown timer directly on the screen, rather than requiring an action from the user.

We then needed to decide how to actually represent the energy bar. Do we simply use boxes, use icons in the boxes, or something else? We decided to model the energy bar similar to battery indicators on mobile devices, hoping that users would associate the representation of battery power with submission energy. Since we wanted to allow an arbitrary number of slots, we were prevented from using off-the-shelf battery icons and instead we used a simple HTML/CSS solution.

One further enhancement was adding a slow fade in/out to indicate the regenerating process occurring in the first empty energy slot. To reduce possible confusion from a quick glance when the next slot is fully faded in, the fully faded-in color was modified to use a lighter shade. After some experimenting, we decided to perform the full color fade loop every four seconds. Figure 1 shows the visual representation of the submission energy bar and how the unit being regenerated is depicted.

Indeed, representing the energy bar turned out to be the main element of the submission energy user interface. To students, this bar appeared on the upper right of the submission page where students could make submissions, and in a similar position on the feedback page showing their most recent results. Beyond that, all interaction with submission energy by students was implicit. When a student made a submission, they could see the updated energy bar in their results, and later

would see it again if they were submitting through the Web-CAT submission upload web page. If a student is out of energy and attempts to make a submission, they receive an error message: "Your submission energy is depleted. Wait until your energy regenerates before submitting." As a result, keeping the student constantly informed of the state of their energy bar is the primary task, and no direct manipulation is needed.

4. EXPERIENCES

After development was complete, we first piloted the submission energy strategy in the Spring 2017 offering of CS1 at Virginia Tech. This initial use helped uncover various implementation issues, and also allowed us to gather student opinions about the limits. It was no surprise that students who already had experience with submitting assignments electronically chafed at the addition of submission energy, although we took this as a positive sign that the system was more likely to affect behavior as students adapted to avoid negative consequences.

During the Fall 2017 and Spring 2018 semesters, we deployed the approach at full scale in CS1 on all out-of-class programming assignments. These programming assignments were assigned once every two weeks, with solutions ranging from 100-750 non-commented lines of source code in size. Students were expected to be able to complete each such assignment within a week, although stronger students with prior experience could complete them much faster. As is typical in beginner courses, programming assignments started easier/smaller at the beginning of the academic term, and increased in size and complexity as the term proceeded.

We also gave students clear information up front on the way submission energy worked and on the goals that motivated its use, including encouraging starting work earlier, avoiding cram sessions, and encouraging more thoughtful time management, with the hope of improving outcomes on assignments. By consistently employing the strategy on every assignment from the beginning, and by clearly explaining the motivation and reasoning behind the strategy, students were more accepting of the modified expectations.

At the same time, it is worth noting that providing this explanation may itself have affected student behavior independently of the submission energy mechanism, although it is not possible to measure this separately in the study because of its design. A future study could provide an equivalent explanation to the control group to provide a better baseline for comparison, however, if there are concerns about the potential impact of the explanation itself.

With IRB approval, we asked permission of students to use their assignment data for research purposes in both semesters. A total of 263 students (out of 961) agreed to participate. We were then able to compare their results to historical data collected from both semesters in a prior year, also under IRB permission. Both the historical control semesters and the treatment semesters used common assignments. All sections of the course across all four semesters in the comparison were used, allowing us to aggregate data across all of the instructors in both groups. While it may be worth considering using a single-semester setup with students randomly assigned to either the treatment or control conditions, that approach is logistically challenging. Because students had the choice of whether or not to participate in the research effort, students who may perceive the intervention as a form of interference in their access to automated assessment could be less likely to consent. Worse still, if we used random assignment to treatment groups within a course section, students may perceive their treatment as unequal (meaning unfair). For these reasons, we chose to apply the treatment to all students in the selected semesters and use historical data as the basis for comparison, relying on use of data from all sections across two semesters to reduce the potential effects of individual instructor differences. We were primarily focused on checking for any indication that adding submission energy was associated with any changes in student submission behaviors.

4.1 Number of Submissions

In comparing students using submission energy against historical data from the same course, we did find that submission energy did somewhat reduce the number of submissions made by students. Without submission energy, students averaged 10.0 submissions per assignment, while with submission energy this dropped to 7.2 submissions per assignment. An analysis of variance with the presence of submission energy limits and the assignment as independent variables, and with students modeled as a random effect, indicated this difference is statistically significant ($F(1, 1539) = 22.6$, $p < 0.0001$). Our experience was that students made somewhat fewer submissions with the energy limits in place.

4.2 Start Time

We also examined when students began working, as approximated by the time of their first submission. Existing research supports this as being a reasonable approximation [1]. We found that without submission energy, students began submitting their work an average of 42.1 hours prior to the deadline, while with submission energy the average time of the first submission was 45.4 hours. While an ANOVA controlling for presence of submission energy, assignment, and individual students (as random effects) indicated this difference to be significant ($F(1, 1621) = 73.3$, $p < 0.0001$), an average difference of only 3 hours is much smaller than hoped.

Following [1], we also examined the total time elapsed between the first and last submission for each student as a way of approximating the total time spent. We found no significant difference in the total elapsed time from first submission to last ($F = 1.1$, $p > 0.29$) between students using submission energy (mean 28.2 hours) and those without (mean 26.2 hours). This is consistent with prior work [1], where students who start earlier do not spend significantly more time on the assignment, and instead tend to finish earlier (see Section 4.4 below).

4.3 Work Sessions

While we directly measured when students made submissions, we did not have an easy way to measure when they began working or stopped working. As a result, we could only attempt to infer this information from submission timestamps to approximate the number of distinct periods during which students worked. As other researchers have done, we used a contiguous series of submissions that were "close enough" together to approximate a single period of work on a given assignment, and treated two consecutive submissions that were much farther apart are marking a break between two different work sessions. Here, we pick a gap size of two hours to mark the boundary between work sessions. Consecutive submissions closer together than this were considered part of the same work session, and consecutive submissions further apart in time were considered to be in separate work sessions.

Using this definition, we found that prior to submission energy, students averaged 2.1 work sessions per assignment, while with submission energy, the average increased to 2.5 work sessions ($F(1, 5146) = 99.7$, $p < 0.0001$). We also examined the number of times students completed an assignment in just a single work session. We might intuitively imagine that this often was the result of a single longer work session on the last day when the assignment was due, although a student who finds an assignment easy might complete it in one sitting well before the due date. We found that without submission energy, student work fell into only one work session 47.6% of the time, while with submission energy, students worked in a single work session only 33.6% of the time ($\chi^2 = 83.6$, $p < 0.0001$).

Of course, submission energy necessarily increases the amount of time between submissions, which might falsely lead to inferring a larger number of work sessions when using an inter-submission time delay to judge work session boundaries. In fact, there was no evidence that students spent more time on assignments, as measured using the difference between the time of first submission and time of last submission. Without submission energy, students spanned an average of 26.2 hours from first submission to last, while with submission energy the average time span was 28.2 hours (not significant, $F(1, 5146) = 1.1$). This suggests the possibility that the difference in inferred work sessions is an artifact of the increased delay between submissions, more than a change in student behavior.

4.4 Finishing Late

One significant issue with student procrastination is that it increases the chances that a student may not finish an assignment on time. Prior work has shown that turning in work late is correlated with lower quality and lower assignment scores [1]. We examined the time of a student's final submission and found that on average, without submission energy students finished 16.7 hours before the deadline, while with submission energy this increased to 16.6 hours ($F(1, 1904) = 36.1$, $p < 0.0001$). Further, without submission energy, we found that 14.4% of the time, student work was turned in late. With submission energy, student work was turned in late 6.8% of the time ($\chi^2 = 52.2$, $p < 0.0001$). Thus, there appeared to be a positive effect on student ability to complete assignments within the time limit.

At the same time, we found that without submission energy, 11.4% of the time students finished during the final hour just before the deadline. With submission energy, students finished during the final hour 14.2% of the time, although this was not significant when controlling for assignments ($\chi^2 = 1.32$, $p = 0.25$). Still, because of the possibility that a 1-hour grace period before the due deadline could also affect student behavior meaningfully, it is important to explore this area further.

4.5 Assignment Scores

Finally, we did examine assignment scores to see if there was any noticeable difference with submission energy. Intuitively, we did not expect noticeable differences here, although it is plausible that if submission energy reduces procrastination (and therefore late submissions) enough, then it might affect assignment scores because of the correlation between late work and lower scores. If we look only at the correctness of student answers, students without submission energy averaged scores of 90.2% while those with submission energy averaged 93.9%, which is significant ($F(1, 1426) = 24.1$, $p < 0.0001$, s.d. = 22.0%). Further, because students were also required to test their own solutions, we can also look at their assignment grades including both correctness of answer and completeness of testing. Then we see that without submission energy, students averaged scores of 87.1%, while with submission energy, they scored an average of 91.6%, a difference that is also significant ($F(1, 1381)$ = 21.6, $p < 0.0001$, s.d. = 23.7%). This difference represents only 0.19 of the whole population's standard deviation, however.

Finally, we examined how many students earned acceptable scores on assignments, using an 80% score as the partition point between successful outcomes and less than successful outcomes on an assignment. Without submission energy, students earned scores above that score 84.9% of the time. With submission energy, students earned scores above that threshold 91.6% of the time. Although the differences are somewhat small, when submission energy limits were used students did earn higher scores across every dimension we checked.

5. STUDENT PERCEPTIONS

At the conclusion of the spring semester, we presented a survey to all students to determine the effectiveness of our user interface design, observance of any submission behavior changes, and overall reactions to the system. The survey consisted of 20 questions, with each question including seven single-option answers ranging from "Strongly Agree" to "Strongly Disagree." 57 students completed the survey.

5.1 User Interface Reactions

Of the respondents, 83% agreed or strongly agreed they were able to easily determine their current submission energy level. In addition, 78% indicated it was easy for them to easily determine when the next energy unit would become available.

One shortcoming of the survey is we did not ask how we could have made the interface better. However, in discussions with students and TAs afterwards, a few students indicated frustrations determining the energy level because the bar was only available while they were on the website. Seeing they were most often working in their programming IDE, they needed to remember to keep the website open.

5.2 Overall Reactions

Another theme quite evident throughout the survey results was overall frustration with the system. A couple of highlights include:

- 71% of respondents agree or strongly agree that submission energy makes them use their time differently.
- 73% agree that they think harder about their changes before each submission.
- 67% believe the recharge time was too long.
- 67% indicated they were frustrated.
- 64% of respondents indicated they made fewer submissions because of the energy bar.
- Only 18% felt their class performance improved as a result.

Overall, it seems students are aware of their own behavior changes in response to the submission energy limits, even if they may not directly observe benefits firsthand. Survey results and discussions with students indicate that students would prefer fewer limits, which is understandable. Indeed, the overall student responses do suggest that students reacted in a mildly negative way to the limits—which, again, should be expected.

However, if the limits are innocuous enough (that is, inconsequential enough) that students are happy with them, it is unlikely that they would be able to produce behavioral change. If changing time management behavior is the goal, then limits must be significant enough that students see a clear need to adjust their behavior to maximize benefits and minimize negative consequences. While answers regarding frustration and recharge time may be viewed as negative, it is clear that students also felt that the think harder about their work before making a submission and felt they made fewer submissions under the limits, which indicates students confirm the limits were pushing them in the direction intended by the mechanism's design.

6. CONCLUSION

After employing this technique at full scale over an entire year with nearly a thousand students, we have learned that it is feasible to apply time management controls like this in an automated way. Managing student expectations, clearly communicating the reasons for the mechanisms, and consistent application will all improve the student experience and improve student acceptance of additional limits.

One goal of this strategy was to encourage students to begin working earlier. While there is evidence students started earlier, the gains were smaller than desired and additional work may be necessary. Another goal was to encourage students to use a larger number of work periods. However, because this strategy encourages longer delays between submissions, measurement issues in determining when work sessions start or stop may interfere with drawing accurate conclusions.

In terms of assignment outcomes, our experience suggests a modest but significant decrease in students turning in assignments late, and a similarly modest but significant increase in scores earned. Both results are promising, and suggest further work is desirable to explore whether adjustments to the strategy can achieve stronger results. It is plausible that these changes are primarily driven by students starting earlier, but that is expected—encouraging earlier start times was one of the goals.

One critical lesson we took away from this experience, however, is that the submission energy limits may have been too soft or too generous. While our goal was to encourage more work sessions, beforehand students were only averaging 10 submissions per assignment across an average of two work sessions spread over an average of about 26 hours. When submission energy was added, we did see the number of submissions drop down to 7.2. However, a student who is making around 5 submissions per evening over two evenings on an assignment may be able to drop back to 4 submissions per night without noticeably changing time management behavior. In CS1, it may be that the scope of assignments is short enough, and the amount of time taken is small enough, that submission limits using the parameters described in this paper do not exert enough influence on student behavior to encourage more substantial changes. Exploring other contexts, either where limits are increased or where assignments take larger amounts of work over a longer period of time, may provide valuable insights into how to achieve the greatest impact.

Based on student feedback, we have determined that the designed user interface meets the needs, but more work can be done to help students benefit. One avenue of exploration is to adapt additional complementary techniques from mobile games, such as combining reward and incentive strategies that synergize with the consumption limiting features. In many mobile games, actions can unlock double recharge rates, an immediate energy recharge, or more. Using the submission energy as a platform, we can also provide rewards to students. These rewards, when utilized, can continue to motivate students to work on the assignment, improving their overall performance.

In a classroom context, other ideas include allowing students to earn energy bonuses for desirable behaviors, or adding special limited-time events where energy recharges faster or where unlimited submissions are allowed during a specific time window may all help make students more aware of their time management choices. While students may experience limits on their freedom as constraining, it seems clear that this friction is necessary in order to prompt a change in behavior. Without this friction, students have no incentive to change.

ACKNOWLEDGMENTS

This work is supported in part by the National Science Foundation under grant DUE-1245334. Any opinions, findings, conclusions, or recommendations expressed in this material are those of the authors and do not necessarily reflect the views of the National Science Foundation.

REFERENCES

[1] Edwards, S.H., Snyder, J., Allevato, A., Perez-Quinones, M.A., Kim, D., and Tretola, B. *Comparing effective and ineffective behaviors of student programmers.* In *Proceedings of the Fifth International Computing Education Research Workshop*, ACM, New York, NY, 2009, pp. 3–14.

[2] S.H. Edwards, J. Martin, and C.A. Shaffer. Examining classroom interventions to reduce procrastination. In *Proc. 2015 ACM Conf. Innovation and Tech. in Comp. Sci. Education (ITiCSE '15)*. ACM, New York, NY, USA, 254-259, 2015.

[3] The Game Theorists, Game theory: Candy Crush, designed to ADDICT, last accessed: August 31, 2018, https://www.youtube.com/watch?v=_BTGgCEFuQw

[4] Hmelo-Silver, C.E. Problem-based learning: What and how do students learn? *Educational Psychology Review*, 16: 235–266, 2004.

[5] Madigan, J. Why you don't burn out on Candy Crush Saga. October 7, 2013. Last accessed: August 31, 2018, http://www.psychologyofgames.com/2013/10/why-you-dont-burn-out-on-candy-crush-saga/

[6] Novotney, A. Procrastination or "intentional delay"? *gradPSYCH*, January, 2010, p. 14.

[7] Spacco, J.W. *Marmoset: A Programming Project Assignment Framework to Improve the Feedback Cycle for Students, Faculty and Researchers*. Ph.D. Dissertation. University of Maryland at College Park, College Park, MD, USA, 2006.

[8] P. Steel. The nature of procrastination: a meta-analytic and theoretical review of quintessential self-regulatory failure. *Psychological Bulletin*, 133(1):65, 2007.

[9] Tice, D.M., and Baumeister, R.F. Longitudinal study of procrastination, performance, stress, and health: The costs and benefits of dawdling. Psychological Science, 8(6): 454-458, November, 1997.

[10] B. W. Tuckman. The development and concurrent validity of the procrastination scale. *Educational and Psychological Measurement*, 51(2):473–480, 1991.

Impact of Open-Ended Assignments on Student Self-Efficacy in CS1

Sadia Sharmin
University of Toronto - OISE
Toronto, ON, Canada
s.sharmin@mail.utoronto.ca

Lisa Zhang
University of Toronto
Mississauga, ON, Canada
lczhang@cs.toronto.edu

Daniel Zingaro
University of Toronto
Mississauga, ON, Canada
daniel.zingaro@utoronto.ca

Clare Brett
University of Toronto - OISE
Toronto, ON, Canada
clare.brett@utoronto.ca

ABSTRACT

A goal of many Computer Science Education (CSE) researchers is reconceptualizing aspects of introductory Computer Science (CS1) to increase student engagement and retention. The measure of self-efficacy, or one's personal judgment about their ability to accomplish a task, is a valuable component of student learning as it affects one's level of effort and perseverance against obstacles. A potential way to restructure aspects of CS1 to increase self-efficacy is by allowing students to have more room for freedom/experimentation within assignments. The purpose of this study is to analyze the impact of a specific, open-ended assignment structure on self-efficacy and academic performance, through a quasi-experimental study involving undergraduate CS1 students. Two concurrent lecture sections (Section A and B) with the same instructor were given two different versions of an assignment — (1) a control version with a typical, standard structure, and (2) an open-ended version with an additional requirement to add enhancements of the student's own choosing to the project. For assignment 1, Section A completed the control assignment, while Section B completed the open-ended assignment. For assignment 2, to counterbalance the groups, Section B completed the control assignment while Section A completed the open-ended one. We found both average self-efficacy and average assignment grades were consistently (although not significantly) higher for students who completed the open-ended versions, and that self-efficacy significantly affected the average grade of both assignments, regardless of the type of assignment structure.

CCS CONCEPTS

• **Social and professional topics** → **CS1**;

KEYWORDS

CS1, self-efficacy, assignments, open-ended

ACM Reference Format:
Sadia Sharmin, Daniel Zingaro, Lisa Zhang, and Clare Brett. 2019. Impact of Open-Ended Assignments on Student Self-Efficacy in CS1. In *ACM Global Computing Education Conference 2019 (CompEd '19), May 17–19, 2019, Chengdu,Sichuan, China*. ACM, New York, NY, USA, 7 pages. https://doi.org/10.1145/3300115.3309532

1 INTRODUCTION

Introductory Computer Science (CS1) is a fundamental course in Computer Science Education (CSE) due to its role in shaping how students understand CS [23]. A key component of CSE research is the examination of how CS1 can be re-conceptualized to increase student engagement and retention [10, 15]. This research is driven by the concern that CS1 often has disappointing levels of student understanding and retention rates, as observed across several years within multiple institutions [15, 23]. Despite continued efforts to improve the structure of CS1 — be it through lecture style, assignment style, or assessments used — determining how to best teach Computer Science remains an ongoing area of interest in CSE.

One way to improve CS1 could be by addressing the lack of creative thinking opportunities within typical introductory CS courses. Through limited, linear assignment structures, CS1 students are often not exposed to the true creative potential that programming knowledge can provide. This causes a disconnect between Computer Science as introduced in CS1 and Computer Science within the innovative, experimental CS work industry [9, 12, 13].

This study explores open-ended assignments as a potential way of allowing CS1 students more creative thinking opportunities. Previous studies examining creativity and assignment structures have attempted to provide students with varying levels of freedom to make their own choices on assignments, such as by building a game where the student could choose their own themes and images [14], or letting the students choose between various assignment options entirely [1]. These studies generally found positive results for student motivation, satisfaction and understanding of material.

The purpose of this study is to build on this area of research in CSE by (1) examining a specific type of open-ended assignment structure that is different from those in prior literature but also meant to allow students freedom to explore/experiment, and (2) gaining a clearer understanding of the relationship between this assignment structure and quantitative measures of grades and self-efficacy. While the previous studies did examine effects on student learning beyond grades — such as motivation, sense of ownership, and levels of interest — none of the studies looked specifically at the concept of self-efficacy. Self-efficacy is an important learning outcome as it can affect a student's level of effort and ability to persevere [2]. This makes self-efficacy a significant factor in a student's success in their courses, and thus an important concept to analyze. Findings from this research can help improve the structure of future CS courses, and deepen instructor understanding of student learning experiences.

The research questions guiding this study are:

- Are there statistically significant differences in measures of self-efficacy between students completing a closed-ended version of an assignment versus a more open-ended version?
- Are there statistically significant differences in student assignment grades between students completing a closed-ended version of an assignment versus a more open-ended version?
- Are these results affected by gender and prior experience with programming?

We hypothesized that the open-ended assignment structure would result in higher self-efficacy, and subsequently, higher grades. We believed the open-endedness should lead to increased levels of comfort with programming by encouraging students to spend time understanding, exploring and experimenting with the relevant concepts, rather than simply following a rigid set of steps toward completion.

2 RELEVANT LITERATURE

The cognitive constructivist view of learning states we each construct our own meaning and knowledge, rather than passively receiving objective knowledge that exists independent of our minds [4, 8]. This view of learning is relevant to the argument that students may benefit from open-ended projects and creative thinking opportunities. Allowing students to form their own knowledge through such projects is reflective of the constructivist belief that meaning-making involves "the process of actively structuring the world" [8].

Existing research on CS assignments that attempt to do this include VanDeGrift [19], who utilized open-ended assignments in an introductory programming course and found increased sense of ownership and creativity among students. Alhazmi et al. [1] studied the impact of providing assignment choices to students as a way of catering to student diversity and increasing motivation, and found this resulted in significantly improved learning outcomes and satisfaction rates for students in a graduate introductory programming course. Schanzer et al. [14] studied a specific assignment that let middle-school and high-school students customize minimal aspects of a game that they designed, and found this increased student engagement with and ownership of their projects. While these studies all consider aspects of freedom and choice in relation to CS assignments, they focus mainly on motivation, satisfaction and sense of ownership as personal learning outcomes. No relevant studies were found concerning self-efficacy and open-ended assignments.

Self-efficacy is defined by Bandura [2] as one's personal judgment about their ability to accomplish a goal or task. This is a valuable learning outcome as those with higher self-efficacy tend to display higher levels of effort in their work, better coping mechanisms during times of difficulty, and stronger perseverance against

obstacles [2]. As Bandura [3] states, "competent functioning requires both skills and self-beliefs of efficacy to use them effectively", making self-efficacy a significant aspect of learning. This study thus focuses on measures of self-efficacy within its analysis of open-ended assignments and their impact on student learning.

Ramalingam and Wiedenbeck [11] developed the widely-used Computer Programming Self-Efficacy Scale (CPSES), which applies self-efficacy theory to the domain of computer programming. It involves thirty-two 7-point Likert-scale questions measuring the following factors: independence and persistence, complex programming tasks, self-regulation, and simple programming tasks [11].

3 METHODS

The data for this study was collected from a CS1 course at a large North American research university in semester 2 (Jan-Apr) 2018, during which two concurrent lecture sections with 245 students in total (116 in Section A, and 129 in Section B) were offered around the same day and time, and taught using the same material by the same instructor. Utilizing a switching replications quasi-experimental design, students in each section experienced two different assignment structures: (1) a control assignment with a typical, standard checklist of requirements, and (2) an open-ended variation of the control assignment with an additional requirement to add enhancements of the student's own choosing to the project. This type of experimental design has high internal validity, allows for two independent measures of the same interventions, and is ethically feasible as it exposes all participants from both groups to the same types of treatment [18].

For Assignment 1, Section A completed the control assignment, while Section B completed the open-ended assignment. Then, to counterbalance the groups, for Assignment 2, Section B completed the control assignment, while Section A completed the open-ended assignment. A control baseline group was not used in this experiment due to it being unethical to give a potential advantage to one set of students over the other. Furthermore, with the current design, students from both Section A and Section B had the opportunity to experience and give feedback on both the traditional and open-ended assignment structures, allowing for two different measures of the results of our intervention. Students from both sections were aware of the fact that they had different versions of the assignments, and that the purpose was to gather student feedback on different assignment structures. The hypothesis of the experiment was not disclosed.

The data gathered for the study consisted of student assignment grades as a measure of academic performance, and student responses to three surveys: (1) a pre-test survey administered at the beginning of the term, (2) a survey administered after the end of the first assignment, and (3) the same survey administered again after the end of the second assignment. Each of these surveys included questions from the Computer Programming Self-Efficacy Scale (CPSES) [11]. The pre-test survey was used to gather information about each student's initial self-efficacy at the start of the course, and the remaining surveys were used to analyze how student self-efficacy was affected following each assignment.

The pre-test survey also asked questions about the student's gender, prior experience with programming, and whether or not they were re-taking CS1 (due to dropping out of, failing, or not earning a desired grade in a previous CS1 offering). This information was collected to (1) determine the similarity of lecture sections for purposes of validity, and (2) add more potential dimensions to our analysis of the predictors that contribute to student self-efficacy and performance.

4 THE ASSIGNMENTS

The two major assignments that were designed to be a part of this study were both projects where students had to build games. The first assignment (Assignment 1) was a text-adventure game, and the second assignment (Assignment 2) was an arcade-style game involving traveling through a two-dimensional grid and trapping monsters.

The length of the entire course was 12 weeks, followed by a final exam. The first assignment was released on Week 7 and due on Week 9. This assignment involved the core topics of: functions, while/for loops, dictionaries, lists and reading/writing text files. The second assignment was released Week 10 and due Week 12, and involved object-oriented programming topics (including composition and inheritance).

For the closed-ended versions of each assignment, the grade was based on completing a set checklist of requirements. For example, for the text-adventure game (Assignment 1), the story and a basic plot was provided to the students, and students had to meet the requirements specified in this plot to complete the assignment. The locations, items, and so on, were all decided by the instructor and laid out in the assignment instructions. Similarly, for the arcade game (Assignment 2), the layout of the grid, images, challenges, and so on, were all laid out in the instructions for the closed-ended version.

For the open-ended versions of each assignment, to keep the two versions of the assignments comparable and as similar as possible, we used the same set of instructions as the closed-ended version but added an extra set of "open-ended" requirements. In the open-ended versions, 80% of the grade came from meeting the checklist of requirements prescribed by the closed-ended versions, and the remaining 20% of the grade came from adding enhancements of the students' own choosing to "make the games their own". For instance, in the text-adventure game, being able to get the game working exactly as described in the given plot accounted for 80% of the grade, and for the remaining 20%, the students were told to add any enhancements they wished (e.g. new locations, extended plot, images, music, new items, etc.). The requirements for the enhancements were left to the students, with the only requirement being that the game should have at least two new additional puzzles of the students' own choice added to it. The open-ended version for the arcade game was similarly structured, with the enhancements section asking students to add their own new types of monsters to the game.

The students were not provided a rubric but were told about the distribution of marks stated above, and informed that their overall grade for the enhancements would be based on creativity and effort. They were asked to hand in a text file with a list of all the enhancements they added or attempted to add. The enhancements were graded using criteria based on the scales used for the Torrance

Tests of Creative Thinking (the most widely used, highly reliable test for measuring creativity [16, 17]). These four scales are fluency – the number of different ideas produced, flexibility – the number of categories of ideas produced (i.e. variations of the same idea will count as one category), originality – the statistical rarity of each idea, and elaboration – how detailed each idea is. Based on these scales, the students were graded on (1) Quantity of ideas, (2) Number of categories of ideas, (3) Originality/uniqueness of ideas, and (4) Complexity of ideas. To keep the grading for this part consistent and eliminate experimenter bias, only one Teaching Assistant (TA) was assigned the responsibility to grade solely the enhancements sections for both assignment 1 and 2, while other TAs were asked to grade the closed-ended parts of the assignments.

5 DATA ANALYSIS AND RESULTS

After Assignment 1 and Assignment 2, survey data was collected from consenting students from both lecture sections (A and B). The sets of data involved are thus (1) Section A (closed-ended) vs. (2) Section B (open-ended) Assignment 1, and (3) Section A (open-ended) vs. (4) Section B (closed-ended) Assignment 2. The Cronbach's alpha reliability for the self-efficacy questionnaire was 0.98.

As this is a quasi-experiment, the students chose which of the two lecture sections to enroll in, rather than being randomly assigned. As such, a pre-test survey was conducted to measure each section's initial self-efficacy rating, and a statistically significant difference was found with Section A having a significantly lower initial mean self-efficacy. Steps taken to mitigate this issue within the study are described next.

5.1 Setting up the Participant Samples

We found that Section A — the section with lower initial mean self-efficacy — also had significantly fewer students re-taking the course, and significantly fewer students with prior programming experience. There was no significant difference in the gender breakdown between the sections.

That is, we found significant differences between lecture sections in three factors: mean self-efficacy, re-taking the course, and prior experience. Correlations between these factors are quite high (r>0.4), and removing the students who are re-taking the course from the dataset reduced these differences to no longer be statistically significant. As such, the rest of the data in this study will only discuss the sample of students from each section who were taking CS1 for the first time.

Furthermore, it was observed that several students failed to submit any attempts for the assignments. These naturally received a zero grade, but failed to provide any useful data about whether or not the students had made any attempt to complete the assignments at all. If the students did not even attempt the assignments, the assignment structure would clearly have no impact on the students' learning, and thus, results would be skewed if this data was included in our analysis. As such, any student who failed to hand in any form of submission for the assignments was excluded from the analysis. It should be noted that the number of students with missing submissions for each section was comparable, with around

10% of students missing submissions for both the open-ended and closed-ended versions of each assignment.

5.2 Mean Self-Efficacy Ratings

Regarding the mean self-efficacy following each assignment, no statistically significant differences were found based on an independent-samples t-test. However, the mean self-efficacy rating was consistently higher for whichever section completed the open-ended version of an assignment. For the first assignment, Section B (the one that completed the open-ended version) had a mean self-efficacy score of 4.53 compared to Section A's 4.47. However, for the second assignment, Section A (who completed the open-ended version) now had the higher mean of 4.68 compared to Section B's 4.63. Details about the t-tests for each assignment are provided in Table 1. Students who did not complete the corresponding post-assignment self-efficacy survey were excluded from this analysis.

Table 1: Independent Samples T-Test Between Mean Self-efficacy Ratings of Section A & B for Assignment 1 & 2

	Section A mean (n)	Section B mean (n)	t	df	p
Assignment 1	(Closed) 4.47 (n=59)	(Open) 4.53 (n=22)	-.14	83	.892
Assignment 2	(Open) 4.68 (n=52)	(Closed) 4.63 (n=22)	-.10	56	.920

Table 2: Independent Samples T-Test Between Mean Assignment Grades of Section A & B for Assignment 1 & 2

	Section A mean (n)	Section B mean (n)	t	df	p
Assignment 1	(Closed) 66% (n=82)	(Open) 73% (n=28)	-1.28	108	.204
Assignment 2	(Open) 78% (n=58)	(Closed) 76% (n=34)	-.10	45	.920

5.3 Student Performance

Independent-samples t-tests found that differences were not statistically significant (p > 0.05) between overall assignment grade for the open- versus closed-ended versions for either assignment. However, similar to the observations made about self-efficacy, the average assignment grade for the open-ended versions were slightly higher for both assignments. For Assignment 1, Section A (who completed the closed-ended version) earned an average grade of 66%, while Section B (who completed the open-ended version) earned an average of 73%. However, for Assignment 2, Section A (who now completed the open-ended version) had a slightly higher average of 78%, while Section B (completing the closed-ended version) had an average of 76%. Details about the t-tests for each assignment are provided in Table 2.

5.4 Effects of Gender and Prior Experience on Self-Efficacy

To explore self-efficacy ratings as affected by gender and prior experience, a multiple regression analysis was performed with SPSS Version 25, on the ability of these factors to predict the mean self-efficacy rating for each assignment.

The only factor that had a statistically significant effect on self-efficacy was prior experience, but this effect was found across both versions of each assignment — that is, those with prior experience had higher self-efficacy overall, regardless of the assignment structure. Details are provided in Table 3.

The self-efficacy ratings for each assignment were not significantly affected by gender nor by which type of assignment (closed-ended or open-ended) the students were assigned. The interaction effects of these factors were also considered, and showed no significant effect (as shown in Table 3).

5.5 Effects of Gender and Prior Experience on Performance

To further analyze the grades, another regression analysis was performed on the ability of gender and prior programming experience, as well as student self-efficacy scores, to predict assignment grade. The interaction effect between each of these factors and the assignment structure was also considered.

The results of the regression analyses for both assignments suggest that the students' self-efficacy ratings had a significant effect (p=0.007 and p=0.04, respectively) on their assignment grade (those with higher self-efficacy earned a higher grade), regardless of which section they were in. Another observation was that students who identified as female earned significantly higher assignment grades on both assignments.

Both the effects of self-efficacy and gender were observed independent of whether a closed-ended or open-ended assignment was used. The type of assignment structure thus had no significant effect on overall assignment grades, including when its interaction with the factors of gender, prior experience, and post-assignment self-efficacy were considered. Details are provided in Table 4.

6 DISCUSSION

6.1 RQ1: Is self-efficacy affected by assignment structure?

To address the first research question regarding the difference between self-efficacy ratings for closed-ended versus open-ended assignments, the summary of mean self-efficacy in Table 1 shows that there was no significant difference between the mean self-efficacy scores based on assignment structure. It may be noted however, that the mean score was consistently slightly higher for whichever section completed the open-ended version of an assignment. Though these differences were not found to be statistically significant, they are suggestive of a potential for open-ended assignments to increase student feelings of self-efficacy, and call for further analysis in future implementations on a larger, or more rigorous, scale.

Table 3: Regression analysis of predictors of mean self-efficacy ratings for Assignment 1 and 2

Variable	Assignment 1 (A-Closed and B-Open)				Assignment 2 (B-Closed and A-Open)			
	b	β	t	p	b	β	t	p
^Section	-.02	-.01	-.07	.946	.08	.03	.20	.845
^Gender	.16	.05	.49	.628	-.24	-.07	-.54	.588
^Prior Experience	1.25	.39	3.68	.000*	.87	.27	2.04	.047*
Section : Gender	-.02	.00	-.02	.981	.72	.11	.80	.430
Section : Prior Exp.	-1.43	-.20	-1.91	.060	1.30	.20	1.49	.143

^ These factors were coded as follows: 1=Open section, 0=Closed section; 1=Female, 0=Male for gender; 1=True, 0=False for having prior experience
* These factors had a significant effect on the regression model (p < 0.05)

Table 4: Regression analysis of predictors of assignment grade for Assignment 1 and 2

Variable	Assignment 1 (A-Closed and B-Open)				Assignment 2 (B-Closed and A-Open)			
	b	β	t	p	b	β	t	p
^Section	8.27	.16	1.69	.096	-2.74	-.07	-.50	.620
^Gender	11.99	.25	2.38	.020*	14.38	.24	2.10	.040*
^Prior Experience	1.68	.04	.33	.739	6.97	.17	1.19	.238
Self-Efficacy	4.22	.29	2.76	.007*	4.40	.25	2.09	.040*
Section : Gender	-8.36	-.08	-.78	.435	6.87	.08	.58	.566
Section : Prior Exp.	11.55	.11	1.10	.274	-4.86	-.06	-.41	.681
Section : Self-Efficacy	-7.61	-.21	-2.06	.053	.94	.04	.26	.796

^ These factors were coded as follows: 1=Open section, 0=Closed section; 1=Female, 0=Male for gender; and 1=True, 0=False for having prior experience
* These factors had a significant effect on the regression model (p < 0.05)

6.2 RQ2: Are assignment grades affected by assignment structure?

The findings related to the second research question are similar to the first, and in need of future analysis. As with the self-efficacy ratings, the differences in assignment grades based on assignment structure were not statistically significant. This means the structure of the assignment had no significant effect on average assignment grades. Yet, similar to the self-efficacy ratings, the average assignment grade for whichever section completed the open-ended version of an assignment was slightly higher, for both assignments.

Again, although not statistically significant, these findings point toward a potential for open-ended assignment structures to have positive effects on student learning; future studies with larger sample sizes, a greater number of assignments, and so on, would help us identify and understand the robustness of these findings.

6.3 RQ3: What is the effect of gender and prior programming experience on self-efficacy, and each of these on assignment grades?

Regarding the third research question, taking the factors of gender and prior experience into consideration, it was found that self-efficacy was not significantly affected by any of these factors other than prior experience. The effect of prior experience occurred regardless of whether the assignment was open- or closed-ended, and is reflective of several previous studies that found prior programming experience to be a valuable asset for student learning within CS1 courses [5, 6, 21, 22].

Regarding the effect of these factors and of self-efficacy ratings on assignment grades, for both assignments, higher self-efficacy ratings were related to higher grades with a statistically significant effect, p<0.05. This implies that students with higher self-efficacy earned higher assignment grades, for both assignments, regardless of the assignment structure. This reinforces the importance of analyzing how student self-efficacy can be affected within a course.

Gender also had a significant effect on the assignment grade, with female students having a higher average grade on both assignments. This finding was not hypothesized by the researchers, although it is reflective of some existing research that finds females perform better academically than males [7, 20].

Overall, these differences were observed across both types of assignments and, as such, do not relate to the effect of the open-ended structure that we aimed to observe, but rather to the general course itself.

7 LIMITATIONS

7.1 Different Students

One of the threats to the validity of a quasi-experimental study is that differences between the population samples being compared are not controlled for. To account for threats to validity posed by the differences among the students within the two lecture sections involved in this study, several measures were taken. Firstly, the two lecture sections were offered on the same day, and around the same time (back-to-back sessions). They were also both taught the same material, at the same pace, and by the same instructor. We hoped this would set the two lecture sections up as comparable to one another, with the attempt to minimize differences between how they are taught except for the aspect being studied — the assignment structures. To further deal with the issue of the two lecture sections having different sets of students, the experiment followed a switching replications design, with both lecture sections having a chance to experience and provide feedback on both assignment structures at alternating times of the semester.

Despite these measures that were taken, the pre-test survey results showed the populations of the two lecture sections were significantly different in terms of how many students in each section were re-taking the course, and in terms of prior experience and self-efficacy ratings. To combat this, this report only considered the first-timers within each section, which reduced these observed differences.

7.2 Small Sample Size

Looking only at the first-timers led to a new concern: reduced sample size, leading to less generalizable results. As such, for the majority of the observations made in this paper, we believe further research is necessary to better understand how significant these observations may be on a wider scale.

7.3 Different Assignments

Another limitation of the study is that the two assignments must necessarily be different, limiting the comparability of the results for each assignment. For instance, the open-ended versions of Assignment 1 and 2 may have not been equal in terms of how open-ended they were, or how much freedom they provided. Furthermore, confounding variables may result from the two assignments taking place at different points of the semester, as the latter will involve more challenging concepts than the former.

To reduce these differences, careful measures were taken to maintain similar contexts (that is, both assignments involved games), and the structure of the assignments in terms of what the open-ended version required (enhancements added to the existing game) was also similar.

8 FUTURE STEPS

As the open-endedness of the assignments is a key factor being analyzed, it is important that the two assignments being compared provide a comparable amount of freedom to students within their open-ended versions. For the next implementation, a collaborative effort involving several experienced instructors in the construction and evaluation of the open-ended assignments may be helpful in mitigating any differences in assignment structure, and in balancing the assignments' difficulty levels.

We will also attempt to replicate this experiment with another large class, as the issues with the differences among the two lecture sections in this study led to smaller sample sizes than we had hoped. The issue with the large number of re-takers is most likely due to the class being offered in the second semester of the year, rather than in the first. Future analyses of the open-ended assignment structure being used in a first-semester class may lead to more concrete results.

Furthermore, having a relatively equal number of re-takers and first-timers among lecture sections being compared would make it possible for us to consider both groups of students and see how the different groups may be affected by the open-ended structure. This was not possible in the current study as the number of re-takers who consented to participate and completed the questionnaires in one of the lecture sections was much too small for analysis (n=15). Analyzing a larger lecture section may combat these issues.

Lastly, further insights could be gained about personal aspects of student learning by incorporating a mixed methods approach in future implementations, so that qualitative data is also collected in addition to the quantitative self-efficacy measures. This could be done by incorporating open-ended survey questions or interviews with students into the study.

9 CONTRIBUTIONS OF THIS STUDY

Despite the above-mentioned limitations with the study, this preliminary research provides a sense of how a study on open-ended assignments can be structured, and highlights potential roadblocks to keep in mind for any future, similar research. This study represents an early step toward investigating a type of pedagogical structure that attempts to positively influence the self-efficacy of students in introductory CS courses. As previously stated, the importance of self-efficacy in relation to student learning is apparent from previous research connecting higher self-efficacy to increased effort and perseverance [2]. As CS1 is often the first CS course a student will take, being able to succeed and persevere within this course will provide students with a stronger foundation for continuing studies in CS. Thus, understanding how self-efficacy may be affected by increased freedom within course assignments, as well as how this is reflected in academic performance, can help improve CS courses and make them more accessible — something that is increasingly important in our digitized age.

REFERENCES

[1] Sohail Alhazmi, Margaret Hamilton, , and Charles Thevathayan. 2018. CS for All: Catering to Diversity of Master's Students through Assignment Choices. In *Proceedings of the 49th ACM Technical Symposium on Computer Science Education.* 38–43.
[2] Albert Bandura. 1977. Self-efficacy: toward a unifying theory of behavioral change. *Psychological review* 84, 2 (1977), 191.
[3] Albert Bandura. 1986. *Social Foundations of Thought and Action.* Prentice Hall, Englewood Cliffs, NJ.
[4] Mordechai Ben-Ari. 2001. Constructivism in computer science education. *Journal of Computers in Mathematics and Science Teaching* 20, 1 (2001), 45–73.
[5] Dianne Hagan and Selby Markham. 2000. Does it help to have some programming experience before beginning a computing degree program? *ACM SIGCSE Bulletin* 32, 3 (2000), 25–28.
[6] Edward Holden and Elissa Weeden. 2003. The impact of prior experience in an information technology programming course sequence. In *Proceedings of the 4th conference on Information technology curriculum.* 41–46.
[7] Heidi Keiser, Paul R. Sackett, Nathan R. Kuncel, and Thomas Brothen. 2016. Why women perform better in college than admission scores would predict: Exploring the roles of conscientiousness and course-taking patterns. *Journal of Applied Psychology* 101, 4 (2016), 569–581.
[8] A. Kent and J. G. Williams. 1996. *Encyclopedia of Computer Science and Technology.* Marcel Dekker Inc., New York, NY.
[9] Maria Knobelsdorf and Carsten Schulte. 2005. Computer biographies-a biographical research perspective on computer usage and attitudes towards informatics. In *Proceedings of the 5th Annual Finnish/Baltic Sea Conference on Computer Science Education.*
[10] Andrew Petersen, Michelle Craig, Jennifer Campbell, and Anya Tafliovich. 2016. Revisiting why students drop CS1. In *Proceedings of the 16th Annual Finnish/Baltic Sea Conference on Computer Science Education.* 71–80.
[11] Vennila Ramalingam and Susan Wiedenbeck. 1998. Development and validation of scores on a computer programming self-efficacy scale and group analyses of

novice programmer self-efficacy. *Journal of Educational Computing Research* 19, 4 (1998), 367–381.

[12] Ralf Romeike. 2007. Applying creativity in CS high school education: criteria, teaching example and evaluation. In *Proceedings of the 7th Annual Finnish/Baltic Sea Conference on Computer Science Education.* 87–96.

[13] Andrea Salgian, Teresa M. Nakra, Christopher Ault, and Yunfeng Wang. 2013. Teaching creativity in computer science. In *Proceedings of the 44th ACM technical symposium on Computer science education.* 123–128.

[14] Emmanuel Schanzer, Kathi Fisler, and Shriram Krishnamurthi. 2018. Assessing Bootstrap: Algebra Students on Scaffolded and Unscaffolded Word Problems. In *Proceedings of the 49th ACM Technical Symposium on Computer Science Education.* 8–13.

[15] Duane F. Shell, Leen-Kiat Soh, Abraham E. Flanigan, and Markeya S. Peteranetz. 2016. Students' initial course motivation and their achievement and retention in college CS1 courses. In *Proceedings of the 47th ACM Technical Symposium on Computer Science Education.* 639–644.

[16] Ellis Paul Torrance. 1990. Torrance tests of creative thinking: Norms-technical manual.

[17] Ellis Paul Torrance. 2000. Research review for the Torrance tests of creative thinking figural and verbal forms.

[18] William Trochim, James P. Donnelly, and Kanika Arora. 2015. *Research methods: The essential knowledge base.* Cengage, Boston, MA.

[19] Tammy VanDeGrift. 2007. Encouraging creativity in introductory computer science programming assignments. In *Proceedings of the American Society for Engineering Education Conference.* 8–13.

[20] Howard Wainer and Linda Steinberg. 1992. Sex Differences in Performance on the Mathematics Section of the Scholastic Aptitude Test: A Bidirectional Validity Study. *Harvard Educational Review* 62 (1992), 323–336.

[21] Susan Wiedenbeck, Deborah Labelle, and Vennila Kain. 2004. Factors affecting course outcomes in introductory programming. In *16th Annual Workshop of the Psychology of Programming Interest Group.* 97–109.

[22] Brenda Cantwell Wilson and Sharon Shrock. 2001. Contributing to success in an introductory computer science course: a study of twelve factors. *ACM SIGCSE Bulletin* 33, 1 (2001), 184–188.

[23] Daniel Zingaro. 2014. Peer instruction contributes to self-efficacy in CS1. In *Proceedings of the 45th ACM technical symposium on Computer science education.* 373–378.

Experience Report: Mini Guest Lectures in a CS1 Course via Video Conferencing

Lisa Zhang
University of Toronto Mississauga
Mississauga, ON
lczhang@cs.toronto.edu

Michelle Craig
University of Toronto
Toronto, ON
mcraig@cs.toronto.edu

Mark Kazakevich
University of Toronto
Toronto, ON
mark@cs.toronto.edu

Joseph Jay Williams
University of Toronto
Toronto, ON
williams@cs.toronto.edu

ABSTRACT

This paper details the experience of bringing an industry perspective to an introductory programming course, via "mini" interviews conducted during lectures using video conferencing. The novelty of this intervention comes from the frequency, duration and diversity of the industrial involvement. The use of video conferencing lowers the participation barrier for industry professionals and enables a broad range of volunteers to contribute. Our primary goal is to communicate the practical relevance of the materials we teach, and to motivate students to learn and practise course material. We discuss student feedback regarding these interviews collected via an optional, post-facto survey. While there was no quantitative evidence of improved learning outcomes, there was suggestive evidence that students found the interviews motivational, and appreciated learning more about available career paths. We conclude with recommendations to instructors who wish to adopt the intervention.

CCS CONCEPTS

• **Social and professional topics** → **Computer science education**; **CS1**;

KEYWORDS

CS1, industry professionals, video-conferenced classroom visits

ACM Reference Format:
Lisa Zhang, Michelle Craig, Mark Kazakevich, and Joseph Jay Williams. 2019. Experience Report: Mini Guest Lectures in a CS1 Course via Video Conferencing. In *ACM Global Computing Education Conference 2019 (CompEd '19), May 17–19, 2019, Chengdu,Sichuan, China.* ACM, New York, NY, USA, 7 pages. https://doi.org/10.1145/3300115.3309511

1 INTRODUCTION

Introductory programming courses teach skills of practical importance. However, it is difficult for a new programmer to appreciate the necessities of testing, the intricacies of naming variables, and even the basic idea of *thinking* before writing code. This report details the experience of bringing industry professionals to a CS1 classroom via short, frequent, video conferenced interviews.

The intervention involved interspersing 10-minute interviews with industry professionals throughout CS1 lectures. These interviews were conducted live via the video conferencing platform Google Hangouts. The professionals were mainly software developers, but also included other professionals who write code on a daily basis. Short, frequent interviews were made viable using video conferencing. The timing of these interviews allowed the instructor to ask professionals questions relevant to a particular week's course material. The professionals answered questions about how they used the material in their day-to-day work, and about their careers.

The primary objective of these interviews was to highlight the relevance of the course content. We hoped that an understanding of how professionals use the course material would motivate students to learn and practice those techniques.

A secondary motivation of these interviews was to showcase diversity in computer science. We interviewed professionals with diverse job titles, backgrounds, ethnicities, and genders. This goal was never explicitly discussed with the students or professionals, to prevent stereotype threat [8].

We conducted a post-facto survey both to collect qualitative student feedback regarding these interviews, and to identify differences between students in a CS1 lecture section that introduced this intervention, and students in a lecture section that did not.

We include in this paper the survey results, insights from the instructor's field notes, and recommendations for fellow computer science instructors who may wish to use a similar intervention.

2 RELATED WORK

Many computer science educators aim to connect students to industry professionals. Beyond a simple guest lecture, educators experiment with involving professional volunteers in a K12 setting [10], and including "industry fellows" in the curriculum development, planning, and delivery of the course as a co-lecturer [11]. Our intervention differs in the involvement and time commitment of the professionals.

Other related interventions include having an industry professional "in residence" [2], especially for the benefit of underrepresented students. Interactions with female professionals is shown to benefit female K12 students [1]. Industry partnerships like "Women in CSE" seminars linked to CS1 courses provide students with an exploration of potential career paths in computer science [7]. The Hour of Code [6] campaign organizes one-hour introductions to Computer Science for a wide variety of audiences. Like in our intervention, professionals can hold video conferences with students, lowering the cost of volunteering. Our intervention requires even less time commitment from the professionals.

The use of video conferencing in education has also become prevalent [9], mostly as a means to connect students and instructors [4]. Still, Celikkan et al. [5] shows how video conferencing can be used to connect nursing students to real-life situations. Our focus is educating CS1 students by exposing them to different professionals.

3 INTERVENTION CONTEXT

The intervention was conducted at a large, research-intensive North American university, during the summer term of 2018. The CS1 course used the programming language Python, and was taught as a "flipped" or "inverted" class [3]. There were two sections of this course, an afternoon (no treatment) and an evening (treatment) section, taught by different instructors. Each section had an enrollment cap of 195 students. The course consisted of 12 weeks of class, with 3 contiguous hours of lecture per week. As part of the inverted-classroom experience, students watched weekly videos and completed exercises before and after lecture. Students also completed three assignments, one term test, and a final exam.

Each section was taught by one instructor and two teaching assistants. The afternoon (no treatment) section was taught by a male instructor, with two female teaching assistants. The evening (treatment) section was taught by a female instructor, with one male and one female teaching assistant. The professionals interviewed belonged to the network of the treatment section instructor, and were more available during the evening lecture times.

We conducted a pre-course survey, not entirely motivated by this research, to better understand our students. The survey was completed by 234/390 students. We found that the summer student demographics were more diverse than those of the same course in traditional semesters. Students' intended major fields of study included Computer Science, Statistics, Mathematics, Life Sciences, and others. More than half of students were taking this course as part of their program requirement. While 47% of respondents intended to take additional CS courses, 40% were unsure.

The demographics in the treatment and non-treatment sections were similar. Some (non-statistically significant) differences include more students in the treatment section taking this course as a program requirement (59% vs 54%), and more students in the treatment section (34% vs 27%) requiring additional computer science courses. Still, even if the student demographics were identical, student self-selection of section would continue to be a confounder. Students

had no prior knowledge about the intervention, but were free to attend whichever lecture section they preferred.

4 INTERVENTION

We interviewed five professionals during the 12 weeks of lectures. The anonymized interview schedule is shown in Table 1.

Each interview began with an introduction of the professional, their job title, and their role in their organization. The interview continued with questions based on that week's lecture topic. The interview concluded with the professional's advice to students, and student questions.

Frequent interviews meant that we could schedule professionals who could most effectively emphasize the corresponding week's lecture topic. The professional A was interviewed first because their organization is known for its strict code quality guidelines. The professional C was chosen for the discussion about problem solving because of their role as a Data Scientist.

Short interviews meant that the timing of the interview within a lecture was also flexible. We interviewed B shortly after providing students with a reference sheet of string methods. Just as students wondered which string methods they should memorize (if any), we asked B about which string functions are most often used. As another example, during week 8 lecture, students spent two hours understanding and modelling a complex coding problem before writing any code. Just as students wondered whether this approach is usual, the interview with C affirmed that, yes, even professionals spend significant time and effort to understand a problem.

Figure 1 provides a sample interview snippet with the professional D. The intention behind the questions about unit tests was to show how pervasive unit testing is in industry. The question about spending time on problem solving was motivated by student surprise in the previous week, when the professional C claimed to spend 30% of time coding versus 70% of time sufficiently understanding the problem.

Scheduling the interviews was not as time consuming as expected. It involved selecting the professionals, asking if they were interested and available, and sending email instructions with potential interview questions. The professionals were very excited to share their expertise and give back to the community. Conducting the interviews via video conferencing was straightforward for the professionals, and allowed us to interview non-local professionals. The professionals were almost always available remotely, so scheduling efforts were minimal.

We recorded the interviews, as part of an initial plan to re-use the videos. All interviewees consented to having the videos recorded

Table 1: Interview Schedule and Topics

Week	Interviewee	Topics
2	A. (Large Co.)	Comments, Naming
4	B. (Medium Co.)	Strings, Constants, Debugging
8	C. (Startup)	Problem Solving, Testing
10	D. (Large Co.)	Testing, Problem Solving
12	E. (Research)	Research, General Next Steps

INSTR: Can you tell us a bit about yourself, what your job title is and what you do?

D: Sure. I've been a software developer since I graduated in 2012, and I am a software development engineer.

INSTR: Very cool! We were talking about testing earlier, can you tell us how you test code where you work?

D: Sure! We write unit tests for each function and module that we write. We have what we call integration tests, where we put multiple functions together and see if they do things together what we want them to do. And then at the very end we load the code up to the device, and then see if it works on the device, because that's what matters the most for customers.

INSTR: So unit tests are what you do first.

D: Yes, that is the most basic test.

INSTR: How often do you write unit tests?

D: Every time I check in code, so every couple days?

INSTR: How often do you run your unit tests?

D: Whenever I make some change to the code, I run tests every few minutes, otherwise I would break something and find out an hour later, I wouldn't know what I changed that caused the break. Also, whenever someone checks in code, there are automatic jobs to run that makes [sic] sure that code didn't break anything else.

...

INSTR: One question from last week where we spent several hours understanding a problem. In your day-to-day work, how much time do you think about a problem versus actually writing code?

D: Me personally, I spend maybe a third of time writing code?

INSTR: One-third writing code, two-thirds thinking.

D: Mostly yes. So the rests are [sic] thinking about different approaches to the problem, and getting others for second opinion.

Figure 1: Sample Interview Snippet

and shared with other CS1 students. However, they were not comfortable with the recorded videos being generally available. Unfortunately, the unedited recordings did not meet the quality expected of a pre-recorded video: the interviews were conducted in a conversational tone, with frequent filter words and pauses that are natural in a live setting but awkward when recorded. We decided not to share the videos with the non-treatment group.

5 DIVERSITY

The instructor made an effort to have a diverse representation in the professionals interviewed. The professionals came from a wide range of ethnic backgrounds. They represented a variety of companies, and a variety of roles within those companies. Two of the five professionals interviewed were women. One professional came from a research background, and the conversation was more related to academic research than industry.

The consideration of diversity was not mentioned to either the professionals or the students. This was intentional, to avoid stereotype threat [8], where being reminded of a stereotype alone may

impact performance. The interview questions were deliberately limited to CS and CS career topics, and avoided diversity related topics. Although there were no explicit instructions to professionals to avoid those topics, they simply did not come up. The intention was to show what diversity in computer science should look like, without drawing any undue attention.

6 KEY LESSONS

This section details the key lessons extracted from a reflective analysis of instructor field notes.

Technical setup. Testing the audio-video system in the lecture room posed some challenges. Fortunately, we did not encounter serious technical difficulties, but could not use the room speakers until the 3rd interview (we used the room microphone with computer speakers, and checked that students could hear). For recording the videos, it was important to record both microphone input (to capture the instructor) and system audio (to capture the professional); not all screen-casting software supports both.

Kicking off. We kicked off the interview with a senior person from a well-known company. Students were impressed by their experience, which captured student attention early on.

Small words. One immediate challenge was that most professionals have little experience speaking to beginning students. After the first interview, the instructor sent clearer instructions to professionals to avoid using jargon, and to avoid topics inaccessible to beginning programmers. After receiving these instructions, the professionals were much more conscious about introducing new material, but still occasionally brought up new concepts. In Figure 3 the professional used the terminologies "integration tests" and "checking in" code.

Short answers. Another challenge was that because the interviews were short, the professional's answers to questions also had to be short. We included in the instructions to professionals to answer questions in about two sentences, and prepare for interruptions. This request was very well taken and followed.

Interview alumni. We found that alumni of our institution were easier for CS1 students to relate to, and generated more honest discussions and better questions. This was true even for alumni who did not take the same CS1 course.

The debugger. During week 4 interviews, B mentioned that even professionals debug on a regular basis. We hoped that this would would motivate students to learn to use the debugger. It is normal for CS1 students to resist learning the debugger due to the high learning curve. There was no evidence that the discussion changed student behaviour.

Smartphone vs Laptop. Some professionals used a smartphone instead of a laptop for video conferencing. Using a smartphone reduced the interviewee's eye contact with students, producing a lower quality, shakier video feed, and reduced student engagement.

Student Questions. Some student questions were especially well thought out. For example, students asked C how much math a data scientist uses on a daily / weekly basis. It was encouraging to see students use the opportunity to interact with professionals by asking questions to which answers are difficult to find elsewhere.

Honesty. There were cases where during the interview, the professional did not respond in the way the instructor had expected.

For example, during the discussion about global variable constants, B explained that constants are discouraged in her work. Though the response foiled the intention behind the question, students seemed to appreciate B's blunt honesty.

Canceling an Interview During week 11, there had been an interview scheduled with a discussion centered around Object Oriented Programming. However, the lecture was progressing slower than expected, so the instructor canceled the interview with around 20 minutes notice. The flexibility to cancel meant we could prioritize learning goals and read the atmosphere of the class. In part, this flexibility comes from using video conferencing rather than arranging travel. Of course, we were lucky to have the relationship with a professional that allowed us to cancel.

7 QUALITATIVE SURVEY RESPONSES

An end-of-term survey (Figure 2) was sent to students of both sections. This survey was longer than the pre-course survey, and was conducted after the course concluded. A total of 56 students completed this survey, 30 from the non-treatment group and 26 from the treatment group. The sample size was small, but offered some insight into student thinking. Students were generally positive about the interviews. We summarize the key themes and include a selection of student responses.

7.1 Highlighting Course Relevance

Recall that our primary objective was to highlight the relevance of course materials through the interviews. Student responses from survey sections 5 and 7 provided suggestive evidence that the interviews fulfilled that objective, though some students (in Section 7.5) disagreed. Quotes from student responses to the open-ended questions that illustrate these themes are:

- I thought [the live interviews] provided perspective for our studies and were inspiring.
- I learned what we study that can be use in the future, and which is mostly [sic] important ...
- Computer science is very useful
- ... Coding can be applied in many different applications. Being a programmer is not just about writing sick code; the process of debugging, styling, commenting and algos is important part too.
- Got tons of advice, and saw that classwork built on industry skills.

7.2 Diversity

No student response mentioned ethnic or gender diversity issues, but students appreciated the career diversity of the professionals:

- Anyone can code; it's all about initiative and practice...
- I [liked that] there were a diverse set of individuals from very different companies and cooperations [sic]
- good from a variety of backgrounds/companies, but find similar vein of thought between them all

7.3 Career exploration

While not an original objective of these interviews, students reported gaining a better understanding of the career paths available

---

1. Consent form Do you consent to participate in this survey?

2. Interest in Computer Sciences To what extend do you agree/disagree with the following? (Strongly Agree / Agree / Neutral / Disagree / Strongly Disagree)

- At the beginning of the term, I intended to take more computer science courses.
- I intend to take more computer science courses.
- I am interested in a career in computer science.
- I believe that anyone, regardless of where they come from, can succeed in computer science.

3. How important do you feel are the following for a programmer? (1-not important; 7-very important)

Coding	Style checker
Commenting	Thinking
Unit tests	String Methods
Classes	Debugging

4. Which Lecture Section Did you Attend?
    o Afternoon (Continue to 8)   o Evening (Continue to 5)

5. Live Interviews If you attended evening section lectures, were you in class when we conducted interviews with ...
What are 3-5 things that you learned from the live interviews? Was there anything you did not expect? [free form responses]

6. Live Interviews To what extent do you agree / disagree with the following? (Strongly Agree / Agree / Neutral / Disagree / Strongly Disagree)

- The interviews helped me understand how material taught in class is relevant to industry professionals.
- The live interviews improved my understanding of what computer science professionals do.
- The live interviews increased my interest in CS.
- The time could have been better spent on other topics (worksheets, shorter class).

7. Live Interviews

- What did you think about the live interviews?
- What did you like?
- What didn't you like?
- Is there anything else we should know?

8. Demographic

- What is your major?
- Do you identify as a woman?
- Do you identify as a person of visible or ethnic minority?

Figure 2: Post-Facto Survey Questions

---

to computer science graduates. Students appreciated the opportunity to meet professionals across a a wide range group of occupations and contexts. For example, students said:

- I like how you took the initiative to show us that [sic] the CS industry is like outside of the classroom. Thank you!
- I learned that computer science can be used in many different fields.
- Really good to see what a future in CS potentially looks like
- Maybe [because] I have not seen it before, it is certainly a new and interesting experience

- [I likeed] hearing about their schooling and how they got into compsci.
- I like [to] talk to people who have experience face to face.
- Liked that these meetings resulted in increased awareness of job applications for future

7.4 Student Questions

A few students mentioned that they found the student question portion of the interview valuable. The quality of student questions varied: some interviews generated insightful questions, and others generated none at all. In the future, students might benefit from guidance on how to ask good questions, or a way to pose questions anonymously.

- Liked how [interviewees] were open to answering questions.
- Well I probably should not say this (since I did not ask any question), but I was hoping my classmates could ask more questions.
- I just like the idea of live interview with computer science professionals (live does make it better).

7.5 Negative Responses

The negative responses pointed to areas for improvement. Since this course included a diverse group of students, many of whom were not CS majors, some students may have felt that learning about careers in this field was uninteresting:

- I think they're all interesting people with interesting career paths but i hate this field and its offputting to me.
- Literally didn't relate to what I want to do in life at all.
- The field is not intriguing to me
- I wasn't particularly interested

Some students did not believe that the interviews helped their learning, or preferred to spend time reviewing core concepts.

- [The interviews were] not super useful [because] I think people would rather have that time spent on going over some materials they're having trouble with.
- [I liked that] they killed some time
- I didn't feel it necessary helped my learning
- They didn't seem to actually promote the lessons which the professor wanted. Often times underplaying the importance of certain aspects; nonetheless it was nice to know that computer scientist/ software engineers still make use of the basic principles which were taught in class.

Other student responses pointed to the professional's difficulty in avoiding complex topics, and the interview logistics.

- Sometimes the interview got too complex and deep within computer science terminology to be helpful.
- Short time allotted to interviews, should have been longer.
- A stronger internet connection or proper [audio] speakers would be nice.

8 QUANTITATIVE SURVEY RESPONSES

In this section we analyze the quantitative survey results, comparing between the non-treatment and treatment sections. Six respondents who were in the treatment section, but who were present for fewer than two interviews were discarded from the data. As a result, the treatment section included 20 data points, and the

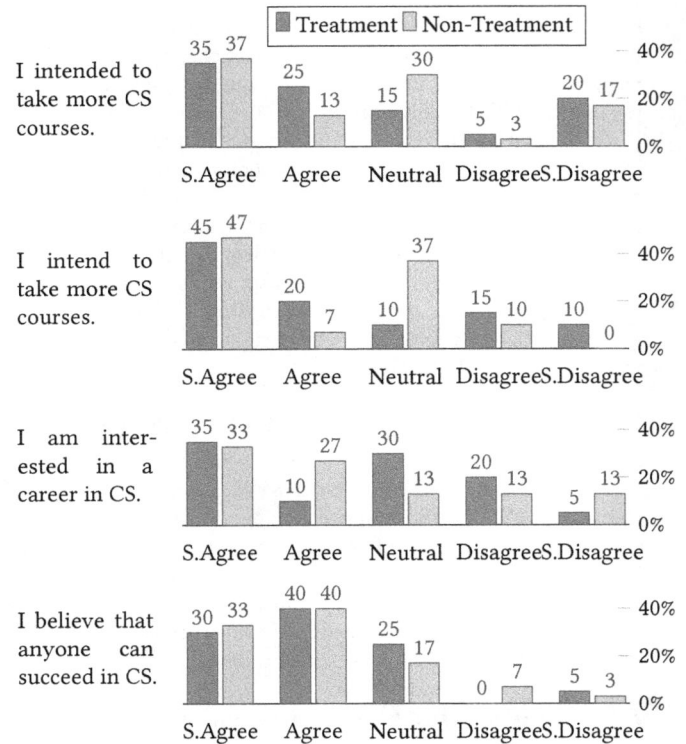

Figure 3: Interest in CS Questions

non-treatment section 30. Out of the survey respondents, 9 of 20 treatment group students and 12 of 30 non-treatment group students identified as a woman.

8.1 Interest in Computer Science

Figure 3 summarizes student responses related to their interest in CS, and their belief that anyone can succeed in the field. The treatment section appears to be more "decisive" (fewer neutral answers) in their intention to take more CS courses, but the difference is not statistically significant (Wilcoxon rank-sum test). There are also no statistically significant differences between the two sections' beliefs that anyone can succeed in computer science.

8.2 Importance of CS Topics

Student response to the importance of CS topics (survey section 3) did not yield interesting results. The interviews emphasized certain topics (commenting, unit tests, style checker, thinking, debugging), omitted other topics (classes), and downplayed others (string methods). However, differences between the two sections were minimal.

8.3 Attendance

Respondents in the evening section (treatment group) attended an average of 3 interviews. As usual, student attendance at the beginning of the term was higher than at the end of the term.

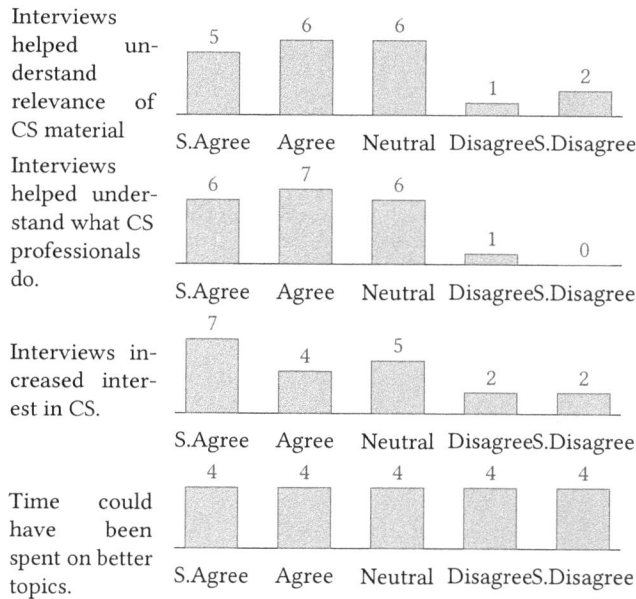

Figure 4: Interview Relevance Questions

8.4 Live Interview

Figure 4 shows that the reactions to the interviews among treatment group respondents were generally positive. There was general agreement that the interviews helped students understand the relevance of course material, and provided an understanding of what professional practitioners do. This result corroborated the written student responses presented in earlier sections.

Students also self-report that the interviews increased their interest in CS, although this result differs from those in Figure 3.

Students were split on whether the time could have been better spent in other ways, again corroborating the qualitative responses.

9 CONCLUSION

We report our experience interspersing short, 10-minute interviews with professional programmers in a CS1 classroom. Survey results show that, in general, students found these engaging, motivating, and appreciated learning about available career paths. Figure 5 summarizes key recommendations for fellow computer science instructors who wish to apply similar interventions.

One key question is whether the trade-off of lost lecture time was worthwhile. Student opinion on the matter was split. The tradeoff depends on available class time and student interest in a CS career. We ended our CS1 course an hour early, suggesting that there was ample lecture time available. However, lecture time was less "tight" near the beginning and end of the course. The intervention would have been more effective if more of our students were CS majors as opposed to non-majors, who would be more interested in learning more about CS career paths.

Another tradeoff is between contact with instructor, and contact with a different type of "authoritative" person. We hoped that professionals may be able to motivate students in ways that instructors

1. Use live video conferencing. Video conferencing simplifies scheduling and lowers the professionals' time commitment.
2. Ask professionals to use a laptop. Using a smartphone instead will produce a shakier and more blurrier video feed with a narrower aspect ratio, and the professional will make less eye contact.
3. Videos won't be reusable. If a reusable video is desired, recording it without the presence of students will increase its quality. Professionals generally consent to being recorded, but not for the recording to be public.
4. Ask professionals to use small words and give short answers. Describe ahead of time concepts students are familiar with, and give examples of concepts to avoid. Shorter responses will keep the conversation moving.
5. Start with a BANG! Kick-off the interview series with a professional from a well-known company, to engage student attention immediately.
6. Interview alumni. Alumni understand students more deeply, and students identify with them.
7. Choose professionals that align with student goals. For example, we chose a data scientist based on observed student interest in artificial intelligence. Ideally, we would have also chosen a medical researcher who programs regularly, since we had many life sciences students.
8. Be intentional about the learning goals. The selection of professionals for each lecture and the timing of the interviews should complement the learning goals. In case class progresses slower than usual, it is beneficial to have the flexibility to cancel.
9. Ask the professionals to be honest. Disagreements between the instructor and the professional engage students.
10. Student questions can be insightful. Students took the opportunity to ask questions that only professionals can answer, and that are difficult to find answers to online.

Figure 5: Recommendations

cannot. Though the survey evidence is not conclusive, the interviews did surprise students in ways that the instructor could not: e.g. just how important it is to understand the problem.

Finally, conducting the interviews via video conferencing was undoubtedly more flexible than doing so in-person. It is difficult to justify asking a professional to travel to campus for a mere 10-minute discussion, so an in-person interview would have required even more lecture time, and likely an entirely different setup.

Given the opportunity to teach a CS1 course comprised mainly of CS majors, we would repeat the intervention, perhaps adjusting the timing and quantity of the interviews to better reflect the learning and career goals for that audience.

ACKNOWLEDGMENTS

We thank Woongbin Kang, Shems Saleh, Pouria Fewzee, and other interviewees who chose to remain anonymous. We also thank Jennifer Campbell and Gregory Rosenblatt for their helpful comments. This work was supported in part by Office of Naval Research award N00014-18-1-2755.

REFERENCES

[1] Catherine Ashcraft, Elizabeth Eger, and Michelle Friend. 2012. Girls in IT: the facts. *National Center for Women & IT. Boulder, CO* (2012).

[2] Legand Burge, Marlon Mejias, KaMar Galloway, Kinnis Gosha, and Jean Muhammad. 2017. Holistic Development of Underrepresented Students through Academic: Industry Partnerships. In *Proceedings of the 2017 ACM SIGCSE Technical Symposium on Computer Science Education*. ACM, 681–682.

[3] Jennifer Campbell, Diane Horton, Michelle Craig, and Paul Gries. 2014. Evaluating an inverted CS1. In *Proceedings of the 45th ACM technical symposium on Computer science education*. ACM, 307–312.

[4] Duygu Candarli and H Gulru Yuksel. 2012. Students' perceptions of video-conferencing in the classrooms in higher education. *Procedia-Social and Behavioral Sciences* 47 (2012), 357–361.

[5] Ufuk Celikkan, Fisun Senuzun, Dilek Sari, and Yasar Guneri Sahin. 2013. Interactive videoconference supported teaching in undergraduate nursing: A case study for ECG. *Journal of Educational Technology & Society* 16, 1 (2013), 286.

[6] Jie Du, Hayden Wimmer, and Roy Rada. 2016. "Hour of Code": Can It Change Students' Attitudes toward Programming? *Journal of Information Technology Education: Innovations in Practice* 15 (2016), 52–73.

[7] Crystal Eney and Crystal Hoyer. 2005. Making a Difference on $10 a Day: Creating a "Women in CSE" Seminar Linked to CS1. In *Proceedings of the American Society for Engineering Education*.

[8] Amruth N Kumar. 2012. A study of stereotype threat in computer science. In *Proceedings of the 17th ACM annual conference on Innovation and technology in computer science education*. ACM, 273–278.

[9] Tony Lawson, Chris Comber, Jenny Gage, and Adrian Cullum-Hanshaw. 2010. Images of the future for education? Videoconferencing: A literature review. *Technology, Pedagogy and Education* 19, 3 (2010), 295–314.

[10] Anthony Papini, Leigh Ann DeLyser, Nathaniel Granor, and Kevin Wang. 2017. Preparing and supporting industry professionals as volunteer high school computer science co-instructors. In *Proceedings of the 2017 ACM SIGCSE Technical Symposium on Computer Science Education*. ACM, 441–446.

[11] Josh Tenenberg. 2010. Industry fellows: bringing professional practice into the classroom. In *Proceedings of the 41st ACM technical symposium on Computer science education*. ACM, 72–76.

Interactive Preparatory Work in a Flipped Programming Course

Lijuan Cao
Department of Software and Information Systems
University of North Carolina Charlotte
Charlotte, NC
lcao2@uncc.edu

Michael Grabchak
Department of Mathematics and Statistics
University of North Carolina Charlotte
Charlotte, NC
mgrabcha@uncc.edu

ABSTRACT

The flipped classroom pedagogy is a popular framework for teaching computing courses. This pedagogy hinges on students completing the preparatory (prep) work before class. This usually requires watching videos or reading several sections from the textbook. To encourage students to do the prep work, a short multiple-choice online quiz is often given. However, despite this incentive, many students do not spend enough time on the prep work. To deal with this challenge, we introduce a new approach that is designed to be more engaging. This approach replaces the regular textbook with an interactive textbook and replaces the multiple-choice quizzes with small programming assignments, which are graded automatically to give students immediate feedback. To test the efficacy of this approach, we offered two sections of the course with the only difference being in the prep work, one (the experimental group) used the proposed approach while the other (the control group) used a standard approach. Our results suggest that students in the experimental group tended to perform better in terms of both the overall mean and the DFW rate, i.e. the proportion of students receiving a D, F, or W (withdraw) as their overall grade in the class. Further, students in the experimental group tended to report more positive attitudes to the prep work and the class overall.

CCS CONCEPTS

• **Social and professional topics** → **Computer science education**.

KEYWORDS

flipped classroom, preparatory work, programming course, interactive textbook

ACM Reference Format:
Lijuan Cao and Michael Grabchak. 2019. Interactive Preparatory Work in a Flipped Programming Course. In *ACM Global Computing Education Conference 2019 (CompEd '19), May 17–19, 2019, Chengdu,Sichuan, China.* ACM, New York, NY, USA, 7 pages. https://doi.org/10.1145/3300115.3309520

1 INTRODUCTION

The flipped classroom pedagogy is a popular framework for teaching computing courses. It is widely used and many positive outcomes have been reported, see for instance [1, 2, 9–11, 15, 17]. In a flipped classroom the entire class time is devoted to problem solving sessions and other hands on activities, and the majority of the content delivery takes place before class, when students complete the preparatory (prep) work. This prep work generally consists of watching online videos or reading the textbook. However, a systematic review of the literature on flipped classrooms, [1], finds that the most commonly reported difficulty with this pedagogy "is students' limited preparation before class time." For instance, in [9], students reported that, on average, they completed only 18.7 out of 26 reading assignments, and watched only 11.6 out of 25 videos. Similarly, another study [18] finds that only 15.5% of students report watching all of the videos, while almost 30% report watching just a few of the videos. Further, in [3] it is shown that asking students to watch videos without additional intervention leads to low compliance. Thus, although the flipped classroom approach hinges on students completing the prep work, studies have found that many students do not complete it in an adequate manner. To deal with these issues, multiple-choice or true-false online quizzes are often used. While this may provide some incentive for students to do the work, [13] found no significant difference in learning outcomes between groups of students who were required to complete the quizzes and those who were not. The authors of that paper conjecture that this may be because this style of quiz can only enforce surface learning, but it cannot promote deep thinking.

In this paper, we propose a new approach for organizing the prep work in a programming course. In our approach, we keep the online videos, but we replace the regular textbook with an interactive textbook and we replace the multiple-choice quizzes with small programming assignments. The interactive textbook that we used breaks the material into short 'bite-sized' sections, which highlight a single topic and contain built-in animations and practice activities. This aims to guide the students, to reinforce the concepts as they are covered, and to make the reading less passive. The programming assignments aim to apply newly learned knowledge and to motivate higher level cognitive learning. Both components are more active and engaging than their more standard counterparts.

We hypothesize that our approach can help to improve student preparedness and, hence, performance in the class. Toward this end, we implemented this approach in a CS1.5 course, which is a second semester programming course that focuses on advanced topics in Java and is taught using the flipped classroom pedagogy. To test the efficacy of this approach, we compared two sections of the course.

The first is a control group, which was taught using standard prep work, while the second is an experimental group, which was taught using our proposed approach. Aside for the prep work, the rest of the courses were taught identically. Our results suggest that students in the experimental group tended to perform better in terms of both the overall mean and the DFW rate. DFW rates are the proportions of students receiving a D, F, or W (withdrawal) as their overall grade in the class. Further, students in the experimental group tended to report more positive attitudes to the prep work and the class overall. Moreover, these students seemed to be engaged by the prep work and almost 60% report that, on average, they completed all of a week's reading assignment.

2 RELATED WORK

2.1 Prep Work

A great deal of research effort has been devoted to understanding and optimizing the flipped classroom pedagogy for computing courses. However, most of this research effort has been focused on improving the in-class component. Far less work has been devoted to best practices for organizing the prep work until quite recently. In this subsection, we discuss two recent approaches introduced in [8, 12], which aim to improve students' preparedness.

In [8], instructors handed out guided practice sheets when assigning the prep work. These sheets included a list of learning objectives and several practice exercises. The list of learning objectives aimed to help students know which aspects of the reading to focus on, while the practice exercises allowed them to test their reading by applying the newly learned knowledge. The authors of that paper indicated a high worksheet completion rate and a positive correlation between individual completion rates and final course grades. However, they also report two limitations due to the fact that the worksheets were submitted on paper. The first is that this leads to grading overhead and the second is that students do not receive immediate feedback. Further, the study was only applied to small and medium size classes.

The study in [12] modified the online quizzes so that, in addition to multiple-choice questions, they also included several programming questions. These questions required students to write "simple expressions or small functions" and were automatically graded by the computer. The students had only one try on the multiple-choice questions, but unlimited tries on the programming questions. However, if a student made a mistake on a programming question, that student would only be told that the "response was incorrect, with no details on the nature of the error." The authors of the paper compared several sections taught using this approach, with ones where the students were not given any quizzes. They found that the students given these quizzes tended to perform better. However, since the class sizes were small, the authors encouraged others to experiment with larger classes.

2.2 Interactive Online Course Materials

With the emergence of MOOCs (Massive Open Online Courses), a lot of interactive online course materials have become available for computing education. In addition, a number of interactive ebooks have been released. For instance, [6] developed an ebook for teaching CS1 and discusses best practices for such ebooks. There are also entire platforms devoted to computing education. Two commonly used platforms are zyBooks [22] and OpenDSA [19].

zyBooks publishes online textbooks, which are integrated with many interactive activities.These include animations, learning questions, and exercises. The questions and exercises allow unlimited attempts and are automatically graded to provide immediate feedback. Further, the platform records each student's grades and reports these to the instructor. A study across four courses at three different universities shows improved student performance using zyBooks as compared to traditional textbooks [5].

OpenDSA is a similar platform, but developed, specifically, for courses in data structures and algorithms. A pilot study compared a course taught on this platform with one taught using traditional course materials [7]. They found a statistically significant increase in the proportion of students getting an A or a B in the class.

All of the studies mentioned here are about the use of these platforms in conjunction with traditional lecture-based classes. However, while it has been suggested that such platforms may be "well-suited" to serve as prep work in a flipped classroom [5], we are aware of no previous studies in this direction.

3 PROPOSED PREP WORK

In this section we discuss how the proposed prep work is organized. Each week the students are required to complete one prep work assignment, which is comprised of three major components that are supposed to be completed in the following order: watch several online videos, read several sections of the interactive online textbook, and complete a small programming assignment. Our approach to the videos is standard and the innovation comes from the other two components.

3.1 Videos

Every prep work assignment has three to five videos, which range in length from five to fifteen minutes. About half of the videos are theoretical and focus on specific concepts, while the other half are more hands on and show a computer screen on which a user types a program while explaining it. Most of the videos are hosted on YouTube and were developed by other educators. Since the videos are not housed locally, we are unable to track how many videos a students watches, nor if he or she watches the complete video.

3.2 Interactive Textbook

The interactive textbook that we adopted is *Programming in Java: Early Objects* [16], which is created by zyBooks. This book has several features, which help to structure the prep work and to engage the students while they read.

The book is highly customizable and allows instructors to change the order of the chapters and to move sections from one chapter to another. Using this feature, we would combine a week's reading into one chapter and assign it to the students. The resulting chapter usually contained five to ten sections. While this may sound like a lot, each section is very short and focuses on just one very specific topic. This way students can clearly see what the main concepts are and focus directly on them.

To actively engage the students, the readings are punctuated by short animations and interactive exercises. The animations help students to visualize the concepts, while the exercises allow them to check their understanding of the key points. While many of the exercises are multiple choice, true/false, or short answer, some require students to write several lines of code. All of the exercises allow unlimited tries and are automatically graded to provide immediate feedback. Further, the book records a student's progress on these exercises, which allows the instructor to assign a grade for this work. This gives students further incentive to complete the reading.

3.3 Programming Assignments

At the end of each prep work, students are asked to complete a small programming assignment. Unlike the exercises in the textbook, which focus on highlighting certain concepts and helping students to memorize and understand newly learned material, the programming assignments aim to motivate higher level cognitive learning. In particular, they synthesize all of the topics covered that week and show how these interact with each other. The programming assignments are open ended and require the students to either write several methods or to complete a class definition. To facilitate this, we used the assignment submission and auto-grading system zyLab, which is part of the zyBooks platform. While zyLab provides several pre-made assignments, it also allows instructors to make their own assignments from scratch. We chose the second option as it allows for more flexibility in both the topics covered and in which aspects are emphasized.

To create an assignment using zyLab, the instructor must provide the problem specification, the program templates, several test cases, and a solution file. The problem specification describes the problem and explains what the students are expected to do. The program templates can be completely empty, but the ones that we provided consisted of partially completed programs, with some of the methods completed, others just defined, and still others only described. We also included comments about what must be added. The test cases are used to evaluate a student's program, and the solution file is used to validate the test cases.

Grades are assigned based on how many and which test cases are passed. If a certain test case is not passed, then the instructor has the option to tell the student where the problem is located and to give any hints desired. This allows for immediate feedback. If a student does not get full marks, she or he can modify the assignment and resubmit. While it is possible to cap the number of submission opportunities, we chose to give students unlimited tries. This is in keeping with the goal of prep work, which is not primarily assessment, but getting the students to think about and engage with the material.

One of the prep work programming assignments that we gave was based on the popular Pokémon video games. In this assignment, we provided two program templates, which were partially completed. The first was the Pokemon class and the second was a driver program. The goal of the assignment was to help students understand the difference between a class and an object and to provide practice working with the related concepts of fields, constructors, accessors, and mutators. The program template for the Pokémon class is given in Figure 1. For this assignment, we created six test cases. The code for one of these is given in Figure 2.

```
1  public class Pokemon {
2      /*Fix (1) Add four fields: name, maxHp, hitPoints, attackPoints*/
3
4
5      /*FIX (2) Add a constructor, which takes three parameters: String n, int max, int ap
6      Initialize name to n, maxHp and hitPoints to max, and attackPoints to ap*/
7
8
9      /*Fix (3) Define the mutator for hitPoints*/
10
11
12      /*Fix (4) Define the mutator for attackPoints*/
13
14
15      /*Fix (5) Define the accessor for name*/
16
17
18      /*Fix (6) Define the accessor for hitPoints*/
19
20
21      /*Fix (7) Define the accessor for attackPoints*/
22
23
24      public void reset() {
25          hitPoints = maxHp;
26      }
27      public void printStat() {
28          System.out.println(name + " has " + hitPoints + " hit points and "
29          + attackPoints + " attack points");
30      }
31  }
```

Current file: Pokemon.java

Figure 1: Program template for the Pokemon class.

```
1. Unit test (1 point)
   Test getHitPoints and setHitPoints
   Hide details ^

1  import java.io.PrintWriter;
2
3  public class zyLabsUnitTest {
4      public boolean passed(PrintWriter testFeedback) {
5          Pokemon p = new Pokemon("Alice", 10, 3);
6          p.setHitPoints(20);
7
8          if(p.getHitPoints() == 20) {
9              System.out.println("Pokemon's hitPoints is correctly set and is accessible.");
10             return true;
11         }
12         else {
13             System.out.println("Pokemon's hitPoints is not correctly set or is not accessible.");
14             System.out.println("Incorrect hitPoints returned: " + p.getHitPoints());
15             return false;
16         }
17     }
18 }
```

Figure 2: A sample test case.

The following week we followed up on this program, which lead to a simple, but complete Pokémon game. That week we covered ArrayLists, and we asked students to create a Player class, where each player had an ArrayList of Pokémon. The players could then select a Pokémon from their ArrayList and have them fight, with the winner determined randomly, but with probabilities based on the Pokémon's attributes.

4 STUDY DESIGN

Our study collected data from two large sections of CS1.5 at a large urban research university. They were taught in Fall 2017 (control group) and Spring 2018 (experimental group). Both sections are large classes (more that 100 students) and were taught by the same instructor, during the same class period, and using the same flipped classroom approach. The only difference in the structure of the two classes was in the prep work. For the control group, each week's prep work asked the students to watch several videos, read several sections from a traditional textbook, and complete an online quiz. The quiz usually consisted of 5 to 10 multiple-choice questions, with students allowed two tries on each. For the experimental group we used the prep work as described in Section 3. The videos used were the same for both sections.

Because students self-select into the courses, the design was quasi-experimental. However, the students were not aware of how the two courses would be taught when they enrolled. This should mitigate any bias caused by self-selection. Another potential cause of bias is the fact that one section was offered in a Fall semester, while the other was offered in a Spring semester. There may be differences in the students who take the course in the different semesters. In particular, in our study there were significantly more students in the Fall section who had either recieved AP credit for CS1 or had recently transferred from a different school.

For both sections, we collected student performance data, and, to check students' attitudes, we conducted an end of semester survey. The research questions that guide this study are as follows:

- Do students taught using the proposed approach rate their experiences higher than students taught using the standard approach?
- Do students taught using the proposed approach have better performance in the course overall?
- Do students taught using the proposed approach complete more readings and prep work assignments?

5 COURSE STRUCTURE

In this section, we describe the structure that was used for both the control and the experimental groups. Both were sections of a CS1.5 course, which is a second semester programming course that requires passing CS1 with a C or better as a prerequisite. It is part of the core curriculum and is required for all Computer Science majors. It covers topics on advanced java programming and includes object oriented design, inheritance, polymorphism, exception handling, GUI, and multi-threading. The course is offered every semester, and the class size ranges between 100 and 120 students. Further, each class splits into several lab sections comprised of between 30 and 60 students. Both the class and the lab session meet once a week, each for two hours and 45 minutes. The class is taught using a flipped classroom structure similar to the one proposed in [14]. In particular, each week is organized as follows:

(1) Prep work: At the beginning of the week, the students complete the prep work, which is due before the week's lab session.

(2) Lab session: Students work in pairs to complete a series of programming tasks, which are designed to allow them to apply knowledge newly acquired from the prep work.

(3) Class: At the end of the week, the students and the instructor meet during the class, where there is Q&A session, peer instruction quiz, group discussions, and additional hands-on activities.

In addition to these day to day items, there are four large scale individual programming assignments and five tests. Aside for the prep work, we did our best to make the two sections as similar as possible to each other. In particular, we used the same labs, programming assignments, and in class hands-on activities in both semesters. Further, while exam questions were slightly different, they covered the same material in very similar ways. In the prep work, the videos used were the same for both semesters.

Table 1: Grading Scheme

Category	Percentage
Prep work	10%
Lab	25%
Peer instruction quizzes	15%
Individual assignments	25%
Tests	25%

Table 2: Means, medians, and standard deviations for the prep work.

Group	Assignment	Mean	Median	Std Dev
Experimental	zyBook	97.39	99.91	5.28
	zyLabs	79.41	100	29.46
Control	Quizzes	90.33	93.68	11.42

The grading scheme for the class is shown in Table 1. Note that, in both sections, the prep work is worth 10% of the final grade. In the control group this was assigned purely on each student's performance on the online quizzes, while in the experimental group it was divided with 7% for the exercises in the interactive textbook and 3% for the zyLab programming assignments.

6 RESULTS

In this section we present the results of a data analysis on both student performance and student feedback. This analysis was performed using the statistical software R [20].

6.1 Student Performance

Table 2 presents the performance of the two groups on the prep work. We can see that students in the experimental group performed very well. In particular, for the zyBook readings both the mean and the median are high, while the standard deviation is low. This suggests that most of the students completed the reading assignments and were engaged by the interactive textbook. For the zyLab programming assignments, the median was 100%, which means that at least half of the students completed all of the programming assignments perfectly. This is especially notable since these assignments are more challenging, but worth only 3% of the final grade. On the other hand, this may have caused some of the students to not engage with this part of the prep work, which may explain why the mean was only 79.41%. To deal with this issue, it may make sense to weight the programming assignments a bit more in the future. Looking at the data from the control group, we see that the students in that section also performed well on the prep work. However, it is more difficult to interpret these results, since the multiple choice quizzes assigned to that section are not a good proxy for completion of the book readings nor do they check for a deeper understanding of the material.

To gauge the effect of the proposed approach on the students' overall performance, we compare the final grades in the two sections. The means and standard deviations for these are presented in Table 3. We can see that the mean of the control group is smaller

Table 3: Means and standard deviations for the final grades in the two sections.

Group	Mean	Std Dev	Sample Size
Control	86.21	13.91	111
Experimental	88.94	11.15	113

Table 4: DFW rates for the two sections.

Group	DFW Rate
Control	14.6%
Experimental	7.5%

than that of the experimental group. To check if this difference is statistically significant, we perform a two-sample z-test. This is appropriate since both sample sizes are large. Here, we test the null hypothesis that $\mu_A = \mu_B$ against the alternative is that $\mu_A < \mu_B$, where μ_A is the theoretical mean of the control group and μ_B is the theoretical mean of the experimental group. We calculate the test statistic to be -1.61, which leads to a p-value of 0.053. Since this value is less than .10, the results are significant at the 90% level. To check if part of this difference can be explained by the grades on the prep work, we also performed this analysis on the grades averaged without the prep work, but the p-value was almost identical in that case.

Aside for considering the average value, it is important to see the effect of the proposed methodology on the lower performing students. For this reason, we compare the DFW rates for the two classes. The DFW rates are presented in Table 4. In both classes, there are more than 5 students receiving a DFW and more than 5 students not receiving a DFW. Thus, the standard rule of thumb for a z-test for proportions is satisfied, see e.g. Section 24.5 in [21]. For this reason, we can perform a z-test for the null hypothesis $p_A = p_B$ against the alternative $p_A > p_B$, where p_A is the theoretical DFW rate for the control group and p_B is the theoretical DFW rate for the experimental group. The test statistics is 1.79, which leads to a p-value of 0.0366. Since this is less than .05, we reject the null hypothesis in favor of the alternative, and conclude that students in the experimental group have a lower DFW rate than those in the control group.

6.2 Student Feedback

To better understand student attitudes to the prep work, an optional and anonymous survey was conducted at the end of each course. This survey was administered and collected by someone who was not an instructor and was not affiliated with the class. Further, it was made clear to the students that the instructor would have no access to the results of the survey until after the final grades for the course were submitted. In total 36 students from the control group and 80 students from the experimental group took the survey. The results can be found in Table 5 and Figures 3 and 4.

The first five questions presented in Table 5 were asked of both groups. The only difference is that Questions 4 and 5 were about the online quizzes when asked of the control group and about the

zyLab programming assignments when asked of the experimental group. These questions use a 5-point Likert-type scale with 1 representing "Strongly Disagree" and 5 representing "Strongly Agree." In all cases, the questions were worded so that 1 suggests negative attitudes and 5 suggests positive attitudes. We can see that, in all cases, the means are higher for the experimental group than the control group. To test if these differences are statistically significant, we preformed a Mann-Whitney U test. This test is similar to a two sample t-test, but is more robust and does not have any distributional assumptions. See [4] for a discussion of the appropriateness of this test for analyzing data on a Likert-type scale.

In our tests, the null hypothesis is that the distributions are the same and the alternative is that the distribution of the control group is stochastically smaller (i.e. tends to take on smaller values) than the distribution of the experimental group. In all cases the p-values are less than .05, and thus all of the null hypotheses are rejected in favor of the alternative. This suggesting that, as a whole, students in the experimental group tended to have more positive attitudes than those in the control group. In particular, students in the experimental group reported that the prep work helped them to learn the material (Q2) and made them better prepared for the in-class activities (Q3). Being well prepared may have made them appreciate the overall structure of the flipped classroom more, leading them to report greater satisfaction with this approach overall (Q1). Further, we see that students in the control group did not find the multiple choice online quizzes to be sufficient for helping them reflect on the material or providing them with adequate incentive to complete the prep work. Students in the experimental group rated the zyLabs higher than students in the control group rated quizzes, suggesting that zyLabs were a better method for helping them to reflect on the material and motivating them to complete the prep work (Q4, Q5). Question 6 on Table 5 was only asked of the experimental group, as it is specific to the proposed prep work. The question asks if students prefer an interactive textbook to a traditional one. The mean for this question is 3.53. Figures 3 and 4 present the responses on two questions, which were not based on a Likert-type scale, but instead asked students to select the choice that they most agree with. The question in Figure 3 was on both surveys, and asks, on average, how much of a week's reading the student completed. We can see that a much larger proportion of the students report doing all of the reading in the experimental group than in the control group. The question in Figure 4 was asked only of the students in the experimental group. It asks which aspect of the prep work the students found to be the most helpful. The proportions of students choosing each of the three are fairly close. However, the interactive textbook had the largest proportion, the zyLabs were in the middle, and the videos had the smallest proportion.

7 CONCLUSIONS

In this paper we compared two large sections of a CS1.5 course, which were taught using the flipped classroom pedagogy. One section was a control group, which used a standard approach to the prep work, while the other was an experimental group and used the proposed prep work. Other than this, the sections were taught using the same structure with as many components as possible

Table 5: Student survey responses.

Survey Questions	Control		Experimental		p-value
	Mean	SD	Mean	Std Dev	
1. I felt that the flipped classroom approach helped me to learn better than the traditional approach.	2.54	1.54	3.10	1.41	0.028
2. Reading the textbook helped me to learn the material.	2.63	1.48	3.30	1.21	0.008
3. Overall, the prep work prepared me adequately for the lab and the class.	2.23	1.37	3.50	1.06	$< 10^{-4}$
4. The online quizzes/zyLabs motivated me to complete the preparatory work.	1.92	1.36	2.99	1.20	$< 10^{-4}$
5. The online quizzes/zylabs made me reflect on what I learned from doing the prep work.	1.97	1.30	3.33	1.03	$< 10^{-4}$
6. I was more motivated to read the interactive textbook than to read a traditional textbook.	–	–	3.53	1.25	–

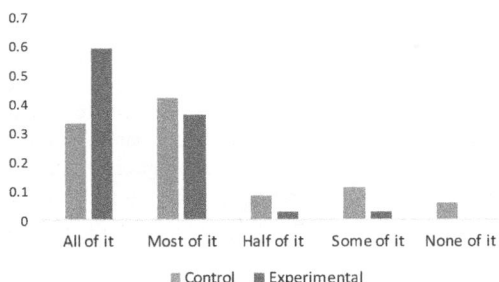

Figure 3: Response to the question: "On average, how much of the reading did you complete in a given week?"

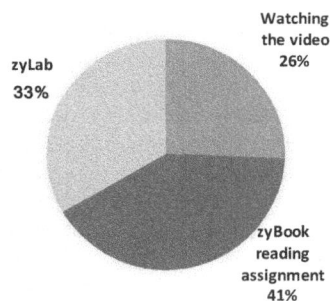

Figure 4: Response to the Question: "Which aspect of the preparatory work was the most helpful for your learning (choose one)?".

kept the same. We saw that students in the experimental group tended to perform better in the class. They had a higher overall mean and a significantly lower DFW rate. Further, students in the experimental group tended to report more positive attitudes to the prep work and the class overall. These students seemed to be engaged by the prep work and almost 60% report that, on average, they completed all of a week's reading assignment. These results suggest affirmative answers to the motivating questions, which were presented in Section 4.

Since we made two major changes to the prep work, it is difficult to disentangle them. However, from Figure 4 we see that large proportions of students found each of them to be useful. To better understand the relative merits of each change, one could introduce them one at a time. However, we feel that both are important and we chose to make both in order to give the students the best possible learning experience.

Aside for the differences in the prep work, we did our best to teach the two sections as similar to each other as possible. This included having the same intructor and using similar course materials. However, there is one confounding variable that we were not able to control for. This is the fact that one section was offered in a fall semester while the other was offered in a spring semester. This raises the question of how much of the difference that we found is caused by the approach used and how much was caused by differences in the student populations. Unfortunately, it is difficult, if not impossible, to answer this question. This is always an issue when comparing data from different semesters. Even data from the same semester may have this issue as there may be differences in the student populations that take the class in the morning instead of the afternoon or evening. The development of approaches for dealing with such issues are an important direction for future research.

After teaching the course using the proposed approach, we found two directions for improvement. First, in our study, the zyLab programming assignments were only worth 3% of a student's final grade. This was done out of a sense to caution, as we were not sure how students would react. Our results suggest that most students tended to do well and seemed to enjoy these assignments. In fact, about a third reported that this was the most helpful aspect of the prep work. However, there were some students who did not seem to engage with these assignments. To help motivate them and to more adequately compensate all students, we feel that this component should be worth a larger proportion of the final grade. In fact, the next time that we teach this class, we plan to make it worth 5%. Second, we were not able to get data on how much time students spend on the prep work, as such information is not currently available through zyBooks. With the development of more interactive textbooks and other platforms, such data could become available and a study of it would be of interest. Further, this would be useful information to make available to instructors.

On the whole, the study of best practices for the prep work in a flipped classroom is in its early stages. It is our hope that this paper, along with other recent studies [8, 12], will stimulate more interest in and research on engaging students with prep work.

ACKNOWLEDGMENTS

The first author's research was supported by a Scholarship of Teaching and Learning (SoTL) grant from UNC Charlotte.

REFERENCES

[1] Gökçe Akçayır and Murat Akçayır. 2018. The flipped classroom: A review of its advantages and challenges. *Computers & Education* 126 (2018), 334–345.
[2] Lijuan Cao and Audrey Rorrer. 2018. An Active and Collaborative Approach to Teaching Discrete Structures. In *Proceedings of the 49th ACM Technical Symposium on Computer Science Education*. ACM, 822–827.
[3] Suzanne L. Dazo, Nicholas R. Stepanek, Robert Fulkerson, and Brian Dorn. 2016. An Empirical Analysis of Video Viewing Behaviors in Flipped CS1 Courses. In *Proceedings of the 2016 ACM Conference on Innovation and Technology in Computer Science Education (ITiCSE '16)*. ACM, New York, NY, USA, 106–111.
[4] Joost CF De Winter and Dimitra Dodou. 2010. Five-point Likert items: t test versus Mann-Whitney-Wilcoxon. *Practical Assessment, Research & Evaluation* 15, 11 (2010), 2.
[5] Alex Edgcomb, Frank Vahid, Roman Lysecky, Andre Knoesen, Rajeevan Amirtharajah, and Mary Lou Dorf. 2015. Student performance improvement using interactive textbooks: A three-university cross-semester analysis. In *2015 ASEE Annual Conference and Exposition*.
[6] Barbara J. Ericson, Mark J. Guzdial, and Briana B. Morrison. 2015. Analysis of Interactive Features Designed to Enhance Learning in an Ebook. In *Proceedings of the Eleventh Annual International Conference on International Computing Education Research (ICER '15)*. ACM, New York, NY, USA, 169–178.
[7] Tommy Färnqvist, Fredrik Heintz, Patrick Lambrix, Linda Mannila, and Chunyan Wang. 2016. Supporting Active Learning by Introducing an Interactive Teaching Tool in a Data Structures and Algorithms Course. In *Proceedings of the 47th ACM Technical Symposium on Computing Science Education (SIGCSE '16)*. ACM, New York, NY, USA, 663–668.
[8] Saturnino Garcia. 2018. Improving Classroom Preparedness Using Guided Practice. In *Proceedings of the 49th ACM Technical Symposium on Computer Science Education (SIGCSE '18)*. ACM, New York, NY, USA, 326–331.
[9] Edward F. Gehringer and Barry W. Peddycord, III. 2013. The Inverted-lecture Model: A Case Study in Computer Architecture. In *Proceeding of the 44th ACM Technical Symposium on Computer Science Education (SIGCSE '13)*. ACM, New York, NY, USA, 489–494.
[10] Michail N. Giannakos, John Krogstie, and Nikos Chrisochoides. 2014. Reviewing the Flipped Classroom Research: Reflections for Computer Science Education. In *Proceedings of the Computer Science Education Research Conference (CSERC '14)*. ACM, New York, NY, USA, 23–29.
[11] Yungwei Hao. 2016. Exploring undergraduates' perspectives and flipped learning readiness in their flipped classrooms. *Computers in Human Behavior* 59 (2016), 82–92.
[12] Lisa L. Lacher, Albert Jiang, Yu Zhang, and Mark C. Lewis. 2018. Including Coding Questions in Video Quizzes for a Flipped CS1. In *Proceedings of the 49th ACM Technical Symposium on Computer Science Education (SIGCSE '18)*. ACM, New York, NY, USA, 574–579.
[13] Lisa L. Lacher and Mark C. Lewis. 2015. The Effectiveness of Video Quizzes in a Flipped Class. In *Proceedings of the 46th ACM Technical Symposium on Computer Science Education (SIGCSE '15)*. ACM, New York, NY, USA, 224–228.
[14] Celine Latulipe, N. Bruce Long, and Carlos E. Seminario. 2015. Structuring Flipped Classes with Lightweight Teams and Gamification. In *Proceedings of the 46th ACM Technical Symposium on Computer Science Education (SIGCSE '15)*. ACM, New York, NY, USA, 392–397.
[15] Kate Lockwood and Rachel Esselstein. 2013. The Inverted Classroom and the CS Curriculum. In *Proceeding of the 44th ACM Technical Symposium on Computer Science Education (SIGCSE '13)*. ACM, New York, NY, USA, 113–118.
[16] Roman Lysecky and Adrian Lizarraga. 2017. *Programming In Java: Early Objects*. zyBook.
[17] Mary Lou Maher, Celine Latulipe, Heather Lipford, and Audrey Rorrer. 2015. Flipped Classroom Strategies for CS Education. In *Proceedings of the 46th ACM Technical Symposium on Computer Science Education (SIGCSE '15)*. ACM, New York, NY, USA, 218–223.
[18] Kurt Nørmark. 2015. The use of video in a mixed classroom approach. In *International Conference on E-learning, E-Learning*.
[19] OpenDSA. Retrieved July 2018 from https://opendsa-server.cs.vt.edu/
[20] R Core Team. 2017. *R: A Language and Environment for Statistical Computing*. R Foundation for Statistical Computing, Vienna, Austria. https://www.R-project.org/
[21] Jerrold H Zar. 2010. *Biostatistical Analysis* (5 ed.). Pearson Prentice-Hall, Upper Saddle River, NJ.
[22] zyBooks. Retrieved July 2018 from www.zyBooks.com

Adaptable Test Design for Collaborative Exams in Computer Science

Qianni Deng
qndeng@sjtu.edu.cn
Shanghai Jiao Tong University
Shanghai, China

ABSTRACT

Group exam is a good way to help students learn theory and concept collaboratively, but the effect of collaborative exam is easily influenced by its design and organization. This poster suggests that the collaborative exams should be carefully designed to be flexible and adaptable to different circumstances and different students for improving their learning gains.

CCS CONCEPTS

• **Applied computing** → **Collaborative learning**.

KEYWORDS

Adaptable Collaborative Test, Zone of Proximal Development

ACM Reference Format:
Qianni Deng. 2019. Adaptable Test Design for Collaborative Exams in Computer Science. In *ACM Global Computing Education Conference 2019 (CompEd '19), May 17–19, 2019, Chengdu,Sichuan, China*. ACM, New York, NY, USA, 1 page. https://doi.org/10.1145/3300115.3312513

1 INTRODUCTION

As a form of group study, collaborative exams, in which students first take the exam individually then immediately complete a similar exam in a group at the second stage, have been adopted in some disciplines including computer science [1]. The exam has been regarded as a learning tool and pedagogy that can help promote student performance.

However, some empirical studies found that the effect of the exams could be impacted by several factors: students in the middle of the class (neither high nor low performers) tend to benefit strongly from the collaborative exam; students in groups with high heterogeneity (different performances) do not gain significant improvement [2]. In our previous research [3], we found that the effect of collaborative exam was influenced by the difficulty of questions: questions with moderate difficulty could lead to a great improvement, on the contrary, high difficulty questions made the cooperation ineffective. A recent study [4] analyzed 16 empirical studies from various disciplines and revealed two key factors that could help explain why some studies found increase in student learning while others did not: (1) the level of impact that students

believe the group portion of an exam will have on their final grade, and (2) the amount of preparation students have to work in groups and whether there is sufficient time for group discussions and debrief after an exam.

According to the famous pedagogic theory: the *zone of proximal development (ZPD)*[5], different students have different ZPDs, the learning plans should be flexible and adaptable for different individuals. This poster suggests that the collaborative exams should be carefully designed to adapte to different circumstances for improving learning gains. We believe that changing the test content and test plans to encourage students at different levels is a more effective and practical way, compared with changing the group compositions.

Since it is very hard to use different exam paper to perform one exam, we designed various plans for the groups after the tests: reorganize the exam by modifying questions what the group want to discuss; design a program to completely solve the problem in the test, complete a concept map which cover the knowledge points in the exam. Each group could select a plan according to their interests and abilities. The purpose of the design is to encourage continuous discussion after the exam.

In our experiment, two classes were both taken the 45-minute-long collaborative exam. In class A, the importance of collaboration was emphasized. An extended work was asked with group mates. Every group should discuss the work both intra-group and inter-group. In class B, the same evaluation regulation was adopted, but the extended work was asked without mandatory inter-group discussion. To gather the difference in learning outcomes, both two classes have taken a class quiz and a final exam.

The result shows that the learning gains of class A is significantly better than class B. The experiment proves that the continuous discussion after the exam, good learning atmosphere and encouragement among team members make students improve.

REFERENCES

[1] Yingjun Cao and Leo Porter. 2017. Evaluating student learning from collaborative group tests in introductory computing. In *Proceedings of the 2017 ACM SIGCSE Technical Symposium on Computer Science Education*. ACM, 99–104.
[2] Yingjun Cao and Leo Porter. 2017. Impact of Performance Level and Group Composition on Student Learning during Collaborative Exams. In *Proceedings of the 2017 ACM Conference on Innovation and Technology in Computer Science Education*. ACM, 152–157.
[3] Qianni Deng and Xinjian Luo. 2018. PipE 2: An Innovative Pipelining Design for Collaborative Two-Stage Exams. In *Proceedings of the 19th Annual SIG Conference on Information Technology Education*. International World Wide Web Conferences Steering Committee, 38–43.
[4] Sandra Ifeatu Efu. 2019. Exams as Learning Tools: A Comparison of Traditional and Collaborative Assessment in Higher Education. *College Teaching* 67, 1 (2019), 73–83.
[5] LF Obukhova and IA Korepanova. 2009. The zone of proximal development: A spatiotemporal model. *Journal of Russian & East European Psychology* 47, 6 (2009), 25–47.

Motivational Factors Affecting Computer Science Enrollment

Lee Kenneth Jones
Curriculum and Instruction
Texas Tech University
Lubbock, TX USA
lee.jones@ttu.edu

Jessica J . Gottlieb
Curriculum and Instruction
Texas Tech University
Lubbock, TX USA
jessica.gottlieb@ttu.edu

ABSTRACT

Internationally, the interest in science, technology, engineering, and math, or STEM, has led many countries to enact education policies aimed at generating more attention to STEM careers among its primary and secondary students. Driven by the supposed need for more STEM field workers, the movement has perhaps failed to look closely at what it is that drives the need and where the actual needs lie. Within the STEM career field lies jobs from nurse to field biologist to civil engineer to computer programmer [7]. However, there is also a large demand for computer science, field that is often swallowed up by the larger STEM interest. According to the Bureau of Labor and Statistics [2], computing jobs will make up 66% of all science, technology, engineering and math (STEM) jobs between 2014–2024 in the United States. However, only 8.48% of college STEM majors are in the computer science (CS) field [2] and there are over 500,000 unfilled computing jobs in the United States alone, but less than 50,000 CS graduates [3].

With the documented need for more CS workers, matched with very little primary and secondary CS education research and slow movements to enact policy, we have reached a critical point where it is important to understand more about what factors motivate students to enter the CS career field and how educators can use these factors to help direct and support more students to fill the important job sector that so desperately needs skilled employees.

Using the expectancy-value theory (EVT) as a framework, this poster presents a study that looks at factors that could serve as predictors for enrollment in high school CS electives. EVT posits that individuals who are given options, particularly around course and career choices, make their decision based on how they expect to perform at the task and what value they see it having in their life. Value can be further broken into utility value, intrinsic value, attainment value, and cost [4, 5, 9]. This framework for understanding student motivations for STEM has been used and validated multiple times [1, 6, 8], so this study hopes to build on that proven reliability to understand student motivations with regard to CS.

Using the High School Longitudinal Study of 2009 (HSLS:2009) This poster presents a work-in-progress that looks at what factors during the ninth grade (first year secondary) year are predictors of a student's enrollment in any CS course during high school.

CCS CONCEPTS

• Social and professional topics ~ K-12 education • Social and professional topics~ Computer science education

KEYWORDS

K-12 education; CS education; motivation theory

ACM Reference format:

Lee Kenneth Jones and Jessica J. Gottlieb. 2019. Motivational Factors Affecting Computer Science Enrollment. In *Proceedings of ACM Global Computing Education Conference (CompEd 2019), May 17, 2019, Chengdu, China*. ACM, New York, NY, USA, 1 page. https://doi.org/10.1145/3300115.3312510

REFERENCES

[1] Andersen, L. and Ward, T. J. Expectancy-value models for the STEM persistence plans of ninth-grade, high-ability students: A comparison between black, hispanic, and white students. Science Education, 98, 2 (2014), 216-242.
[2] Bureau of Labor and Statistics Employment projections. City, 2014.
[3] Code.org Promote Computer Science. Retrieved from https://code.org/promote.
[4] Eccles, J. S. Who Am I and What Am I Going to Do With My Life? Personal and Collective Identities as Motivators of Action. Educational Fsychologist, 44, 2 (2009/05/13 2009), 78-89.
[5] Eccles, J. S., Adler, T. F., Futterman, R., Goff, S. B., Kaczala, C. M. and Meece, J. L. Perspectives on academic achievement and achievement motivation. W.H. Freeman, City, 1983.
[6] Gottlieb, J. J. STEM career aspirations in Black, Hispanic, and White ninth-grade students. Journal of Research in Science Teaching, 55, 10 (2018), 1365-1392.
[7] Rothwell, J. The hidden STEM economy. Metropolitan Policy Program at Brookings, 2013.
[8] Wang, Ming-Te and Degol, J. Motivational pathways to STEM career choices: Using expectancy-value perspective to understand individual and gender differences in STEM fields. Developmental review : DR, 33, 4 (09/13 2013), 10.1016/j.dr.2013.1008.1001.
[9] Wigfield, A. and Eccles, J. S. Expectancy–value theory of achievement motivation. Contemporary Educational Psychology, 25, 1 (2000/01/01/ 2000), 68-81.

Developing Chinese Elementary School Students' Computational Thinking: A Convergent Cognition Perspective*

Yaqin Liu
Dept. of Educational Technology
Jiangnan University, China
yaqin_ll@163.com

Zhiqiang Ma
Dept. of Educational Technology
Jiangnan University, China
mzq1213@gmail.com

Yizhou Qian†
Dept. of Educational Technology
Jiangnan University, China
yqian@jiangnan.edu.cn

ABSTRACT

Computational thinking is considered a fundamental skill of children in the 21st century. In 2017, the new national curriculum standards of China included computational thinking as a core literacy of students. In this poster session, the authors will introduce their research on developing Chinese elementary school students' computational thinking skill. The authors have developed a new information technology course with the focus on computational thinking. The research uses the convergent cognition theory as the theoretical framework. The convergent cognition theory posits that learning computer programming affects students' mathematical thinking and vice versa. The programming environment is Scratch. A group of third grade students and a group of fourth grade students are the participants. Their computational thinking skill and math ability will be measured to see whether this course develops students' computational thinking skill and whether convergent cognition effects exist. Examples from the instructional materials will be presented as part of the poster. The authors will also report on the preliminary results of the course's effectiveness on developing students' computational thinking.

CCS CONCEPTS

• **Social and professional topics~Computational thinking** • Social and professional topics~Student assessment • Social and professional topics~K-12 education

KEYWORDS

Computational Thinking; Convergent Cognition; Chinese Elementary School Students

ACM Reference format:
Yaqin Liu, Zhiqiang Ma and Yizhou Qian. 2019. Developing Chinese Elementary School Students' Computational Thinking: A Convergent Cognition Perspective. In *Proceedings of ACM Global Computing Education Conference 2019 (CompEd'19)*. ACM, New York, NY, USA, 1 page. https://doi.org/10.1145/3300115.3312514

*This work is supported by 2018 Jiangsu Education Informatization Research Grant (No. 20180011) sponsored by Jiangsu Educational Technology Center, China.
† Yizhou Qian is the corresponding author.

1 INTRODUCTION

With the rapid development of computing technologies, computing education gets more and more attention from countries all over the world. In 2006, Professor Wing [3] proposed the concept Computational Thinking, which "involves solving problems, designing systems, and understanding human behavior, by drawing on the concepts fundamental to computer science" (p. 33). She also pointed out that computational thinking is a fundamental skill for everyone in the 21st century. After that, many researchers started to investigate students' computational thinking skill [1]. In 2017, the new national curriculum standards of China included computational thinking as a core literacy of students. In other words, the information technology courses in K-12 schools have started to include content about programming and computational thinking. One significant topic of the research pon computational thinking is to understand the development of students' computational thinking skill. However, few studies have focused on the development of Chinese elementary school students' computational thinking.

This study investigates the development of computational thinking skill of two groups of Chinese elementary school students taking a newly designed information technology course. The research uses the convergent cognition theory [2] as the theoretical framework. The convergent cognition theory posits that learning computer programming affects students' mathematical thinking and vice versa. Hence, the course design is closely aligned with the elementary school math curriculum, and the programming environment is Scratch. A group of third grade students and a group of fourth grade students are the participants. Their computational thinking skill and math ability will be measured to see whether this course develops students' computational thinking skill and whether convergent cognition effects exist. This poster consists of two major components. The first one introduces the background of the research project and demonstrate examples from the instructional materials. The second part presents the preliminary results of the course's effectiveness on developing students' computational thinking.

REFERENCES

[1] Grover, S., & Pea, R. (2013). Computational thinking in K–12: A review of the state of the field. *Educational Researcher, 42*(1), 38-43.
[2] Rich, P. J., Leatham, K. R., & Wright, G. A. (2013). Convergent cognition. *Instructional Science, 41*(2), 431-453.
[3] Wing, J. M. (2006). Computational thinking. *Communications of the ACM, 49*(3), 33-35.

Goal Setting and Self-regulated Experiential Learning in a Paired Internship Program

Lih-Bin Oh
School of Computing
National University of Singapore
Singapore
ohlb@nus.edu.sg

ABSTRACT

Experiential learning is an effective educational approach to improve students' meta-cognitive abilities, enhance their ability to apply information to actual situations, and give them the ability to become self-directed learners [1]. Drawing from the principles of goal-setting and motivation theories [2], a paired internship program was introduced at a large Asian university for business analytics and information systems undergraduate students in 2015. The scope, goals, and learning objectives of each internship were co-defined by the students, host supervisor, and faculty supervisor. The program was designed to be a paired, structured internship where students select their own partner and work full time for 24 weeks. Pair work promotes collaborative peer-learning and allows students to acquire complementary skills.

In order to reap maximum benefits from their internship experience, students need to engage in self-regulated learning by taking control of their own learning through planning, monitoring, and deciding how to spend time on the most important learning activities [3]. Throughout their internship, students submit regular learning logs capturing their reflections of the internship experience. At the end of their internship, they also submit a learning journal by reflecting upon the connection between work and academic experiences, professional skills they have developed, and how theory is translated into practice. These written reflections form the core academic assignments used to enhance the educational value of the internship. Reflective journaling is especially relevant to internships because reflective skills, particularly in work-integrated learning, are critical for fostering students' lifelong learning and professional practice [4].

This research examines the role of goal setting and investigates the effectiveness of the various pedagogical mechanisms used to facilitate self-regulated experiential learning. We performed qualitative content analysis on the document submissions of 74 students to identify evidence of transformative learning in which students show that they can reconcile concrete experiences within a field of theoretical concepts to identify, change, connect, and act differently [5]. We coded the written reflections as either concrete experience (CE), reflective observation (RO), abstract conceptualization (AC), or active experimentation (AE). Besides the qualitative data, we also collected data through two surveys at the start and end of the internship to assess the students' experiential learning styles, motivations, goal-setting behaviors, and goal attainment orientations. We performed quantitative analysis on these measures to uncover further insights.

Overall, the findings indicated positive experience-based learning outcomes from the internship suggesting that designing internship programs based on experiential learning principles can effectively equip students with both technical skills and essential soft skills. Recommendations for incorporating internships in computing curriculum to serve as a form of practice-oriented pedagogy to complement and supplement classroom pedagogy are provided.

CCS CONCEPTS

• Social and professional topics → Professional topics → Computing profession → Computing occupations

KEYWORDS

Internship; experiential learning; goal setting; self-regulation

ACM Reference format:
Lih-Bin Oh. 2019. Goal Setting and Self-regulated Experiential Learning in a Paired Internship Program. In *Proceedings of ACM Global Computing Education Conference, Chengdu, Sichuan, China, May 2019 (CompEd'19)*, 1 page. https://doi.org/10.1145/3300115.3312516

ACKNOWLEDGMENT

This research is supported in part by the Singapore Ministry of Education Academic Research Fund Tier 1.

REFERENCES

[1] A.Y. Kolb and D.A. Kolb. 2006. Learning styles and learning spaces: A review of the multidisciplinary application of experiential learning theory in higher education. In R. R. Sims, & S. J. Sims (Eds.), *Learning styles and learning: A key to meeting the accountability demands in education*, 45-92. New York: Nova Science Publishers.

[2] E.A. Locke and G.P. Latham (2005). Building a practically useful theory of goal setting and task motivation: A 35-year odyssey. American Psychologist, 57(9), 705-717.

[3] D.L. Butler and P.H. Winne (1995). Feedback and self-regulated learning: A theoretical synthesis. Review of Educational Research, 65(3), 245–281

[4] R.R. Rogers (2001). Reflection in higher education: A concept analysis. Innovative Higher Education, 26(1), 37-57.

[5] L. Carson and K. Fisher (2006). Raising the bar on criticality: Students' critical reflection in an internship program. Journal of Management Education, 30(5), 700-723.

University Code Refactoring Practice-Driven Curriculum Instructed by Industry Professionals*

Xiaochun Yang
Shanghai AchieveFun Info Tech
Co., Ltd.
Shanghai, China
janeyungxc@hotmail.com

Jin Zhang*
College of Information Science and
Engineering
Hunan Normal University
Changsha, Hunan, China
jinzhang@hunnu.edu.cn

Qiang Li
College of Information Science and
Engineering
Hunan Normal University
Changsha, Hunan, China
liqiang@hunnu.edu.cn

Meiling Cai
College of Information Science and Engineering
Hunan Normal University
Changsha, Hunan, China
cai.meiling@hunnu.edu.cn

ABSTRACT

As software design and development is engineering technology and art, the design and coding capabilities of software engineers require continuous development and practice. After learning the basic concepts of computers, students need to constantly practice so as to design and develop excellent systems. To assist university teachers to develop software design and code quality curriculums, the authors propose a code refactoring practice-driven curriculum taught by professionals for the university students based on the code refactoring practice case developed for junior engineers. The curriculum uses teacher teaching, student sharing, and teacher summaries, combined with the student's code, through the study and discussion of "refactoring" book, to verify students' object-oriented design ability and coding ability, and help students master and improve the corresponding ability. Firstly, in the guided class, the teacher takes simple cases as examples to guide students to view poor quality code problems, explain the basic principles and common approaches of refactoring. Teacher proposes the reading guide for the Refactoring book for students in preparation for the sharing class. Secondly, in the sharing class, students share one or more knowledge points after reading the book based on their code, and summarize the problems in the code, and introduce the reasons and specific steps to improve the code using each refactoring method. Students can ask relevant questions and advise classroom participants on issues to be aware of in future design and development. Finally, in the summarization class, the teacher summarizes the students' strength and weakness in understanding the object-oriented design and refactoring methods and proposes future goals. This poster emphasizes that the success of this curriculum depends on the teaching ability of the professional and proposes the criteria for selecting the teacher includes profound engineering experience, passion for education, and teaching capabilities. Based on the design and teaching experience of previous coding refactoring curriculum, the first author hopes to cooperate with university teachers to use the excellent engineering practice methodology and pedagogical ideas to inspire and guide students to understand concepts and polish their skills. Together, the authors can make full use of engineering practice and university education concepts to provide a better practical curriculum for university students' software development.

CCS CONCEPTS

• Social and professional topics → Software engineering education

KEYWORDS

Code Refactoring; Object-Oriented Design; Code Quality; Practice-Driven

*Funding agents:1. Hunan Province Postgraduate Education and Teaching Reform Project: JG2018A012; 2. Hunan Province General Higher Education Teaching Reform Research Project: Xiang JiaoTong [2018] No. 436; 3. National Ministry of Education Industry-University Cooperation Collaborative Education Project: 201702001043,201801037136; 4. Hunan Provincial Department of Education Innovation Platform Open Fund Project: 15K082; 5. Hunan Normal University Teaching Reform Research Project, Award number: Xiao Xing FaJiaowu Zi [2018] No. 51, No. 52; 6. Hunan Normal University Degree and Postgraduate Education Teaching Reform Research Project, Award number: 2018 Corresponding Author: Jin Zhang, jinzhang@hunnu.edu.cn

ACM Reference format:

Xiaochun Yang, Jin Zhang and Qiang Li. 2019. University Code Refactoring Practice-Driven Curriculum Instructed by Industry Professionals. In *Proceedings of ACM Global Computing Education Conference 2019(CompEd'19), May17-19,2019, Chengdu, Sichuan, China. ACM, New York, NY, USA, 1 page. https://doi.org/10.1145/3300115.3312509*

Developing and Assessing Educational Games to Enhance Cyber Security Learning in Computer Science

Jinghua Zhang
Department of Computer Science
Winston-Salem State University
Winston-Salem, NC, USA
zhangji@wssu.edu

Xiaohong Yuan
Department of Computer Science
North Carolina A&T State University
Greensboro, NC, USA
xhyuan@ncat.edu

Jinsheng Xu
Department of Computer Science
North Carolina A&T State University
Greensboro, NC, USA
jxu@ncat.edu

Elva J. Jones
Department of Computer Science
Winston-Salem State University
Winston-Salem, NC, USA
jonese@wssu.edu

ABSTRACT

Cyber security is a critical field in Computer Science education today. We need to prepare students for the increasing security challenges they will face in the future. The workforce also needs to have additional cyber security skills to best protect the interests of the nation. Motivating and engaging more students in this field is an important step to meet the needs of future workforce. Games have been successfully used in many areas of education, including Computer Science, to engage students in learning. They provide educational, immersive experiences, which could help underrepresented students gain the confidence to pursue a career or further study in the cyber security field while also inspiring others. The poster will present the three-year project that aims to develop and assess three educational games with in-game assessments to effectively teach cyber security concepts (Access Control, LAN Vulnerabilities and Buffer Overflow). These games will be designed with different levels of difficulty to target students from freshmen to seniors and integrated into the existing computer science curriculum at Winston-Salem State University and North Carolina A&T State University to benefit a wide range of students. In addition, all these games will be portable, self-contained and available for download from the project website.

CCS CONCEPTS

Applied computing → Education → Computer-assisted instruction

KEYWORDS

Cyber Security Education, Game-Based Learning, Simulation

ACM Reference format:
Jinghua Zhang, Xiaohong Yuan, Jinsheng Xu and Elva J. Jones. 2019. Developing and Assessing Educational Games to Enhance Cyber Security Learning in Computer Science. In *Proceedings of ACM Global Computing Education conference (CompEd'19). ACM, New York, NY, USA.* https://doi.org/10.1145/3300115.3312511

ZyCube: An In-House Mini-Cluster for Agilely Developing and Conducting Computer Systems Course Projects

Ke Zhang, Yisong Chang, Mingyu Chen, Yungang Bao, Zhiwei Xu

SKLCA, ICT, Chinese Academy of Sciences; University of Chinese Academy of Sciences (UCAS)

{zhangke,changyisong,cmy,baoyg,zxu}@ict.ac.cn

ABSTRACT

In the new era of AI and IoT, it's crucial to guide students to learn principles of computer systems design with both hardware (HW) and software (SW), or at least equip them with a HW-SW co-design concept. To overcome the lack of hardware reconfigurability in conventionally leveraged single-board computers (SBCs, e.g., Raspberry Pi) in class, this poster delivers ZyCube, a heterogeneous 4-node SoC-FPGA mini-cluster. These four nodes are orchestrated in a manner of on-demand network service to support a dozen of students to agilely and simultaneously conduct computer systems projects. Three capacity-building course projects are shown with ZyCube, which are (1) HW design of a simplified CPU core with performance profiling using C-language microbenchmarks, (2) rapid co-design of a deep neural network inference accelerator with the CPU core, and (3) datapath optimization with a co-designed DMA engine. These projects are believed to help students to obtain a comprehensive perspective of HW-SW coordination and teachers to leverage a similar platform and pedagogy in their courses.

KEYWORDS

FPGA cluster, Computer system, HW-SW co-design

ACM Reference Format:
Ke Zhang, Yisong Chang, Mingyu Chen, Yungang Bao, Zhiwei Xu. 2019. ZyCube: An In-House Mini-Cluster for Agilely Developing and Conducting Computer Systems Course Projects. In *ACM Global Computing Education Conference 2019 (CompEd'19), May 17–19, 2019, Chengdu,Sichuan, China.* ACM, New York, NY, USA, 1 page. https://doi.org/10.1145/3300115.3312515

1 INTRODUCTION

It is an important mission for computer science (CS) educators and instructors to teach students' thinking and practicing capabilities in computer systems and HW-SW co-design. Computer systems experimental curricula and educational tools are of significance in this procedure. Low-cost SBCs are on trial in CS courses. However, this kind of SBCs lacks of hardware reconfigurability and agility, which are of essential necessity for emerging domain-specific acceleration in AI and IoT. Applying FPGA-based platforms [1, 2] in computer systems courses is an alternative approach to provide undergrads with hands-on HW development environments.

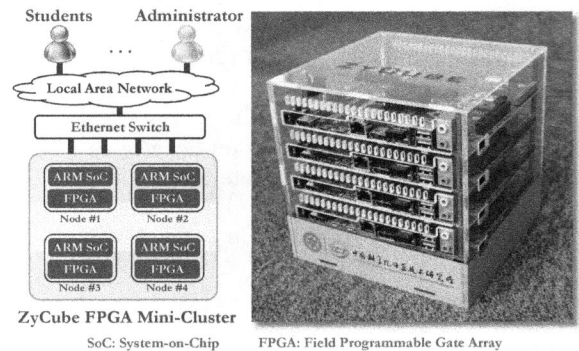

Figure 1: A four-node ZyCube that consist of high-end SoCs, FPGA fabrics and plentiful I/O resources.

2 ZYCUBE: AT A GLANCE

This poster shows an in-house experimental mini-cluster, ZyCube, based on Zynq MPSoC boards used in [3] , which could be useful for students to agilely conduct HW-SW co-design experiments, and easy for other educators to re-design. ZyCube that is composed of four heterogeneous FPGA nodes provides network accessibility for students to simultaneously conduct their experimental projects in a computer lab (Fig. 1). An easy-to-use interface is also built upon the SoC for FPGA configuration and program execution. This in-house appliance will be greatly effective in cultivating students' capabilities in several existing CS courses such as computer organization, computer architecture and operating system.

3 POTENTIAL USERS OF ZYCUBE

Potential users of ZyCube mainly include: (1) educators and instructors; (2) developers interested in creating an agile educaitonal online HW-SW co-design environment; (3) students aiming to improve capabilities in computer systems design and HW-SW programming.

4 ACKNOWLEDGEMENT

This work is partly supported by the National Key Technologies R&D Program of China (2016YFB1000401) and NSF China (61702485).

REFERENCES

[1] M. J. Jipping, S. Henry, K. Ludewig, and L. Tableman. 2006. How To Integrate FPGAs Into a Computer Organization Course. In *Proc. 37th SIGCSE Technical Symposium on Computer Science Education.* 234–238.
[2] D. B. Larkins, W. M. Jones, and H. E. Rickard. 2013. Using FPGAs as a Reconfigurable Teaching Tool Throughout CS Systems Curriculum. In *Proc. 44th SIGCSE Technical Symposium on Computer Science Education.* 397–402.
[3] K. Zhang, Y. Chang, M. Chen, Y. Bao, and Z. Xu. 2019. Computer Organization and Design Course with FPGA Cloud. In *Proc. 50th SIGCSE Technical Symposium on Computer Science Education.* 927–933.

A Platform-as-a-Service System for FPGA Education and Development

Qian Zhao
Kyushu Institute of Technology
680-4 Kawazu, Iizuka, Fukuoka, Japan
cho@ai.kyutech.ac.jp

Takaichi Yoshida
Kyushu Institute of Technology
680-4 Kawazu, Iizuka, Fukuoka, Japan
takaichi@ai.kyutech.ac.jp

ABSTRACT

As a promising technology for the post-Moore era, FPGAs (Field-Programmable Gate Arrays) have been employed in a variety of cloud and edge applications to provide hardware acceleration capability. However, with the introduction of FPGAs, the system architecture and development flow are becoming more complicated. In this work, we propose a PaaS (Platform-as-a-Service) approach to simplify the education and development of an FPGA accelerated system, which allows the FPGA development can be completed with only a browser, and then the PaaS system can automatically perform FPGA compilation and deployment.

KEYWORDS

FPGA education; Platform-as-a-Service; Hardware acceleration

ACM Reference Format:
Qian Zhao and Takaichi Yoshida. 2019. A Platform-as-a-Service System for FPGA Education and Development. In *ACM Global Computing Education Conference 2019 (CompEd '19), May 17–19, 2019, Chengdu,Sichuan, China.* ACM, New York, NY, USA, 1 page. https://doi.org/10.1145/3300115.3312512

1 INTRODUCTION

The HW (Hardware) architecture and the development of a system with FPGAs (Field-Programmable Gate Arrays) is more complicated than a CPU-only system. In this work, we show a in-progress PaaS (Platform-as-a-Service) for simplifying the education and development of an FPGA-attached system, as shown in Fig. 1.

2 CUSTOMIZABLE WEB-BASED IDE

To reduce the requirement of a developer's environment for FPGA development, we propose a server-side compile system that can be utilized through a customizable Web-based IDE (Integrated Development Environment) interface. We set up all mainstream SW (Software) and HW compilers using container technology, which allows us to set up a repository having images of all FPGA CAD tools. To provide a developer-friendly interface, we build a customizable Web-based IDE based on Theia [1]. We propose FPGA development functions such as design simulation, compilation, cluster management as Theia extensions. Besides, the IDE can be customized for the different type of applications such as AI, IoT.

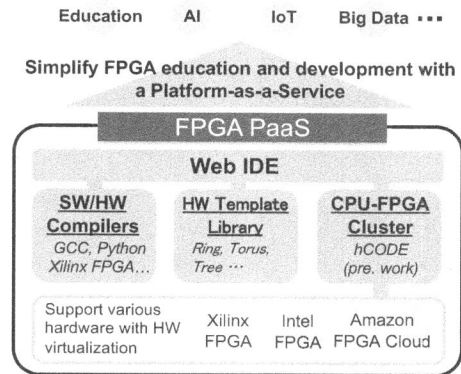

Figure 1: Overview of FPGA PaaS system.

3 TEMPLATE-BASED HW DESIGN MODEL

To improve the reusability and reduce the development cost of HW designs, we propose a template-based HW design model, which divides a design into an application-dependent PE (processing element) logic and an application-independent architecture logic. We propose highly frequent HW architectures such as tree structure and torus structure as reusable templates. Based on a selected template, a developer only has to design an application-dependent PE logic, and then the PaaS can automatically generate a high-performance accelerator project. Besides, as a template organizes PEs in a scalable topology, accelerators can be easily scaled to adapt to FPGA devices of different sizes.

4 FPGA CLUSTER MANAGEMENT

In the FPGA PaaS system, all FPGA-attached servers are organized in a server cluster. The backend of the cluster management is implemented with an FPGA-as-a-Service platform, the hCODE, which is proposed in our previous work [2]. The hCODE platform implements a Shell-and-IP design pattern and an accelerator repository to reduce design and management costs of FPGA projects. Besides, with the FPGA virtualization technique, an accelerator can be scheduled onto an FPGA-attached server node with a policy of a specified target such as fewer resources or higher performance. The front-end provides a graphical interface for the hCODE functions, which is integrated with the web IDE as an extension module.

REFERENCES
[1] THEIA: Cloud & Desktop IDE, Retrieved January 28, 2019 from https://www.theia-ide.org
[2] Q. Zhao, Hendarmawan, M. Amagasaki, M. Iida, M. Kuga, and T. Sueyoshi. 2017. hCODE 2.0: An Open-source Toolkit for Building Efficient FPGA-enabled Clouds. Proc. of ICFPT'17, 267-270. https://doi.org/10.1109/FPT.2017.8280157

Author Index

www.ingramcontent.com/pod-product-compliance
Lightning Source LLC
Chambersburg PA
CBHW061400210326
41598CB00035B/6045